Indian Philosophy in English

GW00994387

Indian Philosophy in English

From Renaissance to Independence

Edited by

NALINI BHUSHAN

JAY L. GARFIELD

OXFORD
UNIVERSITY PRESS

OXFORD
UNIVERSITY PRESS

Oxford University Press, Inc., publishes works that further
Oxford University's objective of excellence
in research, scholarship, and education.

Oxford New York
Auckland Cape Town Dar es Salaam Hong Kong Karachi
Kuala Lumpur Madrid Melbourne Mexico City Nairobi
New Delhi Shanghai Taipei Toronto

With offices in
Argentina Austria Brazil Chile Czech Republic France Greece
Guatemala Hungary Italy Japan Poland Portugal Singapore
South Korea Switzerland Thailand Turkey Ukraine Vietnam

Copyright © 2011 by Oxford University Press, Inc.

Published by Oxford University Press, Inc.
198 Madison Avenue, New York, New York 10016

www.oup.com

Oxford is a registered trademark of Oxford University Press.

All rights reserved. No part of this publication may be reproduced,
stored in a retrieval system, or transmitted, in any form or by any means,
electronic, mechanical, photocopying, recording, or otherwise,
without the prior permission of Oxford University Press.

Library of Congress Cataloging-in-Publication Data
Indian philosophy in English : from renaissance to independence /
edited by Nalini Bhushan and Jay L. Garfield.
p. cm.
Includes bibliographical references.
ISBN 978-0-19-976925-4 (pbk. : alk. paper)
ISBN 978-0-19-976926-1 (hardcover : alk. paper)
1. Philosophy, India—20th century. I. Bhushan, Nalini.
II. Garfield, Jay L., 1955–
B5132. 196 2011
181'. 4—dc22 2010034541

Printed in the United States of America
on acid-free paper

To the memory
of G. C. Pande and Daya Krishna

To whom we owe the very idea for this project.

GROUP PHOTO : FIRST SESSION OF THE INDIAN PHILOSOPHICAL CONGRESS

Sitting on the Floor : J. K. Chakravarthi, A. Nag, ________, R. V. Das, G. R. Malkani, S. S. Suryanarayana Sastri, ________, P. P. S. Sastri, P. G. Dutt, ________,

Chairs : J. R. Banerji, ________, M. N. Tolani, M. R. Oak, A. R. Wadia, R. D. Ranade, Sir W. E. Greaves (*Vice-Chancellor*), G. H. Langley, S. N. Das Gupta, ________, W. S. Urquhart, H. Haldar, Sisir K. Maitra, A. G. Hogg.

Standing (First Row) : ________, S. Radhakrishnan, N. Venkataraman, ________, D. D. Vadekar, S. V. Dandekar, ________, U. C. Bhattacharyya, Kshirode Chandra Mukherji, ________, R. Ramanujachari, ________, E. Ahmed Shah, P. N. Srinivasachari, I. J. S. Taraporewala, N. Sengupta.

Standing (Second Row) : Radhakamal Mukherji, H. S. Bhattacharyya, ________, S. C. Datta, D. M. Datta, S. C. Sinha, ________, H. K. Deb, H. M. Bhattacharyya, B. L. Atreya, P. G. Bridge, B. K. Mullick, ________, J. Mckenzie, S. Sen, ________.

Standing (Third Row) : B. K. Nag, J. N. C. Ganguli, B. S. Guha, P. D. Sastri, R. Kimura, G. C. Chatterji, S. C. Chatterji.

Contents

PART THREE: *Vedānta*

PART FOUR: *Metaphysics and Epistemology*

PART FIVE: *A Session of the Indian Philosophical Congress at Amalner, 1950*

Acknowledgments

THIS PROJECT HAS been in the works for along time, and we have incurred a number of intellectual and personal debts that can never be fully repaid. Our deepest thanks go to the late Professor G. C. Pande and to the late Professor Daya Krishna. Professor Pande initiated this study when he handed us two volumes by his teacher A. C. Mukerji and insisted that there was a lot more where that came from. Conversations with him and with Srimathi Sudha Pande shed more light on our task and led us to Daya Krishna. Daya-ji, despite his initial skepticism about the value of this project, became one its biggest boosters. He gave generously of his time, insight, encyclopedic knowledge and encouragement. Many of the leads we followed we owe to him.

We are also grateful to Professor Kapila Vatsyayan and Professor D. P. Chattopadhyaya for taking time from their busy schedules to speak with us about this period.

Allahabad was an important stop for us. Very special thanks to Professor Arvind Mehrotra. Although he is not a philosopher by trade, he certainly is one by temperament. He instantly developed an enthusiasm for our project and went out of his way both to discover often obscure resources for us and to introduce us to others who could help. Our conversations with him in Dehra Dun were crucial to our developing understanding of Indian intellectual life and aesthetics. Among those in Allahabad who contributed to this project, we note the Rudra sisters, Professor Narendra Singh, Dr. Gauri Chattopadhyaya and Dr. Asha Lal from the Philosophy Department at Allahabad University. Special thanks to Professor Singh for access to A. C. Mukerji's library and for collecting for us all of A. C. Mukerji's published works. We could have never brought this project to completion without this assistance. We are also very grateful to Dr. and Smt. G. N. Mukerji for welcoming us into their home and for their valuable recollections of A. C. Mukerji.

In Kolkata, many more colleagues graciously extended themselves to us. We thank Professor Tapati Guha-Thakurta for a wonderful afternoon of discussion, which helped to frame our thinking about Indian art and its relationship to the development of Indian philosophy. We thank the late Professor P. K. Sen for his reminiscences and insights into the lives and thought of the Bhattaccharyyas. Special thanks to Amit and Rosinka Chaudhuri for stimulating conversation over delicious Bengali cuisine and for lots of encouragement.

Professors Amita Chatterjee, Indrani Sanyal, and Shefali Moitra each generously gave of their time at Jadavpur. Their understanding of the philosophical developments in Bengal contributed much to this project.

In Delhi, we had the distinct pleasure and great good fortune to spend time with Professor Margaret Chatterjee. A great friend and classmate of Daya Krishna, Margaret illuminated the complex social, political, and religious contexts in which these philosophers thought and the network of mutual influences that shaped their work. Her joy in this project was infectious, and her irreverence kept things in perspective. Coming to know Margaret would have made this project worthwhile in itself, and discovering her connection to our own department though her longtime friendship with Alice Ambrose and Morris Lazerowitz was a special treat. We are also grateful to Professor S. R. Bhatt, who welcomed us to his home and whose encyclopedic knowledge of the history of this period filled in many details. We thank Professor Aster Patel, whose discussions with us in Delhi and in Auroville contributed enormously to our understanding of the interaction between Sri Aurobindo and the academic philosophers of the colonial period. Her generosity with her reminiscences and insights was extraordinary. Thanks to Peter Heehs as well for giving generously of his time in Pondicherry.

Some of the essays we present here were first aired in conferences and lectures, including the annual Radha Devi Joshi lecture at the University of Connecticut, sessions of the World Congress of Vedānta, and the American Society of Aesthetics. We thank audiences at those occasions for helpful comments and questions. We are particularly grateful to participants in the conference on Philosophy in Colonial India at the University of Pune in 2009. We gratefully acknowledge the efforts of Professor Sharad Deshpande for organizing that memorable event, and for Dr. Pravesh Golay Jung for his efforts to make the conference a success. A number of eminent scholars presented work on that occasion that we found informative and provided us with valuable critical commentary on our own papers. We note with gratitude the contributions of Professor Deshpande, Professor Shefali Moitra, Professor Amita Chatterjee, Dr. Pravesh Jung, Professor S. K. Dubey, Professor Arindam Chakarabarti, Professor Pradeep Gokhale, Professor Nirmalya Chakrabarty, Professor Godavarish Mishra, Professor Mangesh Kulkarni and Professor S. G. Kulkarni. Professor S. K. Dubey deserves special mention. His hard work editing and collecting the presidential addresses of the Indian Philosophical Congress is a major contribution to the history of Indian philosophy.

Special thanks go to Professor A. Raghuramaraju. His own work on philosophy in colonial India was inspirational to us and influential on our thinking. His contributions at this conference and in our subsequent discussions, including his stimulating visit to Smith College, have been invaluable. It is hard to imagine thinking about colonial Indian philosophy without him.

Smith College has provided a wonderful context in which to pursue this research. Our department has been uniformly supportive of our work, and to them we are always grateful. There could be no better philosophical milieu. President Carol Christ, and Deans Charles Staelin, Susan Bourque, John Davis, and Marilyn Schuster have provided support, both moral and, through generous faculty development grants that funded much of this work, financial. Without that support, none of this could have been accomplished. We also thank Andy Rotman, Rick Millington. and Alan Bloomgarden for valuable critique of numerous grant proposals and early drafts of our work. And thanks to Donna Gunn, the best administrative assistant any department has ever had.

A small army of research assistants has contributed enormously to this project. They have been hard at work tracing hard-to-find documents and references, editing, collating, photocopying, and handling correspondence, and in the innumerable valuable tasks that make research possible. Most importantly, they have all read our work and the texts we proposed to collect with care and have fearlessly and with great insight subjected it to criticism. This volume is much better for their contributions. We thank Francesca King, Kendra Ralston, Margaret Dodge, Shama Rahman, Jennifer De Bernardinis, Mary Kate Long, Noreen Ahsan and Adina Bianchi. We also thank Dr. Pravesh Golay Jung for invaluable research assistance in India, particularly on the early work of Gurudev R. D. Ranade. Thanks to Richard Hayes for help with Sanskrit and special thanks to Lucy Randall and Natalie Johnson at Oxford University Press for painstaking editorial assistance.

Earlier versions of several of our own essays have appeared in print (or in e-print). “Whose Voice? Whose Tongue? Philosophy in English in Colonial India” appears in a slightly different form as “Anglophone Indian Philosophy” (Nalini Bhushan) in the *Oxford Handbook of World Philosophy* (Garfield and Edelglass, Eds.). “Pandits and Professors: The Renaissance of Secular India” appeared in the *Journal of the Indian Council for Philosophical Research* XXVI:1 (2009, published 2010) and in *Essays in Memory of Daya Krishna.* (G. Mishra, Ed.; New Delhi: Indian Council for Philosophical Research, 2010). “An Indian in Paris: Cosmopolitan Aesthetics in India” first appeared as “The Development of a Cosmopolitan Aesthetic in Colonial India” (Nalini Bhushan) in a special issue of *The Journal of Contemporary Aesthetics*, “Aesthetics and Race: New Philosophical Perspectives,” (Special Volume 2, 2009, www.contemparearyaesthetics.org). Curiously, “The Plato of Allahabad: A. C. Mukerji’s Contributions to Indian and to World Philosophy” was originally published in a slightly different version under the title, “Whose Voice? Whose Tongue?

Indian Philosophy in English from Renaissance to Independence" (*Journal of the Indian Council of Philosophical Research* XXV: 2, pp. 89–108, 2008).

Finally, and most important, we thank our families. This project has often taken us away from them for extended periods of time; much of the time we have spent with them has been interrupted by our preoccupation with colonial Indian philosophy. They believed in this project and made it possible. SO, warm thanks to Rick Millington, Ajay Bhushan Rosenfeld, Bharat Bhushan, Dinesh Bhushan and Blaine Garson.

We hope that we haven't forgotten anybody.

INTRODUCTION

*Whose Voice? Whose Tongue? Philosophy in English in Colonial India**

DAYA KRISHNA, ONE of the most eminent Indian philosophers of the 20th century, says of Indian philosophy:

> Anybody who is writing in English is not an Indian philosopher.... What the British produced was a strange species—a stranger in his own country. The Indian mind and sensibility and thinking [during the colonial period] was shaped by an alien civilization.
>
> [The British] created a new kind of Indian who was not merely cut off from his civilization, but was educated in a different way. The strangeness of the species is that their terms of reference are the West.... They put [philosophical problems] in a Western way. (Interview, 2006)

Daya Krishna describes a gulf between philosophy as it was practiced in India during this period and *authentic* Indian philosophy. He characterizes it as follows:

> This picture of Indian philosophy that has been presented by Radhakrishnan, Hiriyanna and others... [each of whom is an *Indian*, writing philosophy in *English* during the colonial period] is not the story of Indian philosophy. We have been fed on the Western presentation of Indian philosophy, which hardly captures the spirit and history of Indian philosophy.... If I were not to know Indian philosophy myself, I would say that [their presentation] is wonderful, that it presents it clearly, with great insight and understanding. Now that I know a little Indian

* Thanks to Margaret Dodge, Francesca King, Kendra Ralston, and Shama Rahman for comments on an earlier draft of this essay and for research assistance on this project.

> philosophy, I say that they did not...They are not concerned with the problems that Indian philosophers were concerned with. (Ibid.)

The view to which Daya Krishna gives voice, despite its prevalence, is deeply mistaken. The intellectual agency and creativity in the domain of Indian philosophy in the nineteenth and early twentieth centuries belongs to Indian thinkers; *they* sustained the Indian philosophical tradition and were the creators of its modern avatar.

From the late 19th century through the middle of the 20th century, important and original philosophy was written *in* English, *in* India, *by* Indians. These philosophers were not cut off from Indian civilization; they were deeply committed to it. Their engagement with Western philosophy was an act of appropriation in the service of a *modern*, indeed cosmopolitan, *Indian* project. The problems they addressed were their own, raised by and for philosophers working in a tradition with roots in India, but who were cognizant of the Western tradition as well.

Daya Krishna may indeed have been wrong about the state of *philosophy* under the Raj, but he gets something deeply right. He correctly characterizes the *experience* of Anglophone Indian intellectuals under colonial rule when he says in the same interview:

> ...The deepest anguish of the Indian intellectual is that he is unrecognized in the West as an equal, or as an intellectual at all. Ibid.

This failure of recognition is tragic. These philosophers wrote in a context of cultural fusion generated by the British colonial rule of India. They were self-consciously writing both as Indian intellectuals for an Indian audience and as participants in a developing global community constructed in part by the British Empire. They pursued Indian philosophy in a language and format that could render it both accessible and acceptable to the Anglophone world abroad. In their attempt to write and to think for *both* audiences they were taken seriously by *neither*. This predicament and this anguish inspire the present volume. We begin by considering the context of Indian academic philosophy.

Anglophone philosophy in colonial India is shaped by three distinct historical phenomena:

(1) Thomas Macaulay's 1835 "Minute on Education" establishes English as the medium of instruction in Indian education and places Protestant missionary professors in charge of philosophical education in Indian colleges and universities;

(2) the Arya and Brahmo Samaj—social and religious reform movements that sweep the country in the late 19th century—which issue in a revaluation of the orthodox Hindu philosophical systems and a return to the original, "purer" Vedas and Upaniṣad; and,
(3) the British occupation itself, which generates a politico-cosmopolitan awareness and a distinctive approach to imagining the modern Indian nation in academic and nonacademic philosophical circles.

The present volume republishes a selection of important philosophical essays written by major figures of this period, together with some of our own reflections on their work. Together they demonstrate the fecundity to which we allude above, the continuity with the classical Indian tradition that renders the philosophy of this place and time distinctively *Indian*, and the cosmopolitan engagement that brings Indian philosophy into modernity.

Many of these articles are long forgotten, even in India, but were influential in their time; they are not, however, mere historical curiosities. Some of the figures we represent are still present in the historical consciousness of most Indian academic philosophers; others, however, will be unfamiliar even to those working in contemporary Indian universities. Very few of these articles are read regularly today, either as part of the syllabus or in professional practice. Nonetheless, they will engage the contemporary reader intellectually, even when their idiom may be somewhat archaic. We present this small selection of a vast literature in order to reinvigorate interest in the philosophy of the Indian colonial period, and to demonstrate that Indian intellectual history is a history of active, creative engagement both with its own past and with the intellectual currents of the broader world.

Philosophy and the Project of Indian National Identity

Anglophone Indian philosophy is coeval with and contributes to the Indian Renaissance. The renaissance was more than a revival of Indian cultural, artistic, and intellectual life after a period of stagnation (indeed, the period of stagnation is itself a problematic myth). The British conquest of India at the same time *unified* a subcontinent that had been a patchwork of large kingdoms and small principalities since the fall of Ashoka's empire and *divided* this newly unified India along caste, communal, and linguistic fault lines enshrined in British administrative law. Paradoxically, as Jawaharlal Nehru so eloquently demonstrates in *The Discovery of India* (1946), their assiduous efforts at division ignited the movement to national unity. And paradoxically as well, their imposition of English as the language of administration and learning facilitated that movement. But Indian nationalism required the construction of a new trajectory for India, grounded in a historical narrative, and aimed at an independent future. The renaissance shaped that trajectory.

Philosophy was central to the renaissance. Colonial philosophers linked classical Indian philosophical concerns to the new social and political movements that swept India. Sri Aurobindo, Mohandas Gandhi, and Krishna Chandra Bhattacharyya, in very different registers, connected classical accounts of individual subjectivity to the emergence of a new Indian collective identity; Ananda Kentish Coomaraswamy, Mulk Raj Anand, and Sister Nivedita linked Indian art and aesthetic theory, grounded in the classical accounts of Bhārata and Abhināvagupta, to the new nationalist ideas of *swaraj* and *swadeshi*; Benoy Kumar Sarkar, Lajpat Rai, Bhagavan Das, and Rabindranath Tagore initiated philosophical debates about the concept of the nation and the relation between nationalism and internationalism.

Aurobindo's "The Renaissance in India" (1918) is a classic from this period. Aurobindo depicts the Indian renaissance as a "reawakening" rather than what he characterizes as an "overturn" or "reversal" in the renaissance of Europe. In solidarity with Young Ireland, he prefers to see in India "a resemblance to the recent Celtic movement in Ireland, the attempt of a reawakened national spirit to find a new impulse of self-expression ... after a long period of eclipsing English influences" (Aurobindo, 1918, this volume, p. 39). Translating individual subjectivity into national subjectivity, Aurobindo writes,

> India can best develop herself and serve humanity by being herself... This does not mean, as some blindly and narrowly suppose, the rejection of everything new that comes to us ... [that] happens to have been first developed or powerfully expressed by the West. Such an attitude would be intellectually absurd, physically impossible, and above all unspiritual; true spirituality rejects no new light, no added means or materials of our human self-development. It means simply to keep our center ... and assimilate to it all we receive, and evolve out of it all we do and create. (Aurobindo, 1918, this volume, p. 64).

A. K. Coomaraswamy worries about the impact of ideas tainted by a legacy of imperialism on the stability of the Indian cultural core of which Aurobindo speaks:

> Our struggle is part of a wider one, the conflict between the ideals of Imperialism and the ideals of Nationalism ... we believe in India for the Indians ... not merely because we want our own India for ourselves, but because we believe that every nation has its own part to play in the

> long history of human progress, and that nations, which are not free to develop their own individuality and own character, are also unable to make the contribution to the sum of human culture which the world has a right to expect of them. (Coomaraswamy, in 1981, p. 2)

Coomaraswamy argues in this essay and throughout his extensive corpus that nationalism is not merely a political, but also a philosophical and cultural imperative, the imperative to preserve the plurality that enriches world culture. He argues that India, like all nations that are custodians of great cultures, has not only a right, but an obligation to preserve, advance, and contribute to a global intellectual and cultural life. The development of an Indian academy is an expression of this obligation and hence part and parcel of the national struggle.

Indian philosophy was not prosecuted only in the academy. Many philosophers were public figures as well, prominently including Tagore and Gandhi. Despite the profound disagreements between Tagore and Gandhi on the concept of nation and on the appropriate route to political independence, they agree about a great deal. Tagore, in his essays on nationalism (1916, 1917), worries about the divisive effects of the idea of Nation on its peoples. He says: "A nation... is that aspect which a whole population assumes when organized for a mechanical purpose. Society as such has no ulterior purpose" (Das, 1996, p. 421). He argues that the very concept of the Nation is oppressive and stultifying. About the British he says: "I have a deep love and a great respect for the British race as human beings... We have felt the greatness of this people as we feel the sun; but as for the Nation, it is for us a thick mist of a stifling nature covering the sun itself" (Das, 1996, p. 424). Gandhi creatively combines the metaphysics of the *Gītā*, the perspectival epistemology of Jain philosophy, with its corresponding prescription of ahiṃsā and Thoreau's notions of a return to nature and the justifiability of civil disobedience, to craft a distinctive philosophical politics for the Indian nation in its struggle for independence. He argues that political freedom (Swaraj as self-government) is genuinely possible only when individuals are free (swaraj as mastery over oneself).

We have seen that Tagore was skeptical about political and cultural arguments in support of nationalism in general, and of the idea of Indian national identity in particular. That skepticism is shared by B. K. Sarkar, who develops a sustained argument for a pluralistic India, criticizing those, such as A. K. Coomaraswamy, who would put forward the "hypothesis as to the 'Indianness' of Indian inspiration, that is, the distinctiveness of Hindu (or Indian?) genius" (Sarkar, 1932, this volume p. 168). Sarkar argues that this would be as bizarre as an Indian physics or chemistry. "There is no one India," he writes, "there are Indias" (Sarkar, 1922, p. 298). He emphasizes the heterogeneity rather than the homogeneity of Indian historical, cultural, and religious experience and articulates a vision of India that is united in virtue of, rather than despite, its plurality.

Sarkar's and Tagore's notions of modern India and of what it means to be authentically Indian contrast markedly from those of Coomaraswamy and Gandhi. Aurobindo occupies a middle ground, for while he argues that India has a center, he sees no need to ensure its protection as a nation or culture, seeing in such efforts a fossilization rather than the much needed rejuvenation.

The Young India movement gave a new urgency to the question of the appropriate form of nationalism in the Indian colonial context. Was national identity to be determined geographically? Culturally? Racially? Does nationalism require independence? Can it justify violence? Lajpat Rai answered these last two questions in the affirmative. His intellectual roots are in the Arya Samaj. He explored these questions in detail in works such as *Young India* (1917), which was banned almost immediately as seditious in nature. Rai was martyred while protesting (nonviolently) the appointment of the Simon commission (a commission of British parliamentarians appointed to design India's government).

Philosophers were not only contributing theoretical foundations to a public political struggle; they were also theorizing the role of philosophy in that struggle, and, more reflexively, the meaning of that struggle for philosophy as a practice. K. C. Bhattacharyya's "Svaraj in Ideas" (Bhattacharyya, 1928, p. 103 of this volume), a talk given to his students in 1928, is the best-known exploration of this issue. This is an intensely personal discussion: Bhattacharyya gives a talk in English in which he laments his own inability to express himself in his native Bengali. He worries about the impact on Indian philosophical thought, creativity, and sense of identity both of the English language and of the emphasis in the colonial academy on education in the Western tradition. This essay gives eloquent voice to the dilemmas facing a philosophy as it was at the same time concerned with its role in the development of an *Indian* tradition and with the positioning of Indian thought and scholarship in a *global* discipline.

We hence see in the period at which the independence struggle came to dominate Indian intellectual life—the 1920s and 1930s—that Coomaraswamy's insight that cultural and political nationalism were but aspects of a single enterprise proved correct. It is important to note in this context that Coomaraswamy's own intellectual focus was always art history and aesthetics. Much of his own work is dedicated to the advancement of Indian aesthetic theory and of an *Indian* eye on Indian art. His work *may* be one of the reasons that aesthetics plays such a central role both in the public discussion of Indian national identity and in academic Indian philosophy of this period. This is a role far greater than that which aesthetic theory plays in Western academic philosophy or in most Western accounts of national self-consciousness and of nationalism.

Aesthetics

Indian aestheticians shared the aim of many Indian philosophers during this period: to demonstrate the relevance of the classical Indian tradition to contemporary philosophical problems, and to develop a modern Indian philosophical idiom continuous with it. Aestheticians of this period hence turned to the classical tradition of Bharata and Abhinavagupta. The central aesthetic concept their work, and in all classical Indian aesthetics, is *rasa*. The term originally denotes the sap or juice of a plant but came to mean both *flavor* and *essence* early on, two meanings curiously merged in its aesthetic use. In this context it evokes the multiple sense of the English word *taste* (as in artistic taste, as well as the experience of savoring, or savor as a property of an object) and that of the essence either of the work of art or of the experience thereof. Preoccupation with the nature of *rasa* originates in Bharata's *Nāṭya Śāstra* (c. 6th century C.E.), a text on dance-drama, regarded by some as a fifth Veda, and famously reinterpreted by Abhinavagupta in the 11th century C.E. Bharata treats *rasa* primarily as a property of the work of art itself to be appreciated by the *rasika*. Abhinavagupta, on the other hand, locates *rasa* in the experience itself, more on the subjective side, and explores the properties of the work as well as those of the observer that jointly contribute to the arising of *rasa* in aesthetic experience. Indian aesthetic debates hence turn not on questions of form and representation but instead on questions about psychological or even soteriological evocation.

Colonial encounters with Indian art often involved the study, characterization, and even its well-meaning advancement informed by a European aesthetic sensibility. The Western gaze often found Indian art primitive, excessive, lascivious, and in general a failed aesthetic project. Indian aestheticians and artists responded to this critique in various ways. Some attempted to Westernize; others sought inspiration elsewhere in Asia, but many, following Coomaraswamy's lead, sought to replace the Western lens that so distorted Indian aesthetic objects and experience with an Indian lens that would present them in a clearer and fairer light. These theorists turned to the classical Indian *rasa* tradition, not as a historical exercise, but as a source of new aesthetic thought and as a contribution from India to global aesthetics. Indian aesthetic theory and art criticism hence moves *rasa*, in a modern voice, to center stage in Indian philosophy in the late 19th and early 20th centuries, particularly in the hands of such theorists as A. K. Coomaraswamy, Aurobindo Ghosh, M. Hiriyanna and K. C. Bhattacharyya.

Ananda K. Coomaraswamy, in a string of essays on Indian aesthetics, takes up the concept of *rasa* with a nationalistic purpose. He argues for the presence of a distinctive Indianness to the best Indian art and identifies that distinctive Indian essence as its evocation of *rasa*. *Rasa*, he argues, can only be evoked by art objects that are traditionally Indian, in a subject immersed in Indian culture and aesthetic theory (Coomaraswamy, "Art and Swadeshi," 1910, present volume; Coomaraswamy, "Swadeshi, True and False," 1910/1994; Coomaraswamy, "Hindu View of Art: Theory of Beauty," 2003; Coomaraswamy, "Indian Music," 2003; Coomaraswamy, "The Theory of Art in Asia, 2004). Aurobindo follows Coomaraswamy in this regard but extends his explorations in two intriguing ways. First, in "The National Value of Art" (1910) he argues that Indian aesthetic theory is not only a better vehicle than Western aesthetic theory for *understanding* classical Indian art; it also provides the key to the rejuvenation and the progressive development of modern Indian art (Aurobindo, 1910). In *The Future Poetry* (1917–1920 / 2000), Aurobindo goes further, using Indian aesthetic theory as an interpretative lens for viewing *Western* art, arguing that Indian aesthetics is not only a better theory for understanding *Indian* art, but that in global philosophical and aesthetic discussion, *rasa* theory belongs in the same conversation with Western aesthetic theory (Aurobindo, 2000).

M. Hiriyanna extends Indian aesthetic theory in a different direction, taking it as a key to Indian philosophical thought as a whole. While acknowledging the centrality of traditional metaphysical and epistemological concerns—of a quest for truth, knowledge, and ultimate reality—he uses the notion of the *jivanmukta* (a person who is free on this earth, rather than in the hereafter) to argue for (both) aesthetic (and ethical) practice as making possible a freedom for an individual that comes not from an extinction or suppression of instincts and interests but rather from their expansion. Consequently, the cultivation of the emotions is one of the aims of art and must be on par with a cultivation of the intellect. In addition, while art does not have anything directly to do with morality so that "a moral aim" is not required as a precondition for aesthetic practice (as it is often required as a precondition for intellectual practice), Hiriyanna argues that art must have "a moral view, if it should fulfill its true purpose" (Hiriyanna, 1954, p. 217 of present volume). This purpose is to free the human being from all strife and secure a form of unique joyful experience. In this way, the metaphysical idea of *mokṣa* (ultimate freedom) gets yoked to the aesthetic, and thereby to the world of the here and now. While Hiriyanna is among the first to underscore the role of the aesthetic in questions concerning freedom, there are many who continue to develop this theme, albeit with different emphases.

Up to this point, we have been considering Indian aestheticians who emphasize the essential *Indianness* of Indian art, and the role of art and aesthetics in the construction of national identity; in their hands, art is central to national revival (and historically, the role of the Bengal School in national self-consciousness lends some support to their view.) But theirs was not the only voice in Indian aesthetics. If Coomaraswamy is the paradigmatic nationalist revivalist, then B. K. Sarkar is India's universalist modernist. In "View-Points in Aesthetics," Sarkar argues against restricting *rasa-vidya* to any specific religious, cultural, or philosophical tradition. While he acknowledges that the significance of a work of art—whether for a religious devotee, an art historian, or a nationalist—depends upon the religion, art historical training, or nation from which the individual springs, he argues that for a *rasika*, one who is to appreciate a work on purely aesthetic grounds, the work is universal. Returning aesthetic debate to the realm of form, he writes, "Paintings and sculptures are . . . universal in their appeal because their spiritual basis is geometry, the most abstract and cosmopolitan of all *vidyas*" (Sarkar, 1922, present volume, p. 187).

Sarkar makes the case for the sculpture of the Tamil Naṭarāja (the god of dance) as one of the permanent glories of the human creative genius in the following way: "Naṭarāja is a most original creation in the ripple of bends and joints. The balancing of diverse masses in motion, the swaying of the volumes away from one another, the construction of imaginary circles within circles, the grouping of unseen parallels in movements and poses, and the gravitation of all the varied shapes to a common center of dynamic rhythm—all these constitute an epoch-making attainment of unity in diversity, of the correlation of matter and motion, which possesses a meaning in the idiom of rupam as much to the Western as to the Eastern artist" (Sarkar, 1922, this volume, p. 189). In this way, Sarkar illustrates the kind of universal language and the universal structural forms that, no matter where and by whose hand they originate, when wielded by the artist in his or her appropriate genre, can evoke *rasa* in the *rasika* who comprehends and appreciates that language.

K. C. Bhattacharyya, in what many regard as the most important academic essay on *rasa* from this period (Bhattacharyya, 1930, "The Concept of Rasa," present volume, 195) provides an analysis of this concept that is striking in its distance from religious or even explicitly Indian philosophical vocabulary. With Sarkar, Bhattacharyya aims for a more universal and less explicitly religious Indian aesthetic theory—a theory that addresses universal aesthetic questions in a philosophical language accessible to any English-speaking philosopher. Nonetheless, his problematic is distinctly Indian. He sides explicitly with Abhinavagupta against Bharata in developing a theory not of the aesthetic object but of the aesthetic experience. Aesthetic enjoyment, on his view, belongs to an abstract level of contemplative feeling. Bhattacharyya calls this feeling the 'heart universal' (*sahṛdaya*). Despite the fact that the feeling is contemplative rather than sympathetic or primary, *rasa* nonetheless has neither an intellectual nor spiritual component, and is to be explicated purely in terms of feeling.

Metaphysics and Epistemology

Colonial Indian philosophy was deeply inflected by the revival of interest in the Vedānta school of thought, inspired by the reformist Arya Samaj and Brahmo Samaj movements. This interest in Vedānta gained encouragement through the coincidental import of British neo-Hegelianism into India by British teachers such as A. C. Hogg and by Indian students who studied in the United Kingdom under T. H. Green, the Cairds, and J. Stirling. The following three critical factors—(1) the broad affinities of Vedānta and post-Kantian German and British idealism, (2) the fact that Vedānta was at the same time authentically Indian and harmonious with the most current metaphysics of the West, and (3) the fact that Vedānta was simultaneously a suitable foundation for new religious movements as well as for secular philosophical thought—propelled Vedānta studies to the center of the philosophical stage. Leading scholars both within and outside of the academy addressed classical Vedānta texts and developed a vibrant neo-Vedānta philosophy, informed by Kant's transcendental idealism, by Hegelian absolute idealism, and by British neo-Hegelianism.

The principal questions addressed by neo-Vedāntins are immediately recognizable: What is the relation between a self and the external world? Is the external world real? Is the self a real entity? Is there a reality beyond the one that we can experience via our senses? If so, what is the relation between the empirical world and that ultimate reality? Can either be known? If so, in what ways? In this literature, methods, vocabularies, and reference points from outside of India are creatively appropriated by philosophers in the service of anchoring, articulating, and rendering accessible to a global audience Indian philosophical issues in a modern context. One of the giants of this period, barely remembered now, was A. C. Mukerji, of Allahabad.

A. C. Mukerji (1888–1968) grapples with issues of subjectivity in his two volumes, *The Nature of Self* (1938) and *Self, Thought and Reality* (1933), and a number of essays published in *Allahabad University Studies*. His focus is on epistemological questions that stem from the egocentric predicament, which he traces past Descartes to the *Bṛhadhāraṇyaka Upaniṣad* and the voice of Yajñavālkya. The problem is this: how does the knower know itself? If knowledge is always of an object, then to know a subject must involve knowledge of a subject as an object and not of subjectivity as such. If so, the subject qua subject must remain unknowable. Mukerji argues that such a subject *can* be known, but not in the way that knowing is traditionally understood; instead, it is a knowing that is direct and nonrelational. (Mukerji, 1933; Mukerji, 1938)

This alternative way of knowing—one that is not reducible to either the intellectual or the perceptual—sometimes called the 'intuitive' or 'direct' or 'nonconceptual' way, is the subject of clarification and further analysis in the work of many Indian thinkers, including, most famously, S. Radhakrishnan (1888–1975), M. Hiriyanna (1871–1950), S. Dasgupta (1887–1952), and R. D. Ranade (1886–1957).

The concepts of 'subject' and 'object', and of the difficult relation between them, are analyzed by perhaps the best-known Indian philosopher of this period, Krishna Chandra Bhattacharyya (1875–1949). His essay "The Concept of Philosophy" (this volume) and his book *The Subject as Freedom* (1930) in particular stand as modern-day Indian classics. Bhattacharyya is particularly interested in the relationship between levels of subjectivity and the corresponding levels of freedoms, both phenomenological and metaphysical, that they make possible. His starting point is often Kantian in sensibility, but his philosophical reflection inevitably takes him to the Upanishads or the Vedas. His resolution of problems he finds in Kant's exposition always involves the integration of ideas from Advaita Vedānta (Bhattacharyya, 1930).

The dichotomy between idealism and realism—two views ordinarily taken to be at opposite ends of the metaphysical spectrum—is rejected by many of these thinkers as a false and pernicious one. This is an important philosophical issue during this period, since of the six orthodox schools of Indian philosophy, Vedānta, and Advaita Vedānta in particular, is often represented as the most idealistic. Creating a neo-Vedānta for the 20th Century required dealing with the apparent metaphysical extravagance, of the ancient philosophical concept *māyā* (often translated as *illusion)*, typically understood as that lens or filter through which alone one typically viewed the world, thereby suggesting that one's grasp of the world was illusory from the start. In the modern context, however, an idealism that regarded the external world as entirely illusory was a nonstarter, as much in the Indian academy as in the West. Consequently, just as Kant did in Europe, Kantian neo-Vedāntins in India worked to take the sting out of idealism.

In arguing for the falsity of the dichotomy between realism and idealism, philosophers from Aurobindo to Mukerji argue for a more nuanced conception of our proper relation to the universe. Mukerji writes: "if we are to retain the terms Idealism and Realism, we must give up the old method of contrasting them, and define Realism as the habit of accepting the facts as out there unconditioned and absolute. Idealism, on the contrary, insists on the conditioned nature of the ordinary facts of experience and holds that apart from their conditions the so-called facts are reduced to non-entities" (Mukerji, 1927, p. 475 of present volume). In his focus on the distinction between the unconditioned and the conditioned as the real source of the debate between the realists and the idealists, he anticipates the arrival on the global metaphysical stage of more nuanced forms of realism that view the conditioned nature of the world as one of its fundamental aspects.

As we noted above, this task required clarification of the central concept of *māyā* in Vedāntic philosophy. Swami Vivekananda and V. Subrahmanya Iyer, among others, make the case for an understanding of *māyā* not as illusion or delusion, but rather, following its meaning as *magic*, as a conceptual veil that distorts our experience. For Vivekananda, *māyā* captures the essential nature of all that we experience—that it is subject to change, to error, to misperception, and that although it is experienced through the mediation of our particular perceptual and conceptual apparatus, values, and interests, we take it to be independent of all of these, self-constituted. *Māyā*, he thus argues, far from being an extravagant metaphysical notion that denies empirical reality, is a commonsense way of capturing our complex and elusive relation to empirical reality (Vivekananda, 1953, p. 219–243).

This modern critical approach to *māyā* led to a debate about the appropriateness of *māyā* in the first place as the central concept of Advaita Vedānta. Aurobindo (1872–1950) in *The Life Divine* (1949/1970) argues for the centrality of *līlā* (play), rather than *māyā* (illusion), as the guiding metaphor for understanding the metaphysical relation between the empirical world and absolute reality, and for understanding the nature of subjectivity.

Aurobindo argues that taking the metaphor of *māyā* as central induces a false dualism, distinguishing a world of reality (the world as it is independent of our experience) from a world we experience, the world of magical play, the world we conjure. This dualism, he urges, despite the fact that it is motivated by the desire to respect the empirical reality of the empirical world, necessarily gives it a second-class ontological status in contradistinction to absolute reality. Instead, he argues, the real spirit of Advaita Vedānta is captured by the metaphor of *līla*—play, or manifestation. This metaphor, he argues, is also more consistent with a modern vision. On this understanding, the empirical world is simply absolute reality as it *plays out* for us, as it is manifested in our experience. It is not illusion, and the world we experience is no different from the world of absolute reality, just as Sir Laurence Olivier is no different from the Hamlet he plays—he is the way Hamlet is played. One consequence of going with a *līlāvāda* rather than a *māyāvāda* emphasis in understanding Advaita philosophy is that it produces an understanding of our presence as selves in the empirical world that is less at odds with what is ultimately required for self-realization. On the *līlāvāda* perspective, the relationship between the realized self and the world is one of immanence rather than of separation, distance, or transcendence (Aurobindo, 1970). Aurobindo's work generated a deep and sustained discussion on this subject among philosophers, finding its most famous scholarly expression in a symposium held by the Indian Philosophical Congress, entitled "Has Sri Aurobindo refuted Maya Vada?" (this volume).

In sum, this period of Anglophone Indian philosophy saw a revisiting of ancient metaphysical and epistemological problems, but with a particular focus, within the context of a university-style philosophical training that required an awareness of habits and styles of philosophizing the world over. There was a will to render accessible to a global audience the problems and arguments and the habits and styles of the Indian philosophical traditions with which they were intimately familiar (in part from informal training in the home as well as from formal teachings by Sanskrit pandits outside of the university setting).

Conclusion

Thomas Macaulay wrote in his minute of 1835 that the goal of education in India, and of the introduction of the English language, in particular was "... to form a class who may be interpreters between us and the millions whom we govern; a class of persons, Indian in blood and color, but English in taste, in opinions, in morals, and in intellect" (Macaulay, 1835). He could not have imagined its consequence: the creation of generations of intellectuals, writing literature, philosophy, history, and in English, transcending their intended status of mere "interpreter" between the British rulers and the Indian masses to become prominent academics in their own right, transforming Indian society and culture, and as a consequence, the global culture in which India participates.

Colonial India was the site of a vibrant, innovative philosophical community, engaging simultaneously with its Vedic roots and with then-current trends in European philosophy. Its problematic was shaped by the political situation in India and the demands for nation building it generated on the one hand and by the Indian intellectual engagement with Europe and modernity on the other. Indian philosophers under the Raj worked quite self-consciously in this environment and produced innovative and valuable philosophical literature. They strove to usher Indian philosophy onto a global stage; they used the English language in order to call attention to Indian philosophy and in an effort to bring India into dialogue with Europe. In prosecuting this project, they did not abandon Indian philosophy but advanced it, bringing Western voices and techniques into its tradition, in the process constructing its modern avatar. Simultaneously, their work enriched Western philosophy with Indian voices and insights. In this process, they brought English into the family of Indian philosophical tongues and have made possible the practice of Indian philosophy in English. Alas, for a variety of historical and political reasons we have addressed elsewhere, their efforts have remained obscure. Nonetheless, we owe them a great debt; their story is a rich and fascinating one, and this anthology is an initial step in bringing their work the attention it deserves.

References

Aurobindo. 1910. "The National Value of Art." www.odinring.de/eng/art.htm.

Aurobindo. 1949/1970. *The Life Divine*. Pondicherry: Sri Aurobindo Birth Centenary Library.

Aurobindo. 1917–1920 / 2000. *The Future Poetry*. Pondicherry: Sri Aurobindo Ashram.

Bhattacharyya, Krishnachandra. 1930. *The Subject as Freedom*. Amalner: The Indian Institute of Philosophy.

Coomaraswamy, Ananda K. 1909/1981. "The Deeper Meaning of the Struggle" in *Essays in National Idealism*, 1–6. New Delhi: Munshiram Manoharlal Publishers Private Limited.

Coomaraswamy, Ananda K. 1910/1994. "Swadeshi, True and False" in *Art and Swadeshi*, 7–18. New Delhi: Munshiram Manoharlal Publishers Private Limited.

Coomaraswamy, Ananda K. 2003. "Hindu View of Art: Theory of Beauty" in *The Dance of Shiva: Fourteen Indian Essays*, 52–60. New Delhi: Munshiram Manoharlal Publishers Private Limited.

Coomaraswamy, Ananda K. 2003. "Indian Music" in *The Dance of Shiva: Fourteen Indian Essays*, 102–114. New Delhi: Munshiram Manoharlal Publishers Private Limited.

Coomaraswamy, Ananda K. 2004. "The Theory of Art in Asia" in *The Transformation of Nature in Art*, 1–57. New Delhi: Munshiram Manoharlal Publishers Private Limited.

Das, Sisir Kumar. 1996. *The English Writings of Rabindranath Tagore, Vol.2*. New Delhi: Sahitya Akademi.

Daya Krishna. May 2006. Personal interview by Bhushan and Garfield. Jaipur.

Macauley, Thomas B. 1835. Minute on Education. Columbia University. http://www.columbia.edu/itc/mealac/pritchett/00generallinks/macaulay/txt_minute_education_1835.html

Mukerji, A.C. 1933. *Self, Thought and Reality*. Allahabad: The Juvenile Press.

Mukerji, A.C. 1938. *The Nature of Self*. Allahabad: The Indian Press, Limited.

Nehru, Jawarharlal. 2004. *The Discovery of India*. New Delhi: Penguin Books.

Rai, Lajpat. 1917. *Young India: An Interpretation and History of the Nationalist Movement From Within*. London: British Auxiliary.

Sarkar, Benoy K. 1922. *The Futurism of Young Asia and Other Essays on the Relations between the East and the West*. Berlin: Julius Springer.

Tagore, Rabindranath. "Nationalism," in *The English Writings of Rabindranath Tagore*, 419–465. Delhi: Macmillan, 1976.

Vivekananda, Swami. 1953. *The Yogas and Other Works*. New York: Ramakrishna-Vivekananda Center.

PART ONE

National Identity

I

Pandits and Professors: The Renaissance of Secular India[*]

IT IS IN philosophy, if anywhere, that the task of discovering the soul of India is imperative for the modern India; the task of achieving, if possible, the continuity of his old self with his present day self, of realizing what is nowadays called the Mission of India, if it has any. Genius can unveil the soul of India in art but it is through philosophy that we can methodically attempt to discover it.[1]

1. Introduction

Philosophy in the West is a highly academic discipline, not often associated with great political and social movements. Philosophy in India has often been associated primarily with religious traditions. Philosophy as pursued in India under the British Raj, particularly that written in English, has had a peculiar reception, typically regarded as either a pale imitation of Western philosophy or as watered-down classical Indian philosophy. It is well worth taking a second look at this body of work and its contribution to Indian culture and to world civilization. In particular, we will argue that Indian philosophy of this period contributes to India what we call "the gift of the secular." We examine specifically a set of strategies that Indian scholars adopted in a range of disciplines—including the social sciences, visual arts, poetics, philosophy, politics, and religion—that led India to a rich an enduring form of secular modernity.

We begin by considering the context within which philosophy was pursued in this period, a context constituted by The British Raj. While Indian philosophy enjoyed a long history prior to the arrival of the British, at least as long as that of Western philosophy, until the late 19th century it was predominantly scholastic. Despite the fact that its *content* was often independent of specifically religious views, its *practice* was closely associated with religious schools.

---

* We thank Margaret Dodge, Francesca King, Kendra Ralston, and Shama Rahman for comments on an earlier draft of this essay and for research assistance on this project.

1. Bhattacharyya, "Svaraj in Ideas," present volume 106.

The British higher education system and the European discipline of Oriental studies brought the practice of philosophy into the secular domain. Universities brought with them departments of philosophy—for the most part focused on Western philosophy, but with some attention to Indian philosophy as well. These departments were staffed by eminent Indian scholars whose work demonstrates their solid training both in Western and in classical Indian philosophy. At the same time, Western Orientalists introduced a systematic and philological secularized study of classical Indian philosophy, producing critical editions and scholarly studies of Sanskrit classics outside of the confines of the *maths.*

The encounter between Indian and Western philosophy as well as that between traditional Indian academic forms and the British university system generated a new self-consciousness in the Indian philosophical world. What had been regarded as a primarily *religious* activity was secularized; what had been regarded as essentially an *Indian* activity came to be seen as but one of several world traditions, at the same time, Indian identity came to be seen as consisting in part in an intellectual and ideological core, distinct from, but coequal with, that of Western culture. This dialectic between the development of a distinct Indian identity and the demand for an equal role for India and Indians on a global stage emerged as a central theme in the development of Indian self-consciousness.

The development of this self-consciousness was the central ideological project in the Indian struggle against British colonialism. This struggle began the moment the East India Company gained its foothold, and developed focus after the rebellion of 1857. This in turn required the creation of a definition of a national identity that could lay claim to such loyalty, requiring the diverse people of the subcontinent, never comprised by a unified nation since the fall of the Ashokan empire, to come to see themselves in *national,* as opposed to regional, religious, or caste terms. Theorizing and prosecuting this struggle preoccupied Indian civil society until independence in 1947.

The development of a narrative of origins, and of the Indian cultural essence, was a promising strategy and was deployed with great success by cultural icons and political leaders alike. But this was a not a single strategy as much as a meta-strategy, implemented in different ways with different agendas by various influential figures in the colonial Indian intelligentsia. We see three important, and importantly different, implementations in the hands of A. K. Coomaraswamy, Aurobindo Ghosh, and Jawarharlal Nehru.

Coomaraswamy (1909) writes:

> The whole of Indian culture is so pervaded with this idea of India as the LAND, that it has never been necessary to insist upon it overmuch, for no-one could have supposed it otherwise....

> And just in such wise, are all of the different parts of India bound together by a common historical tradition and ties of spiritual kinship; none can be spared, nor can any live independent of the others. (pp. 70–71 of present volume)

In this essay, Coomaraswamy develops a narrative of Indian unity grounded in geographical and cultural identity, an identity that links contemporary (that is, colonial) India to Vedic India in an unbroken continuum. Aurobindo Ghosh develops a narrative of Indian unity and identity in a slightly different register. In "Is India Civilized" (1918/1968), while Aurobindo agrees with Coomaraswamy that the foundation of India's identity is to be found in its spiritual link to its Vedic past, he emphasizes neither geographical continuity nor a history of the interdependence of distinct Indian cultures, but rather a persistent spiritual orientation that expresses itself in each embodiment of actual Indian culture:

> India, though its urge is towards the Eternal, since that is always the highest, the eternally real, still contains in her own culture and her own philosophy, a supreme reconciliation of the eternal and the temporal…and she need not seek it from outside. (p. 6)

These spiritual approaches to a narrative of Indian identity contrast dramatically with the narrative developed by Nehru, despite the fact that Nehru shares with Coomaraswamy and Aurobindo a drive to seek that identity in Vedic roots. In *The Discovery of India* (1946), Nehru develops a historical narrative according to which India enjoys a continuous *national, political* identity from the Indus Valley civilization to the present day. The narrative is breathtaking as much for its creativity as for its rhetorical success. For present purposes, it is important to note that Nehru, drawing on the three decades of cultural development that lie between the work of the early nationalists and his own pre-independence meditations, takes up the theme of historical national identity not in religious terms, but in explicitly secular terms. Inasmuch as the canonical origin in all of these nationalist narratives was identified as Vedic culture, and inasmuch as that culture is articulated through a set of philosophical traditions, philosophy had a central role to play in this project. But inasmuch as this project also required a secular identity in order to unite diverse religious communities, philosophy needed secularization.

The creative juxtaposition, and often fusion, of Indian and Western philosophy thus served several purposes at once. First, it enabled the legitimization of Indian philosophy as part of a global enterprise. Second, it provided a model for a secular Indian philosophy independent of the *maths*. Finally, it made possible an ideological dimension to the articulation of Indian national identity. This ideology promised to unify disparate communities behind ideas both distinctively Indian and competitive in a global intellectual economy.

It is therefore not surprising that this period is enormously philosophically fecund, in virtue of the cross-fertilization of classical Indian philosophy, Indian religious revival, revolutionary politics and the infusion into India of Western ideas and models of academic life. It is only surprising that the work of this period is not better known.

2. *Methodological Pluralism and Pluralistic Secularism*

It is instructive in this context to consider James Mill's approach to the study of civilizations in his infamous *The History of British India* (1858). Mill claimed to adopt an *objective* approach to the location of civilizations on the cultural spectrum. As a follower of Jeremy Bentham, he took himself to be a man of science, approaching this question from the privileged perspective of the scientific method. He was the dispassionate observer, intellectually and emotionally independent and distant from any particular culture and civilization (including his own!). From this perspective, the issue of whether, to what extent, or in what respects civilizations were equal or unequal was to be settled objectively by the investigation rather than presupposed at the outset. The goal of the investigation, after all, was the ranking.

While the construction of a league table of cultures might appear to be the epitome of comparison, it is not. Instead, is an exercise in *evaluation*. The questions asked are not about similarities or differences of arguments or positions, with the goal of learning what one culture or tradition might contribute to another, or of what range of differences in perspective are possible on a question. Instead, they are questions about relative sophistication, relative distance from the primitive.

The fatal flaw in this application of the 'objective' method, of course, as was recognized even at the time, consists at least in the fact that it relied on the investigators' own intuitions in selecting and then interpreting the data at hand, simultaneously presupposing the *objectivity* of the external observer and his occupation of the highest rung on the ladder of civilization. The consequence of the deployment of such an apparently objective 'comparative' method by Mill was a reiteration and reinscription of British hegemony. Thus, his 'comparative' method amounted to justifying the expansion of a particular view of culture and civilization. It is ironic that James Mill's *History* was taken up, even by Indians, as the definitive account of British India for many generations to come (Mill, 1817/1858).

B. N. Seal's approach was very different. He introduced comparison as a device in the practice of philosophy. From the perspective of the 21st century, comparison seems a bit quaint and dated as a philosophical method, enshrining archaic Archimedean fulcra and visions of discrete cultures. In the context of the colonial presence in India, however, the strategy of comparison had staggering intellectual and political potential and indeed came to play a formidable role in Indian philosophical thought. Indeed, it was radical, in that it presupposed equality at the outset, and it had the consequence of generating an interest in and respect for cultural pluralism and diversity. "Comparison," Seal argued, "*implies* that the objects compared are of co-ordinate rank" (McEvilley, 2002, p. ix, italics added). His point could hardly be missed. Regardless of the fruits of comparison, the very act of comparison in India *presumed* the equality of Indian and Western philosophy, of Indian and Western culture, in effect anticipating what would become the distinctive approach in anthropology as articulated by Boaz in 1893.

This approach, which involved comparison, was the first step toward a cultural pluralism, and toward what we now recognize as a cosmopolitan attitude to cultures. It is significant that this initial move to comparison was a move away from a prereflective assumption of the truth of one's own beliefs, the rationality of one's own rituals and practices, and led to a valuation both of diversity of practice and ideology and of cultural commonalities. For comparison required a focus on the descriptive details of actual beliefs and practices, which in turn led away from transcendent concerns and toward the daily, the practical. This shift in focus thus led to a greater interest in the similarities between the different societies (among particular Indian communities as well as between India and the West) and in turn contributed to the creation of a shared secular space in which the interests of very different religious, social, and cultural groups coincided and in which they could engage in dialogue.

In India the context for this turn away from orthodoxy to secularity was provided in part by the great social reform movements that swept India at this time, originating in Bengal and in the Punjab, the Brahmo Samaj and the Arya Samaj. Each focused not only on religious questions—doctrinal, hermeneutic, and ritual—but also on the social fabric of daily life in India. Each rejected practices that they deemed unjust, irrational, and unbecoming to an emerging modern India, such as caste restrictions, child marriage, sati, and so on. Each was simultaneously, almost paradoxically, both modernist and deeply traditionalist. On the one hand, they each drew inspiration from liberal democratic ideas and Protestant religious institutions, and on the other hand, each was concerned to develop and reinforce the narrative of Indian culture as constituted by roots in a shared Vedic past, looking to the ancient sacred texts as a purer and richer source of Indian ideas than the subsequent religious and philosophical scholastic texts, which grounded the conservative social institutions these samaj movements were concerned to criticize.

Ram Mohan Roy, founder of the Brahmo Samaj, is simultaneously the founder of the comparative method in the social sciences. In his writings and in his social activism, Roy strove to develop a productive interreligious dialogue between Christianity and Hinduism as well as a new, rationalist approach to Indian religion. His method was always to develop a neutral space in which theological and philosophical debate could occur (in English—despite his fluency in Bengali, Sanskrit, Persian, and Arabic) absent commitment to any particular religious tradition. In an era of missionary activity and state-authorized communal division, Roy pioneered the idea of the secular on the subcontinent. Roy conducted himself not as a Christian, but as a modern thinker, an equal party in debates with the missionaries. He presented Indian ideas so that they might be considered in their own right in a public dialectical space, not simply so that they might be assessed and evaluated by Christians. Roy emphasizes the unity of humanity as well as the distinctive contribution of Indian civilization to modernity, just as does Seal in his advocacy of the comparative method (Collet, 1900/1962; Kotnala, 1975).

The Arya Samaj movement was a cradle for social reformers. Its emphasis on concrete action and service inspired political theorists such as Lajpat Rai, arguably the founder of the Young India movement. This movement was internationalist in character, with important connections to the Young Ireland movement, and ideological foundations both in liberal democratic theory and socialism. Arya Samaj also delivered to India Mulk Raj Anand. Anand is today best known for his fiction—the politically charged novels such as *Untouchable* and *Coolie*—but his oeuvre is much broader, including systematic work in aesthetics (the field of his academic chair) and art criticism (he founded and edited India's leading journal of modern art, *Marg*). Anand's philosophical contributions and contributions to the Indian art world are every bit as important to the development of Indian thought in the preindependence period as are his literary contributions, as again, they develop in a secular space political ideas that have their origins in the Modernism of Dayananda Saraswati's religious reform movement. Through this social and intellectual engagement, what began one Shiva Ratri as a religious reform movement became a pillar of Indian secular society.

In the rise of comparative philosophy in the academy and in the activity of the samaj movements on a broader social and religious scale, we see the same apparently paradoxical objectives, brought together in the service of constructing a modern Indian identity. Continuity with classical Indian ideas is valorized, but modern liberalism and internationalism are also celebrated. Internationalism and liberalism at once provide a context in which

Indian ideas can be seen as coequal with those of the West and a direction in which Indian ideas can receive a trajectory demonstrating their continued vitality. This curious combination of classicism and Modernism introduced by the samaj movements permeated Indian intellectual life, inflecting politics, philosophy, and the visual and literary arts. An examination of its impact in literature is instructive as a background to our consideration of the role of philosophy in this cultural process.

3. *Tagore's Poetics*

Among the most prominent intellectuals to arise from the Brahmo Samaj movement was the first President of the Indian Philosophical Congress, Rabindranath Tagore, who also enjoyed a career on the side as a poet, philosopher, and educator. Tagore's own explicit aesthetic theory represents a fairly straightforward endorsement of the broad outlines of Abhināvagupta's theory of *rasa* and *bhāva*. His greatest philosophical influence, however, derives not from his academic work, but from his poetry and fiction (Das, 1996). Examining this corpus shows how Tagore, reflecting the ideology of the Brahmo Samaj, contributed to a sense of Indian intellectual and artistic life as at once continuous with a classical tradition and engaged with the modern world.

Tagore's synthesis of the classical *kāvya* structure and rhythm with Whitman's transcendentalism and cadences allowed him to present to the world Indian literary art that could claim to be as Indian as that of Tulsidas, as modernist and as forward looking as that of Whitman, and as much a part of the global mainstream as that of Yeats. In Tagore's enormously popular poetic and musical stage dramas, we find a revival of the *mahākāvya* form, albeit often with contemporary thematic material, demonstrating the vitality of this classical Indian dramatic form during the renaissance period. His revival of this classical form in vernacular Bengali placed classical Indian cultural tropes at the centre of his contemporary culture.

Tagore's place in Indian intellectual history underscores the centrality of language to that history. Tagore's native language, and the language in which much, though not all, of his poetry was originally presented, was, of course, Bengali. This was a double-edged sword. On the one hand, it elevated vernacular Indian writing and so assisted in breaking the hold of Sanskrit over high art, helping to usher another dimension of modernity into Indian art. On the other hand, Bengali was a *regional* language, and this meant that for Tagore's work to have *national*, as well as *international* impact, it had to be rendered into what was, ironically, the only *national Indian* language, English. By producing translations of his own work into English, and by writing some originally in English, Tagore transformed that language from a convenient subcontinent *lingua franca* into an instrument of Indian self-expression.

Tagore hence achieved a very public fusion of the Indian classical tradition, the romantic tradition at the center of highbrow English culture, and the democratic, progressive, and prophetic tradition of the new world. This fusion was apparent not only to a Bengali audience, but to a pan-Indian audience, Indian and British alike. Moreover, especially after the Nobel Prize and the subsequent global popularity of *Gitānjali*, it was apparent to a global audience as well. It demonstrated that Indian culture, continuous with its classical tradition, was not degenerate, but flourishing; that its flourishing did not consist in a mere recovery and representation of ancient texts, themes, or forms, but in its progressive development in dialogue with other contemporary global cultural forms; and that India was not isolated from modernity, but part of it, contributing its own voice to world conversations. The English language is thus no mere instrument of expression, or even of colonial domination, but, in the hands of writers from Roy to the present day, becomes the vehicle that enables a literate Indian engagement with modernity. English, paradoxically, enabled a progressive nationalism, and a nationalist progressivism embodied in literary production.

4. The Visual Arts, Artists, and Art Criticism

Revivalism and Modernism, the two major and opposing approaches to art in India, were each motivated by the colonial context. E. B. Havell is the best known of the Revivalists, functioning first as Principal of the Art School in Madras in 1884 and later on as Principal of the Calcutta School in 1896. Havell had very specific ideas about Indian art and art education that captured the core of the Revivalist approach: first, that Indian art was so thoroughly interwoven with Indian philosophy and religion that one could only understand and make Indian art if one were already immersed in these disciplines; second, that traditional Indian art was based fundamentally on idealized images rather than on visual images (Havell, 1964).

Havell's nemesis was the Bombay art school, which, he argued, in adopting the technique of academic realism, revealed a lack of appreciation for the rich and unique heritage of Indian art as it rushed to imitate Western formal painterly techniques. Ravi Varma, one of the Bombay School's most famous alumni, was indicted by the Revivalist art critics like Coomaraswamy and Nivedita on just these points (Coomaraswamy, 1994).

Abanindranath Tagore was the most influential of the Tagores on the Indian visual art scene and a poster child for the Revivalists. This was a form of Revivalism that was quite self-consciously inflected by Indian nationalism. But while Tagore was a Revivalist both in his writings about his artwork and as a member of the Calcutta school sympathetic to Havell's ideas, many of his paintings reveal a borrowing and blending of techniques and a sensibility that is often rather different from his stated views. In A. Tagore's work, we see what would in effect become the self-conscious aesthetic attitude of the modernists who succeeded him like Jamini Roy, Amrita Sher-Gil, and, curiously, his uncle R. Tagore, who took to painting in a serious way in his later years: a more cosmopolitan view of what constituted authentic Indianness in the realm of the arts. Once again, then, we see this curious use of reference to the classical Indian heritage as a vehicle for Modernism.

While Indian Revivalism initially had an important role to play in colonial India, it had a short life span. Not only art historians, but also other intellectuals, took serious issue with Havell's claim of a radical difference between the East and the West in the field of art and aesthetics. This move away from the notion of radical difference in the arts was simultaneously a move toward a more integrated way of viewing the Indian nation and its relation to the rest of the world. B. K. Sarkar, for instance, argued that—far from being radically different in virtue of being essentially tied to philosophy, religion, and culture—art was in fact subject to its own universal laws of form and color, and the mechanisms of color construction, color harmony, spacing, and grouping are among the universal laws of *rasa-vidya* or aesthetics that one finds both in East and West (1932, p. 167 this volume).

Sarkar therefore encouraged artists to experiment with techniques across the global cultural spectrum and rejected the criticism that this amounted to denationalization, arguing to the contrary that this was the way for India *as a nation* to take its rightful place and be a legitimate player in the modern global cultural arena. While some of his views were and remain controversial, Sarkar's criticism of Revivalism in the art world was shown to be right on target. He showed that Modernism ushered in a very different attitude toward Western techniques and subjects. He saw that these techniques were not a threat to Indian art but sources of its enrichment. We explore these themes in greater detail in "An Indian in Paris," later in the present volume.

So far we have been emphasizing diverse strands of the progressive secularization of classical Indian culture in the context of Indian engagement with modernity during the colonial period. We have seen these processes at work in Roy's and Seal's conception of comparison. The comparative project they initiate anticipates the contributions to secularization we have observed in the visual and literary arts and even in the development of social movements whose sources are explicitly religious. We now turn to the role of academic philosophy in this complex social and intellectual process. We will see that professional Indian philosophers, although certainly devoted religious practitioners in their private lives, brought the philosophical ideas that emerge from ancient Indian religious traditions into a secular space in the university.

5. *Public versus Private in Practice*

We noted above both the historical association of philosophy with religious practice in India and the importance of the secularization of philosophy in its role in the broader project of nation building. How did this work out in practice? We know from a variety of sources, including public biographical data (Kulkarni, 1986, 1997; Pandey, 1994) and interviews we have conducted with some of their children and students (G. N. Mukerji, interview with the authors, 2007; P. K. Sen, interview with the authors, 2007), that many of the prominent academic philosophers of this period were devout religious practitioners. R. D. Ranade, for instance, in retirement established and led an ashram. He has religious followers to this day. Gopinath Bhattacharyya is well known for his piety and Hindu orthodoxy. A. C. Mukerji was a stalwart supporter of temples and had a reputation as a singer of *bhajans* at religious festivals.

This private piety, however, is strikingly invisible in the published work and in the academic leadership of Ranade, Mukerji, and Bhattacharyya, and in our interviews, their students report that their religious commitments were never expressed in the classroom. Ranade was a great scholar of classical Greek philosophy and Western philosophy of science, as well as an expert on Buddhist and Vedānta philosophy. His approach to the latter is every bit as philosophical, judicious, and critical as is his approach to the pre-Socratics or early modern Western philosophy. Nothing betrays a life that would lead him later to be referred to as the sainted Gurudev (Kulkarni, 1986, 1997).

A. C. Mukerji built his career in the philosophy of mind and psychology and led the University of Allahabad's department in a mission devoted primarily to the study of the history of Western philosophy. While much of his own philosophical problematic derives from Vedānta, that problematic is pursued in dialogue with Western voices and in the pursuit of purely epistemological and metaphysical questions. His interlocutors are philosophers, including both classical sources such as Śankara and Śriharṣa (Mukerji, 1928), and Indian contemporaries and Western philosophers such as Kant, Caird, and other idealists (Mukerji, 1925, 1931), rather than religious figures in the orthodox tradition. Gopinath Bhattacharyya was renowned for his personal religious orthodoxy but wrote exclusively on Western themes in epistemology and the philosophy of language and founded the Jadavpur philosophy department in Calcutta, for which he designed a predominantly Western curriculum. As Indian philosophy was and is studied in Jadavpur, it is again studied philosophically, not religiously (P. K. Sen, interview with the authors, 2007).

This pattern is common among the major philosophers of this period. Most were personally pious, but academically secular. This double existence can be seen in retrospect to have been valuable at two levels. First, at the ground level, this explicit dissociation of professional Indian philosophy from religious practice was necessary both in order for Indian philosophy to be taken seriously internationally, and in order for Indian philosophy to constitute a unifying force on the subcontinent. If these texts and ideas were to be of more than parochial interest, it was necessary to separate them explicitly from the personal religious commitments and practices of those who were teaching and writing about them.

Their students noticed this. We know this both from memoirs (Kulkarni, 1986, 1997) and from our interviews. Could it be that this double existence itself had demonstrative value? Were these scholars modeling a way of taking up with modernity while maintaining continuity with the Indian traditions in which they were raised? It is hard to know the degree to which this was intentional, but it is hard not to speculate that it was. These philosophers were in the process of creating a liberal civil society, ironically modeled in large part on the libertarian ideas inherited from the British who were so derelict in their conformity to the ideas they bequeathed to India. Their own practice demonstrated the importance of the distinction between the private and public spheres so fundamental to liberal civil society. Given the degree to which so much of the independence movement was dominated by individuals or movements explicitly religious in nature, it was essential to the development of India as a liberal democracy that the academy provide a counterpoint demonstration of the observation of this distinction.

6. *The Jāli between the Math and the Academy*

This distinction, however, was not so much a brick wall as a loosely woven screen, establishing a boundary, but admitting fresh air, and even a bit of unanticipated dust. Much that passed through from the religious side is constitutive of the distinctly Indian character of philosophical work of this period. Our research has revealed that many of the major academic philosophers of the preindependence period, despite their carefully cultivated public secularism, made regular trips to consult with Sri Aurobindo Ghosh, the great exponent of Advaita Vedānta in the early decades of the 20th century, at his ashram in Pondicherry. We don't know what they discussed, and it is possible that the pilgrimages were purely personal, private religious affairs. But there is reason to think that they were more than that.[2]

As we argue in "Bringing Brahman Down to Earth," in the present volume, one of the distinctive features of much of the most creative Indian philosophy in the preindependence period is the revival of Advaita Vedānta and the development of a conversation between Advaita and various strands of Western idealism, including Kantian transcendental idealism and Bradley's absolute idealism. Aurobindo was largely responsible for popularizing the *līlāvāda,* as opposed to *māyāvāda,* most clearly in *The Life Divine.* It is significant that when we examine the way Advaita Vedānta was advanced by such philosophers as Malkani, Nikam, Hiriyanna, Mukerji, and Indrasen, we see that all adopt an approach that fits much more comfortably with the *līlāvāda* rather than with the *māyāvāda* perspective. And most, if not all, traveled to Pondicherry. While we cannot demonstrate that it was Aurobindo's influence that led them to this perspective, the circumstantial evidence is compelling and gains greater strength from the fact that the Indian Philosophical Congress found it important to host an all-India symposium addressing the question, "Has Aurobindo Refuted *Māyāvāda?*" We return to this in detail in our later essay.

This infusion of philosophy with ideas derived from religious leaders and schools is, of course, nothing new. Philosophy in India has, as we noted above, long been prosecuted as a religious activity. Religious institutions and leaders have always contributed to Indian philosophical dialogues, and religious leaders such as Sri Aurobindo and his contemporary Swami Vivekananda and the Ramakrishna Mission contributed a vision of how to develop Advaita in the modern era, and so, by continuing a long tradition of religious involvement in Indian philosophy, helped to keep Indian philosophy, albeit secular, decidedly Indian.

This transition from attention to philosophical texts and ideas in an explicitly religious context to a more abstract and secular presentation of those ideas is characteristic of the development of Indian philosophy in this period and marks the particular way in which the interplay of classical reference and Modernism in the development of Indian cultural identity works itself out in philosophy.

---

2. We know, for instance, from an interview with Professor Indra Sen's daughter, Professor Aster Patel, that Aurobindo specifically charged Indersen with the task of mediating between the religious and academic Vedānta communities; it is also significant that all of the participants in the academic symposium held at the philosophical research center at Amalner under the auspices of the Indian Philosophical Congress were visitors to Pondicherry.

7. *The Politics of Young India and the Construction of a Secular Indian Nation*

So far, we have examined the process of secularization as a means for the creation of a public discourse in the arts and in philosophy. But the whole point of a public discourse in the context of a struggle for national identity is the creation of a shared political space. The artistic and philosophical movements of this period are framed by a coordinate shift from the religious to the secular in the political context. Young India, under the leadership of Lajpat Rai, originated as an activist counterpoint to the then more conservative Indian National Congress. Its history, connections with other nationalist movements, such as Young Ireland and eventual rapprochement with the Congress, need not detain us now. We are, however, interested in how Lajpat Rai, in his stillborn masterpiece *Young India,* rhetorically recruits what might appear to be religious movements for secular nationalist purposes. In a chapter entitled "Types of Nationalists," after scouting what he calls "extremist"(1917, p. 141) positions that advocate armed insurrection, Rai shifts his attention to two, what might be prima facie, surprising types of nationalists: the "mother worshippers" and "Vedāntists," (pp. 144–150).

What is significant about taking "mother worship" to be a specifically nationalist phenomenon in the context of the freedom movement? Rai quotes B. C. Pal, another Young India activist: "The so-called idolatry of Hinduism is also passing through a mighty transfiguration. The process started really with Bankim Chandra, who interpreted the most popular of the Hindu goddesses as symbolic of the different stages of national evolution" (p. 144). After a tour of the iconography of Durga, in which Rai, following Pal, maps the different manifestations of Durga onto distinct moments in Indian nationalism, Rai concludes, "This wonderful transfiguration of the old gods and goddesses is carrying the message of new nationalism to the women and the masses of the country" (146). In this transfiguration we see both the choice of popular *religious* imagery as a rhetorical starting point, and the conscious *secularization* of that imagery in the service of the development of national consciousness.

Rai's discussion of Vedānta follows this model, seeing a transformation of a religious movement into a secular nationalist movement. He begins by asserting the affinities of Vedānta to Hegelianism (pp. 146–147), emphasizing its implications for social life. He concludes "[Vedānta] demands, consequently, a social, an economic, and a political reconstruction... The spiritual note of the present Nationalist Movement in India is entirely derived form this Vedāntic thought" (p. 148). In the discussion that follows, Rai explicitly takes on Swami Vivekananda as a political ally, arguing that he inspired "a slow and silent process of the liberalization of the old social ideas. The old bigotry that anathematized the least deviation from the rules of caste, or the authority of custom, is giving way to a new tolerance. The imperious necessities of national struggle and national life are slowly breaking down, except in ceremonial affairs, the old restrictions of caste" (p. 148).

Once again, Rai's approach, following the lead of Ramakrishna and his followers, is to begin his discourse in the temple, but to end in a public, secular, common ground. Whereas in the case of "mother-worshippers" the transfiguration is iconographic, in the case of the Vedāntists, it is straightforwardly ideological. But in each case, the trajectory is obvious and deliberate. In these discussions, as well as in the subsequent consideration of the politics of the more radical Har Dayal (pp. 151–157), Rai emphasizes constantly the ways in which religious ideas are secularized in the service of nationalism. Indeed, R. D. Ranade, in a bitter screed against Har Dayal, agrees with Rai (who is more favorably disposed) that Har Dayal aims to develop a social theory grounded in Vedānta but at the same time aims to jettison the bhakti tradition he takes as its ground. The kind of secularization Rai applauds Ranade deplores (1956, pp. 166–184). Young India was first and foremost a political movement and an assertion of national identity; although religion played a (complex and problematic) role in the development of this movement, it never adopted religious revival as a route to independence. Instead, it adapted religious ideas to generate secular cultural, literary, and political ideas in order to construct a distinctly pluralistic secular space in the context of British colonial rule.

Despite the plurality of voices involved in the early nationalist movement, a single figure rises to prominence in most discussions of Indian national independence: M. K. Gandhi. Now, it might seem that Gandhi is the obvious icon, not for the *secularization* of Indian philosophy and politics, but for *religious revivalism.* Indeed, he is often read this way, given his regular scriptural references and his justified reputation for orthodox devotion. His central conceptual categories were *swaraj* and *satyāgraha*—*self-rule* and *insistence on* (or *grasping*) *truth.* Each term has distinctly Hindu resonance, harking especially to the *Bhagavad Gītā.* Despite this religious resonance, however, Gandhi's conception of *swaraj* and the method of *satyāgraha* are more plausibly viewed as constituting a distinctly *Indian,* rather than a specifically *religious,* approach to the problem of truth. Gandhi grounds his political philosophy and his conception of the *political* struggle for *swaraj* in his reading of the account of *individual mokṣa* in the *Gītā.* This account draws both on the importance of *karma-yoga* and on the account of the relationship of the individual to a complex cosmos.

The genius of Gandhi was to take these ideas from a text that was deeply *religious,* and to secularize these as *Indian* ideas in an *Indian* political context. The *Gītā's* vision of the unity of the personal self with the cosmos is transformed in Gandhi's hands into a claim that an individual's identity is bound up with that of others, and that *responsibility* is hence universal in scope. The theophany of the *Gītā*, in which the universe is revealed as infinitely complex, becomes Gandhi's insight that, while we all aspire to the truth, none of us can claim to seize much of it, and hence that we never have enough to justify violence, or to allow us to ignore the views of others.

While Gandhi insists on the unity of truth, he also insists on the irreducible multiplicity of perspectives on it. *Karma-yoga* is tied in the *Gītā* via *svādharma* to *varna*. Gandhi releases it from this religious mooring and constructs a *universal svādharma*, a fundamental duty to selfless action that derives from our joint political and social situation. Gandhi hence starts from specifically *Hindu roots* but cultivates a distinctly *Indian* form of nationalism available to *all* Indians, regardless of religious persuasion (Gandhi, 1905/2008).

The Bengali polymath Benoy Kumar Sarkar might at first seem like a counterexample to this account of the centrality of nationalism to the development of Indian secularism. After all, in *The Futurism of Young Asia*, he defends a striking *internationalism*, treating with disdain those who would advance the "hypothesis as to the 'Indianness' of Indian inspiration, that is, the distinctiveness of Hindu (or Indian?) genius," (1922, p. 168 this volume) and urging that this would be as bizarre as an Indian physics or chemistry! His consideration of Indian art in the context of his critique of Indian nationalism is intended to articulate a distinctive vision of a secular Indian *cosmopolitanism*. This vision is apparently grounded not in the evolution of distinctively Indian ideas, but rather on a broad internationalism and a concern to see India as a member of a modern Asian community of nations. Where Gandhi saw *Young India*, Sarkar saw *Young Asia*.

Nonetheless, Sarkar's Asia embraces India, and India as a *nation*. Sarkar develops a sustained argument for a conception of a pluralistic India that rises above "subjectivism, pessimism and religiosity" (1922, p. 297). "There is no one India," he writes, "there are Indias" (1922, p. 298). He documents the heterogeneity of Indian historical, cultural, and religious experience; the distinct approaches to modernity in the different disciplines from chemistry, to literature, to politics; and articulates a vision of an India that is united in virtue of, rather than despite, its heterogeneity, in its hopes for its future as a nation. His pluralism, in the end, is not a *counterpoint* to nationalism, but rather a version of a secular nationalism.

Sarkar and Gandhi, despite their difference regarding an underlying Indian *cultural homogeneity*, hence share a vision of a secular nation constructed on the ground of a public space in which none can claim a privileged position. While Sarkar's enthusiasm for Modernism contrasts starkly with Gandhi's suspicion of modernity, they join in a repudiation of Indian parochialism and a commitment to an ultimately secular interpretation of the political ideas they advance.

8. *Conclusion*

We have argued that India's own intellectuals during the British Raj bequeathed to India the gift of the secular, a secularity that turns out to be an arresting form of modernity. Far from eschewing any link to religion, this form of secular Modernism invites a specific rendering of the relationship of religion to public life and provides an avenue for a religious practice that is as diverse as one might wish for (in one's private life) as it simultaneously facilitates a public discourse that embodies an Indianness grounded in India's diverse religious traditions, but that transcends that very diversity and that religiosity. It is hence a form of secular modernity that is insistent on retaining its ties both to religion and to tradition. The growth of Indian intellectual life consists in a persistent effort to develop what might appear to be parochial insights in the service of the creation of a secular public space.

The cradle of the Indian renaissance is often located in the revival of Vedānta, in the rise of the samaj movements, in the teachings of the great saints of the late 19th and early 20th centuries, in the art of the Bengal school. This is all right as far as it goes. But Indian intellectual life, as we have seen, quickly outgrows that cradle.

References

Aurobindo. 1918/1968. "Is India Civilized?" in *The Foundations of Indian Culture*, 1–41. Pondicherry: Sri Aurobindo Ashram Trust.

Collet, Sophia Dobson. 1900/1962. *The Life and Letters of Raja Rammohun Roy*. Dilip Kumar Biswas and Prabhat Chandra Ganguli, Eds. Calcutta: Sadharan Brahmo Samaj.

Coomaraswamy, Ananda K. 1994. *Art and Swadeshi*. New Delhi: Munshiram Manoharlal Publishers Private Limited.

Das, Sisir Kumar. 1996. *The English Writings of Rabindranath Tagore, Vol. 1–3*. New Delhi: Sahitya Akademi.

Gandhi, MK. 2008. *Hind Swaraj and Other Essays*. Cambridge, UK: Cambridge University Press.

Havell, E.B. 1964. *The Art Heritage of India*. Bombay: D.B. Taraporevala Sons & Company.

Kotnala, M.C. 1975. *Raja Ram Mohun Roy and Indian Awakening*. New Delhi: Gītānjali Prakashan.

Kulkarni, B.R. 1986. *Professor R.D. Ranade as a Teacher and Author*. Bijapur: Shri Gurudev Ranade Samadhi Trust.

Kulkarni, B.R., Ed. 1997. *Gurudev R.D. Ranade: A Glance at His Allahabad University Days and Other Essays*. Maharashtra: Mrs. Sunanda Shintre and Mrs. Ashwini Jog.

McEvilley, Thomas. 2002. *The Shape of Ancient Thought: Comparative Studies in Greek and Indian Philosophies.* New York: Allworth Press.

Mill, James. 1817/1858. *The History of British India.* London: Piper, Stephenson and Spence.

Mukerji, A.C. 1925. "The Realism of David Hume in Relation to Contemporary Philosophy." *Allahabad University Journal* 1: 213–234.

Mukerji, A.C. 1928. "Some Aspects of the Absolutism of Shankaracharya." *Allahabad University Journal* 4: 375–429.

Mukerji, A.C. 1931. "James Ward's Analysis of Experience." *Allahabad University Journal* 7: 336–368.

Mukerji, Dr. G.N. 2007. Personal interview by Bhushan and Garfield. Allahabad.

Nehru, Jawaharlal. 1946/2004. *The Discovery of India.* New Delhi: Penguin Books.

Pandey, S.L. 1994. "The Legacy of Professor A.C. Mukerji." Paper presented at the Inaugural of Professor A.C. Mukerji Memorial Lecture, at University of Allahabad, Allahabad, India.

Rai, Lajpat. 1917. *Young India: An Interpretation and History of the Nationalist Movement from Within.* London: British Auxiliary.

Ranade, R.D. 1956. *Philosophical and Other Essays, Part I.* Jamkhandi: Shri Gurudev Ranade Satkar Samiti.

Sarkar, Benoy K. 1922. *The Futurism of Young Asia and Other Essays on the Relations between the East and the West.* Berlin: Julius Springer.

Sen, P.K. 2007. Personal interview by Bhushan and Garfield. Kolkata.

2

Nationalism in India

OUR REAL PROBLEM in India is not political. It is social. This is a condition not only prevailing in India, but among all nations. I do not believe in an exclusive political interest. Politics in the West have dominated Western ideals, and we in India are trying to imitate you. We have to remember that in Europe, where peoples had their racial unity from the beginning, and where natural resources were insufficient for the inhabitants, the civilization has naturally taken the character of political and commercial aggressiveness. For on the one hand they had no internal complications, and on the other they had to deal with neighbours who were strong and rapacious. To have perfect combination among themselves and a watchful attitude of animosity against others was taken as the solution of their problems. In former days they organized and plundered, in the present age the same spirit continues—and they organize and exploit the whole world.

But from the earliest beginnings of history, India has had her own problem constantly before her—it is the race problem. Each nation must be conscious of its mission and we, in India, must realize that we cut a poor figure when we are trying to be political, simply because we have not yet been finally able to accomplish what was set before us by our providence.

This problem of race unity which we have been trying to solve for so many years has likewise to be faced by you here in America. Many people in this country ask me what is happening as to the caste distinctions in India. But when this question is asked me, it is usually done with a superior air. And I feel tempted to put the same question to our American critics with a slight modification, 'What have you done with the Red Indian and the Negro?' For you have not got over your attitude of caste toward them. You have used violent methods to keep aloof from other races, but until you have solved the question here in America, you have no right to question India.

In spite of our great difficulty, however, India has done something. She has tried to make an adjustment of races, to acknowledge the real differences between them where these exist, and yet seek for some basis of unity. This basis has come through our saints, like Nanak, Kabir, Chaitanya and others, preaching one God to all races of India.

In finding the solution of our problem we shall have helped to solve the world problem as well. What India has been, the whole world is now. The whole world is becoming one country through scientific facility. And the moment is arriving when you also must find a basis of unity which is not political. If India can offer to the world her solution, it will be a contribution to humanity. There is only one history—the history of man. All national histories are merely chapters in the larger one. And we are content in India to suffer for such a great cause.

Each individual has his self-love. Therefore his brute instinct leads him to fight with others in the sole pursuit of his self-interest. But man has also his higher instincts of sympathy and mutual help. The people who are lacking in this higher moral power and who therefore cannot combine in fellowship with one another must perish or live in a state of degradation. Only those peoples have survived and achieved civilization who have this spirit of cooperation strong in them. So we find that from the beginning of history men had to choose between fighting with one another and combining, between serving their own interest or the common interest of all.

In our early history when the geographical limits of each country and also the facilities of communication were small, this problem was comparatively small in dimension. It was sufficient for men to develop their sense of unity within their area of segregation. In those days they combined among themselves and fought against others. But it was this moral spirit of combination which was the true basis of their greatness, and this fostered their art, science and religion. At that early time the most important fact that man had to take count of was the fact of the members of one particular race of men coming in close contact with one another. Those who truly grasped this fact through their higher nature made their mark in history.

The most important fact of the present age is that all the different races of men have come close together. And again we are confronted with two alternatives. The problem is whether the different groups of peoples shall go on fighting with one another or find out some true basis of reconciliation and mutual help; whether it will be interminable competition or cooperation.

I have no hesitation in saying that those who are gifted with the moral power of love and vision of spiritual unity, who have the least feeling of enmity against aliens, and the sympathetic insight to place themselves in the position of others will be the fittest to take their permanent place in the age that is lying before us, and those who are constantly developing their instinct of fight and intolerance of aliens will be eliminated. For this is the problem before us, and we have to prove our humanity by solving it through the help of our higher nature. The gigantic organizations for hurting others and warding off their blows, for making money by dragging others back, will not help us. On the contrary, by their crushing weight, their enormous cost and their deadening effect upon the living humanity they will seriously impede our freedom in the larger life of a higher civilization.

During the evolution of the Nation the moral culture of brotherhood was limited by geographical boundaries, because at that time those boundaries were true. Now they have become imaginary lines of tradition divested of the qualities of real obstacles. So the time has come when man's moral nature must deal with this great fact with all seriousness or perish. The first impulse of this change of circumstance has been the churning up of man's baser passions of greed and cruel hatred. If this persists indefinitely and armaments go on exaggerating themselves to unimaginable absurdities, and machines and store-houses envelop this fair earth with their dirt and smoke and ugliness, then it will end in a conflagration of suicide. Therefore man will have to exert all his power of love and clarity of vision to make another great moral adjustment which will comprehend the whole world of men and not merely the fractional groups of nationality. The call has come to every individual in the present age to prepare himself and his surroundings for this dawn of a new era when man shall discover his soul in the spiritual unity of all human beings.

If it is given at all to the West to struggle out of these tangles of the lower slopes to the spiritual summit of humanity, then I cannot but think that it is the special mission of America to fulfil this hope of God and man. You are the country of expectation, desiring something else than what is. Europe has her subtle habits of mind and her conventions. But America, as yet, has come to no conclusions. I realize how much America is untrammeled by the traditions of the past, and I can appreciate that experimentalism is a sign of America's youth. The foundation of her glory is in the future, rather than in the past; and if one is gifted with the power of clairvoyance, one will be able to love the America that is to be.

America is destined to justify Western civilization to the East. Europe has lost faith in humanity, and has become distrustful and sickly. America, on the other hand, is not pessimistic or blasé. You know, as a people, that there is such a thing as a better and a best; and that knowledge drives you on. There are habits that are not merely passive but aggressively arrogant. They are not like mere walls but are like hedges of stinging nettles. Europe has been cultivating these hedges of habits for long years till they have grown round her dense and strong and high. The pride of her traditions has sent its roots deep into her heart. I do not wish to contend that it is unreasonable. But pride in every form breeds blindness at the end. Like all artificial stimulants its first effect is a heightening of consciousness and then with the increasing dose it muddles it and brings in exultation that is misleading. Europe has gradually grown hardened in her pride of all her outer and inner habits. She not only cannot forget that she is Western, but she takes every opportunity to hurl this fact against others to humiliate them. This is why she is growing incapable of imparting to the East what is best in herself, and of accepting in a right spirit the wisdom that the East has stored for centuries.

In America national habits and traditions have not had time to spread their clutching roots round your hearts. You have constantly felt and complained of its disadvantages when you compared your nomadic restlessness with the settled traditions of Europe—the Europe which can show her picture of greatness to the best advantage because she can fix it against the background of the Past. But in this present age of transition, when a new era of civilization is sending its trumpet call to all peoples of the world across an unlimited future, this very freedom of detachment will enable you to accept its invitation and to achieve the goal for which Europe began her journey but lost herself midway. For she was tempted out of her path by her pride of power and greed of possession.

Not merely your freedom from habits of mind in the individuals but also the freedom of your history from all unclean entanglements fits you in your career of holding the banner of civilization of the future. All the great nations of Europe have their victims in other parts of the world. This not only deadens their moral sympathy but also their intellectual sympathy, which is so necessary for the understanding of races which are different from one's own. Englishmen can never truly understand India because their minds are not disinterested with regard to that country. If you compare England with Germany or France you will find she has produced the smallest number of scholars who have studied Indian literature and philosophy with any amount of sympathetic insight or thoroughness. This attitude of apathy and contempt is natural where the relationship is abnormal and founded upon national selfishness and pride. But your history has been disinterested and that is why you have been able to help Japan in her lessons in Western civilization and that is why China can look upon you with her best confidence in this her darkest period of danger. In fact you are carrying all the responsibility of a great future because you are untrammeled by the grasping miserliness of a past. Therefore of all countries of the earth America has to be fully conscious of this future, her vision must not be obscured and her faith in humanity must be strong with the strength of youth.

A parallelism exists between America and India—the parallelism of welding together into one body various races.

In my country, we have been seeking to find out something common to all races, which will prove their real unity. No nation looking for a mere political or commercial basis of unity will find such a solution sufficient. Men of thought and power will discover the spiritual unity, will realize it, and preach it.

India has never had a real sense of nationalism. Even though from childhood I had been taught that the idolatry of Nation is almost better than reverence for God and humanity, I believe I have outgrown that teaching, and it is my conviction that my countrymen will gain truly their India by fighting against that education which teaches them that a country is greater than the ideals of humanity.

The educated Indian at present is trying to absorb some lessons from history contrary to the lessons of our ancestors. The East, in fact, is attempting to take unto itself a history which is not the outcome of its own living. Japan, for example, thinks she is getting powerful through adopting Western methods, but, after she has exhausted her inheritance, only the borrowed weapons of civilization will remain to her. She will not have developed herself from within.

Europe has her past. Europe's strength therefore lies in her history. We, in India, must make up our minds that we cannot borrow other people's history, and that if we stifle our own, we are committing suicide. When you borrow things that do not belong to your life, they only serve to crush your life.

And therefore I believe that it does India no good to compete with Western civilization in its own field. But we shall be more than compensated if, in spite of the insults heaped upon us, we follow our own destiny.

There are lessons which impart information or train our minds for intellectual pursuits. These are simple and can be acquired and used with advantage. But there are others which affect our deeper nature and change our direction of life. Before we accept them and pay their value by selling our own inheritance, we must pause and think deeply. In man's history there come ages of fireworks which dazzle us by their force and movement. They laugh not only at our modest household lamps but also at the eternal stars. But let us not for that provocation be precipitate in our desire to dismiss our lamps. Let us patiently bear our present insult and realize that these fireworks have splendour but not permanence, because of the extreme explosiveness which is the cause of their power, and also of their exhaustion. They are spending a fatal quantity of energy and substance compared to their gain and production.

Anyhow our ideals have been evolved through our own history and even if we wished we could only make poor fireworks of them, because their materials are different from yours, as is also their moral purpose. If we cherish the desire of paying our all for buying a political nationality it will be as absurd as if Switzerland had staked her existence in her ambition to build up a navy powerful enough to compete with that of England. The mistake that we make is in thinking that man's channel of greatness is only one—the one which has made itself painfully evident for the time being by its depth of insolence.

We must know for certain that there is a future before us and that future is waiting for those who are rich in moral ideals and not in mere things. And it is the privilege of man to work for fruits that are beyond his immediate reach, and to adjust his life not in slavish conformity to the examples of some present success or even to his own prudent past, limited in its aspiration, but to an infinite future bearing in its heart the ideals of our highest expectations.

We must, however, know it is providential that the West has come to India. Yet, some one must show the East to the West, and convince the West that the East has her contribution to make in the history of civilization. India is no beggar of the West. And yet even though the West may think she is, I am not for thrusting off Western civilization and becoming segregated in our independence. Let us have a deep association. If Providence wants England to be the channel of that communication, of that deeper association, I am willing to accept it with all humility. I have great faith in human nature, and I think the West will find its true mission. I speak bitterly of Western civilization when I am conscious that it is betraying its trust and thwarting its own purpose. The West must not make herself a curse to the world by using her power for her own selfish needs, but by teaching the ignorant and helping the weak, by saving herself from the worst danger that the strong is liable to incur by making the feeble to acquire power enough to resist her intrusion. And also she must not make her materialism to be the final thing, but must realize that she is doing a service in freeing the spiritual being from the tyranny of matter.

I am not against one nation in particular, but against the general idea of all nations. What is the Nation?

It is the aspect of a whole people as an organized power. This organization incessantly keeps up the insistence of the population on becoming strong and efficient. But this strenuous effort after strength and efficiency drains man's energy from his higher nature where he is self-sacrificing and creative. For thereby man's power of sacrifice is diverted from his ultimate object, which is moral, to the maintenance of this organization, which is mechanical. Yet in this he feels all the satisfaction of moral exaltation and therefore becomes supremely dangerous to humanity. He feels relieved of the urging of his conscience when he can transfer his responsibility to this machine which is the creation of his intellect and not of his complete moral personality. By this device the people which loves freedom perpetuates slavery in a large portion of the world with the comfortable feeling of pride of having done its duty; men who are naturally just can be cruelly unjust both in their act and their thought, accompanied by a feeling that they are helping the world in receiving its deserts; men who are honest can blindly go on robbing others of their human rights for self-aggrandizement, all the while abusing the deprived for not deserving better treatment. We have seen in our everyday life even small organizations of business and profession produce callousness of feeling in men who are not naturally bad, and we can well imagine what a moral havoc it is causing in a world where whole peoples are furiously organizing themselves for gaining wealth and power.

Nationalism is a great menace. It is the particular thing which for years has been at the bottom of India's troubles. And inasmuch as we have been ruled and dominated by a nation that is strictly political in its attitude, we have tried to develop within ourselves, despite our inheritance from the past, a belief in our eventual political destiny.

There are different parties in India, with different ideals. Some are struggling for political independence. Others think that the time has not arrived for that, and yet believe that India should have the rights that the English colonies have. They wish to gain autonomy as far as possible.

In the beginning of our history of political agitation in India there was not that conflict between parties which there is to-day. In that time there was a party known as the Indian Congress; it had no real programme. They had a few grievances for redress by the authorities. They wanted larger representation in the Council House, and more freedom in the Municipal government. They wanted scraps of things, but they had no constructive ideal. Therefore I was lacking in enthusiasm for their methods. It was my conviction that what India most needed was constructive work coming from within herself. In this work we must take all risks and go on doing our duties which by right are ours, though in the teeth of persecution; winning moral victory at every step, by our failure, and suffering. We must show those who are over us that we have the strength of moral power in ourselves, the power to suffer for truth. Where we have nothing to show, we only have to beg. It would be mischievous if the gifts we wish for were granted to us *right* now, and I have told my countrymen, time and time again, to combine for the work of creating opportunities to give vent to our spirit of self-sacrifice, and not for the purpose of begging.

The party, however, lost power because the people soon came to realize how futile was the half policy adopted by them. The party split, and there arrived the Extremists, who advocated independence of action, and discarded the begging method,—the easiest method of relieving one's mind from his responsibility towards his country. Their ideals were based on Western history. They had no sympathy with the special problems of India. They did not recognize the patent fact that there were causes in our social organization which made the Indian incapable of coping with the alien. What would we do if, for any reason, England was driven away? We should simply be victims for other nations. The same social weaknesses would prevail. The thing we, in India, have to think of is this—to remove those social customs and ideals which have generated a want of self-respect and a complete dependence on those above us,—a state of affairs which has been brought about entirely by the domination in India of the caste system, and the blind and lazy habit of relying upon the authority of traditions that are incongruous anachronisms in the present age.

Once again I draw your attention to the difficulties India has had to encounter and her struggle to overcome them. Her problem was the problem of the world in miniature. India is too vast in its area and too diverse in its races. It is many countries packed in one geographical receptacle. It is just the opposite of what Europe truly is, namely one country made into many. Thus Europe in its culture and growth has had the advantage of the strength of the many, as well as the strength of the one. India, on the contrary, being naturally many, yet adventitiously one has all along suffered from the looseness of its diversity and the feebleness of its unity. A true unity is like a round globe, it rolls on, carrying its burden easily; but diversity is a many-cornered thing which has to be dragged and pushed with all force. Be it said to the credit of India that this diversity was not her own creation; she has had to accept it as a fact from the beginning of her history. In America and Australia, Europe has simplified her problem by almost exterminating the original population. Even in the present age this spirit of extermination is making itself manifest, by inhospitably shutting out aliens, through those who themselves were aliens in the lands they now occupy. But India tolerated difference of races from the first, and that spirit of toleration has acted all through her history.

Her caste system is the outcome of this spirit of toleration. For India has all along been trying experiments in evolving a social unity within which all the different peoples could be held together, yet fully enjoying the freedom of maintaining their own differences. The tie has been as loose as possible, yet as close as the circumstances permitted. This has produced something like a United States of a social federation, whose common name is Hinduism.

India had felt that diversity of races there must be and should be whatever may be its drawback, and you can never coerce nature into your narrow limits of convenience without paying one day very dearly for it. In this India was right; but what she failed to realize was that in human beings differences are not like the physical barriers of mountains, fixed forever—they are fluid with life's flow, they are changing their courses and their shapes and volume.

Therefore in her caste regulations India recognized differences, but not the mutability which is the law of life. In trying to avoid collisions she set up boundaries of immovable walls, thus giving to her numerous races the negative benefit of peace and order but not the positive opportunity of expansion and movement. She accepted nature where it produces diversity, but ignored it where it uses that diversity for its world-game of infinite permutations and combinations. She treated life in all truth where it is manifold, but insulted it where it is ever moving. Therefore Life departed from her social system and in its place she is worshipping with all ceremony the magnificent cage of countless compartments that she has manufactured.

The same thing happened where she tried to ward off the collisions of trade interests. She associated different trades and professions with different castes. It had the effect of allaying for good the interminable jealousy and hatred of competition—the competition which breeds cruelty and makes the atmosphere thick with lies and deception. In this also India laid all her emphasis upon the law of heredity, ignoring the law of mutation, and thus gradually reduced arts into crafts and genius into skill.

However, what Western observers fail to discern is that in her caste system India in all seriousness accepted her responsibility to solve the race problem in such a manner as to avoid all friction, and yet to afford each race freedom within its boundaries. Let us admit in this India has not achieved a full measure of success. But this you must also concede, that the West, being more favourably situated as to homogeneity of races, has never given her attention to this problem, and whenever confronted with it she has tried to make it easy by ignoring it altogether. And this is the source of her anti-Asiatic agitations for depriving the aliens of their right to earn their honest living on these shores. In most of your colonies you only admit them on condition of their accepting the menial position of hewers of wood and drawers of water. Either you shut your doors against the aliens or reduce them into slavery. And this is your solution of the problem of race-conflict. Whatever may be its merits you will have to admit that it does not spring from the higher impulses of civilization, but from the lower passions of greed and hatred. You say this is human nature—and India also thought she knew human nature when she strongly barricaded her race distinctions by the fixed barriers of social gradations. But we have found out to our cost that human nature is not what it seems, but what it is in truth; which is in its infinite possibilities. And when we in our blindness insult humanity for its ragged appearance it sheds its disguise to disclose to us that we have insulted our God. The degradation which we cast upon others in our pride or self-interest degrades our own humanity—and this is the punishment which is most terrible because we do not detect it till it is too late.

Not only in your relation with aliens but also with the different sections of your own society you have not brought harmony of reconciliation. The spirit of conflict and competition is allowed the full freedom of its reckless career. And because its genesis is the greed of wealth and power it can never come to any other end but a violent death. In India the production of commodities was brought under the law of social adjustments. Its basis was cooperation having for its object the perfect satisfaction of social needs. But in the West it is guided by the impulse of competition whose end is the gain of wealth for individuals. But the individual is like the geometrical line; it is length without breadth. It has not got the depth to be able to hold anything permanently. Therefore its greed or gain can never come to finality. In its lengthening process of growth it can cross other lines and cause entanglements, but will ever go on missing the ideal of completeness in its thinness of isolation.

In all our physical appetites we recognize a limit. We know that to exceed that limit is to exceed the limit of health. But has this lust for wealth and power no bounds beyond which is death's dominion? In these national carnivals of materialism are not the Western peoples spending most of their vital energy in merely producing things and neglecting the creation of ideals? And can a civilization ignore the law of moral health and go on in its endless process of inflation by gorging upon material things? Man in his social ideals naturally tries to regulate his appetites, subordinating them to the higher purpose of his nature. But in the economic world our appetites follow no other restrictions but those of supply and demand which can be artificially fostered, affording individuals opportunities for indulgence in an endless feast of grossness. In India our social instincts imposed restrictions upon our appetites,—maybe it went to the extreme of repression,—but in the West, the spirit of the economic organization having no moral purpose goads the people into the perpetual pursuit of wealth;—but has this no wholesome limit?

The ideals that strive to take form in social institutions have two objects. One is to regulate our passions and appetites for harmonious development of man, and the other is to help him in cultivating disinterested love for his fellow-creatures. Therefore society is the expression of moral and spiritual aspirations of man which belong to his higher nature.

Our food is creative, it builds our body; but not so wine, which stimulates. Our social ideals create the human world, but when our mind is diverted from them to greed of power then in that state of intoxication we live in a world of abnormality where our strength is not health and our liberty is not freedom. Therefore political freedom does not give us freedom when our mind is not free. An automobile does not create freedom of movement, because it is a mere machine. When I myself am free I can use the automobile for the purpose of my freedom.

We must never forget in the present day that those people who have got their political freedom are not necessarily free, they are merely powerful. The passions which are unbridled in them are creating huge organizations of slavery in the disguise of freedom. Those who have made the gain of money their highest end are unconsciously selling their life and soul to rich persons or to the combinations that represent money. Those who are enamoured of their political power and gloat over their extension of dominion over foreign races gradually surrender their own freedom and humanity to the organizations necessary for holding other peoples in slavery. In the so-called free countries the majority of the people are not free, they are driven by the minority to a goal which is not even known to them. This becomes possible only because people do not acknowledge moral and spiritual freedom as their object. They create huge eddies with their passions and they feel dizzily inebriated with the mere velocity of their whirling movement, taking that to be freedom. But the doom which is waiting to overtake them is as certain as death—for man's truth is moral truth and his emancipation is in the spiritual life.

The general opinion of the majority of the present day nationalists in India is that we have come to a final completeness in our social and spiritual ideals, the task of the constructive work of society having been done several thousand years before we were born, and that now we are free to employ all our activities in the political direction. We never dream of blaming our social inadequacy as the origin of our present helplessness, for we have accepted as the creed of our nationalism that this social system has been perfected for all time to come by our ancestors who had the superhuman vision of all eternity, and supernatural power for making infinite provision for future ages. Therefore for all our miseries and shortcomings we hold responsible the historical surprises that burst upon us from outside. This is the reason why we think that our one task is to build a political miracle of freedom upon the quicksand of social slavery. In fact we want to dam up the true course of our own historical stream and only borrow power from the sources of other peoples' history.

Those of us in India who have come under the delusion that mere political freedom will make us free have accepted their lessons from the West as the gospel truth and lost their faith in humanity. We must remember whatever weakness we cherish in our society will become the source of danger in politics. The same inertia which leads us to our idolatry of dead forms in social institutions will create in our politics prison houses with immovable walls. The narrowness of sympathy which makes it possible for us to impose upon a considerable portion of humanity the galling yoke of inferiority will assert itself in our politics in creating tyranny of injustice.

When our nationalists talk about ideals, they forget that the basis of nationalism is wanting. The very people who are upholding these ideals are themselves the most conservative in their social practice. Nationalists say, for example, look at Switzerland, where, in spite of race differences, the peoples have solidified into a nation. Yet, remember that in Switzerland the races can mingle, they can intermarry, because they are of the same blood. In India there is no common birthright. And when we talk of Western Nationality we forget that the nations there do not have that physical repulsion, one for the other, that we have between different castes. Have we an instance in the whole world where a people who are not allowed to mingle their blood shed their blood for one another except by coercion or for mercenary purposes? And can we ever hope that these moral barriers against our race amalgamation will not stand in the way of our political unity?

Then again we must give full recognition to this fact that our social restrictions are still tyrannical, so much so as to make men cowards. If a man tells me he has heterodox ideas, but that he cannot follow them because he would be socially ostracized, I excuse him for having to live a life of untruth, in order to live at all. The social habit of mind which impels us to make the life of our fellow-beings a burden to them where they differ from us even in such a thing as their choice of food is sure to persist in our political organization and result in creating engines of coercion to crush every rational difference which is the sign of life. And tyranny will only add to the inevitable lies and hypocrisy in our political life. Is the mere name of freedom so valuable that we should be willing to sacrifice for its sake our moral freedom?

The intemperance of our habits does not immediately show its effects when we are in the vigour of our youth. But it gradually consumes that vigour, and when the period of decline sets in then we have to settle accounts and pay off our debts, which leads us to insolvency. In the West you are still able to carry your head high though your humanity is suffering every moment from its dipsomania of organizing power. India also in the heyday of her youth could carry in her vital organs the dead weight of her social organizations stiffened to rigid perfection, but it has been fatal to her, and has produced a gradual paralysis of her living nature. And this is the reason why the educated community of India has become insensible of her social needs. They are taking the very immobility of our social structures as the sign of their perfection,—and because the healthy feeling of pain is dead in the limbs of our social organism they delude themselves into thinking that it needs no ministration. Therefore they think that all their energies need their only scope in the political field. It is like a man whose legs have become shrivelled and useless, trying to delude himself that these limbs have grown still because they have attained their ultimate salvation, and all that is wrong about him is the shortness of his sticks.

So much for the social and the political regeneration of India. Now we come to her industries, and I am very often asked whether there is in India any industrial regeneration since the advent of the British Government. It must be remembered that at the beginning of the British rule in India our industries were suppressed and since then we have not met with any real help or encouragement to enable us to make a stand against the monster commercial organizations of the world. The nations have decreed that we must remain purely an agricultural people, even forgetting the use of arms for all time to come. Thus India in being turned into so many predigested morsels of food ready to be swallowed at any moment by any nation which has even the most rudimentary set of teeth in its head.

India, therefore has very little outlet for her industrial originality. I personally do not believe in the unwieldy organizations of the present day. The very fact that they are ugly shows that they are in discordance with the whole creation. The vast powers of nature do not reveal their truth in hideousness, but in beauty. Beauty is the signature which the Creator stamps upon his works when he is satisfied with them. All our products that insolently ignore the laws of perfection and are unashamed in their display of ungainliness bear the perpetual weight of God's displeasure. So far as your commerce lacks the dignity of grace it is untrue. Beauty and her twin brother Truth require leisure, and self-control for their growth. But the greed of gain has no time or limit to its capaciousness. Its one object is to produce and consume. It has neither pity for beautiful nature, nor for living human beings. It is ruthlessly ready without a moment's hesitation to crush beauty and life out of them, moulding them into money. It is this ugly vulgarity of commerce which brought upon it the censure of contempt in our earlier days when men had leisure to have an unclouded vision of perfection in humanity. Men in those times were rightly ashamed of the instinct of mere money-making. But in this scientific age money, by its very abnormal bulk, has won its throne. And when from its eminence of piled-up things it insults the higher instincts of man, banishing beauty and noble sentiments from its surroundings, we submit. For we in our meanness have accepted bribes from its hands and our imagination has grovelled in the dust before its immensity of flesh.

But its unwieldiness itself and its endless complexities are its true signs of failure. The swimmer who is an expert does not exhibit his muscular force by violent movements, but exhibits some power which is invisible and which shows itself in perfect grace and reposefulness. The true distinction of man from animals is in his power and worth which are inner and invisible. But the present-day commercial civilization of man is not only taking too much time and space but killing time and space. Its movements are violent, its noise is discordantly loud. It is carrying its own damnation because it is trampling into distortion the humanity upon which it stands. It is strenuously turning out money at the cost of happiness. Man is reducing himself to his minimum, in order to be able to make amplest room for his organizations. He is deriding his human sentiments into shame because they are apt to stand in the way of his machines.

In our mythology we have the legend that the man who performs penances for attaining immortality has to meet with temptations sent by Indra, the Lord of the immortals. If he is lured by them he is lost. The West has been striving for centuries after its goal of immortality. Indra has sent her the temptation to try her. It is the gorgeous temptation of wealth. She has accepted it and her civilization of humanity has lost its path in the wilderness of machinery.

This commercialism with its barbarity of ugly decorations is a terrible menace to all humanity. Because it is setting up the ideal of power over that of perfection. It is making the cult of self-seeking exult in its naked shamelessness. Our nerves are more delicate than our muscles. Things that are the most precious in us are helpless as babes when we take away from them the careful protection which they claim from us for their very preciousness. Therefore when the callous rudeness of power runs amuck in the broad-way of humanity it scares away by its grossness the ideals which we have cherished with the martyrdom of centuries.

The temptation which is fatal for the strong is still more so for the weak. And I do not welcome it in our Indian life even though it be sent by the lord of the Immortals. Let our life be simple in its outer aspect and rich in its inner gain. Let our civilization take its firm stand upon its basis of social cooperation and not upon that of economic exploitation and conflict. How to do it in the teeth of the drainage of our life-blood by the economic dragons is the task set before the thinkers of all oriental nations who have faith in the human soul. It is a sign of laziness and impotency to accept conditions imposed upon us by others who have other ideals than ours. We should actively try to adapt the world powers to guide our history to its own perfect end.

From the above you will know that I am not an economist. I am willing to acknowledge that there is a law of demand and supply and an infatuation of man for more things than are good for him. And yet I will persist in believing that there is such a thing as the harmony of completeness in humanity, where poverty does not take away his riches, where defeat may lead him to victory, death to immortality, and in the compensation of Eternal Justice those who are the last may yet have their insult transmuted into a golden triumph.

Aurobindo Ghosh, "The Renaissance in India" (1918)

Aurobindo Ghosh (later Sri Aurobindo) (1872–1950) was a central political, religious, and philosophical figure in the Indian renaissance. Bengali born and Cambridge-educated, he was trained in Victorian English literature, sat his Cambridge examinations in classics, and taught English at Baroda College. He became involved in radical politics and while imprisoned discovered Indian philosophy. He spent the remainder of his life at his ashram in Pondicherry, producing an enormous volume of religious and philosophical work, including his masterpiece *The Life Divine*. Many Indian philosophers of the colonial period visited him in Pondicherry, and his influence on Indian philosophy is considerable. In this essay he addresses the meaning of the Indian renaissance for India's national identity.

Aurobindo Ghosh

3

The Renaissance in India

I

There has been recently some talk of a Renaissance in India. A number of illuminating essays with that general title and subject have been given to us by a poet and subtle critic and thinker, Mr. James H. Cousins, and others have touched suggestively various sides of the growing movement towards a new life and a new thought that may well seem to justify the description. This Renaissance, this new birth in India, if it is a fact, must become a thing of immense importance both to herself and the world, to herself because of all that is meant for her in the recovery or the change of her time-old spirit and national ideals, to the world because of the possibilities involved in the rearising of a force that is in many respects unlike any other and its genius very different from the mentality and spirit that have hitherto governed the modern idea in mankind, although not so far away perhaps from that which is preparing to govern the future. It is rather the first point of view that I shall put forward at present: for the question what India means to make of her own life must precede the wider question what her new life may mean to the human race. And it is besides likely to become before long an issue of a pressing importance.

There is a first question, whether at all there is really a Renaissance in India. That depends a good deal on what we mean by the word; it depends also on the future, for the thing itself is only in its infancy and it is too early to say to what it may lead. The word carries the mind back to the turning-point of European culture to which it was first applied; that was not so much a reawakening as an overturn and reversal, a seizure of Christianised, Teutonised, feudalised Europe by the old Graeco-Latin spirit and form with all the complex and momentous results which came from it. That is certainly not a type of renaissance that is at all possible in India. There is a closer resemblance to the recent Celtic movement in Ireland, the attempt of a reawakened national spirit to find a new impulse of self-expression which shall give the spiritual force for a great reshaping and rebuilding: in Ireland this was discovered by a return to the Celtic spirit and culture after a long period of eclipsing English influences, and in India something of the same kind of movement is appearing and has especially taken a pronounced turn since the political outburst of 1905. But even here the analogy does not give the whole truth.

We have to see moreover that the whole is at present a great formless chaos of conflicting influences with a few luminous points of formation here and there where a new self-consciousness has come to the surface. But it cannot be said that these forms have yet a sufficient hold on the general mind of the people. They represent an advance movement; they are the voices of the vanguard, the torchlights of the pioneers. On the whole what we see is a giant Shakti who awakening into a new world, a new and alien environment, finds herself shackled in all her limbs by a multitude of gross or minute bonds, bonds self-woven by her past, bonds recently imposed from outside, and is struggling to be free from them, to arise and proclaim herself, to cast abroad her spirit and set her seal on the world. We hear on every side a sound of the slow fraying of bonds, here and there a sharp tearing and snapping; but freedom of movement has not yet been attained. The eyes are not yet clear, the bud of the soul has only partly opened. The Titaness has not yet arisen.

Mr. Cousins puts the question in his book whether the word renaissance at all applies since India has always been awake and stood in no need of reawakening. There is a certain truth behind that and to one coming in with a fresh mind from outside and struck by the living continuity of past and present India, it may be especially apparent; but that is not quite how we can see it who are her children and are still suffering from the bitter effects of the great decline which came to a head in the eighteenth and nineteenth centuries. Undoubtedly there was a period, a brief but very disastrous period of the dwindling of that great fire of life, even a moment of incipient disintegration, marked politically by the anarchy which gave European adventure its chance, inwardly by an increasing torpor of the creative spirit in religion and art,—science and philosophy and intellectual knowledge had long been dead or petrified into a mere scholastic Punditism,—all pointing to a nadir of setting energy, the evening-time from which according to the Indian idea of the cycles a new age has to start. It was that moment and the pressure of a superimposed European culture which followed it that made the reawakening necessary.

We have practically to take three facts into consideration, the great past of Indian culture and life with the moment of inadaptive torpor into which it had lapsed, the first period of the Western contact in which it seemed for a moment likely to perish by slow decomposition, and the ascending movement which first broke into some clarity of expression only a decade or two ago. Mr. Cousins has his eye fixed on Indian spirituality which has always maintained itself even in the decline of the national vitality; it was certainly that which saved India always at every critical moment of her destiny, and it has been the starting-point too of her renascence. Any other nation under the same pressure would have long ago perished soul and body. But certainly the outward members were becoming gangrened; the powers of renovation seemed for a moment to be beaten by the powers of stagnation, and stagnation is death. Now that the salvation, the reawakening has come, India will certainly keep her essential spirit, will keep her characteristic soul, but there is likely to be a great change of the body. The shaping for itself of a new body, of new philosophical, artistic, literary, cultural, political, social forms by the same soul rejuvenescent will, I should think, be the type of the Indian renascence,—forms not contradictory of the truths of life which the old expressed, but rather expressive of those truths restated, cured of defect, completed.

What was this ancient spirit and characteristic soul of India? European writers, struck by the general metaphysical bent of the Indian mind, by its strong religious instincts and religious idealism, by its other-worldliness, are inclined to write as if this were all the Indian spirit. An abstract, metaphysical, religious mind overpowered by the sense of the infinite, not apt for life, dreamy, unpractical, turning away from life and action as *Māya*, this, they said, is India; and for a time Indians in this as in other matters submissively echoed their new Western teachers and masters. They learned to speak with pride of their metaphysics, of their literature, of their religion, but in all else they were content to be learners and imitators. Since then Europe has discovered that there was too an Indian art of remarkable power and beauty; but the rest of what India meant it has hardly at all seen. But meanwhile the Indian mind began to emancipate itself and to look upon its past with a clear and self-discerning eye, and it very soon discovered that it had been misled into an entirely false self-view. All such one-sided appreciations indeed almost invariably turn out to be false. Was it not the general misconception about Germany at one time, because she was great in philosophy and music, but had blundered in life and been unable to make the most of its materials, that this was a nation of unpractical dreamers, idealists, erudites and sentimentalists, patient, docile and industrious certainly, but politically inapt,—"admirable, ridiculous Germany"? Europe has had a terrible awakening from that error. When the renascence of India is complete, she will have an awakening, not of the same brutal kind, certainly, but startling enough, as to the real nature and capacity of the Indian spirit.

Spirituality is indeed the master-key of the Indian mind; the sense of the infinite is native to it. India saw from the beginning,—and, even in her ages of reason and her age of increasing ignorance, she never lost hold of the insight,—that life cannot be rightly seen in the sole light, cannot be perfectly lived in the sole power of its externalities. She was alive to the greatness of material laws and forces; she had a keen eye for the importance of the physical sciences; she knew how to organise the arts of ordinary life. But she saw that the physical does not get its full sense until it stands in right relation to the supra-physical; she saw that the complexity of the universe could not be explained in the present terms of man or seen by his superficial sight, that there were other powers behind, other powers within man himself of which he is normally unaware, that he is conscious only of a small part of himself, that the invisible always surrounds the visible, the suprasensible the sensible, even as infinity always surrounds the finite. She saw too that man has the power of exceeding himself, of becoming himself more entirely and profoundly than he is,—truths which have only recently begun to be seen in Europe and seem even now too great for its common intelligence. She saw the myriad gods beyond man, God beyond the gods, and beyond God his own ineffable eternity; she saw that there were ranges of life beyond our life, ranges of mind beyond our present mind and above these she saw the splendours of the spirit. Then with that calm audacity of her intuition which knew no fear or littleness and shrank from no act whether of spiritual or intellectual, ethical or vital courage, she declared that there was none of these things which man could not attain if he trained his will and knowledge; he could conquer these ranges of mind, become the spirit, become a god, become one with God, become the ineffable *Brahman*. And with the logical practicality and sense of science and organised method which distinguished her mentality, she set forth immediately to find out the way. Hence from long ages of this insight and practice there was ingrained in her her spirituality, her powerful psychic tendency, her great yearning to grapple with the infinite and possess it, her ineradicable religious sense, her idealism, her Yoga, the constant turn of her art and her philosophy.

But this was not and could not be her whole mentality, her entire spirit; spirituality itself does not flourish on earth in the void, even as our mountaintops do not rise like those of an enchantment of dream out of the clouds without a base. When we look at the past of India, what strikes us next is her stupendous vitality, her inexhaustible power of life and joy of life, her almost unimaginably prolific creativeness. For three thousand years at least,—it is indeed much longer,—she has been creating abundantly and incessantly, lavishly, with an inexhaustible many-sidedness, republics and kingdoms and empires, philosophies and cosmogonies and sciences and creeds and arts and poems and all kinds of monuments, palaces and temples and public works, communities and societies and religious orders, laws and codes and rituals, physical sciences, psychic sciences, systems of Yoga, systems of politics and administration, arts spiritual, arts worldly, trades, industries, fine crafts,—the list is endless and in each item there is almost a plethora of activity. She creates and creates and is not satisfied and is not tired; she will not have an end of it, seems hardly to need a space for rest, a time for inertia and lying fallow. She expands too outside her borders; her ships cross the ocean and the fine superfluity of her wealth brims over to Judaea and Egypt and Rome; her colonies spread her arts and epics and creeds in the Archipelago; her traces are found in the sands of Mesopotamia; her religions conquer China and Japan and spread westward as far as Palestine and Alexandria, and the figures of the Upaniṣads and the sayings of the Buddhists are reechoed on the lips of Christ. Everywhere, as on her soil, so in her works there is the teeming of a superabundant energy of life. European critics complain that in her ancient architecture, sculpture and art there is no reticence, no holding back of riches, no blank spaces, that she labours to fill every rift with ore, occupy every inch with plenty. Well, but defect or no, that is the necessity of her superabundance of life, of the teeming of the infinite within her. She lavishes her riches because she must, as the Infinite fills every inch of space with the stirring of life and energy because it is the Infinite.

But this supreme spirituality and this prolific abundance of the energy and joy of life and creation do not make all that the spirit of India has been in its past. It is not a confused splendour of tropical vegetation under heavens of a pure sapphire infinity. It is only to eyes unaccustomed to such wealth that there seems to be a confusion in this crowding of space with rich forms of life, a luxurious disorder of excess or a wanton lack of measure, clear balance and design. For the third power of the ancient Indian spirit was a strong intellectuality, at once austere and rich, robust and minute, powerful and delicate, massive in principle and curious in detail. Its chief impulse was that of order and arrangement, but an order founded upon a seeking for the inner law and truth of things and having in view always the possibility of conscientious practice. India has been preeminently the land of the *Dharma* and the *Śāstra.* She searched for the inner truth and law of each human or cosmic activity, its dharma; that found, she laboured to cast into elaborate form and detailed law of arrangement its application in fact and rule of life. Her first period was luminous with the discovery of the Spirit; her second completed the discovery of the Dharma; her third elaborated into detail the first simpler formulation of the *Śāstra*; but none was exclusive, the three elements are always present.

In this third period the curious elaboration of all life into a science and an art assumes extraordinary proportions. The mere mass of the intellectual production during the period from Aśoka well into the Mahomedan epoch is something truly prodigious, as can be seen at once if one studies the account which recent scholarship gives of it, and we must remember that that scholarship as yet only deals with a fraction of what is still lying extant and what is extant is only a small percentage of what was once written and known. There is no historical parallel for such an intellectual labour and activity before the invention of printing and the facilities of modern science; yet all that mass of research and production and curiosity of detail was accomplished without these facilities and with no better record than the memory and for an aid the perishable palm-leaf. Nor was all this colossal literature confined to philosophy and theology, religion and Yoga, logic and rhetoric and grammar and linguistics, poetry and drama, medicine and astronomy and the sciences; it embraced all life, politics and society, all the arts from painting to dancing, all the sixty-four accomplishments, everything then known that could be useful to life or interesting to the mind, even, for instance, to such practical side minutiae as the breeding and training of horses and elephants, each of which had its *Śāstra* and its art, its apparatus of technical terms, its copious literature. In each subject from the largest and most momentous to the smallest and most trivial there was expended the same all-embracing, opulent, minute and thorough intellectuality. On one side there is an insatiable curiosity, the desire of life to know itself in every detail, on the other a spirit of organisation and scrupulous order, the desire of the mind to tread through life with a harmonised knowledge and in the right rhythm and measure. Thus an ingrained and dominant spirituality, an inexhaustible vital creativeness and gust of life and, mediating between them, a powerful, penetrating and scrupulous intelligence combined of the rational, ethical and aesthetic mind each at a high intensity of action, created the harmony of the ancient Indian culture.

Indeed without this opulent vitality and opulent intellectuality India could never have done so much as she did with her spiritual tendencies. It is a great error to suppose that spirituality flourishes best in an impoverished soil with the life half-killed and the intellect discouraged and intimidated. The spirituality that so flourishes is something morbid, hectic and exposed to perilous reactions. It is when the race has lived most richly and thought most profoundly that spirituality finds its heights and its depths and its constant and many-sided fruition. In modern Europe it is after a long explosion of vital force and a stupendous activity of the intellect that spirituality has begun really to emerge and with some promise of being not, as it once was, the sorrowful physician of the malady of life, but the beginning of a large and profound clarity. The European eye is struck in Indian spiritual thought by the Buddhistic and illusionist denial of life. But it must be remembered that this is only one side of its philosophic tendency which assumed exaggerated proportions only in the period of decline. In itself too that was simply one result, in one direction, of a tendency of the Indian mind which is common to all its activities, the impulse to follow each motive, each specialisation of motive even, spiritual, intellectual, ethical, vital, to its extreme point and to sound its utmost possibility. Part of its innate direction was to seek in each not only for its fullness of detail, but for its infinite, its absolute, its profoundest depth or its highest pinnacle. It knew that without a "fine excess" we cannot break down the limits which the dull temper of the normal mind opposes to knowledge and thought and experience; and it had in seeking this point a boundless courage and yet a sure tread. Thus it carried each tangent of philosophic thought, each line of spiritual experience to its farthest point, and chose to look from that farthest point at all existence, so as to see what truth or power such a view could give it. It tried to know the whole of divine nature and to see too as high as it could beyond nature and into whatever there might be of supradivine. When it formulated a spiritual atheism, it followed that to its acme of possible vision. When, too, it indulged in materialistic atheism,—though it did that only with a side glance, as the freak of an insatiable intellectual curiosity,—yet it formulated it straight out, boldly and nakedly, without the least concession to idealism or ethicism.

Everywhere we find this tendency. The ideals of the Indian mind have included the height of self-assertion of the human spirit and its thirst of independence and mastery and possession and the height also of its self-abnegation, dependence and submission and self-giving. In life the ideal of opulent living and the ideal of poverty were carried to the extreme of regal splendour and the extreme of satisfied nudity. Its intuitions were sufficiently clear and courageous not to be blinded by its own most cherished ideas and fixed habits of life. If it was obliged to stereotype caste as the symbol of its social order, it never quite forgot, as the caste-spirit is apt to forget, that the human soul and the human mind are beyond caste. For it had seen in the lowest human being the Godhead, Nārāyana. It emphasised distinctions only to turn upon them and deny all distinctions. If all its political needs and circumstances compelled it at last to exaggerate the monarchical principle and declare the divinity of the king and to abolish its earlier republican city states and independent federations as too favourable to the centrifugal tendency, if therefore it could not develop democracy, yet it had the democratic idea, applied it in the village, in council and municipality, within the caste, was the first to assert a divinity in the people and could cry to the monarch at the height of his power, "O king, what art thou but the head servant of the demos?" Its idea of the golden age was a free spiritual anarchism. Its spiritual extremism could not prevent it from fathoming through a long era the life of the senses and its enjoyments, and there too it sought the utmost richness of sensuous detail and the depths and intensities of sensuous experience. Yet it is notable that this pursuit of the most opposite extremes never resulted in disorder; and its most hedonistic period offers nothing that at all resembles the unbridled corruption which a similar tendency has more than once produced in Europe. For the Indian mind is not only spiritual and ethical, but intellectual and artistic, and both the rule of the intellect and the rhythm of beauty are hostile to the spirit of chaos. In every extreme the Indian spirit seeks for a law in that extreme and a rule, measure and structure in its application. Besides, this sounding of extremes is balanced by a still more ingrained characteristic, the synthetical tendency, so that having pushed each motive to its farthest possibility the Indian mind returns always towards some fusion of the knowledge it has gained and to a resulting harmony and balance in action and institution. Balance and rhythm which the Greeks arrived at by self-limitation, India arrived at by its sense of intellectual, ethical and aesthetic order and the synthetic impulse of its mind and life.

I have dwelt on these facts because they are apt to be ignored by those who look only at certain sides of the Indian mind and spirit which are most prominent in the last epochs. By insisting only upon these we get an inaccurate or incomplete idea of the past of India and of the integral meaning of its civilisation and the spirit that animated it. The present is only a last deposit of the past at a time of ebb; it has no doubt also to be the starting-point of the future, but in this present all that was in India's past is still dormant, it is not destroyed; it is waiting there to assume new forms. The decline was the ebb-movement of a creative spirit which can only be understood by seeing it in the full tide of its greatness; the renascence is the return of the tide and it is the same spirit that is likely to animate it, although the forms it takes may be quite new. To judge therefore the possibilities of the renascence, the powers that it may reveal and the scope that it may take, we must dismiss the idea that the tendency of metaphysical abstraction is the one note of the Indian spirit which dominates or inspires all its cadences. Its real key-note is the tendency of spiritual realisation, not cast at all into any white monotone, but many-faceted, many-coloured, as supple in its adaptability as it is intense in its highest pitches. The note of spirituality is dominant, initial, constant, always recurrent; it is the support of all the rest. The first age of India's greatness was a spiritual age when she sought passionately for the truth of existence through the intuitive mind and through an inner experience and interpretation both of the psychic and the physical existence. The stamp put on her by that beginning she has never lost, but rather always enriched it with fresh spiritual experience and discovery at each step of the national life. Even in her hour of decline it was the one thing she could never lose.

But this spiritual tendency does not shoot upward only to the abstract, the hidden and the intangible; it casts its rays downward and outward to embrace the multiplicities of thought and the richness of life. Therefore the second long epoch of India's greatness was an age of the intellect, the ethical sense, the dynamic will in action enlightened to formulate and govern life in the lustre of spiritual truth. After the age of the Spirit, the age of the Dhárma; after the Veda and Upaniṣads, the heroic centuries of action and social formation, typal construction and thought and philosophy, when the outward forms of Indian life and culture were fixed in their large lines and even their later developments were being determined in the seed. The great classical age of

Sanskrit culture was the flowering of this intellectuality into curiosity of detail in the refinements of scholarship, science, art, literature, politics, sociology, mundane life. We see at this time too the sounding not only of aesthetic, but of emotional and sensuous, even of vital and sensual experience. But the old spirituality reigned behind all this mental and all this vital activity, and its later period, the post-classical, saw a lifting up of the whole lower life and an impressing upon it of the values of the spirit. This was the sense of the Puranic and Tantric systems and the religions of Bhakti. Later Vaishnavism, the last fine flower of the Indian spirit, was in its essence the taking up of the aesthetic, emotional and sensuous being into the service of the spiritual. It completed the curve of the cycle.

The evening of decline which followed the completion of the curve was prepared by three movements of retrogression. First there is, comparatively, a sinking of that superabundant vital energy and a fading of the joy of life and the joy of creation. Even in the decline this energy is still something splendid and extraordinary and only for a very brief period sinks nearest to a complete torpor; but still a comparison with its past greatness will show that the decadence was marked and progressive. Secondly, there is a rapid cessation of the old free intellectual activity, a slumber of the scientific and the critical mind as well as the creative intuition; what remains becomes more and more a repetition of ill-understood fragments of past knowledge. There is a petrification of the mind and life in the relics of the forms which a great intellectual past had created. Old authority and rule become rigidly despotic and, as always then happens, lose their real sense and spirit. Finally, spirituality remains but burns no longer with the large and clear flame of knowledge of former times, but in intense jets and in a dispersed action which replaces the old magnificent synthesis and in which certain spiritual truths are emphasised to the neglect of others. This diminution amounts to a certain failure of the great endeavour which is the whole meaning of Indian culture, a falling short in the progress towards the perfect spiritualisation of the mind and the life. The beginnings were superlative, the developments very great, but at a certain point where progress, adaptation, a new flowering should have come in, the old civilisation stopped short, partly drew back, partly lost its way. The essential no doubt remained and still remains in the heart of the race and not only in its habits and memories, but in its action it was covered up in a great smoke of confusion. The causes internal and external we need not now discuss; but the fact is there. It was the cause of the momentary helplessness of the Indian mind in the face of new and unprecedented conditions.

It was at this moment that the European wave swept over India. The first effect of this entry of a new and quite opposite civilisation was the destruction of much that had no longer the power to live, the deliquescence of much else, a tendency to the devitalisation of the rest. A new activity came in, but this was at first crudely and confusedly imitative of the foreign culture. It was a crucial moment and an ordeal of perilous severity; a less vigorous energy of life might well have foundered and perished under the double weight of the deadening of its old innate motives and a servile imitation of alien ideas and habits. History shows us how disastrous this situation can be to nations and civilisations. But fortunately the energy of life was there, sleeping only for a moment, not dead, and, given that energy, the evil carried within itself its own cure. For whatever temporary rotting and destruction this crude impact of European life and culture has caused, it gave three needed impulses. It revived the dormant intellectual and critical impulse; it rehabilitated life and awakened the desire of new creation; it put the reviving Indian spirit face to face with novel conditions and ideals and the urgent necessity of understanding, assimilating and conquering them. The national mind turned a new eye on its past culture, reawoke to its sense and import, but also at the same time saw it in relation to modern knowledge and ideas. Out of this awakening vision and impulse the Indian renaissance is arising, and that must determine its future tendency. The recovery of the old spiritual knowledge and experience in all its splendour, depth and fullness is its first, most essential work; the flowing of this spirituality into new forms of philosophy, literature, art, science and critical knowledge is the second; an original dealing with modern problems in the light of the Indian spirit and the endeavour to formulate a greater synthesis of a spiritualised society is the third and most difficult. Its success on these three lines will be the measure of its help to the future of humanity.

The Spirit is a higher infinite of verities; life is a lower infinite of possibilities which seek to grow and find their own truth and fulfilment in the light of these verities. Our intellect, our will, our ethical and our aesthetic being are the reflectors and the mediators. The method of the West is to exaggerate life and to call down as much—or as little—as may be of the higher powers to stimulate and embellish life.[1] But the method of India is on the contrary to discover the spirit within and the higher hidden intensities of the superior powers and to dominate life in one way or another so as to make it responsive to and expressive of the spirit and in that way increase the power of life. Its tendency with the intellect, will, ethical, aesthetic and emotional being is to sound indeed their normal mental possibilities, but also to upraise them towards the greater light and power of their own highest intuitions. The work of the renaissance in India must be to make this spirit, this higher view of life, this sense of deeper potentiality once more a creative, perhaps a dominant

1. Mr. Cousins' distinction between invocation and evocation.

power in the world. But to that truth of itself it is as yet only vaguely awake; the mass of Indian action is still at the moment proceeding under the impress of the European motive and method and, because there is a spirit within us to which they are foreign, the action is poor in will, feeble in form and ineffective in results, for it does not come from the roots of our being. Only in a few directions is there some clear light of self-knowledge. It is when a greater light prevails and becomes general that we shall be able to speak, not only in prospect but in fact, of the renaissance of India.

II

The process which has led up to the renaissance now inevitable, may be analysed, both historically and logically, into three steps by which a transition is being managed, a complex breaking, reshaping and new building, with the final result yet distant in prospect,—though here and there the first bases may have been already laid,—a new age of an old culture transformed, not an affiliation of a new-born civilisation to one that is old and dead, but a true rebirth, a renascence. The first step was the reception of the European contact, a radical reconsideration of many of the prominent elements and some revolutionary denial of the very principles of the old culture. The second was a reaction of the Indian spirit upon the European influence, sometimes with a total denial of what it offered and a stressing both of the essential and the strict letter of the national past, which yet masked a movement of assimilation. The third, only now beginning or recently begun, is rather a process of new creation in which the spiritual power of the Indian mind remains supreme, recovers its truths, accepts whatever it finds sound or true, useful or inevitable of the modern idea and form, but so transmutes and Indianises it, so absorbs and so transforms it entirely into itself that its foreign character disappears and it becomes another harmonious element in the characteristic working of the ancient goddess, the Shakti of India mastering and taking possession of the modern influence, no longer possessed or overcome by it.

Nothing in the many processes of Nature, whether she deals with men or with things, comes by chance or accident or is really at the mercy of external causes. What things are inwardly, determines the course of even their most considerable changes; and timeless India being what she is, the complexity of this transition was predestined and unavoidable. It was impossible that she should take a rapid wholesale imprint of Western motives and their forms and leave the ruling motives of her own past to accommodate themselves to the foreign change as best they could afterwards. A swift transformation scene like that which brought into being a new modernised Japan, would have been out of the question for her, even if the external circumstances had been equally favourable. For Japan lives centrally in her temperament and in her aesthetic sense, and therefore she has always been rapidly assimilative; her strong temperamental persistence has been enough to preserve her national stamp and her artistic vision a sufficient power to keep her soul alive. But India lives centrally in the spirit, with less buoyancy and vivacity and therefore with a less ready adaptiveness of creation, but a greater, intenser, more brooding depth; her processes are apt to be deliberate, uncertain and long because she has to take things into that depth and from its profoundest inwardness to modify or remould the more outward parts of her life. And until that has been done, the absorption completed, the powers of the remoulding determined, she cannot yet move forward with an easier step on the new way she is taking. From the complexity of the movement arises all the difficulty of the problems she has to face and the rather chaotic confusion of the opinions, standpoints and tendencies that have got entangled in the process, which prevents any easy, clear and decided development, so that we seem to be advancing under a confused pressure of circumstance or in a series of shifting waves of impulsion, this ebbing for that to arise, rather than with any clear idea of our future direction. But here too lies the assurance that once the inner direction has found its way and its implications have come to the surface, the result will be no mere Asiatic modification of Western modernism, but some great, new and original thing of the first importance to the future of human civilisation.

This was not the idea of the earliest generation of intellectuals, few in number but powerful by their talent and originative vigour, that arose as the first result of Western education in India. Theirs was the impatient hope of a transformation such as took place afterwards with so striking a velocity in Japan; they saw in welcome prospect a new India modernised wholesale and radically in mind, spirit and life. Intensely patriotic in motive, they were yet denationalised in their mental attitude. They admitted practically, if not in set opinion, the occidental view of our past culture as only a half-civilisation and their governing ideals were borrowed from the West or at least centrally inspired by the purely Western spirit and type of their education. From mediaeval India they drew away in revolt and inclined to discredit and destroy whatever it had created; if they took anything from it, it was as poetic symbols to which they gave a superficial and modern significance. To ancient India they looked back on the contrary with a sentiment of pride, at least in certain directions, and were willing to take from it whatever material they could subdue to their new standpoint, but they could not quite grasp anything of it in its original sense and spirit and strove to rid it of all that would not square with their Westernised intellectuality. They sought for a bare, simplified and rationalised religion, created a literature which imported very eagerly the forms, ideas and whole spirit of their English models,—the value of the other arts was almost entirely ignored,—put their political faith and hope in a wholesale assimilation or rather an exact imitation of the middle-class pseudo-democracy of nineteenth-century England, would have revolutionised Indian society by introducing into it all the social ideas and main features of the European form. Whatever value for the future there may be in the things they grasped at with this eager conviction, their method was, as we now recognise, a false method,—an anglicised India is a thing we can no longer view as either possible or desirable,—and it could only, if pursued to the end, have made us painful copyists, clumsy followers always stumbling in the wake of European evolution and always fifty years behind it. This movement of thought did not and could not endure; something of it still continues, but its engrossing power has passed away beyond any chance of vigorous revival.

Nevertheless, this earliest period of crude reception left behind it results that were of value and indeed indispensable to a powerful renaissance. We may single out three of them as of the first order of importance. It reawakened a free activity of the intellect which, though at first confined within very narrow bounds and derivative in its ideas, is now spreading to all subjects of human and national interest and is applying itself with an increasing curiosity and a growing originality to every field it seizes. This is bringing back to the Indian mind its old unresting thirst for all kinds of knowledge and must restore to it before long the width of its range and the depth and flexible power of its action; and it has opened to it the full scope of the critical faculty of the human mind, its passion for exhaustive observation and emancipated judgment which, in older times exercised only by a few and within limits, has now become an essential equipment of the intellect. These things the imitative period did not itself carry very far, but it cast the germ which we now see beginning to fructify more richly. Secondly, it threw definitely the ferment of modern ideas into the old culture and fixed them before our view in such a way that we are obliged to reckon and deal with them in far other sort than would have been possible if we had simply proceeded from our old fixed traditions without some such momentary violent break in our customary view of things. Finally, it made us turn our look upon all that our past contains with new eyes which have not only enabled us to recover something of their ancient sense and spirit, long embedded and lost in the unintelligent practice of received forms, but to bring out of them a new light which gives to the old truths fresh aspects and therefore novel potentialities of creation and evolution. That in this first period we misunderstood our ancient culture, does not matter; the enforcement of a reconsideration, which even orthodox thought has been obliged to accept, is the fact of capital importance.

The second period of reaction of the Indian mind upon the new elements, its movement towards a recovery of the national poise, has helped us to direct these powers and tendencies into sounder and much more fruitful lines of action. For the anglicising impulse was very soon met by the old national spirit and began to be heavily suffused by its influence. It is now a very small and always dwindling number of our present-day intellectuals who still remain obstinately Westernised in their outlook; and even these have given up the attitude of blatant and uncompromising depreciation of the past which was at one time a common pose. A larger number have proceeded by a constantly increasing suffusion of their modernism with much of ancient motive and sentiment, a better insight into the meaning of Indian things and their characteristics, a free acceptance more of their spirit than of their forms and an attempt at new interpretation. At first the central idea still remained very plainly of the modern type and betrayed everywhere the Western inspiration, but it drew to itself willingly the ancient ideas and it coloured itself more and more with their essential spirit; and latterly this suffusing element has overflooded, has tended more and more to take up and subdue the original motives until the thought and spirit, turn and tinge are now characteristically Indian. The works of Bankim Chandra Chatterji and Tagore, the two minds of the most distinctive and original genius in our recent literature, illustrate the stages of this transition.

Side by side with this movement and more characteristic and powerful there has been flowing an opposite current. This first started on its way by an integral reaction, a vindication and reacceptance of everything Indian as it stood and because it was Indian. We have still waves of this impulse and many of its influences continuing among us; for its work is not yet completed. But in reality the reaction marks the beginning of a more subtle assimilation and fusing; for in vindicating ancient things it has been obliged to do so in a way that will at once meet and satisfy the old mentality and the new, the traditional and the critical mind. This in itself involves no mere return, but consciously or unconsciously hastens a restatement. And the riper form of the return has taken as its principle a synthetical restatement; it has sought to arrive at the spirit of the ancient culture and, while respecting its forms and often preserving them to revivify, has yet not hesitated also to remould, to reject the outworn and to admit whatever new motive seemed assimilable to the old spirituality or apt to widen the channel of its larger evolution. Of this freer dealing with past and present, this preservation by reconstruction Vivekananda was in his life-time the leading exemplar and the most powerful exponent.

But this too could not be the end; of itself it leads towards a principle of new creation. Otherwise the upshot of the double current of thought and tendency might be an incongruous assimilation, something in the mental sphere like the strangely assorted half-European, half-Indian dress which we now put upon our bodies. India has to get back entirely to the native power of her spirit at its very deepest and to turn all the needed strengths and aims of her present and future life into materials for that spirit to work upon and integrate and harmonise. Of such vital and original creation we may cite the new Indian art as a striking example. The beginning of this process of original creation in every sphere of her national activity will be the sign of the integral self-finding of her renaissance.

III

To attempt to penetrate through the indeterminate confusion of present tendencies and first efforts in order to foresee the exact forms the new creation will take, would be an effort of very doubtful utility. One might as well try to forecast a harmony from the sounds made by the tuning of the instrument. In one direction or another we may just detect certain decisive indications, but even these are only first indications and we may be quite sure that much lies behind them that will go far beyond anything that they yet suggest. This is true whether in religion and spirituality or thought and science, poetry and art or society and politics. Everywhere there is, at most, only a beginning of beginnings.

One thing seems at any rate certain, that the spiritual motive will be in the future of India, as in her past, the real originative and dominating strain. By spirituality we do not mean a remote metaphysical mind or the tendency to dream rather than to act. That was not the great India of old in her splendid days of vigour,—whatever certain European critics or interpreters of her culture may say,—and it will not be the India of the future. Metaphysical thinking will always no doubt be a strong element in her mentality, and it is to be hoped that she will never lose her great, her sovereign powers in that direction; but Indian metaphysics are as far removed from the brilliant or the profound idea-spinning of the French or the German mind as from the broad intellectual generalising on the basis of the facts of physical science which for some time did duty for philosophy in modern Europe. It has always been in its essential parts an intellectual approach to spiritual realisation. Though in later times it led too much away from life, yet that was not its original character whether in its early Vedāntic intuitional forms or in those later developments of it, such as the *Gītā*, which belong to the period of its most vigorous intellectual originality and creation. Buddhism itself, the philosophy which first really threw doubt on the value of life, did so only in its intellectual tendency; in its dynamic parts, by its ethical system and spiritual method, it gave a new set of values, a severe vigour, yet a gentler idealism to human living and was therefore powerfully creative both in the arts which interpret life and in society and politics. To realise intimately truth of spirit and to quicken and to remould life by it is the native tendency of the Indian mind, and to that it must always return in all its periods of health, greatness and vigour.

All great movements of life in India have begun with a new spiritual thought and usually a new religious activity. What more striking and significant fact can there be than this that even the new European influence, which was an influence intellectual, rationalistic, so often antireligious and which drew so much of its idealism from the increasingly cosmopolitan, mundane and secularist thought of the eighteenth and nineteenth centuries, precipitated in India from the very first an attempt at religious reformation and led actually to the creation of new religions? The instinct of the Indian mind was that, if a reconstruction of ideas and of society was to be attempted, it must start from a spiritual basis and take from the first a religious motive and form. The Brahmo Samaj had in its inception a large cosmopolitan idea, it was even almost eclectic in the choice of the materials for the synthesis it attempted; it combined a Vedāntic first inspiration, outward forms akin to those of English Unitarianism and something of its temper, a modicum of Christian influence, a strong dose of religious rationalism and intellectualism. It is noteworthy, however, that it started from an endeavour to restate the Vedānta, and it is curiously significant of the way in which even what might be well called a protestant movement follows the curve of the national tradition and temper, that the three stages of its growth, marked by the three churches or congregations into which it split, correspond to the three eternal motives of the Indian religious mind, Jñāna, Bhakti and Karma, the contemplative and philosophical, the emotional and fervently devotional and the actively and practically dynamic spiritual mentality. The Arya Samaj in the Punjab founded itself on a fresh interpretation of the truth of the Veda and an attempt to apply old Vedic principles of life to modern conditions. The movement associated with the great names of Ramakrishna and Vivekananda has been a very wide synthesis of past religious motives and spiritual experience topped by a reaffirmation of the old asceticism and monasticism, but with new living strands in it and combined with a strong humanitarianism and zeal of missionary expansion. There has been too the movement of orthodox Hindu revivalism, more vigorous two or three decades ago than it is now. The rest of India has either felt vibrations of some of these great regional movements or been touched with smaller ones of their own making. In Bengal a strong Neo-Vaishnavic tendency is the most recent development of its religious mind and shows that the preparatory creative activity has not yet finished its workings. Throughout India the old religious sects and disciplines are becoming strongly revitalised, vocal, active, moved to a fresh self-affirmation. Islam has recently shared in the general stirring and attempts to return vitally to the original Islamic ideals or to strike out fresh developments have preceded or accompanied the awakening to life of the long torpid Mussulman mass in India.

Perhaps none of these forms, nor all the sum of them may be definitive, they may constitute only the preparatory self-finding of the Indian spiritual mind recovering its past and turning towards its future. India is the meeting-place of the religions and among these Hinduism alone is by itself a vast and complex thing, not so much a religion as a great diversified and yet subtly unified mass of spiritual thought, realisation and aspiration. What will finally come out of all this stir and ferment, lies yet in the future. There has been an introduction of fresh fruitful impulses to activity: there has been much revival of the vitality of old forms, a new study, rehabilitation, resort to old disciplines and old authorities and scriptures,—we may note that Vedānta, Veda, Purana, Yoga, and recently the same thing is being initiated with regard to the Tantra, have each in their turn been brought back into understanding, if not always yet to a perfect understanding, to practice, to some efficacy on thought and on life; there has been an evolution of enlarging truth and novel forms out of ancient ideas and renewed experience. Whatever the last upshot may be, this spiritual and religious ferment and activity stand out as the most prominent feature of the new India; and it may be observed that while in other fields the tendency has been, until quite recently, more critical than constructive, here every impulse has been throughout powerfully creative. Especially, we see everywhere the tendency towards the return of the spirit upon life; the reassertion of a spiritual living as a foundation for a new life of the nation has been a recognisable impulse. Even asceticism and monasticism are rapidly becoming, no longer merely contemplative, self-centred or aloof, but missionary, educative, humanitarian. And recently in the utterances of the leaders of thought the insistence on life has been growing marked, self-conscious and positive. This is at present the most significant immediate sign of the future. Probably, here lies the key of the Indian renaissance, in a return from forms to the depths of a released spirituality which will show itself again in a pervading return of spirituality upon life.

But what are likely to be the great constructive ideas and the great decisive instruments which this spirituality will take to deal with and govern life, is as yet obscure, because the thought of this new India is still inchoate and indeterminative. Religions, creeds and forms are only a characteristic outward sign of the spiritual impulsion and religion itself is the intensive action by which it tries to find its inward force. Its expansive movement comes in the thought which it throws out on life, the ideals which open up new horizons and which the intellect accepts and life labours to assimilate. Philosophy in India has been the intellectual canaliser of spiritual knowledge and experience, but the philosophical intellect has not as yet decidedly begun the work of new creation; it has been rather busy with the restatement of its past gains than with any new statement which would visibly and rapidly enlarge the boundaries of its thought and aspiration. The contact of European philosophy has not been fruitful of any creative reaction; first because the past philosophies of Europe have very little that could be of any utility in this direction, nothing of the first importance in fact which India has not already stated in forms better suited to her own spiritual temper and genius, and though the thought of Nietzsche, of Bergson and of James has recently touched more vitally just a few minds here and there, their drift is much too externally pragmatic and vitalistic to be genuinely assimilable by the Indian spirit. But, principally, a real Indian philosophy can only be evolved out of spiritual experience and as the fruit of the spiritual seeking which all the religious movements of the past century have helped to generalise. It cannot spring, as in Europe, out of the critical intellect solely or as the fruit of scientific thought and knowledge. Nor has there been very much preparing force of original critical thought in nineteenth century India. The more original intellects have either turned towards pure literature or else been busy assimilating and at most Indianising modern ideas. And though a stronger thought tendency is now beginning, all is yet uncertain flux or brilliantly vague foreshadowing.

In poetry, literature, art, science there have, on the contrary, been definite beginnings. Bengal in these, as in many other directions, has been recently the chief testing crucible or the first workshop of the Shakti of India; it is there she has chosen to cast in the greatest vivacity of new influences and develop her initial forms and inspirations. In the rest of India there is often much activity of production and one hears here and there of a solitary poet or prose-writer of genius or notable talent; but Bengal has already a considerable literature of importance, with a distinct spirit and form, well-based and always developing; she has now a great body of art original, inspired, full of delicate beauty and vision; she has not only two renowned scientists, one of the two world-famous for a central and far-reaching discovery, but a young school of research which promises to count for something in the world's science. It is here therefore that we can observe the trend of the Indian mind and the direction in which it is turning. Especially the art of the Bengal painters is very significant, more so even than the prose of Bankim or the poetry of Tagore. Bengali poetry has had to feel its way and does not seem yet quite definitively to have found it, but Bengal art has found its way at once at the first step, by a sort of immediate intuition.

Partly this is because the new literature began in the period of foreign influence and of an indecisive groping, while art in India was quite silent,—except for the preposterous Ravi Varma interlude which was doomed to sterility by its absurdly barren incompetence,—began in a moment of self-recovery and could profit by a clearer possibility of light. But besides, plastic art is in itself by its very limitation, by the narrower and intense range of its forms and motives, often more decisively indicative than the more fluid and variable turns of literary thought and expression. Now the whole power of the Bengal artists springs from their deliberate choice of the spirit and hidden meaning in things rather than their form and surface meaning as the object to be expressed. It is intuitive and its forms are the very rhythm of its intuition, they have little to do with the metric formalities devised by the observing intellect; it leans over the finite to discover its suggestions of the infinite and inexpressible; it turns to outward life and nature to found upon it lines and colours, rhythms and embodiments which will be significant of the other life and other nature than the physical which all that is merely outward conceals. This is the eternal motive of Indian art, but applied in a new way less largely ideaed, mythological and symbolical, but with a more delicately suggestive attempt at a near, subtle, direct embodiment. This art is a true new creation, and we may expect that the artistic mind of the rest of India will follow through the gate thus opened, but we may expect it too to take on there other characteristics and find other ways of expression; for the peculiar turn and tone given by the Calcutta painters is intimate to the temperament of Bengal. But India is great by the unity of her national coupled with the rich diversity of her regional mind. That we may expect to see reflected in the resurgence of her artistic creativeness.

Poetry and literature in Bengal have gone through two distinct stages and seem to be preparing for a third of which one cannot quite foresee the character. It began with a European and mostly an English influence, a taking in of fresh poetical and prose forms, literary ideas, artistic canons. It was a period of copious and buoyant creation which produced a number of poets and poetesses, one or two of great genius, others of a fine poetic capacity, much work of beauty and distinction, a real opening of the floodgates of Saraswati. Its work was not at all crudely imitative; the foreign influences are everywhere visible, but they are assimilated, not merely obeyed or aped. The quality of the Bengali temperament and its native aesthetic turn took hold of them and poured them into a mould of speech suitable to its own spirit. But still the substance was not quite native to the soul and therefore one feels a certain void in it. The form and expression have the peculiar grace and the delicate plastic beauty which Bengali poetical expression achieved from its beginning, but the thing expressed does not in the end amount to very much. As is inevitable when one does not think or create freely but is principally assimilating thought and form, it is thin and falls short of the greatness which we would expect from the natural power of the poet.

That period is long over, it has lived its time and its work has taken its place in the past of the literature. Two of its creators, one, the sovereign initiator of its prose expression, supreme by combination of original mentality with a flawless artistic gift, the other born into its last glow of productive brilliance, but outliving it to develop another strain and a profounder voice of poetry, released the real soul of Bengal into expression. The work of Bankim Chandra is now of the past, because it has entered already into the new mind of Bengal which it did more than any other literary influence to form; the work of Rabindranath still largely holds the present, but it has opened ways for the future which promise to go beyond it. Both show an increasing return to the Indian spirit in fresh forms; both are voices of the dawn, seek more than they find, suggest and are calling for more than they actually evoke. At present we see a fresh preparation, on one side evolving and promising to broaden out from the influence of Tagore, on the other in revolt against it and insisting on a more distinctively national type of inspiration and creation; but what will come out of it, is not yet clear. On the whole it appears that the movement is turning in the same direction as that of the new art, though with the more flexible utterance and varied motive natural to the spoken thought and expressive word. No utterance of the highest genius, such as would give the decisive turn, has yet made itself heard. But some faint promise of a great imaginative and intuitive literature of a new Indian type is already discernible in these uncertain voices.

In the things of the mind we have then within however limited an area certain beginnings, preparatory or even initially definitive. But in the outward life of the nation we are still in a stage of much uncertainty and confusion. Very largely this is due to the political conditions which have ceased in spirit to be those of the past, but are not yet in fact those of the future. The fever and the strain born from the alternation of waves of aspiration with the reflux of non-fulfilment are not favourable to the strong formulation of a new birth in the national life. All that is as yet clear is that the first period of a superficial assimilation and aping of European political ideas and methods is over. Another political spirit has awakened in the people under the shock of the movement of the last decade which, vehemently national in its motive, proclaimed a religion of Indian patriotism, applied the notions of the ancient religion and philosophy to politics, expressed the cult of the country as mother and Shakti and attempted to base the idea of democracy firmly on the spiritual thought and impulses native to the Indian mind. Crude often and uncertain in its self-expression, organising its effort for revolt against past and present conditions but not immediately successful in carrying forward its methods of constructive development, it still effectively aroused the people and gave a definite turn to its political thought and life, the outcome of which can only appear when the nation has found completely the will and gained sufficiently the power to determine its own evolution.

Indian society is in a still more chaotic stage; for the old forms are crumbling away under the pressure of the environment, their spirit and reality are more and more passing out of them, but the façade persists by the force of inertia of thought and will and the remaining attachment of a long association, while the new is still powerless to be born. There is much of slow and often hardly perceptible destruction, a dull preservation effective only by immobility, no possibility yet of sound reconstruction. We have had a loud proclaiming,—only where supported by religion, as in the reforming Samajes, any strong effectuation,—of a movement of social change, appealing sometimes crudely to Western exemplars and ideals, sometimes to the genius or the pattern of ancient times; but it has quite failed to carry the people, because it could not get at their spirit and itself lacked, with the exceptions noted, in robust sincerity. We have had too a revival of orthodox conservatism, more academic and sentimental than profound in its impulse or in touch with the great facts and forces of life. We have now in emergence an increasing sense of the necessity of a renovation of social ideas and expressive forms by the spirit of the nation awaking to the deeper yet unexpressed implications of its own culture, but as yet no sufficient will or means of execution. It is probable that only with the beginning of a freer national life will the powers of the renaissance take effective hold of the social mind and action of the awakened people.

IV

The renaissance thus determining itself, but not yet finally determined, if it is to be what the name implies, a rebirth of the soul of India into a new body of energy, a new form of its innate and ancient spirit, *prajñā purāṇī*, must insist much more finally and integrally than it has as yet done on its spiritual turn, on the greater and greater action of the spiritual motive in every sphere of our living. But here we are still liable to be met by the remnants of a misunderstanding or a refusal to understand,—it is something of both,—which was perhaps to a little extent justified by certain ascetic or religionist exaggerations, a distrust which is accentuated by a recoil from the excessive otherworldliness that has marked certain developments of the Indian mind and life, but yet is not justified, because it misses the true point at issue. Thus we are sometimes asked what on earth we mean by spirituality in art and poetry or in political and social life,—a confession of ignorance strange enough in any Indian mouth at this stage of our national history,—or how art and poetry will be any the better when they have got into them what I have recently seen described as the "twang of spirituality", and how the practical problems either of society or of politics are going at all to profit by this element. We have here really an echo of the European idea, now of sufficiently long standing, that religion and spirituality on the one side and intellectual activity and practical life on the other are two entirely different things and have each to be pursued on its own entirely separate lines and in obedience to its own entirely separate principles. Again we may be met also by the suspicion that in holding up this ideal rule before India we are pointing her to the metaphysical and away from the dynamic and pragmatic or inculcating some obscurantist reactionary principle of mystical or irrational religiosity and diverting her from the paths of reason and modernity which she must follow if she is to be an efficient and a well-organised nation able to survive in the shocks of the modern world. We must therefore try to make clear what it is we mean by a renaissance governed by the principle of spirituality.

But first let us say what we do not mean by this ideal. Clearly it does not signify that we shall regard earthly life as a temporal vanity, try to become all of us as soon as possible monastic ascetics, frame our social life into a preparation for the monastery or cavern or mountain-top or make of it a static life without any great progressive ideals but only some aim which has nothing to do with earth or the collective advance of the human race. That may have been for some time a tendency of the Indian mind, but it was never the whole tendency. Nor does spirituality mean the moulding of the whole type of the national being to suit the limited dogmas, forms, tenets of a particular religion, as was often enough attempted by the old societies, an idea which still persists in many minds by the power of old mental habit and association; clearly such an attempt would be impossible, even if it were desirable, in a country full of the most diverse religious opinions and harbouring too three such distinct general forms as Hinduism, Islam and Christianity, to say nothing of the numerous special forms to which each of these has given birth. Spirituality is much wider than any particular religion, and in the larger ideas of it that are now coming on us even the greatest religion becomes no more than a broad sect or branch of the one universal religion, by which we shall understand in the future man's seeking for the eternal, the divine, the greater self, the source of unity and his attempt to arrive at some equation, some increasing approximation of the values of human life with the eternal and the divine values.

Nor do we mean the exclusion of anything whatsoever from our scope, of any of the great aims of human life, any of the great problems of our modern world, any form of human activity, any general or inherent impulse or characteristic means of the desire of the soul of man for development, expansion, increasing vigour and joy, light, power, perfection. Spirit without mind, spirit without body is not the type of man, therefore a human spirituality must not belittle the mind, life or body or hold them of small account: it will rather hold them of high account, of immense importance, precisely because they are the conditions and instruments of the life of the spirit in man. The ancient Indian culture attached quite as much value to the soundness, growth and strength of the mind, life and body as the old Hellenic or the modern scientific thought, although for a different end and a greater motive. Therefore to everything that serves and belongs to the healthy fullness of these things, it gave free play, to the activity of the reason, to science and philosophy, to the satisfaction of the aesthetic being and to all the many arts great or small, to the health and strength of the body, to the physical and economical well-being, ease, opulence of the race,—there was never a national ideal of poverty in India as some would have us believe, nor was bareness or squalor the essential setting of her spirituality,—and to its general military, political and social strength and efficiency. Their aim was high, but firm and wide too was the base they sought to establish and great the care bestowed on these first instruments. Necessarily the new India will seek the same end in new ways under the vivid impulse of fresh and large ideas and by an instrumentality suited to more complex conditions; but the scope of her effort and action and the suppleness and variety of her mind will not be less, but greater than of old. Spirituality is not necessarily exclusive; it can be and in its fullness must be all-inclusive.

But still there is a great difference between the spiritual and the purely material and mental view of existence. The spiritual view holds that the mind, life, body are man's means and not his aims and even that they are not his last and highest means; it sees them as his outer instrumental self and not his whole being. It sees the infinite behind all things finite and it adjudges the value of the finite by higher infinite values of which they are the imperfect translation and towards which, to a truer expression of them, they are always trying to arrive. It sees a greater reality than the apparent not only behind man and the world, but within man and the world, and this soul, self, divine thing in man it holds to be that in him which is of the highest importance, that which everything else in him must try in whatever way to bring out and express, and this soul, self, divine presence in the world it holds to be that which man has ever to try to see and recognise through all appearances, to unite his thought and life with it and in it to find his unity with his fellows. This alters necessarily our whole normal view of things; even in preserving all the aims of human life, it will give them a different sense and direction.

We aim at the health and vigour of the body; but with what object? For its own sake, will be the ordinary reply, because it is worth having; or else that we may have long life and a sound basis for our intellectual, vital, emotional satisfactions. Yes, for its own sake, in a way, but in this sense that the physical too is an expression of the spirit and its perfection is worth having, is part of the dharma of the complete human living; but still more as a basis for all that higher activity which ends in the discovery and expression of the divine self in man. *Śarīraṁ khalu dhármasādhanam*, runs the old Sanskrit saying, the body too is our means for fulfilling the dharma, the Godward law of our being. The mental, the emotional, the aesthetic parts of us have to be developed, is the ordinary view, so that they may have a greater satisfaction, or because that is man's finer nature, because so he feels himself more alive and fulfilled. This, but not this only; rather because these things too are the expressions of the spirit, things which are seeking in him for their divine values and by their growth, subtlety, flexibility, power, intensity he is able to come nearer to the divine Reality in the world, to lay hold on it variously, to tune eventually his whole life into unity and conformity with it. Morality is in the ordinary view a well-regulated individual and social conduct which keeps society going and leads towards a better, a more rational, temperate, sympathetic, self-restrained dealing with our fellows. But ethics in the spiritual point of view is much more, it is a means of developing in our action and still more essentially in the character of our being the diviner self in us, a step of our growing into the nature of the Godhead.

So with all our aims and activities; spirituality takes them all and gives them a greater, diviner, more intimate sense. Philosophy is in the Western way of dealing with it a dispassionate enquiry by the light of the reason into the first truths of existence, which we shall get at either by observing the facts science places at our disposal or by a careful dialectical scrutiny of the concepts of the reason or a mixture of the two methods. But from the spiritual view-point truth of existence is to be found by intuition and inner experience and not only by the reason and by scientific observation; the work of philosophy is to arrange the data given by the various means of knowledge, excluding none, and put them into their synthetic relation to the one Truth, the one supreme and universal reality. Eventually, its real value is to prepare a basis for spiritual realisation and the growing of the human being into his divine self and divine nature. Science itself becomes only a knowledge of the world which throws an added light on the spirit of the universe and his way in things. Nor will it confine itself to a physical knowledge and its practical fruits or to the knowledge of life and man and mind based upon the idea of matter or material energy as our starting-point; a spiritualised culture will make room for new fields of research, for new and old psychical sciences and results which start from spirit as the first truth and from the power of mind and of what is greater than mind to act upon life and matter. The primitive aim of art and poetry is to create images of man and Nature which shall satisfy the sense of beauty and embody artistically the ideas of the intelligence about life and the responses of the imagination to it; but in a spiritual culture they become too in their aim a revelation of greater things concealed in man and Nature and of the deepest spiritual and universal beauty. Politics, society, economy are in the first form of human life simply an arrangement by which men collectively can live, produce, satisfy their desires, enjoy, progress in bodily, vital and mental efficiency; but the spiritual aim makes them much more than this, first, a framework of life within which man can seek for and grow into his real self and divinity, secondly, an increasing embodiment of the divine law of being in life, thirdly, a collective advance towards the light, power, peace, unity, harmony of the diviner nature of humanity which the race is trying to evolve. This and nothing more but nothing less, this in all its potentialities, is what we mean by a spiritual culture and the application of spirituality to life.

Those who distrust this ideal or who cannot understand it, are still under the sway of the European conception of life which for a time threatened to swamp entirely the Indian spirit. But let us remember that Europe itself is labouring to outgrow the limitations of its own conceptions and precisely by a rapid infusion of the ideas of the East,—naturally, essential ideas and not the mere forms,—which have been first infiltrating and are now more freely streaming into Western thought, poetry, art, ideas of life, not to overturn its culture, but to transform, enlighten and aggrandise its best values and to add new elements which have too long been ignored or forgotten. It will be singular if while Europe is thus intelligently enlarging herself in the new light she has been able to seize and admitting the truths of the spirit and the aim at a divine change in man and his life, we in India are to take up the cast-off clothes of European thought and life and to straggle along in the old rut of her wheels, always taking up today what she had cast off yesterday. We should not allow our cultural independence to be paralysed by the accident that at the moment Europe came in upon us, we were in a state of ebb and weakness, such as comes some day upon all civilisations. That no more proves that our spirituality, our culture, our leading ideas were entirely mistaken and the best we can do is vigorously to Europeanise, rationalise, materialise ourselves in the practical parts of life,—keeping perhaps some spirituality, religion, Indianism as a graceful decoration in the background,—than the great catastrophe of the war proves that Europe's science, her democracy, her progress were all wrong and she should return to the Middle Ages or imitate the culture of China or Turkey or Tibet. Such generalisations are the facile falsehoods of a hasty and unreflecting ignorance.

We have both made mistakes, faltered in the true application of our ideals, been misled into unhealthy exaggerations. Europe has understood the lesson, she is striving to correct herself; but she does not for this reason forswear science, democracy, progress, but purposes to complete and perfect them, to use them better, to give them a sounder direction. She is admitting the light of the East, but on the basis of her own way of thinking and living, opening herself to truth of the spirit, but not abandoning her own truth of life and science and social ideals. We should be as faithful, as free in our dealings with the Indian spirit and modern influences; correct what went wrong with us; apply our spirituality on broader and freer lines, be if possible not less but more spiritual than were our forefathers; admit Western science, reason, progressiveness, the essential modern ideas, but on the basis of our own way of life and assimilated to our spiritual aim and ideal; open ourselves to the throb of life, the pragmatic activity, the great modern endeavour, but not therefore abandon our fundamental view of God and man and Nature. There is no real quarrel between them; for rather these two things need each other to fill themselves in, to discover all their own implications, to awaken to their own richest and completest significances.

India can best develop herself and serve humanity by being herself and following the law of her own nature. This does not mean, as some narrowly and blindly suppose, the rejection of everything new that comes to us in the stream of Time or happens to have been first developed or powerfully expressed by the West. Such an attitude would be intellectually absurd, physically impossible, and above all unspiritual; true spirituality rejects no new light, no added means or materials of our human self-development. It means simply to keep our centre, our essential way of being, our inborn nature and assimilate to it all we receive, and evolve out of it all we do and create. Religion has been a central preoccupation of the Indian mind; some have told us that too much religion ruined India, precisely because we made the whole of life religion or religion the whole of life, we have failed in life and gone under. I will not answer, adopting the language used by the poet in a slightly different connection, that our fall does not matter and that the dust in which India lies is sacred. The fall, the failure does matter, and to lie in the dust is no sound position for man or nation. But the reason assigned is not the true one. If the majority of Indians had indeed made the whole of their lives religion in the true sense of the word, we should not be where we are now; it was because their public life became most irreligious, egoistic, self-seeking, materialistic that they fell. It is possible, that on one side we deviated too much into an excessive religiosity, that is to say, an excessive externalism of ceremony, rule, routine, mechanical worship, on the other into a too world-shunning asceticism which drew away the best minds who were thus lost to society instead of standing like the ancient Rishis as its spiritual support and its illuminating life-givers. But the root of the matter was the dwindling of the spiritual impulse in its generality and broadness, the decline of intellectual activity and freedom, the waning of great ideals, the loss of the gust of life.

Perhaps there was too much of religion in one sense; the word is English, smacks too much of things external such as creeds, rites, an external piety; there is no one Indian equivalent. But if we give rather to religion the sense of the following of the spiritual impulse in its fullness and define spirituality as the attempt to know and live in the highest self, the divine, the all-embracing unity and to raise life in all its parts to the divinest possible values, then it is evident that there was not too much of religion, but rather too little of it—and in what there was, a too one-sided and therefore an insufficiently ample tendency. The right remedy is, not to belittle still farther the agelong ideal of India, but to return to its old amplitude and give it a still wider scope, to make in very truth all the life of the nation a religion in this high spiritual sense. This is the direction in which the philosophy, poetry, art of the West is, still more or less obscurely, but with an increasing light, beginning to turn, and even some faint glints of the truth are beginning now to fall across political and sociological ideals. India has the key to the knowledge and conscious application of the ideal; what was dark to her before in its application, she can now, with a new light, illumine; what was wrong and wry in her old methods she can now rectify; the fences which she created to protect the outer growth of the spiritual ideal and which afterwards became barriers to its expansion and farther application, she can now break down and give her spirit a freer field and an ampler flight: she can, if she will, give a new and decisive turn to the problems over which all mankind is labouring and stumbling, for the clue to their solutions is there in her ancient knowledge. Whether she will rise or not to the height of her opportunity in the renaissance which is coming upon her, is the question of her destiny.

A. K. Coomaraswamy, "Indian Nationality" (1909)

Ananda Kentish Coomaraswamy (1877–1947) was born in Sri Lanka to a Sri Lankan father and English mother. Most of his life was spent in Boston, where he was curator of Asian art at the Boston Museum of Fine Arts. He was a noted art historian and aesthetician but also addressed Indian national identity and was active in the independence movement. In this essay he argues for an Indian national identity grounded not racially but geographically and culturally.

Ananda Kentish Coomaraswamy

4

Indian Nationality

WHAT ARE THE things which make possible national self-consciousness, which constitute nationality? Certainly a unity of some sort is essential. There are certain kinds of unity, however, which are not essential, and others which are insufficient. Racial unity, for example, does not constitute the Negroes of North America a nation. Racial unity is not even an essential; the British nation is perhaps more composed of diverse racial elements than any other, but it has none the less a strong national consciousness. To take another example, many of the most Irish of the Irish are of English origin; Keating and Emmet, for instance, were of Norman descent; but neither they nor their labours were on that account less a part or an expression of Irish national feeling and self-consciousness. Neither is a common and distinctive language an essential; Switzerland is divided among three languages, and Ireland between two.

Two essentials of nationality there are,—a geographical unity, and a common historic evolution or culture. These two India possesses superabundantly, beside many lesser unities which strengthen the historical tradition.

The fact of India's geographical unity is apparent on the map, and is never, I think, disputed. The recognition of social unity is at least as evident to the student of Indian culture. The idea has been grasped more than once by individual rulers,—Aśoka, Vikramāditya and Akbar. It was recognized before the *Mahābhārata* was written; when Yudhishtira performed the Rājasuya sacrifice on the occasion of his inauguration as sovereign, a great assembly (*sabhā*—simply the *gam-sabhāva*, or village council on a larger scale) was held, and to this assembly came Bhīma, Dhritarashtra and his hundred sons, Subala (King of Gandhāra), etc.... and others from the extreme south and north (Dravida, Ceylon and Kashmir). In legends, too, we meet with references to councils or motes of the gods, held in the Himalayas, whither they repaired to further common ends. No one can say that any such idea as that of a Federated States of India is altogether foreign to the Indian mind. But more than all this, there is evidence enough that the founders of Indian culture and civilization and religion (whether you call them *rishis* or men) had this unity in view; and the manner in which this idea pervades the whole of Indian culture is the explanation of the possibility of its rapid realisation now. Is it for nothing that India's sacred shrines are many and far apart; that one who would visit more than one or two of these must pass over hundreds of miles of Indian soil? Benares is the sacred city of Buddhist and Hindu alike; Samanala in Ceylon is a holy place for Buddhist, Hindu and Muhammadan. Is there no meaning in the sacred reverence for the Himālayas which every Indian feels? Is the *geis* altogether meaningless which forbids the orthodox Hindu to leave the Motherland and cross the seas? Is the passionate adoration of the Indian people for the Ganges thrown away? How much is involved in such phrases as 'The Seven Great Rivers' (of India)! The Hindu in the north repeats the mantram:

> *Om gangē cha yamune chaiva godāvarī, sarasvatī, narmade, sindhu kaverī jale' smin sannidhim kuru.**

when performing ceremonial ablutions; the Buddhist in Ceylon uses the same prayer on a similar occasion. Or take the epics, the foundation of Indian education and culture: or a poem like the *Megha Duta*, the best known and most read work of Kalidasa. Are not these expressive of love for and knowledge of the Motherland? The 'holy land' of the Indian is not a far-off Palestine but the Indian land itself.

The whole of Indian culture is so pervaded with this idea of India as THE LAND, that it has never been necessary to insist upon it overmuch, for no one could have supposed it otherwise. Every province within the vast boundaries fulfils some necessary part in the completion of a nationality. No one place repeats the specialised functions of another. Take, for example, Ceylon (whose people are now the most denationalised of any in India); can we think of India as complete without Ceylon? Ceylon is unique as the home of Pāli literature and Southern Buddhism, and in its possession of a continuous chronicle invaluable as a check upon some of the more uncertain data of Indian Chronology. Sinhalese art, Sinhalese religion, and the structure of Sinhalese society, bring most vividly before us certain aspects of early Hindu culture, which it would be hard to find so perfectly reflected in any other part of modern India. The noblest of Indian epics, the love-story of Rāma and Sītā, unites Ceylon and India in the mind of every Indian, nor is this more so in the south than in the north. In later times, the histories of northern India and Ceylon were linked in Vijaya's emigration, then by Aśoka's missions (contemporaneous with earliest ripples of the wave of Hindu influence which passed beyond the Himalayas to impress its ideals on the Mongolian east); and later still a Sinhalese princess became a Rajput bride, to earn the perpetual love of

---

* "Hail! O ye Ganges, Jamna, Godavari; Sarasvati, Narmada, Sindhu and Kaveri, come and approach these waters."

her adopted people by her fiery death, the death which every Rajput woman would have preferred above dishonour. To this day her name is remembered by the peoples of northern India, as that of one who was the flower and crown of beauty and heroism. And just in such wise are all the different parts of India bound together by a common historical tradition and ties of spiritual kinship; none can be spared, nor can any live independent of the others.

The diverse peoples of India are like the parts of some magic puzzle, seemingly impossible to fit together, but falling easily into place when once the key is known; and the key is that realization of the fact that the parts do fit together, which we call national self-consciousness. I am often reminded of the Cairene girl's lute, in the tale of Miriam and Ali Nur-al-Din. It was kept in a "green satin bag with slings of gold." She took the bag, "and opening it, shook it, whereupon there fell thereout two-and-thirty pieces of wood, which she fitted one into other, male into female, and female into male, till they became a polished lute of Indian workmanship. Then she uncovered her wrists and laying the lute in her lap, bent over it with the bending of mother over babe, and swept the strings with her finger-tips; whereupon it moaned and resounded and after its olden home yearned; and it remembered the waters that gave it drink and the earth whence it sprang and wherein it grew and it minded the carpenters who cut it and the polishers who polished it and the merchants who made it their merchandise and the ships that shipped it; and it cried and called aloud and moaned and groaned; and it was as if she asked it of all these things and it answered her with the tongue of the case." Just such an instrument is India, composed of many parts seemingly irreconcilable, but in reality each one cunningly designed towards a common end; so, too, when these parts are set together and attuned, will India tell of the earth from which she sprang, the waters that gave her drink, and the Shapers that have shaped her being; nor will she be then the idle singer of an empty day, but the giver of hope to all, when hope will most avail, and most be needed.

I have spoken so far only of Hindus and Hindu culture; and if so it is because Hindus form the main part of the population of India, and Hindu culture the main part of Indian culture: but the quotation just made from Arabian literature leads on to the consideration of the great part which Muhammadans, and Persi-Arabian culture have played in the historic evolution of India, as we know it to-day. It would hardly be possible to think of an India in which no Great Mughal had ruled, no Taj been built, or to which Persian art and literature were wholly foreign. Few great Indian rulers have displayed the genius for statesmanship which Akbar had, a greater religious toleration than he. On the very morrow of conquest he was able to dispose of what is now called the Hindu-Muhammadan difficulty very much more successfully than it is now met in Bengal; for he knew that there could be no real diversity of interest between Hindu and Muhammedan, and treated them with an impartiality which we suspect to be greater than that experienced in Bengal to-day. It was not his interest to divide and rule. Like most Eastern rulers (who can never be foreigners in the same way that a Western ruler necessarily must be) he identified himself with his kingdom, and had no interests that clashed with its interests. This has, until modern times, been always a characteristic of an invader's or usurper's rule in India, that the ruler has not attempted to remain in his own distant country and rule the conquered country from afar, farming it like an absentee landlord, but has identified himself with it. The beneficent rule of Elāla, a Tamil usurper in Ceylon two centuries before Christ, was so notorious that deep respect was paid to the site of his tomb more than 2,000 years later; and to mention a more modern case, the 18th century Tamil (Hindu) ruler, Kīrti Srī and his two brothers, so identified themselves with the Sinhalese (Buddhist) people as to have deserved the chronicler's remark that they were "one with the religion and the people." To show that such a situation is still possible, it will suffice to cite the States of Hyderabad, Baroda and Gwalior.

Even suppose the differences that separate the Indian communities to be twice as great as they are said to be, they are nothing compared with the difference between the Indian and the European. Western rule is inevitably alien rule, in a far deeper sense than the rule of Hindus by Muhammadans or the reverse could be. And what does alien rule mean? "The government of a people by itself," says John Stuart Mill, "has a meaning and a reality, but such a thing as the government of one people by another does not and cannot exist. One people may keep another as a warren or preserve for its own use, a place to make money in, a human farm to be worked for the profit of its own inhabitants." No cant of the "white man's burden" alters the stern logic of these facts; to us it appears that the domination of the East by the West is a menace to the evolution of the noblest ideal of humanity; the "white man's burden" translated into the language of Asiatic thought becomes "the white peril;" and this is not because we despise the achievements of Western civilisation, or fail to appreciate the merits of Europeans as such, but because we think that a whole world of Europeans would be a poor place, quite as poor as a whole world of Indians or Chinamen. We feel it then our duty to realise our unity and national self-consciousness in concrete form, as much for the advantage of others as of ourselves; and this without any feeling of bitterness or exclusiveness towards other races, though perhaps for a time such feelings may be inevitable. And to show what spirit moves us we have such a statement of belief in the unity of the Indian people, as the credo of Shiv Narayen; and the beautiful national song, called '*Bande Mātaram*' ('Hail! Motherland') which expresses the aims and the power of the awakened Indian nation, as the

Marseillaise embodied the ideal of awakened France, or as those of Ireland are expressed in the songs of Ethna Carberry.

Their words are not the hysterical utterance of a people uncertain of their unity or doubtful of their future. They express the Indian recognition of the Motherland, their quiet but profound assurance of her greatness and beauty, and their consciousness of the high calling which is hers. They voice the hope of an INDIAN NATION, which shall not be disappointed.

Lajpat Rai, "Reform or Revival?" (1904)

Lajpat Rai (1865–1928) was a major figure in the struggle for independence. Born in the Punjab, he was a leader of the Arya Samaj, a founder of the Young India movement and active in the Indian National Congress. His book *Young India* (1917) was (and still is) banned in the United Kingdom as seditious. Most of his writing is explicitly political, but nonetheless philosophical, providing astute analyses in *Young India* of the varieties of nationalism. He died as a result of injuries sustained protesting the appointment of the Simon Commission on Indian governance. The present essay asks whether India's emergence into modernity requires a reform of Indian culture or a revival of its classical form.

Lajpat Rai

5

Reform or Revival?

WE THOUGHT THAT with the fall of the old class of Pandits we had done with those wars of words which were formerly carried on with all the weight of great learning and accompanied by a demonstrative show of deep erudition, but we had evidently counted without our hosts, the great body of Indian reformers that are the products of English education, who owe nothing to the old school of Pandits and for whom the old school of Pandits have incurred no responsibility whatever. Before the spread of English education in this country there were only two classes of public literary or intellectual entertainments to which the people were treated now and then and which supplied some diversion from the otherwise dull, monotonous or in some places extremely hazardous lives which they generally led. The one was the most popular and useful practice of reciting the *kathās* to mixed and general audience consisting of all classes of people from old men to boys and from old ladies to young girls. The ancient epics of the land—the chronicles of the life of Rama and his consort, and the great *Mahābhārata*—were very often the books that were thus recited.

These *kathās* were greatly instrumental in keeping the national spark alive through so many vicissitudes of national fortune, when on occasions it had almost reached the point of total extinction. The second were the periodical religious discussions, which in most instances originated with the advent of a learned Pandit from the outside.

Very often the new Pandit's discourse had caught the popular ears and the local Pandit or Pandits thought their dignity, prestige and even emoluments were in danger, to prevent which calamity they considered it their duty to come out and give a challenge to the newly arrived, to prove his superiority in the knowledge of the *śāstras* by an open discussion. Or it might be that the newcomer thought his success depended on drawing out the local theologian and giving him a defeat. Be it as it may, the invariable result was that the discussion began with words, the accuracy of certain expressions used by one or the other, the applicability or the non-applicability of certain rules of grammar and ended often if not always in words and sometimes in blows. I am sorry to observe that the present quarrel over "reform or revival" between the reformers seems to me to resemble, at least in parts, the above mentioned wordy polemics between the Pandits. The reformers claim to be the leaders of the community. They have occupied the place of the Pandits and divines of former times. They profess to lay down rules for the guidance of the general mass of people. They are agreed that the state of Hindu society is bad and rotten, that it needs great and radical changes and that without these changes the whole social fabric stands in danger of giving way and burying the nation down in its debris. They have remedies, ready, patent and infallible. On most of these they agree, only to differ on the name by which the same is to be styled. Their agreement as to the remedy disappears in their differences about the wordy habitat to be given to the proposed and contemplated changes. One class of people who have already established a name for themselves do not like to give up the name they have patented and by which they have gained distinction. These latter gentlemen call themselves reformers and insist upon certain social changes being introduced in the name of "reform" and reform only. The other class who have lately come into prominence call themselves "revivalists," and they swear that any change in the social customs and institutions of the community can only be introduced under the shadow of revival. They think they cannot tolerate reform. The result is that while the former taunt the latter as "revivalists and reactionaries" the latter mock the former as "reformers and revolutionists". Both classes contain amongst them great and good men, men with pure motives and noble intentions. They are generally prominent men—well read and deep in the lore of history. Both classes are to all appearances sincere in their convictions and efforts, but to the great misfortune of the country and the nation they cannot join their heads and work amicably. The wordy weapons are sometimes changed, and while the reformers take their stand on "reform on rational lines" the revivalists plead for "reform on national lines." Here for once at least they seem to agree on reform, as the force of the difference is centred on the words "rational" and "national". The result is that much ink and paper are uselessly spent in dilating upon the necessary soundness of reform and the danger and risk of revival, and *vice versa*. Unfortunately no one ever sees and deplores the great waste of valuable time and precious energy which this quarrel involves—time and energy which could be usefully employed in, nay, which is imperatively demanded by so many other things that are the *sine qua non* of national progress and that should be done but are not done from want of working hands. On both sides are arrayed tough warriors armed with the knowledge and experience which is gathered by deep study and growing years. On both sides are arrayed sturdy and stout soldiers possessed of and carried by the enthusiasm of youth, full of ambition, and proud of credentials gained by academical successes and literary achievements. On both sides the pen and the tongue are being used with strength and vigour not totally devoid of grace. It is very perilous to come between such daring, bold and determined fighters specially for a comparatively ill-provided and poorly circumstanced man like myself who can wield neither the pen with the dexterity that comes of practice, nor the tongue with that skill which is the outcome of discipline. In fact I am rather inclined to think that it is positively dangerous for recruits who have not had the advantage of regular lessons in drill or of the discipline that comes out of exercises at the manoeuvres, to interfere between such veteran combatants. But the interests at stake are so great, the field is so vast, the workers in the field are so few and far between, the amount of energy available is so little and the resources are so limited, that on better thought I have decided to take the risk and raise my voice against what to me looks sheer waste of opportunities and misapplication of energy.

I will begin by examining into the respective programmes of reformers and the revivalists and see if there are any vital and real differences which justify so much contemptous talk of each other. On both sides, I believe that the social reform programme begins and very rightly too, with the question of early marriage. I confess. I am unaware of any radical difference between the views of the reformers and the revivalists on the point. In provinces other than the Punjab Mrs. Besant is believed to be the leader of the latter. Now, who does not know that she is opposed to early marriages and denounces them as unshastric and disastrous? She has in fact taken pains not only to definitely pronounce against this evil custom, but to give force to her utterances, has shut the doors of a department of her school at Benares against those who might have been or might be by the improvidence of their guardians married at a tender age. The Arya Samajists also may to a certain extent be called revivalists, but in this matter of early marriage and the marriageable ages of boys and girls they go a step further than even the most radical reformer is prepared to just now. They say and preach, and try to enforce their precept, that no girl be married under 16 and no boy under 25. Now let us ask if there is anything irrational in saying that the institution of child-marriage is not only condemnable by reason, but is actually opposed to the letter as well as the spirit of the *śāstras*. From the question of child-marriage we may proceed to the great evil of the present divisions and sub-divisions of caste. Mrs. Besant and her school have already pronounced against the sub-divisions in the main castes. Her defence of the original Hindu conception of four castes principally coincides with the views of the Aryasamajists in the matter and practically knocks the present caste system on the head, though in theory only. In practice neither the Arya Samajists nor the reformers can go further than denunciation. All of them agree that a beginning should be made with the sub-divisons. The sub-divisions having been swept away (which is not likely to be achieved very soon or very easily) the time will then come to think of the remoulding or the fusion of the main castes on *śāstric* or rational lines. For the present we are all agreed that the existing arrangement is an unmixed evil, and the sooner it is done away with the better. From castes let us proceed to the question of foreign travel, and here again we find a practical unanimity. Of course, there are and there shall continue to be ultra-orthodox people who will not give up their opposition to any of these measures and will continue to say that they are un-Hindu; but just now we are not concerned with them, as we dare say there is no one who can justly or even contemptuously be called a revivalist who condemns foreign travel on the plea of revival and no reform. Then let us take up the great question of female education. I know of no sensible man in the country, not to speak of the revivalists only, who is a man of culture and education, who is opposed to it. The school of Mrs. Besant, the Arya Samajists, and the reformers are all pledged to it. There may be and there are practical difficulties in the way of educating our girls and sisters and wives, but nobody questions the desirability, nay the necessity, of giving, if possible, the very highest education to girls. People may differ on the *modus operandi* or may have different views about schemes of education to be enforced in the case of females, but there are no two opinions on the question of principle. There may be some among the so-called revivalists who are not favourably disposed to an exact copy of European customs and usages relating to females being adopted by the Hindus, but surely there is none who can in the name of revival defend the existing Purdah system or the universal ignorance of women. Similarly we do not think there is much difference of opinion at least so far as practical measures feasible at present are concerned, on the necessity of raising the social status and bettering the condition of low castes, if Hinduism is not bent upon social indifference and mad neglect of vital interests which might result in disastrous consequences. With the exception of some apparently spurious passages in *Manu* and other *Smṛtis*, there is absolutely nothing in the more ancient literature to justify the inhuman and cruel treatment to which the low castes are at present or were till lately subjected. We think we have almost exhausted the list of prominent subjects comprised in the list of reforms advocated by the social reformers, having reserved one important matter to be discussed last, *viz.*, the question of widow remarriage.

On this question there exists undoubtedly real difference of opinion between the so-called reformers and the so-called revivalists. We grant that the question is a very important one; but still we are not prepared to admit that a difference on this single question justifies all that bitterness which characterises the writings of these two classes about one another. The real and important differences are on questions of religion and worship which the social reformers profess to exclude from their curriculum of school and college education. Here in the Punjab, fortunately we have been spared that bitter fight over these words which is going on in the Western and Southern Presidencies, although we are not unaware that of late attempts have not been wanting to introduce it in collegiate and inter-collegiate debates. We cannot but deprecate these unwise attempts and will warn our young men from throwing themselves into the vortex of this absolutely unnecessary and uncalled for fight over words. We may be pardoned for pointing out that to us the fight seems to be generally on the same lines and on the same grounds which marked the polemics of the old class of Pandits. The real truth is that the so-called reformers are mostly in faith and in religion Brahmos. They were the earliest in the field and fought for reform when the revivalists had not yet come into existence. The revivalists are the products of a wider diffusion of Sanskrit literature which has taken place principally within the last quarter of a century. This study has afforded them sufficient and strong evidence of their ancestors having enjoyed a great and glorious civilization from which most of the present evil practices and customs that are the bane of modern Hinduism were absent. They, therefore, naturally look to the past for light and guidance and plead that a revival might lead them into that haven of progress which is the object of all. They have found that most of the social evils existing in their society were not to be found in the ancient Hindu race and they have, therefore, begun to appeal to the authority of the past and the *śāstras* for the introduction of these very reforms for which reformers had been pleading with much force though with scanty success on grounds of utility and natural justice. The revivalists are naturally popular in Hindu society as they take their stand on the authority of the Hindu *śāstras* and thus threaten to oust the reformers from their hard earned position. Then to add insult to injury, their exposition of the popular religious beliefs of the Hindus is so injurious and cunning as to justify a reasonable fear in the minds of the reformers that they are taking the nation back to superstitions and low and debased forms of worship from which English education, contact with Western religion, and a study of the masterminds of the West was just extricating them with so desirable a success. The reformers had thus based their religious propaganda on the same basis on which their social programme rested, *viz.*, grounds of rationality. The revivalists, having taken to the defence of the socalled nation, have extended the same base to the removal of social evils and thus the fight began between "reform on national lines" and "reform on rational lines." But, as I have pointed out above, so far as real social reform is considered, both lines of work lead to a common conclusion. It is not, therefore, fair to entangle social reform in this quarrel which is really based on differences in religious views. Let the 'reformers' by all means if they like, ridicule the religious views of "the revivalists"; and criticise or hold them to derision, but it is not, to say the least, graceful and fair to talk of them contemptuously in matters of social reform. The same should we say to the revivalists. Happily here in the Punjab, as we have already said, there is not much difference between reform and revival. By far the strongest reforming agency in the Punjab appears to accept both. To them reform is revival and revival is reform. It is true they attach much importance to nationality or to national lines, but subject to the important proviso *that they are not irrational.* The Arya-samajists shall have nothing *irrational* though it may even have the look of being national. They want everything national which is rational as well. They even go in for things national if only they [be] not irrational; but no further. According to them nothing can be either national or rational which is against the letter or the spirit of the Vedas. So far there seems to be no danger of the Punjab being involved in this meaningless distinction between reform and revival, but we think it is better to take time by the forelock and sound this note of warning to guard against any contemplated or impending mischief. But over and above that, it is our earnest request to the leaders of the Hindu community in the Western and the Southern provinces to abjure this absurd distinction and to work harmoniously for social reform, at least so far as all are agreed upon. Lately I had occasion to listen to an address on social progress by an esteemed friend of mine who is a pronounced social reformer. In the course of his remarks he treated the revivalists with scant respect and in support of his views read the following quotation from the Amraoti speech of that great reformer—the late Mr. Justice Ranade[1]

"On the other side, some of our orthodox friends find fault with us, not because of the particular reforms we have in view, but on account of the methods we follow. While the new religious sects condemn us for being too orthodox, the extreme orthodox section denounce us for being too revolutionary in our methods. According to these last, our efforts should be directed to revive and not to reform. I have many friends in this camp of extreme orthodoxy and their watchword is that revival and not reform should be our motto. They advocate a return to the old ways, and appeal to the old authorities and the old sanctions. Here also, as in the instance quoted above, people speak without realising the full significance of their own words. When we are asked to revive our institutions and customs, people seem to be very much at sea as to what it is they seem to revive. What particular period of our history is to be taken as the old? Whether the period of the Vedas, of the Smṛítis, of the Puranas, or of the Mahomedan or modern Hindu times? Our usages have been changed from time to time by a slow process of growth, and, in some cases, of decay and corruption, and we cannot stop at a particular period without

1. The source for this quotation has not been found. (eds.)

breaking the continuity of the whole. When my revivalist friend presses his argument upon me, he has to seek recourse in some subterfuge which really furnishes no reply to the question. What shall we revive? Shall we revive the old habits of our people when the most sacred of our caste indulged in all the abominations, as we now understand them, of animal food and drink which exhausted every section of our country's zoology and botany? The men and gods of those old days ate and drank forbidden things to excess in a way no revivalist will now venture to recommend. Shall we revive the twelve forms of sons, or eight forms of marriage which included capture, and recognised mixed and illegitimate intercourse? Shall we revive the Niyoga system of procreating sons on our brothers' wives when widowed? Shall we revive the old liberties taken by the Rishis and by the wives of the Rishis with the marital tie? Shall we revive the hecatombs of animals sacrificed from year's end to year's end, and in which human beings were not spared as propitiatory offerings? Shall we revive the *shakti* worship of the left hand with its indecencies and practical debaucheries? Shall we revive the *sati* and infanticide customs, or the flinging of living men into the rivers, or over rocks, or hook-swinging, or the crushing beneath the Jagannath car? Shall we revive the internecine wars of the Brahmins and Kṣatrīyas or the cruel persecution and degradation of the aboriginal population? Shall we revive the custom of many husbands to one wife or of many wives to one husband? Shall we require our Brahmins to cease to be landlords and gentlemen, and turn into beggars and dependants upon the king as in olden times? These instances will suffice to show that the plan of reviving the ancient usages and customs will not work out salvation, and is not practicable. If these usages were good and beneficial, why were they altered by our wise ancestors? If they were bad and injurious, how can any claim be put forward for their restoration after so many ages? Besides, it seems to be forgotten that in a living organism as society is, no revival is possible. The dead and the buried or burnt are dead, buried, and burnt once for all, and the dead past cannot, therefore, be revived except by a reformation of the old materials into new organised beings."

Now, if it be permissible for a comparatively young and inexperienced man without laying himself open to a charge of disrespect for one of our revered leaders whose great wisdom, deep learning, and general judicial-mindedness are accepted all around, I will, with due deference to the late Mr. Ranade, beg to point out the injustice of the observations quoted above. Cannot a revivalist, arguing in the same strain, ask the reformers into what they wish to reform us? Whether they want us to be reformed on the pattern of the English or the French? Whether they want us to accept the divorce laws of Christian society or the temporary marriages that are now so much in favour in France or America? Whether they want to make men of our women by putting them into those avocations for which nature never meant them? Whether they want us to substitute the legal *niyoga* of the Mahābhārata period with the illegal and immoral *niyoga* that is nowadays rampant in European society? Whether they want us to reform into Sunday drinkers of brandy and promiscuous eaters of beef? In short, whether they want to revolutionise our society by an outlandish imitation of European customs and manners and an undiminished adoption of European vice? The revivalists do not admit that the institutions which they want to revive are dead, burnt and gone. The very fact that they wish to revive them goes to show that they believe that there is still some life left in them and that given the proper remedy, their present unhealthy and abnormal state is sure to disappear and result in the bringing about of the normal and healthy condition of affairs. In fact, in an earlier part of the same address, Mr. Ranade summed up the position of the revivalists in a few well chosen and apt words when he admitted that, "In the case of our society especially, the usages which at present prevail amongst us are admittedly not those which obtained in the most glorious periods of our history. On most of the points which are included in our programme, our own record of the past shows that there has been a decided change for the worse and it is surely within the range of practical possibilities for us to hope that we may work up our way back to a better state of things without stirring up the rancorous hostilities which religious differences have a tendency to create and foster." It is exactly this working up our way back which the revivalists aim at. No revivalist has ever pleaded for the institutions selected by Mr. Justice Ranade as the butt end of his attack against them.

The real significance of these words—"reform" and "revival", if any, seems to be in the authority or authorities from which the reformers and the revivalists respectively seek their inspiration for guidance in matters social. The former are bent on relying more upon reason and the experience of European society, while the latter are disposed to primarily look at their *śāstras* and the past history, and the traditions of their people and the ancient institutions of the land which were in vogue when the nation was at the zenith of its glory. On our part we here in the Punjab are prepared to take our inspiration from both these sources, though we prefer to begin with the latter and call in the assistance of the former mainly to understand and explain what is not clear and ambiguous in the latter. But so long as our conclusions are principally the same, I think the fight is not worth being continued and may be dropped for good.

Bhagavan Das, "The Meaning of Swaraj or Self-Government" (1921)

Bhagavan Das (1869–1958) was a prominent educator and Sankritist, and also active in the Indian National Congress and the Theosophical Society. He lived and taught in Varanasi and wrote on the philosophy of science, political philosophy, and on Vedānta. Here we present an excerpted version of a short book on *swaraj*, or self-rule, written as a position paper for a meeting of the Indian National Congress.

Bhagvan Das

6

The Meaning of Swaraj or Self-government

I

Need for definition of Swa-raj

Among the other items of business and proposals for resolutions which could not be disposed of by the All-India Congress Committee, during its three days sittings in Bombay, on the 28th, 29th and 30th July 1921, but were referred to the Working Committee for disposal, there was one was with regard to the need for some little definition of *Swaraj*…

The settlement of fundamental principles is the first and most urgent and most practical business of all great public movements, as sad experience of other movements shows, and time and trouble stinted from such settlement in the beginning, mean much more time and trouble wasted afterwards. The immense advance made by the country under the inspiration of Mahatma Gandhi in purification of heart in courage of conviction, in peaceful, dignified, undefending resistance of wrong and shaming of the soul of the wrong-doers—this advance, indispensably necessary to the success of the Congress movement, requires more and more to be steadied and confirmed and protected against back-sliding, by a clearer vision of the goal, a clearer knowledge of the aim that the country is striving to achieve. What has been gained by the people's heart should be safeguarded from loss, by the people's head: the clearer their conviction, the greater their courage; knowledge and aspiration, sound principles and noble sentiments, clear ideas and generous emotions, act and re-act on and help each other.

These members were therefore anxious that a preliminary definition of *Swaraj* should not be delayed longer…

The Proposed Resolution

1. Whereas the desire is felt growlingly by many workers of the Indian National Congress that the meaning of the word *Swaraj* (mentioned, but left undefined, in the Creed adopted by the Congress at its last Session in Nagpur) should now receive some definition…

2. And whereas such clearer definition of *Swaraj* will help abate the many misunderstandings and wrong notions now afloat in the country, as to the nature of *Swaraj*.
3. And whereas it is desirable that our opponents, the party now in power and office, should also know what it is that we want, so that they may be able to examine their minds and consult their conscience in the light of that knowledge, and so have a chance of accepting our views.
4. And whereas it is desirable that all concerned should have ready before their minds, the broad outlines of a workable scheme when the change from the present system to the *Swaraj* system comes, lest at that time the change find the people unprepared on the constructible side, and old mistakes be repeated, or, even, the whole country drift into temporary anarchy.
5. And whereas it is desirable to make it clear that while the elective principle is an essential and integral part of *Swaraj*, yet we do not want a blind imitation of the Parliamentary system and methods of election of England, which have not diminished the corruptions of place, power, wealth. And unitarist and navalist ambitions; which have been proved to be failures, so far, by results in respect of securing the general contentment and peace and happiness of even the people of Great Britain and Ireland; which have emphasised and embittered class-differences, promoted extremes of wealth and poverty, and created a hatred between Capital and Labor that is pregnant with disaster; and which, in some essentials, are entirely foreign to the genius and traditions of India and the Indian people.

Therefore, pending fuller and more authoritative definition by the Congress at its next session, be it *Resolved* by the All-India Congress Committee, by virtue of the powers entrusted to it by Art. XXI of the Congress Constitution, as adopted at the Nagpur Congress, 1920,

That the *Swaraj* mentioned in the Creed of the Congress include, as its essential and integral factors, the following main principles:–

(a) All legislators shall be elected, as also all heads of governmental departments; they shall be men and women who have retired from active competitive profession or business of bread-winning or money-making, and who are not representative of any particular interest, but are disinterestedly and wisely benevolent towards all interests and are elected by the trust of the people without any canvassing.
(b) Legislative and executive functions shall not be combined in the same person; nor judicial and executive.

(c) Legislators and heads of government departments shall not receive any salary or cash remuneration for their work, but shall be provided with all requisites necessary for the due discharge of their duties, and shall be paid all out-of-pocket expenses incurred for such discharge, and they shall have precedence over all salaried office-bearers, in the warrants of precedence regulating public functions.
(d) Men and women with full experience of work in the educational, administrative (including landholding and military), commercial, agricultural, and industrial departments of the communal life, and especially persons versed in the knowledge of the psychological and physiological nature of the humane being, and in history, politics and economics, and also honored and trusted by the general public for their upright life, shall be given place in the legislative bodies.
(e) The elected legislature shall make laws as needed, for guiding all departments of the communal life and shall have full control over all departments of the governmental executive and other administration, which shall all be subordinate and responsible to the legislature.
(f) Subject to the above principles, India's *Swaraj* may be within an Indo-British Federation or Commonwealth wherein the Head of the Executive, (Governor-General or Viceroy) may be a member of the British Royal family or such other person as the King of Great Britain may nominate; and
(g) In that case, the British people shall received "Favored Nation" treatment from the Indian People in all dealings with other people as far as may be possible without serious loss to India; and in the appointment of foreign experts...

II

Why the definition of Swa-raj should not be delayed further

That the desire has been present all along in the mind of the public, is evidenced by the fact that, at the Nagpur Session itself, proposals were made to qualify *Swaraj* by the adjective "democratic." That the desire is growing, is evidenced by the repeat query in the papers, and by the fact that Mahatma Gandhi himself has had to say, from time to tome, in reply to such queries, what *Swaraj* means. He has said, for instance, that his own ideal is a spiritual *Swaraj* (implying an individual life of the utmost self-control and the fewest possible wants, and a communal life of primitive simplicity, as indicated in his book on *India Home Rule*): again, that he knows that would not satisfy the many, and that control offers the Police, the Military, the Judiciary, the Finance, etc. would mean *Swaraj*; again (to the Parsi community) that the British Parliamentary system would amount to *Swaraj*; again (to other audiences) that is Rama-raj, or Dhárma-rah; and, yet more recently in the *Hindi Nara-jiran*, he has repeated these ideas in other words, adding others in terms which mention the good fruits of Swa-raj rather than define its nature and manner. No doubt, all these are reconcilable, with the help of some explanations, qualifications, and reservations. But these require to be put forward and, the manner, the nature, of Swa-raj requires to be stated as well as the blessings to result there from. There might have been good reasons for postponing the subject at the Nagpur Congress. An obvious one was the lack for threshing it out. But there is not sufficient [reason] for indefinite further postponement…

Let us examine some objections. Some ask, "Who are we to settle the meaning of *Swaraj*? How do we know that those who come after us will like what we may lay down in the behalf? Should we not leave it to them to decide for themselves? Is it not enough that we achieve *Swaraj*?"

It is not easy to understand this attitude. The counter-questions come up in the mind, "Who are we to try for *Swaraj* at all? How do we know that those who come after us will like *Swaraj*? Should we not to leave it to them to decide for themselves, and they to their next generation, and that to its next, *ad infinitum?* Is it not enough that we mind our own private business now?" The point is this. When we use the word *Swaraj*, when we make it the objective of the Congress Creed, do we use the world with a meaning, or without? If with, then let us make just that meaning tolerably clear, and put it down in black and white. If without, if our business is the good sport of trying to catch the *word Swaraj* first, and then trying to put a *meaning* into it afterwards, then, of course, there is nothing more to say.

But. Perhaps, when people say that the definition of *Swaraj* should be postponed till after *Swaraj* has been achieved, or left to those who come after, probably what they mean is that the details of the form of government should be so left. But that is a matter of course. The details must be so left; and the very purpose of a living legislation is to change and modify such details from time to time, as necessary. But the basic principles, the general outlines of that form, should be decided on, in good time, beforehand, by those who initiate the great change. If they shirk this duty, serious trouble will arise later. The historical Magna Chartas, the Declarations of Independence, the Proclamations, the Rescripts, the Edicts, of the various sovereigns, nations and governments, all endeavor to announce such fundamental principles, according to their lights. And the sounder, the more comprehensive, the more far-seeing the principles uttered by any one of these, the longer-lasting and the smoother-working the system that develops there out.

Another objection. Some think that if a discussion once begins on this subject, there will be no end; there may be serious splits, and the whole movement may come to grief.

This seems to be a peculiarly dangerous position to adopt, a position of false security. It means that we know and feel that there is no real and intelligent unity and unanimity over even the essentials, and that we are held together by a mere meaningless shibboleth. If the apprehension of dissensions be so great now, when there is comparative leisure for quiet exchange of views, and when there is not patent apple of discord, in the shape of power and place and preference, how much greater, how far more serious, will be the danger of internecine conflict, should "the power to do as we please," "self-government," "self-determination," (all very vague phrases, meaning very different things in different mouths, as past and current history shows), come suddenly to the Indian people, and the need to start work should brook no delay for thinking out schemes, and temptations of honor and power and high salaries and monopolies should infuse perverse motives, bitter animus, and acute jealousies, into such hurried conversations as may be indispensable. Rival factions endeavoring to tear down one another, and temporary anarchy, are almost certain, if, at such a time, the workers are not ready prepared with the broad outlines of a workable scheme, the essential principles of which have been generally agreed on beforehand, after due deliberation.

Some Current Misunderstandings

Besides the different things which different thinking persons now understand by the term *Swaraj*, for various plausible though debatable reasons, there are some positive misunderstandings also current in the minds of those who do not bother to think, or are highly prejudiced. And these misunderstandings are causing very mischievous antagonisms between important classes of the community on the one hand, and, on the other, are setting against the Congress Creed, some important and powerful sections, who, if assured that *Swaraj* would not involve wholesale destruction of their interest, might be willing to help the cause. Thus, here and there, some agriculturalist supposes that all land rent will be at once abolished; some tax payer, that no more taxes of any kind will have to be paid; some debaters, that they will not be required to repay; some persons who have lost their lands by action of the law, or whose ancestors lost them in the turmoils of the Sepoy War, that such lands will be restored to them; some imagine that all shall and purchase will cease, and that every body will be able to take or do what he likes; many English and also some Indian persons apparently imagine that it necessarily implies the expulsion of every English person from India; some think it means the partition of what is now

British India, between Muslim Nawabs or Hindu Rajas or both, with their utter autocracy and irresponsibility towards the people, (and, at much present, generally, their servility to the British Resident of Agent, and their worse misgovernment than that of British India, with exceptions). And so on…

The Urgent need to remove the Misunderstandings

Under such circumstances, when the Congress Creed and the Congress movement have spread into the so-called masses, it is very desirable to make it tolerably clear to the world, what it is that the Congress understands by the *Swaraj*; so that false notions, false hopes, false fears, and groundless antagonisms, may be dissipated, on the one hand, and, on the other, those who have to suffer, may know distinctly what it is they are suffering for, and may feel strongly that it is worth suffering for, and so derive strength in their moments of weakness…

The Evils of the Parliamentary System of Swaraj

It seems that most Congress workers of the Nationalist party understand, more or less vaguely and implicitly, by *Swaraj*, the British Parliamentary system and methods of election as also, perhaps, do the members of the Moderate-Liberal party…Yet that system and those methods have on the whole no greater virtues than the system and method now prevailing here. Many thinkers feel that system and those methods to be an utter failure. There ferment, in the West, of the many movements, of Socialism, Anarchism, Collectivism, Communism, Syndicalism, Guild-Socialism, Bolshevism, (each more defective and dangerous than the others, search more discordant with human psychology than the others, except perhaps Guild-Socialism), and the Great European War itself and its increasingly evil consequences, are all patent proofs of the gross failure of the British Parliament and its congeners in other countries, to produce healthy, human, social, economical, and political conditions.

Some of us are therefore very anxious that while we are trying hard to get rid of what has been called slave-mentality (i.e., the tendency to slavishly imitate the West and to regard its ways as the best) in respect of the other aspects and departments of the individual and communal life—we are very anxious that we should not suffer from the very climax and culmination of that "slave-mentality" in respect of the political department of our life.

We are endeavoring to become Swa-deshi in other respects: let us take very great care to be genuinely Swa-deshi in this, which is, at the moment, more important than all other respects…

Though India is governed by the "the Government of India," this latter is the creation of, and is governed by, the Parliament of England, which is the dutiful agent and handmaiden of the capitalist and landed interests of that country. The form in which we have these growing evils here, now, may be somewhat different from that which they show in the West. Here, the form is, primarily, not that of capitalist *versus* laborer as there, but that of the bureaucracy *versus* the people (including rich and poor, but excepting of course such of the rich and the poor as deliberately make themselves subservient to the bureaucracy for the sake of self-aggrandisment—for while English capitalists and aristocrats are the *masters* of the Parliament and the bureaucracy, Indian land-holders, princes, and capitalists are the *servants* of these, because they belong to a subject i.e. 'down-thrown' race). The secondary form of those evils, here, is that of the conflict between the rich and the poor; and this, though daily increasing in acuteness under the influence of the West, continues to be mitigated as yet, by the still persisting remnants of the old customs and traditions as to "biradari" and "bhai-chara" and brotherhood and the duty of supporting poor relations (gone to a wrong extreme in their own way). But if we import the Parliamentary system direct and wholesale, then at least some of us fear greatly, we shall import with them the corresponding abuses and horrors in a more virulent form than they possess there. Imported epidemics rage more fiercely in fresh fields.

Such are the principal reasons for avoiding all further delay in making our minds clear to ourselves and to all concerned, as to what it is that we want when we want *Swaraj*...

The Essential Nature of True Swaraj

Swaraj means "Self-government." But there are two selves in every individual, as well as in every Society or Nation: a higher self and a lower self; a selfish self and an altruistic self; the elements of virtue and the elements of vice. Government by the higher self only is true self-government. Government by the lower self is the same thing as government by another; for this lower self is the worse of foreign tyrants; and all foreign government is, of necessity, and, either frankly or hypocritically tyrannical, because it is government by a selfish self... Government of one race, or nation, or class, by another race, or nation, or class, which keeps itself apart, socially and biologically, can never be government by the higher self, however much it may pretend to be such; for the governor does not identify himself with the higher self of the governed, in reality, and so remains at most a lower and most selfish self, a pretended self, and therefore indeed, doubly dangerous and mischievous.

To secure true Self-government, true *Swaraj*, means, then, to secure the government of a people by its own higher self; and that means, to ensure purity and wisdom of head and hear in its legislators by wise election. And this is the first, most urgent, and most vitally important work, for every Society that desires its own "welfare," that wished to keep "well" and "whole," truly "weal-thy" and "heal-thy"...

The Best Way to Secure Good Legislator

In the case of the legislator, the nearest and most likely way to secure the needed qualifications, namely knowledge and philanthropy, and the third subsidiary but also indispensible qualification of sufficient leisure; the way which is also most in accord with the individuality and the genius of the Indian people, seems to be this. Only such persons should be elected to the office of legislator as occupy, towards the general public, the position that parents, elders, patriarchs, occupy towards their families; who do not take from them, but only give; who are no longer engaged in any competitive, bread wining, or money-making profession or business, but have "retired," not too late in life, but with mental energy unexhausted, after gathering full experience of human affairs in some walks of life who are maintenance on their own savings, directly, or in the shape of "pensions" from their families or friends for whom they have worked in their prime, and to whose new chief or representative they have handed over the business; who will not canvass for their own election, but will take up the burden of office only on pressing request and solicitation by the public; who will not take any cash salary or remuneration from public funds for legislative work; whose life now is almost like that of Vana-prasthas, Sadhus and Faqirs; and who possess the respectful or even the reverent trust of the public in matters political, such as is possessed in India by genuine ascetics in matters spiritual.

The outlook upon life, of such a person, would, so far as is humanely possible, be untainted by selfish ambitions or class-biases; he would have the needed leisure, as well as the needed ripe experience of human affairs; his passions would be spent, or so weakened as to be under control; his powers of thinking un-impaired, and possibly improved; he would be possessed of the conditions that are favourable to philanthropy and to the dispassionate judging of the due proportion that various classes and interests which make up the Organic Social Whole, should bear to each other, in order to make possible and remote the healthy functioning of all; and he would have no personal interest of his own to serve, except perhaps that of continuing to deserve the trust and honor of the public, by beneficent legislation, so long as he is compelled by the solicitation of that public to bear the burden of office...

Is this impossible idealism? But all her ancient law-givers have been Rishis, saints and sages, not kings and courtiers and cabinets, as a fact, is it not? Who are the authors of her Smritis? The legislators of Islam too have been prophets and saints. The recognition of them as saints, the acceptance of their laws, by the public, is their "election" in the old way.

If it is all impossible idealism, then what about that living 'practical mystic' and leader of leaders, Mahatma Gandhi? What about his venerated predecessors, Lokamanya Tilak, and Gokhale, Chief Servant of India? And could not a fair number of others also be named, living leaders, whose long-continued sacrifices for the country, or great, if late, renunciations are almost equally noteworthy, and who would come into the same rank, if they only had a stronger touch of asceticism and of that yearning tenderness of feeling for humanity which marks the saints? And are there not a good many workers of the second rank, who come near the qualifications mentioned, and would develop them in full, once the atmosphere is re-established that is needed for their proper growth, the atmosphere, namely, of a strong, wide-spread, and insistently expressed *public opinion* that only such men are wanted in the legislature?

The courageous suffering of long imprisonments and transportations cheerfully accepted by school-boys, on the one hand, and by Sirdars, Maulanas, Sadhus and Sanyasis, shop-keepers and zamindars, highly educated editors of journals and illiterate tillers of the soil alike, on the other, by hundreds, for the great offence of telling "the true causes of the present discontents," to the public and to the government of the day, unflinchingly—(at times in strong language, without which attention is not received, and which therefore has not always recounted those great defects of the Indian people themselves, which have made their exploitation by others possible, and the persistent recognition of which would engender a just humility, giving a more judicial tone to the language, and a truer direction and a greater firmness to the resolve of *Swaraj*)—this outburst of self-sacrificing idealism, so rapidly evoked by the earnest-minded, sincere-hearted and philanthropy leadership of Mahatma Gandhi, makes the hope, that 'ideal' legislators can and will be produced in sufficient numbers by the same motherland, not so very impossible...

After legislation comes execution. After the laws have been made they require to be enforced. Midway comes the judicial work. India has been crying for long and in vain, for the separation of the judicial and the executive functions. But the separation of the legislative and the executive functions is far more necessary, because the combination of the two is much more radically maleficent. In England the salaried Cabinet, the Chief Executive, is also, for all practical purposes, the Chief Legislative and this is the principal cause of unjust laws...

The ancient tradition, the genius, too, of the country, insists on the separation of the two functions. "The man of thought," the wise and ascetic man, the sage and saint, the priest-scientist, should legislate but exercise no executive power. "The man of action," the king, the soldier, the policeman, should execute the law, but exercise no legislative power. When the two functions are combined, selfish ambition becomes rampant, and benevolent wisdom has no chance. When the two are separate, each helps to check any tendency to error or excess in the other. The same man prince of church and prince of land at the same time, has generally proved to be a prince of darkness.

These two functions are different by nature; they belong to two different temperaments. The business of the man of thought, the man of science, is to 'ascertain facts,' to ascertain what conditions, what allocations of unions, what assignments of rights-and-duties, result in the greatest happiness of the greatest number, and not in the greatest power and glory and cash of the smallest number. The business of the man of action is to enforce the fulfillment of these conditions, the performance of these functions, the exercise of these rights-and-duties, by all concerned. The two businesses should never be combined, any more than the judicial and the executive. The legislative and judicial functions may be combined, if necessary, (though it is desirable, ordinarily, to keep them apart also), because judicial work too is the ascertainment of facts, the facts of a case and of the law applicable to them...

The Function of the State

By ancient indigenous tradition, the work of the State, the functions or duties of the government, fall under four main heads: (a) the right education of the people, (b) their right protection, (c) their right sustentation, (d) their right recreation. Hence we have four main departments, portfolios, or organisations, viz., the Educational, the Protectional, the Economic, and the Recreational. It is worth while to make a regular department of this last, *Panem el circenses*, work and play, are equally necessary: men live not by bread alone, but also by recreation—of body, by play; and of soul, by prayer and religion and communion with the Universal God hidden within the should, the making manifest of Whom within each soul is the work of the priest-educationist, a functionary in importance equal with the legislator.

Of course all four are ever interdependent, though separate, as head, hands, torso, and feet. Each has many sub-departments, some of which may be regarded as midway or connective departments. Thus, public instruction, public morals and religion, public health, public justice, etc.... *i.e.*... the work of "the learned professions," would come under the first; military, police, jails, etc., under the second; agriculture, horticulture, sericulture, forest, mines, cattle-breeding, commerce, finance and revenue, and industries of all kinds, under the third; zoos, museums, theatres, pageants, circuses, festivals, holidays, art-galleries, music-halls, parks and gardens, races and games (without betting), etc., under the fourth. If it were desired to assign legislation also to one of these four, then, obviously, it would go under the first. But it is the business of legislation to govern and co-ordinate these four main departments and all their multifarious sub-divisions, in proper proportion.

The point aimed at by the above is that, generally speaking, four different kinds of temperament are wanted for the proper discharge of the four functions respectively, viz., the man of thought, the man of action, the man of desire, and the artist (varieties of each of the other three, in a sense, together with the artisan)—all under the guidance of the best man of thought, the true scientist-priest, presbyter, elder, the legislator; and that these four functions should be kept apart in four separate pairs of hands, if abuse is to be avoided...

The principle of election is wholesome, and in accord with the traditions of India. It is embodied in the republics of the Buddhist and pre-Buddhist days, and in the village panchyats which are continuously living on into the present day. But the manner of its expression was and is different from that followed in the West. Here, the trusted of the people gradually and almost imperceptibly grew into that position, and came to be recognized as such, more or less unobtrusively, in the course of years, and therefore with certainty as to their character. In the West, in keeping with the whole spirit of its present civilization, the thing is done by challenge, and beat of drum, and rival self-displays of powers of eloquence, heavy expenditures on canvassing, and manifestos of promises of the work that will be done by the candidate, if elected—promises mostly forgotten after election. The heavy expenses also leave behind, naturally, in the mind of the candidate who succeeds, and therefore has opportunities, the wish for recoupment, in some way or other, fair or foul—not a healthy mood for a legislator. And it is obvious that such canvassing and expenditure are not only generally impossible, but degrading and humiliating, for worthy men of the sort we want as legislators, men who have done with the ambitions and luxuries of life, and have retired on a simple competence.

But the *principle of representation*—representation on interests and classes presumed all along to be in conflict with each other, like opposed parties in lawsuits, and requiring to be protected from one another, by the perpetual quarrellings of their respective advocate-representatives in the forum of the legislative assembly; and not presumed to be all interdependent, and capable of being protected only by the harmonizing of all, by dis-interested trustees of the whole community—this principle is unwholesome, and foreign to our genius. It goes with the party-system and all its evils.

This clause makes it clear and unmistakable that all departments of the administration must be subordinate and responsible to the elected legislature, which in turn is responsive to the people as a whole, who exercise their control over it by elective choice. The circle of Self-government is thus completed. No loose end, no one-sidedness is left, as in autocracy, or bureaucracy, or plutocracy, or theocracy, or in democracy (which turns into autocracy after a bout of mobocracy). And the circle of such self-government of the people, for the people, and by the people, is not vicious, but virtuous, because "by the people" means, under such condition, "by the higher self, the wise and virtuous and benevolent self, of the people," when alone the people, of all classes, of all walks of life, can have well-being, can fare well, can be well and whole, truly healthy in the just exercise of all useful functions, and wealthy in the possession of widespread contentment and happiness.

The Indo-British Commonwealth

"Within the British Empire" people feel now, stamps subjectiveness and racial inferiority on the Indian people. The King or Queen of England is only King or Queen, and not Emperor or Empress of England, Scotland, Wales, or Ireland, or of Canada, South Africa, Australia, New Zealand, etc. He or she is Emperor or Empress of India only. Why? "Self-government on *Colonial* lines within the British *Empire*" is a contradiction of terms.

On the other hand, "*Swaraj* or Self-government without the British Empire," i.e. *Swaraj* in absolute separation from England—for without India there is no British *Empire*—is a prospect which also very, very few Congressmen, if any, contemplate as desirable, or as anything but the last alternative. The reasons are plain and need not be dilated here.

Briefly, there is every reason why India should no longer be a "dependency", a mulch-cow of England, to be beaten, starved, and milked at will by torturing processes of forcing. There is also much reason why the friendliest and closest relations between the two should be maintained, to the profit of both and of other countries as well. The way of reconciliation of these two necessities is embodied in these last two clauses, in the shape of "*Swaraj* or Self-government, not on Colonial, but on far better lines, and within, not a British Empire, but an Indo-British or British-Indian Commonwealth or Federation"...

Once British people reconcile themselves to the renunciation of whatever pleasant taste there may be in the arrogance of racial superiority and imperialistic jingoism, and make up their minds to live in India on terms of equality and mutual accommodation with Indians, rank for rank, grade for grade, profession for profession, quality for quality as Punjabis, Bengalis, Marathas, Gujaratis, Tamils, Telugus, Parsis, Indian Christians, Musalmans, Hindus, etc., are living—they will find that they are no worse off than now, financially, in respect of trade-relations, but probably better; and they will certainly be much better off ethically, in respect of mutual good-will and trust and friendliness of social relations. Indian and British, in such circumstance, will be able to help each other by the distinctive qualities and virtues, and supply one another's spiritual and physical lacks much more efficiently. And genuinely sympathetic British persons will be honored in greater degree that Indians of corresponding quality—for, from the latter, more would be expected naturally. If, today, an election were held for some public office of very high trustworthiness, the chances of a sadhu like Mr. C. F. Andrews would be next after those of Mahatma Gandhi only, and as great as those of almost any other Indian leader. British persons have been repeatedly elected Presidents of the Indian National Congress. And always the Inmost Spirit of India has been eclectic, synthetic, all-tolerant, all-gathering, all-reconciling, and not exclusive. Often, in the past, has India slowly converted and incorporated into her body-politic 'foreign' invaders and their companions, transforming them into 'native' priests-scientists-literati, warrior-rulers, agriculturists-tradesmen, and helper-servants according to their natural capacities and functions, without asking them to give up any individual peculiarities that were dear to them and not inconsistent with the well-being of the Indian Social Whole; and India will continue to do so, again and again; for her Inmost Spirit is not racialist or nationalist, but Humanist.

Conclusions

Such I humbly and earnestly believe to be the only way; the way of the great reconciliation, not only of India and England, but of all nations and of all the classes within each nation, with each other...

If this is done by means of wise legislation, which will reconcile the "I" and the "We" that both exist in each human being, the elements of competition and of co-operation that are both indispensable, the individualist initiative and the socialist regulation that are both equally needed for communal health and prosperity; if this is done by means of just and righteous legislation through wisely elected spiritual-minded legislators, then that, for centuries, will be sufficient and true *Swaraj*.

K. C. Bhattacharyya, "Svaraj in Ideas" (1928)

Krishna Chandra Bhattacharyya (1875–1949) is perhaps the best-known academic philosopher of the colonial period. He held the King George V Chair (now the B. N. Seal Chair) in Philosophy at the University of Calcutta and trained many of the eminent philosophers of the post-independence period. He is best known for his highly technical and even forbidding work on metaphysics, epistemology, aesthetics, and the philosophy of Kant. The present essay is actually a transcript of a talk given to students on the practice of philosophy in colonial India and is unusual for its accessibility and personal tone.

Krishna Chandra Bhattacharyya

7

Svaraj In Ideas[*]

1. We speak today of *Svaraj* or self-determination in politics. Man's domination over man is felt in the most tangible form in the political sphere. There is however a subtler domination exercised in the sphere of ideas by one culture on another, a domination all the more serious in the consequence, because it is not ordinarily felt. Political subjection primarily means restraint on the outer life of a people and although it tends gradually to sink into the inner life of the soul, the fact that one is conscious of it operates against the tendency. So long as one is conscious of a restraint, it is possible to resist it or to bear it as a necessary evil and to keep free in spirit. Slavery begins when one ceases to feel the evil and it deepens when the evil is accepted as a good. Cultural subjection is ordinarily of an unconscious character and it implies slavery from the very start. When I speak of cultural subjection, I do not mean the assimilation of an alien culture. That assimilation need not be an evil; it may be positively necessary for healthy progress and in any case it does not mean a lapse of freedom. There is cultural subjection only when one's traditional cast of ideas and sentiments is superseded without comparison or competition by a new cast representing an alien culture which possesses one like a ghost. This subjection is slavery of the spirit; when a person can shake himself free from it, he feels as though the scales fell from his eyes. He experiences a rebirth, and that is what I call *Svaraj* in Ideas.

2. In these days when our political destinies are in the melting pot, one is tempted to express a doubt—till now vaguely felt but suppressed as uncultured—how far generally we have assimilated our western education and how far it has operated as an obsession. Certainly there has been some sort of assimilation—at least by some of us—but even of them it may be asked whether the alien culture has been accepted by them after a full and open-eyed struggle had been allowed to develop between it and their indigenous culture. It is admitted today—what was not sufficiently recognised in the

---

* This discourse was given at a meeting of the students of the Hooghly College of which the writer was Principal, during 1928–30. The present paper was recovered from Dr. Bhattacharyya's unpublished writings.

Subsequently it was published in the *Visva Bharati Journal*, Vol. XX. 1954; pp. 103–114.

earlier days of our western education—that we had an indigenous culture of a high degree of development, the comparative value of which cannot be said to have been yet sufficiently appraised. Under the present system we generally receive western culture in the first instance and then we sometimes try to peer into our ancient culture as a curiosity and with the attitude of foreign oriental scholars and yet we say that this ancient culture of ours is no curiosity. Many of our educated men do not know and do not care to know this indigenous nature of ours. When they seek to know, they do not feel, as they ought to feel, that they are discovering their own self.

3. There is no gainsaying the fact that this western culture—which means an entire system of ideas and sentiments—has been simply imposed upon us. I do not mean that it has been imposed on unwilling minds: we ourselves asked for this education, and we feel, and perhaps rightly, that it has been a blessing in certain ways. I mean only that it has not generally been assimilated by us in an open-eyed way with our old-world Indian mind. That Indian mind has simply lapsed in most cases for our educated men, and has subsided below the conscious level of culture. It operates still in the persisting routine of their family life and in some of their social and religious practices which have no longer, however, any vital meaning for them. It neither welcomes nor resists the ideas received through the new education. It dares not exert itself in the cultural sphere.

4. There can be no vital assimilation, in such case, of the imposed culture. And yet the new ideas are assimilated in a fashion. They are understood and imaginatively realised; they are fixed in language and in certain imposed institutions. A drill in this language and in those institutions induces certain habits of soulless thinking which appear like real thinking. Springing as these ideas do from a rich and strong life—the life of the west—they induce in us a shadow mind that functions like a real mind except in the matter of genuine creativeness. One would have expected after a century of contact with the vivifying ideas of the west that there should be a vigorous output of Indian contribution in a distinctive Indian style to the culture and thought of the modern world,—contribution specially to humane subjects like history, philosophy or literature, a contribution such as may be enjoyed by our countrymen who still happen to retain their vernacular mind and which might be recognized by others as reflecting the distinctive soul of India. Barring the contribution of a few men of genius,—and genius is largely independent of the times,—there is not much evidence of such creative work done by our educated men.

5. I may refer also to more modest forms of creativeness, creativeness such as is evidenced in the daily business of our lives, e.g., in the formation of judgements about our real position in the world. We speak of world movements and have a fair acquaintance with the principles and details of western life

and thought, but we do not always sufficiently realize where we actually stand today and how to apply our bookish principles to our situation in life. We either accept or repeat the judgment passed on us by western culture, or we impotently resent them but have hardly any estimates of our own, wrung from an inward perception of the realities of our position.

6. In the field of politics, for example, we are only today beginning to realize that we have for long wrongly counted on principles that have application only to countries that are already free and already established and have not had sufficient perception of the dark thing they call 'power' which is more real than any logic or political scholarship. In the field of social reform, we have never cared to understand the inwardness of our traditional social structure and to examine how far the social principles of the west are universal in their application. We have contented ourselves either with an unthinking conservatism or with an imaginary progressiveness merely imitative of the west.

7. Then again in the field of learning, how many of us have had distinctively Indian estimates of western literature and thought? It is possible for a foreigner to appreciate the literature of a country, but it is only to be expected that his mind would react to it differently from the mind of a native of the country. A Frenchman, for example, would not, I imagine, appreciate Shakespeare just as an Englishman would do. Our education has largely been imported to us through English literature. The Indian mind is much further removed by tradition and history than the French or the German mind from the spirit of English literature, and yet no Indian, so far as I am aware, has passed judgements on English literature that reflect his Indian mentality.

8. His judgments do not differ materially from the judgment of an English critic and that raises the suspicion whether it is his judgment at all, whether it is not merely the mechanical thinking of the galvanic mind induced in us through our western education.

9. In philosophy hardly anything that has been written by a modern educated Indian shows that he has achieved a synthesis of Indian thought with western thought. There is nothing like a judgment on western systems from the standpoint of Indian philosophy, and although some appraisement of Indian philosophy has been attempted from the western standpoint, there appears to be no recognition yet that a criticism of the fundamental notions of either philosophy is necessary before there can be any useful comparative estimate. And yet it is in philosophy that one could look for an effective contact between Eastern and Western ideas. The most prominent contribution of ancient India to the culture of the world is in the field of Philosophy and if the Modern Indian Mind is to philosophise at all to any purpose, it has to confront Eastern thought and Western thought with one another and attempt

a synthesis or a reasoned rejection of either, if that were possible. It is in philosophy, if anywhere, that the task of discovering the soul of India is imperative for the modern India; the task of achieving, if possible, the continuity of his old self with his present day self, of realising what is nowadays called the Mission of India, if it has any. Genius can unveil the soul of India in art but it is through philosophy that we can methodically attempt to discover it.

10. Our education has not so far helped us to understand ourselves, to understand the significance of our past, the realities of our present and our mission of the future. It has tended to drive our real mind into the unconscious and to replace it by a shadow mind that has no roots in our past and in our real present. Our old mind cannot be wholly driven underground and its imposed substitute cannot function effectively and productively. The result is that there is a confusion between the two minds and a hopeless Babel in the world of ideas. Our thought is hybrid through and through and inevitably sterile. Slavery has entered into our very soul.

11. The hybridisation of our ideas is evidenced by the strange medley of Vernacular and English in which our educated people speak to one another. For the expression of cultural ideas specially we find it very difficult to use the pure Vernacular medium. If I were asked; for example, to conduct today's discourse here in Bengali, I would have to make a particularly strenuous effort. One notices a laudable tendency at the present day to make such an effort. It is not that it is always successful. Perhaps, that is only to be expected in a period of transition. If the language difficulty could be surmounted, it would mean a big step towards the achievement of what I have called Svaraj in Ideas.

12. The hybridisation of ideas brought about by our education and the impact of Western political social and economic institutions on our daily life is one of the most distressing features of present situation. It is unnatural and may be regarded with the same sentiment with which an old world Hindu looks upon varṇ-saṃara. It does not simply mean a confusion in the intellectual region. All vital ideas involve ideals. They embody an entire theory and an insight into life. Thought or reason may be universal, but ideas are carved out of it differently by different cultures according to their respective genius. No idea of one cultural language can exactly be translated in another cultural language. Every culture has its distinctive 'physiognomy' which is reflected in each vital idea and ideal presented by the culture.

13. A patchwork of ideas of different cultures offends against scholarly sense just as much as patchwork of ideals offends against the spiritual sense. There is room indeed for an adjustment and synthesis, within limits of different cultures and cultural ideals. Life means adaptation to varying times and to varying ideals. But we are not always clear about the method of this

adaptation. As we have to live, we have to accept facts and adapt our secular life and secular ideas to the times. We have to alter ourselves here to suit the situation. In spiritual life, however, there is no demand for compromising our ideals in order to have a smooth sailing with the times. Here, if possible and so far as lies in our power, the times have to be adapted to our life and not our life to the times.

14. But the world confronts us not only with aggressive interests but also with aggressive ideals. What response should our traditional ideals make to these imposed ideals? We may respect the new ideals without accepting them, we may attempt a synthesis without compromise, or we may accept them as the fulfilment of our ideals. Different responses may be demanded with respect to different ideals, but in any case a patchwork without adjustment or with a mechanical adjustment, if complacently accepted as a solution, is an evil, as no ideal here gets the entire devotion of the soul. Where different ideals are accepted in the prayerful hope that a synthesis will come, the patchwork is not accepted as a solution and need not be an evil.

15. We talk—a little too glibly perhaps—of a conflict of the ideas and ideals of the West with our traditional ideas and ideals. In many cases it is a confusion rather than a conflict and the real problem is to clear up the confusion and to make it develop in the first instance into a definite conflict. The danger is in the complacent acquiescence in the confusion. The realization of a conflict of ideals implies a deepening of the soul. There is conflict proper only when one is really serious about ideals, feels each ideal to be a matter of life and death. We sometimes sentimentally indulge in the thought of a conflict before we are really serious with either ideal.

16. We speak also a little too readily of the demand for a synthesis of the ideals of the East and the West. It is not necessary in every case that a synthesis should be attempted. The ideals of a community spring from its past history and from the soil: they have not necessarily a universal application, and they are not always self-luminous to other communities. There are ideals of the West which we may respect from a distance without recognizing any specific appeal to ourselves. Then again there are ideals that have a partial appeal to us, because they have an affinity with our own ideals, though still with a foreign complexion. What they prescribe to us is to be worshipped in our own fashion with the ceremonials of our own religion. The form of practical life in which an ideal has to be translated, has to be decided by ourselves according to the genius of our own community. A synthesis of our ideals with western ideals is not demanded in every case. Where it is demanded, the foreign ideal is to be assimilated to our ideal and not the other way. There is no demand for the surrender of our individuality in any case: *Svadharme nidhanaṃ śreyaḥ paradharmo bhayāvahaḥ*. (Perform your own duty, not that of another.)

17. There are those who take this emphasis on the individuality of a historical community to be overstrained. It appears to them to be the expression of national, communal, or racial conceit and the excuse for a perverse obscurantism. They believe in abstract self-luminous ideals for all humanity, in a single universal religion and a single universal reason.

18. There is, however, case for universalism. The progress of a community and of humanity implies a gradual simplification and unification of ideals. This is just the rationalizing movement, the emergence of a common reason. We have to distinguish, however, between two forms of rationalism, two directions of this simplifying movement. In the one, reason is born after the travail of the spirit: rationalism is here the efflux of reverence, reverence for the traditional institutions through which customary sentiments are deepened into transparent ideals. In the other form of rationalism—what is commonly meant by the name, the simplification and generalization of ideals is effected by unregenerate understanding with its mechanical separation of the essential from the inessential. The essential is judged as such here not through reverence, not through deepened spiritual insight, but through the accidental likes and dislikes of the person judging. Customs and institutions bound up with age-long sentiments are brushed aside (in the name of reason) as meaningless and dead without any imaginative effort to realize them in an attitude of humility. Decisions as to what is essential or inessential have indeed to be taken, for time tarries not and mere historical sentimentalism will not avail. In practical life, one may have to move before ideals have clarified; but it is well to recognize the need of humility and patience in the adjustment of the world of ideas. Order is evolved in the world of our ideas through infinite patience and humility. That is the right kind of rationalism: it is only in the wrong and graceless form of rationalism that brusque decisions in the practical manner are taken in the name of reason, in the world of our ideals.

19. There is then a legitimate and obligatory form of rationalism. It is wrong not to accept an ideal that is felt to be a simpler and deeper expression of our own ideas simply because it hails from a foreign country. To reject it would be to insist on individuality for the sake of individuality and would be a form of national conceit and obscurantism. The acceptance of such an ideal is really no surrender of individuality: to serve this foreign god is to serve our own god: the foreign ideal is here in our own ideal. The guru or teacher has to be accepted when he is found to be a real guru, whatever the community from which he comes. But it is not every foreign ideal that is felt to be the soul of our own ideal. Some foreign ideals have affinity with our own, and are really alternative expressions of them in a foreign idiom that has no sacredness for us and there are others which have no real application to our conditions.

20. It is sometimes forgotten by the advocates of universalism that the so-called universalism of reason or of religion is only in the making and cannot be appealed to as an actually established code of universal principles. What is universal is only the spirit, the loyalty to our own ideals and the openness to other ideals, the determination not to reject them if they are found within our ideals and not to accept them till they are so found. The only way to appraise a new ideal is to view it through our actual ideal; the only way to find a new reverence is to deepen our old reverence. Progress in the spiritual world is not achieved by a detached reason judging between an old god and a new god. The way to know facts is not the way to know values.

21. So much for the objection, which is often raised in the name of universalism, to the stress I have laid on the individuality of Indian thought and spirit, on the conservatism of the distinctive values evolved through ages of continuous historical life of Indian society. I have thought it necessary to examine universalism in some detail at the risk of tiring the reader with abstract arguments because this appears to me to be our greatest danger. It is the inevitable result of our 'rootless' education and it stands more than anything else in the way of what I call *Svaraj* in Ideas.

22. The other danger of national conceit and the unthinking glorification of everything in our culture and depreciation of everything in other cultures appears to me, in our circumstances, to require less stressing. Not that it is less serious abstractly considered, but as a matter of fact our educated men suffer more from over-diffidence than from over-confidence, more from a 'rootless' universalism than from clinging particularism. We are more ready to accept others' judgments about us than to resent them. There is the old immemorial habit of regarding what we are taught as sacred learning, and the habit is not easily altered even though the learning imparted is the mere opinion of others—opinion about us, for example, of men who might be presumed to be ignorant of us and unsympathetic to us. There is so much, kind or unkind, written about us and preached to us by others that raises the legitimate question if they have a sufficient perception of the inwardness of our life. Prima facie it is very difficult for a foreigner to understand the mind of a people from whom he is widely removed by tradition and history unless he has intimately participated in their life for a long time. It is only natural that the people in question should receive his judgment about them with a certain amount of mental reserve. It might lead them to self-examination if the foreigner is not obviously ignorant and abusive; but docile acceptance is not certainly demanded in the first instance.

23. Now there is a good deal in the name of learning—history, philosophy or moral sermon—imparted to us through our education which is unconsciously or consciously of a tendentious or propagandist character. They imply a valuation of ourselves, an appraisement of our past history and present position from a foreign standard. Our attitude towards them should be one of critical reserve, and not of docile acceptance. And yet the critical attitude would in many cases be condemned by our foreign teachers and by our own educated men as uncultured and almost as absurdly ignorant as a hesitation to accept the truth of geometry. That is inevitable where the education of a people is undertaken by foreign rulers. There is bound in such a case to be some imposition of foreign valuation on the learner and a discouragement of the critical attitude.

24. The question of imposition does not arise in the case of certain branches of learning—mathematics and the natural sciences, for example, which have no nationality and imply no valuation. Whenever there is valuation, there is the suspicion of a particular point of view—national, communal, or racial, of the person who judges the value. A valuation of our culture by a foreigner from the standpoint of his own culture should be regarded by us as meant not for our immediate acceptance but for our critical examination. It should be a fillip to which we should react. I remember a remark of Sir John Woodroffe to this purpose. That our first impulse here should be one of self-defensive resentment is only natural and need not imply an uncultured self-conceit. Docile acceptance without criticism would mean slavery.

25. The critical attitude is demanded pre-eminently in the field of valuations of ideals. Mere acceptance here makes not only for confusion but for moral evil. But barring the concepts of the sciences—even here there may be some doubt—all concepts and ideas have the distinctive character of the particular culture to which they belong. What should be our reaction to such cultural ideas? They have to be accepted, but metaphors and symbols to be translated into our own indigenous concepts. The ideas embodied in a foreign language are properly understood only when we can express them in our own way. I plead for a genuine translation of foreign ideas into our native ideas before we accept or reject them. Let us everywhere resolutely think in our own concepts. It is only thus that we can think productively on our own account.

26. In politics our educated men have been compelled to realize by the logic of facts that they have absolutely no power for good, though they have much power for evil, unless they can carry the masses with them. In other fields there is not sufficient realization of this circumstance. In the social sphere, for example, they still believe that they can impose certain reforms on the masses—by mere preaching from without, by passing resolutions in social conferences and by legislation. In the sphere of ideas, there is hardly yet any realization that we can think effectively only when we think in terms of

the indigenous ideas that pulsate in the life and mind of the masses. We condemn the caste system of our country, but we ignore the fact that we who have received Western education constitute a caste more exclusive and intolerant than any of the traditional castes. Let us resolutely break down the barriers of this new caste, let us come back to the cultural stratum of the real Indian people and evolve a culture along with them suited to the times and to our native genius. That would be to achieve *Svaraj* in Ideas.

PART TWO

Aesthetics

A. K. Coomaraswamy, "Art and Swadeshi" (1910)

Ananda Kentish Coomaraswamy (1877–1947) was born in Sri Lanka to a Sri Lankan father and English mother. Most of his life was spent in Boston, where he was curator of Asian art at the Boston Museum of Fine Arts. He was a noted art historian and aesthetician. His work addressed Indian national identity and he was active in the independence movement. This essay forms a bridge between the thought about national identity and aesthetic theory, inquiring into the national character of Indian art. It was written initially for an Indian student audience.

Rabindranath Tagore and Ananda Kentish Coomaraswamy

I

Art and Swadeshi[*]

IF YOU GO into one of those shops frequented by tourists in Indian towns, you will find amongst the flimsy wood carving and shallow brass work, the cheap enamels and the overloaded embroideries which are outward manifestations of the degradation of Indian craftsmanship, a few examples of real old Indian manufactures. These things, which used to be common in every market and were at once the wealth of the Indian people and the basis of their export trade for the last three thousand years, are now rare and difficult to obtain; they are called *purani chiz*, 'old things'. They are bought by American connoisseurs and German collectors for museums, for the education of Europe in design and for the benefit of the European manufacturer, for whom, too, they are reproduced in such papers as the *Journal of Indian Art*, and lectured on in Technical Schools and Schools of Art. For while the creative power of the craftsman has been long destroyed by commercialism in the West, it remained alive with us till yesterday, and even today some part of it survives.

Indian design is an inexhaustible treasure-house of fine invention. But have you ever reflected that all this invention belongs to the past—that modern India, Anglicised India, has produced no beauty and romance, but has gone far to destroy the beauty and romance which are our heritage from the past? Go into a *Swadeshi* shop—you will not find the evidences of Indian invention, the wealth of beauty which the Indian craftsman used to lavish on the simplest articles of daily use, the filmy muslins or the flower-woven silks with which we used to worship the beauty of Indian women, the brazen vessels from which we ate and drank, the carpets on which we trod with bare feet or the pictures that revealed to us the love of Radha, or the soul of the eternal snows. You will not find these things, but you will find every kind of imitation of the productions of European commerce, differing only from their unlovely prototypes in their slightly higher price and slightly inferior quality. You will find dingy grey 'shirtings'; other materials dyed with aniline dyes of the loudest and least permanent; travelling trunks that are painted every colour of the rainbow, and if carefully used may hold together for half a year; boot polish,

---

[*] Reprinted from the *Central Hindu College Magazine*. This essay has also appeared in the *Message of the East* which will not be reprinted in its present form.

marking ink, soaps and fountain pens—anything and everything but beauty. It is the outward sign of the merely material ideal of prosperity which is too exclusively striven for by our economists and politicians. I shall show presently how even such an aim defeats itself, but in the meanwhile let us take another view.

You are familiar with the thought that the highest ideal of nationality is service. Have you ever thought that India, politically and economically free, but subdued by Europe in her inmost soul is scarcely an ideal to be dreamt of, or to live, or die, for? "India, vulgarised by modern education, and by the ideals of modern commercialism, will never compensate humanity for India with its knowledge of beauty." Have you ever realised that there are European artists who believe that when a new inspiration comes into European art it will come again from the East? Do you realise that when India was a great political power in Asia, when she colonised Java and inspired China, this also was the period of her greatest achievement in art? Has it never occurred to you that it is as much your duty to make your lives and your environment beautiful as to make them moral, in fact that without beauty there can be no true morality, without morality no true beauty? Look round about you at the vulgarisation of modern India—our prostitution of art to the tourist trade—our use of kerosene tins for water jars, and galvanised zinc for tiles—our caricature of European dress—our homes furnished and ornamented in the style proverbial of seaside lodging houses, with cut glass chandeliers and China dogs and artificial flowers—our devotion to the harmonium and the gramophone—these things are the outward and damning proof of "some mighty evil in our souls."

Try to believe that this callousness of ours, this loss of the fine taste that belonged to classic and mediaeval culture is a sign of weakness, not of strength. Try to believe in the regeneration of India through art, and not by politics and economics alone. A purely material idea will never give to us the lacking strength to build up a great enduring nation. For that we need ideals and dreams, impossible and visionary, the food of martyrs and of artists.

You see, this loss of beauty in our lives is a proof that we do not love India; for India, above all nations, was beautiful once, and that was not long ago. It is the weakness of our national movement that we do not love India; we love suburban England, we love the comfortable bourgeois prosperity that is to be some day established when we have learned enough science and forgotten enough art to successfully compete with Europe in a commercial war conducted on its present lines. It is not thus that nations are made. And so, like Mr. Havell, I would say to you, "Leave off asking Government to revive your art and industries; all that is worth having you must and can do for yourselves; and when you have achieved all that you can do, no Government would refuse to grant you the political rights you desire, for the development of your artistic faculties will give back to India the creative force her people have lost. It will infuse into all your undertakings the practical sense and power of organisation which are now so often wanting."

And now for the practical side of the question, to show, i.e., that the ideal is (as always) the practical *par excellence*. The loss of artistic understanding more than anything else has ruined Indian industries and prevents the possibility of their revival. The neglect of Indian music has taken away the livelihood of the maker of musical instruments, with their hereditary and exquisite skill; has likewise destroyed the livelihood of Indian musicians; and fifteen lakhs worth of foreign instruments are annually imported from abroad! Observe that this is a double loss—material on the one hand, and spiritual on the other, for not only has the community lost wealth in the shape of things, but wealth in the shape of men, men who possessed the cunning and the skill to make them. Were India rich enough to spend a hundred lakhs per year on gramophones and harmoniums, this loss of men would still remain.

So too with the village weaver. Indian colouring and design have not been understood and loved: result, that the weaver's livelihood is gone, and he has to compete in agriculture, or in service in an already overcrowded field. Again, by concentration on the purely material side of the question, but not recognizing the superior workmanship of hand-made and individually designed materials, it has come about that instead of attempting to restore the village weaver and the handloom, we are willing to waste the vital forces of the nation in child-labour and long hours of work under mechanical and unhealthy conditions, transferred from Manchester to India. Remember that it can be said of England that "There is collected a population in our great towns which equals in amount the whole of those who lived in England and Wales six centuries ago; but whose condition is more destitute, whose homes are more squalid, whose means are more uncertain, whose prospects are more hopeless than those of the poorest serf of the middle ages and the meanest drudges of the mediaeval cities." Remember that one-tenth of the English people die in the work-house, the gaol or the lunatic asylum. Therefore learn not to waste the vital forces of the nation in a temporary political conflict, but understand that art will enable you to re-establish all your arts and industries on a surer basis, a basis which will bring well-being to the people themselves; for no lovely thing can be produced in conditions that are themselves unlovely.

Take one concrete case. "The Mirzapur carpets were at one time admired for their fast, bright colour, but are now identified with whatever is inferior in the name of dye or design. Aniline dyes and foreign models are responsible for the decline of a trade which gave fair promise of development not many years ago." Now observe that mere bad taste alone, the lack of artistic understanding, in such a case has destroyed the livelihood of the maker of dyes and the maker of carpets, and ruined even the possibility of an export trade.

The truth is that without artistic understanding, Indian manufacture cannot be effectively restored. It is suicidal to compete with Europe on a basis of cheapness. Competition should be upon a basis of quality.

At the same time the competition in cheapness alone is destructive of the very fibre of the Indian people: for "industry without art is brutality."

Swadeshi must be something more than a political weapon. It must be a religious-artistic ideal. I have heard nationalists exhort each other to sacrifice, in using *Swadeshi* goods. To think that it should need to be called a sacrifice! At least it should not, as now, be a sacrifice both in cost *and* quality. If we loved and understood Indian art we should know that even now the Indian craftsman could, if we would let him, build for us and clothe us in ways of beauty that could not be attained to in modern Europe for any expenditure of money at all. We would if we might, even today, live like the very gods but we lust after the fleshpots of Egypt, and deservedly our economy suffers.

Therefore I say to the well-to-do, that it is better to spend two hundred and fifty rupees on a Benares Sari, dyed with the country dyes, though two hundred would pay for it dyed in aniline, than to subscribe ten times that amount to some *Swadeshi* factory for making nibs or cloth and from which you expect a handsome dividend. And for the poor also in proportion to their ability remembering that "a poor man, by building the smallest temple, is no less meritorious than a wealthy man who builds the largest".*

Remember also that from the standpoint of national wealth, a few possessions that will endure, are better than many that will last only for a day. The builder whose work will last five centuries adds more to the national wealth than he whose work lasts only for fifty years. So, too, the weaver whose fair work is handed on from generation to generation does more for his country than a weaver whose work has soon to be cast aside. Civilisation consists not in multiplying the quantity of our desires, but in the refinement of their quality.

But let us not love art because it will bring to us prosperity; rather because it is a high function of our being, a door for thoughts to pass from the unseen to the seen, the source of those high dreams and the embodiment of that enduring vision that is to be the Indian nation; not less, but more strong and more beautiful than ever before, and the gracious giver of beauty to all the nations of the earth.

---

* *Agni Purana*, ch. XXVIII.

Aurobindo Ghosh, "The Future Poetry" (1917–1918)

Aurobindo Ghosh (later Sri Aurobindo) (1872–1950) was a central political, religious, and philosophical figure in the Indian renaissance. Bengali born and Cambridge-educated, he was trained in Victorian English literature, sat his Cambridge examinations in classics, and taught English at Baroda College. He became involved in radical politics and while imprisoned discovered Indian philosophy. He spent the remainder of his life at his ashram in Pondicherry, producing an enormous volume of religious and philosophical work, including his masterpiece *The Life Divine*. Many Indian philosophers of the colonial period visited him in Pondicherry, and his influence on Indian philosophy is considerable. In *The Future Poetry*, of which we present the first five chapters, Aurobindo advances a bold new aesthetic for poetry, grounded in Indian aesthetic and poetic theory, through which he assesses English poetry of the Victorian period.

2

The Future Poetry

I

The Mantra

It is not often that we see published in India literary criticism which is of the first order, at once discerning and suggestive, criticism which forces us both to see and think. A book which recently I have read and more than once reperused with a yet unexhausted pleasure and fruitfulness, Mr. James Cousins' *New Ways in English Literature,* is eminently of this kind. It raises thought which goes beyond the strict limits of the author's subject and suggests the whole question of the future of poetry in the age which is coming upon us, the higher functions open to it—as yet very imperfectly fulfilled,—and the part which English literature on the one side and the Indian mind and temperament on the other are likely to take in determining the new trend. The author is himself a poet, a writer of considerable force in the Irish movement which has given contemporary English literature its two greatest poets, and the book on every page attracts and satisfies by its living force of style, its almost perfect measure, its delicacy of touch, its fineness and depth of observation and insight, its just sympathy and appreciation.

For the purpose for which these essays have been, not indeed written, but put together, the criticism, fine and helpful as it is, suffers from one great fault,—there is too little of it. Mr. Cousins is satisfied with giving us the essential, just what is necessary for a trained mind to seize intimately the spirit and manner and poetic quality of the writers whose work he brings before us. This is done sometimes in such a masterly manner that even one touch more might well have been a touch in excess. The essay on Emerson is a masterpiece in this kind; it gives perfectly in a few pages all that should be said about Emerson's poetry and nothing that need not be said. But some of the essays, admirable in themselves, are too slight for our need. The book is not indeed intended to be exhaustive in its range. Mr. Cousins wisely takes for the most part,—there is one notable exception,—writers with whom he is in close poetical sympathy or for whom he has a strong appreciation; certain names which have come over to our ears with some flourish of the trumpets of renown, Thompson, Masefield, Hardy, do not occur at all or only in a passing allusion.

But still the book deals among contemporary poets with Tagore, A. E. and Yeats, among recent poets with Stephen Phillips, Meredith, Carpenter, great names all of them, not to speak of lesser writers. This little book with its 135 short pages is almost too small a pedestal for the figures it has to support, not, be it understood, for the purposes of the English reader interested in poetry, but for ours in India who have on this subject a great ignorance and, most of us, a very poorly trained critical intelligence. We need something a little more ample to enchain our attention and fix in us a permanent interest; a finger-post by the way is not enough for the Indian reader, you will have to carry him some miles on the road if you would have him follow it.

But Mr. Cousins has done a great service to the Indian mind by giving it at all a chance to follow this direction with such a guide to point out the way. The English language and literature is practically the only window the Indian mind, with the narrow and meagre and yet burdensome education given to it, possesses into the world of European thought and culture; but at least as possessed at present, it is a painfully small and insufficient opening. English poetry for all but a few of us stops short with Tennyson and Browning, when it does not stop with Byron and Shelley. A few have heard of some of the recent, fewer of some of the contemporary poets; their readers are hardly enough to make a number. In this matter of culture this huge peninsula, once one of the greatest centres of civilisation, has been for long the most provincial of provinces; it has been a patch of tilled fields round a lawyer's office and a Government cutcherry, a cross between a little district town and the most rural of villages, at its largest a dried-up bank far away from the great stream of the world's living thought and action, visited with no great force by occasional and belated waves, but for the rest a bare field for sluggish activities, the falsest possible education, a knowledge always twenty-five or fifty years behind the time. The awakening brought by the opening years of the twentieth century has chiefly taken the form of a revival of cultural patriotism, highly necessary for a nation which has a distinctive contribution to make to the human spirit in its future development, some new and great thing which it must evolve out of a magnificent past for the opening splendours of the future; but in order that this may evolve rapidly and surely, it needs a wide and sound information, a richer stuff to work upon, a more vital touch with the life and master tendencies of the world around it. Such books as this will be of invaluable help in creating what is now deficient.

The helpfulness of this suggestive work comes more home to me personally because I have shared to the full the state of mere blank which is the ordinary condition of the Indian mind with regard to its subject. Such touch as in the intellectual remoteness of India I have been able to keep up with the times, had been with contemporary continental rather than contemporary

English literature. With the latter all vital connection came to a dead stop with my departure from England a quarter of a century ago; it had for its last events the discovery of Meredith as a poet, in his *Modern Love*, and the perusal of *Christ in Hades*,—some years before its publication,—the latter an unforgettable date. I had long heard, standing aloof in giant ignorance, the great name of Yeats, but with no more than a fragmentary and mostly indirect acquaintance with some of his work; A. E. only lives for me in Mr. Cousins' pages; other poets of the day are still represented in my mind by scattered citations. In the things of culture such a state of ignorance is certainly an unholy state of sin; but in this immoral and imperfect world even sin has sometimes its rewards, and I get that now in the joy and light of a new world opening to me all in one view while I stand, Cortez-like, on the peak of the large impression created for me by Mr. Cousins' book. For the light we get from a vital and illuminative criticism from within by another mind can sometimes almost take the place of a direct knowledge.

There disengages itself from these essays not so much a special point of view as a distinctive critical and literary temperament, which may be perhaps not so much the whole mind of the critic as the response to his subject in a mind naturally in sympathy with it. Mr. Cousins is a little nervous about this in his preface; he is apprehensive of being labelled as an idealist. The cut and dried distinction between idealism and realism in literature has always seemed to me to be a little arbitrary and unreal, and whatever its value in drama and fiction, it has no legitimate place in poetry. What we find here is a self-identification with what is best and most characteristic of a new spirit in the age, a new developing aesthetic temper and outlook,—or should we rather say, inlook? Its mark is a greater (not exclusive) tendency to the spiritual rather than the merely earthly, to the inward and subjective than the outward and objective, to the life within and behind than to the life in front, and in its purest, which seems to be its Irish form, a preference of the lyrical to the dramatic and of the inwardly suggestive to the concrete method of poetical presentation. Every distinctive temperament has naturally the defect of an insufficient sympathy, often a pronounced and intolerant antipathy towards all that departs from its own motives. Moreover contemporary criticism is beset with many dangers; there is the charm of new thought and feeling and expression of tendency which blinds us to the defects and misplaces or misproportions to our view the real merits of the expression itself; there are powerful cross-currents of immediate attraction and repulsion which carry us from the true track; especially, there is the inevitable want of perspective which prevents us from getting a right vision of things too near us in time. And if in addition one is oneself part of a creative movement with powerful tendencies and a pronounced ideal, it becomes difficult to get away from the standpoint it creates to a larger critical outlook. From these reefs and shallows Mr. Cousins' sense of measure and justice of appreciation largely, generally indeed, preserve him, though not, I think, quite invariably. But still it is not a passionless, quite disinterested criticism which we get or want from this book, but a much more helpful thing, an interpretation of work which embodies the creative tendencies of the time by one who has himself lived in them and helped both to direct and to form.

Mr. Cousins' positive criticism is almost always fine, just and inspired by a warm glow of sympathy and understanding tempered by discernment, restraint and measure; whatever the future critic, using his scales and balance, may have to take away from it, will be, one would imagine, only by way of a slight alteration of stress here and there. His depreciations, though generally sound enough, are not, I think, invariably as just as his appreciations. Thus his essay on the work of J. M. Synge, "The Realist on the Stage", is, in sharp distinction from the rest of the book, an almost entirely negative and destructive criticism, strong and interesting, but written from the point of view of the ideals and aims of the Irish literary movement against a principle of work which seemed entirely to depart from them; yet we are allowed to get some glimpse of a positive side of dramatic power which the critic does not show us, but leaves us rather to guess at. Mr. Cousins seems to me to take the dramatist's theory of his own art more seriously than it should be taken; for the creator can seldom be accepted—there may of course be exceptions, rare instances of clairvoyant self-sight—as a sound exponent of his own creative impulse. He is in his central inspiration the instrument of a light and power not his own, and his account of it is usually vitiated, out of focus, an attempt to explain the workings of this impersonal power by motives which were the contribution of his own personal effort, but which are often quite subordinate or even accidental side-lights of the lower brain-mind, not the central moving force.

Mr. Cousins' has pointed out clearly enough that art can never be a copy of life. But it is also true, I think, that that is not the secret object of most realism, whatever it may say about itself; realism is in fact a sort of nether idealism, or, perhaps more correctly, sometimes an inverse, sometimes a perverse romanticism which tries to get a revelation of creative truth by an effective force of presentation, by an intensity, often an exaggeration at the opposite side of the complex phenomenon of life. All art starts from the sensuous and sensible, or takes it as a continual point of reference or, at the lowest, uses it as a symbol and a fount of images; even when it soars into invisible worlds, it is from the earth that it soars; but equally all art worth the name must go beyond the visible, must reveal, must show us something that is hidden, and in its total effect not reproduce but create. We may say that the artist creates an ideal world of his own, not necessarily in the sense of ideal perfection, but a world that exists in the idea, the imagination and vision of the creator. More truly, he throws into significant form a truth he has seen, which may be truth of hell or truth of heaven or an immediate truth behind things terrestrial or any other, but is never merely the external truth of earth. By that ideative truth and the power, the perfection and the beauty of his presentation and utterance of it his work must be judged.

Some occasional utterances in this book seem to spring from very pronounced idiosyncrasies of its distinctive literary temperament or standpoint and cannot always be accepted without reservation. I do not myself share its rather disparaging attitude towards the dramatic form and motive or its comparative coldness towards the architectural faculty and impulse in poetry. When Mr. Cousins tells us that "its poetry and not its drama, will prove to be the thing of life" in Shakespeare's work, I feel that the distinction is not sound all through, that there is a truth behind it, but it is overstated. Or when still more vivaciously he dismisses Shakespeare the dramatist to "a dusty and reverent immortality in the libraries" or speaks of the "monstrous net of his life's work" which but for certain buoys of line and speech "might sink in the ocean of forgetfulness," I cannot help feeling that this can only be at most the mood of the hour born of the effort to get rid of the burden of its past and move more freely towards its future, and not the definitive verdict of the poetic and aesthetic mind on what has been so long the object of its sincere admiration and a powerful presence and influence. Perhaps I am wrong, I may be too much influenced by my own settled idiosyncrasies of an aesthetic temperament and being impregnated with an early cult for the work of the great builders in Sanskrit and Greek, Italian and English poetry. At any rate, this is true that whatever relation we may keep with the great masters of the past, our present business is to go beyond and not to repeat them, and it must always be the lyrical motive and spirit which find a new secret and begin a new creation; for the lyrical is the primary poetical motive and spirit and the dramatic and epic must wait for it to open for them their new heaven and new earth.

I have referred to these points which are only side issues or occasional touches in Mr. Cousins' book, because they are germane to the question which it most strongly raises, the future of English poetry and of the world's poetry. It is still uncertain how that future will deal with the old quarrel between idealism and realism, for the two tendencies these names roughly represent are still present in the tendencies of recent work. More generally, poetry always sways between two opposite trends, towards predominance of subjective vision and towards an emphasis on objective presentation, and it can rise too beyond these to a spiritual plane where the distinction is exceeded, the divergence reconciled. Again, it is not likely that the poetic imagination will ever give up the narrative and dramatic form of its creative impulse; a new spirit in poetry, even though primarily lyrical, is moved always to seize upon and do what it can with them,—as we see in the impulsion which has driven Maeterlinck, Yeats, Rabindranath to take hold of the dramatic form for self-expression as well as the lyrical in spite of their dominant subjectivity. We may perhaps think that this was not the proper form for their spirit, that they cannot get there a full or a flawless success; but who shall lay down rules for creative genius or say what it shall or shall not attempt? It follows its own course and makes its own shaping experiments. And it is interesting to speculate whether the new spirit in poetry will take and use with modifications the old dramatic and narrative forms, as did Rabindranath in his earlier dramatic attempts, or quite transform them to its own ends, as he has attempted in his later work. But after all these are subordinate issues.

It will be more fruitful to take the main substance of the matter for which the body of Mr. Cousins' criticism gives a good material. Taking the impression it creates for a starting-point and the trend of English poetry for our main text, but casting our view farther back into the past, we may try to sound what the future has to give us through the medium of the poetic mind and its power for creation and interpretation. The issues of recent activity are still doubtful and it would be rash to make any confident prediction; but there is one possibility which this book strongly suggests and which it is at least interesting and may be fruitful to search and consider. That possibility is the discovery of a closer approximation to what we might call the *mantra* in poetry, that rhythmic speech which, as the Veda puts it, rises at once from the heart of the seer and from the distant home of the Truth,—the discovery of the word, the divine movement, the form of thought proper to the reality which, as Mr. Cousins excellently says, "lies in the apprehension of a something stable behind the instability of word and deed, something that is a reflection of the fundamental passion of humanity for something beyond itself, something that is a dim shadowing of the divine urge which is prompting all creation to unfold itself and to rise out of its limitations towards its Godlike possibilities." Poetry in the past has done that in moments of supreme elevation; in the future there seems to be some chance of its making it a more conscious aim and steadfast endeavour.

II

The Essence of Poetry

What then is the nature of poetry, its essential law? what is the highest power we can demand from it, what the supreme music that the human mind, reaching up and in and out to its own widest breadths, deepest depths and topmost summits, can extract from this self-expressive instrument? and how out of that does there arise the possibility of its use as the *mantra* of the Real? Not that we need spend any energy in a vain effort to define anything so profound, elusive and indefinable as the breath of poetic creation; to take the myriad-stringed harp of Saraswati to pieces for the purpose of scientific analysis is a narrow and barren amusement. But we stand in need of some guiding intuitions, some helpful descriptions which will serve to enlighten our search; to fix in that way, not by definition, but by description, the essential things in poetry is neither an impossible, nor an unprofitable endeavour.

We meet here two common enough errors, to one of which the ordinary uninstructed mind is most liable, to the other the too instructed critic or the too intellectually conscientious artist or craftsman. To the ordinary mind, judging poetry without really entering into it, it looks as if it were nothing more than an aesthetic pleasure of the imagination, the intellect and the ear, a sort of elevated pastime. If that were all, we need not have wasted time in seeking for its spirit, its inner aim, its deeper law. Anything pretty, pleasant and melodious with a beautiful idea in it would serve our turn; a song of Anacreon or a plaint of Mimnermus would be as satisfying to the poetic sense as the Oedipus, Agamemnon or Odyssey, for from this point of view they might well strike us as equally and even, one might contend, more perfect in their light but exquisite unity and brevity. Pleasure, certainly, we expect from poetry as from all art; but the external sensible and even the inner imaginative pleasure are only first elements. For these must not only be refined in order to meet the highest requirements of the intelligence, the imagination and the ear; but afterwards they have to be still farther heightened and in their nature raised beyond even their own noblest levels, so that they may become the support for something greater beyond them; otherwise they cannot lead to the height on which lives the Mantra.

For neither the intelligence, the imagination nor the ear are the true or at least the deepest or highest recipients of the poetic delight, even as they are not its true or highest creators; they are only its channels and instruments: the true creator, the true hearer is the soul. The more rapidly and transparently the rest do their work of transmission, the less they make of their separate claim to satisfaction, the more directly the word reaches and sinks deep into the soul, the greater the poetry. Therefore poetry has not really done its work, at least its highest work, until it has raised the pleasure of the instrument and transmuted it into the deeper delight of the soul. A divine *Ānanda,*[1] a delight

1. *Ānanda*, in the language of Indian spiritual experience, is the essential delight which the Infinite feels in itself and in its creation. By the infinite Self's *Ānanda* all exists, for the Self's *Ānanda* all was made.

interpretative, creative, revealing, formative,—one might almost say, an inverse reflection of the joy which the universal Soul felt in its great release of energy when it rang out into the rhythmic forms of the universe the spiritual truth, the large interpretative idea, the life, the power, the emotion of things packed into an original creative vision,—such spiritual joy is that which the soul of the poet feels and which, when he can conquer the human difficulties of his task, he succeeds in pouring also into all those who are prepared to receive it. This delight is not merely a godlike pastime; it is a great formative and illuminative power.

The critic—of a certain type—or the intellectually conscientious artist will, on the other hand, often talk as if poetry were mainly a matter of a faultlessly correct or at most an exquisite technique. Certainly, in all art good technique is the first step towards perfection; but there are so many other steps, there is a whole world beyond before you can get near to what you seek; so much so that even a deficient correctness of execution will not prevent an intense and gifted soul from creating great poetry which keeps its hold on the centuries. Moreover, technique, however indispensable, occupies a smaller field perhaps in poetry than in any other art,—first, because its instrument, the rhythmic word, is fuller of subtle and immaterial elements; then because, the most complex, flexible, variously suggestive of all the instruments of the artistic creator, it has more—almost infinite—possibilities in many directions than any other. The rhythmic word has a subtly sensible element, its sound value, a quite immaterial element, its significance or thought value, and both of these again, its sound and its sense, have separately and together a soul value, a direct spiritual power, which is infinitely the most important thing about them. And though this comes to birth with a small element subject to the laws of technique, yet almost immediately, almost at the beginning of its flight, its power soars up beyond the province of any laws of mechanical construction: and this form of speech carries in it on its summits an element which draws close to the empire of the ineffable.

Poetry rather determines its own form; the form is not imposed on it by any law mechanical or external to it. The poet least of all artists needs to create with his eye fixed anxiously on the technique of his art. He has to possess it, no doubt; but in the heat of creation the intellectual sense of it becomes a subordinate action or even a mere undertone in his mind, and in his best moments he is permitted, in a way, to forget it altogether. For then the perfection of his sound-movement and style come entirely as the spontaneous form of his soul: that utters itself in an inspired rhythm and an innate, a revealed word, even as the universal Soul created the harmonies of the universe out of the power of the word secret and eternal within him, leaving the mechanical work to be done in a surge of hidden spiritual excitement by the subconscient part of his Nature. It is this highest speech which is the supreme poetic utterance, the immortal element in his poetry, and a little of it is enough to save the rest of his work from oblivion. *Svalpam apyasya dharmasya!*

This power makes the rhythmic word of the poet the highest form of speech available to man for the expression whether of his self-vision or of his world-vision. It is noticeable that even the deepest experience, the pure spiritual which enters into things that can never be wholly expressed, still, when it does try to express them and not merely to explain them intellectually, tends instinctively to use, often the rhythmic forms, almost always the manner of speech characteristic of poetry. But poetry attempts to extend this manner of vision and utterance to all experience, even the most objective, and therefore it has a natural urge towards the expression of something in the object beyond its mere appearances, even when these seem outwardly to be all that it is enjoying.

We may usefully cast a glance, not at the last inexpressible secret, but at the first elements of this heightening and intensity peculiar to poetic utterance. Ordinary speech uses language mostly for a limited practical utility of communication; it uses it for life and for the expression of ideas and feelings necessary or useful to life. In doing so, we treat words as conventional signs for ideas with nothing but a perfunctory attention to their natural force, much as we use any kind of common machine or simple implement; we treat them as if, though useful for life, they were themselves without life. When we wish to put a more vital power into them, we have to lend it to them out of ourselves, by marked intonations of the voice, by the emotional force or vital energy we throw into the sound so as to infuse into the conventional word-sign something which is not inherent in itself. But if we go back earlier in the history of language and still more if we look into its origins, we shall, I think, find that it was not always so with human speech. Words had not only a real and vivid life of their own, but the speaker was more conscious of it than we can possibly be with our mechanised and sophisticated intellects. This arose from the primitive nature of language which, probably, in its first movement was not intended,—or shall we say, did not intend,—so much to stand for distinct ideas of the intelligence as for feelings, sensations, broad indefinite mental impressions with minute shades of quality in them which we do not now care to pursue. The intellectual sense in its precision must have been a secondary element which grew more dominant as language evolved along with the evolving intelligence.

For the reason why sound came to express fixed ideas, lies not in any natural and inherent equivalence between the sound and its intellectual sense, for there is none,—intellectually any sound might express any sense, if men were agreed on a conventional equivalence between them; it started from an indefinable quality or property in the sound to raise certain vibrations in the life-soul of the human creature, in his sensational, his emotional, his crude mental being. An example may indicate more clearly what I mean. The word wolf, the origin of which is no longer present to our minds, denotes to our intelligence a certain living object and that is all, the rest we have to do for ourselves: the Sanskrit word *vṛka*, "tearer", came in the end to do the same thing, but originally it expressed the sensational relation between the wolf and man which most affected the man's life, and it did so by a certain quality in the sound which readily associated it with the sensation of tearing. This must have given early language a powerful life, a concrete vigour, in one direction a natural poetic force which it has lost, however greatly it has gained in precision, clarity, utility.

Now, poetry goes back in a way and recovers, though in another fashion, as much as it can of this original element. It does this partly by a stress on the image replacing the old sensational concreteness, partly by a greater attention to the suggestive force of the sound, its life, its power, the mental impression it carries. It associates this with the definitive thought value contributed by the intelligence and increases both by each other. In that way it succeeds at the same time in carrying up the power of speech to the direct expression of a higher reach of experience than the intellectual or vital. For it brings out not only the definitive intellectual value of the word, not only its power of emotion and sensation, its vital suggestion, but through and beyond these aids its soul-suggestion, its spirit. So poetry arrives at the indication of infinite meanings beyond the finite intellectual meaning the word carries. It expresses not only the life-soul of man as did the primitive word, not only the ideas of his intelligence for which speech now usually serves, but the experience, the vision, the ideas, as we may say, of the higher and wider soul in him. Making them real to our life-soul as well as present to our intellect, it opens to us by the word the doors of the Spirit.

Prose style carries speech to a much higher power than its ordinary use, but it differs from poetry in not making this yet greater attempt. For it takes its stand firmly on the intellectual value of the word. It uses rhythms which ordinary speech neglects, and aims at a general fluid harmony of movement. It seeks to associate words agreeably and luminously so as at once to please and to clarify the intelligence. It strives after a more accurate, subtle, flexible and satisfying expression than the rough methods of ordinary speech care to compass. A higher adequacy of speech is its first object. Beyond this adequacy it may aim at a greater forcefulness and effectiveness by various devices of speech, by many rhetorical means for heightening the stress of its intellectual appeal. Passing beyond this first limit, this just or strong, but always restrained measure, it may admit a more emphatic rhythm, more directly and powerfully stimulate the emotion, appeal to a more vivid aesthetic sense. It may even make such a free or rich use of images as to suggest an outward approximation to the manner of poetry; but it employs them decoratively, as ornaments, *alaṁkāra,* or for their effective value in giving a stronger intellectual vision of the thing or the thought it describes or defines; it does not use the image for that profounder and more living vision for which the poet is always seeking. And always it has its eye on its chief hearer and judge, the intelligence, and calls in other powers only as important aids to capture his suffrage. Reason and taste, two powers of the intelligence, are rightly the supreme gods of the prose stylist, while to the poet they are only minor deities.

If it goes beyond these limits, approaches in its measures a more striking rhythmic balance, uses images for sheer vision, opens itself to a mightier breath of speech, prose style passes beyond its normal province and approaches or even enters the confines of poetry. It becomes poetical prose or even poetry itself using the apparent forms of prose as a disguise or a loose apparel. A high or a fine adequacy, effectivity, intellectual illuminativeness and a carefully tempered aesthetic satisfaction are the natural and proper powers of its speech. But the privilege of the poet is to go beyond and discover that more intense illumination of speech, that inspired word and supreme inevitable utterance, in which there meets the unity of a divine rhythmic movement with a depth of sense and a power of infinite suggestion welling up directly from the fountain-heads of the spirit within us. He may not always or often find it, but to seek for it is the law or at least the highest trend of his utterance, and when he can not only find it, but cast into it some deeply revealed truth of the spirit itself, he utters the *mantra.*

But always, whether in the search or the finding, the whole style and rhythm of poetry are the expression and movement which come from us out of a certain spiritual excitement caused by a vision in the soul of which it is eager to deliver itself. The vision may be of anything in Nature or God or man or the life of creatures or the life of things; it may be a vision of force and action, or of sensible beauty, or of truth of thought, or of emotion and pleasure and pain, of this life or the life beyond. It is sufficient that it is the soul which sees and the eye, sense, heart and thought-mind become the passive instruments of the soul. Then we get the real, the high poetry. But if what acts is too much an excitement of the intellect, the imagination, the emotions, the vital activities seeking rhythmical and forceful expression, without that greater spiritual excitement embracing them, or if all these are not sufficiently sunk into the soul, steeped in it, fused in it, and the expression does not come out purified and uplifted by a sort of spiritual transmutation, then we fall to lower levels of poetry and get work of a much more doubtful immortality. And when the appeal is altogether to the lower things in us, to the mere mind, we arrive outside the true domain of poetry; we approach the confines of prose or get prose itself masking in the apparent forms of poetry, and the work is distinguished from prose style only or mainly by its mechanical elements, a good verse form and perhaps a more compact, catching or energetic expression than the prose writer will ordinarily permit to the easier and looser balance of his speech. It will not have at all or not sufficiently the true essence of poetry.

For in all things that speech can express there are two elements, the outward or instrumental and the real or spiritual. In thought, for instance, there is the intellectual idea, that which the intelligence makes precise and definite to us, and the soul-idea, that which exceeds the intellectual and brings us into nearness or identity with the whole reality of the thing expressed. Equally in emotion, it is not the mere emotion itself the poet seeks, but the soul of emotion, that in it for the delight of which the soul in us and the world desires or accepts emotional experience. So too with the poetical sense of objects, the poet's attempt to embody in his speech truth of life or truth of Nature. It is this greater truth and its delight and beauty for which he is seeking, beauty which is truth and truth beauty and therefore a joy for ever, because it brings us the delight of the soul in the discovery of its own deeper realities. This greater element the more timid and temperate speech of prose can sometimes shadow out to us, but the heightened and fearless style of poetry makes it close and living and the higher cadences of poetry carry in on their wings what the style by itself could not bring. This is the source of that intensity which is the stamp of poetical speech and of the poetical movement. It comes from the stress of the soul-vision behind the word; it is the spiritual excitement of a rhythmic voyage of self-discovery among the magic islands of form and name in these inner and outer worlds.

III

Rhythm and Movement

The Mantra, poetic expression of the deepest spiritual reality, is only possible when three highest intensities of poetic speech meet and become indissolubly one, a highest intensity of rhythmic movement, a highest intensity of interwoven verbal form and thought-substance, of style, and a highest intensity of the soul's vision of truth. All great poetry comes about by a unison of these three elements; it is the insufficiency of one or another which makes the inequalities in the work of even the greatest poets, and it is the failure of some one element which is the cause of their lapses, of the scoriae in their work, the spots in the sun. But it is only at a certain highest level of the fused intensities that the Mantra becomes possible.

It is from a certain point of view the rhythm, the poetic movement that is of primary importance; for that is the first fundamental and indispensable element without which all the rest, whatever its other value, remains inacceptable to the Muse of poetry. A perfect rhythm will often even give immortality to work which is slight in vision and very far from the higher intensities of style. But it is not merely metrical rhythm, even in a perfect technical excellence, which we mean when we speak of poetic movement; that perfection is only a first step, a physical basis. There must be a deeper and more subtle music, a rhythmical soul-movement entering into the metrical form and often overflooding it before the real poetic achievement begins. A mere metrical excellence, however subtle, rich or varied, however perfectly it satisfies the outer ear, does not meet the deeper aims of the creative spirit; for there is an inner hearing which makes its greater claim, and to reach and satisfy it is the true aim of the creator of melody and harmony.

Nevertheless metre, by which we mean a fixed and balanced system of the measures of sound, *mātrā*, is not only the traditional, but also surely the right physical basis for the poetic movement. A recent modern tendency—that which has given us the poetry of Whitman and Carpenter and the experimentalists in *vers libre* in France and Italy,—denies this tradition and sets aside metre as a limiting bondage, perhaps even a frivolous artificiality or a falsification of true, free and natural poetic rhythm. That is, it seems to me, a point of view which cannot eventually prevail, because it does not deserve to prevail. It certainly cannot triumph, unless it justifies itself by supreme rhythmical achievements beside which the highest work of the great masters of poetic harmony in the past shall sink into a clear inferiority. That has not yet been done. On the contrary, *vers libre* has done its best when it has either limited its aim in rhythm to a kind of chanting poetical prose or else based itself on a sort of irregular and complex metrical movement which in its inner law, though not in its form, recalls the idea of Greek choric poetry.

Milton disparaging rhyme, which he had himself used with so much skill in his earlier, less sublime, but more beautiful poetry, forgot or ignored the spiritual value of rhyme, its power to enforce and clinch the appeal of melodic or harmonic recurrence which is a principal element in the measured movement of poetry, its habit of opening sealed doors to the inspiration, its capacity to suggest and reveal beauty to that supra-intellectual something in us which music is missioned to awake. The Whitmanic technique falls into a similar, but wider error. When mankind found out the power of thought and feeling thrown into fixed and recurring measures of sound to move and take possession of the mind and soul, they were not discovering a mere artistic device, but a subtle truth of psychology, of which the conscious theory is preserved in the Vedic tradition. And when the ancient Indians chose more often than not to throw whatever they wished to endure, even philosophy, science and law, into metrical form, it was not merely to aid the memory,—they were able to memorise huge prose Brahmanas quite as accurately as the Vedic hymnal or the metrical Upaniṣads,—but because they perceived that metrical speech has in itself not only an easier durability, but a greater natural power than unmetrical, not only an intenser value of sound, but a force to compel language and sense to heighten themselves in order to fall fitly into this stricter mould. There is perhaps a truth in the Vedic idea that the Spirit of creation framed all the movements of the world by *Chandas* , in certain fixed rhythms of the formative Word, and it is because they are faithful to the cosmic metres that the basic world-movements unchangingly endure. A balanced harmony maintained by a system of subtle recurrences is the foundation of immortality in created things, and metrical movement is nothing else than creative sound grown conscious of this secret of its own powers.

Still there are all sorts of heights and gradations in the use of this power. General consent seems indeed to have sanctioned the name of poetry for any kind of effective language set in a vigorous or catching metrical form, and although the wideness of this definition is such that it has enabled even the Macaulays and Kiplings to mount their queer poetic thrones, I will not object: catholicity is always a virtue. Nevertheless, mere force of language tacked on to the trick of the metrical beat does not answer the higher description of poetry; it may have the form or its shadow, it has not the essence. There is a whole mass of poetry,—the French metrical romances and most of the mediaeval ballad poetry may be taken as examples,—which relies simply on the metrical beat for its rhythm and on an even level of just tolerable expression for its style; there is hardly a line whose rhythm floats home or where the expression strikes deep. Even in later European poetry, though the art of verse and language has been better learned, essentially the same method persists, and poets who use it have earned not only the popular suffrage, but the praise of the critical mind. Still the definitive verdict on their verse is that it is nothing more than an effective jog-trot of Pegasus, a pleasing canter or a showy gallop. It has great staying-power,—indeed there seems no reason why, once begun, it should not go on for ever,—it carries the poet easily over his ground, but it does nothing more. Certainly, no real soul-movement can get easily into this mould. It has its merits and its powers; it is good for metrical romances of a sort, for war poetry and popular patriotic poetry, or perhaps any poetry which wants to be an "echo of life"; it may stir, not the soul, but the vital being in us like a trumpet or excite it like a drum. But after all the drum and the trumpet do not carry us far in the way of music.

But even high above this level we still do not get at once the greater sound-movement of which we are speaking. Poets of considerable power, sometimes even the greatest in their less exalted moments, are satisfied ordinarily with a set harmony or a set melody, which is very satisfying to the outward ear and carries the aesthetic sense along with it in a sort of even, indistinctive pleasure, and into this mould of easy melody or harmony they throw their teeming or flowing imaginations without difficulty or check, without any need of an intenser heightening, a deeper appeal. It is beautiful poetry; it satisfies the aesthetic sense, the imagination and the ear; but there the charm ends. Once we have heard its rhythm, we have nothing new to expect, no surprise for the inner ear, no danger of the soul being suddenly seized and carried away into unknown depths. It is sure of being floated along evenly as if upon a flowing stream. Or sometimes it is not so much a flowing stream as a steady march or other even movement: this comes oftenest in poets who appeal more to the thought than to the ear; they are concerned chiefly with the thing they have to say and satisfied to have found an adequate rhythmic mould into which they can throw it without any farther preoccupation.

But even a great attention and skill in the use of metrical possibilities, in the invention of rhythmical turns, devices, modulations, variations, strong to satisfy the intelligence, to seize the ear, to maintain its vigilant interest, will not bring us yet to the higher point we have in view. There are periods of literature in which this kind of skill is carried very far. The rhythms of Victorian poetry seem to me to be of this kind; they show sometimes the skill of the artist, sometimes of the classical or romantic technician, of the prestigious melodist or harmonist, sometimes the power of the vigorous craftsman or even the performer of robust metrical feats. All kinds of instrumental faculties have been active; but the one thing that is lacking, except in moments or brief periods of inspiration, is the soul behind creating and listening to its own greater movements.

Poetic rhythm begins to reach its highest levels, the greater poetic movements become possible when, using any of these powers but rising beyond them, the soul begins to make its direct demand and yearn for a profounder satisfaction: they awake when the inner ear begins to listen. Technically, we may say that this comes in when the poet becomes, in Keats' phrase, a miser of sound and syllable, economical of his means, not in the sense of a niggardly sparing, but of making the most of all its possibilities of sound. It is then that poetry gets farthest away from the method of prose-rhythm. Prose-rhythm aims characteristically at a general harmony in which the parts are subdued to get the tone of a total effect; even the sounds which give the support or the relief, yet to a great extent seem to be trying to efface themselves in order not to disturb by a too striking particular effect the general harmony which is the whole aim. Poetry on the contrary makes much of its beats and measures; it seeks for a very definite and insistent rhythm. But still, where the greater rhythmical intensities are not pursued, it is only some total effect that predominates and the rest is subdued to it. But in these highest, intensest rhythms every sound is made the most of, whether in its suppression or in its swelling expansion, its narrowness or its open wideness, in order to get in the combined effect something which the ordinary harmonic flow of poetry cannot give us.

But this is only the technical side, the physical means by which the effect is produced. It is not the artistic intelligence or the listening physical ear that is most at work, but something within that is trying to bring out the echo of a hidden harmony, to discover a secret of rhythmic infinities within us. It is not a labour of the devising intellect or the aesthetic sense which the poet has achieved, but a labour of the spirit within itself to cast something out of the surge of the eternal depths. The other faculties are there in their place, but the conductor of the orchestral movement is the soul suddenly and potently coming forward to get its own work done by its own higher and unanalysable methods. The result is something as near to wordless music as word-music can get, and with the same power of soul-life, of soul-emotion, of profound supra-intellectual significance. In these higher harmonies and melodies the metrical rhythm is taken up by the spiritual; it is filled with or sometimes it seems rolled away and lost in a music that has really another unseizable and spiritual secret of movement.

This is the intensity of poetic movement out of which the greatest possibility of poetic expression arises. It is where the metrical movement remains as a base, but either enshrines and contains or is itself contained and floats in an element of greater music which exceeds it and yet brings out all its possibilities, that the music fit for the Mantra makes itself audible. It is the triumph of the embodied spirit over the difficulties and limitations of the physical instrument. And the listener seems to be that other vaster and yet identical eternal spirit whom the Upanishad speaks of as the ear of the ear, he who listens to all hearings; "behind the instabilities of word and speech" it is the profound inevitable harmonies of his own thought and vision for which he is listening.

IV

Style and Substance

Rhythm is the premier necessity of poetical expression because it is the sound-movement which carries on its wave the thought-movement in the word; and it is the musical sound-image which most helps to fill in, to extend, subtilise and deepen the thought impression or the emotional or vital impression and to carry the sense beyond itself into an expression of the intellectually inexpressible,—always the peculiar power of music. This truth was better understood on the whole or at least more consistently felt by the ancients than by the modern mind and ear, perhaps because they were more in the habit of singing, chanting or intoning their poetry while we are content to read ours, a habit which brings out the intellectual and emotional element, but unduly depresses the rhythmic value. On the other hand modern poetry has achieved a far greater subtlety, minute fineness and curious depth of suggestion in style and thought than was possible to the ancients,—at the price perhaps of some loss in power, height and simple largeness. The ancients would not so easily as the moderns have admitted into the rank of great poets writers of poor rhythmic faculty or condoned, ignored or praised in really great poets rhythmic lapses, roughnesses and crudities for the sake of their power of style and substance.

In regard to poetic style we have to make, for the purpose of the idea we have in view, the starting-point of the Mantra, precisely the same distinctions as in regard to poetic rhythm,—since here too we find actually everything admitted as poetry which has some power of style and is cast into some kind of rhythmical form. But the question is, what kind of power and in that kind what intensity of achievement? There is plenty of poetry signed by poets of present reputation or lasting fame which one is obliged to consign to a border region of half-poetry, because its principle of expression has not got far enough away from the principle of prose expression. It seems to forget that while the first aim of prose style is to define and fix an object, fact, feeling, thought before the appreciating intelligence with whatever clearness, power, richness or other beauty of presentation may be added to that essential aim, the first aim of poetic style is to make the thing presented living to the imaginative vision, the responsive inner emotion, the spiritual sense, the soul-feeling and soul-sight. Where the failure is to express at all with any sufficient power, to get home in any way, the distinction becomes palpable enough, and we readily say of such writings that this is verse but not poetry. But where there is some thought-power or other worth of substance attended with some power of expression, false values more easily become current and even a whole literary age may dwell on this borderland or be misled into an undue exaltation and cult for this half-poetry.

Poetry, like the kindred arts of painting, sculpture, architecture, appeals to the spirit of man through significant images, and it makes no essential difference that in this case the image is mental and verbal and not material. The essential power of the poetic word is to make us see, not to make us think or feel; thought and feeling[2] must arise out of the sight or be included in it, but

2. I speak here of the outer emotional or sensational feeling, not of the spiritual sense and soul-stir which is the invariable concomitant of the soul's sight.

sight is the primary consequence and power of poetic speech. For the poet has to make us live in the soul and in the inner mind and heart what is ordinarily lived in the outer mind and the senses, and for that he must first make us see by the soul, in its light and with its deeper vision, what we ordinarily see in a more limited and halting fashion by the senses and the intelligence. He is, as the ancients knew, a seer and not merely a maker of rhymes, not merely a jongleur, rhapsodist or troubadour, and not merely a thinker in lines and stanzas. He sees beyond the sight of the surface mind and finds the revealing word, not merely the adequate and effective, but the illumined and illuminating, the inspired and inevitable word, which compels us to see also. To arrive at that word is the whole endeavour of poetic style.

The modern distinction is that the poet appeals to the imagination and not to the intellect. But there are many kinds of imagination; the objective imagination which visualises strongly the outward aspects of life and things; the subjective imagination which visualises strongly the mental and emotional impressions they have the power to start in the mind; the imagination which deals in the play of mental fictions and to which we give the name of poetic fancy; the aesthetic imagination which delights in the beauty of words and images for their own sake and sees no farther. All these have their place in poetry, but they only give the poet his materials, they are only the first instruments in the creation of poetic style. The essential poetic imagination does not stop short with even the most subtle reproductions of things external or internal, with the richest or delicatest play of fancy or with the most beautiful colouring of word or image. It is creative, not of either the actual or the fictitious, but of the more and the most real; it sees the spiritual truth of things,—of this truth too there are many gradations,—which may take either the actual or the ideal for its starting-point. The aim of poetry, as of all true art, is neither a photographic or otherwise realistic imitation of Nature, nor a romantic furbishing and painting or idealistic improvement of her image, but an interpretation by the images she herself affords us, not on one but on many planes of her creation, of that which she conceals from us, but is ready, when rightly approached, to reveal.

This is the true, because highest and essential aim of poetry; but the human mind arrives at it only by a succession of steps, the first of which seems far enough from its object. It begins by stringing its most obvious and external ideas, feelings and sensations of things on a thread of verse in a sufficient language of no very high quality. But even when it gets to a greater adequacy and effectiveness, it is often no more than a vital, an emotional or an intellectual adequacy and effectiveness. There is a strong vital poetry which powerfully appeals to our sensations and our sense of life, like much of Byron or the less inspired mass of the Elizabethan drama; a strong emotional poetry which stirs our feelings and gives us the sense and active image of the passions; a strong intellectual poetry which satisfies our curiosity about life and its mechanism, or deals with its psychological and other "problems", or shapes for us our thoughts in an effective, striking and often quite resistlessly quotable fashion. All this has its pleasures for the mind and the surface soul in us, and it is certainly quite legitimate to enjoy them and to enjoy them strongly and vividly on our way upward; but if we rest content with these only, we shall never get very high up the hill of the Muses.

The style of such poetry corresponds usually to its substance; for between the word and the vision there tends to be, though there is not by any means perfectly or invariably, a certain equation. There is a force of vital style, a force of emotional style, a force of intellectual style which we meet constantly in poetry and which it is essential to distinguish from the language of the higher spiritual imagination. The forceful expression of thought and sentiment is not enough for this higher language. To take some examples, it is not enough for it to express its sense of world-sorrow in a line of cheap sentimental force like Byron's

> There's not a joy the world can give like that it takes away,

or to voice an opposite truth in the sprightly-forcible manner of Browning's

> God's in his heaven,
> All's right with the world,

or to strike the balance in a sense of equality with the pointed and ever quotable intellectuality of Pope's

> God sees with equal eyes as lord of all
> A hero perish or a sparrow fall.

This may be the poetical or half-poetical language of thought and sentiment; it is not the language of real poetic vision. Note that all three brush the skirts of ideas whose deeper expression from the vision of a great poet might touch the very heights of poetic revelation. Byron's line is the starting-point in the emotional sensations for that high world-pessimism and its spiritual release which finds expression in the *Gītā*'s

> *Anityam asukhaṁ lokam imaṁ prāpya bhajasva mām;*[3]

---

3. "Thou who hast come to this transient and unhappy world, love and turn to Me."

and one has only to compare the manner of the two in style and rhythm, even leaving the substance aside, to see the difference between the lesser and the greater poetry. Browning's language rises from a robust cheerfulness of temperament, it does not touch the deeper fountain-heads of truth in us; an opposite temperament may well smile at it as vigorous optimistic fustian. Pope's actually falsifies by its poetical inadequacy that great truth of the Gītā's teaching, the truth of the divine equality, because he has not seen and therefore cannot make us see; his significant images of the truth are, like his perception of it, intellectual and rhetorical, not poetic figures.

There is a higher style of poetry than this which yet falls below the level to which we have to climb. It is no longer poetical language of a merely intellectual, vital or emotional force, but instead or in addition a genuinely imaginative style, with a certain, often a great beauty of vision in it, whether objective or subjective, or with a certain, often a great but indefinite soul-power bearing up its movement of word and rhythm. It varies in intensity: for the lower intensity we can get plenty of examples from Chaucer, when he is indulging his imagination rather than his observation, and at a higher pitch from Spenser; for the loftier intensity we can cite at will for one kind from Milton's early poetry, for another from poets who have a real spiritual vision like Keats and Shelley. English poetry runs, indeed, ordinarily in this mould. But this too is not that highest intensity of the revelatory poetic word from which the Mantra starts. It has a certain power of revelation in it, but the deeper vision is still coated up in something more external; sometimes the poetic intention of decorative beauty, sometimes some other deliberate intention of the poetic mind overlays with the more outward beauty, beauty of image, beauty of thought, beauty of emotion, the deeper intention of the spirit within, so that we have still to look for that beyond the image rather than are seized by it through the image. A high pleasure is there, not unspiritual in its nature, but still it is not that point where pleasure passes into or is rather drowned in the pure spiritual *Ānanda*, the ecstasy of the creative, poetic revelation.

That intensity comes where everything else may be present, but all is powerfully carried on the surge of a spiritual vision which has found its inspired and inevitable speech. All or any of the other elements may be there, but they are at once subordinated and transfigured to their highest capacity for poetic light and rapture. This intensity belongs to no particular style, depends on no conceivable formula of diction. It may be the height of the decorative imaged style as often we find it in Kalidasa or Shakespeare; it may be that height of bare and direct expression where language seems to be used as a scarcely felt vaulting-board for a leap into the infinite; it may be the packed intensity of language which uses either the bare or the imaged form at will, but fills every word with its utmost possible rhythmic and thought suggestion. But in itself it depends on none of these things; it is not a style, but poetic style itself, the Word; it creates and carries with it its elements rather than is created by them. Whatever its outward forms, it is always the one fit style for the Mantra.

V

Poetic Vision and the Mantra

This highest intensity of style and movement which is the crest of the poetical impulse in its self-expression, the point at which the aesthetic, the vital, the intellectual elements of poetic speech pass into the spiritual, justifies itself perfectly when it is the body of a deep, high or wide spiritual vision into which the life-sense, the thought, the emotion, the appeal of beauty in the thing discovered and in its expression—for all great poetic utterance is discovery,—rise on the wave of the culminating poetic inspiration and pass into an ecstasy of sight. In the lesser poets these moments are rare and come like brilliant accidents, angels' visits; in the greater they are more frequent outbursts; but in the greatest they abound because they arise from a constant faculty of poetic vision and poetic speech which has its lesser and its greater moments, but never entirely fails these supreme masters of the expressive word.

Vision is the characteristic power of the poet, as is discriminative thought the essential gift of the philosopher and analytic observation the natural genius of the scientist. The Kaví[4] was in the idea of the ancients the seer and revealer of truth, and though we have wandered far enough from that ideal to demand from him only the pleasure of the ear and the amusement of the aesthetic faculty, still all great poetry instinctively preserves something of that higher turn of its own aim and significance. Poetry, in fact, being Art, must attempt to make us see, and since it is to the inner senses that it has to address itself,—for the ear is its only physical gate of entry and even there its real appeal is to an inner hearing,—and since its object is to make us live within ourselves what the poet has embodied in his verse, it is an inner sight which he opens in us, and this inner sight must have been intense in him before he can awaken it in us.

Therefore the greatest poets have been always those who have had a large and powerful interpretative and intuitive vision of Nature and life and man and whose poetry has arisen out of that in a supreme revelatory utterance of it. Homer, Shakespeare, Dante, Vālmīki, Kālidāsa, however much they may

---

4. The Sanskrit word for poet. In classical Sanskrit it is applied to any maker of verse or even of prose, but in the Vedic it meant the poet-seer who saw the Truth and found in a subtle truth-hearing the inspired word of his vision.

differ in everything else, are at one in having this as the fundamental character of their greatness. Their supremacy does not lie essentially in a greater thought-power or a more lavish imagery or a more penetrating force of passion and emotion; these things they may have had, one being more gifted in one direction, another in others, but these other powers were aids to their poetic expression rather than its essence or its source. There is often more thought in a short essay of Bacon's than in a whole play of Shakespeare's, but not even a hundred cryptograms can make him the author of the dramas; for, as he showed when he tried to write poetry, the very nature of his thought-power and the characteristic way of expression of the born philosophic thinker hampered him in poetic expression. It was the constant outstreaming of form and thought and image from an abundant inner vision of life which made Shakespeare, whatever his other deficiencies, the sovereign dramatic poet. Sight is the essential poetic gift. The archetypal poet in a world of original ideas is, we may say, a Soul that sees in itself intimately this world and all the others and God and Nature and the life of beings and sets flowing from its centre a surge of creative rhythm and word-images which become the expressive body of the vision. The great poets are those who repeat in some measure this ideal creation, *kavayaḥsatyaśrutaḥ*, seers of the poetic truth and hearers of its word.

The tendency of the modern mind at the present day seems to be towards laying a predominant value on the thought in poetry. We live still in an age which is in a great intellectual trouble and ferment about life and the world and is developing enormously the human intelligence,—often at the expense of other powers which are no less necessary to self-knowledge,—in order to grapple with life and master it. We are seeking always and in many directions to decipher the enigma of things, the cryptogram of the worlds which we are set to read, and to decipher it by the aid of the intellect; and for the most part we are much too busy living and thinking to have leisure to be silent and see. We expect the poet to use his great mastery of language to help us in this endeavour; we ask of him not so much perfect beauty of song or largeness of creative vision as a message to our perplexed and seeking intellects. Therefore we hear constantly today of the "philosophy" of a poet, even the most inveterate beautifier of commonplaces being forcibly gifted by his admirers with a philosophy, or of his message,—the message of Tagore, the message of Whitman. We are asking then of the poet to be, not a supreme singer or an inspired seer of the worlds, but a philosopher, a prophet, a teacher, even something perhaps of a religious or ethical preacher. It is necessary therefore to say that when I claim for the poet the role of a seer of Truth and find the source of great poetry in a great and revealing vision of life or God or the gods or man or Nature, I do not mean that it is necessary for him to have an intellectual philosophy of life or a message for humanity, which he chooses to express in verse because he has the metrical gift and the gift of imagery, or that he must give us a solution of the problems of the age, or come with a mission to improve mankind, or, as it is said, "to leave the world better than he found it." As a man, he may have these things, but the less he allows them to get the better of his poetic gift, the happier it will be for his poetry. Material for his poetry they may give, an influence in it they may be, provided they are transmuted into vision and life by the poetic spirit, but they can be neither its soul nor its aim, nor give the law to its creative activity and its expression.

The poet-seer sees differently, thinks in another way, voices himself in quite another manner than the philosopher or the prophet. The prophet announces the Truth as the Word, the Law or the command of the Eternal, he is the giver of the message; the poet shows us Truth in its power of beauty, in its symbol or image, or reveals it to us in the workings of Nature or in the workings of life, and when he has done that, his whole work is done; he need not be its explicit spokesman or its official messenger. The philosopher's business is to discriminate Truth and put its parts and aspects into intellectual relation with each other; the poet's is to seize and embody aspects of Truth in their living relations, or rather—for that is too philosophical a language—to see her features and, excited by the vision, create in the beauty of her image.

No doubt, the prophet may have in him a poet who breaks out often into speech and surrounds with the vivid atmosphere of life the directness of his message; he may follow up his injunction "Take no thought for the morrow," by a revealing image of the beauty of the truth he enounces, in the life of Nature, in the figure of the lily, or link it to human life by apologue and parable. The philosopher may bring in the aid of colour and image to give some relief and hue to his dry light of reason and water his arid path of abstractions with some healing dew of poetry. But these are ornaments and not the substance of his work; and if the philosopher makes his thought substance of poetry, he ceases to be a philosophic thinker and becomes a poet-seer of Truth. Thus the more rigid metaphysicians are perhaps right in denying to Nietzsche the name of philosopher; for Nietzsche does not think, but always sees, turbidly or clearly, rightly or distortedly, but with the eye of the seer rather than with the brain of the thinker. On the other hand we may get great poetry which is full of a prophetic enthusiasm of utterance or is largely or even wholly philosophic in its matter; but this prophetic poetry gives us no direct message, only a mass of sublime inspirations of thought and image, and this philosophic poetry is poetry and lives as poetry only in so far as it departs from the method, the expression, the way of seeing proper to the philosophic mind. It must be vision pouring itself into thought-images and not thought trying to observe truth and distinguish its province and bounds and fences.

In earlier days this distinction was not at all clearly understood and therefore we find even poets of great power attempting to set philosophic systems to music or even much more prosaic matter than a philosophic system, Hesiod and Virgil setting about even a manual of agriculture in verse! In Rome, always a little blunt of perception in the aesthetic mind, her two greatest poets fell a victim to this unhappy conception, with results which are a lesson and a warning to all posterity. Lucretius' work lives only, in spite of the majestic energy behind it, by its splendid digressions into pure poetry, Virgil's *Georgics* by fine passages and pictures of Nature and beauties of word and image; but in both the general substance is lifeless matter which has floated to us on the stream of Time, saved only by the beauty of its setting. India, and perhaps India alone, managed once or twice to turn this kind of philosophic attempt into a poetic success, in the *Gītā*, in the Upaniṣads and some minor works modelled upon them. But the difference is great. The *Gītā* owes its poetical success to its starting from a great and critical situation in life, its constant keeping of that in view and always returning upon it, and to its method which is to seize on a spiritual experience or moment or stage of the inner life and throw it into the form of thought; and this, though a delicate operation, can well abide within the limits of the poetic manner of speech. Only where it overburdens itself with metaphysical matter and deviates into sheer philosophic definition and discrimination, which happens especially in two or three of its closing chapters, does the poetic voice sink under the weight, even occasionally into flattest versified prose. The Upaniṣads too, and much more, are not at all philosophic thinking, but spiritual seeing; these ancient stanzas are a rush of spiritual intuitions, flames of a burning fire of mystic experience, waves of an inner sea of light and life, and they throw themselves into the language and cadence of poetry because that is their natural speech and a more intellectual utterance would have falsified their vision.

Nowadays we have clarified our aesthetic perceptions sufficiently to avoid the mistake of the Roman poets; but in a subtler form the intellectual tendency still shows a dangerous spirit of encroachment. For the impulse to teach is upon us, the inclination to be an observer and critic of life,—there could be no more perilous definition than Arnold's poetic "criticism of life", in spite of the saving epithet,—to clothe, merely, in the forms of poetry a critical or philosophic idea of life to the detriment of our vision. Allegory with its intellectual ingenuities, its facile wedding of the abstract idea and the concrete image, shows a tendency to invade again the domain of poetry. And there are other signs of the intellectual malady of which we are almost all of us the victims. Therefore it is well to insist that the native power of poetry is in its sight, not in its intellectual thought-matter, and its safety is in adhering to this native principle of vision; its conception, its thought, its emotion, its presentation, its structure must rise out of that or else rise into it before it takes its finished form. The poetic vision of things is not a criticism of life, not an intellectual or philosophic view of it, but a soul-view, a seizing by the inner sense. The Mantra too is not in its substance or its form a poetic enunciation of philosophic verities, but a rhythmic revelation or intuition arising out of the soul's sight of God and Nature and itself and of the world and of the inner truth—occult to the outward eye—of all that peoples it, the secrets of their life and being.

In the attempt to fix the view of life which Art must take, distinctions are constantly laid down, such as the necessity of a subjective or an objective treatment or of a realistic or an idealistic view, which mislead more than they enlighten. Certainly, one poet may seem to excel in the concrete presentation of things and falter or be less sure in his grasp of the purely subjective, while another may move freely in the more subjective worlds and be less at home in the concrete; and both may be poets of a high order. But when we look closer, we see that just as a certain objectivity is necessary to make poetry live and the thing seen stand out before our eyes, so on the other hand even the most objective presentation starts from an inner view and subjective process of creation or at least a personal interpretation and transmutation of the thing seen. The poet really creates out of himself and not out of what he sees outwardly: that outward seeing only serves to excite the inner vision to its work. Otherwise his work would be a mechanical construction and putting together, not a living creation.

Sheer objectivity brings us down from art to photography; and the attempt to diminish the subjective view to the vanishing-point so as to get an accurate presentation is proper to science, not to poetry. We are not thereby likely to get a greater truth or reality, but very much the reverse; for the scientific presentation of things, however valid in its own domain, that of the senses and the observing reason, is not true to the soul. It is not the integral truth or the whole vision of things, for it gives only their process and machinery and mechanic law, but not their inner life and spirit. That is the error in realism,—in its theory, at least, for its practice is something other than what it intends or pretends to be. Realistic art does not and cannot give us a scientifically accurate presentation of life, because Art is not and cannot be Science. What it does do, is to make an arbitrary selection of motives, forms and hues, here of dull blues and greys and browns and dingy whites and sordid yellows, there of violent blacks and reds, and the result is sometimes a thing of power and sometimes a nightmare. Idealistic art makes a different selection and produces either a work of nobly-coloured power or soft-hued beauty or else a high-pitched and false travesty or a specious day-dream. In these distinctions there is no safety; nor can any rule be laid down for the poet, since he must necessarily go by what he is and what he sees, except that he should work from the living poetic centre within him and not exile himself into artificial standpoints.

From our present point of view we may say that the poet may do as he pleases in all that is not the essential matter. Thought-matter may be prominent in his work or life-substance predominate. He may proceed by sheer force of presentation or by direct power of interpretation. He may make this world his text, or wander into regions beyond, or soar straight into the pure empyrean of the infinite. To arrive at the Mantra he may start from the colour of a rose, or the power or beauty of a character, or the splendour of an action, or go away from all these into his own secret soul and its most hidden movements. The one thing needful is that he should be able to go beyond the word or image he uses or the form of the thing he sees, not be limited by them, but get into the light of that which they have the power to reveal and flood them with it until they overflow with its suggestions or seem even to lose themselves and disappear into the revelation and the apocalypse. At the highest he himself disappears into sight; the personality of the seer is lost in the eternity of the vision, and the Spirit of all seems alone to be there speaking out sovereignly its own secrets.

But the poetic vision, like everything else, follows necessarily the evolution of the human mind and according to the age and environment, it has its ascents and descents, its high levels and its low returns. Ordinarily, it follows the sequence of an abrupt ascent pushing to a rapid decline. The eye of early man is turned upon the physical world about him, the interest of the story of life and its primary ideas and emotions; he sees man and his world only, or he sees the other worlds and their gods and beings, but it is still his own physical world in a magnified and heightened image. He asks little of poetry except a more forceful vision of familiar things, things real and things commonly imagined, which will help him to see them more largely and feel them more strongly and give him a certain inspiration to live them more powerfully. Next,—but this transition is sometimes brief or even quite overleaped,—there comes a period in which he feels the joy and curiosity and rich adventure of the expanding life-force within him, the passion and romance of existence and it is this in all its vivid colour that he expects art and poetry to express and satisfy him through the imagination and the emotions with its charm and power. Afterwards he begins to intellectualise, but still on the same subject-matter; he asks now from the poet a view of things enlightened by the inspired reason and beautifully shaped by the first strong and clear joy of his developed aesthetic sense. A vital poetry appealing to the imagination through the sense-mind and the emotions and a poetry interpretative of life to the intelligence are the fruit of these ages. A later poetry tends always to return on these forms with a more subtilised intellect and a richer life-experience. But, having got so far, it can go no farther and there is the beginning of a decadence.

Great things may be done by poetry within these limits and the limited lifetime it gives to a literature; but it is evident that the poet will have a certain difficulty in getting to a deeper vision, because he has to lean entirely on the external thought and form; he must be subservient to them because they are the only safe support he knows, and he gets at what truth he can that may be beyond them with their veil still thickly interposing between him and a greater light. A higher level can come, bringing with it the possibility of a renewed and prolonged course for the poetic impulse, if the mind of man begins to see more intimately the forces behind life, the powers concealed by our subjective existence. The poet can attempt to reveal these unsuspected ranges and motives and use the outward physical and vital and thought symbol only as a suggestion of greater things. Yet a higher level can be attained, deeper depths, larger horizons when the soul in things comes nearer to man or when other worlds than the physical open themselves to him. And the entire liberation of the poetic vision to see most profoundly and the poetic power to do its highest work will arrive when the spiritual itself is the possession of the greatest minds and the age stands on the verge of its revelation.

Therefore it is not sufficient for poetry to attain high intensities of word and rhythm; it must have, to fill them, an answering intensity of vision and always new and more and more uplifted or inward ranges of experience. And this does not depend only on the individual power of vision of the poet, but on the mind of his age and country, its level of thought and experience, the adequacy of its symbols, the depth of its spiritual attainment. A lesser poet in a greater age may give us occasionally things which exceed in this kind the work of less favoured immortals. The religious poetry of the later Indian tongues has for us fervours of poetic revelation which in the great classics are absent, even though no mediaeval poet can rank in power with Vālmīki and Kālidāsa. The modern literatures of Europe commonly fall short of the Greek perfection of harmony and form, but they give us what the greatest Greek poets had not and could not have. And in our own days a poet of secondary power in his moments of inspiration can get to a vision far more satisfying to the deepest soul within us than Shakespeare's or Dante's. Greatest of all is the promise of the age that is coming, if the race fulfils its highest and largest opening possibilities and does not founder in a vitalistic bog or remain tied in the materialistic paddock; for it will be an age in which all the worlds are beginning to withdraw their screens from man's gaze and invite his experience, and he will be near to the revelation of the Spirit of which they are, as we choose, the obscuring veils, the significant forms and symbols or else the transparent raiment. It is as yet uncertain to which of these consummations destiny is leading us.

Rabindranath Tagore, "Pathway to Mukti" (1925)

Rabindranath Tagore (1861–1941) was a prolific and accomplished poet, novelist, and playwright, and is perhaps best known for his literary output, a massive corpus comprising superb writing in both Bengali and English. He was awarded the Nobel Prize for Literature in 1913 for his *Gitānjali*, a cycle of prose poems. Tagore was also a prominent educator, founding Visva Bharati University at Shantiniketan, a university noted for its internationalism and strength in the arts, now a leading university in India. Tagore is less well known as a philosopher but indeed contributed importantly to the development of Indian philosophy in the early 20th century. It is a sign of his impact that he was invited to be the inaugural President of the Indian Philosophical Congress. This presidential address considers the role of philosophy in Indian culture and re- ects Tagore's poetic and cultural sensibilities as well.

3

Pathway to Mukti

MY TIMIDITY MAKES it difficult for me properly to enjoy the honour you have done me today by offering a chair which I cannot legitimately claim as my own. It has often made me wonder, since I had my invitation, whether it would suit my dignity to occupy such a precarious position on an ephemeral eminence, deservedly incurring anger from some and ridicule from others. While debating in my mind as to whether I should avoid this risk with the help of the doctor's certificate, it occurred to me that possibly my ignorance of philosophy was the best recommendation for this place in a philosopher's meeting,—that you wanted for your president a man who was blankly neutral and who consciously owed no allegiance to any particular system of metaphysics, being impartially innocent of them all. The most convenient thing about me is that the degree of my qualification is beyond the range of a comparative discussion,—it is so utterly negative. In my present situation, I may be compared to a candlestick that has none of the luminous qualities of a candle and, therefore, suitable for its allotted function, which is to remain darkly inactive.

But, unfortunately, you do not allow me to remain silent even in the circumstance when silence was declared to be prudent by one of our ancient sages. The only thing which encourages me to overcome my diffidence, and give expression in a speech to my unsophisticated mind, is the fact that in India all the vidyas,—poesy as well as philosophy,—live in a joint family. They never have the jealous sense of individualism maintaining the punitive regulations against trespass that seem to be so rife in the West.

Plato as a philosopher decreed the banishment of poets from his ideal Republic. But, in India, philosophy ever sought alliance with poetry, because its mission was to occupy the people's life and not merely the learned seclusion of scholarship. Therefore, our tradition, though unsupported by historical evidence, has no hesitation in ascribing numerous verses to the great Śaṅkarāchārya, a metaphysician whom Plato would find it extremely difficult to exclude from his Utopia with the help of any inhospitable Immigration Law. Many of these poems may not have high poetical value, but no lover of literature ever blames the sage for infringement of propriety in condescending to manufacture verse.

According to our people, poetry naturally falls within the scope of a philosopher, when his reason is illumined into a vision. We have our great epic *Mahābhārata*, which is unique in world literature; not only because of the marvellous variety of human characters, great and small, discussed in its pages in all variety of psychological circumstances, but because of the case with which it carries in its comprehensive capaciousness all kinds of speculation about ethics, politics and philosophy of life. Such an improvident generosity on the part of poesy, at the risk of exceeding its own proper limits of accommodation, has only been possible in India where a spirit of communism prevails in the different individual groups of literature. In fact, the *Mahābhārata* is a universe in itself in which various spheres of mind's creation find ample space for their complex dance rhythm. It does not represent the idiosyncrasy of a particular poet but the normal mentality of the people who are willing to be led along the many branched path of a whole world of thoughts, held together in a gigantic orb of narrative surrounded by innumerable satellites of episodes.

The numerous saints that India successively produced during the Mohamedan rule have all been singers whose verses are aflame with the fire of imagination. Their religious emotion had its spring in the depth of a philosophy that deals with fundamental questions,—with the ultimate meaning of existence. That may not be remarkable in itself; but when we find that these songs are not specially meant for some exclusive pandits' gathering, but that they are sung in villages and listened to by men and women who are illiterate, we realize how philosophy has permeated the life of the people in India, how it has sunk deep into the subconscious mind of the country.

In my childhood I once heard from a singer, who was a devout Hindu, the following song of Kabir:

> When I hear of a fish in the water dying of thirst, it makes me laugh.
> If it be true that the infinite Brahma pervades all space.

What is the meaning of the places of pilgrimage like Mathurā or Kāśī?

This laughter of Kabir did not hurt in the least the pious susceptibilities of the Hindu singer; on the contrary, he was ready to join the poet with his own. For he, by the philosophical freedom of his mind, was fully aware that Mathurā or Kāśī, as sites of God, did not have an absolute value of truth, though they had their symbolical importance. Therefore, while he himself was eager to make a pilgrimage to those places, he had no doubt in his mind that, if it were in his power directly to realize Brahma as an all-pervading reality, there would have been no necessity for him to visit any particular place for the quickening of his spiritual consciousness. He acknowledged the psychological necessity for such shrines, where generations of devotees have chosen to gather for the purpose of worship, in the same way as he felt the special efficiency for our mind of the time-honoured sacred texts made living by the voice of ages.

It is a village poet of East Bengal who in his songs preaches the philosophical doctrine that the universe has its reality in its relation to the Person. He sings:

> The sky and the earth are born of mine own eyes.
> The hardness and softness, the cold and the heat are the products of
> mine own body;
> The sweet smell and the bad are of mine own nose.

This poet sings of the Eternal Person within him, coming out and appearing before his eyes just as the Vedic Ṛṣī speaks of the Person, who is in him, dwelling also in the heart of the Sun.

> I have seen the vision,
> The vision of mine own revealing itself,
> Coming out from within me.

The significant fact about these philosophical poems is that they are of rude construction, written in a popular dialect and disclaimed by the academic literature; they are sung to the people, as composed by one of them who is dead, but whose songs have not followed him. Yet these singers almost arrogantly disown their direct obligation to philosophy, and there is a story of one of our rural poets who, after some learned text of the Vaiṣṇava philosophy of emotion was explained to him, composed a song containing the following lines:

> Alas, a jeweller has come into the flower garden!
> He wants to appraise the truth of a lotus by rubbing it against his
> touchstone.

The members of the Baül sect belong to that class of the people in Bengal who are not educated in the prevalent sense of the word. I remember how troubled they were, when I asked some of them to write down for me a collection of their songs. When they did venture to attempt it, I found it almost impossible to decipher their writing—the spelling and lettering were so outrageously unconventional. Yet their spiritual practices are founded upon a mystic philosophy of the human body, abstrusely technical. These people roam about singing their songs, one of which I heard years ago from my roadside window, the first two lines remaining inscribed in my memory.

Nobody can tell whence the bird unknown
Comes into the cage and goes out.
I would feign put round its feet the fetter of my mind,
Could I but capture it.

This village poet evidently agrees with our sage of the Upaniṣad who says that our mind comes back baffled in its attempt to reach the Unknown Being; and yet this poet like the ancient sage does not give up his adventure of the infinite thus implying that there is a way to its realization. It reminds me of Shelley's poem in which he sings of the mystical spirit of Beauty.

The awful shadow of some unseen Power
Floats, though unseen, among us; visiting
This various world with as inconstant wing
As summer winds that creep from flower to flower.
Like moonbeams that behind some piny mountain shower,
It visits with inconstant glance
Each human heart and countenance.

That this Unknown is the profoundest reality, though difficult of comprehension, is equally admitted by the English poet as by the nameless village singer of Bengal in whose music vibrate the wing-beats of the unknown bird,—only Shelley's utterance is for the cultured few, while the Baül song is for the tillers of the soil, for the simple folk of our village households, who are never bored by its mystic transcendentalism.

All this is owing to the wonderful system of mass education which has prevailed for ages in India, and which today is in danger of becoming extinct. We have our academic seats of learning where students flock round their famous teachers from distant parts of the country. These places are like lakes, full of deep but still water, which have to be approached through difficult paths. But the constant evaporation from them, forming clouds, is carried by the wind from field to field, across hills and dales and through all the different divisions of the land. Operas based upon legendary poems, recitations and story-telling by trained men, the lyrical wealth of the popular literature distributed far and wide by the agency of mendicant singers—these are the clouds that help to irrigate the minds of the people with the ideas which in their original form belonged to difficult doctrines of metaphysics. Profound speculations contained in the systems of Sāṃkhya, Vedānta and Yoga are transformed into the living harvest of the people's literature, brought to the door of those who can never have the leisure and training to pursue these thoughts to their fountainhead.

In order to enable a civilized community to carry on its complex functions, there must be a large number of men who have to take charge of its material needs, however onerous such task may be. Their vocation gives them no opportunity to cultivate their mind. Yet they form the vast multitude, compelled to turn themselves into unthinking machines of production, so that a few may have the time to think great thoughts, create immortal forms of art and to lead humanity to spiritual altitudes.

India has never neglected these social martyrs, but has tried to bring light into the grim obscurity of their life-long toil, and has always acknowledged its duty to supply them with mental and spiritual food in assimilable form through the medium of a variety of ceremonies. This process is not carried on by any specially organized association of public service, but by a spontaneous social adjustment which acts like circulation of blood in our bodily system. Because of this, the work continues even when the original purpose ceases to exist.

Once when I was on a visit to a small Bengal village, mostly inhabited by Mohamedan cultivators, the villagers entertained me with an opera performance the literature of which belonged to an obsolete religious sect that had wide influence centuries ago. Though the religion itself is dead, its voice still continues preaching its philosophy to a people who in spite of their different culture are not tired of listening. It discussed according to its own doctrine the different elements, material and transcendental, that constitute human personality, comprehending the body, the self and the soul. Then came a dialogue during the course of which was related the incident of a person who wanted to make a journey to Brindāvan, the Garden of Bliss, but was prevented by a watchman who started him with an accusation of theft. The thieving was proved when it was shown that inside his clothes he was secretly trying to smuggle into the garden the self, passing it on as his own and not admitting that it is for his master. The culprit was caught with the incriminating bundle in his possession which barred for him his passage to the supreme goal. Under a tattered canopy held on bamboo poles and lighted by a few smoking kerosene lamps, the village crowd, occasionally interrupted by howls of jackals in the neighbouring paddy fields, attended with untired interest, till the small hours of the morning, the performance of drama, that discussed the ultimate meaning of all things in a seemingly incongruous setting of dance, music and humorous dialogue.

These illustrations will show how naturally, in India, poetry and philosophy have walked hand in hand, only because the latter has claimed its right to guide men to the practical path of their life's fulfilment. What is that fulfilment? It is our freedom in truth, which has for its prayer:

> Lead us from the unreal to Reality.
> For *satyam* is *ānandam*, the real is joy.

From my vocation as an artist in verse, I have too my own idea about the joy of the real. For to give us the taste of reality through freedom of mind is the nature of all arts. When in relation to them we talk of aesthetics we must know that it is not about beauty in its ordinary meaning, but in that deeper meaning which a poet has expressed in his utterance: "Truth is beauty, beauty truth". An artist may paint a picture of a decrepit person not pleasant to look at, and yet we call it perfect when we become intensely conscious of its reality. The mind of the jealous women in Browning's poem, watching the preparation of poison and in imagination gloating over its possible effect upon her rival, is not beautiful; but when it stands vividly real before our consciousness, through the unity of consistency in its idea and form, we have our enjoyment. The character of Karna, the great warrior of the *Mahābhārata*, gives us a deeper delight through its occasional outbursts of meanness, than it would if it were a model picture of unadulterated magnanimity. The very contradictions which hurt the completeness of a moral ideal have helped us to feel the reality of the character, and this gives us joy, not because it is pleasant in itself, but because it is definite in its creation.

It is not wholly true that art has its value for us because in it we realize all that we fail to attain in our life; but the fact is that the function of art is to bring us with its creations, into immediate touch with reality. These need not resemble actual facts of our experience, and yet they do delight our heart because they are made true to us. In the world of art, our consciousness being freed from the tangle of self-interest, we gain an unobstructed vision of unity, the incarnation of the real which is a joy forever.

As in the world of art, so in God's world, our soul waits for its freedom from the ego to reach that disinterested joy which is the source and goal of creation. Its cries for its *mukti* into the unity of truth from the mirage of appearances endlessly pursued by the thirsty self. This idea of *mukti*, based upon metaphysics, has affected our life in India, touched the springs of our emotions, and supplications for its soar heavenward on the wings of poesy. We constantly hear men of scanty learning and simple faith singing in their prayer to Tārā, the Goddess Redeemer:

For what sin should I be compelled to remain in this dungeon of the world of appearances?

They are afraid of being alienated from the world of truth, afraid of their perpetual drifting amidst the froth and foam of things, of being tossed about by the tidal waves of pleasure and pain and never reaching the ultimate meaning of life. Of these men, one may be a carter driving his cart to market, another a fisherman plying his net. They may not be prompt with an intelligent answer, if questioned about the deeper import of the song they sing, but they have no doubt in their mind, that the abiding cause of all misery is not so much in the lack of life's furniture as in the obscurity of life's significance. It is a common topic with such to decry an undue emphasis upon me and mine, which falsifies the perspective of truth. For, have they not often seen men, who are not above their own level in social position or intellectual acquirement, going out to seek Truth, leaving everything that they have behind them?

They know that the object of these adventures is not betterment in wordly wealth and power,—it is *mukti*, freedom. They possibly know some poor fellow villager of their own craft, who remains in the world carrying on his daily vocation, and yet has the reputation of being emancipated in the heart of the Eternal. I myself have come across a fisherman singing with an inward absorption of mind, while fishing all day in the Ganges, who was pointed out to me by my boatmen, with awe, as a man of liberated spirit. He is out of reach of the conventional prices which are set upon men by society, and which classify them like toys arranged in the shop-windows according to the market standard of value.

When the figure of this fishermen comes to my mind, I cannot but think that their number is not small who with their lives sing the epic of the unfettered soul, but will never be known in history. These unsophisticated Indian peasants know that an Emperor is a decorated slave remaining chained to his Empire, that a millionaire is kept pilloried by his fate in the golden cage of his wealth, while this fisherman is free in the realm of light. When, groping in the dark, we stumble against object, we cling to them believing them to be our only hope. When light comes we slacken our hold, finding them to be mere parts of the all to which we are related. The simple man of the village knows what freedom is—freedom from the isolation of self from the isolation of things which imparts a fierce intensity to our sense of possession. He knows that this freedom is not in the mere negation of bondage, in the bareness of belongings, but in some positive realisation which gives pure joy to our being, and he sings:

To him who sinks into the deep, nothing remains unattained.

He sings:

> Let my two minds meet and combine
> And lead me to the City Wonderful.

When the one mind of ours which wanders in search of things in the outer region of the varied, and the other seeks the inward vision of unity, are no longer in conflict, they help us to realise the *ajab*, the *anirvacanīya*, the ineffable. The poet saint Kabir has also the same message when he sings:

> By saying that Supreme Reality only dwells in the inner realm of spirit we shame the outer world of matter and also when we say that he is only in the outside we do not speak the truth.

According to these singers, truth is in unity and therefore freedom is in its realization. The texts of our daily worship and meditation are for training our mind to overcome the barrier of separateness from the rest of existence and to realize *advaitam*, the Supreme Unity which is *anantam*, infinitude. It is philosophical wisdom having its universal radiation in the popular mind in India that inspires our prayer, our daily spiritual practices. It has its constant urging for us to go beyond the world of appearances in which facts as facts are alien to us, like the mere sounds of a foreign music; it speaks to us of an emancipation in the inner truth of all things in which the endless Many reveals the One, as the multitude of notes, when we understand them, reveal to us the inner unity which is music.

But because this freedom is in truth itself and not in an appearance of it, no hurried path of success, forcibly cut out by the greed of result, can be a true path. And an obscure village poet, unknown to the world of a recognized respectability untrammelled by the standardised learning of the Education Department, sings:

> O cruel man of urgent need, must you scorch with fire the mind which still is a bud? You want to make the bud bloom into a flower and scatter its perfume without waiting! Do you see that my lord, the Supreme Teacher, takes ages to perfect the flower and never is in a fury of haste? But because of your terrible greed you only rely on force, and what hope is there for you, O man of urgent need? Prithee, says Madan the poet, Hurt not the mind of my Teacher. Lose thyself in the simple current, after hearing his voice, O man of urgent need.

This poet knows that there is no external means of taking freedom by the throat. It is the inward process of losing ourselves that leads us to it. Bondage in all its forms has its stronghold in the inner self and not in the outside world; it is in the dimming of our consciousness, in the narrowing of our perspective, in the wrong valuation of things.

The proof of this we find in the modern civilization whose motive force has become a ceaseless urgency of need. Its freedom is only the apparent freedom of inertia which does not know how and where to stop. There are some primitive people who have put an artificial value on human scalps and they develop an arithmetical fury which does not allow them to stop in the gathering of their trophies. They are driven by some cruel fate into an endless exaggeration which makes them ceaselessly run on an interminable path of addition. Such a freedom in their wild course of collection is the worst form of bondage. The cruel urgency of need is all the more aggravated in their case because of the lack of truth in its object. Similarly it should be realized that a mere addition to the rate of speed, to the paraphernalia of fast living and display of furniture, to the frightfulness of destructive armaments, only leads to an insensate orgy of a caricature of bigness. The links of bondage go on multiplying themselves, threatening to shackle the whole world with the chain forged by such unmeaning and unending urgency of need.

The idea of *mukti* in Christian theology is liberation from a punishment which we carry with our birth. In India it is from the dark enclosure of ignorance which causes the illusion of a self that seems final. But the enlightenment which frees us from this ignorance must not merely be negative. Freedom is not in an emptiness of its contents, it is in the harmony of communication through which we find no obstruction in realizing our own being in the surrounding world. It is of this harmony, and not of a bare and barren isolation, that the Upaniṣad, speaks, when it says that the truth no longer remains hidden in him who finds himself in the All.

Freedom in the material world has also the same meaning expressed in its own language. When nature's phenomena appeared to us as manifestations of an obscure and irrational caprice, we lived in an alien world never dreaming of our *svarāj* within its territory. With the discovery of the harmony of its working with that of our reason, we realize our unity with it and, therefore freedom. It is *avidyā*, ignorance, which causes our disunion with our surroundings. It is *vidyā*, the knowledge of the Brahma manifested in the material universe that makes us realize *advaitaṃ*, the spirit of unity in the world of matter.

Those who have been brought up in a misunderstanding of this world's process, not knowing that it is his by his right of intelligence, are trained as cowards by a hopeless faith in the ordinance of a destiny darkly dealing its blows, offering no room for appeal. They submit without struggle when human rights are denied them, being accustomed to imagine themselves born as outlaws in a world constantly thrusting upon them incomprehensible surprises of accidents.

Also in the social or political field, the lack of freedom is based upon the spirit of alienation, on the imperfect realization of *advaitaṃ*. There our bondage is in the tortured link of union. One may imagine that an individual who succeeds in dissociating himself from his fellows attains real freedom in as much as all ties of relationship imply obligation to others. But we know that, though it may sound paradoxical, it is true that in the human world only a perfect arrangement of interdependence gives rise to freedom. The most individualistic of human beings, who own no responsibility, are the savages who fail to attain their fulness of manifestation. They live immersed in obscurity, like an ill-lighted fire that cannot liberate itself from its envelope of smoke. Only those may attain their freedom from the segregation of an eclipsed life, who have the powers to cultivate mutual understanding and co-operation. The history of the growth of freedom is the history of the perfection of human relationship.

The strongest barrier against freedom in all departments of life is the selfishness of individuals or groups. Civilization, whose object is to afford humanity its greatest possible opportunity of complete manifestation, perishes when some selfish passion, in place of a moral ideal, is allowed, to exploit its resources unopposed, for its own purposes. For the greed of acquisition and the living principle of creation are antagonistic to each other. Life has brought with it the first triumph of freedom in the world of the inert, because it is an inner expression and not merely an external fact, because it must always exceed the limits of its substance, never allowing its materials to clog its spirit, and yet ever keeping to the limits of its truth. Its accumulation must not suppress its harmony of growth, the harmony that unites the in and the out, the end and the means, what is and what is to come.

Life does not store up but assimilates; its spirit and its substance, its work and itself, are intimately united. When the non-living elements of our surroundings are stupendously disproportionate, when they are mechanical and hoarded possessions, then the mutual discord between our life and our world ends in the defeat of the former. The gulf thus created by the receding stream of soul we try to replenish with a continuous shower of wealth which may have the power to fill but not the power to unite. Therefore the gap is dangerously concealed under the glittering quicksands of things which by their own accumulating weight cause a sudden subsidence, while we are in the depth of our sleep.

But the real tragedy does not lie in the destruction of our material security, it is in the obscuration of man himself in the human world. In his creative activities man makes his surroundings instinct with his own life and love. But in his utilitarian ambition he deforms and defiles it with the callous handling of his voracity. This world of man's manufacture, with its discordant shrieks and mechanical movements, reacts upon his own nature, incessantly suggesting to him a scheme of universe which is an abstract system. In such a world there can be no question of *mukti*, because it is a solidly solitary fact, because the cage is all that we have, and no sky beyond it. In all appearance the world to us is a closed world, like a seed within its hard cover. But in the core of the seed there is the cry of life for *mukti* even when the proof of its possibility is darkly silent. When some huge temptation tramples into stillness this living aspiration after *mukti*, then does civilization die like a seed that has lost its urging for germination.

It is not altogether true that the ideal of *mukti* in India is based upon a philosophy of passivity. The *Īśopaniṣad* has strongly asserted that man must wish to live a hundred years and go on doing his work; for, according to it, the complete truth is in the harmony of the infinite and the finite, the passive ideal of perfection and the active process of its revealment; according to it, he who pursues the knowledge of the infinite as an absolute truth sinks even into a deeper darkness than he who pursues the cult of the finite as complete in itself. He who thinks that a mere aggregation of changing notes has the ultimate value of unchanging music, is no doubt foolish; but his foolishness is exceeded by that of one who thinks that true music is devoid of all notes. But where is the reconciliation? Through what means does the music which is transcendental turn the facts of the detached notes into a vehicle of its expression? It is through the rhythm, the very limit of its composition. We reach the infinite through crossing the path that is definite. It is this that is meant in the following verse of the *Īśa*:

> He who knows the truth of the infinite and that of the finite both united together, crosses death by the help of *avidyā*, and by the help of *vidyā* reaches immortality.

The regulated life is the rhythm of the finite through whose very restrictions we pass to the immortal life. This *amṇtaṃ*, the immortal life is not a mere prolongation of physical existence, it is in the realization of the perfect, it is in the well-proportioned beautiful definition of life which every moment surpasses its own limits and expresses the Eternal. In the very first verse of the *Īśa*, the injunction is given to us: '*mā gṛdhah*'; Thou shalt not covet. But why should we not? Because greed, having no limit, smothers the rhythm of life—the rhythm which is expressive of the limitless.

The modern civilization is largely composed of *ātmahanojanāḥ* who are spiritual suicides. It has lost its will for limiting its desires, for restraining its perpetual self- exaggeration. Because it has lost its philosophy of life, if loses its art of living. Like poetasters it mistakes skill for power and realism for reality. In the Middle Ages when Europe believed in the kingdom of heaven, she struggled to modulate her life's forces to effect their harmonious relation to this ideal, which always sent its call to her activities in the midst of the boisterous conflict of her passions. There was in this endeavour an ever present scheme of creation, something which was positive, which had the authority to say: Thou shalt not covet, thou must find thy true limits. Today there is only a furious rage for raising numberless brick-kilns in place of buildings. The great scheme of the master-builder has been smothered under the heaps of brick-dust. It proves the severance of *avidyā* from her union with *vidyā* giving rise to an unrhythmic power, ignoring all creative plan, igniting a flame that has heat but no light.

Creation is in rhythm,—the rhythm which is the border on which *vidyāṁ ca avidyāṁca*, the infinite and the finite, meet. We do not know how, from the indeterminate, the lotus flower finds its being. So long as it is merged in the vague it is nothing to us, and yet it must have been everywhere. Somehow from the vast it has been captured in a perfect rhythmical limit, forming an eddy in our consciousness, arousing within us a recognition of delight at the touch of the infinite which finitude gives. It is the limiting process which is the work of a creator, who finds his freedom through his restraints, the truth of the boundless through the reality of the bounds. The insatiable idolatry of material that runs along an everlengthening line of extravagance, is inexpressive; it belongs to those regions which are *andhena tamasāvrtāḥ*, enveloped in darkness, whichever carry the load of their inarticulate bulk. The true prayer of man is for the Real, not for the big, for the light which is not in incendiarism but in illumination, for Immortality which is not in duration of times but in the eternity of the perfect.

Only because we have closed our path to the inner world of *mukti*, the outer world has become terrible in its exactions. It is a slavery to continue to live in a sphere where things are, yet where their meaning is obstructed. It has become possible for men to say that existence is evil, only because in our blindness we have missed something in which our existence has its truth. If a bird tries to soar in the sky with only one of its wings, it is offended with the wind for buffeting it down to the dust. All broken truths are evil. They hurt because they suggest something which they do not offer. Death does not hurt us, but disease does, because disease constantly reminds us of health and yet withholds it from us. And life in a half world is evil, because it feigns finality when it is obviously incomplete, giving us the cup, but not the draught of life. All tragedies consist in truth remaining a fragment, its cycle not being completed.

Let me close with a Baül song, over a century old, in which the poet sings of the eternal bond of union between the infinite and the finite soul, from which there can be no *mukti*, because it is an interrelation which makes truth complete, because love is ultimate, because absolute independence is the blackness of utter sterility. The idea in it is the same as we have in Upanisad, that truth is neither in pure *vidyā* not in *avidyā*, but in their union:

> "It goes on blossoming for ages, the soul-lotus in which I am bound, as well as thou, without escape. There is no end to the opening of its petals, and the honey in it has such sweetness that thou like an enchanted bee canst never desert it, and therefore thou art bound, and I am, and *mukti* is nowhere."

B. K. Sarkar, "Viewpoints in Aesthetics" (1922)

Benoy Kumar Sarkar (1887–1949) was a polymath. Trained in English and History, he held a chair in Economics and lectured widely (in English, French, German, and Italian as well as Bengali) not only on economics but also on political theory, art history and aesthetics. He was well known in colonial India but is largely forgotten today. We present a selection excerpted from his book *The Futurism of Young Asia* interrogating the role of nationalism in aesthetic theory (1922).

4

View-Points in Aesthetics

1. Two Specimens of Art-Appreciation

A gifted Indian painter writes to me from Calcutta (March 9, 1921): "If I had spent years among the museums and exhibitions of Paris I could never have reproduced a replica of that art in an Indian city."

The artist's argument is thus worded: "People—including our greatest men—come back from Europe with a changed point of view which they cannot adjust to Indian conditions. Our ideas must live and grow on Indian conditions—however much our education and outlook may be finished and enlarged by foreign travels and intimate contact with the living phases of a living civilisation."

The writer is not only an artist of distinction but is also the author of writings on several phases of Indian painting and sculpture. He is familiar, besides, with the art-history of the world in both its Asian and European developments.

Almost in the same strain Mr. "Agastya" gives his reactions to the "art of a Bengali sculptor" in the *Modern Review* for May 1921. Says he: "Though the subject is Indian there is nothing in it which could not come from the chisel of a non-Indian sculptor. Indeed our grievance is that in Mr. Bose's (Fanindra Nath) works we search in vain for the revelation of the Indian mind of an Indian artist, the peculiarity of his point of view, and the traditions of his great heritage."

"Agastya" also, like my friend the painter, attacks the problem from the standpoint of a "question larger than the merits of his (Bose's) individual works." "What is the value", asks he, "of a long training in a foreign country which disqualifies an artist from recognizing and developing his own national and racial genius? A nation can no more borrow its art from abroad than its literature."

The problem is explicitly stated by "Agastya" in the following terms. "We are told," writes he, "that Mr. Bose perfected his training by his travels in France and Italy. We are not told if he ever studied the masterpieces of old Indian sculpture and extracted from them the lessons which no Greek marble or bronze could teach him." Further, "an Indian artist," as we are assured by "Agastya", "is destined to tread a path not chosen by artists of other nationalities."

From his communication in the *Modern Review* Mr. "Agastya" appears to be "an authority on Indian sculpture." He is at present, as may be gathered, engaged in deciphering with his "old eyes dim with age" some of the worm eaten palm-leaves on image making now rotting in the archives of the Palace Library at Tanjare. Consequently he claims to be resting "in a place of telescopic distance" and to "have a more correct perspective and a wider and a dispassionate view of things, unattached by temporary values or local considerations." It must be added that "Agastya" also has cared to devote attention to Ruskin, Leighton and other Westerns.

2. *The Current Standard of Aesthetic Appraisal*

These statements, coming as they do from two authorities, might be strengthened by passages from the writings of other Indian writers who are known to be connoisseurs and art-historians or art-critics. For, virtually with no exception the field of art-appreciation is being dominated in India by one and only one strand of thought. And this "monistic" critique of aesthetic values which our archaeologists and essayists have chosen to advocate in season and out of season is essentially none other than what Eur-American "orientalists" and "friends of the Orient" have propagated in regard to the "ideals" of Asian art and civilisation.

There are two conceptions underlying each of the above specimens of art-appraisal.

First, there runs a hypothesis as to the "Indianness" of Indian inspiration, i.e., the distinctiveness of Hindu (or Indian?) genius, or, in other words, as to the alleged antithesis between the "ideals of the East" and those of the West.

Secondly, both writers have pursued certain canons in regard to the very nature and function of art itself. In their appreciation of paintings and sculptures they seem to be guided exclusively by the subjects painted and carved, in other words, by the story, legend, or literature of the pictorial and plastic arts. That is, while travelling in the realms of art they continue to be obsessed by the results of their studies in history, literary criticism, and anthropology.

This methodology of art-appreciation has long awaited a challenge. It is the object of the present essay to offer this challenge.

3. *The Boycott of Western Culture*

Let us follow the first point in the current standard of art-appreciation systematically and comprehensively to its furthest logical consequences.

If the exhibitions of paintings, sculptures and decorative arts conducted under the auspices, say, of a *Salon* like the *Société des Artistes Français*, in Grand

Palais (Paris) every spring, or the collections of Assyro-Babylonian cylinders, Greek vases, Roman sarcophagi, Etruscan urns, the safety-pins of Roman Gaul, the keys of Saalburg, Renaissance bronzes, and the mosaics, coins, and *terra cottas* of different epochs in the museums of Europe and America, and the studies concerning these monuments published in the monographs of learned societies, or, visits of investigation to the edifices of Moscow, the basilica of Algeria, the Byzantine sphere of influence in Asia Minor and Eastern Europe, not to speak of the Acropolis and the Gothic Cathedrals should have to be ruled out as of questionable importance in regard to the spiritual equipment of an Indian creator of art-forms because in sooth the East is postulated always to have been and ever in the future to remain different from the West, can we not dogmatize with the same emphasis that writers of novels, dramas and lyric poetry in modern Marathi, Urdu, Bengali, Hindi, Tamil and other Indian languages are not likely to imbibe any inspiration or derive any creative suggestions from Whitman, Browning, Sudermann, Ibsen, Dostoyevski, and Hervieu? And yet what else is Indian literature of the last two generations but the product of India's intimate aquaintance with and assimilation of Western literary models?

If the frescoes of Ajanta and the bas-reliefs of Bharhut, if the South Indian bronzes and Rajput-Pahari illustrations, if the *gopurams*, the *shikharas* and the Indo-Moslem domes and minars are to exclude from India's aesthetic vision the superb architectural immensities engineered by the American designers of sky-scrapers, the styles of Kiev and Novogorod, the glories of Florence and Ravenna, the Parthenon and the Notre Dame, why should not Kural, Kalidas, Vidyāpati, Tukārām and Tulsidās monopolize the imagination of every rising genius in the field of Indian letters? Should Hari Narayan Apte have produced another volume of *Abhangs*? Should the creator of *Bande Mātaram* have compiled another *Kathā-saritsāgara*?

Pursuing the current logic of art-appreciation we should have to dictate that Indians must by all means avoid the contact of Lavoisier and his disciples, of Humboldt, Pasteur, Agassiz, Maxwell, and Einstein because in order to be true to Hindu "heritage" it is necessary to boycott everything that has appeared in the world since Leibnitz, Descartes and Newton! No Indian, therefore, we must accordingly advise, should investigate the acoustics of the violin because not much on this subject is to be found in the mediaeval *Sangita-ratnākara*! And since the only mechanical engineering of which our great encyclopaedia, the *Brihat Samhitā*, is aware is the dynamics of the bullock cart, no Indian if he wishes to remain a loyal Indian must pry into the mysteries of the printing press, wireless telegraphy, the Zeppelin, and long-distance phones!

From the identical standpoint the student of Hindu heritage in polity should be asked to come forward with the message that India's Indianness is to be found only in Kautilya or that from the great vantage ground of the *Arthaśāstra* and of the Tamil inscription discovered at Uttaramallur. Young India can afford to declare a contraband of Rousseau, Washington, Mill, Mazzini, Treitschke, and Lenin!

Perhaps the advocates of the current method in art-appreciation will consider our students of philosophy to be the best representatives of Indianness and of the distinctive Hindu spirit because during the period of over half a century they have failed to produce anything superior to mere paraphrases, translations and commentaries of the ancient *darśanas* and have thus marvellously succeeded in demonstrating that they were incapable of assimilating and extending the thought-world exhibited by masters from Bacon to James and Wundt.

And certainly the apostles of Indianness of the Indian mind will as a matter of course fail to appreciate the achievement, whatever be its worth, of Vivekananda simply because on account of his Western leavening this Carlyle of Young India happened to realize and exploit the dynamic possibilities of the Vedānta such as were undreamt of by Saṅkaracārya.

The absurdity of the current methodology in the appraisal of life's values is patent on the surface.

4. *Achievements of the Modern Mind*

Our Vishvakarma had succeeded in inventing a bullock cart. He could not hit upon the steam engine. Is this why the bullock cart is to stand for "spirituality" and the steam engine for gross materialism? Is this why the bullock cart should be regarded as the symbol of Hindu genius, and the railway and all that has followed it of the Western?

But how old is the steam engine in the West as an aid to transportation or manufacture? This machine was unknown to the Vishvakarmas of Greece and Rome and of Europe down to the French Revolution. The difference between the East and the West in materialism is then not a difference in "ideals" but only a difference in time which can be measured by decades.

What the bullock cart is to the steam engine, that is all that Hindu genius had produced during the epochs of its creative history to all that Western genius has produced during, roughly speaking, the last two hundred years. Previous to the advent of the recent phase of civilisation East and West ran parallel, nay, identical in the "point of view", in "genius", in "spirit".

Here is a test case. The music of Beethoven, nay, the "harmonies", "symphonies" and "overtures" of modern Europe would have been as unintelligible in the Middle Ages, to Dante and his predecessors for instance, as they are still unintelligible to us in Asia simply because we have not advanced further than the discoveries of our forefathers in the thirteenth century.

If today an Indian *ostad*, but one who is conversant with the theory of Indian music,—a condition perhaps very difficult to fulfil in the present state of the art—were to attempt mastering the technique of the great "composers"—a class of artists probably unknown in Indian tradition—of this new West and on the strength of that equipment proceed to improvise some novel forms for our own *rāgas* and *rāginis* should he be condemned as a dilettante or should he be appreciated as the true disciple of our own *swadeshi* Bharata and Dhananjaya? And if a failure, should he not be honoured as the first term in a long series of pioneering experiments?

The instance of music is offered as a typical problem for Young India because music is perhaps *the* line of creative activity in which Indian "genius" has taken the least step forward in centuries. Even the elementary work of matching appropriate "chords" to the notes of a melody or of devising a musical notation has not been attempted as yet.

5. *The Alleged Indian Point of View*

From achievements let us pass on to the analysis of ideals, the same problem, in fact, turned inside out. The question may reasonably be asked: What is the Indian spirit? What is the distinctive Hindu or Oriental ideal?

Is it to be detected in the *charkhā*, the handloom, and in cottage industry? But previous to the "industrial revolution" mankind nowhere knew of weaving factories, a Massachusetts Institute of Technology, and the Krupp Workshops.

In the "village communities", those so-called rural republics, as every Indian has learned to repeat *ad nauseam* since the publication of Metcalfe's *Report*? But England also should appear to be quite possessed of the Hindu spirit because there, says Gomme the anthropologist and historian of civics, the "localities" have "survived all shocks, all revolutions, all changes, and their position on the map of England is as indestructible as the country itself." Has Metcalfe said anything more or different about India, the country *sui generis* of *panchāyat* and "local government?"

In agriculture? But all through the ages civilization has fundamentally been agricultural. And today not only in France, Russia and Germany, but even in the United States agriculture (including *go-sevā* or cow-"worship") is the greatest single occupation of the people.

In land-revenue as the principal item of public finance? But the backbone of the national treasury even under the Roman Empire was furnished by the realizations from land, nay, from crown-land.

In the *shrenis, ganas,* corporations or gilds? But these economico-political unions have served the same social, religious, ethical, literary and artistic functions of the Europeans in the Middle Ages as in India.

In monasticism and *sādhuism?* But in a religious map, say, of England in the sixteenth century, previous to the dissolution of monasteries the country will appear to have been dotted over almost with as many cathedrals, churches, *āshrams, mathas, tapovans,* "forests", as our own *punya-bhumi,* sacred Motherland.

In the sanctity of the home and in the reverence for the female sex? But even in 1921 entire Latin Europe, as we understand from Joseph Barthélemy, the liberal suffragist, in his *Le Vote des Femmes,* is disposed, although without *purdāh* (veil), to look with disfavor on the public and political activities of women. And in the Anglo-Saxon world, even in go-ahead America[1], although the tremendous economic developments of the last century have inevitably led on to the recognition of the independent status of the woman in law and politics, it is the "society" obsessed as it is with the ideal of the *Hausfrau* which still rules the "proprieties" of the "eternal feminine" in the daughter, the bride, the wife, and the mother.

What, then, are the elements in the Indian "atmosphere" which differentiate it, whether item by item or *ensemble,* from other atmospheres? Where are to be discovered the specifically Indian "traditions" of human evolution?

In the "enlightened despotism" and *pax sârva-bhaumica* (peace of the world empire) of the Mauryas, Guptas, Pālas, Cholas, Moghuls, and Marathas? But one has only to envisage Versailles or study the seventeenth century of European civilisation with open mind in order to be convinced that there has not occurred anything in the history of the world since the days of the ancient Egyptians more dehumanizing and demoralizing than were the autocracy, intolerance, luxury, effeminacy, and licentiousness which Europe has exhibited under her Bourbon and other pharaohs.

6. *Race-Ideals in Fine Arts*

Perhaps here one should be interrupted with the remark that the *rasas* or emotions with which paintings and sculptures deal belong to a category altogether distinct from the psychological processes involved in the making of exact science, industrial technique, material invention, and social or political institution. It might be suggested, in other words, that although the sciences may be

1. Cf. the position of the woman in the colonial period and since in Calhoun's *Social History of the American Family* (1918).

conceded to be universal, international, cosmopolitan, or human, fine arts are on the contrary essentially racial, national, local or regional.

For the present we need not enter into a discussion as to the correct physiological and psychological basis of the mentalities operating in the different orders of creation. We shall only single out certain types from the art-history of the world at random and examine if they really point to any psychological diversity, any divergence in *rasa* between race and race.

Let us consider the epochs of European art previous to the moderns, say, previous to Da Vinci, Rembrandt, and Velazquez. The sociology of that Western art will be found to be governed by the same *rasas*, the same ideals, whatever they be, as that of the Hindu. We have only to visit the galleries or go around the world with eyes open, i.e. with an eye to the pragmatic meaning of the diverse art-forms in the life's scheme of the different peoples.

The sculptures of Greece and their Roman copies do not tell any story different from the images of the Hindu gods and goddesses. The art of Catholic Europe (both Roman and Greek Church), embodied in the architecture, painting, stained glass, mosaic, bas relief, and statue, is one continuous worship of the Unknown, the Infinite, and the Hereafter, which the Hindu or the Buddhist considers to be a monopoly of his own *shilpa-śāstra* and temple paraphernalia.

Ecclesiastical art was practically the only art of Europe until about three centuries ago. From an intensive study of the Notre Dame alone (such as the orientalists and archaeologists are used to bestow on our Ajantas and Bharhuts), from an analysis of the elongated statues, the design of parallels, the transcendentalized anatomies, the morals on the façade, the chimerical animals on the roofings, the ritualistic basis of its internal arrangements, and the metaphysics of its mystical theology any Asian can satisfy himself as to the existence in Western civilisation of everything which he considers to be essential to "spirituality."

To what extent has this old religious mentality or superstitious attitude disappeared from modern Europe? Even today a Catholic priest is shocked to see the nudes in the Museum of Fine Arts at Boston or in the Luxembourg galleries at Paris. While examining the paintings and sculptures of the saints or the illustrations of the Biblical stories, should he chance to come across a "modern" treatment somewhere hard by, he knows that he has committed a sin against the most important commandment. This is the attitude also of every "decent" Christian woman, especially among Catholics,—the more so in the villages. What more does Indian "intuition" demand? And catholicism is still the predominant religion in Eur-America.

Cornelius, Overbeck and other painters of German romanticism in the early years of the last century must have out-Hindued the Hindu in their practice of *dhyāna* yoga meditation. In order to derive inspiration they renounced their family ties and came all the way to Italy, because, verily, they believed, as says Lewes in his *Life of Goethe*, that highest art was not achievable except by *sādhus, sanyasis*, Capucins and Rosicrucians.

Even in the "idealistic" interpretation of art-philosophy it is possible to find the alleged Hindu principles in Western speculation. If Croce's Italian *Aesthetic* is too contemporaneous, one can cite Schiller from Germany of a few generations ago. For, says he in his *Use of the Chorus in Tragedy*: "The aim of art is to make us absolutely free; and this it accomplishes by awakening, exercising and perfecting in us a power to remove to an objective distance the sensible world." Here then we have a European philosopher preaching the Hindu doctrine of *mukti, mokṣa*, freedom.

Nay, the art of Bolshevism counts among its spiritual antecedents the same "Hindu" mentality. As can be gathered from Reau's *Russie: Art Ancien*, for about two decades previous to the Sovietic revolution of 1917 the art and craft circles of Young Russia had carried on a propaganda in favour of going back to religious paintings, images, and so forth.

It is indeed absolutely necessary for every student of a so-called Hindu type of inspiration in art to be familiar with the Christian iconography and symbolism in the researches of Martin, Cahier, and Didron. More modern and novel eye-openers from the same standpoint will be Male's *Art religieux du XIIIe siècle* (available in English) and *Art religieux de la fin du moyen âge*.

Should we still have to suspect a difference in life's attitudes between the East and the West as exhibited in art-structures, let us observe the Napoleonic *Arc de Triomphe* at Paris. The arch is a *jaya-stambha*—like the one our own Raghu constructed on the Gangetic delta in Eastern Bengal—consecrated to the victories of the *grande armée* from 1792 to 1815. The sculptures illustrate the scene in the history of revolutionary France with special reference to Austerlitz (1806).

No man of common sense will dare remark that in this memorial of military glories Napoleon or the French nation intended to display a characteristically French or European ideal of civilisation. The obelisks and pylons of Luxor and Karnak had anticipated the same ideals of mankind three thousand years ago. We may come to the Persia of Darius or even nearer home and say that if a monument in stone were erected by Samudragupta's (c 370 C.E.) architects and sculptors in order to illustrate the lengthy literary monument composed by Harishena in honour of the emperor's *digvijaya* (conquest of the quarters) the descendants of this Hindu Napoleon would have always seen in their own Rome the solid testimony to the same Egyptian or French *rasa* (emotion).[2]

2. Albert Hoffmann: *Denkmäler*. 2 vols. (1906), in *Handbuch der Architektur* Series, Stuttgart. Sarkar, *The Futurism of Young Asia*.

Where, then, are the distinctive racial traits and psychological attitudes in the world's architecture, sculpture, and painting? Nowhere. Such differences have never existed in the mentality of which history furnishes the objective evidence.

7. *Aesthetic Revolution*

But in the first place the moderns in Eur-America have succeeded in profoundly secularizing the arts. In the second place they have attained certain conspicuous results in technique and treatment of the material. It is questionable if we can credit them with the creation or discovery of an essentially new *rasa*, a characteristically modern emotion,—except what is automatically implied in the new subjects of secular experience.

Whether there have emerged some new emotions or not, the advance of the creative mind in technique is already too obvious. And continuing the previous parallelism, one may almost remark, although with great caution in regard to the application and interpretation of the analogy in the field of aesthetics, that what the fishing canoe is to the submarine, that is all Classic and Christian art to the art of the last two hundred years, and that is all Hindu art to European art since the Renaissance.

This revolution in fine arts is indicated by Professor Lewis in a public lecture on the "Logical in Music" given at Harvard University in the summer of 1917. While analyzing the "First Movement" in Beethoven's *Third Symphony* this lecturer on musical appreciation remarks: "The logical development of the thematic material in the first section to the climax has the same place in the history of music as the French Revolution in world's history. It swept away the 'Classical' in music by establishing the influence of the 'individual passage.' Measures 280–283 are epoch-making. Herein is born the 'romantic movement' which gives rise to 'modern beauty.'"

Perhaps these words do not convey any sense to the ordinary Asian student of art. This is all the more corroborative of the fact that in art technique as in everything else India, nay, Asia has failed independently to evolve this last epoch of human attainments.

For Young India today to appreciate and assimilate the new achievements of mankind in aesthetics as in the utilitarian sciences and arts is not tantamount to inviting an alleged denationalization. That is, on the contrary, one of the chief means of acquiring strength in order that the Orient may push forward the creative urge of life and contribute to the expansion of the human spirit as the offsprings of Māyā and Vishvakarmā should be able to do.

8. Historical Art-Criticism

But all this analysis of sociological ideals, *Weltanschauungen*, and other philosophical platitudes in the style of a Hegel or a Taine is the least part in the appreciation of art. It is the most irrelevant and the most superficial element in genuine *shilpaśāstra*. We are thus led to the discussion of the second point in traditional art-criticism, viz. the question of the importance of the story, the legend, or the theme in sculptures and paintings, and in aesthetics generally.

It must be admitted at the outset that in this respect the methodology of art-appreciation prevalent in India or Japan is but an echo of the conventional manner in which art-products are usually evaluated in the *bazaars* and learned societies of Eur-America. The method consists in describing the pieces limb by limb, telling the subject matter, counting the number of figures, trees or utensils, naming the animal, directing attention to the costume, and finally, if old, ascertaining the date.

The manner is familiar to those who have to use the catalogues of museums, expositions, show-rooms, and art dealers' salons. This is the "method in archaeology" as described by Reinach in *De la méthode dans les sciences*. Essays which appear in newspapers and magazines and even in such reviews as are devoted exclusively to fine arts hardly ever rise above this descriptive plane. The traditional method is thus one adapted to the kindergarten stage of art-education.

Equipped with this canon the art connoisseur comes to study in the Notre Dame the economic organization of the French *shrenis* (gilds) of masons and glass-cutters in the thirteenth century just as he tries to reconstruct the dress, manners, jokes, funeral ceremonies, dance, rural institutions, and commercial activities of ancient India in the bas-reliefs of Sanchi. In the Venuses and Apollos of Classical Europe the conventional art-critic studies perhaps the physiognomies of the Aegeans, Pelasgians, Cretans, Ionians, Etruscans, Florentines, and others, in the Madonnas he will detect the faces of the wives of the Italian Renaissance painters, Spanish or Russian nuns or the milkmaids and peasant women of the Netherlands, in the Buddhas he marks the Afghan, Central-Asian, Punjabi, Nepalese, Mongolo-Dravidian, Chinese, Javanese, Siamese or Japanese types, and within the Indian boundaries he tabulates the goddess Shakti according to her aboriginal, Kashmiri, Bengali, Tamil and other features.

Such studies are important in themselves. Their value as aid to identification and "classification in a series" is unquestionable. They offer material contributions also to the geography of art-migration, the science of ritual, superstition, and religious observances, economic history, ethnography, and to the study of many other phases of human civilisation. Readers of Michaelis'

Ein Jahrhundert kunstarchäologischer Entdeckungen could never dare suspect the utility of such investigations.

But how much of these studies is real analysis of *rasa*, genuine art-criticism? Absolutely nothing.

9. Philosophical Art-Criticism

Not all art critics, however, are exclusively interested in these descriptive, historical, economic, anthropological or sociological aspects of fine arts. There are connoisseurs who try to attack the problem from what may be called the psychological point of view. They analyze the ideas, the ideals, the "nine *rasas*", the message, or the philosophy of the paintings and sculptures.

When these art-philosophers see the landscapes of Sesshiu, the great Japanese master of the fourteenth century, they read in the *rasa* of his pines the symbolism for longevity, in that of his bamboos the allegory of chastity, and in that of his plums all that is implied by taste and elegance in *belles lettres.*

If they come across Chinese silks depicting mountain scenes with snows and pines or perhaps a solitary man seated in a certain pose these metaphysicians of aesthetics will discover therein the cool contemplative calm of Chinese consciousness conducive to the quest of the Beyond.

In the same manner they would have interpreted at least half a dozen works of Corot (1796–1875)—his mornings, evenings, shepherds playing on the flute in moonlight—as philosophical allegories pointing to quiescence, passivity, and the communion of the soul with nature, were it not for the fact that Corot happens to be a Frenchman and a European and that *ergo* the "message of the forest" must by no means be attributed to a beef-eating materialistic Westerner!

Likewise will these philosophical connoisseurs find a mystery in the paintings illustrating Radha and Krishna simply because by their conventional pose and dress such as are described in literature the figures can easily be identified as the sacred persons of semi-mythical tradition. With equal energy do such critics run into ecstasy over a Giotto's (1276–1337) *St. Francis receiving the wounds of Jesus on his own person* or over a Murillo the Spanish master's (1616–1682) *Immaculate Conception* and *Angel's Kitchen* because these stories possess a spiritual "polarization" in the folk-psychology.

And in the portraits of a Rash Behari Ghosh or an Andrew Carnegie or in the statues of a Ranade or a Clemenceau the metaphysicians of *rasa* will manage to discover the idea, the soul, the allegory of the person, so to speak, and try to point it out in a language which satisfies none but the initiated, in the facial expression, in the eyes, in the forehead, in the jaw-bones, in the lips and in the chin.

It is out of such Hegelian analysis of the "souls" of paintings and sculptures that critics have generalized as to the fundamental distinction in spirit between the East and the West.

These are clever investigations undoubtedly, and perhaps not unnecessary. But here, again, we ask: How much of all these is art-criticism? Absolutely nothing.

10. The Themes of Art

Both the historical and the philosophical art critics are focusing their attention on one thing, viz. the legend, the story, the theme. While evaluating the workmanship, the *shilpa*, of the artist they are not at all studying the *shakti*, the genius of the sculptor or the painter as creator of beauties nor the magic touch of technique by which he has been able to produce the *rasa*, whatever it be. They are interested in everything else, i.e., all that lies outside the sphere of beauty and the artist's *rasa*. They are concerning themselves with the history, the literature, the geography and the biography of the themes with which they are already familiar or about which, maybe, they wish to derive some new information.

Of what avail, from the standpoint of aesthetic enjoyment, is it to know that Cimabue (1240–1302), the "father of modern painting", was the first artist to paint from the living model or to be told that the expression of a portrait is exactly what one knows of the person? Do we gain anything in art appreciation by indicating that certain pictures on *terra cottas* or certain bas reliefs on walls or on sarcophagi are vivid illustrations of the armageddons in the *Iliad* or the *Purānas*? Similarly to emphasize that the message of Omar Khayyam has found the aptest expression in certain paintings is nothing but beating about the bush, promenading far beyond the vestibule of the temple of art. All this is like reading the description at the bottom of a piece and on that strength announcing that over here there is the picture of a mouse.

Such descriptions or expressions (i.e., interpretations) are the minimum expected of every painter and sculptor. One or other of the so-called nine or of the thousand and one *rasas* (emotions) may be postulated about every piece of work, Oriental or Occidental, ancient or modern. But when we enter the sphere of art we must take care not to insult the artist by asking such puerile, elementary and extraneous questions. We come to understand him in his own language, in his own idiom, in his own technique.

And that language, that idiom, that technique are absolutely independent of the theme, the legend, the story, the message. The art-world is a sphere by itself with its own "conditions of temperature and pressure", its own zones of influence, its own canons, statutes and bye-laws. It can only betray our naive simplicity if we obtrude our knowledge of history, biography, psychology, drama, lyric and epic upon the productions of the painter and the sculptor when we come to interrogate them.

11. Swaraj *in* Shilpa

It is now time to cast aside the negatives and enunciate our position in as positive a manner as possible. What are we to understand by the emancipation that is being advocated here of art from the despotism of literary criticism, historical or philosophical analysis, ethical or religious studies, and democratic, bolshevistic or nationalistic propaganda? What is the meaning of the thesis that we should have to conceive *shilpa* as a *swaraj* in itself, i.e. to treat art or the creation of "beauties" as a self-determined entity in human experience? In what sense is it possible to concede to painting and sculpture an absolute autonomy whether as modes of objective description or subjective expression?

The problem will become lucid if we take an analogy from the domain of music. If I say that *behag* is a melody which is played at midnight or that it is suggestive of the depths of mountain solitude, or that it is evocative of the emotions, the *rasas*, of a pensive mood, am I using the language of music? None at all.

Or, if in order to illustrate the beauty of *behag* I begin to sing a song which is tuned to that melody and then point out the exquisiteness of the words and the charm of the ideas in them, am I using the language of music? None at all.

All this at best is but literary criticism which does not touch the stuff of which music is made.

If I am to appreciate *behag* as the master devised it I must have the capacity to analyze the sounds and the "phrases of sounds", and discover the integral and "organic" concatenation of sounds. I should be in a position to point out the logic of these sound-combinations and detect the consistency in the development of the "sound-sentence" and the sound-paragraph from beat to beat, rhythm to rhythm, phrase to phrase. It should be necessary, for instance, to explain why a "phrase" from *todi* melody can serve but to create a melodic inconsistency in the system of *behag*.

There is a logical "necessity" in the order and sequence of the rhythm constituting each "musical form". It is the function of musical appreciation to deal with that organic necessity in the creation of sound-structures.

The sense of the sounds, thus grasped, possesses an independent existence. It must not be confounded with the sense of the subject matter of a song which is set to that sound-structure. Music itself has absolutely no connection with the meaning of the words, the significance of the song, the philosophy of the poetry. Indeed to confound music with song is a sign of puerilism in an individual, and if committed by a race it can only point to the primitive stage of development so far as this particular art is concerned.

Let us now illustrate the autonomy of art in the domain of poetry. If I say that Jogindra Nath Bose has produced a great epic because it deals with Shivaji, a historic hero, or because his *Prithvirāj* is a call to national unity, or that Rajani Kanta Sen is a great poet because he writes devotional hymns, or that the poets of Young Bengal are performing great things in poetry because they sing to the country, to nationalism, and to democracy, am I using the language of poetry? None at all.

The message does not make poetry. The subject matter does not make poetry great.

The subject matter, the message, the philosophy, the social ideal, the "criticism of life" may have to be appreciated or condemned on their own merits. But poetry itself will have to stand on its own dignity. You may condemn the *rasas* dealt with in a work, i.e., the message of the author from your particular ethical point of view and yet you may worship him as a great poet.

One does not have to be a Roman Catholic in order to feel that the author of the *Divine Comedy* is a first class creator of characters and situations, of problems and possibilities. *Paradise Lost* does not depend for its strength on the cult of militant puritanism on which it is reared. Men who are the furthest removed from the religious controversies and political *rasas* of the English people in the seventeenth century or of the Italians in the thirteenth can feel in the atmosphere of these two creations the Titanic might of Himalayan upheavals.

Whatever be the subject matter, the poet will have to be judged *as poet* solely by his manipulations, his treatment of the material, the machinery he has invented in order to make the material speak, the individuality and fruitfulness of his technique. We need only ask: "What new personalities have been manufactured by the author? What new attitudes and rearrangements of ideas? What devices, what complexities, what surprises? Are the creations attempted important, integral, and organic enough to enrich human experience?"

The autonomy of poetry as a mode of literary expression depends on the "artistic necessity" pervading, as it must, the organism of vital situations and ideas. Not to create this artistic necessity through the medium of language is not to be a poet. To fail to discover and appreciate this artistic necessity is to fail in understanding poetry.

12. The Art-In-Itself or Pure Art

We should now be able to analyze and understand the artistic necessities in painting and sculpture.

Let us begin with a simple query in regard to modern French paintings: How do the Cézannes differ from the Corots in so far as both Cézanne and Corot are landscapists? If you wish to detect a Chinese *Tao* or a Wordsworthian "Nature's holy plan" you are at liberty to interpret both these masters alike. But wherein lies the individuality of each as *shilpin*, as artist? How has each created his own beauties, his own "message of the forest"? Here then we have to find some new criterion of art. The problem lies in the *how*.

Indeed, when we are face to face with one thousand landscapes executed by several hundred painters and get used to viewing them from different angles and in different moods all those descriptive, historical, philosophical and idealistic criticisms are bound to disappear. We are forced to meditate upon the art-in-itself, the only feature in all these productions which is of supreme importance to the painters themselves, in other words, upon "pure" art.

The same problem arises when we are in a gallery of sculptures where the exhibits are to be counted by hundreds, and including the miniatures, by thousands. The question of photographic likeness or the symbolism of the executions then retires into the background; and even in spite of ourselves real aesthetic criticism makes its appearance. We begin to discuss the "hows" of each masterpiece.

It is possible for some while to remain satisfied with cataloguing the Natarājas as South Indian and Sinhalese, the Buddhas and Tārās in terms of latitude and longitude, the Apollos and Venuses according to the cities where they were unearthed, and the Madonnas according as their pose agrees with or varies from the Cimabue patent. One may also enjoy a diversion by classifying the distortions in anatomy as much from the Pharaonic, the Aegean, Korean, Japanese and Hindu executions as from the statues on the facade of the treasury at Delphi or from those on the portals and tympanum of the cathedrals in France.

But the multitude of specimens and the plurality of types, inevitable as they are, compel us at last to come down to the fundamentals of beauty and truth in *shilpa* and to try to decipher the alphabet of plastic and pictorial art.

13. The Alphabet of Beauty

Drawing, painting, bas relief and sculpture deal with the subject matter of anatomy, botany, and the other branches of natural history, but they are not governed by these sciences. These arts are regulated by the science of space, geometry, the *vidyā* of *rupam*, the knowledge of form, morphology.

The language of the painter and the sculptor is, therefore, point, line, angle, cone, square, curve, mass, volume. The creators of beauty speak the vocabulary of positions, magnitudes, dimensions, perspectives. If we are to associate with the manipulators of these forms we must learn how to employ the terminology of obliques and parallelograms, prisms and pentagons. We must also have to practise understanding the message, which in every instance is spiritual, of the lumps, patches, contours, balls, depths, and heights.

We can only make ourselves a nuisance in the company of painters and sculptors if we speak a jargon which is utterly incomprehensible to them. Such jargons, not to be found in the dictionary of art, are the technical terms known as the tibia, the clavicle, the cerebellum, the stirnum, the pelvic girdle. Other jargons like these are the dicotyledons, the conifers, the palmates, the pinnates. More such jargons are love, anger, hatred, malice, compassion, and the rest of the *rasas,* whatever be their number according to the latest experiments in "individual psychology."

To a *shilpin* there is only one organ of sense, and that is the eye. The artist does not, however, view the world as a theatre of minerals, plants, and animals, nor of the races of men with their physical, mental or emotional characteristics. In the geology and anthropo-geography of art there are recorded only the forms (and also the colours). The optic nerves, or for that matter, the entire sensibility of the artist *as artist* cannot respond to anything but these shapes and hues,—the most fundamental "generalizations" that can be deduced out of the world's structure.

And what does the artist create? Not necessarily the doubles or replicas nor even the interpretations or symbolisms of the forms which arrest his eyes, but whatever his form-sense, his *rasa-jñāna,* dictates to him as worth creating. If out of his readings of the crystallography of the universe he can give birth to a type by his constructive will he is an artist. If he can render his types readable, i.e. intelligible to the eyes of his fellowmen, in other words, if he can make his creations, the progeny of his form-sense, live in the imagination even of a section of his community he is a master.

The creators of Apollos, Buddhas, Madonnas, Natarājas, Radhas, Shaktis, Venuses, and Vishnus happen to be masters because their *rasa-jñāna* bodied forth these types out of "airy nothings" endowing a "local habitation and a name" to "things unknown", and because these formations will talk to human beings as long as the world endures,—even when the dialects of the human language cease to be spoken, even when Greek mythology, Buddhism, Mariolatry, and the other conventional religious systems of mankind become things of the past.

The painter and the sculptor do not construct leaves, trunks, branches, arms, lips, thighs, loves, angers, hatreds. They are interested solely in the juxtaposition of forms, in the intermarriage of shapes, in the permutation and combination of masses and surfaces.

There is a blank wall, or a blank sheet of paper, silk, or canvas. The function of the artist is to fill it with designs, necessarily of geometry, but not necessarily the Euclid of the class-room. It is a geometry which serves the form-sense of the *shilpin.*

Or, there is a log of wood, a lump of clay, or block of stone. The function of the sculptor simply is to fashion out of this dead mass an organism of objects in space. The structure will naturally be made of cones, cavities, flats.

Perhaps we have already before us a Natarāja of Ceylon, a Venus of Melos, a Buddhist or Christian animal in prayer, or an Immaculate Conception. But the "reality" of these formations from the painter's or sculptor's geometry is not to be tested by their resemblance with or divergence from the types that are known to exist on earth. These *rupams* have a validity all their own.

The geometry of Māyā or Vishvakarmā has architectured a new world the denizens of which are *ipso facto* as real as anything of flesh and blood, or sap and tissue. The artist's creations are born on their own anatomy and physiology, on their own statics and dynamics. The solar system of *shilpa* moves independently of the solar system of nature.

The creations of mass in space are problems in themselves. And a "message" is immanent in each problem, in each contour in each coexistence of forms, in each treatment of colour. No *rupam,* however irregular, "unnatural", abnormal, nebulous, hazy, vague, or dim without its specific *meaning in space.* Not a bend without a sense, not a lump without its philosophy, not a bit of coloured space without its significance—in the scheme of art geometry. We do not have to wander away from these lines, surfaces, curves, and densities in order to discover the "ideals" of the maker. The ideals are right there speaking to my eyes.

A "still life", a few slices of cucumber on a plate, the struggle of a fish in a net, the drunkard on a donkey, a pose of the arm, the leaning of a head,—things which are not at all counted in an inventory of "spiritual" assets, Hindu or Christian—can still awaken awe, curiosity, wonder, in short, can possess a most profound spiritual mission through the sheer influence of mass, volume, position, or colour-arrangement. And, on the other hand, the thousand times memorized subjects of religious history, howsoever propped up by social inertia, may fail to excite even a thrill in our vascular organism and may thus leave our personality absolutely indifferent to their call simply because of an amateurish handling of patches and lumps.

One may have an emotional prejudice or unfavorable reaction of *rasa* against certain eye-types, certain lips and jaw-bones, certain other racial physiognomies, and of course, against certain distortions and multiplicities of limbs. But one must not import the reactions, responses and experiences of one's life-history into the world of art and make them the criterion of art products.

If I condemn a face in sculpture or an arm in bas-relief on such grounds I shall only be betraying impatience with the artist. In order that I may be competent to condemn a shape executed in *shilpa* I must be qualified enough to advance the sculptural or pictorial grounds, the grounds which belong to the sphere of the *shilpin's* experience.

In the world of art it is irrelevant to urge that in Bombay the female types are different or dress themselves differently from those known in Bengal. Nor does it help anybody in the creation or appreciation of art to proceed to psychoanalyze the sensibilities of a young man of Kashmir and declare that a Madras beauty is likely to fall flat on his aesthetic personality.

Whatever be the type created by the artist, whether it be a Japanese Hachiman or the ten-handed Rāvana, the supreme question for him as well for us is its consistency on sculptural or pictorial reasons. What we are to seek in his forms, normal or abnormal, is nothing but their organic synthesis in accordance with the logic of aesthetics. What may be considered to be abnormals or absurdities in the world of nature may happen to be quite justified by the grounds of art.

14. Structural Composition or Morphology of Art

These aesthetic grounds are the foundations of artistic necessity. They constitute the "spiritual" basis of paintings and sculptures (as of music and poetry) considered as structural organisms or vital entities, i.e. as contrasted with mere mechanical manipulations.

The space on the canvas is naturally to be divided into different sections and subsections. The problem is to divide it in such a manner that the different parts from one harmonious whole,—limbs of an integral entity. Easier said than done!

The same problem of "grouping" is the essential feature in the sculptor's art. He stands or falls on the organic necessity he can evoke of the different limbs for one another in the structural whole.

The form-sense, the *rasa-jñāna,* is thus ultimately the sense of "composition". This sense of composition, which is the soul of the geometry of beauty, does not defy analysis, as a mystic in art-appreciation might rashly assert. It can be analyzed almost as exactly, as positively, as objectively, as anything that is thought out or otherwise accomplished by man. It is on the possibility of such analysis that an "experimental psychology of beauty" can come into existence.

But this sense of composition can, however, be realized or analyzed only after the *rupam* has been created, i.e. only after a thing of beauty has been manufactured to add to the known forms in the universe. It can hardly be taught from mouth to mouth in a school of arts nor communicated from master to disciple in the studio of the artist.

The sculptor and the painter are not before me to explain with a compass, as it were, the warps and woofs of their art-texture, why, for instance, their spacing is such and such, or how they have been led to conceive such and such proportions in their handiwork. No, the formations must explain themselves. The key to the crystallography of art is contained in the very specimens.

And their sole language is the voice of *rupam*, the vocabulary of masses, volumes and poses, and the necessary lights and shades. If these forms do not convey any meaning to me about their morphology or structural composition, either I have no eye for art (an eye which certainly is very rare among men and women), or the artist himself is a quack.

From the standpoint taken in the present thesis, literary descriptions, howsoever short, which it has been the custom to tag at the bottom of art-objects, are in almost every instance a hindrance to genuine art-appreciation. Invariably they serve to shunt off the eye and the mind from the track of *rasa*, *shilpa*, and *shakti* (genius) of the artist to absolutely irrelevant and extraneous matters.

15. The Idiom of Painting

Up till now it has been possible to speak of painting and sculpture in a parallel manner, as if they were the same arts. But these two arts are not identical as modes of creation. The language of the painter is substantially different from that of the sculptor. In the appreciation of art accordingly, in *shilpa-śāstra*, we have to employ two different languages adapted to the two spheres.

So far as composition or art-crystallography is concerned, so far as artistic necessity is sought, so far as the organic consistency of the whole is the object of our investigation, painting and sculpture can be treated in one and the same breath. But this composition, this organic consistency, this logical necessity in the art-texture is achieved in sculpture in a manner quite different from that in painting.

The sculptor speaks essentially the language of dimensions. The painter's language is essentially that of colour. The permutation and combination of *rupams* and their harmonic synthesis are brought about by the sculptor through his three-dimensional solids; whereas for the same object the painter depends almost exclusively on the mixing of tints and gradation of colour.

It is not only the perspective that evokes volume in the painter's work. Painting becomes "sculpturesque" or three-dimensioned through colour also. The American Max Weber's blues have the solid texture of Chinese porcelains. The French Renoir's metallic red brings forth the volumes of human flesh.

The brush can achieve what the chisel does, viz, manufacture a structural composition. The *vidyā* of *rupam*, the science of form, the geometry of aesthetics, thus bifurcates itself in two directions: the composition of plastic arts and the art of colour-construction.

16. Form and Volume in Colour

The question may naturally be asked: What does one mean when one says that colour is laid at the service of form? How can *rupam* be constructed out of colour?

Ordinarily colour is known merely to influence us with its tints. The agreeableness or disagreeableness of the effects on optic nerves is the sole quality we generally attribute to the combination of hues produced by the painter's artistic chemistry.

In Asia especially it is difficult to take colour in any other association and conceive the mechanics of hues in any other light. Because Oriental art-history does not make us familiar with very many "pure paintings."

The paintings of ancient and mediaeval India, for instance, should not be called paintings in the strictest sense of the term. Most of these specimens are really "drawings", but coloured drawings.

Hindu artists were primarily draftsmen. They made lines and constructed shapes with the pen or the pencil as it were. These "pencil-sketches" or designs were the most important elements in the workmanship of the *shilpins*. To them colour was very secondary. It was added almost as a second thought, so to speak, on the background or the surface prepared by the drawing.

Shall we call such pieces of old Indian *shilpa* paintings on the ground that they possess a variety of tints and also display a remarkable discretion in the selection and treatment of these tints? We can do so if we please only in the same manner, however, in which we are entitled to describe the coloured bas-reliefs in pharaonic tombs at Dehrel-bahri and other sites as paintings.

Be this as it may, the point to notice especially in connection with the handling of colour is that, neither in coloured bas-reliefs nor in coloured drawings can we find the mass, the depth, the volume, in short, the "architectural" or sculpturesque quality, which comes to our attention as soon as we view a work in which the drawing is nowhere but in which the artist uses his brush and practically nothing but the brush. It is this exclusive employment of the brush and the consequent manipulation of paintings without the support and background of drawings, which is one of the greatest contributions of the modern, especially of the contemporary Occident to the achievements of mankind in *rupam.*

In such "pure paintings" the idiom that the artist speaks is that of colour and nothing but colour. It is with colour that he constructs shapes, erects forms, brings about light and shade, arranges the perspective, and redistributes the forces of nature for the world of art. Colour alone has thus been made to evolve the dimensions of sculpture on canvas and to produce the harmony of structural composition.

17. The Geometry of Sculpture

Paintings and sculptures are then universal in their appeal simply because their spiritual basis is geometry, the most abstract and cosmopolitan of all *vidyās,* which is known to be the groundwork of all knowledge in the Platonic grammar of science. Curiously enough, anthropologically speaking, the primitive patterns and designs of all races (including the "savages" of to-day and the prehistoric forefathers of the "civilised" nations of history) are preponderantly geometrical, strictly so called. The specimens of decorative arts,—Peruvian, American-Indian, Maori, Central-African,—with which we are familiar in the ethnological museums of the world, point overwhelmingly to the manipulation of lines, triangles, squares, hexagons etc. (animal and plant devices must not be overlooked however) in a manner for which a comparatively modern parallel is to be sought in the "arabesque" of Saracenic fine arts. The same universal principles of aesthetics can be watched (allowance to be made for the master's creative *rasa-jñāna*) in all epochs of art-development, no matter whatever be the latitude and longitude, whatever be the subject matter, the superstition and the *esprit des lois.*

Take Plate III, *Le Sommeil des Femmes* in Mallon's *Quatorze Sculptures Indiennes* (Paris, 1920).

This piece of bas-relief consists of two horizontal sections, one-third at the top being devoted to two semi-circles enclosing an inner triangle with the vertex cut out.

The principal two-thirds is divided, again, vertically into two sections, two-thirds of which at the left forms a square. This square is divided horizontally into two sections, of which the lower rectangle is more full than the upper.

The figure seated erect helps making a small square to the left and an agreeable rectangle with the reclining form to the right. It reaches right up to the parallelogram at the top with a ball. It serves also with a cross to connect the shapes in the rectangle at the bottom with the top.

The vertical parallelogram at the right consists of two figures, of which one is erect. The lower half of this figure is covered by a parabolic shape, thoroughly supple and pliant, the two extremities of which are firmly fixed on to a semi-elliptical cylinder.

We do not have to examine the piece anatomically or anthropologically. From top to bottom, from right to left we are here viewing nothing but a drama of forms and the interplay of light and shade. Every curve tells a story to the eyes, every wave brings its message to the spirit. We do not care to know if it is a Buddha seated or a Yasodhara sleeping, or the women of the concert party enjoying repose on the spot. We do not have to inquire if the piece comes from Afghanistan, if the artists are Central-Asian, Hellenistic, or Indian, if the legend is derived from the *Jātakas*.

We feel that the sculptor has contributed to the experiences of our life another creation of shapes, another truth in patterns and designs, another thing of beauty which is a joy forever and to all mankind. One may view the piece from any angle, to be extreme, even upside down. It will not lose its quality of composition in any event. The melody of rhythmic contours in this bas-relief is constant and perpetual.

The composition here is very simple, almost elementary. Perhaps this is the reason why the pattern of this structure is to be found in its essential details as much in "pagan" Greece as in Christian cathedrals. Morphologically it is indeed an A. B. C. in art formations. It is a real "primitive" of art-technique.

A very close resemblance to this type is furnished by Plate V, *Le Parinirvâna*. There, among other things a special significance is to be attached to the oblique in the centre, which to the reader of the story is meant to indicate a person lying on the bed. But the artist's *rasa-jñāna* has counselled him to the effect that an ordinary horizontal would not provide the desired effect. He wants to create an aesthetic diversion in the midst of the monotonous group of parallel verticals.

A religious devotee will perhaps see in this piece one of the most solemn incidents visualized in stone. But in art-appreciation, in *shilpa-śāstra*, it is nothing but the "mystery" of an inclined plane which has been exploited by the sculptor in an exquisite manner. Where is the artist or the art-critic who will have to be told the story of the Great Passing Away in order to be responsive to the call of these universals in sculptural geometry?

We can then understand easily why Natarāja is one of the most signal contributions of India to the history of world's sculpture. To the anthropologist it is perhaps a Dravidian devil in his bacchanalian orgies, to the mystic it is an emblem of the cosmic music of the world-process, or, may be, of something in tune with the Infinite, to the student of literature it is but a Tamil embodiment in bronze of a Shaiva story.

But to the sculptor with his *rasa-jñāna*, his sense of form and composition, wherever he be, but to one who speaks his own language and is true to his *shilpa*, Natarāja is a most original creation in the ripple of bends and joints. The balancing of diverse masses in motion, the swaying of the volumes away from one another, the construction of imaginary circles within circles, the grouping of unseen parallels in movements and poses, and the gravitation of all the varied shapes to a common centre of dynamic rhythm—all these constitute an epoch-making attainment of unity in diversity, of the correlation of matter and motion, which possesses a meaning in the idiom of *rupam* as much to the Western as to the Eastern artist.

To a student of the geometry of dance the fantasy of forms exhibited by the Sinhalese or South Indian Natarāja will not fail to suggest the design of the group of dancing figures on the façade of the Opera at Paris (for which, by the bye, American millionaires are said to have offered a price worth its weight in gold). The Tamil Natarāja type of sculpture-formation is one of the permanent glories of man's creative *shakti*.

18. The Mechanism of Colour-Construction

We shall now mention some achievements in colour construction to illustrate the universal in artistic geometry.

Every painter has an idiom of his own in the matter of spacing and grouping. Among the moderns Cézanne, for instance, has created a type of composition, almost a formula, which he has followed in almost all his major works. Whether the shapes be trees, or fruits or human figures, this master begins by dividing his canvas by a vertical structure almost into two equal divisions. The right and the left as well as the top and the bottom are then filled in with such details as will evoke a sense of their balancing and belonging to each other.

Cézanne's anatomies are always questionable like those of the old Spanish master Greco (sixteenth century). But his colour-masses have an undeniable effect as much because of his symmetry of construction as on account of the sense of proportion he observes in the handling of different tints.

Corot's geometry is altogether different. The parts of his canvas do not balance one another as in a symmetrical scheme. He produces his volumes invariably by dark greys of which nearly the entire gamut is laid under contribution. The harmony of shapes thus created possesses a characteristic individuality which marks off the maker from other designers of landscapes.

But let us sample out some of the great masters of old, Andrea Del Sarto (1487–1531) has a piece at the bottom of which there is the caption, *Charity*. But what will a person see here who does not know how to read, whose sole capital is his eye-sight? A Hindu pearl merchant who was present in one of my trips to the Louvre remarked: "The face looks quite Italian, doesn't it?"—especially because he can read French and knows that the picture is exhibited in the Italian rooms. My guide-book says that the model for the artist's figure was always "his beautiful but dissolute wife who ruined and then deserted him."

What, now, is the art-value of this piece? As in reproduction we cannot watch the effects of colour-harmony we have to be satisfied in the present examination exclusively with noting the structural composition in the abstract. If we want a parallel from the Indian side we may point out one of those family pictures of the Shaiva pantheon in which Durgā is seated with her children on both sides. But this analogy does not carry us any way nearer to the aesthetic.

An artist with his *rasa-jñāna* will find in the entire construction of this piece the form of a pyramid. It is made up by the stately pose not of a thoroughly perpendicular figure but of one slightly curved, like the leaning tower, from the vertical towards the right. From the extremities indicating the toes of the child at the base to the apex of the coiffure the inclined plane is quite obvious. The parallels of the masses—arms and thighs—introduce variety in structure, while as is noticeable even in the reproduction the white patches of different shades at the top and at the bottom to the right and to the left set off the light blue of the drapery.

We do not really have to know if the figure is that of a man or of a woman. If instead of human babies we had here a bunch of guinea-pigs or puppies, and if instead of a woman seated straight with legs stretched towards the right and eyes gazing towards the left we had a boulder of granite or alabaster in the same pose and architectured into groups of the same contrasts as in the present piece we should still have the harmony of, say, a mountain scenery, of a composite triangle of masses and hues. This is a symphony of shapes comparable in its general morphology to the *chāli of Durgā* worshipped every autumn in the villages and towns of Bengal or to the composition of the miniatures described as *Vishnu with attendants* among the exhibits of the *Bangiya Sāhitya Sammilan* or of the Varendra Research Society of Rajsahi.

Almost to the Sarto-type belongs Murillo's *Holy Family* which also can hardly fail to suggest to the Hindu his own pantheon. This of course is more complex in design than the Sarto. Here the group in the centre is linked up with the one at the right by an oblique line and with the other at the top by a bird device. The corners at the top are not kept empty and the centre in the left is filled in with dark. From the apex with its parabolic arch made by the extension of arms in a rounded form down to the greyish neat lump of animal structure at the bottom in the middle the whole constitutes one organic piece of workmanship.

The *Birth of the Virgin* by the same painter is likewise another exquisite masonry work in colour. It possesses the most remarkable design of a right-angled triangle, placed at an agreeable distance from both ends of the canvas, as the pattern for a cluster of human masses. The tall straight figure at the right is the perpendicular. From the apex to the tip of the tail formation at the left there is the hypotenuse. The whole makes a solid geometry of shapes in all possible poses.

We do not have to know if the shapes are he or she or it. Luckily, the Asian has no "polarization" in regard to the legend. We are therefore free from the tyranny of tradition and can enjoy the *rasa-jñāna* of the master all the better.

Corresponding to the Sarto and closely following the pyramid-type there is a Da Vinci (1452–1519) known as *Virgin, Infant Jesus and St. Anne*. A special feature to note in this piece is the absence of the self-conscious fore-finger which according to the present writer is so conspicuous a blemish in Da Vinci's *Bacchus* and *St. John the Baptist*. That is a mannerism which is not justified by the composition of the forms. But the typical *Mona Lisa* coquetry (?) is obvious in the two faces of the piece under discussion.

Altogether, however, as a structural design this is not only among the best that Da Vinci has produced but may be considered to be among the masterpieces of composition in painting, although perhaps not listed as such in the conventional catalogues of art-wonders. Anybody with a sense of colour and of light and shade will find here a diversity of forms laid out in a harmonious device.

It must be understood that the mechanism of colour in painting can after all be very vaguely described in language either by the terminology of colour-chemistry or of prismatic analysis. The most minute investigation will fail to reach the processes of creative metabolism in the master's *rasa-jñāna*. There is accordingly no recipe, no formula for the manipulation of beauties in colour, although their objective background is unquestionable. The manufacture of beauty is the *shilpin's* "trade secret". Only in this sense can there be a mysticism in art.

These four specimens, all drawn from Europe, are universal masterpieces because their geometric composition is superb and because the interlacing of *rupam* achieved in these happens to be brought about by the most delightful magic of colour harmony. You may be unfamiliar with the legends, you may not know how to philosophize about *rasa*, spirit or idea, you may eliminate the racial elements in the human faces, if you please; but you will feel that the creators of these forms in colour have a message even for you whether as artist or as student of art.

Such are the universal laws of *rasa-vidyā* or aesthetics, such the most generalized canons of *shilpa-śāstra*, such the fundamental art-geometry of *rupam* (i.e. of form and colour), such the positive foundations of beauty, such the absolute principles of the mechanics of creation to which Young India invites both the East and the West.

K. C. Bhattacharyya, "The Concept of Rasa" (1930)

Krishna Chandra Bhattacharyya (1875–1949) is perhaps the best-known academic philosopher of the colonial period. He held the King George V Chair (now the B. N. Seal Chair) in Philosophy at the University of Calcutta and trained many of the eminent philosophers of the postindependence period. He is best known for his highly technical and even forbidding work on metaphysics, epistemology, aesthetics and the philosophy of Kant. The present essay is one of his best-known articles, in which he takes up the classical Indian aesthetic construct of *rasa*, (taste, essence) and provides a very nonclassical analysis.

5

The Concept of Rasa

I

Artistic Enjoyment

1. Indian aesthetics presents the characteristic concept of *rasa* for which it is difficult to find an English equivalent. Literally '*rasa*' means two things among others—it means essence and it means what is tasted or felt. The aesthetic conception of *rasa* combines the two senses and signifies the essence of a feeling, which is indifferently taken either as an eternal feeling or as the object of it, an eternal value that is felt. 'Essence', however, is an intellectual concept and the phrase 'essence of feeling' requires explanation. 'Essence' here is not taken in the sense of a logical universal. There is no suggestion in the Indian theory of art, as in certain other theories, that the same universal that is known as the essence of things is apprehended in feeling in a confused way as rasa. The logical universal has sometimes been identified with the ideal for life and the aesthetic essence has been conceived as the ideal that is felt or the feeling of the ideal. *Rasa* in the Indian conception is not identified with the Idea or universal truth, or with the ideal to be realised or as realised. It is understood purely through feeling and in terms of feeling; and if it is to be called essence or ideal, it can only be by way of metaphor. There is danger, however, of making too much of the metaphors both in the general theory of art and in the actual criticism of particular works of art. (Aesthetics—to start with at any rate—should not assume any speculative or religious postulates). What appears valuable to artistic feeling need not so appear—at least to the same degree—to the intellect or to the will, and feeling here should have the final say.

2. *Rasa* means either aesthetic enjoyment or that which is aesthetically enjoyed. The significance of the concept is best interpreted by the orientation of aesthetic enjoyment in reference to other feelings. As will be explained presently, the artistic sentiment is not merely a feeling among feelings but the feeling par excellence, standing as it does on a new grade or level altogether as compared with other feelings. The place of a feeling is sometimes assigned in reference to the truth or known content with which it is bound up or to the order of its emergence in mental evolution. It, however, does not help

us far to find the significance or distinctive value of the feeling. This is best understood by the determination of the level or mental plane to which the feeling belongs.

3. We may begin by distinguishing between the direct feeling of an object and sympathy with such feeling. We speak of enjoying an object. What is the implication of the transitive use of the verb 'to enjoy'? It does not mean—at least to the enjoyer—that the object is only a means to the enjoyment: he feels no distinction between his enjoyment and the object. In this sense the clear-cut contrast of subject and object becomes obscured for feeling. The subject of the enjoyment unconsciously affects and is affected by the object. The object does not appear to him as a mere fact but as having a value, an enjoyable look or expression. The subject, too, does not feel his detachment from the object: he feels attracted into or weighed down by the object.

4. Consider next a feeling of which the direct object is another feeling, say, in a separate mind. This feeling of a feeling is to be distinguished from the mere understanding of it as a fact, which may leave one cold. Neither should it be confused with merely having a like feeling on the occasion of another's feeling. To sympathise with a person is to feel *him* feeling: only in this sense is his feeling the direct object of my feeling. We refer specially to sympathy, as it is the most familiar form of the feeling of feeling.

5. In sympathising with a child enjoying his toy, I am not interested like the child in the toy itself but in his enjoyment. Sympathy with joy is also joy but it is freer than the primary joy. I do not unconsciously project the joyous look or expression on the toy. I do not *see* it there like the child: I at best feel like *imagining it*. Nor do I like him feel fascinated by the toy, feel attracted into or glued down as it were to the toy. Not that I am altogether free in my sympathy, for I am still affected by the child's joy as a fact though not by the object of it, attracted by the particular feeling of the individual child as a compelling subjective fact. Even here, however, I do not lose the sense [of the difference] between my feeling and the child's feeling in the sense the child loses it between his feeling and the object of it.

6. By reason of this freedom then, feeling of feeling—of which we take sympathy as the type—may be taken as constituting a higher level than the feeling of an object. We have next to consider if artistic enjoyment does not belong to a higher level still. That it has at least something of the freedom of sympathy can hardly be disputed. But it may be said that we seem to directly enjoy the beauty of an object and the beauty appears to be just as much *seen there* in the object as the terrible look of an object to one who feels terror. Where, it may be asked, is the distinction between such enjoyment and an ordinary object-feeling like terror? How does the former stand on a higher level—the level at least of sympathy? How sympathy with a feeling affects

the object of the feeling requires first to be considered. Every feeling affects its object by lending a look or value to it. Sympathy does not indeed affect the object of the feeling sympathised with. To a person afraid of an object, the object has a terrible look but not one who sympathises with his fear. But the sympathiser, although he does not *see* the expression there, tends consciously to project something similar, to imagine seeing it there. The look or aspect that is consciously imagined differs from that which appears to be seen. The latter is presented as one with the given fact, as adjectival to it; whereas the former is presented as detached from the fact—as floating on it or as shining beyond it. The freedom of the sympathetic feeling, in fact, is reflected in the object as this detachment of expression from given fact, as expression 'in the air' without a substratum.

7. Now the beauty of an object, though not consciously projected on it by artistic feeling, does not appear to such feeling, as a quality or adjective of the object in the way the terrible aspect of an object does to one in fear. It is presented as a floating or transcendent expression like that which is consciously projected by sympathy on the object of the feeling sympathised with. The circumstance that beauty is not consciously projected but appears to be seen does indeed make a difference, to be explained presently. But that beauty is not presented as an adjective or quality of the object distinguishes it from the reflex of an object-feeling. That is why aesthetic enjoyment is taken to belong to a higher level than object-feeling. The question remains if it belongs to a level higher than sympathy.

8. We have pointed out that sympathy though unaffected by the object of feeling sympathised with, is still affected by and limited to the particular feeling and the individual subject to it. In sympathy, the detachment is felt from objective fact but not from subjective fact, though the distinction from the subject sympathised with is not observed. But there may be such a feeling as sympathy with sympathy. One may sympathise, for example, with a mother feeling for her child suffering. Just as my sympathy with a person's feeling of an object is unaffected by the object, so my sympathy with a person's sympathy for a third person's feeling is unaffected by the feeling. It is thus on the level of this duplicated sympathy that a feeling can be emotionally contemplated in a detached way, felt as dissociated from its character as a given subjective fact, realised as self-subsisting value. To simple sympathy with a feeling, the object of the feeling has already a detached expression which, however, lacks reality by reason of the detachment. To this duplicated sympathy, the expression of the object is not only detached but self-subsisting, having a felt independent reality of which the given object is only a kind of symbol. Since it is altogether detached from the particularity of fact, it is a kind of eternal reality, a real eternal value.

9. Beauty, we hold, is just such an eternal value and aesthetic enjoyment accordingly belongs to the level of duplicated sympathy—sympathy with sympathy. That the beauty of an object appears to be seen rather than imagined shows that to feeling it has a reality not inferior to that of the object as a given fact. That it is not seen as a quality or adjective of the object and is yet not presented as another object side by side with it implies that it is reality to which the *object* is somehow adjectival or subordinate. As, however, there would be no sense in saying that the object is a quality of the beauty, the adjectivity of the object here has to be recognised as a peculiar relation—the relation of the symbol to the symbolised, an analogue in the sphere of feeling of the logical relation between a word and its meaning.

10. Aesthetic enjoyment thus stands on a level higher than ordinary sympathy which again constitutes a level higher than primary object-feeling. The artistic sentiment may in some cases be literally taken as sympathy with sympathy. I may, for example, enjoy contemplating an old man affectionately watching his grandchild playing with a toy. Contrast here the child's joy in the toy with the grand-father's sympathetic joy and this again with my contemplative joy. Although the old man is not immersed like the child in the enjoyment of the toy, his feeling is not yet of the artistic character: it is still a personal selective interest in the particular child and his feeling. My contemplative joy has no such personal complexion. I am interested in the child's feeling reflected in the grand-father's heart as an eternal emotion or value. I enjoy the essence of the emotion, get immersed in it even like the child in the toy, without, however, being affected by it and thus losing my freedom. I no longer feel the distinction between my feeling and the child's feeling, as the old man does between his feeling and the child's feeling. My personality is, as it were, dissolved and yet I am not caught in the object like the child. I freely become impersonal.

11. In the above example, my aesthetic enjoyment is feeling for another actual person feeling for a third actual person. But one or both of these persons sympathised with may be imaginary. Consider a case where the second person is imaginary. I may aesthetically contemplate a poor waif in the street. The waif is beautiful to me not as a dirty child but as it may be somebody's darling. I contemplate what the child would be to its mother, had she been living. The mother is here an imaginary person. A case in which the third person is imaginary would be where I contemplate a mother treasuring up the toys of her child who is no more. She sees the same value in the toys as though the child were living and playing with them. The child is here the imaginary person but the mother's emotion is still actual or personal and it is to me alone who contemplate the emotion a beautiful theme of art. Again both the persons are imaginary when, for example. I contemplate a character in a drama. The character is here the

imaginary third person or primary subject; but who it may be asked is the sympathising second person?

12. There is a difference between imagining an object as actual and imagining it as imaginary. In the former, the object is imagined as presented to an actual feeling of the person imagining as, for example, a savoury dish imagined by a hungry person. In the latter, the feeling bodying forth the image is itself imaginary: the object is imagined as what would be imagined by another person having the actual feeling. Now the character in the drama is not imagined by me as an actual person: I imagine some one imagining the character as an actual person and I sympathise with this imaginary 'some one' as the second person. The imaginary second person is not one particular person but *some one* or *any one* person. He has the value of a concept of a person in general: only here we have in the concept an efflux of feeling and not of the intellect. This person is felt—not thought—by me who am aesthetically contemplating. The felt-person-in-general may be semi-mythologically called the Heart Universal. Every feeling that is depicted in art is contemplated as reflected in or sympathised with by this Heart Universal and the person who contemplates the feeling merges his personal or private heart in this ubiquity. Artistic enjoyment is not a feeling of the enjoyer on his own account; it involves a dropping of self-consciousness, while the feeling that is enjoyed—the feeling of the third person—is freed from its reference to an individual subject and eternalised in the Heart Universal.

13. Can we keep up the scheme of three persons or three grades of feeling—contemplative, sympathetic and primary—in the case of the enjoyment of the beauty of a natural object ? Here also we may take the second and the third persons as imaginary and implicitly intervening between the contemplator and the object. Only here the third person is evanescent—some person rather than a particular imaginary person like the character in the drama spoken of. When I appreciate the beauty of a natural object, I imagine in the first place a particular primary feeling —say, joy or sorrow or fear—according as the object has a joyous or melancholy or fearful expression. This feeling is imagined as the feeling of 'some one', of an indefinite third person. The indefiniteness here, like the conceptual character of the second person referred to, is felt and not thought, It implies that the third person is indifferent to me: I am interested less in him than in his feeling. This feeling is next idealised by being contemplated as felt by or reflected in the second person—the Heart Universal. Lastly, I, the first person, feel this idealised feeling as my direct object.

14. Is this an artificial analysis? We have indicated that the beauty of an object does not appear as a mere fact—a quality of the object like its colour but as an expression or value. The expression, however, unlike the reflex of

a primary feeling, is not seen as one with the object or adjectival to it but as floating on it or as irradiating beyond it. At the same time it is not presented like the reflex of a sympathetic feeling as an expression 'in the air': it is to aesthetic feeling a real eternal value. The beauty of an object, thus, implies three characters distinguishing it from mere fact—expression, detachment from the object and eternity. These three can only be understood in the object as the respective projections of primary feeling, sympathetic feeling, and contemplative feeling. The feelings have to be understood as the feelings of three persons who may, however, all be in one person, viz., the aesthetic enjoyer in three different emotional levels at the same time. Since the last grade of feeling comprehends the other two, we have taken aesthetic enjoyment as not merely a feeling among feelings but as the feeling *par excellence*.

15. The conception of *rasa* or aesthetic essence may thus be interpreted entirely in terms of feeling, without any reference to the intellectual Idea or the spiritual ideal. We have indicated the place and significance of aesthetic joy by determining the level or grade of feeling to which it belongs. A further elaboration is necessary to bring out the distinctive flavour of the Indian concept. Artistic enjoyment is conceived not merely as *free* from the entanglement of fact but as the *realisation* of an eternal value, as an identification with the aesthetic essence without loss of freedom. What is the precise sense in which this realisation or identification is understood? To answer the queston, we have to consider first certain features of primary feeling and sympathy.

16. We have pointed out that in a primary feeling—say, sensuous enjoyment of an object, the distinction of feeling and the object is obscured: the object gets an expression and the feeling loses its subjective detachment. Yet the confused unity of the object-immersed feeling has two alternative directions, the objective and the subjective. In the objective direction the self-feeling lapses: the object alone is perceived as with the expression adjectival to it. But the subject need not be in the perceiving or objective attitude; it may retain the feeling-attitude, while the object perceived gets indefinite and melts away, much as to a drowsy person the fixed world appears to swim and shimmer away into nought. This would be the subjective direction. Instead of the subject forgetting itself in the object, we have the object here getting dissolved in the subjective feeling. To understand it, we have to remember how in respect of an object in one's clasp, there is a difference between trying to enjoy it and actually enjoying it. When one is only trying to enjoy, the feeling has indeed begun; but there is a constant sense of not being able to enjoy, of the object refusing to be enjoyed, to melt into the feeling. This tantalizing experience constitutes the unreal character that attaches to the incipient feeling. To successfully enjoy, to have the object dissolved in one's feeling, is

to get rid of the felt unreality. The feeling here becomes subjectively real: it stands by consuming the object.

17. Two forms of sympathy may be distinguished corresponding to these two directions of object-feeling. Although in sympathy, the distinction between the sympathiser and the person sympathised with is never lost, the two subjects do not simply stand side by side. The sympathiser either feels through the other person's heart or feels the other person within his own heart. In the former case I feel *out* towards the other person, feel my detachment from him to be an evil, seek to forget myself, to feel as though I were the other person feeling and to become the other person in this sense. In the latter case, I feel my sympathy with him to be unreal so long as the other person is foreign and his feeling a mere fact which I cannot feel as mine. In the former I resent my detachment, in the latter his foreignness. In both I strive to feel freedom; in the former by expanding, by projecting myself outwards and in the latter by assimilating or drawing in, feeling his feeling as mine. We may accordingly call these the projective and the assimilative types of sympathy.

18. Similarly the identification with the object in the aesthetic enjoyment has two alternative directions—the projective or creative direction and the assimilative or abstractive direction. What is enjoyed in the object is its beauty which we have taken as an eternal self-subsisting value to which the object is related as a symbol. The symbolising function in the aesthetic sphere is of two kinds. The object that is the symbol may retain its definite character of fact and express a value as its transcendent significate, or its fact-character may get evanescent while the value symbolised gets defined out as a subtile spirit-form, as a dream floating in the ether of the heart and nowhere in space and time. Either way the enjoyer identifies himself with the eternal value. But whereas in the former he enters into the object freely, overcomes its opacity and sees himself as the soul of it, the heart of its reality; in the latter, he dissociates himself from the object as mere fact which accordingly tends to dissolve, to have its hard outlines softened away, and feels rather than sees the soul of it freeing itself and merging in his enjoyment. In the former, the feeling becomes objective but does not get entangled in the given fact: it transfigures the fact into a value. In the latter, the detachment of the subject does not imply a feeling of unreality: the value or soul of the object is drawn out as it were and reposefully enjoyed. In the former, there is freedom in spite of enjoying contact: and in the latter, enjoyment or reality in spite of detaching freedom.

19. Indian art is prevailingly abstractive or contemplative in character and not dynamically creative: and in the Indian theory of art, the aesthetic essence is conceived as a subjective absolute or *rasa* rather than as an objective absolute or beauty.

II

The Beautiful and the Ugly

20. In the previous part, I did not distinguish between the feeling for the beautiful and the feeling for the ugly. I was concerned there mainly with the general level or grade to which both these feelings belong. In the present part, I have endeavoured to bring out the specific nature of the feeling for the ugly and the varying aesthetic values of ugliness as an objective expression.

21. As in the previous part, so here I rule out the question as to what there is in the object that makes it appear beautiful or ugly. Formal characters like symmetry or unity in variety, such as are ordinarily spoken of as constituting beauty, are not only inadequate for a definition but appear to presuppose the aesthetic feeling from which they derive their specific meaning. For one thing, an important element of beauty is subjective association: the objective formal element is not all. Besides, what does symmetry or unity in variety mean? Any geometrical symmetry is not beautiful: what particular symmetrical form is beautiful depends on the intuition of the artist and thus presupposes the artistic feeling. Similarly as to unity in variety: it all depends on what the artist *feels* to be the satisfying unity. The formal characters in their generality, apart from the particularising feeling of the artist, mean almost nothing. Certain forms in certain contexts may indeed appear beautiful in many cases, though not in all cases. This, however, is a matter of technique which is but a summary of particular artistic experiences. A general theoretic discussion of the objective characters of beauty and ugliness appears to me, therefore, to be unprofitable. Not that I deny that there is something in the object that determines the aesthetic feeling. I believe, in fact, that the aesthetic attitude does not create but only discovers beauty or ugliness, and that while an object that appears indifferent to others has an aesthetic value to one already in the attitude, there are objects which perforce induce the attitude in many souls, if not in all. At the same time I hold that the objective aesthetic quality cannot be discovered except through the aesthetic feeling, that it is only by this feeling and not by any merely intellectual investigation that we can analyse beauty or ugliness in the object, and that the analysis can only be of a piecemeal character in the form of particular intuitions and can never be exhausted by any objective formula. So, as in the previous part, I confine myself here to an analysis of the mental attitude.

22. All feeling implies an identification of subject and object. Contrast the thought of an object with the feeling of it. The former implies a detachment from the object, the latter an intimacy with it. To thought, the intimacy appears to be a confusion, while to feeling the detachment means inanity or unreality of the subject. The subject feels itself real when it is filled with the

object, when it feels the object united or identified with itself. What to thought is but a confusion is to feeling a real identity.

23. Identity with the object is felt in all feeling. Is distinction from the object also felt? Not in the grade of primary feeling. In some sense, indeed, all feeling of pain is a feeling of distinction between subject and object, but in the grade of primary feeling, the distinction is not explicitly felt as such. In the grade of sympathetic feeling, the distinction from the object of the feeling sympathized with is explicitly felt while the identity continues to be felt with the primary feeling, The two attitudes, however, do not enter into any relation in this stage: the feeling of identity here is only implicit and is completely merged in the explicit feeling of difference. In the contemplative feeling, both the feelings of identity and difference are explicit. The subject freely merges into the object and the object tends to get dissolved in the subject. That is the identity. The object gets idealised into a standing expression, into a sort of objective mind and the subject feels real in joy by consuming the object. At the same time the feeling of identity is a process. There survive aspects of the object which stand out un-idealised as full fact and there is a persistent sense of not being able to enjoy along with the joy that has begun. The feeling (as un-idealised fact) of the inability to enjoy is the feeling of distinction between subject and object. It is still a feeling on the aesthetic plane because it would not arise but for the idealisation or enjoyment, the identity that is already felt.

24. If the feeling of identity be called enjoyment, the feeling of of difference may be taken as a pain, both the feelings being on the artistic or contemplative level. Now enjoyment and pain cannot simply stand together side by side: one is subordinated to the other, subordination being a unique relation in the sphere of feeling. When the pain is subordinate to the enjoyment, we have the feeling of beauty. Where the enjoyment is subordinate to pain, there emerges the feeling of ugliness and its congeners.

25. To explain. Take the artistic contemplation of sorrow. A well-told tale of sorrow moves one to tears who yet gets exquisite enjoyment out of it. The pain is here subordinate to the enjoyment. The pain is still explicitly felt and felt in fact more exclusively, though not, it may be, more intensely than by the primary subject of the sorrow. Sorrow to the primary subject has its distraction and has, more often than not, an admixture of other and sometimes quite incompatible feelings such as the subject may be ashamed to confess. But the contemplative subject is absorbed in the sorrow in its purity, stripped of all its accidents. That does not mean that he contemplates the mere feeling of sorrow and has no interest in its objective setting: that would be only logical abstraction. He contemplates the setting also—such circumstances as bring out the feeling and are suffused with the feeling-value, though there is a

difference still between the centre of interest and the setting like that between a flame and its halo or irradiated light. But the primary subject of sorrow has not only the sorrow and its aesthetically relevant setting presented to him but also other feelings and objective circumstances along with them which have no affinity of tone with the sorrow. These are what I call 'accidents'. The aesthetic enjoyer contemplates the painful feeling of sorrow stripped of such accidents. To aesthetically realise or contemplate a person's sorrow is to *feel* the *sorrow*, not to think it, though it is to feel it as a pure eternal value such as the person himself is not privileged to feel. I say 'privileged', because though the sorrow is a more exquisite or penetrating (though not more intense) pain to the contemplator than to the primary subject, the former does not in the feeling lose his freedom like the latter, but feels himself more real as a spirit through the pain than if he did not experience it. So even where the pain is not itself artistically enjoyed, it is no mere evil to be avoided: its purity and depth are in themselves a spiritual value.

26. But the artistic contemplation of sorrow is an enjoyment. The sorrow is felt as an exquisite pain but it is still the object of the enjoyment and in this sense subordinate to it. As a felt object it is one with the enjoyment, turned into it, transfigured. As an object of contemplative feeling, it is still distinct, the sorrow continuing to be felt in its purity within the enjoyment. This relation of 'within' or subordination has only to be accepted as a matter of experience; it can only be explicated, not disputed. So any kind of primary feeling in its purity may be the object of enjoyment and subordinated to it; when the primary feeling is itself an enjoyment, it is completely merged in the contemplative feeling, merging being the limit of subordination.

27. But while any feeling may be subordinated to aesthetic joy, it *need* not be. That depends, so far as the subject is concerned, on the depth of his artistic realisation. Potentially, I believe the artistic spirit can swallow and assimilate every kind of feeling, subordinate the most refractory of feelings to itself, transmute all painful feelings into enjoyment. As a matter of fact, however, it cannot or does not in many cases transmute the presented feeling: it lacks either the energy or the transparency of the soul requisite for it, this being entirely a matter of inborn gift or previous discipline. Artistic feeling represents a new depth of the spirit: contemplative level is deeper than the level of primary feeling or sympathy. But there are varying depths within the contemplative level and a primary feeling which stands out untransmuted in one grade of aesthetic feeling may be transmuted into joy in a deeper grade. Where a primary feeling presented to the aesthetic attitude is not assimilated, the joy of the attitude is present but gets subordinated to the presented feeling. The presented feeling is here a pain, a feeling that emerges in the joyous aesthetic attitude as distinct from it. So in the artistic contemplation of sorrow

just considered, the sorrow is presented as distinct, as a pain to start with. But the pain is there the object of the joy while in the present case the joy is the object of the pain. The joy of the aesthetic attitude is here itself a torture which lends a new value to pain. But for the joy, in fact, the pain would not take the form of disgust. That is the sense in which I understand the subordination of enjoyment to pain. When the aesthetic feeling, unable to assimilate a presented primary feeling, gets thus subordinated to it, it turns into the feeling of ugliness. The implications of this account of ugliness have to be brought out. The primary feeling is here present to the aesthetic feeling. That means it is raised to the contemplative grade, stripped of accidents, isolated in its purity. A fact viewed in the scientific or practical attitude is neither beautiful nor ugly. It is only when it is aesthetically contemplated that it appears beautiful or ugly. When so contemplated, the fact as such retires into the back-ground and its expression or value as due to a primary feeling comes into prominence, this being viewed through the double medium of sympathy, as indicated in the previous part. The primary feeling as presented to the aesthetic attitude is thus itself turned into a contemplative feeling.

28. Next this contemplative feeling enters into a relation with the aesthetic feeling to which it is presented. The aesthetic attitude is in itself a joy, not merely an expectation of joy: it is joyous expectancy waiting to turn by its alchemy any new experience into joy. But the alchemy may not be potent enough. The new experience may be refractory and then the joyous expectancy is turned into bitterness or disgust so that the refractory experience gets an extra painful value, viz., the repulsive or disgusting value. The experience itself as a contemplative presentation is not repulsive: it is so only because of there being baffled expectation of joy.

29. When repulsion is thus felt on the contemplative level, there are many alternative ways in which the spirit saves itself. The contemplative attitude may be withdrawn altogether and there may be a simple relapse to the normal practical attitude. Or it may happen that the spirit keeps on the contemplative level and the artistically refractory experience is side-tracked into contemplative channels other than the artistic. Received first in the artistic attitude as an un-welcome kill-joy, the experience may be presently draped off for philosophic or religious contemplation. The aesthetic expectancy is retracted but the spirit may be overborne by the hideousness of the world. The ordinary spirit is not artistic enough to stand ugliness for any length of time, to maintain the joy of the aesthetic attitude while either shaking off the repulsive experience or transmuting it into joy with the patience and faith of a courageous love. Yet there are spirits where joy is too deep to be killed by a repulsive experience and whose artistry is potent enough to evolve a beauty rich and strange out of presented ugliness. The aesthetic attitude survives the feeling

of ugliness in two ways. It may, in the first place, turn into the feeling of the ludicrous which is just the joy of detaching oneself from or shaking off the repulsive experience. The feeling of ugliness is itself a contemplative feeling but the artistic spirit may retire to a deeper level and rejoicingly contemplate the ugly in an attitude of superior detachment. It rejoices either in having eluded its touch and in being able to watch it from a secure distance or in the sense of power to blow it away and turn it into thought—I mean the explosive power of laughter, these being the two directions of the feeling of the ludicrous. The other aesthetic attitude in which ugliness can be negotiated is what I have characterised as the patient faith of courageous love. The faith that the ugly can be transmuted into beauty is familiar enough in the artistic sphere. It is in fact what makes aesthetic education possible. No one will condemn more than the artist the conceit—which is unfortunately common to-day—that refuses to admit the need of educating the taste and the possibilities of realising what immediately appears ugly as beautiful through such education. It is this faith then that sustains what we may call aesthetic effort—the effort to deepen the feeling of ugliness into an enjoyment, to perceive the immediately ugly in its infinite setting and thus to realise it as beautiful. During the effort, the ugly remains ugly but becomes tremulous with the shimmer of expectant delight; the faith becomes objective as the suggestion of a beauty that is not yet manifest. And then as the aesthetic faith turns into vision and attainment, there emerges a Beauty Triumphant in which ugliness is itself realised in its quintessence as an object of enjoyment. This enjoyed quintessence of ugliness is just what Indian aesthetic daringly recognises as a *rasa* viz., the *bībhatsa-rasa*. Such recognition does credit to the virility of Indian art and to the Indian theory of art.

M. Hiriyanna, "Indian Aesthetics 2," "Art Experience 2" (1951)

Mysore Hiriyanna (1871–1950) is best known as a historian of Indian philosophy. His text *Outlines of Indian Philosophy* (1932) is still a standard text worldwide. He also made important contributions to Vedānta studies and to ethics and aesthetics. Hiriyanna taught for many years at Mysore University. Here we present two chapters from his book *Art Experience* in which he examines the aesthetics of the literary arts as well as the connection between aesthetics and ethics.

Mysore Hirayanna

6

Indian Aesthetics 2

IT IS USUAL for every prominent philosopher in the West to regard the question of beauty as a part of the problem he is attempting to solve. Hence aesthetics has come to be recognised there as a regular part of philosophy. The intrinsic relation implied in this between aesthetics and philosophy is not denied in India; but the former of these studies is carried on by a distinct class of thinkers—*alaṃkārikas,* as they are called or literary critics—who are not, generally speaking, professional philosophers. This separation of aesthetic problems, in the matter of investigation, from those of general philosophy may at first sight appear not only strange but also defective; a little reflection, however, will show that it is not really so. Before explaining this point, however, it is necessary to state that when we say that Indian philosophers have not troubled themselves with questions of beauty, what is meant is only that they do not deal with beauty in art and not also beauty in nature. The latter is certainly included; but, while it is explicit in some systems, it is only implicit in others. The exact view which they hold in this respect will become clear as we proceed. As regards their neglect of beauty in art, the reason is that its pursuit cannot, according to them, directly minister to the attainment of the final goal of life, which is the prime concern of Indian philosophers. Perhaps some among them thought that its pursuit might even tend to lead man away from that goal, in which case their attitude towards art would be like that of Plato towards the same.

So far from being a defect, the separation of aesthetics in this sense from general philosophy has many positive advantages. It has thereby been able to get rid of the constraint which particular types of metaphysical thought may impose upon it. When a philosopher holds a particular view of reality, he is bound to square his theory of art, if he formulates one, with it; and the consequence is that we have as many theories of art in the West as there are theories of reality. This cannot be helped in the case of beauty in nature, but there is no reason for acquiescing in such diversity of views in a theory of art. That is the view of Indian aestheticians. Thus the postulation by Indian aestheticians of what is called *vyaṅgyārtha,* which is not only not recognised by any school of philosophy but is definitely opposed, shows the freedom with which aesthetic investigation has been carried on in India. They have succeeded in this in evolving a theory of meaning which, as we shall try to point out, certainly sheds new light on the nature of art. Where it is not necessary to devise such a new theory, Indian aestheticians select one or other of the views held by the philosophic schools according to the needs of the case. Such eclecticism results in a more detached view (from the aesthetic standpoint) than would be the case if a particular philosophic point of view were adopted in its entirety. This does not, however, mean that there is a dull uniformity in the Indian theory of art. There is as much diversity in it as in any Western treatment of the subject; but the important point is that the diversity is based upon purely artistic considerations and is therefore more genuine.

There is another reason to support the Indian practice. Reality, as represented in art, as is generally admitted, is a unity in diversity, so that there is no room for any divergence of opinion in regard to it, so far as art is concerned. The aim of art is not to discover the nature of reality but to secure for us the highest experience of life. It does not pronounce any final opinion on the tenability or otherwise of the view of reality it thus uses. In other words, aesthetics, unlike ethics for instance, is alogical. While it is closely connected with psychology it regards logic, or more properly epistemology, as irrelevant to its purpose. Art is a short cut to the ultimate value of life, by-passing logic. Even supposing it is not admitted that reality, as represented in art, is necessarily a unity in diversity, the view of reality that may be accepted in its stead does not matter, for it is to serve but as the medium through which the value is realised, art being concerned less with facts than with values.

1. Nature and Art

We have distinguished nature from art. The question will naturally arise here whether there is any need for seeking beauty in art, if it is found in nature. As G. E. Moore has stated in his *Principia Ethica*, when other things are the same, beauty which is found in actual objects is decidedly better than that in imaginary ones. It is therefore necessary to point out why art is necessary, though in certain respects the beauty which it presents may be inferior to that in nature. As regards the latter, two views are possible.

(i) We may hold, with the idealists, that nature as a whole is beautiful, but that when it is looked at in parts, it may or may not be so. That is, though nature may, in reality, be beautiful, there may appear ugliness in it when we take a partial view of it as, ordinarily speaking, we are bound to do. This means that, though in the case of those few who can take a synoptic view of nature, art may be superfluous, it is not so in the case of the many. As an old Vedāntic stanza has it, it is only 'when man has overcome selfishness and realised the highest truth, he will be in rapt ecstasy wherever he may turn', for he sees the glory of Being everywhere. Till then therefore he can have an experience of complete beauty only in art. Further, even as regards the parts that appear beautiful in nature, there is no certainty that they will continue to be so for long. For there may come to be a change in our attitude towards them, when their appeal will become non-aesthetic. Or the situations in nature may themselves so change in course of time that they will cease to appear beautiful. Hence it is that we require the creations of art which are not subject to these defects—a change in the presentations of nature or in our attitude towards them. This is the need for art according to the idealistic view of nature.

(ii) The second view of nature is that though it may be beautiful, that feature is inevitably associated with ugliness and that the latter element cannot be eliminated from it without, at the same time, eliminating the former also. According to this pessimistic view, art becomes even more necessary. In fact, it is the *sole* means, in this view, of satisfying the quest for unmixed joy which somehow actuates all men or, to state the same otherwise, the need for escaping from the struggles and perplexities of everyday life.

Whatever the worth of these two metaphysical theories in themselves may be, the point that is important for us now is that there is a need for art in either case. To state this need in terms applicable to both the views, it is the presence, on the one hand, of evil in life and, on the other, of an ideal within us that has led to the invention of art. Here we may observe, in passing, we have another instance of Indian aesthetics transcending the differences that characterise the metaphysical schools. Art is a device for the provisional attainment of the final ideal of life, whether or not we look forward to a state which eventually renders it superfluous.[1]

2. *Art Experience*

The aim of art is implicit in what we have said so far. It is to secure for man a unique form of experience which, according to one view, can never be attained in actual life and, according to the other, can be attained only when self-perfection is achieved. But either way, it is an ultimate value in the sense that it is sought for its own sake and not as a means to anything else.[2] The characteristics of this art experience are two:

---

1. There is an ultimate ideal according to the second view also; but it is a state transcending joy as well as suffering. Positivistically speaking, this means that man may cultivate detachment to such an extent that he will ignore nature altogether. But there is nothing resembling aesthetic pleasure then, unless we understand the aesthetic end itself in an uncommon way.

2. Self-realisation in Advaita is value-realisation, for the Self is the ultimate value.

(1) The first is unselfishness. It is true that all or nearly all men, in virtue of their social nature, show more or less of unselfishness in their behaviour; but it may be the result of habit or of prudential, and therefore eventually of selfish, considerations. Such outward unselfishness is not what is meant here. Even when it is spontaneous and therefore quite genuine, it is not complete. The selfishness signified by art experience, on the other hand, is not only spontaneous but also complete. Man grows so unselfish then that he becomes virtually unconscious of his private self. This is the meaning of saying that art experience consists in the disinterested contemplation of beauty. The intrusion of any personal aim is sure to vitiate it, and make the pursuit of art unsuccessful.

(2) The second characteristic, which is probably a consequence of the first, is that it yields a kind of joy which is pure and untainted by even the least pain. This is a further indication of the transcendental character of art experience; and it shows that the aesthetic attitude stands higher than that of common or everyday life which is invariably characterised by more or less of mental tension.

On account of these excellences, art experience is regarded as identifiable with the ultimate goal of life as it is conceived by the idealists. When we take the ideal of life, as it is conceived by others, art experience affords the same escape from worldly concerns as that ideal, when attained, does; but it also does more for, while the latter does not represent a state of supreme joy, the former does. According to both, it is one of the only two such values recognised by Indians—*ātmānanda* and *rasānubhava.*

The Content of Art

But what is the means whereby the artist is able to secure for us such experience? All art is a blend of form and content; and it is through certain excellences characterising either, that he succeeds in inducing in us the artistic attitude. In the case of poetry, for example, the content is constituted by the figurative ideas and sentiments it expresses; and the form, by the musical language through which they find expression. Of these, the form varies much from one art to another; and it is also technical. We shall not refer to it here at any length, and shall confine our attention mainly to the content. We shall only observe, in passing, that the legitimate function of form is to subserve the content; and if it assumes greater importance, the work in which it does so marks a lapse from the best type of art.

The content of art may be defined generally as the meaning which it expresses. The excellences that may characterise it are many, and they have been classified in various ways. But these details, while they are undoubtedly helpful in indicating to us their character in a concrete manner, can never be exhaustively enumerated. As one Indian literary critic observes,[3] they can only be indicated generally. This general character of the content of art is that it must be drawn from actual life, but that it should also be judiciously idealised. The purpose of the idealisation is two-fold: In the first place, it is that, having its source in the artist's imagination, it may appeal to the same faculty in the spectator and not to his intellect merely. In the second place, it is that the particular things of common experience may thereby be transformed into general ones, and thus readily induce a detached attitude in the spectator which, as we have pointed out, is a salient feature of all art experience. But it is necessary to add that the things represented in art will not become false or fictitious through such idealisation. For a spectator to mistake them for real objects, as we do in illusions, will be to lapse from the truly aesthetic attitude, because he will then cease to remain detached. But at the same time, they cannot be viewed as unreal or false because then they will cease to interest him. Thus the things depicted in art assume a unique character which the spectator can describe as neither real nor unreal. In brief, we do not take a logical view of them. We neither believe nor disbelieve in their reality. We merely entertain them.[4]

This is the general view of the content of art which is prevalent everywhere. Indian aestheticians also held the same opinion for a long time; but a profound change in this respect, the germs of which seem to have been there all along, was introduced about the ninth century A.D. The change was to look upon what had so far been regarded as the content of art, *viz.*, the meaning also as only the outer vesture of art and to take emotion as its true content.[5] When the meaning in general was regarded as the content, it might be emotion or might not be; but now it is laid down that it should be only emotion. We have stated that the appeal of art should be to the imagination; and imagination always implies the presence of emotion in some degree or other. But it is not this emotion that we should think of now. It is the emotional character of the situation depicted by the artist that constitutes the true content of art, and the type of experience to which it gives rise in the spectator is called *rasa*. A consequence of this change in the idea of the content of art was to deny that the expressed meaning can have any excellences of its own and to assert that, like the form, it also has them only in relation to the emotion which it

3. *Cf. Vāgabhatālaṁkāra*, p. 77.

4. Cf. 'Poetic Truth'.

5. [Poetry was] brought nearer music thereby.

is intended to subserve. The excellences of meaning may be the very best, according to earlier standards; but yet they may produce the exact opposite of artistic feeling in the spectator, if they are out of harmony with the emotion depicted. This rightly introduces a relativistic view into art criticism; and neither form nor meaning was thenceforward regarded as beautiful in itself. The standards by which they were judged remained more or less the same, but they ceased to be taken as absolute.

We may point out before concluding this topic that the earlier view of art as consisting in the excellences characterising its form and meaning was not abandoned. That view also was retained; but works answering to that description came to be assigned an inferior status. It is designated *citra*, a term which, in all probability signifies that its merit lies more in skill which appeals to our intellect rather than in affecting our life or soul.

The Method of Art

Now emotions cannot be directly communicated. We can, of course, talk of (say) love or fear; but these words, when used by themselves, merely convey the idea of the corresponding feeling and do not communicate it to the listener. Such communication of it is possible only through a proper portrayal of select aspects of its causes and consequences. That is, the artist is obliged, if he is to succeed in what is his foremost aim, to adopt an indirect method in dealing with his material. This method is called *dhvani*; and secondarily, the work of art also, which is characterised by it, is designated by the same term. It had always been recognised as important for the artist, but only as one of those at his disposal for conveying the appropriate sentiment to the spectator. We may instance, as illustrating this point, *alaṃkāras* like *paryāyokta* and *samāsokti*, which are mentioned in the earliest *alaṃkāra* works. The discovery that was made later was that it was the *sole* method of the best type of art. This we may add, was the direct consequence of recognising *rasa* to be the aim *par excellence* of the artist. The method of art is thus as unique as its aim.

The method of *dhvani* has naturally been extended to other spheres of art where direct communication is possible, *viz.*, *alaṃkāras*; and has led to a preference being shown to them when they are indirectly suggested, instead of being directly expressed. Owing, however, to the intimate connection between imagination on which *alaṃkāras* are chiefly based and emotion on which *rasa* is, the difference between them is not always quite definite. The one may easily pass into another. Hence the decision in any particular case depends upon the view one takes of it; and it accordingly becomes personal, illustrating the well-known saying that tastes differ. Another extension of this theory of *dhvani* is to those poetic representations, which can be regarded neither as *rasa* nor as *alaṃkāra* and are therefore indefinitely designated as *vastu*. The innovation thus introduced by the *dhvani* canon here, like that in the case of *alaṃkāras*, we may observe, is more in rearranging conclusions that had already been reached than in making any new additions. The above statements enable us to divide the subject of first-rate art in a triple way. It may be emotion, when the resulting experience is called *rasa-dhvani*; it may be any other imaginative situation, in which case it will be *alaṃkāradhvani*; or it may be a matter-of-fact representation, in which case it will be *vastu-dhvani*.

The discovery that the *dhvani* method is the secret of true art furnishes another instance of what we described above as the alogical character of art. The conclusions suggested by this method vary according to the persons concerned and the contexts to which they belong, although the premises given are the same. At best, the mental process involved resembles analogical reasoning. Some of the erroneous views current before the method of *dhvani* was formulated or after are due to mistaking the method of art to be logical. Thus Mahima Bhaṭṭa tried to make out that the process involved in the so-called *dhvani* was nothing but inferential; and others like Mukula Bhaṭṭa represented the secondary senses of words as derived through the *pramāṇa* known as *arthāpatti*. Both forgot that the *dhvani* lacks the element of necessity, which is essential to what is strictly a logical process.

3. Art and Morality

We have referred to two views of reality in explaining the need for art. Whichever of them we may adopt, the implication is the presence of evil in life. According to one of these views, evil is finally removable; according to the other also it is so, only its removal involves the removal of good as well along with it. Overlooking this distinction which is really irrelevant for art, we may ask what the bearing of art is on the problem of evil, which it thus implicitly postulates.[6]

It may appear that art cannot be unconnected with morality, since the experience which it yields is, as we have pointed out, essentially disinterested; and disinterestedness is the very root of all morality. It is therefore necessary to examine what precisely the significance of this attitude is. To begin with, the ethical attitude is more than one of mere detachment. It is essentially active; but activity is, from the very nature of the case, wholly excluded from art experience. Or to state the same otherwise, the ethical attitude is orientated

6. It is the problem of evil that gives rise to art as well as to philosophy.

towards some purpose, while the artistic is quite the reverse, its sole purpose being the transcendence of all purpose. It is an attitude of contemplation rather than of achievement. Even as regards the unselfishness, which it shares with the ethical attitude, there is a vital distinction. There are two points to be noted in connection with it. In the first place, the aesthetic attitude is induced by an external stimulus. When once it has arisen, it may be quite genuine; but we cannot overlook the fact that it is due to an external influence. Morality which springs from fear of punishment or hope of reward is really no morality at all. The unselfishness characterising the ethical attitude, on the other hand, springs from inside and is quite spontaneous. It is only when it is the result of an inner urge that it will be of an enduring influence on life. But this later feature is lacking in the case of the art attitude, which we chiefly owe to the power that all true works of art possess. That such an exalted attitude can be produced, without any arduous trouble on the part of the spectator, is indeed an excellence of it; but it is unfortunately fugitive. Sooner or later, it comes to an end for it cannot last longer than the outside stimulus which has evoked it. Even such short-lived experience may, through refining emotions, leave some good influence behind; but the point to be noted is that there is no guarantee that it will. In the second place, the disinterestedness of the aesthetic attitude marks a reaction to an imaginary situation and not to a real one. It results from the contemplation not of actual but fictitious situations created by the artist. Fiction facilitates detachment. The consequence of this again is unfavourable to true morality, whose proper sphere is actual life. Thus even though perfect selflessness may be a prominent mark of art experience, its influence on the moral side of man may be very little. When that experience ceases he may lapse into the former state of tension and perplexity, which has its source in a selfish outlook on life.

According to some, this is no defect at all; for art, they maintain, has nothing to do with morality and is ethically neutral. But if that is so, it ceases to be a human value; and its recognition of evil as a fact of life becomes virtually meaningless.[7] There has been much controversy in this respect among art critics; but if we take a comprehensive view of man's nature and his aims, it seems that art cannot be altogether divorced from morality.[8] Art is, no doubt, for its own sake. But, in the result, it should be more by being a criticism of

7. It would also then cease to appeal to the whole being of man which, as an ultimate value, it is expected to do.

8. It would then amount to a selfish escape from the tedium of life—a view as blameworthy as pure asceticism is in ethics. Both are at bottom egoistic, being preoccupied with oneself and not caring in the least for society.

life's values. This explains, for instance, the double standard of our judging a character appearing in a work of art. To take the case of Iago, as an example, we not only speak of him as a perfect creation of Shakespeare but also condemn him as wicked in the extreme. The practice of the best artists is our support here. And the close alliance, again, of art with religion in all countries and in all times appears to be for saving art from possible degeneration by its separation from morality.[9] Art, correctly conceived, cannot be merely a selfish escape from life; it must also influence life permanently or, at least, tend to do so. But the view that art is not connected with morality is not altogether baseless. The truth underlying it is that art has nothing *directly* to do with morality. It should influence character indirectly; and what is discountenanced is only direct instruction in that regard, for it will militate against the primary purpose of art which is to raise man above all strife and secure a form of unique joyful experience.[10]

When even the primary aim of art is to be attained indirectly, it is natural to ask: What is this indirect connection between art and morality? It cannot be due to the method of art, for fables and parables teach morality indirectly but are not art. It must be through the characters which it introduces or, what comes to the same thing, through the general significance of the plot, that art can exercise moral influence on the spectators.[11] The implied outlook of these characters on life and the world should be moral. 'That is a true poem', says an old Indian authority, 'which treats of the doings of the good and the great'. The best examples of this are to be found in the great epics of the *Rāmāyaṇa* and the *Mahābhārata* whose indirect influence on Indian men and women has all along been greater than that of any other single factor. In a work of art where no such characters are found, say, a lyric poem, it is the artist's outlook on what he portrays that counts. The conclusion to be drawn from this is that art should not have a moral *aim*, but most necessarily have a moral *view*, if it should fulfil its true purpose.[12] This is not to make art didactic, for morality does not form either its content or its purpose according to this view.

In addition to this general moral view, there may be some aspect of the moral idea dominating the conduct of the hero or of other characters, and

9. The association of art with religion, in all probability, is primarily to make the latter attractive; but it has undoubtedly helped to prevent the former from deteriorating.

10. In this sense, the following statement of Bhaṭṭa Nāyaka is correct: *Kavye rasayitā sarvo na boddhā na niyoga-bhāk*. [Quoted in *DA*. (com.), p. 12.] We shall herafter refer to this work as DA., and our references will be to the first edition of it printed at Bombay in 1891.

11. It is not what the characters say that counts; but what they are and what they do.

12. No artist will present characters like Iago as examples to be followed. But this negative attitude towards them is not enough. He should do his best to leave the impression on us that they are warnings.

be thus intimately woven into the structure of the plot.[13] It will then become an organic part of the content of art. A very good example of it is found in Bhavabhūti's drama, *Uttararāma-carita*. Here, as in any other great work of art, there is a general moral view pervading the whole piece. It includes not a single character which leads to any lapse from the high level that is expected in a play of which Rama is the hero. But over and above this, there is Rama's sense of public duty (as interpreted by him, of course) and his determination that it should have priority over all private obligations, which forms the very pivot on which the whole of the story here dramatised turns.[14] Unlike the general moral view, this is in the foreground of the picture. But it must be added that it, in no way, encroaches upon the artistic function of the play which is to awaken in us the emotion of love—not as the source of all life's joy, but as leading to pathos which so often and so inexplicably comes in its wake. This emphasis on the importance of public duty may be the main lesson of the story. But the story is not the end in dramatic art; it is only a means to the communication to the spectators of the *rasa* in question.

That is, the creations of art must leave a moral influence on the spectator without his knowing that he is being so influenced. Though theoretically, the theme of art may be anything which has a basis in life, this additional requirement makes it necessary to restrict the scope of the artist's choice to the higher aspects of life. Otherwise, art not only ceases to exert any moral influence; it may turn out in the end to be a means of corrupting character and degrading ideals.

---

13. This is the meaning of Indian critics saying that any of the *puruṣārthas* may be the content of art. When either *artha* or *kāma* forms the content, a general moral view is expected to prevail; when *dharma* becomes the content, there is this additional emphasis on morality.

14. There is no hesitation whatever before the dictate of reason that a ruler must put public good before private inclination and there is a majestic sadness in the banishment of Sita as a consequence.

7

Art Experience 2

OF THE INDIAN theories of art the most important is the one known as the *Rasa* theory. References to it are found in very early Sanskrit works, but it was not formulated and clearly expounded until the ninth century A.D.[1] In various directions, it marks an advance on the earlier theories and has virtually superseded them. In one respect, *viz.*, its conception of the aim of art, it is quite unique. The purpose of the present article is to explain the nature of this conception, and briefly to indicate wherein its uniqueness lies. Though the theory applies equally to all the fine arts, it has been particularly well-developed in relation to poetry and the drama; and we shall therefore consider it here mainly from that standpoint. But before we proceed to do so, it is desirable, for the sake of contrast, to make a reference to the general Indian view of poetry so far as it bears on the topic we are to consider.

I

There are two points of view from which the aim of poetry may be considered—one, of the poet, and the other, of the reader of poetry.[2] But for us, in explaining the distinctive feature of the view taken of it in the *Rasa* school, it is the latter that is more important. Let us therefore begin by asking the question: What is the use of poetry to its reader? The answer that is almost universally given to this question by Indian writers is pleasure (*prīti*).[3] It may have other uses also for him. For example, it may have some lesson or criticism of life to convey to him; but they are all more or less remote, unlike pleasure which is its immediate use[4] or value for him. But pleasure here is not to be taken in the abstract; rather, to judge from the explanation given of its nature in Indian works, it stands for a state of the self or a mode of experience of which it is a constant and conspicuous feature. Hence pleasure, by itself, does not constitute the whole of

1. This formulation is found in the *Dhvanyāloka* of Ānandavardhana. It was authoritatively commented upon in the tenth century A.D. by Abhinavagupta.

2. It is not meant by this that the two view-points necessarily differ in every respect.

3. See, e.g. Vāmana's *Kāvyālaṁkāra-sūtra*, I. i. 5.

4. Cf. the term *sadyaḥ* ('instantly') used in describing the aim of poetry in *Kāvya-prakāśa* (Bombay Sanskrit Series), p. 8: *sadyaḥ paranirvṛti*. This work will be referred to as *KP.*, hereafter.

what is experienced at the time of poetic appreciation, but is only an aspect of it. The immediate value of poetry for the reader then is the attainment of this enjoyable experience and not mere pleasure. That is its primary use, and any other use it may have for him is a further good which poetry brings.

But pleasure, even when thus understood, is an end that is associated with many kinds of activities such, for example, as eating or bathing which none would place on the same level as poetry. It is therefore necessary to distinguish between the two. The distinction depends chiefly on the fact that, though art may eventually be based upon Nature, we are, in appreciating the objects it depicts, concerned more with their appearance than with their actual existence. In art, as it has been stated, 'we value the semblance above the reality'. So the artist selects only those among the features of the object to be depicted that are necessary for making his representation appear like it, and omits all the rest. A painter, for example, does not actually show us the thickness or depth of the things he paints, but yet succeeds in giving us an idea of their solidity. Art objects have consequently no place in the everyday world of space and time; and, owing to this lack of spatio-temporal position or physical status, the question of reality does not apply to them. This does not mean that they are unreal; it only means that the distinction of existence and non-existence does not arise at all in their case.[5]

But we should not think that these objects may therefore be of no interest to the reader. They have their own attraction for him, because a certain element of novelty enters into their representation. We have stated that the artist selects those features of the object he deals with which will make it retain its resemblance to the real. But that is not the whole truth, for he has also recourse often to fresh invention. Thus an Indian poet, in referring to the appearance of the earth on a moonlit night, represents it as 'carved out of ivory'. Almost all the writers on poetics lay down that *pratibhāna*, which may be rendered in English as 'creative fancy', is an indispensable condition of genuine poetry. It is 'the seed of poetry' (*kavitva-bīja*) according to them. But the Sanskrit word further connotes that the object so fancied is experienced *as if* it is being actually perceived—'like a globular fruit', it is said, 'placed on the palm of one's own hand'. But such invention does not mean the introduction of new features for their own sake. They are not merely pleasant fictions. When a poet, for instance, pictures fairies as dwelling in flowers or a cloud as carrying a message of love, he does so in strict conformity to the total imaginative vision

5. Cf. *KP.*, pp. 102–3, where this point is illustrated by the example of a 'painted horse' (*citra-turaga*).

which has inspired him to the creation of the particular work of art. The art object is thus much more than an appearance of the actual. It involves a good deal of mental construction and far surpasses in quality its counterpart in Nature.[6] In other words, the poet idealises the objects in depicting them; and it is in this process that they are raised to the level of art and acquire aesthetic significance and, though not real, come to be of interest to the reader.

As a result of their idealised character, art objects lose their appeal to the egoistic or practical self and appear the same to all. That is, art appreciation is indifferent not only to the distinction between the real and the unreal, but also to that between desire and aversion. They become impersonal in their appeal, and therefore enjoyable in and for themselves.[7] It is the complete detachment with which, in consequence, we view them, that makes our attitude then one of pure contemplation. But we must be careful to remember that by describing this attitude as contemplative, we do not mean that it is passive and excludes all activity. The very fact that it is an *appreciative* attitude implies that it is active. The belief that it is passive is the result of mistaking the disinterested for what is totally lacking in interest. But, as we have seen, the art object has its own interest to the spectator; and, so long as his mind is under the selective control of interest, it can by no means be regarded as passive. All that is meant by saying that the art object makes no appeal to the practical self is that our attention then is confined wholly to that object, and that it is not diverted therefrom by any thought of an ulterior use to which it may be put.

This transcendence of the egoistic self in the contemplation of art profoundly alters the nature of the pleasure derived from it. Being altogether divorced from reference to personal interests, one's own or that of others', art experience is free from all the limitations of common pleasure, due to the prejudices of everyday life such as narrow attachment and envy. In a word, the contemplation being disinterested, the pleasure which it yields will be absolutely pure. That is the significance of its description by Indian writers as 'higher pleasure' (*para-nirvṛti*).[8] And art will yield such pleasure, it should be observed, not only when its subject-matter is pleasant, but even when it is

6. The following anecdote narrated about a famous painter of modern times brings out this feature very well. When the artist had painted a sunset, somebody said to him, 'I never saw a sunset like that'; and he replied, 'Don't you wish you could?'

7. Cf. *K.P.*, p. 107. This does not, however, mean that the response to them will be the same in the case of all. It will certainly vary, but only according to the aesthetic sensibilities of particular individuals and not according to their other personal peculiarities.

8. See note 4 above on p. 34. Cf. the explanation of *prīti* as *alaulika-camatkāra* in *DA.*, p. 203 (com.). In view of this higher character, it would be better to substitute for it a word like 'joy' or 'delight'. But for the sake of uniformity, we shall generally use the word 'pleasure' itself.

not, as in a tragedy with its representation of unusual suffering and irremediable disaster. The facts poetised may, as parts of the actual world, be the source of pain as well as pleasure; but, when they are contemplated in their idealised form, they should necessarily give rise only to the latter. It is for this reason that pleasure is represented in Indian works as the *sole* aim of all art.[9] It means that the spectator, in appreciating art, rises above the duality of pain and pleasure as commonly known, and experiences pure joy. Here we see the differentia of poetic pleasure or, more generally, aesthetic delight.

II

The *Rasa* school agrees with the above conception of the poetic aim, but it distinguishes between two forms of it; and, since the distinction depends upon the view which the school takes of the theme of poetry, we have first to indicate the nature of that view. The theme of poetry, according to the general Indian theory, may be anything. One of the oldest writers on poetics in Sanskrit remarks that there is nothing in the realm of being or in that of thought which does not serve the poet's purpose.[10] Nor is any distinction made there between one topic and another as regards fitness for poetic treatment. One subject is as good as another, and there is none on which a fine poem might not be written. The *Rasa* school also admits the suitability of all themes for poetic treatment, but it divides them into two classes—one comprising those that are *dominated* by some emotion, particularly an elemental one like love or pathos, and the other all the remaining ones; and it holds that, for the purpose of poetic treatment, the first is superior to the second.[11] The exact significance of this bifurcation of themes will become clear as we proceed. For the present, it will suffice to say that there are two types or order of poetry, according to this school, one dealing with 'emotional situations' in life, as we may describe them, and the other,[12] dealing with the other situations in life or with objects of external nature; and that the latter is reckoned as relatively inferior poetry. It is in justifying this discrimination that the *Rasa* school makes the differentiation in the purpose of poetry to which we have just referred. But before attempting to explain it, it is desirable to draw attention to one or two important points concerning emotional situations regarded as the theme of poetry.

---

9. *KP.*, i. 1 (p. 2): (*hlādaikamayī*). Since no pleasure, as commonly known, answers to this description, it is not a hedonistic view of art, in the accepted sense, that we have here.

10. Bhāmaha's *Kāvyālamkāra*, v. 4.

11. *DA.*, p. 28; pp. 20–7 (com.).

12. This class is further divided in a twofold way, but the division is not of importance for us here.

A poem of the higher type, we have stated, depicts a situation which is predominantly emotional. This emphasis on the emotional character of the theme may lead one to suppose that the type resembles lyrical poetry, as distinguished (say) from the epic and the drama. The expression 'lyrical poetry' does not seem to have any very definite significance. But if, as implied by common usage, it stands for a particular class of poetry and signifies the expression by the poet of his own feelings,[13] we must say that, on neither of these considerations, is the above supposition correct:

In the first place, emotional situations may here to be the chief theme of *any* kind of poetry. In fact, their importance is discussed in the works of the school, particularly with reference to the drama; and the adoption of such a method is fully supported by the facts of India's literary history. Thus it is a situation of love that is dramatised by Kālidāsa in his famous play the *Śakuntalā*; and, in the case of the equally famous play of Bhavabhūti, the *Uttara-rāma-carita* which treats of the desertion of Sita by her royal husband, it is one of deep pathos. It is not merely dramas that may choose such topics for treatment; even extensive epics are not precluded from doing so. Thus the emotional element serves here as the basis for contrasting different *grades*, rather than different *forms* of poetry. We may adopt any classification of it we like. Every one of the resulting classes, according to the present view, will comprise two grades of poetry—one the higher, in which the theme is predominantly emotional, and the other the lower, in which it is not so.

In the next place, the poet's own feeling, according to the *Rasa* view, is *never* the theme of poetry. This point is usually explained by reference to the episode narrated in the beginning of the *Rāmāyaṇa* about the birth of Sanskrit classical poetry. The details of the episode are attractive enough to bear repetition, and they are briefly as follows: On a certain day, in a beautiful forest bordering on his hermitage, Vālmīki, the future author of the epic, it is said, chanced to witness a fowler killing one of a pair of lovely birds that were disporting themselves on the branch of a tree. The evil-minded fowler had singled out the male bird, and had brought it down at one stroke. Seeing it lie dead on the ground, all bathed in blood, its companion began to wail in plaintive tones. The soft-hearted sage was moved intensely by the sight; and he burst into song which was full of pathos and which, according to tradition, became the prelude to the composition of the first great epic in Sanskrit.

The poetic utterance is apt to be viewed as the expression of the sage's sorrow at the sight he witnessed; but writers of the *Rasa* school point out that

13. Cf. 'Lyric poetry is the expression by the poet of his own feelings': Ruskin.

it cannot really be so,[14] for the utterance of personal feeling would be quite different. It is hardly natural, they say, for one that is tormented by grief to play the poet.[15] The sage is not preoccupied with his own immediate reaction to what he saw, but with something else, *viz.*, the objective scene itself. He is less concerned with his own feelings than with what has stirred them, and the song gives expression to the poignancy of the latter. But, as in the case of other poetic themes, it is not the emotional situation as it actually was (*laukika*) that is represented in it. That would by no means constitute art. It is the situation as it is in the poet's vision,[16] or as it has been transfigured by his sensitive nature and imaginative power (*alaukika*). In other words, the situation is idealised. Absorption in such a situation, for the reason already set forth, means transcending the tensions of ordinary life, and thereby attaining a unique form of experience. It is when the poet is fully under the spell of such experience that he spontaneously expresses[17] himself in the form of poetry.

III

To explain now the nature of the differentiation which the *Rasa* school makes in the aim of poetry: We have stated that poems may be of two kinds—one with an emotional theme and the other in which the theme is different, like (say) natural scenery:

(1) In the latter, there are the words of the poem; and the thoughts and images which they convey[18] form its essential content. It is the disinterested contemplation of them that gives rise to the joy of poetry. This contemplation, as a mental state, involves a subjective as well as an objective factor; and it is the total absorption in the objective factor, forgetting the subjective, that constitutes poetic experience here.

---

14. *Na tu muneḥ śoka iti mantavyam: DA.*, pp. 27–8 (com.).

15. [In another paper called 'The Idea of *Rasa*' which was not published and which seems to be an earlier and shorter version of the present one, Professor Hiriyanna has, at this place, the following footnote: 'This should not be taken to mean the elimination of all lyric poetry which, as ordinarily understood, gives expression to the poet's own feeling. It may well do so; only we have to look upon that feeling also as treated *objectively* by him in it. Cf. Wordsworth's saying, "Poetry springs from emotion recollected" (and, we should add, "sublimated") "in tranquility".'—Ed.]

16. Indian writers describe this as 'in the poem' (*kāvya-gata*) to distinguish it from the fact poetised, which is outside it. See *DA.*, p. 56 (com.).

17. *Yāvat pūrṇo na caitena tāvan naiva vamaty amum: DA.*, p. 27 (com.).

18. It is not meant that words in a poem always or necessarily form only the medium of conveying thoughts or images. They may, and often do contribute directly to the beauty of the poem. We are overlooking that point since our purpose here is to bring out the distinction in aim in the case of the two types of poetry we are considering, and not to explain the nature of either completely.

(2) But the case is altogether different in the other type of poetry. For the central feature of the situation to be portrayed in it is an emotion; and no emotion is, in its essence, directly describable. The poet cannot therefore communicate it, as he can a thought or image.[19] He can only suggest it[20] to the reader, who has already had personal experience of it (for it cannot be made known to any other), by delineating its causes and consequences or, in other words, the objects that prompt it and the reactions which they provoke. That is, the emotional aspect of the situation can be indicated only in an indirect or mediate sense, the media being the thoughts and images, as conveyed by the poet's words, of the objective constituents of that situation. Thus what, by themselves, form the content in the other type of poetry here become the means to its suggestion. They accordingly occupy a place here similar to the one occupied by words there;[21] and the final aesthetic fact in this type of poetry thereby comes to be, not thoughts and images as in the other, but the emotional mood which they help to induce in the reader. Now, as an emotion is a phase of our own being and not a presentation, this mood cannot be *contemplated*, but can only be *lived through*;[22] and it is this inner process of experiencing that is the ultimate meaning or aim in this type of poetry. There is a presentational element involved in this case also, as certainly as there is in the other, and it has, of course, its own poetic quality of beauty, if we like to put it so; but reduced, as it becomes here, to merely a condition of suggesting the emotion, it slides into the margin in our consciousness, instead of occupying the focus as it does there.[23]

Thus the experience for which poetic appreciation stands here is vastly different from that for which it does in the other type of poetry. It also connotes

---

19. The use of words like 'love' and 'anger' may convey to a person, who knows their meaning, an idea of the corresponding emotion; but it will be only an *idea* of them, while what is meant here is a *felt* emotion. See *DA.*, pp. 24–6.

20. To use technical terms, it will necessarily be *vyaṅgya*. Thoughts and images also may be suggested; but they are, at the same time expressible and therefore *vācya* also.

21. See *DA.*, pp. 31–2, 190–1.

22. The same may appear to hold good of the other phases of mind also, but it does not. To consider the case of 'thought', the only one of them that has a bearing on our subject (see next note): According to the Indian conception, the term 'thought' (*jñāna*) means 'what reveals' (*prakāśaka*); and thought, in this sense, is always intimately connected with 'what is revealed' by it (*prakāśya*), *viz.*, the object. Hence the *process of thinking*, apart from reference to some presentation, is meaningless. When it has meaning, i.e. 'when it is considered along with the presentational element', it becomes expressible and can also be contemplated. Cf. *Arthenaiva viśeṣo his nirākāratayā dhiyām.*

23. Ordinarily an emotion, no doubt, is also directed upon some object; but here, as aesthetic activity is not practical in its usual sense, this element is lacking.

detached joy; but, while the other experience takes the form of contemplating the poetic object, this one takes the form entirely of an inward realisation. The distinction will become clear, if we consider one or two examples. Let us contrast the example, already cited, of imagining the moonlit earth as 'carved out of ivory', with the appreciation of Kālidāsa's *Cloud Messenger*, which depicts the forlorn state of a lover exiled from his home. In the former, there is plainly an external object in the focus of our attention; but in the latter, though it abounds in exquisite pictures of external nature, we have finally to look within in order to appreciate properly its ultimate meaning, *viz.*, the deep anguish of forced separation from the beloved. To take another pair of illustrations, let us compare Milton's description, in the *Nativity Hymn*, of the rising sun as 'in bed curtained with cloudy red' and as pillowing 'his chin upon an orient wave', and Tennyson's well-known lyric, *Break, break, break*, with its poignant lament for lost love, heightened by a knowledge of the difference of the world, as a whole, to the suffering of the individual. In the former, the reader is engrossed in an object outside himself; but, in the latter, he has to retreat, as it were, into his inner self to realise its final emotional import. Both varieties of experience, as being aesthetic, are marked by a temporary forgetting of the self. But while in one case, the objective factor is *integral* to the ultimate poetic experience; in the other, it is not so,[24] because it has, as we have seen, only a marginal significance. That is, the emotion is experienced here virtually by itself, and the experience may accordingly be said to transcend, in a sense, the subject-object relation, and therefore to be of a higher order[25] than the mere contemplation of the other kind of poetry. It is this higher experience, that is called '*Rasa*'.

The word '*Rasa*' primarily means 'taste' or 'savour', such as sweetness; and, by a metaphorical extension, it has been applied to the type of experience referred to above. The point of the metaphor is that, as in the case of a taste like sweetness, there is no knowing of *Rasa* apart from directly experiencing it.[26] This experience, in addition to having its own affective tone or feeling of pleasure which is common to all aesthetic appreciation, is, as we know, predominantly emotional; and it is the latter feature, *viz.*, the predominance of its emotional quality, that distinguishes it from the experience derivable from the other type of poetry, dealing with a subject like natural scenery. It

24. Cf. *Rasādir artho hi sahaiva vācyenāvabhāsate: DA.*, p. 67. See also pp. 182–7.

25. It will be noticed that, in thus ascribing a superior status to *Rasa* experience, the value of neither the subjective nor the objective factor is denied, since the need for it of personal experience (remotely) and of appropriate objective accompaniments (externally) is fully recognised.

26. Cf. *āsvādyamānatā-prāṇatayā bhānti: DA.*, p. 24 (com.).

naturally differs according to the specific kind of emotion portrayed—love, pathos, fear, wonder and the like; and, on the basis of this internal difference, *Rasa* experience is ordinarily divided into eight or nine kinds. But it is not necessary for our present purpose to enter into these details. Besides, *Rasa* is, in its intrinsic nature, but *one* according to the best authorities;[27] and its so-called varieties are only different forms of it, due to a difference in their respective psychological determinants. In its fundamental character, it signifies a mood of emotional exaltation which, on the ground of what has been stated so far, may be characterised as quite unique.

It is necessary to dwell further on the nature of this experience, if what is meant by *Rasa* is to be properly understood. We have shown that when a poet treats of an emotional theme, he never depicts his own feeling, but only that which distinguishes the objective situation occasioning that feeling. This should not be taken to mean that it is the awareness (to revert to our earlier illustration) of the bird's sorrow at the loss of its mate, even in its idealised form, which constitutes *Rasa* experience.[28] As already implied, it consists in an ideal revival (*udbo-dhana*) in the reader's mind of a like emotion which, being elemental by hypothesis, may be expected to lie latent in all. Being a revival, it necessarily goes back to his past experience; but it is, at the same time, very much more than a reminiscence. In particular, the emotional situation, owing to the profound transformation which it undergoes in the process of poetic treatment, will throw a new light on that experience, and reveal its deeper significance for life as, for instance, in the case of love, in Kālidāsa's *Śakuntalā*, which appears first as the manifestation of a natural impulse but is transformed before the play concludes into what has been descried as 'a spiritual welding of hearts'. To realise such significance fully, the reader's own efforts become necessary in the way of imaginatively reproducing in his mind the whole situation as it has been depicted by the poet. *Rasa* experience is thus the outcome more of reconstruction than of remembrance. The whole theory is based on the recognition of an affinity of nature between the poet and the reader of poetry; and, on the basis of this affinity, it is explained that appreciation of poetry is essentially the same as the creation of it.[29] The need for presupposing past experience arises from the peculiar nature of emotion, to which we have already drawn attention, *viz.*, its essential privacy owing to which it remains opaque, as it were, to all

27. Cf. *Abhinava-bhāratī*, I, pp. 273–4, 293.

28. *DA.*, pp. 56–7 (com.).

29. *Nāyakasya kaveḥ srotuḥ samānonubhavaḥ*. *DA.*, p. 20 (com.). Cf. 'To listen to a harmony is to commune with its composer'.

those who have not personally felt it. But past experience serves merely as the centre round which the reconstruction takes place; and, in this reconstructed form, it is anything but personal.[30]

The point to be specially noticed here is that emotions are not *communicated* by the poet to the reader, as it is often assumed.[31] In fact, they *cannot* be communicated according to the present theory. All that the poet can do is to awaken in him an emotion similar to the one he is depicting. Even this awakening, it should be noted, is not the result of any conscious purpose on the part of the poet. The spontaneous character of all poetic utterance precludes such a supposition. The poet is intent, not upon influencing the reader in this or that way, but upon giving expression, as best he can, to his unique experience. It is this expression, that is primary, and the kindling up or waking to life of the emotion in the mind of the reader is more in the nature of its consequence than the result of any set purpose behind it. The reader starts from the poet's expression; and, if he is competent, that is, if he is sufficiently sensitive and sympathetic, he succeeds in capturing for himself the experience which it embodies. The process whereby such ideal awakening takes place is described:[32] Briefly, the mind of the responsive reader first becomes attuned to the emotional situation portrayed (*hṛdaya-saṁvāda*), through one or more of the knowing touches which every good poem is sure to contain; is then absorbed in its portrayal (*tanmayī-bhavana*); and this absorption, in the deeper sense already explained, results in the aesthetic rapture of *Rasa* (*rasānubhava*).

If this type of poetry were identical with lyrical and with short poems, we might have a relatively simple emotion as its characteristic feature. But when its scope is widened as here, the emotions involved may be very complex, indeed. In an epic, for example, practically all the familiar emotions are likely to appear at one stage or another; and, if they are not well co-ordinated, the aesthetic value of the poem will suffer. Hence the exponents of the *Rasa* view lay down that the treatment of the theme by the poet should be such as to secure the unity of the different emotions suggested—a unity which, they insist, is as important a canon of poetic composition here, as the unity of action is admitted to be in the case of all poetry.[33] Only a single emotion should be represented in a poem as dominant on the whole; and its progressive development from the moment of its emergence to its natural culmination should

30. *Tat-kāla-vigalita-parimita-pramātṛ-bhāva: KP.*, p. 108.

31. Cf. What has been described as the 'infection theory' of Tolstoy.

32. See, e.g. *DA.*, pp. 11, 15, 24 and 27 (com.).

33. *DA.*, pp. 170–1.

be methodically delineated. Its many and varied manifestations should be properly related to it, so that its portrayal may become internally coherent. Where other emotions, not altogether incompatible with it, enter the situation, they should all be synthetically related to it. Everything else also, like the construction of the plot, the interludes, characterisation and the poetic imagery in which the artist clothes his ideas should be oriented towards the ruling emotion. Even the diction and the other refinements of style must be appropriate to its nature. In one word, fitness (*aucitya*) of everything that has any bearing on it is the life-breath of *Rasa*.[34] This topic occupies considerable space in the works of the school; but, in view of its uniform recognition of the spontaneity of all poetic utterance, the rules formulated in this connection are to be looked upon more as aids in appraising the worth of a poem of this type than as restraints placed upon the freedom of the poet.

But the intrinsic worth of a poem is not all that is needed for its true appreciation. The reader also should be properly equipped for it. No doubt, the emotion depicted in this type of poetry is elemental, and therefore familiar to all. But that only signifies the universality of its appeal. It means that nobody is excluded from appreciating it, merely by virtue of its theme. The reader, in addition to possessing a general artistic aptitude specially qualified, if he is to appraise and enjoy a poem of the present type.[35] These qualifications are compendiously indicated by saying that he should be a *sa-hṛdaya*,[36] a word which cannot easily be rendered in English. It literally means 'one of similar heart', and may be taken to signify a person whose insight into the nature of poetry is, in point of depth, next only to that of the poet. In the absence of adequate equipment, he may lose sight of the *Rasa* aspect and get absorbed in the objective details portrayed by the poet which also, as we said, have a poetic qualify of their own. We would then be preferring the externals of true poetry to its essence; or, as Indian critics put it, he would mistake the 'body' (*śarīra*) of poetry for its 'soul' (*ātman*).[37] To cite a parallel from another of the fine arts, he will be like a person who, in looking on a statue of Buddha in meditative posture, remains satisfied with admiring the beauty, naturalness and proportion of its outward features, but fails to realise the ideal of serenity and calm depicted there, which constitutes its ultimate meaning. It is on this basis, *viz.*, that it is not merely the intrinsic excellence of a poem that is required for attaining *Rasa* experience but also a special capacity for it in the

34. *DA.*, p. 145.

35. *DA.*, pp. 18–19 (com.).

36. *DA.*, p. 11 (com.).

37. *DA.*, p. 13 (com.).

reader, that the present school explains how, though great poets like Kalidasa have tacitly endorsed the *Rasa* view by the place of supremacy they have given to emotion in their best works, it took so long for theorists to discover that they had done so.

Such, in brief outline, is the *Rasa* view advocated by what is known as the 'later' (*navīna*) school of art critics in India, as distinguished from the 'earlier' (*prācīna*). We have already drawn attention to one or two important points in the *Rasa* theory, in which it differs from the generality of aesthetic views. For example, it rejects the very common view that a poet may, and often does, give expression to his own feelings in poetry. Here is another point which is far more important, *viz.*, the discovery that there is an order of poetry which requires a deeper form of appreciation and yields a higher kind of aesthetic experience than is ordinarily acknowledged; and in this discovery, we may say, consists one of the chief contributions of India to the general philosophy of art.

8

An Indian in Paris: Cosmopolitan Aesthetics in Colonial India

1. Introduction

What is the fundamental question that animates Indian aesthetics during the colonial period? It is the question of authenticity. What makes Indian art *authentically* Indian? And how can one remain authentically Indian while being creative, modern and relevant to the art world as a whole? Discourse invoking the trope of the authentic placed aesthetic and even political demands on artists and their artwork and defined the emerging aesthetic sensibility in the late 19th and early 20th century. In this essay we examine how these demands were met, and also how they were sometimes simply sidestepped.

Race can always be recruited in service of authenticity, and indeed Indian aestheticians, art critics, and artists were happy to do so. The primal fantasy of the racialized authentic is often the tacit presupposition underlying more explicit discourse framed in the more acceptable vocabulary of cultural or national identity. We see this clearly in the Indian colonial context. Indian artists were challenged by the following sorts of questions: Is your art non-Western enough? Is it national enough? These innocent sounding questions often really meant "Is it brown enough? Is it native enough?" Aesthetic discourse then asks how much of each of these ingredients is enough to warrant the seal of authenticity.

On the other hand, artists in India, just as artists anywhere, faced the following questions: Is your art creative enough to be *art*? Is it modern enough? Is it distanced enough? Is it sufficiently universal to be *real art*? And aestheticians in India, just as aestheticians anywhere, asked how much of *these* is enough to warrant the seal of authentic *art*. In the Indian colonial context, these two apparently complementary sets of demands turned out to be almost impossible to satisfy jointly. An artist could be either authentic (authentically Indian but uncreative) or creative (aesthetically authentic but un-Indian). Either way, we are left with one more failed attempt by a local native to join and to address the global public.

There were, however, notable exceptions in colonial Indian art. A chosen few somehow achieved the impossible: they transcended the dichotomy to become *cosmopolitan* Indian artists. That is, they came to be viewed both by Western critics and Indian *rasikas* as universal: producing art beyond the parochial boundaries of nation, race, ethnicity, and religion. They came to be seen as cosmopolitan despite the fact that their art was recognized as rooted in fundamentally Indian soil. How was this possible? We consider three artists from this period; the reception of each of their works and techniques; and the rich and complicated network of reasons and emotional attitudes that, in retrospect—if not when they lived—established them as great cosmopolitan artists of colonial India.

We consider the projects of Ravi Varma (1848–1906) and Abanindranath Tagore (1871–1951) on the one hand and that of Amrita Sher-Gil (1913–1941) on the other. Varma and Tagore (very different from one another in some respects, but in others deeply implicated in the same ideology), we will argue, achieve a certain cosmpolitanism—that is, each of them produces work responsive to global aesthetic trends, and each achieves recognition as an *Indian artist*. Nonetheless, we will show, neither of them succeeds in transcending a racialized aesthetic, and hence neither fully escapes the dilemma scouted above. Their work, while it reveals their cosmopolitan sensibilities, remains rooted in an ideology shared by many Indians and British alike: the colonial fantasy of the authentic that insists on a central role for race in the aesthetic enterprise.

Sher-Gil's aesthetic, in contrast, succeeds in being genuinely cosmopolitan. That is, she succeeds in transcending the racialized aesthetic that traps Varma and Tagore, despite their success in other dimensions. Sher-Gil's own struggles with authenticity have little to do with the colonial fantasy of race. Since she does not get caught up in the ideology of the authentic to begin with, she is freed from its constraint, in her work, and in her sensibility as an artist. This very freedom, however, raises—for a brief—moment—the issue of her authenticity as an *Indian* artist, as we shall see.

2. *Varma and Tagore*[1]

The fundamental challenge for artists and art enthusiasts in India in the 1850s was to move Indian art into the modern era while retaining its Indian character. But how was one to create art that was at once genuinely artistic and authentically Indian? Traditional Indian art was viewed by Indian and Western

1. Portions of this section of the essay appear in our "Whose Voice? Whose Tongue? Indian Philosophy in English from Renaissance to Independence" in the *Journal of the Indian Council for Philosophical Research*. XXV: 2, pp. 89–108, 2008.

aesthetes alike as either "monstrous and barbaric" (Guha-Thakurta 1992, p. 184), guilty of undisciplined excess, as evidenced, for instance, in the paintings of the Kalighat school (figure 1), and symbolic of an untamed Other, or as mere imitative shopwork, as in the case of the Company School (figure 2).[2]

The early work of Raja Ravi Varma (of Kerala), in the period from 1900 to 1907 was initially seen as successfully overcoming this problematic dichotomy. Varma used techniques from the Company School in the style of academic realism but evoked Botticelli and Renoir in style and sensibility. Varma's artwork, in its subject matter, represented Indian virtue (domesticity) and female beauty (figure 3); it was historically continuous with ancient art subjects, depicting figures such as Sita (figure 4), central to the epic *Rāmāyaṇa*, and Indian mythological and religious themes (figure 5). Varma initially achieved enormous success as an Indian cosmopolitan artist, viewed as being both authentic and creative. His art transcended local community boundaries and was immediately popular throughout India (indeed, judging by the frequency of display, he must certainly be rated *today* as the most popular artist in India).

The immense popularity of Varma's art and resonance of the classical themes and values it espoused were, despite the deprecation of certain aesthetes, genuinely efficacious in generating national consciousness and so contributed to the nation-building effort. But his stature—as an artist able to be at once both contemporary and Indian—was ultimately unstable. For an "Indian Renoir" was, in the end, a Renoir manqué *who happened to be* Indian. And so, his art came to be disparaged by most Indian and Western art critics as inauthentic—as mere imitation of a colonial model. He came to be regarded as expressing at best an Indian enthusiasm, that, while genuine, was superficial, *merely reporting* on Indian mythological themes rather than *artistically rendering* them. Thus, Ravi Varma, in the end, was impaled on both horns of the dilemma: incapable not only of being *both* authentic and creative in his work but incapable of being *either*.

This deprecation of Ravi Varma's work went hand in hand with the evolution of a different approach to Indian art, starting around 1910, focused instead on "idealism and spirituality" (Guha-Thakurta, 1992, p. 183) as the key to its authenticity. Art critics such as A. K. Coomaraswamy and Sister Nivedita explicitly contrast Ravi Varma's work with that of Abanindranath Tagore, arguing that, in the work of Tagore (figures 6, 7, and 8), one finally finds a recovery of genuine tradition, transformed as the exotic, disciplined, ideal,

2. The British set up art schools in the major metropolitan areas (Bombay, Calcutta, Madras) in order to train Indian artists in Western art techniques. Artists who graduated from these schools and/or who deployed the techniques taught in these schools were called Company School artists.

and spiritual Other to the West's realist, practical, and material artistic sensibility as it is imitated in the work of Ravi Varma.

Within this new critical perspective, one grounded in Indian *rasavidyā* as an alternative aesthetic framework to that imposed by Western aesthetes, modern Indian art is revealed not as condemned to *failed representation*, but as capable, in the hands of Tagore, of *successful evocation*. Nivedita (1907) writes, "An Indian painting, if it is to be really Indian . . . must appeal to the Indian heart in an Indian way . . ." (quoted in Guha-Thakurta, 1992, p. 187). Ravi Varma, we now learn, got it all wrong. The buxom female body depicted by Varma is a distraction from divine womanly virtue, evoking, at best, the wrong *bhāva*. Indian purity and spirituality are undermined by Varma's *realistic* depictions of women, men, children—and gods, for that matter—represented, despite their idealization, without the symbolic markers that would lead the viewer beyond the concrete work to a contemplation of the transcendental ideal, the *Indian* ideal. This world beyond appearance, where the ineffable soul of India is revealed by Indian artistic genius, is immanent for the first time in the work of Abanindranath Tagore.

Nivedita's critique echoes the response of Coomaraswamy and Aurobindo to Varma's work. Coomarswamy writes, ". . . Ravi Varma's divinities, in spite of their many arms, are very human, and often not very noble human types. At best the goddesses are 'pretty': stronger condemnation of what should be ideal religious art would be hard to find. . . . Theatrical conceptions, want of imagination, want of restraint, anecdotal aims, *and a lack of Indian feeling* in the treatment of sacred and epic subjets are his faults. *His art is not truly national*—he merely plays with local color. . . . Ravi Varma's pictures . . . are such as any European student could paint, after only a superficial study of Indian life and literature." (Coomaraswamy, 1981, pp. 78–79). Aurobindo puts it this way ". . . From the point of view of art, Ravi Varma's images of gods and goddesses are as ugly as the pictures in the Bat-tala novels . . . such pictures are as repugnant to the sadhu's spiritual sensibility as to the moralist's sense of decency and decorum, as also to the artist's sense of beauty" (Guha-Thakurta, 1992, p. 307). Aurobindo conceives the artist as a *rishi*, Nivedita art as spiritual exercise.

In terms of their artwork alone, it is hard to justify issuing the seal of authenticity to Tagore and withholding it from Varma. It is clear that Varma was appropriating the styles of the European masters in rendering Indian themes and was wildly successful with the Indian *public*, for whom Indian art became salient as the authentic expression of Indian sensibility as never before. (Indeed, there is terrible irony here: it is precisely Varma's success with the Indian masses that undermined his acceptance by the Anglophone, British-educated Bengali elite who came to be the arbiters of high taste, and of Indian identity.) On the other hand, it is clear that Tagore was appropriating Japanese and Mughal miniature styles in his work (along with French impressionism) in rendering Indian themes. He was wildly successful with the Indian *art elite*, for whom Indian art became salient as the authentic expression of *Indian* sensibility as never before, despite its inaccessibility to the average Indian and its failure to penetrate India beyond the Calcutta salon. Each appropriates non-Indian techniques; each uses them to represent Indian themes; each appeals to *an* Indian public, and indeed Varma's public was arguably *more* Indian than Tagore's.

So why is Varma's work eventually judged to be discontinuous with the deepest Indian sensibility, while Tagore's work is seen as continuous with it? The answer to this question, of course, is not entirely clear. The influential contemporary art critic, A. K. Coomaraswamy (1907), bases his criticism of Varma's work quite explicitly on Varma's training lineage. The Bombay and Madras Schools of Art, on his view, train their artists to simply mimic Western styles, so that while the subject matter of the artwork may well be Indian, it is distinctly "un-Indian" in its style and evocation. In contrast, the Calcutta School, again, on his view, explicitly rejects such mimicry, with a record of seeking newness in Asia, looking to Japanese art style and sensibility, rather than to Europe. But as Guha-Thakurta observes, "[In the end], it was... Orientalist and nationalist propaganda which established him [Abanindranath Tagore] as a cult figure of 'national art' and defined a 'New School of Indian Painting' around him" (p. 189).

We have suggested an alternative explanation. The Bengali Abanindranath Tagore was far more closely connected to the arbiters of high taste in Calcutta than was Ravi Varma, who was an interloper, from Kerala, in the South, and a popular and "cheap lithographer" at that. This explanation suggests that we take seriously the very real possibility that, in the end, matters *extraneous* to the quality of the art itself determine the evaluation of the work. These include matters such as *whose* art lineage is more expressive of continuity with the Indian tradition; *what* subjects are evocative of Indian virtue; *which* forms best express Indian spirituality; *which class* is the appropriate consumer of real art; *which other* is an appropriate artistic reference point, and which is *not;* and, last, but certainly not least, *who* counts as the quintessentially Indian artist. All of these commitments are expressive of political, social, and personal dimensions of the authentic, and it is *these* matters that may explain Varma and Tagore's relative evaluation in the contest for the artist who is most accurately to capture the aesthetic soul, the *rasa*, the essence, of colonial India.

Last, but not least, having noted the ironic role of class in establishing authenticity, it is worth noting another weird irony in the discourse of Indian authenticity, which is replete with racial overtones. Varma draws his stylistic image from the white race, while Tagore looks to the nonwhite (Asian). Tagore gets to be an authentically Indian by imitating the Japanese. One is forced to wonder about the role of the strange coterie of hybrid aesthetes—the mixed Coomaraswamy in Boston, Sister Nivedita (European by birth but Indian by choice), and the Protestant Anglophone Unitarian Brahmo Samaj reformers in Calcutta—in deciding what it is to be *purely* Indian.

3. An Indian in Paris: Amrita Sher-Gil

Let us return to that crucial remark by the influential art critic Nivedita (1907) that set up the artistic challenge for that period: "An Indian painting, if it is to be really Indian... must appeal to the Indian heart in an Indian way..."

Nivedita is expressing the *invention* of a distinct category of art, of artist, and of audience in India, for the very first time: *Indian* art by an *Indian* artist for an *Indian* audience. The category INDIA is occasioned by the British colonial encounter with a multinational subcontinent but is taken up, articulated, and transformed in the creative Indian response to British rule and to the fantasies that animated it.[3] Varma and Tagore each invented *an* Indian artistic tradition; each was a complex weave of nation, race, tradition, and aspiration to authenticity. Each tried in his own way to be free. But in neither case was their art free from explicit consciousness of this purpose, that is, of the deliberate inquiry into what it meant to be an Indian artist; in each case, it drove their oeuvre and its reception. In neither case did their cosmopolitanism as artists transcend the racialized aesthetic of colonial consciousness.

Sher-Gil's work provides an illuminating contrast. Born in Hungary in 1913 (died at age 28, in 1941), she was of mixed pedigree, with an Indian Sikh aristocratic father and a Hungarian Jewish aristocratic mother. She spent the first eight years of her life in Hungary, moving to Simla, India with her parents for the next eight years. She was trained in Paris in the style of academic realism but was profoundly influenced by Cézanne, Gauguin, and Van Gogh (as well as the philosopher-poet Baudelaire). Upon her return to India from Paris, these influences were joined by the Ajanta and Cochin frescoes, the sculpture of Mahabalipuram, and Rajput miniatures. These facts—personal, social, and professional—are all relevant to Sher-Gil's artistic style and sensibility.

Because she was mixed racially, she was forcibly freed from a crucial dimension of the essentialized and racialized authentic in the Indian context.

---

3. India, prior to the arrival of the British, was not one nation but a number of different principalities. Nonetheless, Jawarharlal Nehru, in his *The Discovery of India* (1946), finds it necessary in the course of undermining British authority to invite his readers to participate, via his own narrative, in an imaginative viewing of India as an eternal unity, both adopting and subverting that of the British.

In her *Self-Portrait as Tahitian* (figure 9) she plays with the category of race even as she undermines its pretensions to essentialist purity. In many of her works (figures 10 and 11), she calls attention to the fact of racial difference, as marked by color (or caste marks), but as a *contingent* topic for artistic exploration, rather than as a representation of (idealized) eternal truth.

Moreover, in virtue of her mixed roots, her *taste* for different traditions arises from the ground up, or *organically*, in virtue of her contact from a very early age with a wide variety of works, peoples, and tastes reflecting different cultural contexts. This is also true of her *training* (Budapest, the Hungarian countryside in Zebegeny, the Latin quarter in Paris and the Beaux Arts school, the Ajanta caves, the Punjab countryside and the trip to South India). This taste and training conditions not so much a reflective and deliberative response as a deeply visceral, mostly nonconscious response to aesthetic variety. In her choices of artistic subject matter, her attention to difference is nuanced, as is her attention to similarity. She calls attention both to ways in which color and form *differ* in figure and landscape in different geographical, racial, economic, and cultural contexts, and to ways in which they are inextricably *intertwined* (as we see in the interweaving of race in her own case, and documented in the body of her work, which is diverse in technique and subject matter). This diversity of form and subject matter (self-portrait, landscape, and European and Indian human subjects, in a variety of attitudes and tones) contrasts with the striking uniformity of thematic content in the work of Tagore and Varma—the former emphasizing the spiritual and ethereal, the latter the concrete and realistic.

Sher-Gil's multiple roots nourish a unique artistic perspective that allows her, in contrast to her artistic contemporaries, a freedom to appropriate styles and to blend them in such a way as to fashion her own artistic signature. Her unique background also provides Sher-Gil with a cosmopolitan lens that allows her to see subjects in their particularity; the multiplicity of categories she invokes, and her awareness of their fluidity, overlap, and even interpenetration prevents her from essentializing them. Indeed, it is this strikingly individualistic cosmopolitan streak that initially rendered Sher-Gil's work simultaneously provocative and suggestive of a promising Indian modernity and suspect as authentically Indian. Even her contemporaries who championed her paintings wondered, for instance, about her fascination with the subjects of poverty and the dark, emaciated body, viewing her choices as at best sentimental and, at worst un-Indian, at best the work of an outsider and at worst a betrayal of her "heritage." (Dalmiya (2006)

It is instructive to contrast the kinds of attacks launched against Sher-Gil with the attack on Varma. Recall that Varma was paradoxically rendered un-Indian in contrast with the standard-bearer of Indian authenticity, Tagore, because he appealed too much to *Indians* of the *wrong class* (common folk as opposed to sophisticated *rasikas*) and because he borrowed technique from the *wrong culture* (European academic realism as opposed to Japanese inkwash painting). Sher-Gil's critical attention was very different. In her case, it was not a matter of her *appealing to* the wrong class as much as it was *portraying* the wrong class, and in an inappropriate way. She did not portray the Indian body as buxom, fair, and elegantly robed, which was Varma's artistic failing, but instead portrayed it as dark, emaciated, and only partially clothed, emphasizing not sensuality, but deprivation—deprivation of all the prerequisites of material life. This was taken to be equally problematic as an honest depiction of a basic Indian sensibility, replacing Varma's domestication of Indian prosperity and religious imagery with a European exoticization of Indian poverty and mundane life (Sher-Gil, 2007).

One of Sher-Gil's early champions was the art critic Charles Fabri, who rejected the view of Indian art as essentially spiritual: "This search for religion and philosophy, this tendency to interpret all Indian art in terms of spiritual experience stood between the sensitive and aesthetically inclined student and a proper feeling for Indian art like a hazy, misty curtain, that veiled the truth: indeed, hid the sheer loveliness of Indian works" (quoted in Dalmia, 2006, p. 101). Responding to Fabri's concern, Yashodhara Dalmia (2006) approvingly describes the artistic attitude of Sher-Gil as follows: "She [Sher-Gil] melded the Western and Indian idioms and did not, like many other artists of her time, attempt to find an authentic 'Indian' mode or weave together a nationalist agenda" (p. 91). Sher-Gil herself said: "Modern art has led me to the comprehension and appreciation of Indian painting and sculpture. It seems paradoxical, but I know for certain that had we not come away to Europe, I should perhaps never have realized that a fresco from Ajanta.... is worth more than the whole Renaissance!" (p. 43).

It is impossible to ignore B. K. Sarkar's striking interpretation of the statue of Natarāja (see p. xxi, pp. xxi–xxii, present volume) in the context of Sher-Gil's "paradoxical" observation that exposure to Western techniques enriched rather than tainted her insights about the splendor of Indian art. For while Sarkar interprets this quintessentially Indian art object purely in terms of line, color, and harmony of form, using no vocabulary from *rasa theory*, his description evokes a powerful and viscerally immediate *experience* of *rasa* (See "Whose Voice? Whose Tongue?" p. xxi, present volume). Sarkar shares Sher-Gil's cosmopolitan suspicion of nationalist Indian essentialism in aesthetics. But he also shares with her an aesthetic depth, and an understanding that even a cosmopolitan gaze, reflecting an education in the world's aesthetic history, theory, and culture, reveals an artistic object both in its own cultural context, and in the context of the theoretical framework through which the artist intends to communicate with the connoisseur. In the Indian case, this is the *rasa* theory.

But that anticipation, he and Sher-Gil would agree, neither demands an essentialism with respect to style nor an essentialism with respect to the gaze of the viewer. It would be tragic to interpret Sher-Gil's perspective on Indian art and sculpture or her own artistic production as that of an outsider (the Western-returned aesthete/artist). On the contrary, it is her experience and training outside of India that allows her a freedom to approach the works of art in India without the nationalist frame that was at one level imposed and at another level consciously adopted—though in different registers and with different kinds and degrees of success—by Varma and Tagore.

In much of her work, Sher-Gil explicitly explores the human body and various forms of human intimacy, including both feminine intimacy (figure 12) and intimacy with one's own self (figure 9). Here gender is relevant to her style of cosmopolitanism, particularly when interwoven with her mixed racial heritage. For our bodies—which are inextricably bound up with who we are—are indeed colored, while spirits and minds are not. Sher-Gil takes her physical identity seriously, in her life and in her work. This serious engagement with embodiment and its implications in Indian and in Europe explains in part her interest in exploring this central aspect of human existence in her artwork, not as a voyeur surfing a fantasy or as an outsider interested in the exotic, but as an intimate participant.

Sher-Gil's early training with nude models in Paris no doubt contributes to her interest in this subject (and this is an aspect of her Modernism). But whereas the respective receptions of Varma and Tagore as artists is explained in part by the added dimension of an Indian ideological lineage, in the case of Sher-Gil this kind of ideological lineage is notably absent. Sher-Gil is an individual woman artist, not easily classifiable as belonging to a particular race, nation, ethnicity, religion, or sexual orientation (though she is of a certain class), and certainly not essentially so. In any case, she attempts in her artwork to make sense of the range of actual experiences she has in the country she loves, India, and with which she so strongly identifies.

This makes her a cosmopolitan artist, but what makes her Indian? At the very least the following two facts. First, she *took herself to be* Indian. This was not justified on grounds of racial purity, nationalist loyalty, or even a continued presence in India but was, rather, due to a host of interlocking causal factors mentioned earlier, not one of which was necessary or sufficient for her being Indian but which together enabled a sensibility and a sense of belonging to the actual and imaginary space of India. Second, India *has come to claim her as one of its own.* Her works are proudly exhibited in the national gallery in New Delhi, and reports of their sales for astronomical figures are touted in the Indian press as evidence of appreciation of *Indian* art.

IV

Conclusion

This essay explores some of the complex ways in which race and aesthetics are coimplicated in the British–Indian colonial encounter. We have distinguished between Amrita Sher-Gil's art and artistic sensibility and that shared—despite their differences—by Ravi Varma and Abanindranath Tagore, as well as by many of the most influential art critics and aestheticians of colonial India. Specifically, we have argued that their cosmopolitanism embodies a self-consciousness about race, in the guise of a concern for something else, namely,

1

2

3

Fig. 1. Kalighat Painting (oil, anonymous, n.d.).
Fig. 2. The Bird (Company School).
Fig. 3. Here Comes Papa, 30" x 20," c. 1890s, oil on canvas (Ravi Varma).
Fig. 4. Sita Vanavasa, c. 1890s, oleograph. (Ravi Varma). Collection of the Trustees of the Wellcome Trust, London.
Fig. 5. Radha, Krishna, Rukmani, c. 1890s (Ravi Varma).
Fig. 6. Abhisarika, c. 1900, water color, (Abanindranath Tagore), Indian Museum, Calcutta.
Fig. 7. The Passing of Shah Jahan, 1902, oil on wood (Abanindranath Tagore).
Fig. 8. Sita in Captivity in Lanka, c. 1906-07, water color (Abanindranath Tagore).
Fig. 9. Self-Portrait as Tahitian, 1934, oil on canvas, 90 x 56 cm, (Amrita Sher-Gil). Collection: Vivan and Navina Sundaram, New Delhi.
Fig. 10. Brahmacharis, 1937, oil on canvas, 145.5 x 88 cm (Amrita Sher-Gil). Collection: National Gallery of Modern Art, New Delhi.
Fig. 11. Bride's Toilet, 1937, oil on canvas, 145.5 x 88 cm (Amrita Sher-Gil). Collection: National Gallery of Modern Art, New Delhi.
Fig. 12. Two Girls, 1939, oil on canvas, 158 x 90 cm (Amrita Sher-Gil). Collection: Vivan and Navina Sundaram, New Delhi.

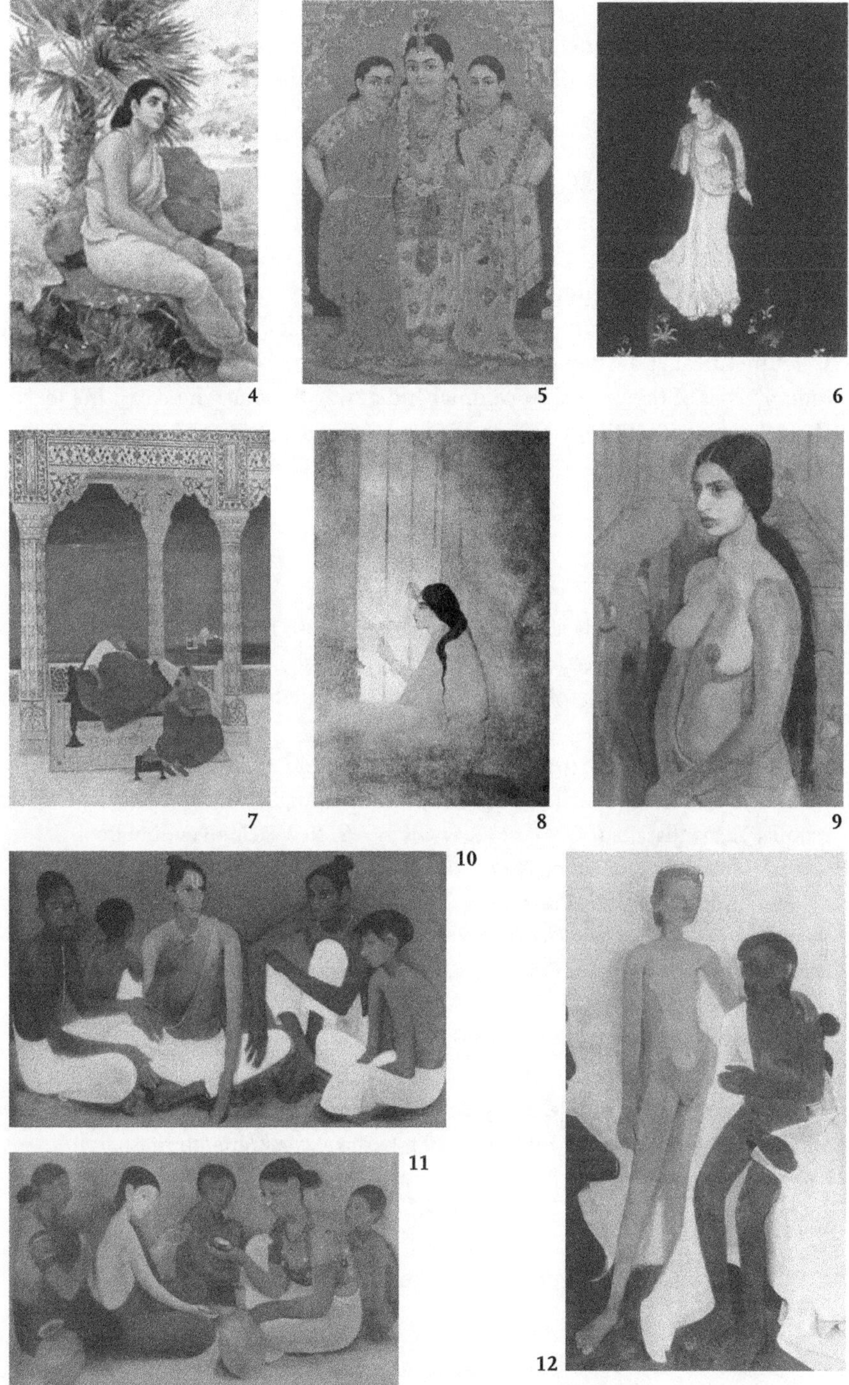
4
5
6
7
8
9
10
11
12

authenticity. Once race is *named*—as Indian—it begins to get used in a particular way, as a tool that demarcates certain works of art as legitimate aesthetic objects (i.e., as truly expressive of the "race" in question) but excludes others. Here we see that race is not merely expressed or explored but functions instead to patrol the boundary of the aesthetic.

The case of Amrita Sher-Gil reveals another way of being cosmopolitan. In her case, the aesthetic is used to rethink, or at least to situate, race differently in the colonial context. In the case of her artworks, we see race explored, with racial identity functioning as an aesthetic subject to be itself interrogated, rather than as an instrument used to delineate what does and does not count as (authentically) aesthetic. It is ironic that Sher-Gil, arguably the greatest Indian artist of this period in colonial India, was the one who cared the least about being authentically Indian, and who cared the least about an Indian *racial* identity.

References

Bhushan, Nalini, and Garfield, Jay. "Whose Voice? Whose Tongue? Indian Philosophy in English from Renaissance to Independence" present volume.

Coomaraswamy, Ananda. 1981. *Essays in National Idealism*. New Delhi: Munshiram Manoharlal Publishers.

Coomaraswamy, Ananda. (1907). "The Present State of Indian Art. Part I: Painting and Sculpture," *The Modern Review. Vol. 2, No. 2,* Aug.

Dalmia, Yashodhara. 2006. *Amrita Sher-Gil: A Life*. New Delhi: Penguin Books.

Guha-Thakurta, Tapati. 1992. *The Making of a New 'Indian' Art*. London: Cambridge University Press.

Nehru, Jawaharlal. (1946). *The Discovery of India*. New Delhi: Penguin.

Nivedita. (1907). "The Function of Art in Shaping Nationality, Part I.," *The Modern Review. Vol.* 8, No. 2, Jan.-Feb.

Amrita Sher-Gil. 2007. *An Indian Artist Family in the Twentieth Century*. (A book based on an exhibition of Sher-Gil's work in 2007, held in Munich and at the Tate Gallery, London.) Germany: Schirmer/Mosel.

Shikh Art. "Amrita Shergil." http//www.sikh-heritage.co.uk/arts/amritashergil/amritashergill.html

PART THREE

Vedānta

R. D. Ranade, "The Problem of Ultimate Reality in the Upanishads" (1926)

Ramchandra Dattatraya Ranade (1886-1957) was Professor of Philosophy at the University of Allahabad. He specialized initially in classical Greek philosophy (Aurobindo read Ranade, and reports that he learned his Greek philosophy from Ranade), with special attention to the pre-Socratics, but was also an eminent scholar of the Upaniṣads. His *Constructive Survey of Upaniṣadic Philosophy* (1926) from which the present selection is excerpted, is widely regarded as a classic in the field. Ranade's presentation is noteworthy in that he emphasizes the centrality of a psychological approach, as opposed to a theological approach, to understanding ultimate reality. Ranade is also widely revered as a religious leader. In retirement he founded an ashram, which is still active today.

Ramchandra Dattatraya Ranade

I

The Problem of Ultimate Reality in the Upaniṣads

The Supreme Philosophical Problem

1. In the midst of all the metaphysical conflicts that we have witnessed in the last chapter, there arises one supreme question—what, if any, is the core of Upaniṣadic teaching? Shall our minds be only tossed on the waves of philosophical conflicts, or can we have a ballast which will give the necessary poise to our philosophical speculations? Shall our minds be only sunk in the mire of the metaphysical conflicts of Pluralism, Qualified Monism, and Monism as we find them in the Upaniṣads? Is there not, at the basis of these various attempts at the solution of the central metaphysical problem, one fundamental conception, which will enable us to string together the variegated philosophical speculations of the Upaniṣads? This raises a very important problem—the problem of Ultimate Reality as understood by the Upaniṣadic seers. As we shall notice in this chapter, the Upaniṣadic philosophers solved the problem by taking recourse to the conception of *Ātman* a word which originally signified the breathing principle in man, but which came in the end to denote the essence of the Universe. Readers of Greek philosophy need hardly be reminded of the close parallel that exists between this Upaniṣadic conception of *Ātman* and the Platonic conception of the *ατὸ καθ' ατό*. The *Ātman* as we shall see in the course of this chapter, is the ultimate category of existence to the Upaniṣadic seers. How they arrived at this conception, and what use they made of it in the solution of the fundamental philosophical problem will form the theme of the present discourse.

The three approaches to the Problem in the history of thought: cosmological, theological, psychological

2. If we look at the history of philosophic thought, we shall see that there are various ways in which the problem of Ultimate Reality has been approached. The three chief types of approach are the Cosmological, the Theological, and the Psychological. Dr. Caird has said, that, by the very constitution of man's

mind, there have been only three ways of thinking open to man: "He can look outward upon the world around him; he can look inward upon the Self within him; and he can look upward to the God above him, to the Being who unites the outward and inward worlds, and who manifests himself in both."[1] According to him, the consciousness of objects is prior in time to self-consciousness, and the consciousness of both subject and object is prior to the consciousness of God. As he also elsewhere expresses it: "Man looks outward before he looks inward, and he looks inward before he looks upward."[2] The question arises: Is this account of the development of the consciousness of Reality ultimately valid? Is it necessary that man must look at the outside world before he looks within, and must he always look within before he can look up to God? The solutions which the history of philosophy gives to this problem are not exactly as Caird would have them. The Cartesian solution does not start by saying that the outside world is real. For Descartes, the Self is the primary reality, self-consciousness the primary fact of existence, and introspection the start of the real philosophical process. From the Self, says Descartes, we arrive at the conception of God, who is the cause of the Self, and whom we must therefore regard as more perfect than the Self. Finally, it is from God that we arrive at the world which we started by negating, by regarding as the creation of a deceptive evil spirit. On the other hand, to the God-intoxicated philosopher, Spinoza, neither the Self nor the world is the primary reality. To him, God is the be-all and the end-all of all things, the alpha and the omega of existence. From God philosophy starts, and in God philosophy ends. The manner of approach of the Upaniṣadic philosophers to the problem of ultimate reality was neither the Cartesian nor the Spinozistic one. The Upaniṣadic philosophers regarded the Self as the ultimate existence and subordinated the World and God to the Self. The Self, to them, is more real than either the World or God. It is only ultimately that they identify the Self with God, and thus bridge over the gulf that exists between the theological and psychological approaches to Reality. They start, no doubt, by looking out into the world, but they find that the solution of the ultimate problem cannot come from the world without: it is necessary for us, they say, to go back to the psychological category. Then they try another experiment: they go by the theological approach to the problem of reality, but they find that also to be wanting. Finally, they try the psychological approach, and arrive at the solution of the problem of ultimate existence. We thus see that the problem of ultimate Reality to the Upaniṣadic philosophers is a cosmo-theo-psychological problem: finding both the cosmological

1. *Evolution of Religion*, I. 77.

2. *Evolution of Religion*, II. 2.

and theological approaches deficient, they take recourse to the psychological approach and arrive at the conception of the Self, which they call the *Ātman*. We shall proceed to show at length in this chapter how the Upaniṣadic philosophers regarded the cosmological and theological approaches as only ancillary, and the psychological approach as the only true approach to the ultimate solution.

I—The Cosmological Approach

Regress from the cosmological to the physiological categories

3. We shall first discuss the cosmological approach, and see how it was found deficient. The naive mind of the natural man is likely to consider the forces of nature as ultimate realities; but a deeper speculation and a greater insight into events show that the phenomenal forces cannot be taken to be ultimate realities. This fact is illustrated by a story in the *Chhāndogya Upaniṣad*, where we are told how one student, Upakosala, lived for instruction with his preceptor, Satyakāma Jābāla, and served him assiduously for twelve years; how even though the ordinary period of tutelage was over, his teacher would not leave him; how the wife of the teacher asked her husband why it was that he would not leave this one disciple while he had left the others; how, when Upakosala had once gone to the forest, the three sacrificial Fires, whom he had assiduously served in his master's house, rose in bodily form before him; how the first, namely Gāhrapatya, told him that the ultimate reality was to be found in the sun; how the second, namely Anvāhāryapachana, told him that it was to be found in the moon; how, the last, namely Āhavanīya, told him that it was to be found in the lightning; how, in fact, Upakosala seemed to be temporarily satisfied with the instruction imparted to him by the three Fires; how, when he returned home, his teacher asked him why it was that his face shone as if with spiritual illumination; how the student told him that the spiritual illumination, if at all, was due to the instruction imparted to him by the three Fires; how the teacher replied that the teaching imparted to him by the Fires was deficient and inferior to the teaching which he himself knew; how he ultimately imparted that teaching to his disciple, which consisted in saying that the ultimate reality was to be found neither in the sun, nor in the moon, nor in the lightning, but in the image of the person reflected in the human eye. "It is this image," said Satyakāma Jābāla, "which is the *Ātman*. It is this image which is fearless, and the ultimate reality. It is this image which brings all blessings. It is this image which is the most resplendent thing in all the worlds. He who knows it to be so will himself be resplendent in the worlds" (S. 1). This

passage evidently indicates a regress from the cosmological to the physiological category. Not satisfied with objective existences being regarded as ultimate reality, Satyakāma declares that ultimate reality is to be found in a physiological category, namely, the eye. This, in itself, as we shall see later on, is only an inferior truth, though evidently it has the merit of taking us from the outside world to the physiological sphere. In a similar spirit, in another passage of the *Chāndogya Upaniṣad*, we are told how the light "which shines in the high heavens in transcendent space is the same light which is within man, and of this we have tactual proof, namely, when we feel the warmth in the body, and audible proof when after closing our ears we hear what may be regarded as the thunder of heaven, or the bellowing of an ox, or the sound of a burning fire. He who meditates on ultimate reality as thus dwelling in the human body becomes himself conspicuous and celebrated" (S. 2. a). This same idea is expressed in the *Maitrī Upaniṣad* when the author of that Upaniṣad speaks of the ultimate reality in man as being verily the sound which a man hears after shutting his ears (S. 2. b). We thus see that in these passages we have a regress from the cosmological to the physiological categories, namely, the eye, or bodily warmth, or the sound that man hears after closing his ears. The cosmological approach has been tried and found wanting. It seems necessary for the Upaniṣadic philosophers to halt at the caravansary of the physiological categories[3] before they can proceed to the psychological destination.

Regress from the cosmological and physiological to the psychological categories

4. In a passage which occurs both in the *Kauṣītakī* and the *Bṛhadāraṇyaka* Upaniṣads, we are told how both the cosmological and physiological categories must be regarded as deficient, and how they must, therefore, necessarily pave the way for the psychological category. There is here a discussion as to how the proud Bālāki once went to Ajātatśatru, the king of Kāśī, and how he tried to impose upon him by saying that he would impart superior wisdom to him; how Ajātaśatru welcomed this great man who told him that he would impart superior knowledge; how the proud Bālāki began by saying that true wisdom consisted in regarding the sun as ultimate reality; how he went on to say that the ultimate reality was to be found, one after another, in such objects as the moon, the lightning, the thunder, the wind, the sky, the fire, the water, the mirror, the image, the echo, the sound, the body, the right eye and the left

3. There is the same distinction between physiology and psychology as Matthew Arnold would say between the poetries of Byron and Wordsworth.

eye; how ultimately Bālāki's mouth was gagged when he could proceed no further in his peculiar way of philosophising; how Ajātaśatru took Bālāki by the hand, went to a man who had fallen in deep sleep, and called upon him saying 'Thou great one, clad in white raiment, O king Soma'; how the man, who had fallen in deep sleep, still remained lying; how he rose at once when Ajātaśatru pushed him with his stick; and how, finally, Ajātaśatru told Bālāki that in the person who had gone to sleep, the sleeping consciousness may be regarded as ultimate reality (S. 3). In this passage we have evidently the deficiency of both the cosmological and physiological categories brought out in favour of the psychological category, namely, the deep-sleep consciousness. We shall see later how even this is an inferior answer to the problem that has been raised; and, therefore, we shall not stop at this place to discuss the final psychological answer of the Upaniṣadic philosophers on this head.

The cosmological argument for the existence of God: God is all-powerful

5. The cosmological approach has been tried and found wanting in favour either of physiological or psychological categories. But it does not by any means follow that the cosmological speculations of the Upaniṣadic philosophers did not lead them independently to the positing of Absolute Existence. If we look deeper, we shall find in them the same kind of cosmological proof for the existence of the Absolute, as we find, for example, in the history of Greek Philosophy. A passage of the *Taittirīya Upaniṣad* declares that behind the cosmos there must be an existence which must be regarded as responsible for its origin, sustenance, and absorption: "that from which all these beings come into existence, that by which they live, that into which they are finally absorbed, know that to be the eternal verity, the Absolute" (S. 4. a). And, again, a cryptic formula of the *Chāndogya Upaniṣad* declares that a man must compose himself in the belief that the world has come out of, lives in, and is finally absorbed in the Absolute. The philosopher of this Upaniṣad expresses this whole conception by means of a single word *tajjalān*, which means that it is from the Absolute that the world has sprung, it is into it that it is dissolved, and it is by means of it that it lives (S. 4. b). This "cosmological" proof for the existence of an eternal verity behind the cosmos by reference to the origin, existence, and destruction of the world is known to all students of philosophy, and we find the same thing in the Upaniṣads also. It is true that the same kind of objections that were advanced by Kant against the traditional cosmological argument may likewise be advanced against this way of argumentation in the Upaniṣads; but the fact cannot be gainsaid that the argument is there. When once an eternal verity behind the cosmos has

been postulated, the Upaniṣadic philosophers have no hesitation in making it the fount and source of all power whatsoever. They consider it to be the source of Infinite Power which is only partially exhibited in the various phenomena of Nature. Thus the forces of Nature that we are aware of are ultimately only partial manifestations of the power that is in the Absolute. There is a very interesting parable in the *Kenopaniṣad* which tells us how this is so. Parables and myths in philosophical works are to be understood as merely allegorical representations of philosophical truths, and it is thus that the story in that Upaniṣad of Brahman, the eternal Verity, showing its prowess against the arrogant godlings of Nature, must be understood. The story runs, that there was, once upon a time, a great fight between the gods and the demons, and the gods were successful. The gods thought that the success was due entirely to their own power, and forgetting that this power was only a manifestation of the power of Brahman in them, they became proud. The Brahman, knowing this, suddenly made its appearance before them, and the gods were greatly wonderstruck, not knowing what it was. Then they sent forth one of them, namely, the god of fire, as an emissary to Brahman, and charged him with the task of learning the real nature of that Great Being. The god of fire ran in pride to Brahman. Brahman asked him who he was, and the god of fire proudly answered that he was Jātavedas, in whom lay the power of burning the whole of the earth if he pleased. Then Brahman threw before him a small blade of grass, and asked him to burn it if he could. The god of fire was unable to burn it with all his might. He became disappointed and returned to the gods. Then the gods sent another godling of nature, the god of wind, and charged him with the same mission. The god of wind ran in pride to Brahman, and, being asked who he was, said that he was Mātariśvan, in whom lay the power of blowing away anything from off the surface of the earth. Brahman again threw a blade of grass before him. Not with all his might was the god of wind able to move it to an infinitesimal distance. Then the god of wind returned in shame, not being able to know the nature of that Great Being. Then the gods sent Indra and charged him with the same mission. Indra was a more modest god than either the god of fire or the god of wind. He ran to Brahman to know its nature, and Brahman disappeared from his sight, for the simple reason, it seems, that Indra was more humble than either of the gods previously sent. Then suddenly sprang before Indra one very beautiful celestial damsel, from whom Indra inquired what that Great Being was, which had made its sudden disappearance from before him. Then that damsel told him that it was Brahman, and said further, that it was due to the power of the Brahman that the gods had gained victory over the demons, and not to their own personal power. God Indra was shrewd enough and understood that the power of the gods was only a manifestation of the power of the Absolute. It was on account of this humility, which made it possible for him to go to Brahman and touch him nearest, that he became the foremost of the gods. "It is verily the power of Brahman which flashes forth in the lightning and vanishes again. It is the power of Brahman which manifests itself as the motion of the soul in us and bethinks itself" (S. 5. a). This parable tells us that all physical as well as mental power is to be regarded merely as a manifestation of the power of Brahman. We thus see how the philosopher of the *Kenopaniṣad* arrives cosmologically at the conception of an unmanifested Power which lies at the back of the so-called manifest powers of nature and mind, and which must therefore be understood as the primary reality.

God is supreme resplendence

6. It is not merely that all the power in the world is ultimately due to Brahman: the very resplendence and illumination that we meet with in the world are also to be regarded as manifestations of the great unmanifest luminosity of the Absolute. "Does the sun shine by his own power?" asks the *Kaṭhopaniṣad* a "Do the moon and the stars shine by their own native light? Does the lightning flash forth in its native resplendence?—Not to speak of the paltry earthly fire, which obviously owes its resplendence to something else?" Shall we say that all these so-called resplendent things are resplendent in their own native light, or must we assert that they derive their power of illumination from a primal eternal verity which lies at the back of them all, and whose illumination makes possible the illumination of the so-called luminous objects of nature? "Before Him the Sun does not shine, before Him the moon and the stars do not shine, before Him the lightning does not shine; far less this earthly fire. It is only when the Absolute shines first, that all these objects shine afterwards. It is by His luminosity that they become luminous" (S. 5. b).

God is the subtle essence underlying phenomenal existence

7. The Brahman, therefore, which must be posited as the fount and source of all existence, and which must be regarded as the origin of all power and resplendence, must also be taken, say the Upaniṣadic thinkers, as the subtle essence underlying all the gross manifestations that we meet with in the world. Another parable, this time from the *Chāndogya Upaniṣad*, tells us how in the conversation that took place between a teacher and his pupil, the teacher, in order to convince his pupil of the subtlety of the underlying essence, directed him to bring to him a small fruit of the Nyagrodha tree;

how, when the disciple had brought one, the teacher directed him to break it open; how, when it was broken open, he asked him to see what was inside the fruit of the tree; how, when the disciple looked into it, he saw that there were seeds infinite in number, and infinitesimal in size; how when the teacher again directed him to break open one of those seeds, the disciple did so, and, being asked to see further what was there, said "Nothing, Sir", upon which the teacher told him, "My dear boy, it is of the very subtle essence that you do *not* perceive there—it is of this very essence that the great Nyagrodha tree is made. Believe it, my dear boy" (S. 6). This parable tells us how the underlying essence of things is to be regarded as subtle and unmanifest, and how the gross and manifested objects are to be understood as merely phenomenal appearances. There is, however, a further point in the parable which we must duly notice. When the teacher told his disciple that behind the Nyagrodha tree there lay a subtle essence which was unmanifest, he also told him that it was to be identified with the Self, and further, that the disciple must identify himself with it (S. 6). We see here the limitation of the mere cosmological conception of an underlying essence of things, and it seems as if cosmology must invoke the aid of psychological categories once more before the essence underlying the cosmos could be identified with the essence that lies at the back of the human mind. Thus the whole Universe becomes one, only when we suppose that there is the same subtle essence underlying both the world of nature and the world of mind.

The physico-theological argument

8. The cosmological argument, as it happens in the history of thought, seems also to take the help of the physico-theological proof and the two together seem to offer a formidable front to the thinking mind. Likewise does it happen in the case of Upaniṣadic philosophy. The argument from design and the argument from order are merely the personal and impersonal aspects of the physico-theological argument. Those who believe in God believe in design. Those who believe in an impersonal Absolute believe only in order. Very often, as in the case of the Upaniṣadic thinkers, the personal and impersonal aspects are fused together, and we are told how the Self as personal existence is yet "an impersonal bund which holds the river of existence from flowing by. Neither night nor day, neither age nor death, neither grief nor good nor evil, are able to transgress this eternal bund of existence" (S. 7. a). "It is at the command of this imperishable existence," says the *Bṛhadāraṇyaka Upaniṣad*, "that the sun and the moon stand bound in their places. It is due to the command of this Absolute that the heaven

and the earth stand each in its own place. It is due to the command of this imperishable Brahman that the very moments, the hours, the days, the nights, the months, the seasons, and the years have their appointed function in the scheme of things. It is at the command of this Brahman that some rivers flow to the east from the snow-clad mountains, while others flow to the west" (S. 7. b). We shall not try to disentangle here the personal and impersonal aspects of the physico-theological proof, the aspect of design and the aspect of order. Suffice it to say that the physico-theological proof is present in the Upaniṣads, pointing out that the Absolute must be regarded as the ballast of the cosmos, preventing it from rocking to and fro at the slightest gust of chance.

Regress from polytheism to monotheism

II—The Theological Approach

9. We shall now see how the Upaniṣadic philosophers went by the theological approach to the conception of reality. They began by inquiring how many gods must be supposed to exist in the universe. They could not rest content until they arrived at the idea of one God, who was the ruler of the whole universe. Ultimately, they identified this God with the inner Self in man. In this way did theological categories become subservient to the psychological category of the Self. We shall see how this happens. In the controversy which took place between Vidagdha Śākalya and the sage Yājñavalkya as reported in the *Bṛhadāraṇyaka*, we are told that the former asked Yājñavalkya how many gods must be regarded as existing in the world, to which the first answer of Yājñavalkya was "three and three hundred," Yājñavalkya closely following upon this by saying that there were "three and three thousand." Not satisfied with the answers, Śākalya asked again how many gods there were. Yājñavalkya replied there were thirty-three gods. Śākalya was again dissatisfied and asked again. Yājñavalkya replied there were six gods. In answer to further inquiries from Śākalya, Yājñavalkya went on to say that there were three gods, and then two gods, and even one-and-a-half (!) god, and finally that there was only one God without a second. Yājñavalkya was merely testing the insight of Śākalya as to whether he would rest satisfied with the different answers that he first gave, and when Śākalya did not seem satisfied, he finally said that there was only one God. By mutual consent, Śākalya and Yājñavalkya came to the conclusion that He alone is the God of the Universe, "whose body the earth is, whose sight is fire, whose mind is light, and who is the final resort of all human souls" (S. 8. a).

The theistic conception of God and His identification with the Self

10. The *Śvetāśvatara Upaniṣad* develops this conception of a personal God. In a theistic vein it declares how the one God, whom it calls Rudra, beside whom there is no second, and who rules the worlds with his powers, stands behind all persons, creates all the worlds, and, in the end of time, rolls them up again. He has his eyes everywhere, and his face everywhere; his hands and feet are also omnipresent. He creates the men of earth and endows them with hands. He creates the fowl of air and endows them with wings. He is the only God who has created the heaven and the earth (S. 8. b). In a later passage of the same Upaniṣad, the author inquires further into the nature and attributes of this God. He calls him the only Lord of the universe, the creator, the preserver, and the destroyer of all. He ends by declaring that it is only to those who regard this God as identical with the Self within,—to those belongs eternal happiness, to none else: "Some so-called wise men, being under a great philosophic delusion, regard Nature, and others Time, as the source of being. They forget that it is the greatness of the Lord, which causes the wheel of Brahman to turn round. It is by Him that all this has been covered. He is the only knower, he is death to the god of death, the possessor of all qualities and wisdom. It is at His command that creation unfolds itself, namely, what people call earth, water, fire, air and ether. He is the permanent as well as the accidental cause of unions. He is beyond the past, the present, and the future, and is truly regarded as without parts. That universal God, who is immanent in all these beings, should be meditated upon as dwelling in our minds also—that God who is the Lord of all gods, who is the Deity of all deities, who is the supreme Master of all masters, and who is the adorable Ruler of the universe. There is no cause of Him, nor any effect. There is none equal to Him, nor any superior. The great power inherent in Him manifests itself alike in the form of knowledge and action. There is no master of Him in this world, nor any ruler, nor is there anything which we might regard as His sign. He is the only Cause, the Lord of all those who possess sense-organs. There is no generator of Him, nor any protector. He is the self-subsistent mover of the unmoving manifold, who causes the one seed to sprout in infinite ways. It is only to those who regard this Universal Being as immanent in their own Selves, to them belongs eternal happiness, to none else" (S. 8. c). In this theistic description of the *Svetāśvatara Upaniṣad* we are told how God is the only cause of the world, and how ultimately he is to be regarded as identical with the Self within. Here again the purely theological category becomes subservient to the psychological category of the Self; and it seems as if the ultimate category of existence to the Upaniṣadic philosophers is God-*Ātman*.

The immanence-transcendence of God

11. The Upaniṣads are not without reference to the immanence and transcendence of God. There are some passages which declare merely his immanence, others merely his transcendence; others again bring together the two aspects of the immanence and transcendence of God. Thus, for example, we are told in the *Śvetāśvatara Upaniṣad* that "God is to be regarded as being present in fire and in water, in all the universe, in the herbs and plants." In the *Bṛhadāraṇyaka Upaniṣad* we are told how God-*Ātman* is immanent in us from top to toe, as a razor is entirely closed up within the razor-box, or again, as a bird is pent up within its nest. A story from the *Chāndogya Upaniṣad* also brings into relief this aspect of the immanence of God. We are told there how the disciple was asked by his teacher to place a small piece of salt in water at night, and come to him in the morning; how the disciple did as he was commanded; how, when the teacher asked him what had become of the salt, the disciple could not find it out because it had already melted in the water; how when the teacher asked him to taste the water from the surface, then from the middle, and then from the bottom, the disciple replied that it was salt in all places; then how the teacher told him that the salt, even though it seemed to have disappeared in the water, was thoroughly present in every part of it. Thus, verily, says the clever teacher, is that subtle *Ātman* immanent in the universe, whom we may not be able to see, but whom we must regard as existing as the supreme object of faith (S. 9. a). All these passages speak of the thorough immanence of God. A passage from the *Kaṭhopaniṣad*, which reminds us of a similar one from the *Republic* of Plato, which speaks of the Sun of the world of Ideas, tells us how the universal Self is to be regarded as beyond all the happiness and the misery of the world—"like the celestial Sun who is the eye of all the universe and is untouched by the defects of our vision" (S. 9. b). Here the transcendence of God is clearly brought into relief. In other passages, we are also told how God is to be regarded as having "filled the whole world and yet remained beyond its confines." "Like the fire and the wind which enter the world and assume various forms, the universal *Ātman* is immanent in every part of the universe and protrudes beyond its confines." "Verily motionless like a lone tree does this God stand in the heaven and yet by Him is this whole world filled." This is how the *Śvetāśvatara Upaniṣad* declares the transcendence and immanence of God (S. 9. c). We see from all these passages how God-*Ātman* is to be regarded as having filled every nook and cranny of the Universe, and yet having overflowed it to a limitless extent. In any case, the God in the universe is to be regarded as identical with the Self within us: it is only when this identification takes place that we arrive, according to the Upaniṣadic philosophers, at the ultimate conception of Reality.

III—The Psychological Approach

The conception of the Self reached by an analysis of the various physiological and psychological categories

12. Let us now proceed to see how the Upaniṣadic philosophers reached the idea of ultimate reality by the psychological method. In a conversation which took place between King Janaka and Yājñavalkya as reported in the *Bṛhadāraṇyaka Upaniṣad*, we find that Yājñavalkya asked Janaka as to what psychological doctrines he had heard about the nature of ultimate reality. Janaka was a very inquisitive and philosophically inclined king, and he had therefore known all the opinions on that head which had been imparted to him by different sages. He proceeded to tell Yājñavalkya the opinions of these various philosophers. "Jitvan Śailini told me," said king Janaka, "that speech was the ultimate reality." Yājñavalkya answered that this was merely a partial truth. Then king Janaka told him that Udaṅka Śaulbāyana had said to him that breath was the ultimate reality. This also, said Yājñavalkya, was only a partial truth. Varku Vārshṇi had told him, said Janaka, that the eye was the final reality. This again, said Yājñavalkya, was only a partial truth. Then the king went on to say how Gardabhī-vipīta Bhāradvāja had told him that the ear was the final reality; how Satyakāma Jābāla had said that the mind was the final reality; how Vidagdha Śākalya had told him that the heart was the final reality;—all of which opinions, said Yājñavalkya, were only partial truths (S. 10. a). In this enumeration of the opinions of different Upaniṣadic philosophers as regards the various physiological or psychological categories as constituting the ultimate reality, and in Yājñavalkya's rejection of each one of them in turn, there lies implicitly the conception that ultimate reality can be found only in the Self, and not in the accidental adjuncts with which the Self may come to be clothed. This same idea has been developed in the *Kenopaniṣad* where we are told that "the Self must be regarded as the ear of ear, as the mind of mind, as the speech of speech, as the breath of breath, as the eye of eye. Those who know the Self thus are released from this world and become immortal." "That which speech is unable to give out, but that which itself gives out speech, know that to be the ultimate reality, not that which people worship in vain. That which the mind is unable to think, but which thinks the mind, know that to be the ultimate reality; that which the eye is unable to see, but that which enables us to see the eye, know that to be the ultimate reality; that which the ear does not hear, but that which enables us to perceive the ear, that which breath is not able to breathe, but that by which breath itself is breathed, know that to be the final reality" (S. 10. b.). In this passage we are told that the Self must be regarded as the innermost

existence, while all the physiological and psychological elements are only external vestures, which clothe reality but which do not constitute it.

The states of consciousness: waking-consciousness, dream-consciousness, sleep-consciousness, Self-consciousness

13. We now come to a very famous parable in the *Chāndogya Upaniṣad* which unmistakably tells us how we must arrive at the conception of the Self-conscious Being within us as constituting the ultimate reality. In a very clever analysis of the psychological states through which a man's soul passes, the author of that Upaniṣad brings out how the ultimate reality must not be mistaken with bodily consciousness; how it must not be confused with the dream-consciousness; how it transcends even the deep-sleep-consciousness; how, finally, it is the pure Self-consciousness, which is beyond all bodily or mental limitations. We are told in the *Chāndogya Upaniṣad* that the gods and demons were, once upon a time, both anxious to learn the nature of final reality, and they therefore went in pursuit of it to Prajāpati. Prajāpati had maintained that "that entity, which is free from sin, free from old age, free from death and grief, free from hunger and thirst, which desires nothing, and imagines nothing, must be regarded as the ultimate self." The gods and demons were anxious to know what this Self was. So the gods sent Indra and the demons Virochana as their emissaries to learn the final truth from Prajāpati. They dwelt there as pupils at first for a period of thirty-two years, which condition was necessary before a master could impart spiritual wisdom to his disciples. Then Prajāpati asked them what it was that had brought them there. Indra and Virochana told him that they had come to him in order that they might know the nature of the Self. Now Prajāpati would not immediately tell them the final truth. He tried to delude them by saying first that the Self was nothing more than the image that we see in the eye, in water, or in a mirror. It was this, he said, which must be regarded as the immortal and fearless Brahman. Indra and Virochana became complacent in the belief that they had understood the nature of the Self. They bedecked themselves by putting on excellent clothes and ornaments, cleaned themselves, looked into a water-pan, and imagined they had visualised the ultimate Self, and went altogether composed in mind. Virochana told the demons that he had been in possession of the ultimate secret, namely, that the so-called Self was no other than the image that one sees in the eye, in a mirror, or in a pan of water, thus identifying the Self with the mere image of the body. The Upaniṣad tells us how there are a certain set of people who take this as final gospel, which it calls the gospel of the Asuras. There must be a slight reference here to those, who, like the later

Cārvākas, maintained that the Self was nothing more than the mere consciousness of body. Indra, however, unlike Virochana, bethought himself that Prajāpati must not have given him the final answer in the matter of the knowledge of ultimate reality. There was this difficulty that pressed itself before him. "It is true," he said, "that, when the body is well adorned, the Self is well adorned; when the body is well dressed, the Self is well dressed; when the body is well cleaned, the Self is well cleaned; but what if the body were blind, or lame, or crippled? Shall not the Soul itself be thus regarded as blind, or lame, or crippled"? He thought that there was this great difficulty in the teaching that had been imparted to him by Prajāpati, and so he went back again to Prajāpati to request him once more to tell him what ultimate reality was. Prajāpati advised him to practise penance once more for thirty-two years, and, when Indra had performed that penance, Prajāpati supplied him with another piece of knowledge. "The true Self is he," said Prajāpati, "who moves about happy in dreams. He is the immortal, the fearless Brahman." In fact, Prajāpati told him that dream-consciousness must be regarded as identical with the Self. This seemed to please Indra and he went back; but before he reached the gods, he saw again that there was another difficulty in the information that had been imparted to him by Prajāpati. "Do we not feel," he asked himself, "as if we are struck, or chased in our dreams? Do we not experience pain, and do we not shed tears in our dreams? How can we account for this difficulty if the Self were to be identified with dream-consciousness?" So he went back to Prajāpati again, and told him that the knowledge which he had imparted to him could not be final, inasmuch as the dream-consciousness seemed to him to be affected with feelings of pain and fear. The true Self could experience neither pain nor fear. Prajāpati saw that Indra was a pupil worthy to know better things, and so he asked him once more to practise penance for another thirty-two years, at the end of which time he imparted to him another piece of knowledge which was yet not the highest knowledge, namely, when he said, that the true Self must be regarded as identical with the deep-sleep consciousness in which there is perfect repose and perfect rest. Indra was satisfied with the answer which Prajāpati had given and returned. But before he reached the gods, he again saw that the real Self could not be identified even with deep-sleep consciousness for the simple reason that in deep-sleep we are conscious neither of our own selves nor of objects. In fact, in deep-sleep we are as if we were only logs of wood. There is neither consciousness of self nor consciousness of the objective world. Feeling this great difficulty in the teaching that had been imparted to him by Prajāpati, he went back again and told him that he could not be satisfied with the knowledge which had been imparted to him, namely that the ultimate Self was to be found in the consciousness of deep-sleep. For, he said, in that state there was neither self-consciousness, nor any consciousness of the objective world; and it seemed as if the soul was entirely annihilated in that state. This could not be regarded, said Indra, as the final wisdom. Prajāpati now saw that Indra by his shrewd insight had made himself worthy of receiving the highest knowledge. So he asked Indra once more, and this time finally, to practise penance for five years again. Indra practised penance for five years, thus completing the round of penance for a hundred and one years. At the end of that period, he went in all humility to Prajāpati and implored him to give him an insight into the final knowledge. Prajāpati said, "Verily, O Indra, this body is subject to death, but it is at the same time the vesture of an immortal Soul. It is only when the Soul is encased in the body, that it is cognisant of pleasure and pain. There is neither pleasure nor pain for the Soul once relieved of its body. Just as the wind and the cloud, the lightning and the thunder, are without body, and arise from heavenly space and appear in their own form, so does this serene being, namely, the Self, arise from this mortal body, reach the highest light, and then appear in his own form. This Serene Being, who appears in his own form is the highest Person." There is here an indication of the true nature of ultimate reality as being of the nature of self-consciousness. That which sees itself by itself, that which recognises itself as identical with itself in the light of supreme knowledge—that must be regarded as the final reality. The final reality, therefore, according to the *Chāndogya Upaniṣad*, is reached in that theoretic, ecstatic, self-spectacular state in which the Self is conscious of nothing but itself. (S. 11). There is a great meaning which runs through this parable. By an analysis of the different states of consciousness, the philosopher of the *Chhāndogya Upaniṣad* points out that the bodily consciousness must not be mistaken for final reality nor the consciousness in dreams, nor that in deep sleep. The Soul is of the nature of pure self-consciousness, the Kantian "I am I." Those who mistake the ultimate Self as identical with bodily consciousness are the materialists. Those who identify it with the consciousness in the dream-state rise a little higher no doubt, but they mistake the Self for what the modern Theosophists call the "etheric double." Those, on the other hand, who regard the Self as identical with deep-sleep consciousness also misunderstand its nature, because there is in that state no consciousness either of the object world or of the Self. The true Self could only be the self-conscious Being, shining in his own native light, thinking of nothing but his own thought, the νοησις νοήσεως of Aristotle, the supreme theoretic Being, the eternal Self-spectator.

The ontological argument for the existence of the Self

14. We have hitherto seen how the philosopher of the *Chāndogya Upaniṣad* arrives at the conception of Self-consciousness as constituting the ultimate

reality. We have seen also how the Upaniṣadic philosophers generally regard God as identical with this pure self-consciousness. The philosopher of the *Taittirīya Upaniṣad* gives us certain characteristics of this final reality which enable us to regard his argument as almost an ontological characterisation of reality. "The Absolute," he says, "is Existence, Consciousness, and Infinity" (S. 12. a). In this identification of the Absolute with Consciousness, we have again the real nature of the *Ātman* brought out in bold relief. Existence to that philosopher means Consciousness. The same idea is repeated elsewhere in the *Aitareya Upaniṣad*, where the author of that Upaniṣad speaks "of the gods of the heaven and the beings of the earth, whether produced from eggs, or embryo, or sweat, or from the earth, everything that moves, or flies, or is stationary—Self-consciousness is the eye of all these. They are rooted in Self-consciousness. Self-consciousness is the eye of the world; it is Self-consciousness which is the Absolute" (S. 12. b). Here we have unmistakably the ontological argument, namely, that ultimate Existence must be identified with Self-consciousness. Thus by a survey of the different approaches to the problem of Reality, namely, the cosmological, the theological, and the psychological, we see that the Upaniṣadic philosophers try to establish Reality on the firm footing of Self-consciousness. Self-consciousness to them is the eternal verity. God to them is not God, unless he is identical with Self-consciousness. Existence is not Existence if it does not mean Self-consciousness. Reality is not reality, if it does not express throughout its structure the marks of pure Self-consciousness. Self-consciousness thus constitutes the ultimate category of existence to the Upaniṣadic philosophers.

IV—The Significance of Self-consciousness

Self-consciousness: its epistemological and metaphysical significance contrasted with the mystical

15. The great question that now confronts the Upaniṣadic seeker after truth is: if Self-consciousness is the final reality, how would it be possible for us to realise it? Can bare intellect suffice to give us a vision of this final reality, or is there any other process beyond the reach of intelligence which has the power of taking us within the portals of pure Self-consciousness? The Upaniṣadic answer is that mere intellect would be lame to enable us to realise pure Self-consciousness. Pure Self-consciousness could only be reached in a state of mystic realisation. Whether the mystical faculty, which may be called intuition, is higher than, analogous to, or included in the faculty of intellect, whose product all philosophy is, we shall not stop here to consider. It raises a large problem which does not lie within the scope of this work.

We shall, however, try to describe it partly in our last Chapter on "The Intimations of Self-Realisation," where we shall see how it would be possible mystically to realise Self-consciousness. Our answer there would evidently be the super-sensuous and the super-intellectual answer. Intuition, as we shall see, is a superior faculty to either mere sensuous perception, or intellective apprehension. At present, however, we are concerned merely with the "philosophic" aspect of pure Self-consciousness, which may be looked at from two different points of view, the epistemological and the metaphysical. We shall see first what the epistemological aspect of Self-consciousness is according to the Upaniṣads, and then shall end this chapter by bringing out its full metaphysical significance, reserving the mystical aspect of it for our last chapter.

The Epistemology of Self-consciousness

16. Epistemologically, we are told in various passages of the Upaniṣads, it would not be possible for us to know the Self in the technical meaning of the word "knowledge." Our readers might bring to mind the fact that Kant equally well regarded Reality, as consisting of God and the Self, as technically unknowable. These were, he said, merely matters of faith. The Upaniṣadic answer is that it is true that God and the Self are unknowable, but they are not merely objects of faith, they are objects of mystical realisation. Then, again, the Upaniṣads do not regard the Self as unknowable in the agnostic sense of the word, for example, in the sense in which Spencer understands it. Rather, it is "unknowable" from the standpoint of philosophic humility.

(i) The *Ātman*, say the Upaniṣadic philosophers, is unknowable in his essential nature. "That, from which our speech turns back along with mind, being unable to comprehend its fulness, is the ultimate reality," says the *Taittirīya Upaniṣad*. "That where the eye is unable to go, where neither speech nor mind is able to reach—what conception can we have of it, except that it is beyond all that is known, and beyond all that is unknown!" says the *Kenopaniṣad*. The philosopher of that Upaniṣad says in an Augustinian mood that he who thinks he knows does not know, while he who thinks he does not know does really know. *Cognoscendo ignorari, et ignorando cognosci*. The *Kaṭhopaniṣad* in a similar vein says that "the Self is not in the first instance open to the hearing of men, but that even having heard him, many are unable to know him. Wonderful is the man, if found, who is able to speak about him; wonderful, indeed, is he who is able to comprehend him in accordance with the instruction of a teacher" (S. 13. a). We see in all these passages how the *Ātman* is to be regarded as unknowable in his essential nature.

(ii) There is, however, another side to the subject of the unknowability of *Ātman*. The *Ātman* is unknowable because He is the Eternal Subject who knows. How could the Eternal Knower, ask the Upaniṣads in various places, be an object of knowledge? "The *Ātman* is the Great Being," says the *Śvetāśvatara Upaniṣad* "who knows all that is knowable; who can know him who himself knows?" In the *Bṛhadāraṇyaka Upaniṣad*, in various passages, we are put in possession of the bold speculations of the philosopher Yājñavalkya. "That by whom everything is known, how could he himself be known? It is impossible to know the knower." "It would not be possible for us to see the seer, to hear the hearer, to think the thinker, and to apprehend him by whom everything is apprehended." "He is the eternal seer without himself being seen; he is the eternal hearer without himself being heard; he is the only thinker without himself being thought; he is the only comprehender without any one to comprehend him; beyond him there is no seer, beyond him there is no hearer, beyond him there is no thinker, beyond him there is no being who comprehends" (S. 13. b.) We thus see that the question of the unknowability of *Ātman* has another aspect also, namely, that He is unknowable because He is the Eternal Subject of knowledge, and cannot be an object of knowledge to another beside Him.

(iii) But this raises another fundamental question. Granted that the Self is the eternal knower of objects, granted also there is no other knower of him, would it be possible for the knower to know himself? This very subtle question was asked of Yājñavalkya in another passage of the *Bṛhadāraṇyaka Upaniṣad*, and here again we see the brilliant light which the sage Yājñavalkya throws on the problem. It *is* possible, he says, for the knower to know himself. In fact, Self-knowledge or Self-consciousness is the ultimate category of existence. The Self can become an object of knowledge to himself. According to the philosophy of Yājñavalkya, nothing is possible, if self-consciousness is not possible. Self-consciousness is the ultimate fact of existence. We see here how boldly Yājñavalkya regards both introspection and self-consciousness as the verities of experience. We also see the nudity of the doctrines of Kant and Comte when they try to deny the fact of introspection. Introspection is a psychological process corresponding to Self-consciousness as a metaphysical reality. Self-consciousness is possible only through the process of introspection. The Self is endowed with the supreme power of dichotomising himself. The empirical conditions of knowledge are inapplicable to the Self. The Self can divide himself into the knower and the known. It is wonderful how Kant should have posited the "I am I" as the supreme metaphysical category, which he called the transcendental, original, and synthetic unity of apperception, and yet should have denied the reality of the corresponding psychological process of introspection. The answer of Yājñavalkya is that Self-consciousness *is* possible, and is not only possible, but alone real. King Janaka asked Yājñavalkya what was the light of man. Yājñavalkya first said that the light of man was the sun. It is on account of the sun that man is able to sit and to move about, to go forth for work, and to return. "When the sun has set, O Yājñavalkya," asked king Janaka "what is the light of man?" Yājñavalkya said that then the moon was the light of man. For, having the moon for light, man could sit, and move about, and do his work, and return. "When both the sun and the moon have set," asked king Janaka, "what is the light of man?" "Fire indeed," said Yājñavalkya, "is man's light. For having fire for his light, man can sit and move about, do his work, and return." "When the sun has set, when the moon has set, and when the fire is extinguished, what is the light of man?" asked Janaka. "Now, verily," says Yājñavalkya, "you are pressing me to the deepest question. When the sun has set, when the moon has set, and when the fire is extinguished, the Self alone is his light" (S. 13. c.). Yājñavalkya is here clearly positing what Aristotle called "*theoria*," the act of pure self-contemplation in which the Self is most mysteriously both the subject and object of knowledge,

The Metaphysics of Self-consciousness

17. We have seen, hitherto, the epistemological significance of the conception of pure Self-consciousness in the Upaniṣads. We have seen that the Self is regarded as unknowable in his essential nature, as well as because he cannot be an object of knowledge. We have seen also that he can dichotomise himself and make himself at once the knower and the known. It remains for us now to discourse on what may be called the metaphysical significance of the conception of Self-consciousneess. In the preceding Chapter we have seen how the whole field of philosophic thought was torn by the conflicts of the metaphysicians, some regarding the Self as entirely distinct from the Absolute, others regarding it as a part of the Absolute, and yet others regarding the Self and the Absolute as entirely identical. These constitute respectively the fundamental positions of the three great metaphysical schools—the dualistic, the quasi-monistic, and the monistic. Never has any land possibly experienced such bitter and prolonged argumentative battles as were witnessed in India throughout the history of its thought. The question arises: Is there any way out of the difficulty? How is it that each of these different metaphysical

schools comes to interpret the same Upaniṣadic passages as confirming its own special metaphysical doctrines? Shall we not say that the Upaniṣads are higher than the Commentators? Is there not a common body of metaphysical doctrine in the Upaniṣads which each of the metaphysical schools has only partially envisaged? Is the utterance of that greatest of Indian philosophers to be regarded as vain, when he said that the Schools may battle among themselves, but yet that Philosophy is above the Schools? May we not find a supreme clue to the reconciliation of these different battling doctrines? We must go back to the Upaniṣads themselves, with our mind entirely purged of all scholastic interpretation. Let us make our mind a *tabula rasa*, an unwritten slate upon which there is no hurtful imprint of scholastic superstition, and we shall see that there is a clue through the labyrinth and mazes of the philosophic conflicts. It is true that the reconciliation of the different schools must come, if at all, only through mystical experince. It is only in mystic experience that each school and each doctrine can have its own appointed place and level. But it may also be granted to us to look even philosophically at the problem, to go back to the texts of the Upaniṣads themselves, to arrange them in a serial order of developing philosophical propositions, and finally to see a vista of supreme reconciliation spreading out before us among the battling forces.

The Ladder of Spiritual Experience

18. We may arrange the different stages of spiritual experience, as developed in the Upaniṣads, philosophically interpreted, in a series of five developing propositions. We may regard them as constituting the ladder of spiritual experience with a series of five ascending steps. The first stage of spiritual experience would consist, according to *Bṛhadāraṇyaka Upaniṣad*, in realising the Self, in mystically apprehending the glory of the Self within us, as though we were distinct from him (S. 14. a). Now comes the second stage. Another passage from the *theoria* tells us that the Being, which calls itself the "I" within us, must be identified with the Self that is hithertofore realised. We must experience that we are really the very Self, and that we are neither the bodily, or the sensuous, or the intellectual, or the emotional vestures; that we are in our essential nature entirely identical with the pure Self. This is the second stage (S. 14. b). In the third stage of spiritual experience, we must come to realise, according to *theoria*, that the Self that we have realised is identical with the Absolute. This same identification of the Ātman and the Brahman, of the Individual Spirit and the Universal Spirit, of the Self and the Absolute, is also proclaimed by the epistolary stanza of the *Īśa* and its cognate Upaniṣads, where we are told that the *Ātman* must be regarded as verily the Brahman, that the *Ātman* is infinite in its nature

as also the Brahman, that the *Ātman* derives its being from Brahman, that subtracting the infinity of the *Ātman* from the infinity of the Brahman, the residuum is even infinite. Thus does that epistolary stanza pile infinities over infinities, and, taking the mathematical lead, speak as if when the infinity of the *Ātman* is deducted from the infinity of the Brahman, the remainder itself is infinite. The inner meaning of this assertion is that we should see that there is no difference between the Self and the Absolute. This constitutes the third stage (S. 14. c). Now comes the fourth. If the Being that calls itself the "I" within us is the *Ātman* according to our second proposition, and if it is to be entirely identified with the Brahman according to our third proposition; that is, in other words, if I am the Self, and the Self is the Absolute; then, it follows syllogistically that I am the Absolute. This is unmistakably inculcated by a passage of *Bṛhadāraṇyaka Upaniṣad*, where we are told that we must identify the "I" with the Absolute. Another aspect of the same doctrine is proclaimed in the *Chāndogya Upaniṣad*, where the "Thou" comes also to be "projectively" identified with the Absolute. This constitutes the fourth stage (S. 14. d.). If now the "I" is the Absolute, and if also the "Thou" is equally the Absolute, if, in other words, both the subject and object are the Absolute, then it follows that everything that we see in this world, Mind and Nature, the Self and the not-Self, equally constitute the Absolute. Whatever falls within the ken of apprehension, equally with whatever we are, goes to make up the fulness of the Absolute. The Brahman according to the *Chāndogya Upaniṣad* is verily the "ALL" (S. 14. e). To such a giddy height does the philosophic ladder take us on the rising steps of philosophic thought. This is verily the position of Absolute Monism. Whether this state of Absolute Monism is to be merely intellectually apprehended, or mystically realised, depends upon whether we are by nature destined to be merely torch-bearers or mystics in the spiritual pilgrimage. That we should prefer the second alternative will be evident in our last Chapter on the "Intimations of Self-Realisation."

Vivekananda, Jñāna Yoga (1915)

Swami Vivekananda (1863–1902) was born Narendranatha Dutta. He became the principal disciple of the Advaita Vedānta scholar/saint Sri Ramakrishna, was founder of the Ramakrishna mission, and was one of the principal exponents of Advaita Vedānta in the late 19th century. Vivekananda came to international prominence following his dramatic addresses to the World Parliament of Religions in Chicago in 1893. He introduced Vedānta philosophy to the United States and Europe, where he taught extensively and established Vedānta societies. The present essay is a remarkable exposition of the concept of *māyā* in Vedānta philosophy, demonstrating both its relevance to ordinary experience and how to interpret this doctrine in the context of modernity.

Swami Vivekananda

2

Jñāna–Yoga

THE REAL NATURE OF MAN

(Delivered in London)

GREAT IS THE tenacity with which man clings to the senses. Yet, however substantial he may think the external world in which he lives and moves, there comes a time in the lives of individuals and of races when, involuntarily, they ask, "Is this real?" To the person who never finds a moment to question the credentials of his senses, whose every moment is occupied with some sort of sense-enjoyment—even to him death comes, and he also is compelled to ask, "Is this real?" Religion begins with this question and ends with its answer. Even in the remote past, where recorded history cannot help us, in the mysterious light of mythology, back in the dim twilight of civilisation, we find the same question was asked, "What becomes of this? What is real?"

One of the most poetical of the Upaniṣads, the *Kaṭhopaniṣad*, begins with the inquiry: "When a man dies, there is a dispute. One party declares that he has gone for ever, the other insists that he is still living. Which is true?" Various answers have been given. The whole sphere of metaphysics, philosophy, and religion is really filled with various answers to this question. At the same time, attempts have been made to suppress it, to put a stop to the unrest of mind which asks, "What is beyond? What is real?" But so long as death remains, all these attempts at suppression will always prove to be unsuccessful. We may talk about seeing nothing beyond and keeping all our hopes and aspirations confined to the present moment, and struggle hard not to think of anything beyond the world of senses; and, perhaps, everything outside helps to keep us limited within its narrow bounds. The whole world may combine to prevent us from broadening out beyond the present. Yet, so long as there is death, the question must come again and again, "Is death the end of all these things to which we are clinging, as if they were the most real of all realities, the most substantial of all substances?" The world vanishes in a moment and is gone. Standing on the brink of a precipice beyond which is the infinite yawning chasm, every mind, however hardened, is bound to recoil and ask, "Is this real?" The hopes of a lifetime, built up little by little with all the energies of a great mind, vanish in a second. Are they real? This question must be answered. Time never lessens its power; on the other hand, it adds strength to it.

Then there is the desire to be happy. We run after everything to make ourselves happy; we pursue our mad career in the external world of senses. If you ask the young man with whom life is successful, he will declare that it is real; and he really thinks so. Perhaps, when the same man grows old and finds fortune ever eluding him, he will then declare that it is fate. He finds at last that his desires cannot be fulfilled. Wherever he goes, there is an adamantine wall beyond which he cannot pass. Every sense-activity results in a reaction. Everything is evanescent. Enjoyment, misery, luxury, wealth, power, and poverty, even life itself, are all evanescent.

Two positions remain to mankind. One is to believe with the nihilists that all is nothing that we know nothing, that we can never know anything either about the future, the past, or even the present. For we must remember that he who denies the past and the future and wants to stick to the present is simply a madman. One may as well deny the father and mother and assert the child. It would be equally logical. To deny the past and future, the present must inevitably be denied also. This is one position, that of the nihilists. I have never seen a man who could really become a nihilist for one minute. It is very easy to talk.

Then there is the other position—to seek for an explanation, to seek for the real, to discover in the midst of this eternally changing and evanescent world whatever is real. In this body which is an aggregate of molecules of matter, is there anything which is real? This has been the search throughout the history of the human mind. In the very oldest times, we often find glimpses of light coming into men's minds. We find man, even then, going a step beyond this body, finding something which is not this external body, although very much like it, much more complete, much more perfect, and which remains even when this body is dissolved. We read in the hymns of the *Ṛgveda*, addressed to the God of Fire who is burning a dead body, "Carry him, O Fire, in your arms gently, give him a perfect body, a bright body, carry him where the fathers live, where there is no more sorrow, where there is no more death."

The same idea you will find present in every religion. And we get another idea with it. It is a significant fact that all religions, without one exception, hold that man is a degeneration of what he was, whether they clothe this in mythological words, or in the clear language of philosophy, or in the beautiful expressions of poetry. This is the one fact that comes out of every scripture and of every mythology that the man that is is a degeneration of what he was. This is the kernel of truth within the story of Adam's fall in the Jewish scripture. This is again and again repeated in the scriptures of the Hindus: the dream of a period which they call the age of truth, when no man died unless he wished to die, when he could keep his body as long as he liked, and his mind was pure and strong. There was no evil, and no misery; and the present age is a corruption of that state of perfection.

Side by side with this, we find everywhere the story of the deluge. That story itself is a proof that this present age is held by every religion to be a corruption of a former age. It went on becoming more and more corrupt until the deluge swept away a large portion of mankind and again the ascending series began. It is going up slowly again, to reach once more that early state of purity. You are all aware of the story of the deluge in the Old Testament. The same story was current among the ancient Babylonians, the Egyptians, the Chinese, and the Hindus.

Manu, a great ancient sage, was praying on the bank of the Ganges, when a little minnow came to him for protection, and he put it into a pot of water he had before him. "What do you want?" asked Manu. The little minnow declared that it was pursued by a bigger fish and wanted protection. Manu carried the little fish home with him. By morning the fish had become as big as the pot and he said, "I cannot live in this pot any longer." Manu put him in a tank, and the next day he was as big as the tank and declared he could not live there any more. So Manu had to take him to a river, and in the morning the fish filled the river. Then Manu put him in the ocean, and he declared, "Manu, I am the Creator of the universe. I have taken this form to come and warn you that I will deluge the world. You build an ark and in it put a pair of every kind of animals, and let your family enter the ark, and there will project out of the water my horn. Fasten the ark to it; and when the deluge subsides, come out and people the earth." So the world was deluged, and Manu saved his own family and two of every kind of animal and seeds of every plant. When the deluge subsided, he came and peopled the world; and we are all called "man", because we are the progeny of Manu.

Now, human language is the attempt to express the truth that is within. I am fully persuaded that a baby whose language consists of unintelligible sounds is attempting to express the highest philosophy, only the baby has not the organs to express it nor the means. The difference between the language of the highest philosophers and the utterances of babies is one of degree and not of kind. What you call the most correct, systematic, mathematical language of the present time, and the hazy, mystical, mythological languages of the ancients, differ only in clarity. Both of them have a grand idea behind, which is, as it were, struggling to express itself; and often behind these ancient mythologies are nuggets of truth; and often, I am sorry to say, behind the fine, polished phrases of the moderns is arrant trash. So, we need not throw a thing overboard because it is clothed in mythology, because it does not fit in with the notions of Mr. So-and-so or Mrs. So-and-so of modern times. If people should laugh at religion because most religions declare that men must believe in mythologies taught by such and such a prophet, they ought to laugh more at these moderns. In modern times, if a man quotes a Moses or a Buddha or a Christ, he is laughed at; but let him give the name of a Huxley, a Tyndall, or a Darwin, and it is swallowed without salt. "Huxley has said it", that is enough for many. We are free from superstitions indeed! That was a religious superstition, and this is a scientific superstition; only, in and through that superstition came life-giving ideas of spirituality; in and through this modern superstition come lust and greed. That superstition was worship of God, and this superstition is worship of filthy lucre, of fame or power. That is the difference.

To return to mythology. Behind all these stories we find one idea standing supreme—that man is a degeneration of what he was. Coming to the present times, modern research seems to repudiate this position absolutely. Evolutionists seem to contradict entirely this assertion. According to them, man is the evolution of the mollusc; and, therefore, what mythology states cannot be true. There is in India, however, a mythology which is able to reconcile both these positions. The Indian mythology has a theory of cycles, that all progression is in the form of waves. Every wave is attended by a fall, and that by a rise the next moment, that by a fall in the next, and again another rise. The motion is in cycles. Certainly it is true, even on the grounds of modern research, that man cannot be simply an evolution. Every evolution presupposes an involution. The modern scientific man will tell you that you can only get the amount of energy out of a machine which you have previously put into it. Something cannot be produced out of nothing. If a man is an evolution of the mollusc, then the perfect man—the Buddha-man, the Christ-man—was involved in the mollusc. If it is not so, whence come these gigantic personalities? Something cannot come out of nothing.

Thus we are in the position of reconciling the scriptures with modern light. That energy which manifests itself slowly through various stages until it becomes the perfect man cannot come out of nothing. It existed somewhere; and if the mollusc or the protoplasm is the first point to which you can trace it, that protoplasm, somehow or other, must have contained the energy.

There is a great discussion going on as to whether the aggregate of materials we call the body is the cause of manifestation of the force we call the soul, thought, etc., or whether it is the thought that manifests this body. The religions of the world of course hold that the force called thought manifests the body, and not the reverse. There are schools of modern thought which hold that what we call thought is simply the outcome of the adjustment of the parts of the machine which we call body. Taking the second position that the soul or the mass of thought, or however you may call it, is the outcome of this machine, the outcome of the chemical and physical combinations of matter making up the body and brain, leaves the question unanswered. What makes the body? What force combines the molecules into the body form? What force is there which takes up material from the mass of matter around and forms my body one way, another body another way, and so on? What makes these infinite distinctions? To say that the force called soul is the outcome of the combinations of the molecules of the body is putting the cart before the horse. How did the combinations come; where was the force to make them? If you say that some other force was the cause of these combinations, and soul was the outcome of that matter, and that soul—which combined a certain mass of matter—was itself the result of the combinations, it is no answer. That theory ought to be taken which explains most of the facts, if not all, and that without contradicting other existing theories. It is more logical to say that the force which takes up the matter and forms the body is the same which manifests through that body.

To say, therefore, that the thought forces manifested by the body are the outcome of the arrangement of molecules and have no independent existence has no meaning; neither can force evolve out of matter. Rather it is possible to demonstrate that what we call matter does not exist at all. It is only a certain state of force. Solidity, hardness, or any other state of matter can be proved to be the result of motion. Increase of vortex motion imparted to fluids gives them the force of solids. A mass of air in vortex motion, as in a tornado, becomes solid-like and by its impact breaks or cuts through solids. A thread of a spider's web, if it could be moved at almost infinite velocity, would be as strong as an iron chain and would cut through an oak tree. Looking at it in this way, it would be easier to prove that what we call matter does not exist. But the other way cannot be proved.

What is the force which manifests itself through the body? It is obvious to all of us, whatever that force be, that it is taking particles up, as it were, and manipulating forms out of them—the human body. None else comes here to manipulate bodies for you and me. I never saw anybody eat food for me. I have to assimilate it, manufacture blood and bones and everything out of that food. What is this mysterious force? Ideas about the future and about the past seem to be terrifying to many. To many they seem to be mere speculation. We will take the present theme. What is this force which is now working through us?

We know how in old times, in all the ancient scriptures, this power, this manifestation of power, was thought to be of a bright substance having the form of this body, and which remained even after this body fell. Later on, however, we find a higher idea coming—that this bright body did not represent the force. Whatsoever has form must be the result of combinations of particles and requires something else behind it to move it. If this body requires something which is not the body to manipulate it, the bright body, by the same necessity, will also require something other than itself to manipulate it. So, that something was called the soul, the *Ātman*, in Sanskrit. It was the *Ātman* which through the bright body, as it were, worked on the gross body outside. The bright body is considered as the receptacle of the mind, and the *Ātman* is beyond that. It is not the mind even; it works the mind, and through the mind, the body. You have an *Ātman*, I have another, each one of us has a separate *Ātman* and a separate fine body, and through that we work on the gross external body. Questions were then asked about this *Ātman*, about its nature. What is this *Ātman*, this soul of man, which is neither the body nor the mind? Great discussions followed. Speculations were made, various shades of philosophic inquiry came into existence; and I shall try to place before you some of the conclusions that have been reached about this *Ātman*.

The different philosophies seem to agree that this *Ātman*, whatever it be, has neither form nor shape, and that which has neither form nor shape must be omnipresent. Time begins with mind, space also is in the mind. Causation cannot stand without time. Without the idea of succession there cannot be any idea of causation. Time, space, and causation, therefore, are in the mind, and as this *Ātman* is beyond the mind and formless, it must be beyond time, beyond space, and beyond causation. Now, if it is beyond time, space, and causation, it must be infinite. Then comes the highest speculation in our philosophy. The infinite cannot be two. If the soul be infinite, there can be only one Soul, and all ideas of various souls—you having one soul, and I having another, and so forth—are not real. The Real Man, therefore, is one and infinite, the omnipresent Spirit. And the apparent man is only a limitation of that Real Man. In that sense the mythologies are true that the apparent man, however great he may be, is only a dim reflection of the Real Man who is beyond. The Real Man, the Spirit, being beyond cause and effect, not bound by time and space, must, therefore, be free. He was never bound, and could not be bound. The apparent man, the reflection, is limited by time, space, and causation, and is, therefore, bound. Or in the language of some of our philosophers, he appears to be bound, but really is not. This is the reality in our souls, this omnipresence, this spiritual nature, this infinity. Every soul is infinite, therefore there is no question of birth and death.

Some children were being examined. The examiner put them rather hard questions, and among them was this one: "Why does not the earth fall?" He wanted to evoke answers about gravitation. Most of the children could not answer at all; a few answered that it was gravitation or something. One bright little girl answered it by putting another question: "Where should it fall?" The question is nonsense. Where should the earth fall? There is no falling or rising for the earth. In infinite space there is no up or down; that is only in the relative. Where is the going or coming for the infinite? Whence should it come and whither should it go?

Thus, when people cease to think of the past or future, when they give up the idea of body, because the body comes and goes and is limited, then they have risen to a higher ideal. The body is not the Real Man, neither is the mind, for the mind waxes and wanes. It is the Spirit beyond, which alone can live for ever. The body and mind are continually changing, and are, in fact, only names of series of changeful phenomena, like rivers whose waters are in a constant state of flux, yet presenting the appearance of unbroken streams. Every particle in this body is continually changing; no one has the same body for many minutes together, and yet we think of it as the same body. So with the mind; one moment it is happy, another moment unhappy; one moment strong, another weak; an ever-changing whirlpool. That cannot be the Spirit which is infinite. Change can only be in the limited. To say that the infinite changes in any way is absurd; it cannot be. You can move and I can move, as limited bodies; every particle in this universe is in a constant state of flux, but taking the universe as a unit, as one whole, it cannot move, it cannot change. Motion is always a relative thing. I move in relation to something else. Any particle in this universe can change in relation to any other particle; but take the whole universe as one, and in relation to what can it move? There is nothing besides it. So this infinite Unit is unchangeable, immovable, absolute, and this is the Real Man. Our reality, therefore, consists in the Universal and not in the limited. These are old delusions, however comfortable they are, to think that we are little limited beings, constantly changing.

People are frightened when they are told that they are Universal Being, everywhere present. Through everything you work, through every foot you move, through every lip you talk, through every heart you feel. People are frightened when they are told this. They will again and again ask you if they are not going to keep their individuality. What is individuality? I should like to see it. A baby has no moustache; when he grows to be a man, perhaps he has a moustache and beard. His individuality would be lost, if it were in the body. If I lose one eye, or if I lose one of my hands, my individuality would be lost if it were in the body. Then, a drunkard should not give up drinking because he would lose his individuality. A thief should not be a good man because he would thereby lose his individuality. No man ought to change his habits for fear of this. There is no individuality except in the Infinite. That is the only condition which does not change. Everything else is in a constant state of flux. Neither can individuality be in memory. Suppose, on account of a blow on the head I forget all about my past; then, I have lost all individuality; I am gone. I do not remember two or three years of my childhood, and if memory and existence are one, then whatever I forget is gone. That part of my life which I do not remember, I did not live. That is a very narrow idea of individuality.

There is no individuality except in the Infinite. That is the only condition which does not change. Everything else is in a state of flux. We are not individuals yet. We are struggling towards individuality, and that is the Infinite, that is the real nature of man. He alone lives whose life is in the whole universe, and the more we concentrate our lives on limited things, the faster we go towards death. Those moments alone we live when our lives are in the universe, in others; and living this little life is death, simply death, and that is why the fear of death comes. The fear of death can only be conquered when man realises that so long as there is one life in this universe, he is living. When he can say, "I am in everything, in everybody, I am in all lives, I am the universe," then alone comes the state of fearlessness. To talk of immortality in constantly changing things is absurd. Says an old Sanskrit philosopher: It is only the Spirit that is the individual, because it is infinite. No infinity can be divided; infinity cannot be broken into pieces. It is the same one, undivided unit for ever, and this is the individual man, the Real Man. The apparent man is merely a struggle to express, to manifest this individuality which is beyond. Evolution is not in the Spirit.

These changes which are going on—the wicked becoming good, the animal becoming man, take them in whatever way you like—are not in the Spirit. They are evolution of nature and manifestation of Spirit. Suppose there is a screen hiding you from me, in which there is a small hole through which I can see some of the faces before me, just a few faces. Now suppose the hole begins to grow larger and larger, and as it does so, more and more of the scene before me reveals itself, and when at last the whole screen has disappeared, I stand face to face with you all. You did not change at all in this case; it was the hole that was evolving, and you were gradually manifesting yourselves. So it is with the Spirit. No perfection is going to be attained. You are already free and perfect.

What are these ideas of religion and God and searching for the hereafter? Why does man look for a God? Why does man, in every nation, in every state of society, want a perfect ideal somewhere, either in man, in God, or elsewhere? Because that idea is within you. It was your own heart beating and you did not know; you were mistaking it for something external. It is the God within your own self that is propelling you to seek for Him, to realise Him. After long searches here and there, in temples and in churches, in earths and in heavens, at last you come back, completing the circle from where you started, to your own soul and find that He for whom you have been seeking all over the world, for whom you have been weeping and praying in churches and temples, on whom you were looking as the mystery of all mysteries shrouded in the clouds, is nearest of the near, is your own Self, the reality of your life, body, and soul.

That Self is your own nature. Assert it, manifest it. Not to become pure, you are pure already. You are not to be perfect, you are that already. Nature is like that screen which is hiding the reality beyond. Every good thought that you think or act upon is simply tearing the veil, as it were; and the purity, the Infinity, the God behind, manifests Itself more and more. This is the whole history of man. Finer and finer becomes the veil, more and more of the light behind shines forth, for it is its nature to shine.

That Self cannot be known; in vain we try to know it. Were it knowable, it would not be what it is, for it is the eternal subject. Knowledge is a limitation, knowledge is objectifying. He is the eternal subject of everything, the eternal witness in this universe, your own Self. Knowledge is, as it were, a lower step, a degeneration. We are that eternal subject already; how can we know it?

The infinite Self is the real nature of every man, and he is struggling to express it in various ways; otherwise, why are there so many ethical codes? Where is the explanation of all ethics? One idea stands out as the centre of all ethical systems, expressed in various forms, namely, doing good to others. The guiding motive of mankind should be charity towards men, charity towards all animals. But these are all various expressions of that eternal truth that, "I am the universe; this universe is one." Or else, where is the reason? Why should I do good to my fellowmen? Why should I do good to others? What compels me? It is sympathy, the feeling of sameness everywhere. The hardest hearts feel sympathy for other beings sometimes. Even the man who gets frightened if he is told that this assumed individuality is really a delusion, that it is ignoble to try to cling to this apparent individuality, that very man will tell you that extreme self-abnegation is the centre of all morality. And what is perfect self-abnegation? It means the abnegation of this apparent self, the abnegation of all selfishness.

This idea of "me and mine"—*ahaṁkāra* and *mamat*—is the result of past superstition, and the more this present self passes away, the more the real

Self becomes manifest. This is true self-abnegation, the centre, the basis, the gist of all moral teaching; and whether man knows it or not, the whole world is slowly going towards it, practising it more or less. Only, the vast majority of mankind are doing it unconsciously. Let them do it consciously. Let them make the sacrifice, knowing that this "me and mine" is not the real Self, but only a limitation. But one glimpse of that infinite reality which is behind—one spark of that infinite fire that is the All—represents the present man; the Infinite is his true nature.

What is the utility, the effect, the result, of this knowledge? In these days, we have to measure everything by utility—by how many pounds, shillings, and pence it represents. What right has a person to ask that truth should be judged by the standard of utility or money? Suppose there is no utility, will it be less true? Utility is not the test of truth. Nevertheless, there is the highest utility in this. Happiness, we see, is what everyone is seeking for, but the majority seek it in things which are evanescent and not real. No happiness was ever found in the senses. There never was a person who found happiness in the senses or in enjoyment of the senses. Happiness is only found in the Spirit. Therefore the highest utility for mankind is to find this happiness in the Spirit.

The next point is that ignorance is the great mother of all misery, and the fundamental ignorance is to think that the Infinite weeps and cries, that He is finite. This is the basis of all ignorance that we, the immortal, the ever pure, the perfect Spirit, think that we are little minds, that we are little bodies; it is the mother of all selfishness. As soon as I think that I am a little body, I want to preserve it, to protect it, to keep it nice, at the expense of other bodies; then you and I become separate. As soon as the idea of separation comes, it opens the door to all mischief and leads to all misery. This is the utility that if a very small fractional part of human beings living today can put aside the idea of selfishness, narrowness, and littleness, this earth will become a paradise tomorrow; but with machines and improvements of material knowledge only, it will never be. These only increase misery, as oil poured on fire increases the flame all the more. Without the knowledge of the Spirit, all material knowledge is only adding fuel to fire, only giving into the hands of selfish man one more instrument to take what belongs to others, to live upon the life of others, instead of giving up his life for them.

Is it practical?—is another question. Can it be practised in modern society? Truth does not pay homage to any society, ancient or modern. Society has to pay homage to truth or die. Societies should be moulded upon truth, and truth has not to adjust itself to society. If such a noble truth as unselfishness cannot be practised in society, it is better for man to give up society and go into the forest. That is the daring man.

There are two sorts of courage. One is the courage of facing the cannon. And the other is the courage of spiritual conviction. An Emperor who invaded India was told by his teacher to go and see some of the sages there. After a long search for one, he found a very old man sitting on a block of stone. The Emperor talked with him a little and became very much impressed by his wisdom. He asked the sage to go to his country with him. "No," said the sage, "I am quite satisfied with my forest here." Said the Emperor, "I will give you money, position, wealth, I am the Emperor of the world." "No," replied the man, "I don't care for those things." The Emperor replied, "If you do not go, I will kill you." The man smiled serenely and said, "That is the most foolish thing you ever said, Emperor. You cannot kill me. Me the sun cannot dry, fire cannot burn, sword cannot kill, for I am the birthless, the deathless, the ever-living, omnipotent, omnipresent Spirit." This is spiritual boldness, while the other is the courage of a lion or a tiger.

During the Mutiny of 1857 there was a Swami, a very great soul, whom a Mohammedan mutineer stabbed severely. The Hindu mutineers caught and brought the man to the Swami, offering to kill him. But the Swami looked up calmly and said, "My brother, thou art He, thou art He!" and expired. This is another instance. What good is it to talk of the strength of your muscles, of the superiority of your Western institutions, if you cannot make Truth square with your society, if you cannot build up a society into which the highest Truth will fit? What is the good of this boastful talk about your grandeur and greatness, if you stand up and say, "This courage is not practical." Is nothing practical but pounds, shillings, and pence? If so, why boast of your society? *That society is the greatest, where the highest truths become practical.* That is my opinion; and if society is not fit for the highest truth, make it so; and the sooner, the better.

Stand up, men and women, in this spirit, dare to believe in the Truth, dare to practise the Truth! The world requires a few hundred bold men and women. Practise that boldness which dares know the Truth, which dares show the Truth in life, which does not quake before death, nay, welcomes death, makes a man know that he is the Spirit, that, in the whole universe, nothing can kill him. Then you will be free. Then you will know your real Soul.

"This *Ātman* is first to be heard, then thought about, and then meditated upon." There is a great tendency in modern times to talk too much of work and decry thought. Doing is very good, but that comes from thinking. Little manifestations of energy through the muscles are called work. But where there is no thought, there will be no work. Fill the brain, therefore, with high thoughts, highest ideals, place them day and night before you, and out of that will come great work. Talk not about impurity, but say that we are pure. We have hypnotised ourselves into this thought that we are little, that we are born, and that we are going to die, and into a constant state of fear.

There is a story about a lioness, who was big with young, going about in search of prey; and seeing a flock of sheep, she jumped upon them. She died in the effort; and a little baby lion was born, motherless. It was taken care of by the sheep, and the sheep brought it up, and it grew up with them, ate grass, and bleated like the sheep. And although in time it became a big full-grown lion, it thought it was a sheep. One day another lion came in search of prey and was astonished to find that in the midst of this flock of sheep was a lion, fleeing like the sheep at the approach of danger. He tried to get near the sheep-lion, to tell it that it was not a sheep but a lion; but the poor animal fled at his approach. However, he watched his opportunity and one day found the sheep-lion sleeping. He approached it and said, "You are a lion." "I am a sheep," cried the other lion and could not believe the contrary but bleated. The lion dragged him towards a lake and said, "Look here, here is my reflection and yours." Then came the comparison. It looked at the lion and then at its own reflection, and in a moment came the idea that it was a lion. The lion roared, the bleating was gone.

You are lions, you are souls, pure, infinite, and perfect. The might of the universe is within you. "Why weepest thou, my friend? There is neither birth nor death for thee. Why weepest thou? There is no disease nor misery for thee, but thou art like the infinite sky; clouds of various colours come over it, play for a moment, then vanish. But the sky is ever the same eternal blue."

Why do we see wickedness? There was a stump of a tree, and in the dark, a thief came that way and said, "That is a policeman." A young man waiting for his beloved saw it and thought that it was his sweetheart. A child who had been told ghost stories took it for a ghost and began to shriek. But all the time it was the stump of a tree. We see the world as we are. Suppose there is a baby in a room with a bag of gold on the table and a thief comes and steals the gold. Would the baby know it was stolen? That which we have inside, we see outside. The baby has no thief inside and sees no thief outside. So with all knowledge.

Do not talk of the wickedness of the world and all its sins. Weep that you are bound to see wickedness yet. Weep that you are bound to see sin everywhere, and if you want to help the world, do not condemn it. Do not weaken it more. For what is sin and what is misery, and what are all these, but the results of weakness? The world is made weaker and weaker every day by such teachings. Men are taught from childhood that they are weak and sinners: Teach them that they are all glorious children of immortality, even those who are the weakest in manifestation. Let positive, strong, helpful thought enter into their brains from very childhood. Lay yourselves open to these thoughts, and not to weakening and paralysing ones. Say to your own minds, "I am He, I am He." Let it ring day and night in your minds like a song, and at the point of death declare, "I am He." That is the Truth; the infinite strength of the world is yours. Drive out the superstition that has covered your minds. Let us be brave. Know the Truth and practise the Truth. The goal may be distant, but awake, arise, and stop not till the goal is reached.

MĀYĀ AND ILLUSION

(Delivered in London)

ALMOST ALL OF you have heard of the word *Māyā*. Generally it is used, though incorrectly, to denote illusion, or delusion, or some such thing. But the theory of *Māyā* forms one of the pillars upon which the Vedānta rests; it is, therefore, necessary that it should be properly understood. I ask a little patience of you, for there is a great danger of its being misunderstood.

The oldest idea of *Māyā* that we find in Vedic literature is the sense of delusion; but then the real theory had not been reached. We find such passages as, "Indra through his *Māyā* assumed various forms." Here it is true that the word *Māyā* means something like magic, and we find various other passages, always taking the same meaning. The word *Māyā* then dropped out of sight altogether. But in the meantime the idea was developing. Later, the question was raised: "Why can't we know this secret of the universe?" And the answer given was very significant: "Because we talk in vain, and because we are satisfied with the things of the senses, and because we are running after desires; therefore, we, as it were, cover the Reality with a mist." Here the word *Māyā* is not used at all, but we get the idea that the cause of our ignorance is a kind of mist that has come between us and the Truth. Much later on, in one of the latest Upaniṣads, we find the word *Māyā* reappearing, but this time, a transformation has taken place in it, and a mass of new meaning has attached itself to the word. Theories had been propounded and repeated, others had been taken up, until at last the idea of *Māyā* became fixed. We read in the *Svetāśvatara Upaniṣad*, "Know nature to be *Māyā* and the Ruler of this *Māyā* is the Lord Himself."

Coming to later philosophers, we find that this word Māyā has been manipulated in various fashions, until we come to the great Śankarāchārya. The theory of Māyā was manipulated a little by the Buddhists too, but in the hands of the Buddhists it became very much like what is called Idealism, and that is the meaning that is now generally given to the word *Māyā*.

When the Hindu says the world is *Māyā*, at once people get the idea that the world is an illusion. This interpretation has some basis, as coming through the Buddhistic philosophers, because there was one section of philosophers who did not believe in the external world at all. But the *Māyā* of the Vedānta, in its last developed form, is neither Idealism nor Realism, nor is it a theory. It is a simple statement of facts—what we are and what we see around us.

As I have told you before, the minds of the people from whom the Vedas came were intent upon following principles, discovering principles. They had no time to work upon details or to wait for them; they wanted to go deep into the heart of things. Something beyond was calling them, as it were, and they could not wait. Scattered through the Upaniṣads, we find that the details of subjects which we now call modern sciences are often very erroneous, but, at the same time, their principles are correct. For instance, the idea of ether, which is one of the latest theories of modern science, is to be found in our ancient literature in forms much more developed than is the modern scientific theory of ether today, but it was in principle. When they tried to demonstrate the workings of that principle, they made many mistakes. The theory of the all-pervading life principle, of which all life in this universe is but a differing manifestation, was understood in Vedic times; it is found in the *Brāhmanas*. There is a long hymn in the *Samhītas* in praise of *prāna* of which all life is but a manifestation. By the by, it may interest some of you to know that there are theories in the Vedic philosophy about the origin of life on this earth very similar to those which have been advanced by some modern European scientists. You, of course, all know that there is a theory that life came from other planets. It is a settled doctrine with some Vedic philosophers that life comes in this way from the moon.

Coming to the principles, we find these Vedic thinkers very courageous and wonderfully bold in propounding large and generalised theories. Their solution of the mystery of the universe, from the external world, was as satisfactory as it could be. The detailed workings of modern science do not bring the question one step nearer to solution, because the principles have failed. If the theory of ether failed in ancient times to give a solution of the mystery of the universe, working out the details of that ether theory would not bring us much nearer to the truth. If the theory of all-pervading life failed as a theory of this universe, it would not mean anything more if worked out in detail, for the details do not change the principle of the universe. What I mean is that in their inquiry into the principle, the Hindu thinkers were as bold, and in some cases, much bolder than the moderns. They made some of the grandest generalisations that have yet been reached, and some still remain as theories, which modern science has yet to get even as theories. For instance, they not only arrived at the ether theory, but went beyond and classified mind also as a still more rarefied ether. Beyond that again, they found a still more rarefied ether. Yet that was no solution, it did not solve the problem. No amount of knowledge of the external world could solve the problem.

"But," says the scientist, "we are just beginning to know a little: wait a few thousand years and we shall get the solution." "No," says the Vedāntist, for he has proved beyond all doubt that the mind is limited, that it cannot go beyond certain limits—beyond time, space, and causation. As no man can jump out of his own self, so no man can go beyond the limits that have been put upon him by the laws of time and space. Every attempt to solve the laws of causation, time, and space would be futile, because the very attempt would have to be made by taking for granted the existence of these three. What does the statement of the existence of the world mean, then? "This world has no existence." What is meant by that? It means that it has no absolute existence. It exists only in relation to my mind, to your mind, and to the mind of everyone else. We see this world with the five senses, but if we had another sense, we would see in it something more. If we had yet another sense, it would appear as something still different. It has, therefore, no real existence; it has no unchangeable, immovable, infinite existence. Nor can it be called non-existence, seeing that it exists, and we have to work in and through it. It is a mixture of existence and non-existence.

Coming from abstractions to the common, everyday details of our lives, we find that our whole life is a contradiction, a mixture of existence and non-existence. There is this contradiction in knowledge. It seems that man can know everything, if he only wants to know; but before he has gone a few steps, he finds an adamantine wall which he cannot pass. All his work is in a circle, and he cannot go beyond that circle. The problems which are nearest and dearest to him are impelling him on and calling, day and night, for a solution, but he cannot solve them, because he cannot go beyond his intellect. And yet that desire is implanted strongly in him. Still we know that the only good is to be obtained by controlling and checking it. With every breath, every impulse of our heart asks us to be selfish. At the same time, there is some power beyond us which says that it is unselfishness alone which is good. Every child is a born optimist; he dreams golden dreams. In youth he becomes still more optimist. It is hard for a young man to believe that there is such a thing as death, such a thing as defeat or degradation. Old age comes, and life is a mass of ruins. Dreams have vanished into the air, and the man becomes a pessimist. Thus we go from one extreme to another, buffeted by nature, without knowing where we are going.

I am reminded of a celebrated song in the *Lalita Vistara*, the biography of Buddha. Buddha was born, says the book, as the saviour of mankind, but he forgot himself in the luxuries of his palace. Some angels came and sang a song to rouse him. And the burden of the whole song is that we are floating down the river of life which is continually changing with no stop and no rest. So are our lives, going on and on without knowing any rest. What are we to do? The man who has enough to eat and drink is an optimist, and he avoids all mention of misery, for it frightens him. Tell not to him of the sorrows and the sufferings of the world; go to him and tell that it is all good. "Yes, I am safe," says he. "Look at me! I have a nice house to live in, I do not fear cold and hunger; therefore do not bring these horrible pictures before me." But, on the other hand, there are others dying of cold and hunger. If you go and teach *them* that it is all good, they will not hear you. How can they wish others to be happy when they are miserable? Thus we are oscillating between optimism and pessimism.

Then, there is the tremendous fact of death. The whole world is going towards death; everything dies. All our progress, our vanities, our reforms, our luxuries, our wealth, our knowledge, have that one end—death. That is all that is certain. Cities come and go, empires rise and fall, planets break into pieces and crumble into dust, to be blown about by the atmospheres of other planets. Thus it has been going on from time without beginning. Death is the end of everything. Death is the end of life, of beauty, of wealth, of power, of virtue too. Saints die and sinners die, kings die and beggars die. They are all going to death, and yet this tremendous clinging on to life exists. Somehow, we do not know why, we cling to life; we cannot give it up. And this is *Māyā*.

The mother is nursing a child with great care; all her soul, her life, is in that child. The child grows, becomes a man, and perchance becomes a blackguard and a brute, kicks her and beats her every day; and yet the mother clings to the child; and when her reason awakes, she covers it up with the idea of love. She little thinks that it is not love, that it is something which has got hold of her nerves, which she cannot shake off; however she may try, she cannot shake off the bondage she is in. And this is *Māyā*.

We are all after the Golden Fleece. Everyone of us thinks that this will be his. Every reasonable man sees that his chance is, perhaps, one in twenty millions, yet everyone struggles for it. And this is *Māyā*.

Death is stalking day and night over this earth of ours, but at the same time we think we shall live eternally. A question was once asked of King Yudhishthira. "What is the most wonderful thing on this earth?" And the king replied, "Every day people are dying around us, and yet men think they will never die." And this is *Māyā*.

These tremendous contradictions in our intellect, in our knowledge, yea, in all the facts of our life, face us on all sides. A reformer arises and wants to remedy the evils that are existing in a certain nation; and before they have been remedied, a thousand other evils arise in another place. It is like an old house that is falling; you patch it up in one place and the ruin extends to another. In India, our reformers cry and preach against the evils of enforced widowhood. In the West, non-marriage is the great evil. Help the unmarried on one side; they are suffering. Help the widows on the other; they are suffering. It is like chronic rheumatism: you drive it from the head, and it goes to the body; you drive it from there, and it goes to the feet. Reformers arise and preach that learning, wealth, and culture should not be in the hands of a select few; and they do their best to make them accessible to all. These may bring more happiness to some, but, perhaps, as culture comes, physical happiness lessens. The knowledge of happiness brings the knowledge of unhappiness. Which way then shall we go? The least amount of material prosperity that we enjoy is causing the same amount of misery elsewhere. This is the law. The young, perhaps, do not see it clearly, but those who have lived long enough and those who have struggled enough will understand it. And this is *Māyā*.

These things are going on, day and night, and to find a solution of this problem is impossible. Why should it be so? It is impossible to answer this, because the question cannot be logically formulated. There is neither *how* nor *why* in fact; we only know that it *is* and that we cannot help it. Even to grasp it, to draw an exact image of it in our own mind, is beyond our power. How can we solve it then?

Māyā is a statement of the fact of this universe, of how it is going on. People generally get frightened when these things are told to them. But bold we must be. Hiding facts is not the way to find a remedy. As you all know, a hare hunted by dogs puts its head down and thinks itself safe; so, when we run into optimism, we do just like the hare, but that is no remedy. There are objections against this, but you may remark that they are generally from people who possess many of the good things of life. In this country (England) it is very difficult to become a pessimist. Everyone tells me how wonderfully the world is going on, how progressive; but what he himself is is his own world. Old questions arise; Christianity must be the only true religion of the world, because Christian nations are prosperous! But that assertion contradicts itself, because the prosperity of the Christian nations depends on the misfortune of non-Christian nations. There must be some to prey on. Suppose the whole world were to become Christian, then the Christian nations would become poor, because there would be no non-Christian nations for them to prey upon. Thus the argument kills itself. Animals are living upon plants, men upon animals and, worst of all, upon one another, the strong upon the weak. This is going on everywhere. And this is *Māyā*.

What solution do you find for this? We hear every day many explanations, and are told that in the long run all will be good. Taking it for granted that this is possible, why should there be this diabolical way of doing good? Why cannot good be done through good, instead of through these diabolical methods? The descendants of the human beings of today will be happy; but why must there be all this suffering now? There is no solution. This is *Māyā*.

Again, we often hear that it is one of the features of evolution that it eliminates evil, and this evil being continually eliminated from the world, at last only good will remain. That is very nice to hear; and it panders to the vanity of those who have enough of this world's goods, who have not a hard struggle to face every day and are not being crushed under the wheel of this so-called evolution. It is very good and comforting indeed to such fortunate ones. The common herd may suffer, but they do not care; let them die, they are of no consequence. Very good, yet this argument is fallacious from beginning to end. It takes for granted, in the first place, that manifested good and evil in this world are two absolute realities. In the second place, it makes a still worse assumption that the amount of good is an increasing quantity and the amount of evil is a decreasing quantity. So, if evil is being eliminated in this way by what they call evolution, there will come a time when all this evil will be eliminated and what remains will be all good. Very easy to say, but can it be proved that evil is a lessening quantity?

Take, for instance, the man who lives in a forest, who does not know how to cultivate the mind, cannot read a book, has not heard of such a thing as writing. If he is severely wounded, he is soon all right again; while we die if we get a scratch. Machines are making things cheap, making for progress and evolution, but millions are crushed, that one may become rich; while one becomes rich, thousands at the same time become poorer and poorer, and whole masses of human beings are made slaves. That is the way it is going on.

The animal man lives in the senses. If he does not get enough to eat, he is miserable; or if something happens to his body, he is miserable. In the senses both his misery and his happiness begin and end. As soon as this man progresses, as soon as his horizon of happiness increases, his horizon of unhappiness increases proportionately. The man in the forest does not know what it is to be jealous, to be in the law courts, to pay taxes, to be blamed by society, to be ruled over day and night by the most tremendous tyranny that human diabolism ever invented, which pries into the secrets of every human heart. He does not know how man becomes a thousand times more diabolical than any other animal, with all his vain knowledge and with all his pride. Thus it is that, as we emerge out of the senses, we develop higher powers of enjoyment, and at the same time we have to develop higher powers of suffering too. The nerves become finer and capable of more suffering. In every society, we often find that the ignorant, common man, when abused, does not feel much, but he feels a good thrashing. But the gentleman cannot bear a single word of abuse; he has become so finely nerved. Misery has increased with his susceptibility to happiness. This does not go much to prove the evolutionist's case.

As we increase our power to be happy, we also increase our power to suffer, and sometimes I am inclined to think that if we increase our power to become happy in arithmetical progression, we shall increase, on the other hand, our power to become miserable in geometrical progression. We who are progressing know that the more we progress, the more avenues are opened to pain as well as to pleasure. And this is *Māyā*.

Thus we find that *Māyā* is not a theory for the explanation of the world: it is simply a statement of facts as they exist, that the very basis of our being is contradiction, that everywhere we have to move through this tremendous contradiction that wherever there is good, there must also be evil, and wherever there is evil, there must be some good, wherever there is life, death must follow as its shadow, and everyone who smiles will have to weep, and vice versa. Nor can this state of things be remedied. We may verily imagine that there will be a place where there will be only good and no evil, where we shall only smile and never weep. This is impossible in the very nature of things; for the conditions will remain the same. Wherever there is the power of producing a smile in us there lurks the power of producing tears. Wherever there is the power of producing happiness, there lurks somewhere the power of making us miserable.

Thus the Vedānta philosophy is neither optimistic nor pessimistic. It voices both these views and takes things as they are. It admits that this world is a mixture of good and evil, happiness and misery, and that to increase the one, one must of necessity increase the other. There will never be a perfectly good or bad world, because the very idea is a contradiction in terms. The great secret revealed by this analysis is that good and bad are not two cut-and-dried, separate existences. There is not one thing in this world of ours which you can label as good and good alone, and there is not one thing in the universe which you can label as bad and bad alone. The very same phenomenon which is appearing to be good now, may appear to be bad tomorrow. The same thing which is producing misery in one, may produce happiness in another. The fire that burns the child, may cook a good meal for a starving man. The same nerves that carry the sensations of misery carry also the sensations of happiness.

The only way to stop evil, therefore, is to stop good also; there is no other way. To stop death, we shall have to stop life also. Life without death and happiness without misery are contradictions, and neither can be found alone, because each of them is but a different manifestation of the same thing.

What I thought to be good yesterday, I do not think to be good now. When I look back upon my life and see what were my ideals at different times, I find this to be so. At one time my ideal was to drive a strong pair of horses; at another time I thought, if I could make a certain kind of sweetmeat, I should be perfectly happy; later I imagined that I should be entirely satisfied if I had a wife and children and plenty of money. Today I laugh at all these ideals as mere childish nonsense. Vedānta says, there must come a time when we shall look back and laugh at the ideals which make us afraid of giving up our individuality. Each one of us wants to keep this body for an indefinite time, thinking we shall be very happy, but there will come a time when we shall laugh at this idea.

Now, if such be the truth, we are in a state of hopeless contradiction—neither existence nor non-existence, neither misery nor happiness, but a mixture of them. What, then, is the use of Vedānta and all other philosophies and religions? And, above all, what is the use of doing good work? This is a question that comes to the mind. If it be true that you cannot do good without doing evil, and whenever you try to create happiness there will always be misery, people will ask you, "What is the use of doing good?" The answer is, in the first place, that we must work for lessening misery, for that is the only way to make ourselves happy. Every one of us finds it out sooner or later in our lives. The bright ones find it out a little earlier, and the dull ones a little later. The dull ones pay very dearly for the discovery and the bright ones less dearly. In the second place, we must do our part, because that is the only way of getting out of this life of contradiction. Both the forces of good and evil will keep the universe alive for us, until we awake from our dreams and give up this building of mud pies. That lesson we shall have to learn, and it will take a long, long time to learn it.

Attempts have been made in Germany to build a system of philosophy on the basis that the Infinite has become the finite. Such attempts are also made in England. And the analysis of the position of these philosophers is this, that the Infinite is trying to express itself in this universe, and that there will come a time when the Infinite will succeed in doing so. It is all very well, and we have used the words *Infinite* and *manifestation* and *expression*, and so on, but philosophers naturally ask for a logical fundamental basis for the statement that the finite can fully express the Infinite. The Absolute and the Infinite can become this universe only by limitation. Everything must be limited that comes through the senses, or through the mind, or through the intellect; and for the limited to be the unlimited is simply absurd, and can never be.

Vedānta, on the other hand, says that it is true that the Absolute or the Infinite is trying to express itself in the finite, but there will come a time when it will find that it is impossible, and it will then have to beat a retreat, and this beating a retreat means renunciation which is the real beginning of religion. Nowadays it is very hard even to talk of renunciation. It was said of me in America that I was a man who came out of a land that had been dead and buried for five thousand years, and talked of renunciation. So says, perhaps, the English philosopher. Yet it is true that that is the only path to religion. Renounce and give up. What did Christ say? "He that loseth his life for my sake shall find it." Again and again did he preach renunciation as the only way to perfection.

There comes a time when the mind awakes from this long and dreary dream—the child gives up its play and wants to go back to its mother. It finds the truth of the statement, "Desire is never satisfied by the enjoyment of desires, it only increases the more, as fire when butter is poured upon it." This is true of all sense-enjoyments, of all intellectual enjoyments, and of all the enjoyments of which the human mind is capable. They are nothing, they are within *Māyā*, within this network beyond which we cannot go. We may run therein through infinite time and find no end, and whenever we struggle to get a little enjoyment, a mass of misery falls upon us. How awful is this! And when I think of it, I cannot but consider that this theory of *Māyā*, this statement that it is all *Māyā*, is the best and only explanation.

What an amount of misery there is in this world, and if you travel among various nations, you will find that one nation attempts to cure its evils by one means, and another by another. The very same evil has been taken up by various races, and attempts have been made in various ways to check it, yet no nation has succeeded. If it has been minimised at one point, a mass of evil has been crowded at another point. Thus it goes.

The Hindus, to keep up a high standard of chastity in the race, have sanctioned child-marriage, which in the long run has degraded the race. At the same time, I cannot deny that this child-marriage makes the race more chaste. What would you have? If you want the nation to be more chaste, you weaken men and women physically by child-marriage. On the other hand, are you in England any better off? No, because chastity is the life of a nation. Do you not find in history that the first death-sign of a nation has been unchastity? When that has entered, the end of the race is in sight. Where shall we get a solution of these miseries then? If parents select husbands and wives for their children, then this evil is minimised. The daughters of India are more practical than sentimental. But very little of poetry remains in their lives. Again, if people select their own husbands and wives, that does not seem to bring much happiness. The Indian woman is generally very happy; there are not many cases of quarrelling between husband and wife. On the other hand, in the United States, where the greatest liberty obtains, the number of unhappy homes and marriages is large.

Unhappiness is here, there, and everywhere. What does it show? That, after all, not much happiness has been gained by all these ideals. We all struggle for happiness, and as soon as we get a little happiness on one side, on the other side there comes unhappiness.

Shall we not work to do good then? Yes, with more zest than ever, but what this knowledge will do for us is to break down our fanaticism. The

Englishman will no more be a fanatic and curse the Hindu. He will learn to respect the customs of different nations. There will be less of fanaticism and more of real work. Fanatics cannot work, they waste three-fourths of their energy. It is the level-headed, calm, practical man who works. So, the power to work will increase from this idea. Knowing that this is the state of things, there will be more patience. The sight of misery or of evil will not be able to throw us off our balance and make us run after shadows. Therefore, patience will come to us, knowing that the world will have to go on in its own way. If, for instance, all men have become good, the animals will have in the meantime evolved into men, and will have to pass through the same state, and so with the plants.

But only one thing is certain; the mighty river is rushing towards the ocean, and all the drops that constitute the stream will in time be drawn into that boundless ocean. So, in this life, with all its miseries and sorrows, its joys and smiles and tears, one thing is certain, that all things are rushing towards their goal, and it is only a question of time when you and I, and plants and animals, and every particle of life that exists must reach the Infinite Ocean of Perfection, must attain to Freedom, to God.

Let me repeat, once more, that the Vedāntic position is neither pessimism nor optimism. It does not say that this world is all evil or all good. It says that our evil is of no less value than our good, and our good of no more value than our evil. They are bound together. This is the world, and knowing this, you work with patience.

What for? Why should we work? If this is the state of things, what shall we do? Why not become agnostics? The modern agnostics also know there is no solution of this problem, no getting out of this evil of *Māyā*, as we say in our language; therefore they tell us to be satisfied and enjoy life. Here, again, is a mistake, a tremendous mistake, a most illogical mistake. And it is this. What do you mean by life? Do you mean only the life of the senses? In this, every one of us differs only slightly from the brutes. I am sure that no one is present here whose life is only in the senses. Then, this present life means something more than that. Our feelings, thoughts, and aspirations are all part and parcel of our life; and is not the struggle towards the great ideal, towards perfection, one of the most important components of what we call life? According to the agnostics, we must enjoy life as it is. But this life means, above all, this search after the ideal; the essence of life is going towards perfection. We must have that, and, therefore, we cannot be agnostics or take the world as it appears. The agnostic position takes this life, *minus* the ideal component, to be all that exists. And this, the agnostic claims, cannot be reached, therefore he must give up the search.

This is what is called *Māyā*—this nature, this universe. All religions are more or less attempts to get beyond nature—the crudest or the most developed, expressed through mythology or symbology, stories of gods, angels or demons, or through stories of saints or seers, great men or prophets, or through the abstractions of philosophy—all have that one object, all are trying to get beyond these limitations. In one word, they are all struggling towards freedom.

Man feels, consciously or unconsciously, that he is bound; he is not what he wants to be. It was taught to him at the very moment he began to look around. That very instant he learnt that he was bound, and he also found that there was something in him which wanted to fly beyond, where the body could not follow, but which was as yet chained down by this limitation. Even in the lowest of religious ideas, where departed ancestors and other spirits—mostly violent and cruel, lurking about the houses of their friends, fond of bloodshed and strong drink—are worshipped, even there we find that one common factor, that of freedom. The man who wants to worship the gods sees in them, above all things, greater freedom than in himself. If a door is closed, he thinks the gods can get through it, and that walls have no limitations for them. This idea of freedom increases until it comes to the ideal of a Personal God, of which the central concept is that He is a Being beyond the limitation of nature, of *Māyā*.

I see before me, as it were, that in some of those forest retreats this question is being discussed by those ancient sages of India; and in one of them, where even the oldest and the holiest fail to reach the solution, a young man stands up in the midst of them, and declares, "Hear, ye children of immortality, hear, ye who live in the highest places, I have found the way. By knowing Him who is beyond darkness we can go beyond death."

This *Māyā* is everywhere. It is terrible. Yet we have to work through it. The man who says that he will work when the world has become all good and then he will enjoy bliss is as likely to succeed as the man who sits beside the Ganga and says, "I will ford the river when all the water has run into the ocean." The way is not *with Māyā*, but *against* it. This is another fact to learn. We are not born as helpers of nature, but competitors with nature. We are its bond-masters, but we bind ourselves down. Why is this house here? Nature did not build it. Nature says, go and live in the forest. Man says, I will build a house and fight with nature, and he does so. The whole history of humanity is a continuous fight against the so-called laws of nature, and man gains in the end. Coming to the internal world, there too the same fight is going on, this fight between the animal man and the spiritual man, between light and darkness; and here too man becomes victorious. He, as it were, cuts his way out of nature to freedom. We see, then, that beyond this *Māyā* the Vedāntic philosophers find something which is not bound by *Māyā*; and if we can get there, we shall not be bound by *Māyā*. This idea is in some form or other the common property of all religions. But, with the Vedānta, it is only the beginning of religion and not the end. The idea of a Personal God, the Ruler and Creator of this universe, as He has been styled, the Ruler of *Māyā*, or nature, is not the end of these Vedāntic ideas; it is only the beginning. The idea grows and grows until the Vedāntist finds that He who, he thought, was standing outside, is he himself and is in reality within. He is the one who is free, but who through limitation thought he was bound.

MĀYĀ AND THE EVOLUTION OF THE CONCEPTION OF GOD

(Delivered in London, 20th October 1896)

WE HAVE SEEN how the idea of *Māyā*, which forms, as it were, one of the basic doctrines of the Advaita Vedānta, is, in its germ, found even in the Samhitās, and that in reality all the ideas which are developed in the Upaniṣads are to be found already in the *Samhītas* in some form or other. Most of you are by this time familiar with the idea of *Māyā*, and know that it is sometimes erroneously explained as illusion, so that when the universe is said to be *Māyā*, that also has to be explained as being illusion. The translation of the word is neither happy nor correct. *Māyā* is not a theory; it is simply a statement of facts about the universe as it exists, and to understand *Māyā* we must go back to the *Samhītas* and begin with the conception in the germ.

We have seen how the idea of the Devas came. At the same time we know that these Devas were at first only powerful beings, nothing more. Most of you are horrified when reading the old scriptures, whether of the Greeks, the Hebrews, the Persians, or others, to find that the ancient gods sometimes did things which, to us, are very repugnant. But when we read these books, we entirely forget that we are persons of the nineteenth century, and these gods were beings existing thousands of years ago. We also forget that the people who worshipped these gods found nothing incongruous in their characters, found nothing to frighten them, because they were very much like themselves.

I may also remark that that is the one great lesson we have to learn throughout our lives. In judging others we always judge them by our own ideals. That is not as it should be. Everyone must be judged according to his own ideal, and not by that of anyone else. In our dealings with our fellow-beings we constantly labour under this mistake, and I am of opinion that the vast majority of our quarrels with one another arise simply from this one cause that we are always trying to judge others' gods by our own, others' ideals by our ideals, and others' motives by our motives. Under certain circumstances I might do a certain thing, and when I see another person taking the same course I think he has also the same motive actuating him, little dreaming that although the effect may be the same, yet many other causes may produce the same thing. He may have performed the action with quite a different motive from that which impelled me to do it. So in judging of those ancient religions we must not take the standpoint to which we incline, but must put ourselves into the position of thought and life of those early times.

The idea of the cruel and ruthless Jehovah in the Old Testament has frightened many—but why? What right have they to assume that the Jehovah of the ancient Jews must represent the conventional idea of the God of the present day? And at the same time, we must not forget that there will come men after us who will laugh at our ideas of religion and God in the same way that we laugh at those of the ancients. Yet, through all these various conceptions runs the golden thread of unity, and it is the purpose of the Vedānta to discover this thread. "I am the thread that runs through all these various ideas, each one of which is like a pearl," says the Lord Krishna; and it is the duty of Vedānta to establish this connecting thread, however incongruous or disgusting may seem these ideas when judged according to the conceptions of today.

These ideas in the setting of past times were harmonious, and not more hideous than our present ideas. It is only when we try to take them out of their settings and apply to our own present circumstances that the hideousness becomes obvious. For the old surroundings are dead and gone. Just as the ancient Jew has developed into the keen, modern, sharp Jew, and the ancient āryan into the intellectual Hindu, similarly Jehovah has grown, and Devas have grown. The great mistake is in recognising the evolution of the worshippers, while we do not acknowledge the evolution of the Worshipped. He is not credited with the advance that his devotees have made. That is to say, you and I, as representing ideas, have grown; these gods also, as representing ideas, have grown.

This may seem somewhat curious to you—that God can grow. He cannot. He is unchangeable. In the same sense the real man never grows. But man's ideas of God are constantly changing and expanding. We shall see later on how the real man behind each one of these human manifestations is immovable, unchangeable, pure, and always perfect; and in the same way the idea that we form of God is a mere manifestation, our own creation. Behind that is the real God who never changes, the ever pure, the immutable. But the manifestation is always changing, revealing the reality behind more and more. When it reveals more of the fact behind, it is called progression, when it hides more of the fact behind, it is called retrogression. Thus, as we grow, so the gods grow. From the ordinary point of view, just as we reveal ourselves as we evolve, so the gods reveal themselves.

We shall now be in a position to understand the theory of *Māyā*. In all the religions of the world the one question they propose to discuss is this: Why is there disharmony in the universe? Why is there this evil in the universe? We do not find this question in the very inception of primitive religious ideas, because the world did not appear incongruous to the primitive man. Circumstances were not inharmonious for him; there was no clash of opinions; to him there was no antagonism of good and evil. There was merely a feeling in his own heart of something which said yea, and something which said nay. The primitive man was a man of impulse. He did what occurred to him, and tried to bring out through his muscles whatever thought came into his mind, and he never stopped to judge, and seldom tried to check his impulses. So with the gods, they were also creatures of impulse. Indra comes and shatters the forces of the demons. Jehovah is pleased with one person and displeased with another, for what reason no one knows or asks. The habit of inquiry had not then arisen, and whatever he did was regarded as right. There was no idea of good or evil. The Devas did many wicked things in our sense of the word; again and again Indra and other gods committed very wicked deeds, but to the worshippers of Indra the ideas of wickedness and evil did not occur, so they did not question them.

With the advance of ethical ideas came the fight. There arose a certain sense in man, called in different languages and nations by different names. Call it the voice of God, or the result of past education, or whatever else you like, but the effect was this that it had a checking power upon the natural impulses of man. There is one impulse in our minds which says, do. Behind it rises another voice which says, do not. There is one set of ideas in our mind which is always struggling to get outside through the channels of the senses, and behind that, although it may be thin and weak, there is an infinitely small voice which says, do not go outside. The two beautiful Sanskrit words for these phenomena are *Pravṛtt* and *Nivṛtti*, "circling forward" and "circling inward". It is the circling forward which usually governs our actions. Religion begins with this circling inward. Religion begins with this "do not". Spirituality begins with this "do not". When the "do not" is not there, religion has not begun. And this "do not" came, causing men's ideas to grow, despite the fighting gods which they had worshipped.

A little love awoke in the hearts of mankind. It was very small indeed, and even now it is not much greater. It was at first confined to a tribe, embracing perhaps members of the same tribe; these gods loved their tribes and each god was a tribal god, the protector of that tribe. And sometimes the members of a tribe would think of themselves as the descendants of their god, just as the clans in different nations think that they are the common descendants of the man who was the founder of the clan. There were in ancient times, and are even now, some people who claim to be descendants not only of these tribal gods, but also of the Sun and the Moon. You read in the ancient Sanskrit books of the great heroic emperors of the solar and the lunar dynasties. They were first worshippers of the Sun and the Moon, and gradually came to think of themselves as descendants of the god of the Sun, of the Moon, and so forth. So when these tribal ideas began to grow there came a little love, some slight idea of duty towards each other, a little social organisation. Then, naturally, the idea came: How can we live together without bearing and forbearing? How can one man live with another without having sometime or other to check his impulses, to restrain himself, to forbear from doing things which his mind would prompt him to do? It is impossible. Thus comes the idea of restraint. The whole social fabric is based upon that idea of restraint, and we all know that the man or woman who has not learnt the great lesson of bearing and forbearing leads a most miserable life.

Now, when these ideas of religion came, a glimpse of something higher, more ethical, dawned upon the intellect of mankind. The old gods were found to be incongruous—these boisterous, fighting, drinking, beef-eating gods of the ancients—whose delight was in the smell of burning flesh and libations of strong liquor. Sometimes Indra drank so much that he fell upon the ground and talked unintelligibly. These gods could no longer be tolerated. The notion had arisen of inquiring into motives, and the gods had to come in for their share of inquiry. Reason for such-and-such actions was demanded and the reason was wanting. Therefore man gave up these gods, or rather they developed higher ideas concerning them. They took a survey, as it were, of all the actions and qualities of the gods and discarded those which they could not harmonise, and kept those which they could understand, and combined them, labelling them with one name, Deva-deva, the God of gods. The god to be worshipped was no more a simple symbol of power; something more was required than that. He was an ethical god; he loved mankind, and did good to mankind. But the idea of god still remained. They increased his ethical significance, and increased also his power. He became the most ethical being in the universe, as well as almost almighty.

But all this patchwork would not do. As the explanation assumed greater proportions, the difficulty which it sought to solve did the same. If the qualities of the god increased in arithmetical progression, the difficulty and doubt increased in geometrical progression. The difficulty of Jehovah was very little beside the difficulty of the God of the universe, and this question remains to the present day. Why under the reign of an almighty and all-loving God of the universe should diabolical things be allowed to remain? Why so much more misery than happiness, and so much more wickedness than good?

We may shut our eyes to all these things, but the fact still remains that this world is a hideous world. At best, it is the hell of Tantalus. Here we are with strong impulses and stronger cravings for sense-enjoyments, but cannot satisfy them. There rises a wave which impels us forward in spite of our own will, and as soon as we move one step, comes a blow. We are all doomed to live here like Tantalus. Ideals come into our head far beyond the limit of our sense-ideals, but when we seek to express them, we cannot do so. On the other hand, we are crushed by the surging mass around us. Yet if I give up all ideality and merely struggle through this world, my existence is that of a brute, and I degenerate and degrade myself. Neither way is happiness. Unhappiness is the fate of those who are content to live in this world, born as they are. A thousand times greater misery is the fate of those who dare to stand forth for truth and for higher things and who dare to ask for something higher than mere brute existence here.

These are facts; but there is no explanation—there cannot be any explanation. But the Vedānta shows the way out. You must bear in mind that I have to tell you facts that will frighten you sometimes, but if you remember what I say, think of it, and digest it, it will be yours, it will raise you higher, and make you capable of understanding and living in truth.

Now, it is a statement of fact that this world is a Tantalus's hell, that we do not know anything about this universe, yet at the same time we cannot say that we do not know. I cannot say that this chain exists, when I think that I do not know it. It may be an entire delusion of my brain. I may be dreaming all the time. I am dreaming that I am talking to you, and that you are listening to me. No one can prove that it is not a dream. My brain itself may be a dream, and as to that no one has ever seen his own brain. We all take it for granted. So it is with everything. My own body I take for granted. At the same time I cannot say, I do not know.

This standing between knowledge and ignorance, this mystic twilight, the mingling of truth and falsehood—and where they meet—no one knows. We are walking in the midst of a dream, half sleeping, half waking, passing all our lives in a haze; this is the fate of every one of us. This is the fate of all sense-knowledge. This is the fate of all philosophy, of all boasted science, of all boasted human knowledge. This is the universe.

What you call matter, or spirit, or mind, or anything else you may like to call them, the fact remains the same: we cannot say that they are, we cannot say that they are not. We cannot say they are one, we cannot say they are many. This eternal play of light and darkness—indiscriminate, indistinguishable, inseparable—is always there. A fact, yet at the same time not a fact; awake, and at the same time asleep. This is a statement of facts, and this is what is called *Māyā*.

We are born in this *Māyā*, we live in it, we think in it, we dream in it. We are philosophers in it, we are spiritual men in it, nay, we are devils in this *Māyā*, and we are gods in this *Māyā*. Stretch your ideas as far as you can, make them higher and higher, call them infinite or by any other name you please, even these ideas are within this *Māyā*. It cannot be otherwise, and the whole of human knowledge is a generalisation of this *Māyā*, trying to know it as it appears to be. This is the work of *Nāma-Rūpa*—name and form. Everything that has form, everything that calls up an idea in your mind, is within *Māyā*; for everything that is bound by the laws of time, space, and causation is within *Māyā*.

Let us go back a little to those early ideas of God and see what became of them. We perceive at once that the idea of some Being who is eternally loving us—eternally unselfish and almighty, ruling this universe—could not satisfy. Where is the just, merciful God? asked the philosopher. Does He not see millions and millions of His children perish, in the form of men and animals; for who can live one moment here without killing others? Can you draw a breath without destroying thousands of lives? You live because millions die. Every moment of your life, every breath that you breathe, is death to thousands; every movement that you make is death to millions. Every morsel that you eat is death to millions. Why should they die? There is an old sophism that they are very low existences. Supposing they are—which is questionable, for who knows whether the ant is greater than the man, or the man than the ant—who can prove one way or the other? Apart from that question, even taking it for granted that these are very low beings, still why should they die? If they are low, they have more reason to live. Why not? Because they live more in the senses, they feel pleasure and pain a thousandfold more than you or I can do. Which of us eats a dinner with the same gusto as a dog or wolf? None, because our energies are not in the senses; they are in the intellect, in the spirit. But in animals, their whole soul is in the senses, and they become mad and enjoy things which we human beings never dream of, and the pain is commensurate with the pleasure. Pleasure and pain are meted out in equal measure. If the pleasure felt by animals is so much keener than that felt by man, it follows that the animals' sense of pain is as keen, if not keener, than man's. So the fact is, the pain and misery men feel in dying is intensified a thousandfold in animals, and yet we kill them without troubling ourselves about their misery. This is *Māyā*.

And if we suppose there is a Personal God like a human being, who made everything, these so-called explanations and theories which try to prove that out of evil comes good are not sufficient. Let twenty thousand good things come, but why should they come from evil? On that principle, I might cut the throats of others because I want the full pleasure of my five senses. That is no reason. Why should good come through evil? The question remains to be answered, and it cannot be answered. The philosophy of India was compelled to admit this.

The Vedānta was (and is) the boldest system of religion. It stopped nowhere, and it had one advantage. There was no body of priests who sought to suppress every man who tried to tell the truth. There was always absolute religious freedom. In India the bondage of superstition is a social one; here in the West society is very free. Social matters in India are very strict, but religious opinion is free. In England a man may dress any way he likes, or eat what he likes—no one objects; but if he misses attending church, then Mrs. Grundy is down on him. He has to conform first to what society says on religion, and then he may think of the truth. In India, on the other hand, if a man dines with one who does not belong to his own caste, down comes society with all its terrible powers and crushes him then and there. If he wants to dress a little differently from the way in which his ancestor dressed ages ago, he is done for. I have heard of a man who was cast out by society because he went several miles to see the first railway train. Well, we shall presume that was not true! But in religion, we find atheists, materialists, and Buddhists, creeds, opinions, and speculations of every phase and variety, some of a most startling character, living side by side. Preachers of all sects go about teaching and getting adherents, and at the very gates of the temples of gods, the Brāhmins—to their credit be it said—allow even the materialists to stand and give forth their opinions.

Buddha died at a ripe old age. I remember a friend of mine, a great American scientist, who was fond of reading his life. He did not like the death of Buddha, because he was not crucified. What a false idea! For a man to be great he must be murdered! Such ideas never prevailed in India. This great Buddha travelled all over India, denouncing her gods and even the God of the universe, and yet he lived to a good old age. For eighty years he lived, and had converted half the country.

Then, there were the Cārvākas, who preached horrible things, the most rank, undisguised materialism, such as in the nineteenth century they dare not openly preach. These Cārvākas were allowed to preach from temple to temple, and city to city, that religion was all nonsense, that it was priestcraft, that the Vedas were the words and writings of fools, rogues, and demons, and that there was neither God nor an eternal soul. If there was a soul, why did it not come back after death drawn by the love of wife and child? Their idea was that if there was a soul it must still love after death, and want good things to eat and nice dress. Yet no one hurt these Cārvākas.

Thus India has always had this magnificent idea of religious freedom, and you must remember that freedom is the first condition of growth. What you do not make free, will never grow. The idea that you can make others grow and help their growth, that you can direct and guide them, always retaining for yourself the freedom of the teacher, is nonsense, a dangerous lie which has retarded the growth of millions and millions of human beings in this world. Let men have the light of liberty. That is the only condition of growth. We, in India, allowed liberty in spiritual matters, and we have a tremendous spiritual power in religious thought even today. You grant the same liberty in social matters, and so have a splendid social organisation. We have not given any freedom to the expansion of social matters, and ours is a cramped society. You have never given any freedom in religious matters but with fire and sword have enforced your beliefs, and the result is that religion is a stunted, degenerated growth in the European mind. In India, we have to take off the shackles from society; in Europe, the chains must be taken from the feet of spiritual progress. Then will come a wonderful growth and development of man. If we discover that there is one unity running through all these developments, spiritual, moral, and social, we shall find that religion, in the fullest sense of the word, must come into society, and into our everyday life. In the light of Vedānta you will understand that all sciences are but manifestations of religion, and so is everything that exists in this world.

We see, then, that through freedom the sciences were built; and in them we have two sets of opinions, the one the materialistic and denouncing, and the other the positive and constructive. It is a most curious fact that in every society you find them. Supposing there is an evil in society, you will find immediately one group rise up and denounce it in vindictive fashion, which sometimes degenerates into fanaticism. There are fanatics in every society, and women frequently join in these outcries, because of their impulsive nature. Every fanatic who gets up and denounces something can secure a following. It is very easy to break down; a maniac can break anything he likes, but it would be hard for him to build up anything. These fanatics may do some good according to their light, but much more harm. Because social institutions are not made in a day, and to change them means removing the cause. Suppose there is an evil; denouncing it will not remove it, but you must go to work at the root. First find out the cause, then remove it, and the effect will be removed also. Mere outcry will not produce any effect unless indeed it produces misfortune.

There were others who had sympathy in their hearts and who understood the idea that we must go deep into the cause; these were the great saints. One fact you must remember, that all the great teachers of the world have declared that they came not to destroy but to fulfil. Many times this has not been understood, and their forbearance has been thought to be an unworthy compromise with existing popular opinions. Even now, you occasionally hear that these prophets and great teachers were rather cowardly and dared not say and do what they thought was right; but that was not so. Fanatics little understand the infinite power of love in the hearts of these great sages who looked upon the inhabitants of this world as their children. They were the real fathers, the real gods, filled with infinite sympathy and patience for everyone; they were ready to bear and forbear. They knew how human society should grow, and patiently, slowly, surely, went on applying their remedies, not by denouncing and frightening people, but by gently and kindly leading them upwards step by step. Such were the writers of the Upaniṣads. They knew full well how the old ideas of God were not reconcilable with the advanced ethical ideas of the time; they knew full well that what the atheists were preaching contained a good deal of truth, nay, great nuggets of truth; but at the same time, they understood that those who wished to sever the thread that bound the beads, who wanted to build a new society in the air, would entirely fail.

We never build anew, we simply change places; we cannot have anything new, we only change the position of things. The seed grows into the tree, patiently and gently; we must direct our energies towards the truth, and fulfil the truth that exists, not try to make new truths. Thus, instead of denouncing these old ideas of God as unfit for modern times, the ancient sages began to seek out the reality that was in them. The result was the Vedānta philosophy, and out of the old deities, out of the monotheistic God, the Ruler of the universe, they found yet higher and higher ideas in what is called the Impersonal Absolute; they found oneness throughout the universe.

He who sees in this world of manifoldness that One running through all, in this world of death he who finds that One Infinite Life, and in this world of insentience and ignorance he who finds that One Light and Knowledge, unto him belongs eternal peace. Unto none else, unto none else.

MĀYĀ AND FREEDOM

(Delivered in London, 22nd October 1896)

"TRAILING CLOUDS OF glory we come," says the poet. Not all of us come as trailing clouds of glory however; some of us come as trailing black fogs; there can be no question about that. But every one of us comes into this world to fight, as on a battle-field. We come here weeping to fight our way, as well as we can, and to make a path for ourselves through this infinite ocean of life; forward we go, having long ages behind us and an immense expanse beyond. So on we go till death comes and takes us off the field—victorious or defeated, we do not know. And this is *Māyā.*

Hope is dominant in the heart of childhood. The whole world is a golden vision to the opening eyes of the child; he thinks his will is supreme. As he moves onward, at every step nature stands as an adamantine wall, barring his future progress. He may hurl himself against it again and again, striving to break through. The further he goes, the further recedes the ideal till death comes, and there is release, perhaps. And this is *Māyā.*

A man of science rises, he is thirsting after knowledge. No sacrifice is too great, no struggle too hopeless for him. He moves onward discovering secret after secret of nature, searching out the secrets from her innermost heart, and what for? What is it all for? Why should we give him glory? Why should he acquire fame? Does not nature do infinitely more than any human being can do?—and nature is dull, insentient. Why should it be glory to imitate the dull, the insentient? Nature can hurl a thunderbolt of any magnitude to any distance. If a man can do one small part as much, we praise him and laud him to the skies. Why? Why should we praise him for imitating nature, imitating death, imitating dullness, imitating insentience? The force of gravitation can pull to pieces the biggest mass that ever existed; yet it is insentient. What glory is there in imitating the insentient? Yet we are all struggling after that. And this is *Māyā.*

The senses drag the human soul out. Man is seeking for pleasure and for happiness where it can never be found. For countless ages we are all taught that this is futile and vain, there is no happiness here. But we cannot learn;

it is impossible for us to do so, except through our own experiences. We try them, and a blow comes. Do we learn then? Not even then. Like moths hurling themselves against the flame, we are hurling ourselves again and again into sense-pleasures, hoping to find satisfaction there. We return again and again with freshened energy; thus we go on, till crippled and cheated we die. And this is *Māyā*.

So with our intellect. In our desire to solve the mysteries of the universe, we cannot stop our questioning, we feel we must know and cannot believe that no knowledge is to be gained. A few steps, and there arises the wall of beginningless and endless time which we cannot surmount. A few steps, and there appears a wall of boundless space which cannot be surmounted, and the whole is irrevocably bound in by the walls of cause and effect. We cannot go beyond them. Yet we struggle, and still have to struggle. And this is *Māyā*.

With every breath, with every pulsation of the heart, with every one of our movements, we think we are free, and the very same moment we are shown that we are not. Bound slaves, nature's bond-slaves, in body, in mind, in all our thoughts, in all our feelings. And this is *Māyā*.

There was never a mother who did not think her child was a born genius, the most extraordinary child that was ever born; she dotes upon her child. Her whole soul is in the child. The child grows up, perhaps becomes a drunkard, a brute, ill-treats the mother, and the more he ill-treats her, the more her love increases. The world lauds it as the unselfish love of the mother, little dreaming that the mother is a born slave, she cannot help that. She would a thousand times rather throw off the burden, but she cannot. So she covers it with a mass of flowers, which she calls wonderful love. And this is *Māyā*.

We are all like this in the world. A legend tells how once Nārada said to Krishna, "Lord, show me *Māyā*." A few days passed away, and Krishna asked Nārada to make a trip with him towards a desert, and after walking for several miles, Krishna said, "Nārada, I am thirsty; can you fetch some water for me?" "I will go at once, sir, and get you water." So Nārada went. At a little distance there was a village; he entered the village in search of water and knocked at a door, which was opened by a most beautiful young girl. At the sight of her he immediately forgot that his Master was waiting for water, perhaps dying for the want of it. He forgot everything and began to talk with the girl. All that day he did not return to his Master. The next day, he was again at the house, talking to the girl. That talk ripened into love; he asked the father for the daughter, and they were married and lived there and had children. Thus twelve years passed. His father-in-law died, he inherited his property. He lived, as he seemed to think, a very happy life with his wife and children, his fields and his cattle, and so forth. Then came a flood. One night the river rose until it overflowed its banks and flooded the whole village. Houses fell, men and animals were swept away and drowned, and everything was floating in the rush of the stream. Nārada had to escape. With one hand he held his wife, and with the other two of his children; another child was on his shoulders, and he was trying to ford this tremendous flood. After a few steps he found the current was too strong, and the child on his shoulders fell and was borne away. A cry of despair came from Nārada. In trying to save that child, he lost his grasp upon one of the others, and it also was lost. At last his wife, whom he clasped with all his might, was torn away by the current, and he was thrown on the bank, weeping and wailing in bitter lamentation. Behind him there came a gentle voice, "My child, where is the water? You went to fetch a pitcher of water, and I am waiting for you; you have been gone for quite half an hour." "Half an hour!" Nārada exclaimed. Twelve whole years had passed through his mind, and all these scenes had happened in half an hour! And this is *Māyā*. In one form or another, we are all in it. It is a most difficult and intricate state of things to understand. It has been preached in every country, taught everywhere, but only believed in by a few, because until we get the experiences ourselves we cannot believe in it. What does it show? Something very terrible. For it is all futile.

Time, the avenger of everything, comes, and nothing is left. He swallows up the saint and the sinner, the king and the peasant, the beautiful and the ugly; he leaves nothing. Everything is rushing towards that one goal, destruction. Our knowledge, our arts, our sciences, everything is rushing towards it. None can stem the tide, none can hold it back for a minute. We may try to forget it, in the same way that persons in a plague-stricken city try to create oblivion by drinking, dancing, and other vain attempts, and so becoming paralysed. So we are trying to forget, trying to create oblivion by all sorts of sense-pleasures. And this is *Māyā*.

Two ways have been proposed. One method which everyone knows, is very common, and that is, "It may be very true, but do not think of it. 'Make hay while the sun shines,' as the proverb says. It is all true, it is a fact, but do not mind it. Seize the few pleasures you can, do what little you can, do not look at the dark side of the picture, but always towards the hopeful, the positive side." There is some truth in this, but there is also a danger. The truth is that it is a good motive power. Hope and a positive ideal are very good motive powers for our lives, but there is a certain danger in them. The danger lies in our giving up the struggle in despair. Such is the case with those who preach, "Take the world as it is; sit down as calmly and comfortably as you can, and be contented with all these miseries. When you receive blows, say they are not blows but flowers; and when you are driven about like slaves, say that you are free. Day and night tell lies to others and to your own souls, because that is the only way to live happily."

This is what is called practical wisdom, and never was it more prevalent in the world than in this nineteenth century; because never were harder blows hit than at the present time, never was competition keener, never were men so cruel to their fellowmen as now; and, therefore, must this consolation be offered. It is put forward in the strongest way at the present time; but it fails, as it always must fail. We cannot hide a carrion with roses; it is impossible. It would not avail long; for soon the roses would fade, and the carrion would be worse than ever before. So with our lives. We may try to cover our old and festering sores with cloth of gold, but there comes a day when the cloth of gold is removed, and the sore in all its ugliness is revealed.

Is there no hope then? True it is that we are all slaves of *Māyā*, born in *Māyā*, and live in *Māyā*. Is there then no way out, no hope? That we are all miserable, that this world is really a prison, that even our so-called trailing beauty is but a prison-house, and that even our intellects and minds are prison-houses, have been known for ages upon ages. There has never been a man, there has never been a human soul, who has not felt this sometime or other, however, he may talk. And the old people feel it most, because in them is the accumulated experience of a whole life, because they cannot be easily cheated by the lies of nature. Is there no way out?

We find that with all this, with this terrible fact before us, in the midst of sorrow and suffering, even in this world where life and death are synonymous, even here, there is a still small voice that is ringing through all ages, through every country and in every heart: "This My *Māyā* is divine, made up of qualities, and very difficult to cross. Yet those that come unto Me, cross the river of life." "Come unto Me all ye that labour and are heavy laden, and I will give you rest." This is the voice that is leading us forward. Man has heard it, and is hearing it all through the ages. This voice comes to men when everything seems to be lost and hope has fled, when man's dependence on his own strength has been crushed down, and everything seems to melt away between his fingers, and life is a hopeless ruin. Then he hears it. This is called religion.

On the one side, therefore, is the bold assertion that this is all nonsense, that this is *Māyā*, but along with it, there is the most hopeful assertion that beyond *Māyā*, there is a way out. On the other hand, practical men tell us, "Don't bother your heads about such nonsense as religion and metaphysics. Live here; this is a very bad world indeed, but make the best of it." Which put in plain language means, live a hypocritical, lying life, a life of continuous fraud, covering all sores in the best way you can. Go on putting patch after patch, until everything is lost, and you are a mass of patchwork. This is what is called practical life. Those that are satisfied with this patchwork will never come to religion.

Religion begins with a tremendous dissatisfaction with the present state of things, with our lives, and a hatred, an intense hatred, for this patching up of life, an unbounded disgust for fraud and lies. He alone can be religious who dares say, as the mighty Buddha once said under the Bo-tree, when this idea of practicality appeared before him and he saw that it was nonsense, and yet could not find a way out. When the temptation came to him to give up his search after truth, to go back to the world and live the old life of fraud, calling things by wrong names, telling lies to oneself and to everybody, he, the giant, conquered it and said, "Death is better than a vegetating ignorant life; it is better to die on the battle-field than to live a life of defeat." This is the basis of religion.

When a man takes this stand, he is on the way to find the truth, he is on the way to God. That determination must be the first impulse towards becoming religious. I will hew out a way for myself. I will know the truth or give up my life in the attempt. For on this side it is nothing, it is gone, it is vanishing every day. The beautiful, hopeful, young person of today is the veteran of tomorrow. Hopes and joys and pleasures will die like blossoms with tomorrow's frost. That is one side; on the other, there are the great charms of conquest, victories over all the ills of life, victory over life itself, the conquest of the universe. On that side men can stand. Those who dare, therefore, to struggle for victory, for truth, for religion, are in the right way; and that is what the Vedas preach. Be not in despair; the way is very difficult, like walking on the edge of a razor; yet despair not, arise, awake, and find the ideal, the goal.

Now, all these various manifestations of religion, in whatever shape and form they have come to mankind, have this one common central basis. It is the preaching of freedom, the way out of this world. They never came to reconcile the world and religion, but to cut the Gordian knot, to establish religion in its own ideal, and not to compromise with the world. That is what every religion preaches, and the duty of the Vedānta is to harmonise all these aspirations, to make manifest the common ground between all the religions of the world, the highest as well as the lowest. What we call the most arrant superstition and the highest philosophy really have a common aim in that they both try to show the way out of the same difficulty, and in most cases this way is through the help of some one who is not himself bound by the laws of nature, in one word, some one who is free. In spite of all the difficulties and differences of opinion about the nature of the one free agent, whether he is a Personal God, or a sentient being like man, whether masculine, feminine, or neuter—and the discussions have been endless—the fundamental idea is the same. In spite of the almost hopeless contradictions of the different systems, we find the golden thread of unity running through them all, and in this philosophy, this golden thread has been traced, revealed little by little to our view, and the first step to this revelation is the common ground that all are advancing towards freedom.

One curious fact present in the midst of all our joys and sorrows, difficulties and struggles, is that we are surely journeying towards freedom. The question was practically this: "What is this universe? From what does it arise? Into what does it go?" And the answer was: "In freedom it rises, in freedom it rests, and into freedom it melts away." This idea of freedom you cannot relinquish. Your actions, your very lives will be lost without it. Every moment nature is proving us to be slaves and not free. Yet, simultaneously rises the other idea, that still we are free. At every step we are knocked down, as it were, by *Māyā*, and shown that we are bound; and yet at the same moment, together with this blow, together with this feeling that we are bound, comes the other feeling that we are free. Some inner voice tells us that we are free. But if we attempt to realise that freedom, to make it manifest, we find the difficulties almost insuperable. Yet, in spite of that, it insists on asserting itself inwardly, "I am free, I am free." And if you study all the various religions of the world you will find this idea expressed.

Not only religion—you must not take this word in its narrow sense—but the whole life of society is the assertion of that one principle of freedom. All movements are the assertion of that one freedom. That voice has been heard by everyone, whether he knows it or not, that voice which declares, "Come unto Me all ye that labour and are heavy laden." It may not be in the same language or the same form of speech, but in some form or other, that voice calling for freedom has been with us. Yes, we are born here on account of that voice; every one of our movements is for that. We are all rushing towards freedom, we are all following that voice, whether we know it or not; as the children of the village were attracted by the music of the flute-player, so we are all following the music of the voice without knowing it.

We are ethical when we follow that voice. Not only the human soul, but all creatures from the lowest to the highest have heard the voice and are rushing towards it; and in the struggle are either combining with each other or pushing each other out of the way. Thus come competition, joys, struggles, life, pleasure, and death, and the whole universe is nothing but the result of this mad struggle to reach the voice. This is the manifestation of nature.

What happens then? The scene begins to shift. As soon as you know the voice and understand what it is, the whole scene changes. The same world which was the ghastly battle-field of *Māyā* is now changed into something good and beautiful. We no longer curse nature, nor say that the world is horrible and that it is all vain; we need no longer weep and wail. As soon as we understand the voice, we see the reason why this struggle should be here, this fight, this competition, this difficulty, this cruelty, these little pleasures and joys; we see that they are in the nature of things, because without them there would be no going towards the voice, to attain which we are destined, whether we know it or not. All human life, all nature, therefore, is struggling to attain to freedom. The sun is moving towards the goal, so is the earth in circling round the sun, so is the moon in circling round the earth. To that goal the planet is moving, and the air is blowing. Everything is struggling towards that. The saint is going towards that voice—he cannot help it, it is no glory to him. So is the sinner. The charitable man is going straight towards that voice, and cannot be hindered; the miser is also going towards the same destination; the greatest worker of good hears the same voice within, and he cannot resist it, he must go towards the voice; so with the most arrant idler. One stumbles more than another, and him who stumbles more we call bad, him who stumbles less we call good. Good and bad are never two different things, they are one and the same; the difference is not one of kind, but of degree.

Now, if the manifestation of this power of freedom is really governing the whole universe—applying that to religion, our special study—we find this idea has been the one assertion throughout. Take the lowest form of religion where there is the worship of departed ancestors or certain powerful and cruel gods; what is the prominent idea about the gods or departed ancestors? That they are superior to nature, not bound by its restrictions. The worshipper has, no doubt, very limited ideas of nature. He himself cannot pass through a wall, nor fly up into the skies, but the gods whom he worships can do these things. What is meant by that, philosophically? That the assertion of freedom is there, that the gods whom he worships are superior to nature as he knows it. So with those who worship still higher beings. As the idea of nature expands, the idea of the soul which is superior to nature also expands until we come to what we call monotheism, which holds that there is *Māyā* (nature), and that there is some Being who is the Ruler of this *Māyā*.

Here Vedānta begins, where these monotheistic ideas first appear. But the Vedānta philosophy wants further explanation. This explanation—that there is a Being beyond all these manifestations of *Māyā*, who is superior to and independent of *Māyā*, and who is attracting us towards Himself, and that we are all going towards Him—is very good, says the Vedānta, but yet the perception is not clear, the vision is dim and hazy, although it does not directly contradict reason.

Just as in your hymn it is said, "Nearer my God to Thee", the same hymn would be very good to the Vedāntist, only he would change a word, and make it, "Nearer my God to me." The idea that the goal is far off, far beyond nature, attracting us all towards it, has to be brought nearer and nearer, without degrading or degenerating it. The God of heaven becomes the God in nature, and the God in nature becomes the God who is nature, and the God who is nature becomes the God within this temple of the body, and the God dwelling in the temple of the body at last becomes the temple itself, becomes the soul and man—and there it reaches the last words it can teach. He whom the sages have been seeking in all these places is in our own hearts; the voice that you heard was right, says the Vedānta, but the direction you gave to the voice was wrong. That ideal of freedom that you perceived was correct, but you projected it outside yourself, and that was your mistake. Bring it nearer and nearer, until you find that it was all the time within you, it was the Self of your own self. That freedom was your own nature, and this *Māyā* never bound you.

Nature never has power over you. Like a frightened child you were dreaming that it was throttling you, and the release from this fear is the goal; not only to see it intellectually, but to perceive it, actualise it, much more definitely than we perceive this world. Then we shall know that we are free. Then, and then alone, will all difficulties vanish, then will all the perplexities of the heart be smoothed away, all crookedness made straight, then will vanish the delusion of manifoldness and nature; and *Māyā*, instead of being a horrible, hopeless dream, as it is now, will become beautiful, and this earth, instead of being a prison-house, will become our playground; and even dangers and difficulties, even all sufferings, will become deified and show us their real nature, will show us that behind everything, as the substance of everything, He is standing, and that He is the one real Self.

THE ABSOLUTE AND MANIFESTATION

(Delivered in London, 1896)

THE ONE QUESTION that is most difficult to grasp in understanding the Advaita philosophy and the one question that will be asked again and again and that will always remain is: How has the Infinite, the Absolute, become the finite? I will now take up this question, and, in order to illustrate it, I will use a figure.

Here is the Absolute (*a*), and this is the universe (*b*). The Absolute has become the universe. By this is not only meant the material world, but the mental world, the spiritual world—heavens and earths, and in fact, everything that

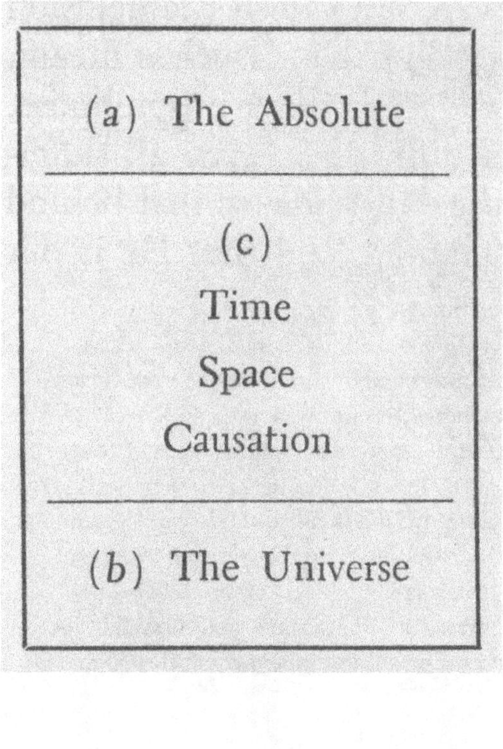

(a) The Absolute
(c) Time Space Causation
(b) The Universe

exists. Mind is the name of a change, and body the name of another change, and so on, and all these changes compose our universe. This Absolute (*a*) has become the universe (*b*) by coming through time, space, and causation (*c*). This is the central idea of Advaita. Time, space, and causation are like the glass through which the Absolute is seen, and when It is seen on the lower side, It appears as the universe. Now we at once gather from this that in the Absolute there is neither time, space, nor causation. The idea of time cannot be there, seeing that there is no mind, no thought. The idea of space cannot be there, seeing that there is no external change. What you call motion and causation cannot exist where there is only One. We have to understand this, and impress it on our minds, that what we call causation begins after, if we may be permitted to say so, the degeneration of the Absolute into the phenomenal, and not before; that our will, our desire, and all these things always come *after* that.

I think Schopenhauer's philosophy makes a mistake in its interpretation of Vedānta, for it seeks to make the will everything. Schopenhauer makes the will stand in the place of the Absolute. But the Absolute cannot be presented as will, for will is something changeable and phenomenal, and over the line drawn above time, space, and causation, there is no change, no motion; it is only below the line that external motion and internal motion, called thought, begin. There can be no will on the other side, and will, therefore, cannot be the cause of this universe. Coming nearer, we see in our own bodies that will is not the cause of every movement. I move this chair; my will is the cause of this movement, and this will becomes manifested as muscular motion at the other end. But the same power that moves the chair is moving the heart, the lungs, and so on, but not through will. Given that the power is the same, it only becomes will when it rises to the plane of consciousness, and to call it will before it has risen to this plane is a misnomer. This makes a good deal of confusion in Schopenhauer's philosophy.

A stone falls and we ask, why? This question is possible only on the supposition that nothing happens without a cause. I request you to make this very clear in your minds, for whenever we ask why anything happens, we are taking for granted that everything that happens must have a why, that is to say, it must have been preceded by something else which acted as the cause. This precedence and succession are what we call the law of causation. It means that everything in the universe is by turn a cause and an effect. It is the cause of certain things which come after it, and is itself the effect of something else which has preceded it. This is called the law of causation and is a necessary condition of all our thinking. We believe that every particle in the universe, whatever it be, is in relation to every other particle.

There has been much discussion as to how this idea arose. In Europe, there have been intuitive philosophers who believed that it was constitutional in humanity, others have believed it came from experience, but the question has never been settled. We shall see later on what the Vedānta has to say about it. But first we have to understand this: that the very asking of the question "why" presupposes that everything round us has been preceded by certain things and will be succeeded by certain other things.

The other belief involved in this question is that nothing in the universe is independent, that everything is acted upon by something outside itself. Interdependence is the law of the whole universe. In asking what caused the Absolute, what an error we are making! To ask this question we have to suppose that the Absolute also is bound by something, that It is dependent on something; and in making this supposition, we drag the Absolute down to the level of the universe. For in the Absolute, there is neither time, space, nor causation; It is all one. That which exists by itself alone cannot have any cause. That which is free cannot have any cause; else it would not be free, but bound. That which has relativity cannot be free. Thus we see the very question, why the Infinite became the finite, is an impossible one, for it is self-contradictory.

Coming from subtleties to the logic of our common plane, to common sense, we can see this from another side, when we seek to know how the Absolute has become the relative. Supposing we knew the answer, would the Absolute remain the Absolute? It would have become relative. What is meant by knowledge in our common-sense idea? It is only something that has become limited by our mind, that we know, and when it is beyond our mind, it is not knowledge. Now if the Absolute becomes limited by the mind, It is no more Absolute; It has become finite. Everything limited by the mind becomes finite. Therefore, to know the Absolute is again a contradiction in terms. That is why this question has never been answered, because if it were answered, there would no more be an Absolute. A God known is no more God; He has become finite like one of us. He cannot be known, He is always the Unknowable One.

But what Advaita says is that God is more than knowable. This is a great fact to learn. You must not go home with the idea that God is unknowable in the sense in which agnostics put it. For instance, here is a chair, it is known to us. But what is beyond ether, or whether people exist there or not is possibly unknowable. But God is neither known nor unknowable in this sense. He is something still higher than known; that is what is meant by God being unknown and unknowable. The expression is not used in the sense in which it may be said that some questions are unknown and unknowable. God is more than known. This chair is known, but God is intensely more than that, because in and through Him we have to know this chair itself.

He is the Witness, the eternal Witness of all knowledge. Whatever we know we have to know in and through Him. He is the Essence of our own Self. He is the essence of this ego, this I, and we cannot know anything excepting in and through that I. Therefore you have to know everything in and through the Brahman. To know the chair you have to know it in and through God. Thus God is infinitely nearer to us than the chair, but yet He is infinitely higher. Neither known, nor unknown, but something infinitely higher than either. He is your Self. "Who would live a second, who would breathe a second in this universe, if that Blessed One were not filling it?" Because in and through Him we breathe, in and through Him we exist. Not that He is standing somewhere and making my blood circulate. What is meant is that He is the Essence of all this, the Soul of my soul. You cannot by any possibility say you know Him; it would be degrading Him. You cannot get out of yourself, so you cannot know Him.

Knowledge is objectification. For instance, in memory you are objectifying many things, projecting them out of yourself. All memory, all the things which I have seen and which I know are in my mind. The pictures, the impressions of all these things, are in my mind, and when I would try to think of them, to know them, the first act of knowledge would be to project them outside. This cannot be done with God, because He is the Essence of our souls; we cannot project Him outside ourselves. Here is one of the profoundest passages in Vedānta: "He that is the Essence of your soul, He is the Truth, He is the Self, thou art That, O Śvetaketu." This is what is meant by "Thou art God." You cannot describe Him by any other language. All attempts of language, calling Him father, or brother, or our dearest friend, are attempts to objectify God, which cannot be done. He is the Eternal Subject of everything. I am the subject of this chair; I see the chair; so God is the Eternal Subject of my soul. How can you objectify Him, the Essence of your souls, the Reality of everything?

Thus, I would repeat to you once more, God is neither knowable nor unknowable, but something infinitely higher than either. He is one with us; and that which is one with us is neither knowable nor unknowable, as our own self. You cannot know your own self; you cannot move it out and make it an object to look at, because you *are* that and cannot separate yourself from it. Neither is it unknowable, for what is better known than yourself? It is really the centre of our knowledge. In exactly the same sense, God is neither unknowable nor known, but infinitely higher than both; for He is our real Self.

First, we see, then, that the question, "What caused the Absolute?" is a contradiction in terms, and secondly, we find that the idea of God in the Advaita is this Oneness; and, therefore, we cannot objectify Him, for we are always living and moving in Him, whether we know it or not. Whatever we do is always through Him.

Now the question is: What are time, space, and causation? Advaita means non-duality; there are no two, but one. Yet we see that here is a proposition that the Absolute is manifesting Itself as many, through the veil of time, space, and causation. Therefore it seems that here are two, the Absolute and *māyā* (the sum total of time, space, and causation). It seems apparently very convincing that there are two. To this the Advaitist replies that it cannot be called two. To have two, we must have two absolute independent existences which cannot be caused. In the first place, time, space, and causation cannot be said to be independent existences. Time is entirely a dependent existence; it changes with every change of our mind. Sometimes in dream one imagines that one has lived several years; at other times several months were passed as one second. So, time is entirely dependent on our state of mind. Secondly, the idea of time vanishes altogether, sometimes. So with space. We cannot know what space is. Yet it is there, indefinable, and cannot exist separate from anything else. So with causation.

The one peculiar attribute we find in time, space, and causation is that they cannot exist separate from other things. Try to think of space without colour, or limits, or any connection with the things around—just abstract space. You cannot; you have to think of it as the space between two limits or between three objects. It has to be connected with some object to have any existence. So with time; you cannot have any idea of abstract time, but you have to take two events, one preceding and the other succeeding, and join the two events by the idea of succession. Time depends on two events, just as space has to be related to outside objects. And the idea of causation is inseparable from time and space. This is the peculiar thing about them: they have no independent existence. They have not even the existence which the chair or the wall has. They are as shadows around everything which you cannot catch. They have no real existence; yet they are not non-existent, seeing that through them all things are manifesting as this universe.

Thus we see, first, that the combination of time, space, and causation has neither existence nor non-existence. Secondly, it sometimes vanishes. To give an illustration, there is a wave on the ocean. The wave is the same as the ocean certainly, and yet we know it is a wave, and as such different from the ocean. What makes this difference? The name and the form; that is, the idea in the mind and the form. Now, can we think of a wave-form as something separate from the ocean? Certainly not. It is always associated with the ocean idea. If the wave subsides, the form vanishes in a moment, and yet the form was not a delusion. So long as the wave existed the form was there, and you were bound to see the form. This is *māyā*.

The whole of this universe, therefore, is, as it were, a peculiar form; the Absolute is that ocean, while you and I, and suns and stars, and everything else are various waves of that ocean. And what makes the waves different? Only the form, and that form is time, space, and causation, all entirely dependent on the wave. As soon as the wave goes, they vanish. As soon as the individual gives up this *māyā*, it vanishes for him, and he becomes free. The whole struggle is to get rid of this clinging on to time, space, and causation, which are always obstacles in our way.

What is the theory of evolution? What are the two factors? A tremendous potential power which is trying to express itself, and circumstances which are holding it down, the environments not allowing it to express itself. So, in order to fight with these environments, the power is taking new bodies again and again. An amoeba, in the struggle, gets another body and conquers some obstacles, then gets another body and so on, until it becomes man. Now, if you carry this idea to its logical conclusion, there must come a time when that power that was in the amoeba and which evolved as man will have conquered all the obstructions that nature can bring before it and will thus escape from all its environments. This idea expressed in metaphysics will take this form: there are two components in every action, the one the subject, the other the object, and the one aim of life is to make the subject master of the object. For instance, I feel unhappy because a man scolds me. My struggle will be to make myself strong enough to conquer the environment, so that he may scold and I shall not feel. That is how we are all trying to conquer. What is meant by morality? Making the subject strong by attuning it to the Absolute, so that nature ceases to have control over us. It is a logical conclusion of our philosophy that there must come a time when we shall have conquered all the environments, because nature is finite.

Here is another thing to learn. How do you know that nature is finite? You can only know this through metaphysics. Nature is that Infinite under limitations. Therefore it is finite. So, there must come a time when we shall have conquered all environments. And how are we to conquer them? We cannot possibly conquer *all* the objective environments. We cannot. The little fish wants to fly from its enemies in the water. How does it do so? By evolving wings and becoming a bird. The fish did not change the water or the air; the change was in itself. Change is always subjective. All through evolution you find that the conquest of nature comes by change in the subject. Apply this to religion and morality, and you will find that the conquest of evil comes by the change in the subjective alone. That is how the Advaita system gets its whole force, on the subjective side of man. To talk of evil and misery is nonsense, because they do not exist outside. If I am immune against all anger, I never feel angry. If I am proof against all hatred, I never feel hatred. This is, therefore, the process by which to achieve that conquest—through the subjective, by perfecting the subjective.

I may make bold to say that the only religion which agrees with, and even goes a little further than modern researches, both on physical and moral lines is the Advaita, and that is why it appeals to modern scientists so much. They find that the old dualistic theories are not enough for them, do not satisfy their necessities. A man must have not only faith, but intellectual faith too. Now, in this latter part of the nineteenth century, such an idea as that religion coming from any other source than one's own hereditary religion must be false shows that there is still weakness left, and such ideas must be given up. I do not mean that such is the case in this country alone, it is in every country, and nowhere more than in my own. This Advaita was never allowed to come to the people. At first some monks got hold of it and took it to the forests, and so it came to be called the "Forest Philosophy." By the mercy of the Lord, the Buddha came and preached it to the masses, and the whole nation became Buddhists. Long after that, when theists and agnostics had destroyed the nation again, it was found out that Advaita was the only way to save India from materialism.

Thus Advaita has twice saved India from materialism. Before Buddha came, materialism had spread to a fearful extent, and it was of a most hideous kind, not like that of the present day, but of a far worse nature. You see, I myself am a materialist in a certain sense, because I believe that there is only One. That is what the materialist wants you to believe, only he calls it matter and I call it God. The materialists admit that out of this matter all hope and religion and everything have come. I say that all these have come out of Brahman. But the materialism that prevailed before Buddha's time was that crude sort of materialism which taught: "Eat, drink, and be merry. There is no God, soul, or heaven. Religion is a concoction of wicked priests." It taught the morality that so long as you live, you must try to live happily; eat, though you have to borrow money for the food, and never mind about repaying it. That was the old materialism, and that kind of philosophy spread so much that even today it goes by the name of "popular philosophy." Buddha brought Vedānta to light, gave it to the people, and saved India.

A thousand years after his death a similar state of things again prevailed. The mob, the masses, and various races coming from outside had been converted to Buddhism; naturally the teachings of the Buddha became in time degenerated, because most of the people were very ignorant. Buddhism taught no God, no Ruler of the universe; so gradually the masses brought their gods and devils and hobgoblins out again, and a tremendous hotchpotch was made of Buddhism in India. Again materialism came to the fore, taking the form of licence with the higher classes and superstition with the lower. Then Śankarāchārya arose and once more revivified the Vedānta philosophy. He made it a rationalistic philosophy. In the Upaniṣads the arguments are often very obscure. By Buddha the moral side of the philosophy was laid stress upon, and by Śankarācārya, the intellectual side. Śaṅkara worked out, rationalised, and placed before men the wonderful coherent system of Advaita.

Materialism prevails in Europe today. You may pray for the salvation of the modern sceptics, but they do not yield, they want reason. The salvation of Europe depends on a rationalistic religion, and Advaita—the non-duality, the Oneness, the idea of the Impersonal God—is the only religion that can have any hold on any intellectual people. It comes whenever religion seems to disappear and irreligion seems to prevail, and that is why it has taken ground in Europe and America.

I would say one thing more in connection with this philosophy. In the old Upaniṣads we find sublime poetry; their authors were poets. Plato says, inspiration comes to people through poetry, and it seems as if these ancient Rishis, seers of truths, were raised above humanity to show these truths through poetry. They never preached or philosophized or wrote. Music came out of their hearts. In Buddha we had a great, universal heart and infinite patience, making religion practical and bringing it to everyone's door. In Śankarācārya we saw tremendous intellectual power, throwing the searching light of reason upon everything. We want today that bright sun of intellectuality joined with the heart of Buddha, the wonderful, infinite heart of love and mercy. This union will give us the highest philosophy. Science and religion will meet and shake hands. Poetry and philosophy will become friends. This will be the religion of the future, and if we can work it out, we may be sure that it will be for all times and peoples.

This is the one thing that will prove acceptable to modern science, for it has almost come to it. When a scientist makes the assertion that all objects are the manifestation of one force, does it not remind you of the God of whom you hear in the Upaniṣads? "As the one fire entering into the universe expresses itself in various forms, even so that one Soul is expressing Itself in every soul and yet is infinitely more besides." Do you not see whither science is tending? The Hindu nation proceeded through the study of the mind, through metaphysics and logic. The European nations start from external nature, and now they too are coming to the same results. We find that searching through the mind we at last come to that Oneness, that Universal One, the Internal Soul of everything, the Essence and Reality of everything, the Ever-Free, the Ever-Blissful, the Ever-Existing. Through material science we come to the same Oneness. Science today is telling us that all things are but the manifestation of one energy which is the sum total of everything which exists, and the trend of humanity is towards freedom and not towards bondage. Why should men be moral? Because through morality is the path towards freedom, and immorality leads to bondage.

Another peculiarity of the Advaita system is that from its very start it is non-destructive. This is another glory, the boldness to preach, "Do not disturb the faith of any, even of those who through ignorance have attached themselves to lower forms of worship." That is what it says, do not disturb, but help everyone to get higher and higher; include all humanity. This philosophy preaches a God who is a sum total. If you seek a universal religion which can apply to everyone, that religion must not be composed of only the parts, but it must always be their sum total and include all degrees of religious development. This idea is not clearly found in any other religious system. They are all parts equally struggling to attain to the whole. The existence of the part is only for this.

So, from the very first, Advaita had no antagonism with the various sects existing in India. There are dualists existing today, and their number is by far the largest in India, because dualism naturally appeals to less educated minds. It is a very convenient, natural, commonsense explanation of the universe. But with these dualists, Advaita has no quarrel. The one thinks that God is outside the universe, somewhere in heaven, and the other, that He is his own Soul, and that it will be a blasphemy to call Him anything more distant. Any idea of separation would be terrible. He is the nearest of the near. There is no word in any language to express this nearness except the word Oneness. With any other idea the Advaitist is not satisfied just as the dualist is shocked with the concept of the Advaita, and thinks it blasphemous. At the same time the Advaitist knows that these other ideas must be, and so has no quarrel with the dualist who is on the right road. From his standpoint, the dualist will have to see many. It is a constitutional necessity of his standpoint. Let him have it. The Advaitist knows that whatever may be his theories, he is going to the same goal as he himself. There he differs entirely from the dualist who is forced by his point of view to believe that all differing views are wrong.

The dualists all the world over naturally believe in a Personal God who is purely anthropomorphic, who like a great potentate in this world is pleased with some and displeased with others. He is arbitrarily pleased with some people or races and showers blessing upon them. Naturally the dualist comes to the conclusion that God has favourites, and he hopes to be one of them. You will find that in almost every religion is the idea, "We are the favourites of our God, and only by believing as we do, can you be taken into favour with Him." Some dualists are so narrow as to insist that only the few that have been predestined to the favour of God can be saved; the rest may try ever so hard, but they cannot be accepted. I challenge you to show me one dualistic religion which has not more or less of this exclusiveness. And, therefore, in the nature of things, dualistic religions are bound to fight and quarrel with each other, and this they have ever been doing. Again, these dualists win the popular favour by appealing to the vanity of the uneducated. They like to feel that they enjoy exclusive privileges.

The dualist thinks you cannot be moral until you have a God with a rod in His hand, ready to punish you. The unthinking masses are generally dualists, and they, poor fellows, have been persecuted for thousands of years in every country; and their idea of salvation is, therefore, freedom from the fear of punishment. I was asked by a clergyman in America, "What! You have no Devil in your religion? How can that be?"

But we find that the best and the greatest men that have been born in the world have worked with that high impersonal idea. It is the Man who said, "I and my Father are One," whose power has descended unto millions. For thousands of years it has worked for good. And we know that the same Man, because he was a non-dualist, was merciful to others. To the masses who could not conceive of anything higher than a Personal God, he said, "Pray to your Father in heaven." To others who could grasp a higher idea, he said, "I am the vine, ye are the branches", but to his disciples to whom he revealed himself more fully, he proclaimed the highest truth, "I and my Father are One."

It was the great Buddha, who never cared for the dualist gods, and who has been called an atheist and materialist, who yet was ready to give up his body for a poor goat. That Man set in motion the highest moral ideas any nation can have. Wherever there is a moral code, it is a ray of light from that man.

We cannot force the great hearts of the world into narrow limits and keep them there, especially at this time in the history of humanity, when there is a degree of intellectual development such as was never dreamt of even a hundred years ago, when a wave of scientific knowledge has arisen which nobody, even fifty years ago, would have dreamt of. By trying to force people into narrow limits you degrade them into animals and unthinking masses. You kill their moral life. What is now wanted is a combination of the greatest heart with the highest intellectuality, of infinite love with infinite knowledge. The Vedāntist gives no other attributes to God except these three: Infinite Existence, Infinite Knowledge, and Infinite Bliss; and he regards these three as one. Existence without Knowledge and Love cannot be; Knowledge without Love, and Love without Knowledge, cannot be. What we want is the harmony of Existence, Knowldege, and Bliss Infinite. For that is our goal. We want harmony, not one-sided development. And it is possible to have the intellect of a Śaṅkara with the heart of a Buddha. I hope we shall all struggle to attain to that blessed combination.

A. C. Mukerji, "Absolute Consciousness" (1938)

Anukul Chandra Mukerji (1888–1968) succeeded R. D. Ranade as Professor of Philosophy at Allahabad. He was a scholar of Western and Indian philosophy and specialized in epistemology, with a special interest in idealism and the problem of self-knowledge. He published two books during his life: *The Nature of Self* (1933), and *Self Thought and Reality* (1938). The present essay, a chapter of *The Nature of Self,* deploys the insights of British neo-Hegelians, such as Caird and Greene, to gain insight into Śaṅkara's account of absolute consciousness.

Anukul Chandra Mukerji

3

Absolute Consciousness

THE POSITION WE have so far reached under the guidance of Śaṅkara, Kant, Green, Haldane, and Bradley is that an unchanging, unobjectifiable, immediate, consciousness must be postulated for explaining the poorest type of knowledge and the facts of experience. Truth emerges from mutual supplementation and correction of different interpretations of experience; and it is, therefore, necessary, for a further development of our position, to examine its strength in resolving some of the difficulties that have been repeatedly pointed out by the critics of modern absolutism which in many respects, as we have seen above, is an unconscious exposition of the advaita doctrine.[1]

Bradley's supra-relational immediate experience in which "the experienced and the experience are one," and Prof. Alexander's formulation of the knowledge of mind as an enjoyment which is an "experienced experiencing," are, as we have contended in the last chapter, unexpected confirmations of the advaita theory of self from the realistic and the idealistic quarters respectively. Its further elaboration may now be attempted through Śaṅkara's theory of the Absolute; and it will incidentally dissipate the wide-spread illusion that the advaita Absolute is an altogether transcendent Principle, sitting, like an oriental potentate, out of all connections with our finite experiences. Such a transcendent Absolute may inspire the sentiments of adoration and admiration like a colossal marble structure, but what it cannot precisely do is to serve as an explanatory principle of our finite experience.

We must resist here the temptation to examine the current view that Śaṅkara's position was essentially anticipated by the Buddhistic idealists, and that "looked at from that point of view there would be very little which could be regarded as original in Śaṅkara."[2] There can be no two opinions in respect of the fact that some Buddhists, such as, Aśvaghoṣe, Asaṅga, Vasubandhu,

1. For instance, Bradley's doctrine of immediate experience has provoked much criticism, and, therefore, to depend upon Bradley would be like leaning upon a broken reed. One of the most cautious examinations of Bradley's theory has been recently furnished by Prof. G. Watts Cunningham in *The Idealistic Argument in Recent British and American Philosophy*, pp. 382–407. His contentions seem, on the whole, not unjustifiable; and it will be, therefore, necessary to see how far our position may be kept free from the main difficulties in the theory of immediate experience.

2. Dr. S. N. Das Gupta, *Indian Idealism*, p. 195.

Sthiramati, and others, were eminent absolutists who taught a type of monistic philosophy that cannot be easily distinguished from that of Śaṅkara. Particularly, the *Vijñaptimātra* of Vasubandhu can be hardly distinguished from the *Brahman* of Śaṅkara. In fact, no philosopher can expound an entirely original doctrine without being indebted in any way to his predecessors. The originality of a philosopher consists in his capacity for an intelligent appropriation of the previously formulated doctrines and their development in new directions, rather than in shooting a new bullet from a newly manufactured pistol. But when it is remarked that "Śaṅkara does not try to prove philosophically the existence of the pure self as distinct from all other things," and that he "is satisfied in showing" it to be the teaching of the Upaniṣads, it may not be easy for everyone to subscribe to this view.[3] Such a remark, though made by many modern orientalists, requires justification at least in view of the contrary opinion of P. Deussen that Śaṅkara "makes a far more extensive use" of philosophical reflection as an aid than might appear from his antirational expressions, and that it is "not merely theological, but also in the highest degree philosophical."[4] It is true that he does sometimes claim the privilege of flouting logic by appealing to the Upaniṣads; but the philosophical analysis that is avoided at one place is supplied at another. The Absolute, he says explicitly, is not to be realised through mere scriptural texts, on the contrary, it can be understood only through the threefold stage of authority, reasoning, and contemplation.[5] Even in his principal work, the object of the Vedānta is said at the beginning to be to prove the identity of the individual self with the Absolute; because there are conflicting opinions on the nature of the self. And all the non-advaita theories may be refuted, as he says explicitly, *independently of the scriptural texts*.[6] The fact is that the Vedānta, far from faring without logic, has to remove "all doubts arising out of conflicting opinions" (*vipratipattyāśankā*) as a necessary part of its discipline, even when the scriptures fail to provide appropriate texts.

The very first thing to be noted in expounding Śaṅkara's theory of Absolute Self is the contrast which his method of approach offers to that of modern absolutism. In the latter, the finite self is a self-discrepant reality which forces thought to transcend it; the finite self, that is, has no logical stability, though it is the highest reality, the most consistent reality, among the finite things of

---

3. *Ibid.*, p. 163, and *History of Indian Philosophy I*, p. 435.

4. *The System of the Vedānta*, p. 96. Dr. Das Gupta appears to attach much importance to the opinions of such scholars as Dr. Th. Stcherbatsky who has supposed that Śaṅkara "does not accept the authority of logic as a means of cognising the Absolute, but he deems it a privilege of the Vedānta to fare without logic since he has Revelation to fall back upon."—*The Conception of Buddhist Nirvāṇa*, p. 38.

5. *Nānyathā śravaṇamātreṇa—Com. on the Bṛh. Up. IV. 2. 5.*

6. *Iha tu vākyanirapekṣaḥ etc. S. B. II. 2. 1.*

the world. The Absolute, on the other hand, is a perfect system, a perfectly consistent whole, and, as such, it is the resting place of thought, it is the Idea in which thought finds its fullest satisfaction. In sharp contrast with this method of approach, Śaṅkara seeks to discover the Absolute, not by transcending the finite self, but by a deeper analysis of the self in us which is erroneously taken to be anything less than the Absolute; it is, in other words, the method of discovering the Absolute by removing the erroneous notions about our self which, though in fact the Absolute, is falsely taken to be finite and relative. The Absolute, he says, exists and is real in the highest sense, because it is the self in us which none can deny.[7] The latter does not possess a particular degree of reality, as distinct from the former, but it *is* the highest reality. There is essentially no distinction between the two; and, consequently, the problem which a philosopher must set to himself in respect of the Absolute is, not to prove the Absolute from the relative, but to account for the rise of the relative from the Absolute.

In view of this contrast of the advaita method with that of modern absolutism, it will be evident that what we have so far said about the foundational consciousness is as much true of the finite self as of the Absolute Self. If the finite self is essentially an unchanging, immediate non-objectifiable, consciousness, the same must be true of the Absolute Self. Hence, an exposition of the Absolute will necessarily mean a further development and clarification of the principle of unchanging, immediate, consciousness.

The Absolute Self, for Śaṅkara, may be negatively defined as that which is diametrically opposed to an object, it has none of the characteristics which belong to the objects. It is neither a quality, nor a substance; neither a cause nor an effect; neither the creator nor the created; in fact all categories are applicable to the world of objects, and not to the Absolute. All categories are relational, and, therefore, are inapplicable to what is non-relational. But this must not be interpreted as leading to the doctrine that the Absolute is pure nothing, a mere thing-in-itself in the Kantian sense. The agnostic's Reality is in fact a self-contradictory reality, if it can be called a reality at all; it falls entirely beyond our human faculties, inconceivable, unthinkable, and perfectly unknowable. Thus, as we have remarked frequently, Śaṅkara's doctrine of self is one which is developed by a careful avoidance of the opposite fallacies of pan-objectivism and agnosticism. On the one hand, he is anxious to emphasise that the self is distinct from the not-self as light is distinct from darkness, that the conditions under which the objects stand are inapplicable to the subject. But lest the self should be misunderstood as a pure nothing, he adds, sometimes immediately, that what is thus beyond the conditions of the

7. *S. B. I. 1. 1.*

knowable objects is our very self. The self in this sense is said to be beyond the known and above the unknown.

Most of the self-theories, either in India or the West, have succumbed to pan-objectivism; while those which have successfully withstood this fatal materialistic tendency have lost themselves in mysticism and agnosticism. Some of these we have examined in the foregoing pages; but to do it exhaustively would be neither possible within the limits of this work nor necessary for our purpose. What must have been clear by now is that no theory of self can stand logical scrutiny if it fails to avoid these two extremes of pan-objectivism and agnosticism. The self, as we have urged, is a reality which is both undefinable and undeniable. This peculiar character of the self has been missed partly because it has been supposed that whatever is undefinable must be also unintelligible and a pure nothing, and largely because the very grammatical forms of the language in which we are to express our thought have encouraged the conception of a self as something like the table or the chair, or, as a man looking, to put it after an Indian philosopher, through the windows of the sense-organs.

But we have seen very clearly that the self is not something like a table possessing different qualities of hardness, colour, and weight; it is, in other words, a reality that cannot be brought under the categories of substance and attribute; on the contrary, the self *is* consciousness, and not a substance possessing consciousness. And it should be, therefore, clear why it must be both undefinable as well as undeniable. That it is undeniable seems to be so evident a fact that any imposing array of dialectical weapons for proving it would look like wasting philosophical ingenuity on a trifle. You may deny or doubt everything, as Śaṅkara and Descartes urged, but you cannot deny the fact of consciousness.

As for the other alternative, it will be enough to remember Śaṅkara's analysis of definition which always consists in bringing what is defined under a generic unity with specific difference through the attributes by which it is differentiated from other things belonging to the same genus. But consciousness cannot be so defined inasmuch as it is the ultimate presupposition of all knowable objects. Whatever is known, as we have observed repeatedly, must be presented to consciousness, and in this sense it is the universal presupposition of all things and of all interobjective relations. In order to be defined, consciousness must be brought under a higher genus, and also differentiated from things other than itself belonging to the same genus. But this would be to contradict the assertion that it is the ultimate presupposition of all knowable objects. It will also commit ourselves to the absurd position that consciousness has an attribute by which it may be distinguished from things other than itself. Once, therefore, it is admitted that consciousness is *sui generis*, it must also be conceded that it cannot be defined in the ordinary way. It may be very interesting to note here that at least one of the modern philosophers has come to admit the essential truth of our contentions. Thinking as well as knowing, willing and desiring, it has been remarked by J. Cook Wilson, are activities of consciousness. "This, therefore, is a case where the ordinary idea of definition is not applicable. Ordinary definition is a statement of the general kind (genus) to which the thing to be defined belongs and of the characteristics of the particular sort (species), that is the differentiation of the kind (genus), to which the thing to be defined belongs."[8] The process of definition, it is further remarked, must end in something "which cannot be defined, in the given sense of definition, or the process would never end. Definition in fact itself presupposes the ending of the process in elements which cannot be themselves defined, in so-called ultimate distinctions explicable from themselves alone. This does not leave our notions indefinite, because the nature of such undefinable universals is perfectly definite and is apprehended by us in the particular instances of them."

How far these remarks of Wilson on the nature of consciousness are but a confirmation of the views we have so far explained is too clear to require any special comment. It is of the nature of the undefinable universals which are yet perfectly definite, and intelligible. To ask to define consciousness, therefore, Wilson continues, would be to commit "the fallacy of asking an unreal question, a question which is such in verbal form only and to which no real questioning in thought can correspond." In professing to explain, therefore, such a term as consciousness, the result will be "identical statements, for we should use in our explanation the very notion we professed to explain, disguised perhaps by a change of name or by the invention of some new term, say cognition or some similar imposture." Wilson then concludes: "Our experience of knowing then being the presupposition of any enquiry we undertake, we cannot make knowing itself a subject of enquiry in the sense of asking what knowing is."

Here we find an excellent formulation, from an unexpected quarter, of the essentials of our contentions about the foundational character of consciousness, as well as about its undefinable nature. Incidentally, it exposes the fallacy of presentationism which clings to the unwarranted assumption that whatever is real must be a definable object of thought. The truth is that Reality is wider than the world of definable objects, though Kant supposed that it was limited to what he called the phenomenal world. The categories are certainly applicable to the objects of experience alone, but from this it does not follow that whatever does not conform to them must necessarily be a mere 'x.' Kant could not catch the self and turned round and round it in a perpetual circle, because he wanted to catch it, like the empiricists, as a definable object. His assumption here was identical with that of the rational psychologists whom

8. *Statement and Inference*, p. 38.

he was criticising. The self, again, does not reduce itself to something "completely empty of all content," simply on the ground that it is not conformable to the categories. It is true, says Śaṅkara, that by 'the known' we mean "whatever is the object of special knowledge, and as all such objects can be known somewhere, to some extent and by someone, and so forth, the whole world is meant by the term 'the known.' " But the self is something entirely different (*anyadeva*). From this we must not conclude that it is unknown.[9] The objects must conform to the categories of genus, action, etc. (*Jāti, kriyā,* etc.). But the self cannot be unknown simply because it does not conform to the categories; and to draw such a conclusion would be as absurd as that of a man "who fails to see, though near, the existence of himself, which completes the number, when closely engaged in counting the persons other than himself."[10]

The empiricists like Locke, James and the Indian realists who tried to discover the self through introspection made a similarly futile attempt. Is not the self, asks Śaṅkara, known at all, and, if so, does not the scripture contradict itself when it says: "You should not try to know the thinker of thought and the knower of knowledge?" Certainly, Śaṅkara replies, this would be contradictory "if he is to be directly perceived like joy, etc."[11] But the self is neither an object of external nor of internal perception, yet its reality cannot be denied.

Enough perhaps has been said in explication of the undefinability of the self as consciousness. But this fact does not make it unintelligible through human faculties; we need not appeal to any extra-human or extraordinary intuition for understanding the nature of consciousness. Because it is perfectly intelligible, though undefinable. It will help a further clarification of the nature of the self if we now turn to Śaṅkara's explanation of the Absolute or *Brahman,* and, we believe, it will be clear that consciousness is not only immediate in the sense that it is ever known though not known as an object, but it is necessarily absolute. In this sense, if the self is given in an immediate experience, it is also an Absolute Immediate Experience.[12]

---

9. *Com. on the Kenopaniṣad I.* 3.

10. *Com, on the Tait. Up. Brahmaballī.*

11. Summary of the *Ch. IV. of the Ait. Up.*

12. It may be emphasised here that the advaita term '*aparokṣ ānubhūti*' does not necessarily mean mystic intuition, though many have still the tendency to interpret it as an extraordinary perception of the character of the religious ecstasy. But this point need not be pressed very much, as every instructed student of the advaita philosophy knows that Śaṅkara uses the word '*aparokṣa*' at the very beginning of his principal work in the ordinary sense of immediate experience. The term, in fact, means any immediate perception not arising from the senses when it is used in connection with our knowledge of the self. But it is also used in a wider sense to include immediate sense-perception as well as any other type of immediate knowledge not originating from the senses. The term is clearly explained in *Outlines of Indian Philosophy*, p. 545, by Prof. M. Hiriyanna.

The Absolute, we must repeat, is not, for Śaṅkara, something essentially different from the self which we know immediately, and, consequently, the method of establishing its reality is that of a further analysis of our own self which is consciousness. The contrast of the advaita conception of the difference between the individual self and the Absolute with that of the Hegelian idealists may be very well seen from the remarks of an Indian Hegelian. In spite of the divergence of opinion on a number of subjects connected with Hegel's philosophy, we are told by Dr. Hiralal Haldar, the leading exponents of absolutism agree that the Absolute is a concrete whole, it is "the unity which realises *itself* in the differences;" and not a unity in which all differences are lost. But how do we come to posit the reality of such an Absolute? The logic of this type of absolutism, it is replied, lies in the conviction that the conception of an individual including in its knowledge the whole of Reality which at the same time it excludes is not a satisfying concept. "It is a contradictory conception pointing to the solution of it in the inclusion of the individuals in a wider unity, where it and other selves like it come together and are commingled without loss of their individuality."[13] The finite is supposed to be a "contradictory self," though it resolves the greater contradictions which are in the not-selves, such as matter, when regarded in abstraction from the finite self. Nothing can be external to consciousness; but as consciousness exists through its opposition to the 'other,' which it at the same time annuls, and as the unity of my consciousness does not exercise this double function completely, there must be an Absolute Unity.

In view of a strong tendency in contemporary Indian philosophy to obscure the difference between modern idealism and the advaita absolutism, it will be useful to follow Dr. Haldar's formulation of the former a little further. The Absolute, he adds, is not a mere aggregate, it is a conscious organic unity, and though not personal as man is personal, it is super-personal, because it must be conscious or rather a self-conscious unity realised in the self-consciousness of each individual. The absolutists before McTaggart, it is continued, did not emphasise the fact that the self-differentiations of the Absolute are themselves persons. McTaggart, on the other hand, while rightly emphasising that each of the differentiations of the Absolute must be a spirit, shrinks from the position that the Absolute must also be a person. The Absolute, we are told in another context, is not the synthesis of finite experiences; it is the finite selves, on the contrary, which arise out of the limitation of the Absolute life and experience."[14] Our knowledge of the Absolute, however, is bound to

---

13. *Neo-Hegelianism*, p. 466.

14. *Essays*, p. 117.

be imperfect, yet it is a "necessary corollary of Hegel's theory" that the Absolute, as a harmonious Whole cannot be other than blissful. Thus, the True, the Good, the Beautiful—"this must ever remain the fittest description of the Absolute."[15]

Thus, it is clear that Dr. Haldar's difference from the other British Hegelians centres round the problem of personality, but he agrees with them in respect of the main outlines of the nature of the Absolute and that of the finite self, and he clearly shows why thought must transcend the finite self and find satisfaction in an Absolute Experience. "The basis of my thought," he admits, "is undoubtedly Hegelian," though it has been modified in later years.[16] It is evident then that there is a deep chasm between the advaita absolutism and its modern type. Immediate experience is the very heart of Śaṅkara's absolutism, whereas Hegel would never tolerate pure immediacy in absolutism, and this was at the root of his well-known criticism of the *unmittelbares Wissen* of Jacobi. It is true that there was a stage in the development of Hegel's thought when he accepted as the ultimate criterion of truth some type of immediacy to which reason was supposed to be unable to rise; but this was only a stage which he overgrew, and as a result, he broke off his friendship with Schelling. The strength of Hegelian idealism is in its conception of the concrete universal, the mediated unity, whereas Śaṅkara's absolutism is nothing if it is shorn of immediate experience. Other interesting points of difference will suggest themselves automatically as we proceed to expound his doctrine of the Absolute Self.

One of the places where Śaṅkara formulates clearly his doctrine of the Absolute is the *Brahmaballī* of the *Tait. Up*. The Absolute (*Brahman*), he starts by saying, is Existence, Knowledge, and Infinity. These, however, are not attributes of the Absolute, they are rather the Absolute itself; they do not define the Absolute in the ordinary sense of the term 'definition.' Because definition which is always through generic unity and specific difference cannot be applied to what is not a finite thing among other finite things, like the blue lotus. Yet just as Space (*ākāśa*) may be indirectly indicated by giving its peculiarity, when, *e.g.*, it is said that the space is what gives room, the *Brahman* also may be defined in this sense by the three indicative terms. These three indicative epithets, it is said as a warning against possible misinterpretations, are not to be taken as three distinct categories; they do not indicate the Absolute when taken severally, but they can indicate it only "by virtue of their combined connotation in which the meaning of each controls, and is controlled by, the

15. *Essays*, p. 42.

16. *Contemporary Indian Philosophy*, p. 216.

meaning of the other."[17] That is, though each of these categories is ordinarily used independently of the other, yet, they, when used in their combined connotation, may differentiate the Absolute from all finite things, like the blue lotus. It is true that the Absolute is indescribable; but, in spite of this, it may be indirectly described by using the highest categories of thought when the latter are not taken in their individual meanings.

We do not intend to discuss here how far Śaṅkara's interpretation of the agnostic tendency of some of the expressions of the Upaniṣads is more or less true than that of the other nonadvaita thinkers, such as Rāmānuja; nor need we raise here the interesting problem of the comparative faithfulness of Śaṅkara and Rāmānuja respectively to the philosophical significance of the *Vedānta Sūtra* of Bādarāyaṇa. What is clear from the above explanations by Śaṅkara of the Upaniṣadic agnosticism is that he was not an agnostic in the same sense as Kant or Spencer. And a little exposition of his contentions will show the profundity of his philosophical insight as well as the baselessness of the common charge that his absolutism offers no aid for any new interpretation of experience.

Being, like knowledge, is foundational; it is as meaningless to deny existence or being, as to refute consciousness or knowing. The attempt to contrast being with non-being presupposes the existence of non-being, much as the attempt to contrast knowledge with ignorance presupposes that ignorance is known. In this sense, being is as irrepressible a category as consciousness. Even illusions and dreams exist, and if these are unreal, the very contrast between the real and the unreal would be impracticable without their common basis in the category of being. A real appearance, that is, can be distinguished from an illusory or mere appearance, like the dream-experience, only in so far as the category of being is immanent in both. Being in this sense "is the root of the universe; and all these creatures—movable and immovable—have their root in Being; and not only have they their root in Being, but during their continuance too, they reside in Being, much as apart from the clay, the jar does not exist."[18] It is true that the dream-experiences are unreal in comparison with our waking experience, "the objects perceived in dreams are false for the awakened man," but "the falsity is not by itself, but only in comparison with waking cognition." Even when some experiences are condemned as false, they are false "only in their character of specific forms; in their character of pure Being, these too are true."[19]

17. *Evaṁsatyādiśabdā itaretarasaṅnidhāvanyonyaniya-myaniyāmaka santaḥ—loc. cit.*

18. Śaṅkara's *Commentary on the Ch. Up. VI. 8. 5.*

19. *Ibid. VIII. 5. 4.*

Modern thought is already familiar with such arguments. Green, for instance, remarks that "the illusive appearance, as opposed to the reality, of any event is what *that* event really is not; but at the same time it really is something."[20] Green, therefore, warns against the crude logic of Plato in supposing that there are objects which stand in the same relation to ignorance as to knowledge, and other objects which stand in a corresponding relation to mere opinion; the distinction of the real from the unreal is, therefore, "a distinction between one particular reality and another."[21] It is true that "we may confuse the two kinds of object. We may take what is really of the one kind to be really of the other. But this is not a confusion of the real with the unreal. The very confusion itself, the mistake of supposing what is related in one way to be related in another, has its own reality. It has its history, its place in the development of a man's mind, its causes and effects; and, as so determined, it is as real as anything else." It is thus in vain, concludes Green, "that we seek to define the real by finding, either in the work of the mind or elsewhere, an unreal to which it may be opposed." All things, in the language of Śaṅkara, are in this sense rooted in being, have their cause in being, and rest on and reside in being.[22]

In view of this foundational character of Being which is emphasised by Śaṅkara, it will be surely doing a grave injustice to him to say that both Śaṅkara and Nāgārjuna strike on the same rock, as both "explain experience in such a way that the experience to be explained has no longer any reality."[23] But, continues Mr. Thomas, though experience has to be denied explicitly, "yet the experience itself is the basis of the negative conclusion." The real difference between Śaṅkara and Nāgārjuna or Candrakīrti has been rightly emphasised by Dr. Das Gupta, in so far as he points out that, for Nāgārjuna, the appearance of the world "is like the appearance of mirages or dreams which have no reality of their own, but still present an objective appearance of reality."[24] Though the world, according to Nāgārjuna and Candrakīrti, has only a relative truth, yet "there is no reality on which these appearances rest or are imposed." But Śaṅkara differed from the Buddhists at this place; both Gauḍapāda and Śaṅkara think that "even false creations must have some basis in truth."[25] If

20. *Prolegomena*, p. 27.

21. *Loc. cit.*

22. They are *sanmūlāḥ, satkāraṇ āḥ, sadāyatanāḥ, and sadāśrayāḥ—Com. on the Ch. Up. VI.* 8. 4.

23. Mr. E. J. Thomas, *History of Buddhist Thought*, p. 256.

24. *History of Indian Philosophy, Vol. II*, p. 5.

25. *Ibid.*, p. 7.

then the originality of Śaṅkara consisted in this "fundamental doctrine" that "there was one reality, the Brahman," this, we believe, was no mean originality, as Dr. Das Gupta seems to think.[26] The comprehension of the foundational character of Being is one of the greatest achievements of modern idealism; Being, as rightly urged by Hegel, is immanent in all other categories, however poor and indeterminate it might be in comparison with the other categories. In spite of their fundamental differences in other respects, Śaṅkara and Hegel are so far in agreement with each other that Being is the most irrepressible category of all things.

The foundational character of Being is contrasted in another context with the concept of being in the other systems of philosophy. Existence or Being, it is urged, is pure, subtle, undefinable, all-pervading, one, taintless, indivisible, knowledge.[27] It is not a class-concept, as held by the Vaiśeṣika thinkers. It is true that they accept being as a class-concept pervading substances, qualities, actions, etc. But they miss the foundational character of Being inasmuch as they accept a doctrine of causation according to which every effect is a new creation which did not exist in the cause. Such a view of causation (known technically as the *asatkāryavāda*), to explain Śaṅkara's meaning, arises out of the confusion between the ultimate presupposition of all knowable things and the empirical concept of being. "Nor do they admit of the reality of a single Being." In other words, the category of being, as a universal, must be one, while the empirical concept of being, as a class-concept, is abstracted from the actually perceived things.

Again, the Naiyāyikas hold that "the reality is both being and non-being," one being the contradictory of the other; while the Buddhists do not admit of any other reality except the negation of being. Śaṅkara's criticism of the Buddhistic doctrine of pure negation brings out clearly the meaning of his theory of foundational being. "If the nihilists contend that prior to creation, there was a mere negation of being, how is it that they speak of it as *existing* prior to creation, and being one only, without a second, asserting thereby its relations with time and number?" Again, the theory of pure negation would amount to the denial of "the existence of the theoriser himself." It may no doubt be retorted that all apparent beings are due to a mistake (*saṁvṛti*); but "what is this *mistake* itself? Is it an entity or a non-entity?" If the mistake be a non-entity, its existence cannot be proved by any example. So it must be admitted that "the fact of Being never ceases." And even when it is said that the *idea* of the clay is the cause of the *idea* of the jar (*e.g.*, by the Buddhist idealists), it

26. *Indian Idealism*, p. 195.

27. *Com. on the Ch. Up. VI. 2. 1.*

must be admitted that "only an *existing* idea of clay is the cause of the *existing* idea of the jar. Being in this sense is an ultimate category, and even an effect coming out of a cause must so far be called "being in another form," much as the different things produced from the clay, though differing among themselves, are yet "the same in respect of the clay."

Thus, to put it briefly, the category of being is an ultimate and universal category presupposed by all conceivable things, including the concepts of substance, attribute, cause, effect, idea, illusion, and error. The Absolute, therefore, far from being a transcendent Principle out of all relation to the world of our experience, is immanent through and through in all that exists. It is not a mere class-concept, nor is it an empirical concept limited in its application to one group of things to the exclusion of another group. It is the immanent principle which is so foundational that no conceivable entity can stand without it. Some of the problems which arise here must be considered below. Meanwhile, it will be useful to consider Śaṅkara's doctrine of the Absolute as Infinite.

Infinity, for Śaṅkara, is three-fold; namely, infinity in respect of time, infinity in respect of space, and infinity in respect of substance. A finite thing may be either limited in time, or limited in space, or, again, it may be limited by the existence of something external to itself. The Absolute, on the contrary, is neither limited in space or time nor by something distinct from itself. Hence, the infinity of the Self is the highest type of infinity, and its truth is the highest truth.[28] Space, for example, has a kind of infinity, in so far as all particular spaces are within one unlimited space; but it cannot be called infinite in respect of time and substance. (*Natu kālataśca ānantyam vastutaśca ākāśasya.*) The infinity of the Absolute is, therefore, not like the spatial infinity. A finite thing, on the other hand, is always limited by the existence of things different from itself. (*Bhinnaṁ hi vastu vast-vantarasyānto bhavati.*) "It is the existence of a thing different from a given thing that limits the latter." Every object of thought is limited by that other object from which thought turns away; as, for instance, "our knowledge of the cow is reflected away from our knowledge of the horse, and consequently the concept of cow is limited by the concept of horse." Such limitations are not applicable to the Absolute.

From these explanations of the nature of the Absolute, as offered by Śaṅkara, arises a rather puzzling question which is not brought to the prominence it deserves in modern philosophy. That each category has implicit in it an 'other' is a recognised tenet of modern absolutism. It is also admitted that the objects that are opposed to each other presuppose a common basis

28. *Ato niratiśayam Ātmana ānantyam*, and it has *niratiśayasatyatvam*—*Com. on the Tait. Up. loc. cit.*

or unity underlying the opposition. But, do these rules of determinate knowledge apply to the Absolute? Here we arrive at the parting of the way between modern absolutism and its earlier type. For the former, all knowledge, including the Absolute Experience, is a whole, a unity-in-difference. The Absolute, according to it, is a Spiritual Principle which expresses itself in the different parts, and not a bare identity that excludes all difference. The Infinite, therefore, is a concrete universal which manifests or realises itself in the finite individuals.

For Śaṅkara, on the contrary, the rules of determinate knowledge are inapplicable to the Absolute; because their application would mean that the Absolute has something different from itself belonging to a common genus with it, and that the Absolute has an attribute by which it is differentiated from the other 'something.' The ultimate unity, therefore, must be, for Śaṅkara, what J. Cook Wilson calls an undefinable universal. This position, however, develops another puzzle. "Words signify counter-realities in the objective world."[29] The discursive understanding (*Buddhi*) comprehends everything through specific relations of it to things different from itself. How can, then, the Absolute be even *named*? To name is to differentiate and delimit, but to delimit the Absolute is to bring it under relations. We are thus caught on the horns of a dilemma. Either the Absolute is something that can be named and talked about; in this case, it cannot be absolutely beyond all relational categories. Or, it may be taken as being above all relations, an *ens absolute indeterminatum*, and as such, beyond all speech and thought; in that case, there can be no philosophical discourse about the Absolute, for, like Kant's Thing-in-itself, it can then neither be proved nor disproved.

The former alternative is accepted by many modern absolutists, while the latter has been favoured by some Buddhist absolutists. The modern idealists, in spite of their internal differences, draw their inspiration from the Hegelian tenet that Pure Being is Pure Nothing, that is, existence, when divorced from character, is indistinguishable from a mere naught. The Absolute, therefore, it is insisted, must be in some sense a determinate Being. The Buddhist absolutists, on the other hand, found that whatever was determinate was relative, and, consequently, a determinate Absolute would be a relative Absolute which was a contradiction in terms. The result was that they condemned as futile all reasoned discourse on the Absolute. Not only this, but they sometimes gave themselves up to universal scepticism and declared that all logical or reasoned knowledge was altogether futile and purposeless, and if they themselves were drawn into a logical refutation of a given thesis, the reason was not that they

29. *Com. on the Ch. Up. VI. 2. 1.*

had any definite position of their own, but because this was necessary for convincing an unwise public of the futility of all logical disquisitions. Thus, for instance, Candrakīrti, the distinguished exponent of Nāgārjuna, had to prescribe silence as the only wise course for a philosopher, and this might be taken as the *reductio ad absurdum* of extreme scepticism represented also by the Greek sceptic, Pyrrho.

The anti-agnostic tendency of Hegel, as well as the agnostic attitude of the Buddhist absolutists, despite their antithetical outlooks, have implicit in them a common assumption, namely, that everything which is real for us must be either determinate and definable or pure nothing. From this identical assumption, mutually contradictory conclusions are drawn by Hegel and Nāgārjuna respectively. The logical method is apotheosized by the former and anathematized by the latter; but both leave the initial assumption unquestioned and unchallenged.

The strength of Hegelian absolutism, as we have contended above, lies in its doctrine of the concrete universal. The empiricists supposed that whatever could not be known by the inductive and experimental method was neither real nor true; this attitude ended inevitably in scepticism. Over against this, it was rightly urged by Kant and the post-Kantian thinkers that the universal, though not derivable from experience, was yet the indisputable background of all knowledge, including the knowledge of inductive origin. You cannot, for example, handle a universal law as you handle the stick or the brickbat, but this does not warrant the conclusion that the law is less real than the stick. Similarly, the pattern according to which the parts of a watch are adjusted, the biological laws that govern the functions of a living body, or the mathematical principle that regulates the different sections of a hyperbola,—these are not less real than the parts they govern. To have raised thought from the world of mere particulars to that of the true universal must be considered as a great achievement of the post-Kantian idealists.

The strength of the Buddhist absolutists, on the other hand, lies in their insight into the conditions of discursive thinking. To think is to distinguish, and to know is to contrast; hence it is urged that those who are tied to words do not understand the Absolute Truth. All knowledge, according to them, is vitiated by the exigencies of language, which is always discriminative. Consequently, the pure *Garbha*, according to the Mahāyāna Buddhists, is like a pure gem concealed under a soiled garment, and this garment is linguistic knowledge.[30] The concepts of matter and mind, subject and object, phenomenon and noumenon, cause and effect, are grasped in mutual exclusion and

30. See, e.g., Suzuki, *Studies in the Lankāvatāra Sūtra*, p. 107.

correlativity; thus, relativity and conditionality (called *śūnya* by the Mādhyamika Buddhists) are implicit in all our categories.

If, however, we look at Hegel with the eye of the Buddhists, and *vice versa*, it would appear that the only escape from the horns of the dilemma consists in challenging their common assumption that whatever is real must be either definable or pure nothing. No philosophy can be worth the name if it has to admit the suspension of all judgments to be the highest state of wisdom, and if logical thinking is to be substituted by purely mystic intuition. The modern absolutists, therefore, are here right over against the Buddhists. If the Absolute, which is variously called the *Tathatā*, the *Garbha*, or the *Dharmakāya*—has to be understood by a perfectly anti-logical method, all talks about the philosophical establishment of the Absolute are purely empty and meaningless. Even the so-called perfect knowledge (*pariniṣpannam jñānam*) would in that case reduce itself to an unmeaning word, because its meaning is understood only by contrasting it with imperfect knowledge (*parikalpita*), and if the latter is to be condemned as meaningless, the former cannot escape a similar disaster. In fact, philosophy cannot afford to abandon logical thinking. The Buddhists, on the other hand, are surely right, over against Hegel, in their insight that the Absolute falls beyond relational categories. All our categories are shot through and through with relativity, and, consequently, to identify the Absolute with a category would be to deny in a roundabout way that there is an Absolute at all, because a relational Absolute is a contradiction in terms.

The whole difficulty is clearly envisaged by Śaṅkara in his exposition of the Absolute by the following remarks. If the Absolute cannot be known as we know a lotus, then it might be objected that the definition of the Absolute as Existence, Consciousness, and Infinite, is as meaningless as the assertion that "having bathed in the waters of the mirage, crowned with a garland of sky-flowers, this son of the barren woman is going, armed with a bow made of a hare's horn."[31] But, replies Śaṅkara, the Absolute is not a meaningless naught, though it cannot be defined in the same way as the lotus: because the terms, such as existence, knowledge, etc., are not meaningless, and they retain their original meaning even when they are used for defining the Absolute. It is a mistake to suppose that "whatever is, is capable of being perceived through the medium of the senses by means of its peculiar attribute, such as, e.g., a pot, and what is not so perceived is like the horn of a hare." The Absolute being the presupposition of all finite and determinate things, including even such a thing as space, its reality cannot be denied.

---

31. *Com. on the Tait. Up. loc. cit.*

What Śaṅkara is driving at is evidently this that the self *for* which all objects have a meaning, cannot be itself meaningless, though it cannot be defined in the same way in which a finite thing is defined; consciousness *to* which all objects are presented, cannot be meaningless, though it is not itself presented to something else, though, that is, it is not itself a presentation or an idea. To put it in a different way, the self is not a finite thing along with other finite things, and, consequently, it cannot be defined in accordance with the ordinary rule of definition which consists in distinguishing the thing defined from other things belonging to the same genus by means of its peculiar attributes.

The mistake of the Buddhists, it is now evident, lies in the assumption that whatever is not definable in the ordinary way is as unreal as the hare's horn; and, consequently, it is presumed by them that the Absolute, which cannot be defined *per genus et differentiam*, is as good as nothing for us, and has to be, therefore, apprehended through a type of mystical intuition. What is to be urged against such a view is that the rule of definition cannot be applied to the highest genus inasmuch as it cannot be brought under a higher unity, nor can it be differentiated from any other correlative unities belonging along with it to a higher unity. But this does not reduce the highest unity to a mere nothing, it is rather the ultimate presupposition of all subordinate unities. In this respect, it has been rightly urged by Kant that the unity of consciousness, "which precedes any conception of combination," must not "be confused with the category of unity;" and, for an explanation of this qualitative unity, "we must go further back, and seek it in that which, as the ground of the unity of various conceptions in judgment, is implied in the possibility even of the logical use of understanding."[32] There is one conception, he contends in another context, "that we must now put along with the transcendental conceptions contained in the table of categories, but without in any way changing or adding to the table. This is the conception, or, if it is preferred, the judgment, 'I think.' It is easy to see, that 'I think' is the common vehicle of all conceptions, and therefore of transcendental as well as empirical conceptions. As the vehicle of transcendental conceptions it is itself transcendental, but it cannot claim a special place in the list of these transcendental conceptions, because it merely serves to indicate that all thought belongs to consciousness."[33]

All our categories, it is rightly seen by the Buddhists, are relational and conditional. Substance, attribute, cause, effect, etc., are correlative to one another; but this correlativity among the categories presupposes an ultimate unity which cannot be reduced to any one of these correlated categories.

32. Watson's *Selections*, p. 64.

33. *Ibid.*, p. 145.

The categories of existence and knowledge are generally used in connection with the finite things and the fragmentary knowledge-events, and, as such, they are no doubt in perfect correlativity with the other things and the other knowledge-events from which they are differentiated. But the foundational existence and the foundational knowledge cannot be correlated with anything outside themselves. They are rather the ground of all correlated categories, and, consequently, undefinable yet undeniable. Whatever can be *named* has no doubt to be differentiated from things other than itself, but it cannot be urged that the ultimate and foundational principle itself must be differentiated from other things, because that would be to deny that it is foundational. In this sense, therefore, the ultimate principle is beyond speech and thought, and it may so far be rightly urged that all relational categories, such as, "existence or non-existence, one or many, conditioned or unconditioned, intelligent or dull, active or passive, fruitful or fruitless, produced or causeless, happy or miserable, inside or outside, negative or positive, distinct or non-distinct, are inapplicable to the Absolute."[34] But the difficulty of naming the Absolute can be removed when our ordinary categories are used, not in their individual and mutually exclusive meanings, but "in their combined connotation in which the meaning of each controls and is controlled by the meaning of the other." In other words, the categories of existence, knowledge, and infinity, can indicate the Absolute, only when they are not used as relational categories, but as one single principle in which their relational meanings are merged.

> The only interpreter who has emphasised this aspect of Śaṅkara's position aright, as far as we know, is René Guénon. Some of his remarks on the Vedānta conception of Self are of invaluable importance for avoiding misinterpretations of the advaita doctrine. He has, for instance, rightly warned that when the Self is said to be the universal principle, "the distinction between the Universal and the individual must not be regarded as a correlation, since the second of these two terms, being strictly annulled in respect of the first, cannot in any way be opposed to it."—*L'Homme et son Devenir selon le Vêdânta*, English translation, p. 31.

It may be now seen that Bradley's doctrine of immediate experience, in spite of all that has been said against it, has an important value for working out a true theory of self. The "direct awareness" which is taken to be non-relational, must be recognised to be the ultimate presupposition of all relational knowledge. "A relation," he rightly remarks, "exists only between terms,

34. Śaṅkara's *Summary of the fourth chapter of the Ait. Up.*

and those terms, to be known as such, must be objects." Hence we cannot strictly speak "of a relation, between immediate experience and that which transcends it, except by a licence." It is no doubt necessary, while describing this direct awareness, to speak of it as that *for* which all objects exist; but "if all metaphors are to be pressed, then I, and I think all of us, in the end must keep silence." On some matters, it is necessary to use metaphors which, it is added almost in the language of Śaṅkara, "conflict with and correct each other."[35] It is true that Bradley would not agree to use the term 'self' for this "direct awareness" or immediate experience, because he uses the terms 'self' as well as 'consciousness' in the relational sense. The Absolute, he urges, must not be called a self, or *vice versa,* because that would be "to postulate in the teeth of facts, facts which go to show that the self's character is gone when it ceases to be relative."[36] But this is after all a matter of terminology, and we have seen ample justification in the foregoing pages to find the real character of the self beyond all relations. And as a matter of fact he himself does not hesitate to use the term subject for immediate experience, only it is added that the subject is felt, and, as such, "neither itself, nor its actual distinction from the object, can be got out and placed before it as an object."

So far as Bradley's theory of self and his doctrine of absolute experience is concerned, we need not enter here upon any detailed examination of them, as this has been done by many able critics, particularly by Dr. H. Haldar.[37] But we believe that Bradley's critics have not entirely succeeded in avoiding the mistake of throwing away the baby with the bath. It is unfortunate that Bradley should have used the same term 'feeling' for the sub-relational as well as for the ultra-relational experience. So far as the former is concerned, it is surely a hypothetical state, and, as such, there is ample room here for dispute. And it has been, as a matter of fact, a subject of heated controversy in Indian philosophy between the Naiyāyikas and the Buddhists. (It is called *nirvikalpa pratyakṣa* or *ālocana.*) But Bradley means by immediate experience, not only a stage that is transcended, but also the felt subject which is ever present at all the stages of experience, and in which there is no distinction between the experienced and the experience. The latter is the ultimate epistemological presupposition of all relational knowledge, like J. Ward's pure subject which, though last in the order of knowledge, is yet first in the order of existence. It is, in the language of Śaṅkara, *Vijñānaghana* in which there is no distinction between existence and knowledge. "He who would maintain that *Brahman*

35. *Truth and Reality*, p. 196.

36. *Appearance and Reality, p. 497.*

37. See his *Neo-Hegelianism, pp. 247–256.*

is characterised by thought different from existence, and at the same time by existence different from thought, would virtually maintain that there is a plurality in *Brahman*."[38] The truth is that in respect of the Absolute, existence is thought, and thought is existence. (*Sattaiva bodho bodha eva ca sattā.*) The Absolute, so characterised, is not a mere stage of experience which is *psychologically a priori* to the relational stage, but it is the *epistemologically a priori* principle presupposed by the relational experience.[39]

It is of course very misleading to say that thought seeks its satisfaction in an immediate experience in entering which thought commits suicide and where it would be present as a higher intuition.[40] The undeniable fact is that thought wants consistency, it has always a nisus to a systematic whole. Equally unquestionable is its essentially discursive nature; nothing can be thought of, which cannot be distinguished from its 'other.' But, then, it must also be taken as incontrovertible that "I think" is the presupposition of all discursive thinking; that is, I can distinguish between two given terms, only because I am not myself one of the terms that are distinguished. The distinction of 'a' from 'b' has a meaning for me, only because I am the common presupposition of both, and, as such, not identifiable with any one of them. The perplexities provoked by Bradley's doctrine of immediate experience are certainly due, at least partly, to his use of the terms 'self' and 'consciousness' in the relational sense, and his consequent belief that the self is nothing more than an appearance and consciousness is not something original. He should have seen a little more clearly why his fellow-idealists had insisted that the self was the ultimate presupposition of all known and knowable things. If the Absolute is neither a self nor a conscious principle, it cannot surely be distinguished from Kant's 'Thing-in-itself,' in spite of all the efforts Bradley has made in that direction.

But, none the less, he was certainly right in emphasising the need of an immediate experience for a systematic philosophy. Consistency requires that the relation of distinction presupposes a common principle that cannot be reduced to any of the terms distinguished. Even the relation of one particular

---

38. *S. B. III. 2. 21.*

39. Prof. Cunningham does little justice to this epistemological priority of immediate experience which Bradley intends to signify by his doctrine, though it must be admitted that the latter has made himself open to misinterpretations by the confused way in which he talks of the immediate experience in the epistemological as well as in the psychological sense. Relational experience is self-contradictory, not because a non-relational whole is inconceivable, but because such an experience, when taken apart from immediate experience, leads to the contradiction of an infinite regress, as Bradley rightly contends. Apart from the self as *aparokṣa* and *svaprakāśa*, as put by Śaṅkara, a theory of self must lead to the perplexities of the Naiyāyikas whose doctrine of infinite *anuvyavasāyas* has ever remained as a sad commentary on their logical insight and analytic accomplishments.

40. Bradley, *Appearance and Reality*, p. 152.

to another is not equivalent to the relation of the particulars to the universal. And when one universal is distinguished from another universal, this relation between two universals cannot be identical with the relation in which both stand to the foundational principle which is their common presupposition. In other words, all distinctions are between objects and objects, and if we speak of the distinction between the conscious subject and the objects we should at least guard ourselves against identifying this relation with any relation between one object and another. The 'I think,' in other words, is the presupposition of all relational categories, and, therefore, as Kant puts it, this conception does not add to the list of the categories through which the objects exist for us.

Some remarks of Prof. Gentile are so pertinent to the subject under discussion that they may bear a reference here. We must not, he insists, put together the unity of mind with the multiplicity of things, because "the multiplicity of things does not stand in the same rank with the unity of the ego, for multiplicity belongs to things in so far as all together are gathered into the unity of consciousness."[41] It is, therefore, contended that the unity of mind which lives in the immediate intuition of the spiritual life is "unmultipliable and infinite unity."[42] Determinateness is "essentially and fundamentally multiplicity, it is the particularity of the determinations by which each is what it is, and reciprocally excludes the others." The unity of the mind, on the other hand, "is infinite;" it cannot be "limited by other realities and still keep its own reality. Its unity implies its infinity. The mind is not a multiplicity; nor is the whole, of which it is a part, multiple, the part being a unity." The conclusion which he draws is: "A unique and infinite thing would not be knowable, because to know is to distinguish one thing from another. *Omnis determinatio est negatio.*"

As the conception of the Infinite is one of the most interesting subjects upon which modern speculations are still divided, a student of the advaita philosophy will naturally feel encouraged to find in Prof. Gentile's contentions an unconscious corroboration by a modern thinker of the advaita theory of self as infinite. The self, as we have seen above, is unlike the finite things which are necessarily determined from outside. Being the ultimate presupposition of all finite things, the self cannot be limited by something other than itself. It is well known, remarks Śaṅkara, that "that is infinite which cannot be divided from anything else; and if the Absolute be a knowing agent, then, it is divided from knowledge and the knowable object, and, as such, cannot be infinite."[43]

41. *Mind as Pure Act*, p. 52.

42. *Ibid.*, p. 26.

43. *Com. on the Tait. Up. Brahmaballī.*

The Absolute, therefore, is Knowledge *within* which there is no distinction. The Infinite, it is said in another context, is that "where one sees nothing else, hears nothing else, understands nothing else."[44] The finite, on the contrary, is that "where one sees something else, hears something else, understands something else." The infinite (*bhūmā*), as put elsewhere, "is something quite different from all notions of duality."[45] It being the presupposition of all known and knowable things, the Infinite may be said to "rest in its own greatness," or, to put it more strictly, "the Infinite is without any resting place or support." All objects, that is, presuppose the Absolute Self, though the latter has no presupposition.

It does not matter much whether the ultimate presupposition of all knowledge is called the conscious subject, or the unity of mind, or the pure ego, provided it is remembered that it is not itself either one thing among other things or one category among other categories. Without such a foundational principle, every analysis of knowledge will be confronted by the paradox of infinite regress. When, therefore, the ultimate principle is described even as a universal, we must guard ourselves against interpreting this ground-universal in the sense in which a universal is correlative with a particular. Similarly, again, when it is described as immediate experience, we must with equal care avoid the mistake of thinking that immediate experience is one type of experience by the side of all other types of experience. So far Bradley is altogether right in his remark that even the term 'for' has only a metaphorical significance when all relational knowledge is said to be *for* immediate experience. All criticisms directed against the doctrine of immediate experience, in so far as they start with the assumption that the relation of this experience to the objects is identical with an inter-objective relation, must be altogether irrelevant.

The Buddhistic agnosticism, as we have remarked above, arose out of drawing from a true premise a false conclusion. It is certainly true that all our categories are relational and so far finite. But this circumstance by itself does not guarantee the conclusion that the Absolute falls altogether beyond the limits of human comprehension. If it is true that the principle of relativity is called upon by the nihilists in order to destroy all theories and to replace them by "direct mystic intuition," as we are told by Dr. Th. Stcherbatsky,[46] then it must be said, in the words of E. Caird, that if the philosopher assumes prophetic airs or speaks to ordinary men from the height of 'an immediate insight' or 'transcendental intuition,' from which they are excluded, then, he

44. *S. B. I.* 3. 8.

45. *Com. on the Ch. Up. VII.* 24. 1.

46. *Nirvāna*, p. 49.

is pretending "to be of a different species from other men" and is so far "trampling the roots of humanity under foot."[47]

The confusion between Śaṅkara's absolutism and the Buddhistic agnosticism must, it should be emphasised once more, be avoided by every sympathetic interpreter of the advaita philosophy. Yet this confusion was started by no less an authority than Paul Deussen who has done so much for the spread of the Vedānta teachings. And since then this confusion has remained unchallenged, and the subsequent interpreters of Śaṅkara's philosophy have implicitly accepted his interpretation. Recollecting the phenomenalism of Kant, Deussen remarks that the "central thought" of the Vedānta consists in this that the *Brahman* is "theoretically unknowable; because in all knowing, it is the knowing subject, it can never be an object of knowledge for us." It must, therefore, be "grasped practically."[48] We need not here examine Deussen's criticism of "the weakness and frailty of man's intellect" that, according to him, is shared by Śaṅkara with the Greek and modern philosophers in so far as Śaṅkara, like Descartes, could not "go so far" as to see that what remains of the self when all notions of the not-self are withdrawn from it is, not consciousness, but something unconscious.[49] What is suggested here is evidently this that it is the Will and not consciousness which is more fundamental than the other. Such an interpretation, as we have contended in the last chapter, would put Śaṅkara's position in an extremely misleading light. There is an important sense in which consciousness is the ultimate presupposition of all fragmentary and relative experiences.

But what should be challenged in the present context is Deussen's assimilation of Śaṅkara's position to that of Kant. The real value of Kant's contribution to a sound theory of knowledge consists in his insistence that the categories are the logical presuppositions of all objects that we know. But his theory of an unknowable and inconceivable Thing-in-itself has been rightly rejected by all subsequent idealists from Fichte to Bradley. In this respect Kant's position is more akin to that of Candrakīrti and other Buddhist agnostics than to the position of Śaṅkara. The Absolute, for Śaṅkara, is our very self which none can deny; it is the pre-established ground (*svayamsiddha*) of all proof and disproof, though it cannot be known in the same way in which an object is known. The Absolute is like the light which manifests all objects, and which, consequently, does not require another light for its own revelation. To contend, therefore, that there can be no theoretical knowledge of the Absolute,

---

47. *Hegel*, p. 57.

48. *The System of the Vedānta*, p. 143.

49. *Ibid.*, p. 135.

as it is contended by Deussen, would be as absurd as the assertion that light cannot be known theoretically because it illumines the objects while it itself is not revealed by another light.

These thoughts are put very clearly in the commentary on the Gītā. How can there be, it is asked, a cognition of the Absolute Self? How is the constant meditation of self-knowledge possible if the self as well as knowledge be formless? The answer runs as follows:—

There is a sense in which it is unnecessary to impart the knowledge of the self; because it is invariably comprehended in association with all objects of perception. The *Brahman*, though eminently evident, intimately known, very near, and essentially the self, appears to the undiscriminating people as obscure, difficult to know, remote, and different from the self. But to those whose intellect (*Buddhi*) has been withdrawn from the external things, there can be nothing so blissful, so evident, so easily comprehensible, and so near.[50] All that is necessary, therefore, for knowing the real self is to avoid its false identification with the pseudo-egos, such as, the intellect, mind, body, etc. It is only some self-conceited thinkers who suppose that the intellect cannot comprehend the self on account of its being formless. In reality, however, "the self is not a thing unknown to anybody at any time, it is not a thing to be reached, or abandoned, or acquired. If the self be unknown, all actions for the attainment of an object would be meaningless." Knowledge though formless, must be admitted to be as immediate as pleasure, since objects are apprehended because of the reality of knowledge.[51]

Deussen's misinterpretation of Śaṅkara's theory of Self on the agnostic lines seems to be due to the fact that he construes such phrases as "not knowable as an object," and "unknown as an object," as equivalents of "entirely inconceivable and unknowable." But this would surely be a mistake; and in fact, Śaṅkara anticipates such a confusion of his theory of the Absolute with the agnostic position, and often carefully distinguishes between the two. It is true, he says, that the Absolute transcends all speech and thought, but it "certainly does not mean that *Brahman* is a mere naught."[52] The negative judgment has no meaning apart from a positive background. Consequently, all that the *Bṛh. Up.* means by the negative description of the Absolute is this that it does not fall within the category of object (*aviṣayāntaḥpāti*); for, it is "the innermost self whose nature is eternal, pure and eternally free consciousness."

---

50. *Sukham, suprasiddham, suvijñeyam, āsannam.—Com. on the Gītā* XVIII. *50*.

51. *Jñānavaśenaiva jñeyamavagati iti jñānam atyantam prasiddham sukhādivadeva—loc. cit. Cp.* also *Ibid. II. 18*.

52. *S. B. III. 2. 22*.

Indeed, the assertion that the Absolute is theoretically incomprehensible would be as absurd as that there can be no theoretical knowledge of space on the ground that all spaces that are ever known are limited spaces, or that light is theoretically unknowable because what is known directly is an illumined object. The truth, on the contrary, is that our knowledge of particular spaces and that of illumined objects presuppose the reality of an infinite space and of the source of illumination respectively. Similarly, the foundational consciousness which is presupposed by all particular conscious activities cannot be itself said to be a mere naught for our thought. The Absolute, in this sense, far from being entirely unknowable, is knowable *par excellence.*

In interpreting the advaita system, it is of primary importance to remember that this particular philosophy is not a mere speculative adventure of purely theoretical interest. On the contrary, it is a practical discipline designed for the attainment of what its founders considered to be the highest state of spiritual evolution. This highest stage was supposed by them to be realised through three stages, known technically as *śravaṇa, manana*, and *nididhyāsana*, each stage being as indispensable as the rest. Misconceptions, therefore, are surely to arise when one of them is taken to be unnecessary, when, for instance, it is said that Śaṅkara fares entirely without logic and has no other evidence for his conclusions than an appeal to the Upaniṣads. It is an equally serious error to think that the highest stage of spiritual realisation, according to Śaṅkara, can be attained without a theoretically satisfactory philosophy of the Absolute. That would be to ignore the importance of the second stage of reasoned knowledge. The fact is that a theoretically satisfactory position reached by refuting all rival theories which excite doubts and suspicions in the mind is an indispensable preliminary to the attainment of the last stage of self-realisation. This, according to Śaṅkara, cannot be attained by the absurd method of proving the incompetency of thought by means of thought itself, as Bradley, for instance, supposed. The anti-rational and sceptical attitude may breed despair, but cannot be a necessary stage in a spiritual discipline.

Śaṅkara's method of knowledge, we believe, is more correctly analysed by another distinguished exponent of mysticism than what is offered by Deussen. In comparing the method of Śaṅkara with that of Eckhart, it is remarked by Prof. Rudolf Otto that their mysticism is "no mysticism in the usual sense of the term."[53] Theirs is the method of an "intellectual and not of an emotional mysticism." Both of them seek to give "a knowledge which is to be translated into a comprehensible doctrine with all the aids of proof, scholarly presentation and keen dialectic."[54] But even Prof. Otto seems sometimes to

53. *Mysticism East and West*, p. 29.

54 *Ibid.*, p. 31.

underestimate the contribution of Śaṅkara to a philosophical interpretation of experience, when, for instance, it is remarked that the "intuitus mysticus" is "a first-hand and immediate fact and possession of the mystical mind" in the case of Śaṅkara as well as Eckhart. So far as the former is concerned, we believe, we have been able to show clearly in the foregoing pages that Śaṅkara's works are full of illuminating analysis of knowledge which will be acceptable to all, and not simply to the mystical minds. The discovery of the *a priori* conditions of knowledge does not certainly require a mystical mind, otherwise we shall have to admit that all the philosophers from Kant to Hegel and the modern absolutists are mystics. There is no doubt a place for mysticism in Śaṅkara's doctrine of self-realisation; but his theory of knowledge, we believe, is free from any mystical element. Reasoned knowledge is an indispensable stage in the advaita method of self-realisation; and no reasoned refutation of rival doctrines can be promoted by an appeal to mystical intuition.

Our conclusion, therefore, is that Śaṅkara's doctrine of the Absolute Self is based on an analysis of experience, and, as such, it is different from the agnostic method of the Buddhists. The self, when rightly understood, is an undefinable, yet perfectly intelligible, principle presupposed by all experience. It is, in other words, consciousness, the peculiar character of which is that here there is no distinction between the experienced and the experiencing. In fact, the whole of Śaṅkara's discussions on the Self may be viewed as an able and comprehensive analysis of *consciousness*.

It will be interesting here to add a few remarks on the place of the negative dialectic method in the development of the advaita philosophy,—a method which has been recently introduced into modern thought by Bradley. A short comparison between Bradley, Nāgārjuna and Śaṅkara may remove what seems to us another misapprehension of the method of Śaṅkara which has particularly led to the belief that the Absolute in the advaita philosophy is a transcendent principle.

Bradley starts his destructive criticism of all appearances in the spirit of Nāgārjuna, which was wrongly infused into Śaṅkara's philosophy by Śrīharṣa at a later age. But while following the same dialectic method, Bradley tried to steer clear of Nāgārjuna's agnosticism by means of the Hegelian doctrine of degrees in truth and reality. But, as has been rightly contended by Dr. Haldar, he has failed to bring this doctrine into accord with his destructive criticism.[55] His transition from appearance to the Absolute is so abrupt that it "takes one's breath away, and savours too much of the incomprehensible process by which the mystic is transported beyond the region of ordinary experience."[56]

55. *Neo-Hegelianism*, p. 250.

56. *Ibid.*, p. 251.

In fact, the mere negative criticism of all the categories of thought must lead inevitably to Nāgārjuna's agnosticism which is equivalent to universal scepticism, and so the Absolute which emerges out of such a negative method must emerge abruptly; and, consequently, Nāgārjuna's *Dharmakāya* as well as Bradley's Absolute must have the appearance of, as put by Dr. Haldar in respect of the latter, being "shot out of a pistol."[57]

We must, therefore, be on our guard when it is remarked that there is a great "family likeness between the dialectical method of Hegel and Nāgārjuna's dialectics."[58] The truth is that this family likeness exists between the dialectic method of Bradley and that of Nāgārjuna, and neither Śaṅkara nor Hegel would subscribe to the position of universal scepticism which follows necessarily from the method of the former. A category, for Hegel, as we have remarked elsewhere, "is no doubt self-discrepant, but this is due to its forced abstraction from the higher category in which the inconsistencies of the lower category are reconciled. For Bradley, on the other hand, every category of knowledge can give us only appearance, and in this regard, one category is as bad as another."[59] And in transplanting the Buddhistic dialectic method on the advaita soil,—which process really began as early as the beginning of the ninth century with Maṇḍana Miśra, and was completed by Ānandajñāna, Śrīharṣa and Citsukha—the advaita dialecticians have put Śaṅkara's position in an extremely misleading light. Śaṅkara, as we have seen, is very definite in his polemic against absolute nihilism. Being, for him, is the most fundamental category, and the world of appearance, howsoever unreal, does not militate against the possibility of a systematic philosophy. The entire complex of phenomenal existence, he admits, is true in a certain sense, and so far there "is no reason why the ordinary course of secular and religious activity should not hold undisturbed".[60] The negative dialectic of the Buddhists, on the contrary, is entirely incompatible with any fixed criterion of truth and reality. Nāgārjuna, it has been rightly urged by M. Anesaki, pursued the negative dialectic "till he reached a complete denial of any definite thought about anything."[61] If then Śrīharṣa fell a prey to the allurements of negative dialectic, he really did a great disservice to Śaṅkara's

57. *Ibid.*, p. 249.

58. Dr. Th. Stcherbatsky, *Nirvāna*, p. 53.

59. See *infra, Appendix.*

60. *S. B. II. 1.* 14.

61. *Encyclopædia of Religion and Ethics, Vol. IV*, p. 838.

position by ignoring the fact that the latter had great respect for reasoned knowledge.[62]

It was this incompatibility of the negative dialectic with the genuinely advaita position which was responsible, at least partly, for Śaṅkara's silence over his indebtedness to the Buddhist thought; his silence cannot be attributed entirely to "sectarian animosity" or "extreme hatred," as Dr. Th. Stcherbatsky seems to suppose.[63] And if Śrīharṣa acknowledged his indebtedness, that was because he was actually influenced by the Buddhistic speculations to a degree which was not in harmony with the position of Śaṅkara. While Śrīharṣa thinks that the Absolute can be well established by a negative criticism of all categories and declaring, like Candrakīrti, that he has no particular thesis to prove in respect of the phenomenal world, Śaṅkara begins with the declaration that the object of the Vedānta is to furnish a positive proof for the identity of the individual and the Absolute Self. Such a positive proof would be impossible if he had started with the attitude of universal scepticism. Nor does it appear to be a mere irony that is responsible for Śaṅkara's polemic against the nihilists, as suggested by Prof. S. Radhakrishnan.[64] If we follow the interpretation of Nāgārjuna as offered by Candrakīrti as distinct from what is offered by other Buddhists, such as, Bhāvaviveka, then, the term '*śunya*' cannot be identified with Śaṅkara's empirical existence. The world of appearance, for Śaṅkara, is not entirely false; Being is immanent in the world of appearance. On the contrary, Nāgārjuna's conception does not leave any reality for the phenomenal world which, for him, is as unreal as the horn of a hare.[65]

It is true that the Madhyamaka philosophers employ many terms (such as, *nirvikalpa, niṣprapanca, vyavahāra, paramārtha*, etc.), that are also used by Śaṅkara. But they are used by the latter with very important changes in their connotations. The Absolute, according to Candrakīrti, for instance, repels all predicates, including those of being and non-being; and Candrakīrti complains that his position should have been taken to be identical with the doctrine of non-being.[66] But the difficulty is that such an Absolute can neither be

---

62. It is a pity that many modern interpreters of Śaṅkara have the tendency to make him consistent by reading into his position the thoughts of his followers who made the mistake of thinking that the position of Śaṅkara could be developed by the Buddhistic method of criticism.

63. *Buddhist Logic, Vol. I*, p. 22.

64. *Indian Philosophy I*, p. 669.

65. This distinction has been accentuated rightly by many, such as, Poussin in *The Journal of the Royal Asiatic Society*, 1910, p. 129, and Prof A. B. Keith in his *Buddhistic Philosophy*, p. 261.

66. *Mūla-Madhyamaka-Kārikās*, ed. by Poussin, p. 499.

refuted nor established; and we cannot be said to advance a single step in the way of establishing the truth of the Absolute by raising it entirely above all categories. Śaṅkara's Absolute, on the other hand, as we have seen, is not such a transcendent principle, though it is not definable in the ordinary way; and he seeks to prove its reality by a careful analysis of knowledge and experience.

Ras Bihari Das, "The Falsity of the World" (1940)

Ras Bihari Das (1886–1945) specialized in Advaita Vedānta studies and the philosophy of Whitehead. He was influenced by Hiralal Haldar, B. N. Seal, and K. C. Bhattacharyya. He published commentaries on Kant and Whitehead. This essay reflects his distinctively realistic interpretation of Vedānta, a position often read as idealistic.

4

The Falsity of the World

'THE WORLD IS false.' This astounding statement is made by advaitism in all seriousness, and some very sensible people seem to believe it quite honestly. Before one can accept the statement as true or reject it as false, it is necessary that one should understand its proper meaning. We can neither believe nor disbelieve a statement truly without understanding beforehand what it really means. The present statement is so comprehensive in its scope and so far-reaching in its intent that our first attempts at understanding its meaning seem to end in failure.

Let us first of all try to understand what the term 'the world' stands for, what it is exactly that is roundly said to be false. The world does not mean merely the external visible world with its sensible qualities. It means this and more than this. Our bodies are also included in the world, and our mental states too are not excluded from it. In fact whatever can be presented to us either externally or internally, to the mind or the senses, forms part of the world which as a whole as well as every item in it is said to be false. Falsity is thus asserted of everything that we can sense or feel, think of or imagine as an object.

One way of understanding a theory or a belief is to see how one is led to it from the facts of common experience. Now, illusion is a familiar fact of common experience and in this experience we become acquainted with a falsity which we certainly associate with a visible appearance. May we not pass quite easily from this notion of falsity connected with some appearances to the notion of the falsity of all appearances, seeing that there is nothing to distinguish one appearance as appearance from another? Such passage, however far from being easy does not even seem possible, because in the first place, the cases of recognised illusion are not so plentiful in life as to give us the impression that everything is illusory, and, secondly, it is not true that we cannot and do not distinguish between one appearance and another. The discredited appearance of a snake in the place of a rope is certainly not put on a par with the appearance which we take to be a rope. Apart from some religious or mystical interest, it does not seem possible on the basis of common experience, on the basis, that is, of the sporadic cases of recognised illusion which we meet with in life, to arrive at the notion that the whole world is false.

But although psychologically we may not be able to trace the origin of a theory or a belief in our common everyday experience, we may still see the logical grounds which go to support it, and that would also be a way, and a better way, of understanding it. Tracing the origin of a belief or a theory would decide nothing as to its validity or invalidity, whereas the logical grounds in support of it, if we can see them, would at once win for it at least our intellectual assent. Now what can be the logical ground of the statement that the world is false? The ground that is generally assigned is that the world is an appearance. But why should an appearance, because it is an appearance, be false? The answer we get is that we know cases of appearance which are clearly false, such as that of silver in place of a piece of shell or that of a snake in place of a rope, and there is no difference of kind or character between such appearances and the world as a whole. All are appearances and since appearances are known to be false, everything that is an appearance must be false.

We must confess that this argument, so far as it is an argument, is highly unconvincing. We are even persuaded that it is quite fallacious. Put in the logical form, the argument simply amounts to saying 'Because some appearances are false, and the world is an appearance, therefore it is false.' This argument clearly involves the fallacy of undistributed middle. It says, in short, 'because some appearances are false, therefore all appearances are false.' There is no logical connection here between the premiss and the conclusion, in the sense that from the truth of the premiss ('some appearances are false') nothing can be inferred as to the truth or falsity of the conclusion ('all appearances are false'). When we recognise some appearances as false, we certainly observe a distinction between these appearances and others that are not recognised as false. This distinction between a false appearance and a true one, between a false snake and a true rope, is entirely denied in the conclusion which says all appearances are false. Can we regard an argument as valid in any sense which denies in the conclusion what is implied in the premiss?

We cannot suppose that the connection between falsity and appearance is analytical, that is, the idea of falsity is involved in the idea of appearance. If such were the case, nobody would need to point to certain special cases of appearance (rope-snake etc.) in order to persuade us that all appearance is false; in recognising anything as appearance, we should recognise it as false. We know this is not the case. When you say that you cannot distinguish one appearance as appearance from another, this only means that the ground of falsity of an appearance does not lie in its character as an appearance, but in something else. An appearance as such is neither true nor false. It is condemned as false only when it cannot stand light of examination. We judge it to be true or false only in consideration of certain other characteristics than that of being an appearance merely.

Moreover the falsity of an illusory appearance is not arrived at by means of an argument. Its falsity lies in its disappearing of itself from the place of its appearance. But the world is a standing appearance. It shows no tendency to disappear from the field of our view. The world therefore is not certainly false in the sense in which the illusory snake is false. Thus it appears that there is no logical ground for the statement that the world is false.

We have so far assumed that the statement as a whole as well as each of its terms has an intelligible meaning, even though we have failed to find any rational basis for it, whether psychological or logical. But if we examine carefully we shall find that what is asserted in the statement (viz. the falsity of the world) has no intelligible meaning. The notion of falsity is significant only within the world in regard to some particular item in it which is superseded by another. The notion has no intelligible sense when we take it out of its proper sphere and apply it to the world as a whole. It is the rope that makes the snake false. What is it that can possibly make the world false? There is nothing. You cannot say that it is the *Brahman* which makes the world false, because the *Brahman* is never put in the place of the world, the *Brahman* is never seen or conceived objectively. When we say that the snake is false, we mean that there was no snake at all in the place where it appeared to be but something else, viz, a rope. The idea of falsity is mainly a negative idea, with a positive basis, which gives it its significance. Everything that is recognised as false must have this positive basis. Even a hallucination is not possible without a background or surrounding. In the case of the illusory snake which is false the positive basis is supplied by the rope in the place of which it was seen or by the ground to which it was referred But when we are called upon to think of the world as false, our mind gets no positive basis to support this absolute negation which therefore remains utterly non-significant. Really speaking such a proposition is literally unthinkable. The world which is declared to be false is not merely the world of physical existence. But whatever can be thought of as an objective content is included in the world, so that to say that the world is false is to say that there is really no objective content. But can we exactly think of or conceive a situation in which there is no objective content? All thinking is objective thinking, and no thought is possible without some objective content. Therefore to say that the world is false is to deny all thought, and the denial of all thought can be no proper thought at all. It is like saying that my mother is childless or that I am quite dumb. Thus we find that the proposition that the world is false is not literally intelligible, because it involves self-contradiction and cannot be thought; because what it asserts has no proper significance, and lastly because, even assuming that it has a sense, we can find no rational basis for it.

But still we cannot help supposing that there must be some good sense in this apparently nonsensical (in the modern positivistic sense) proposition, otherwise so many sensible people could never believe in its truth. Let us try to find out if this statement can be made to yield any intelligible sense.

1. To be able successfully to bring out the meaning of this proposition we must realise first of all that when any thing is declared to be false by the advaitist he does not mean that the thing in question is absolutely nothing. Even an illusory appearance is not for him the manifestation of an unreal thing (*asat-khyati*). That which is an absolute nought has not the capacity to show itself forth. A hare's horn or a flower in the sky is never seen. An illusory appearance then for the advaitist is something that cannot be described either as real or as unreal. By real he means real as the unchanging eternal *Brahman* is real, and by unreal he means something that is never an object of apprehension, as for instance, the horn of a hare. When the world is declared to be false, we must understand it to be indescribable (*anirvacaniya*) in this particular sense. It is neither real like the *Brahman* nor unreal like a hare's horn. In this sense the falsity of the world is quite an intelligible notion. The world is not simply and totally denied, it is merely described in terms of its difference from absolute reality and absolute unreality, and this description does not contain any unintelligible concept. In this view the world seems to enjoy a sort of reality. But will it not militate against the monistic character of the advaitic reality if we grant some kind of reality to the world? The advaitist does not think so, because the reality which the world enjoys is not of the same grade as that of the *Brahman*. The unity of the *Brahman* would have been affected if the world were real in the sense in which the *Brahman* is real. But it is not so. Just as the rope which underlies the appearance of a snake is not affected by the apparent snake, so is the *Brahman* quite unaffected by the world. This, I suppose is the easiest way of understanding the so-called falsity of the world.

2. In another way we may try to make the concept of the falsity of the world intelligible. To say that the world is false is to say that is has been judged by a standard and has been found wanting. Self-subsistence or independence is a fairly good criterion of reality. If a thing depends on something else for its existence, then it is not real in itself. We may well conceive that the whole world is sustained by a unitary principle, so that every item in it as well as the whole is maintained in being only by the sustaining power of this principle. In such a case the world may be said to be false, as enjoying only dependent existence; it is false as any abstraction is false. Even Whitehead says that the world which is studied by science is an abstraction, as it is conceived apart from the subjective relation in which it is actually given. The world conceived in dissociation

from the subjective relation or apart from God or the *Brahman* is false in a quite intelligible sense. This does not mean that the world is nothing even when we grant its dependence on God or the *Brahman*. To be dependent, it must be something. If it were nothing, there could be no question of its dependence or independence. The world is not a baseless show; it has a very good basis in the *Brahman*.

3. From this we may easily pass on to the view that the world is a mere appearance which is another intelligible meaning of the assertion that the world is false. To arrive at this view we are considerably helped by the instance of an illusory object. From such instances we learn that when we apprehend an appearance we do not and cannot apprehend by the same act the physical or empirical existence of the thing which appears. Even contemporary philosophy in the West makes it abundantly clear that when a sensum is given, the corresponding physical reality is not given in the same way. While the sensum is known, the physical or spatio-temporal reality is constructed, believed or merely accepted as real. This construction, belief or acceptance is different from knowledge. From the point of view of knowledge, then, the world is a mere appearance. In itself it is neither real nor unreal and is not given as either in direct awareness. We attribute reality or unreality to it from our practical points of view. But apart from this attribution, belief or assertion, the world is neither real nor unreal. This is its falsity which is different from utter negation. This is an intelligible view of the falsity of the world. Merely by philosophising we cannot reduce the world any farther. Philosophy cannot reduce the presentation of the world to utter nought, which is the ideal of advaitic spiritual discipline. But at the level of philosophy this ideal is scarcely intelligible.

4. Although the three different ways in which I have tried to make the notion of the falsity of the world intelligible are not, I believe without some support in authoritative texts, they do not bring out, in my opinion, the most important point in the whole notion. If the recognition of the falsity of the world does not at all affect my beliefs and practices of daily life. I have not certainly grasped all that the advaitic teachers seek to convey when they condemn the world as false. It seems perfectly possible for me to retain all my empirical beliefs and carry on my worldly practices in the same passionate way as before, even when I recognise quite clearly that the reality of the world is different in kind from that of the *Brahman*, that the world depends for its existence on some unitary principle and is a mere appearance from the point of view of direct awareness. To say that the world is merely an appearance for direct knowledge is not to support or oppose any of our empirical beliefs which may remain just as they are.

> I can hardly suppose that advaitism, which proposes to transform all our valuations of things and revolutionise our whole outlook on life and the world can be content with such a position.

We have said that the world is an appearance from the point of view of direct awareness. But that is an ideal or abstract point of view. We are no mere ghostly spectators without any personal interests of our own. Our knowledge is guided and collected by our interests and the object of our actual knowledge is never a mere appearance but always something or other with causal efficiency. The point of view of mere apprehension is impossible of realisation for us so long as we are in the body. We are thoroughly identified with our bodies and, through them, are connected in an intimate manner with the rest of the physical world, so that the object of knowledge always affects us in a favourable or unfavourable way. When I see my body approached by a snake, I do not merely take note of the approach of one appearance by another, myself their spectator remaining quite unaffected. No, I am thrown into a great agitation of mind and body and even run for my life. Thus the world which I actually know is intimately connected with me and every object of my knowledge reacts favourably or unfavourably on my will and feeling. That is, the objects of my knowledge are objects of my interest and I am bound to recognise as real what touches my interest. It would be sheer mockery and a sad travesty of the advaitic position if I were to say that the world is false when all my interests in the world remained quite intact. The reality for me (though not in itself) is defined by my interests and so long as I retain the least interest in the things of the world I cannot truly and honestly say that the world is false. Because our present interests are mainly about the body, about food and raiment, therefore the physical reality or matter is the highest reality for us. We are all materialists in this sense. We must get rid of this materialism if we are to achieve any true understanding of the advaitic position.

The first requisite condition for being eligible (*adhikari*) for a study of the advaitic philosophy as any authority on the subject would tell us, is the state of utter detachment (*vairagya*) in regard to all worldly things. We are born with many worldly interests, and we can understand and appreciate the advaitic position, that is, realise the falsity of the world, only to the extent we are able to extricate ourselves from the grip of these interests. The falsity of the world then means, to begin with, its utter unimportance or irrelevance for spiritual interests. To recognise the falsity of the world is not merely to correct a theoretical error of judgment which takes place only on the intellectual plane, but really to rectify a fundamental spiritual defect of our nature which colours our whole life and thought. Thus it is clear that to realise this kind of falsity merely theoretical argument provided by philosophy is not enough. We must practically raise ourselves to a level of spiritual intensity in which material interests have no appeal whatsoever. Then and then only can we realise what it really means to say that the world is false. What we mean is that one must get rid of one's worldly interests in order to realise the falsity of the world. But getting rid of worldly interests is a practical proposition, not a theoretical problem to be solved by logical arguments. It involves a turning of the whole direction of our willing and feeling which is different from correcting an intellectual error. True, the recognition of falsity is ultimately a cognitive act, but this is preceded and conditioned by a discipline of the mind which involves the purification of our will and feeling.

The real problem is to get rid of our worldly interests. And this can not be brought about merely by wishing. We can not give up all interests at once. To give up all interests is hardly compatible with life itself. We can however lessen our worldly interests by cultivating certain other-worldly or spiritual interests. Our worldly interests diminish with the increase of our spiritual interests and vice versa. Through art, morality and religion we may achieve a chastening of the mind which will enable us to see more reality in spiritual things than in physical matter.

For the artist beauty of form is certainly a greater reality than the matter which embodies that form. Whatever importance the matter has for the artist, it derives it from the circumstance that it can be made to represent a particular beautiful form. For ordinary people form or beauty is adjectival, whereas the matter, in which the form is embodied, is substantive. To the artist with his mind concentrated on the contemplation of the form, it is the matter that takes a secondary place and may be considered adjectival. To him the form is the reality or substance while the matter is an accident.

In moral life we clearly recognise a reality which may not and indeed does not have a material being. In leading a moral life we pledge our unswerving loyality to an ideal, to an ought, which is nowhere seen on earth, on sea or land. Although it has no material embodiment, it enables us to defy all earthly powers.

Religion expressly draws our mind away from all visible things to an invisible reality. Our spiritual nature certainly gains in strength through these activities of art, morality and religion. As our spiritual life deepens and we are more and more imbued with a lively feeling for things invisible and divine, the sense of reality which is now associated with the physical world and which is so oppressive begins to wear quite thin till the whole visible world becomes a shadowy appearance, and may at last even fade out of sight.

The falsity of the world then, according to the advaitists, as far as I understand them, is not a mere theoretical idea but a concept of spiritual valuation which can be realised in its full significance only as a result of spiritual discipline. When I do not believe in the falsity of the world, it is not because my understanding is dull, and I cannot follow your philosophic argument, but because I lack the requisite spiritual culture, or outlook. I can however, well imagine a level of spiritual exaltation from which the whole material world may be realised not only as a thing of no importance but as altogether lost to spiritual sight.

S. S. Suryanarayana Sastri, "Advaita, Causality and Human Freedom" (1940)

S. S. Suryanarayana Sastri (1893–1942) headed the University of Madras Department of Philosophy from 1927 to 1942. He was principally a scholar of Advaita Vedānta. The present essay explores specific metaphysical problems as they are addressed in the advaita system.

5

Advaita, Causality and Human Freedom

IT WILL BE the aim of this paper to treat in some detail the notion of causality as set out in and criticised by the Advaita Vedānta, consider its affinities if any with the conception of cause in modern science and discuss the bearing of these views on the problem of human freedom. In the course of the discussion I shall specifically refer to two books—Prof. Stebbing's *Philosophy and the Physicists*[1] and Dr. Brahma's *Causality and Modern Science*.[2] I have neither the time nor the ability to discuss the former in full; I shall content myself with a consideration of the tenth chapter on 'Human Freedom and Responsibility'. The second book presents more a point of view than a detailed exposition; and with this, though in agreement to a large extent, I have to express dissatisfaction in some measure.

The Advaitin's ontological position has been often stated and requires little repetition. Reality is non-dual; it is consciousness or experience, self-luminous by nature; it is eternal and free. On this are super-imposed as appearances duality, inertness, cognisability in dependence on another, dependence, impermanence, and so on. The super-imposition is the work of nescience. This is not real as then there could not even be the realisation of it as nescience, leading to its sublation; it is not unreal, since duality and dependence are facts of immediate experience in no wise comparable to the impossible barren woman's son or even to the barely possible, but not actual, hare's horn; it is therefore considered indeterminable, not characterisable as real or as unreal, *anirvācya*. All limitations, and all relations among the limited fall within the realm of this nescience, which is neither co-eval with reality nor falls outside of it. Finitude and plurality being phenomenal, the relations among the diverse, such as time, space and cause are also phenomenal. They cannot claim to hold good absolutely, whether for all or everywhere.

Though such a position is not attractive or convincing on the face of it, a little consideration would seem to make it acceptable in the case of space

1. Methuen, 1937.

2. Allen and Unwin, 1939.

and time. Analysis of these reveals two sets of difficulties. We seem unable to set limits to space and time though, obviously, spatial and temporal characteristics belong only to the finite. What is bounded in space, and what has a beginning or end, these are certainly finite. Space itself, however, cannot be bounded; what lies outside space? If it is more space, it means we have not so far come to the limits of space; if it is non-space, we have to admit that the spatial finitude of our experience derives from something determined, if at all, in the last resort by something which is not space; and this, in effect, will not differ from conceding the phenomenality of space. One may contend that space is infinite though spaces are finite. This again will be the admission of Advaita in another way—the admission of the possibility of finitude being an appearance of the infinite, limitation an appearance of the limitless, the many an appearance of the one. It may still be argued that while the advaitin considers the many and the finite to be appearances, the opponent treats them as real just as much as the one and the infinite. To maintain in the same breath the reality of opposed qualities like infinitude and finitude is to fly in the face of the law of contradiction and refuse to think. Justification based on the category of identity-indifference will prove but a broken reed, as will be seen presently. It may be said that an infinite cause may have finite effects; with this contention we shall have to deal in the consideration of causality. This possibility excepted, there seems no way of avoiding the phenomenality of space. So also of time.

The other set of considerations mentioned relates to experiences like dreams. The contents of these experiences are actual enough and enjoy spatial and temporal properties very much at variance with the setting of the dreamer in what we call actual, i.e. waking, life. While the dreamer's body lies in Madras, the dream relates to Benares or to the battle-front. While the dream occupies what corresponds to a few minutes of our waking time, the dreamer often grows up, gets married, achieves success and even dies within that period. There would thus seem to be different and conflicting spatial and temporal systems within our experience. Even within waking experience, consider the phenomenon of reverie. In the course of a few minutes we run through a course of events which occupied a considerably longer interval of time. Is the latter contained in the former? If so, how can this be unless the interval which seems so variable is also negligible as ultimate reality, unless time is phenomenal?

Similar considerations may be raised in regard to causality too. It has been argued that causal efficiency is no proof of reality; the dream food satisfies dream hunger though not waking hunger. But these arguments are not quite conclusive in regard to causality being phenomenal. The causal efficiency of the dream content has indeed been used in the reverse way by realists like the Mādhvas to establish the reality of that content. Further, though he who dreams of Māhiṣmatī does not wake up there, he who dreams of a snake wakes up often with actual trembling; the victim of a nightmare actually cries out; and the physiological consequences of an erotic dream belong to the waking order of experience. It was also noticed that an appeal may be made to causality in order to exhibit the reconcilability of one and many, finite and infinite. The notion of cause, therefore, seems to stand on a slightly better footing than space and time, from the point of view of the anti-phenomenalist; and it deserves a fuller consideration.

The Advaitin, like the follower of the Sāṁkhya holds to *satkārya-vāda*, the doctrine that the effect is not a creation *de novo*, but is prefigured in the cause. The Sāṁkhya arguments for the position are well known. Either there is or there is not a time interval between cause and effect. If there is, does the cause wholly cease to exist, before the effect comes into being? In that case, the immediate antecedent of the product would be a non-existence; and though we may in speech distinguish non-existence of X from non-existence of Y, there is in reality no way of distinguishing one non-existence from another. Thus, so far as the immediate antecedent goes, we have no explanation why X is the effect, not Y; theoretically any effect may follow from any cause; sand may produce oil, and water curds; for between the alleged cause and sought effect, there is interposed a non-existence, whose character can be but homogeneous. Yet in practice we do not get curds out of water; we treat the effect as derivable only from a potent cause. What can this potency be except the pre-existence of the effect in the cause, in a latent form? If, however, no time-interval be admitted between cause and effect, we have to take them as either identical or as wholly different; in neither case is the cause-effect relation possible; cow is not the cause of itself; nor is it the cause of a horse; co-existent differents are no more cause and effect than the two horns of a bull.

With this line of Sāṁkhya criticism of the Vaiśeṣika creationist position, the advaitin has great sympathy. He will not, however, subscribe to the ultimacy of the causal concept; for if the Sāṁkhya criticism is pressed to its limits, the concept has to be abandoned. The critic of the creationist view can admit the pre-existence of the effect only in a latent form; the causal operation serves to make it patent or manifest. The questions raised about the effect may be raised about its manifestation too. Is that pre-existent or not? If pre-existent, it could be only as manifest, since it is absurd to say there is manifestation, but as non-manifest; and if manifestation is pre-existent, it amounts to the admission of the effect as fully pre-existent, not merely as a potentiality; and such an effect needs no explanation in terms of causal operation. On the other alternative of manifestation being produced *de novo* by the operation, what is the special virtue of this effect, that it alone is susceptible of creation, not the effects which become manifest? It seems legitimate to conclude that the Sāṁkhya while envisaging a difficulty has, instead of solving it, only pushed it back one stage. And the difficulty seems insoluble so long as we stick to the distinctness of cause and effect. We seem nearer a solution, if we deny the distinctness treating cause and effect as appearances of the same reality. This is in effect what the Advaitin does. The non-distinctness is asserted not as between finite causes and effects in the world, but as between the world and its cause, *Brahman*. The causal relationship is to be understood as between the substrate and the super-imposed, the rope and the snake; but for the rope there would be no snake-delusion there; it is present only so long as the rope is there and disappears into the rope, when the latter is truly known as such. The effect, the delusion, is nothing other than the cause, though it appears to be different. The causal relation is based on this delusive difference. It is, so to speak, subjective; and this subjectivity will, one may expect, infect all derivative finite causal relations too. The advaitin, however, maintains the relative objectivity of finite causal relationships. Causality is no doubt a product of nescience; but so long as we live in a world of nescience, without rising above it to that which is neither cause nor effect, we have no right to impugn causality; it is as objective as the world is; even for the transcendence of nescience we depend on this concept, since we have to depend on means like instruction, reflection, contemplation, etc. If these were not well-settled causes, they could not be depended on by us in our laudable endeavour to realise ourselves; and yet when we do realise, the very means which furthered our endeavours appear delusive. The needs of science and metaphysics seem to be equally satisfied by the invocation of two worlds. Whether causal rigidity in the empirical world is consistent with denial of causality in the transcendental world is a problem which we shall have to pose in the course of this paper. The orthodox Advaita position would seem to admit of some improvement.

We have to note in the meantime that the cause would seem to find no logical resting place short of *Brahman*; and in *Brahman* it seems to annul itself along with the effect. This is how. The concept in question is an attempt to understand change. It attempts to explain what is fleeting and limited in time, what was not, but is and may cease to be, what in other words is occasional and impermanent. The presumption in any such explanation is that the permanent and the unchanging is self-explanatory; by being related thereto the transient may be made intelligible. A mere relation of one thing to another does not satisfy *per se*. It will no doubt be said that explanation consists in relating the unknown to the known, not the fleeting to the permanent; even in this way of conceiving explanation it must be remembered that the known implies a relatively unified and relatively permanent system; and the permanence of the knowing self at least is in most cases assumed. Without the relation to something more permanent or fundamental, no phenomenon finds explanation. The goal of explanation would seem to be therefore the exhibition of the relation of the changing to that which is above change. Hence it is that *pradhāna* and primal atoms alike are conceived as unborn and eternal. Where the world is declared to arise out of a First Cause, such cause is itself not a product and is conceived as above space and time. This indeed is the merit of the causal concept, that, however inconsistently, it rises above the very limitations and diversities which lead to its invocation and seeks to reach infinitude and unity. The relating of one phenomenon to another may give some temporary or practical satisfaction; but we cannot logically stop short of the noumenon above the phenomena.

And when we do get to the noumenon, whether by reasoning or testimony or both, we still seem to be no better off logically. The noumenon, *Brahman*, the supreme and sole reality, is the cause. The effect cannot be spoken of as such unless there is some difference from the cause. Hence the world though differing from *Brahman* in respect of finitude, inertness etc., may well because of this very difference be the effect of *Brahman*. The world is not eternal and constant; else it would not be an effect; nor would it require explanation, as the eternal is self-explanatory. It is not real in the way that *Brahman* is real. Nor is it unreal, as in that case it would have nothing at all in common with *Brahman* and could not be its product. The effect shares with the cause the negation of unreality; it differs from the cause in falling short of reality by which we understand what is always and for ever. The phenomenon in other words is indeterminable as real or as unreal; hence its relation to the noumenon can have no better status; that too, must be but indeterminable or phenomenal. The Advaitin does assert the non-otherness of effect from cause; he does not however assert their identity in such wise as to deduce for the effect the reality of the cause; the negation of otherness amounts only to this—that the effect has no reality other than that of the cause.[3] Hence, it is that the promissory statements of *śruti* can be justified as to the knowledge of all (effects) through knowledge of the one (cause).

It is worth while sparing some attention here to the notion of identity-in-difference as connected with the causal concept. Identity and difference may appear *prima facie* irreconcilable contraries; but their co-existence, one may contend, is both possible and actual, as will be seen if we look at the many transformations of a single cause. Hail and snow are different; so are bracelet and ear-ring; yet these differences co-exist with the fundamental identity of each pair, in the causal aspect, i.e., as water and as gold. As cause there is

3. Cf.: "*na khalv ananyatvam ity abhedam brūmaḥ kiṃ tu bhedaṃ vyāsedhāmaḥ*"—*Bhāmatī*, II, i, 14.

identity; as effect there is difference. One has to ask what the relationship is between the cause and the effects. Is it identity or difference? If identity, then, what holds good in the causal aspect should equally hold good in the effect-aspect too, so that there is no propriety in restricting the identity of hail and snow only to their causal aspect; they must be identical even as products, a conclusion commendable neither to common-sense nor to the opponent. Suppose, however, there is difference between cause and effects; then between hail which is different from water and snow also different from water, how can there be identity in the causal, i.e., water-aspect? We shall have to resort here again to identity-in-difference, a procedure tainted with the charge of self-dependence or infinite regress. Further, when because of identity-in-difference there is intermixture between the causal and effect-aspects, how can there be the restriction of identity to one of these aspects? We are again faced with the violation of common-sense.

The real is the cause; the effect may not be identical therewith nor different therefrom; nor is difference *cum* non-difference intelligible; the effect is neither real nor unreal; one term of the causal relation being thus indeterminable, the relation itself is indeterminable.

This conclusion may be due to our illegitimate attempt to extend the causal concept beyond the phenomenal realm, where alone it can be legitimately invoked. Phenomenal causality knows nothing of these transcendental difficulties. The relation between one phenomenon and another can be so refined as to be invariable and unconditional; and with this all reasonable ambitions of causal explanation will have been satisfied. In answer to such an objection let us undertake a still closer investigation of the causal concept.

The Advaitin's examination of cause as conceived by the realists of the time is very instructive and can perhaps be hardly improved upon. The cause is usually conceived as an antecedent in time. Of course, not any antecedent will do, e.g. a donkey standing by the potter's shed is not a cause in respect of the production of a pot. We refine the notion by the qualification of invariability; we know that the donkey is not an invariable antecedent. But our difficulties seem to be just beginning. Those who enumerate causes admit causal efficacy not merely for distinct events in time, but also for certain common conditions like time, space, *Iśvara*, etc. *Iśvara* is above time, hence not an antecedent in time. Time itself is not in time and hence cannot be treated as such an antecedent. An ingenious attempt will claim that though there are no temporal distinctions for time, they may be understood through adjuncts, just as the Advaitin claims that, because of adjuncts, distinctions are introduced in the distinctionless. Priority and posteriority for time would be due to the priority and posteriority of the adjuncts. But how are the adjuncts distinguished as prior or posterior? Because of time; and because of the adjuncts so determined time itself is to be characterised as prior or posterior; a clear case of self-dependence. If time were not the determinant of sequence among adjuncts, all of them would be simultaneous, making all empirical usage impossible. This very impossibility would be a ground for treating time and cause as phenomenal, not for admitting sequence among adjuncts and claiming at the same time that it is not temporally determined. This is only to recognise under another name, time as a distinct adjunct determinative of sequence; and one of the two postulates, either this adjunct or time, is clearly superfluous. Even were differentiation by adjuncts possible, it could not be said that time qualified by one of these exists in another time differently qualified, since in any case time cannot exist *in* itself. We do not indeed say that Devadatta who wears glasses exists *in* Devadatta who wears a suit.

This kind of difficulty may not appeal to those who refuse to recognise general causes. Even these will realise that invariable antecedence in time is over-pervasive of symptoms and co-effects, which are not causes. Day is not the cause of night. A persistent low temperature symptomatic of tuberculosis is not the cause of the patient's subsequent decline. We have to introduce further refinements in our understanding of invariable antecedence; and we seem nowhere near success in doing this. We may thus seek to dismiss symptoms and co-effects on the ground of their being *anyathāsiddha*, like the donkey or like the all-pervasive ether. The donkey's presence where the pot is made is due to other causes. Neither its presence nor the cognition of its presence is linked up *as a cause* with the cognition of the pot. Given its own causes the presence of the donkey would be fully accounted for, without any reference to the production of pot. So too in the case of ether, its presence is inevitable because of its pervasiveness, not because it accounts for the pot-production. Similarly the day is the effect of the rotation of the earth round the sun; it may be invariably associated in our minds with night, but its presence and cognition are adequately accounted for by its own cause without reference to night; so also the low persistent fever is accounted for by the tubercle bacillus without a necessary reference to the subsequent decline. Thus co-effects and symptoms may be ruled out.

But, we ask, do you mean to rule out all conditions that are accounted for by their own causes or are inevitable? In that case you would be ruling out most if not all accepted causes. The pervasive ether is admitted to be the cause of sound, and the pervasive self of happiness, etc. It may be you are not prepared to admit their pervasiveness and *anyathāsiddhatva*. The difficulty, however, persists in the case of admitted causes. The clay and the wheel and the staff are undoubted causes of the pot. Are not these causal conditions sufficiently accounted for in their turn by their own antecedents? Perhaps, you think, they are not fully accounted for without reference to their purpose, the production of the pot, their final cause. There are at least two difficulties in such a view. You as a conscious being may consider the lack of final purpose to be a defect and may be inclined to read it in whatever you cognise; but that of itself will be no justification for reading this purpose into inert objects and determining their causality or non-causality thereby. Further this purpose is not an antecedent in time, but what is to be fulfilled in time, while what we seek to do here is to clear up the notion of an invariable antecedent. Again, what is it that we try to understand? Is it not the causality of clay, wheel etc., in relation to pot? The notion of pot as the final cause of the wheel, etc., how does that help us in this? In any case, it is difficult to maintain that clay is not understandable except with reference to a pot to be produced. It may be where it is by accident or design; and the design may relate to pots or dolls or a nature-cure plaster. The antecedents of its presence can be definite, not the purposes which it may serve; and because of the definiteness of the former, it does not cease to be a cause of pot etc. Of course, clay present in a potter's house is different from clay in Mahatma Gandhi's. In the former case, its causality of pot or basin is exceedingly likely; but it is only likely; the probability approximates to certainty when you see it in the potter's hands; even then there is an element of uncertainty; he may change his mind and throw it away or fashion something else; the certainty is greater when a rough shape has been given and you watch it on the wheel; it is greatest when the pot has been finished; you can then say the clay of the pot is the cause of the pot, a proposition perilously near tautology. Again, in the case of earth, water, light, and seed, each of which is accounted for by its own causes and is known without a necessary reference to the growth of crops, can the causality in respect of crops be denied? The notion of *ananyathāsiddhatva* turns out to be a frail reed incapable of sustaining the causal concept.

You may now demand of the alleged cause that it should be helpful in producing the effect. But wherein lies helpfulness? And what degree of it is required? In any particular case of pot the donkey may be helpful; from contemplating its utility the potter may have derived extra cheerfulness and succeeded in finishing off a better pot than usual. This extra psychical stimulus may be provided by different causes for different pots; the potter may dream of his wife or his gains; though because of variability no one of these can be the cause of pot in general, causality in respect of each particular pot seems difficult, if not impossible, to deny.

Assuming for a moment all such objections to be fanciful, let us see whether there is any definite way of understanding the helpfulness of the cause. It is not that the effect is invariably present where the cause is; or the presence of seed is not invariably attended by the shoot. Of course, it will be said, seed alone is not the cause, but seed together with accessories. But it is in determining these accessories that we have all the trouble just noted; the donkey and the potter's wife are clamant in their demand for inclusion though with a show of logic we insist on excluding them. The only legitimate ground for their exclusion is that though present they are not present as causal. Our difficulty however is just what constitutes causal presence and it is no help to refer to accessories with a need for excluding what are not causal.

In any case, it is clear that the semi-popular usage of 'cause' has to be abandoned; for this can produce the effect only in dependence on auxiliaries; and those auxiliaries do, properly speaking, enter into the very cause of the effect in question. We cannot legitimately separate the alleged cause from the auxiliaries; and any attempt to include them seems to end only when we come right down to the effect itself.

It may be said that nothing can be simpler than to determine the true auxiliaries, on the ground of co-presence and co-absence, *anvaya* and *vyatireka*. Whatever has this generic quality is a cause, not any other. There are some merely technical objections to such a view; e.g. a genus, since it cannot possess another genus, can never be a cause. Since clay which is co-present and co-absent with pot has the genus substance-ness and this is shared by donkey etc., these too would be causes. If this genus be considered too wide and remote and a narrower more proximate genus insisted on, e.g. clayiness or earthiness, then such non-distinctive causes as ether, time, space etc., would be wholly excluded from the causal category, whereas time and space are always conceded to be causes. This is also the reason for our failure to understand *anvaya* and *vyatireka*. Is the co-presence in time, or space, or both? In the first case, time cannot be a cause since it is not present in time; in the second case, space cannot be a cause since it is not present in space, and since neither is present in *both* space and time, neither can be a cause in the third case. Nor is the difficulty merely fanciful or terminological. For no cause is such in the abstract, but only as occurring in certain spatial and temporal conditions; and these cannot be ignored in reckoning causal efficiency; rains at harvest-time cannot be the cause of plenty.

We have still to face the ancient bugbear known as plurality of causes. Fire may be caused by a match-stick, or a burning-glass or by a steel and tinder. No one of these is the invariable antecedent of fire, yet each is said to cause fire. Our logicians in their wisdom say such usage is due to ignorance and lack of analysis. Where the alleged cause and effect are sufficiently refined by analysis it will be found the same cause has only the same effect and the same effect has the same cause. Where the fire in the oven has been lit by one of these alternative modes, what, one wonders, will the analysis of the effect lead us to? Our perception does not acquaint us with any difference in the fires. It may be said that if we look at the fires armed with the knowledge of their causes, we are enabled to distinguish the products too. In a class of young boys not old enough to be invested with the sacred thread and all looking more or less alike we distinguish a brahmin boy by his parentage from the rest; so too in the case of the fire and other similar effects alleged to result from a plurality of causes. The illustration is not suitable. For reasons, sound and unsound, we admit the brahmin parentage of the particular boy and then deduce or admit his brahminhood. Here, however, which is the cause is the very point at issue; and the matter we say is unsettled, because of the inconstancy of the antecedents of fire at different times. To the reply that the fires too are different we oppose their practical indistinguishability. It is no answer to this to offer their distinguishability in the light of their distinct causes. Granted their causality the effects would be distinguishable; granted the distinguishability the alleged causes would be really such: thus we have flagrant reciprocal dependence.

Nor is this due to the apparent puerility of the instance chosen. Though death, in popular speech, may be due to many causes, any particular instance of death will on analysis prove traceable only to one of such causes. Interference with the respiratory system is not the same as interference with the circulatory system. Drowning interferes with respiration; certain varieties of snake poison clot the blood and arrest the circulation. Both are vital functions. The arrest of one leads to the suspension of the other also, resulting in what we call death. In respect of the final cessation of all functions, is there any difference? None we can discover. In the preliminaries thereto there are differences: one may get black in the face, or have the wind-pipe or spinal column broken, or the respiratory passage filled with water, or one's blood-vessels choked up with clotted blood; but this is just what we too affirm; in the face of such divergent antecedents how can we deny plurality of causes or affirm a distinction in the effects, except at the risk of such tautologies, as "Drowning is the cause of death by drowning"? Analysis is a good servant, but a bad master. The man in the street does not analyse and has perhaps little faith in the infallibility of causal relations; the logically trained person analyses, but that does not justify his pathetic faith in the perfect causal relation; if the process of analysis is pressed forward rigorously instead of being allowed to stop short to contemplate its triumphs, it will find itself under the necessity to transcend the causal concept.

Again, since, where we do not arrive at a non-difference of cause from effect, we have to distinguish between the cause and its auxiliaries, may we not, even on the assumption of effects being distinguishable, attribute the distinctness to the auxiliary rather than to the cause? Drowning and shooting are both causes of death, we may say; there is no doubt of this difference in the effects, that there is water in the respiratory passages in one case and a hole through the heart in the other; but this is due to the mode in which the different causes function to their accessories; it cannot detract from the possibility of different causes to produce the same effect. Not a very sound argument, perhaps, but a plausible one.

Our difficulties, it may be thought, are due to the persistence of the popular notion that the cause is a single condition, whereas it is in truth a complex of conditions. We should not confuse ourselves with the notion of a cause and its auxiliaries, but should always envisage a causal complex, any member of which may figuratively, and for strictly limited purposes, be called a cause. A cause is that which is a member of a causal complex. This does not, however, take us very far, since, as we have already seen, our difficulty is to determine how much to include in this complex and what to exclude. The only answer we get is that we should include all causes and only causes; but this is to go round in a circle. Further, being a member of the complex, is it the very nature (*svarūpa*) of each of the components? Then each should produce the effect. Even if aggregation be not the *svarūpa* it may be eternal; in such a case the effect should be constant, instead of appearing and disappearing. If, however, the aggregation is adventitious and occasional, how does *that* come about? If it is due to another cause, that will involve another complex and we shall have an infinite regress; or our notion of the first complex would itself turn out to be defective because of the non-inclusion of this factor which accounts for its own being. And when this cause of the complex can itself explain the effect, why postulate an intermediate complex? The complex should be accounted for by its own constituents. Is each then distributively the cause? Then, since some one element of it, e.g. space, will be constant, the complex should be constant, and also the effect. If to avoid this we say that the factors collectively account for the aggregation, we are in the old round of explaining collectiveness by itself. To postulate another complex or aggregate of course leads to infinite regress.

Why all this difficulty about aggregation? All conditions that are proximate constitute the complex; what is remote does not enter into it. The matter is not so simple, as we have difficulties parallel to those in understanding co-presence and co-absence. If the proximity be in time alone or space alone, time would be excluded in the former case and space in the latter; proximity in both would exclude both from causal conditions. If you mean not such contiguity, but either conjunction or inherence of one condition or set of conditions in the other or others, then conjunction and inherence would not be causes, since for them there is not another conjunction or inherence. That there is a single complex may be determined from the production of a single effect; but this is to beg the question as to what it is that produces the effect.

Our troubles have been due to conceiving cause statically. The factors not merely exist but also function in producing the effect. This functioning (*vyāpāra*) we call aggregation or complication; and the effect results therefrom. We are still in the woods; for is this functioning extrinsic or intrinsic to the factors? If intrinsic, we have to determine whether it belongs to each factor distributively or to all collectively. In the former case we have the old difficulty that some factors being constant, the operation and the effect would also be constant. To conceive function as intrinsic to the aggregate does not help, since our present efforts are directed only to the understanding of aggregation. If the functioning be extrinsic to the factors, another functioning would have to be interposed between that and the factors, and there would be infinite regress. If, however, the function of complication can be arrived at without intermediate function, why may not the factors produce the effect itself without the interposition even of complication?

When the conception of functioning fares thus, it is no help to define cause as that which has function. Other difficulties apart, this would exclude the final function from the cause, since that function has not another function. And since function cannot be defined except in terms of generating i.e. causing,[4] we are again involved in a vicious circle. Further, the possession of function cannot be interpreted as inherence or as generation. The latter involves self-dependence while the former is contrary to what is known. Sacrifice is said to be instrumental to heavenly enjoyment through the function of an unseen potency (*apūrva*); but this *apūrva* is not inherent in the sacrifice; for the sacrifice perishes while the *apūrva* survives and results in the enjoyment hereafter.

Enough of this juggling, you may say; it may be that I cannot define cause; but you cannot disprove it. For, living as we do in a world of finite particulars that come and go, the recognition of cause is inevitable; else there would be but constancy, neither appearance nor disappearance; what is uncaused is eternal, like ether or the self. The average realist who urges this is not quite aware of his own presuppositions. The Indian logician, for instance, holds that the non-existence of an effect prior to its production is uncaused; but it is not eternal, terminable as it is by the coming into being of the effect. Again, a barren woman's son is not caused; nor is he eternal. Even if you protest against this reference to non-entities, what are the positive instances on which you base your pervasion? Neither the existence nor the eternality of ether and the self is universally admitted. The rejection alike of eternality and of the absence of causation cannot avail as the ground of pervasion; for the materialist who admits all things to be transient yet denies the validity of inference or causation. One who delights in the bare bones of logic may attempt the following

4. The function is what is generated by the cause and generates the effect produced by the cause.

inference. What is in dispute is caused, since it has prior non-existence; what is uncaused has no prior non-existence, like the self; since the uncaused self is admitted by the Vedāntins, and the present argument is addressed to them alone, the example is unquestionable. But there is a more fundamental defect; the *probandum* must be something known; it must not be a wholly unknown predicate or one whose nature is in doubt; it must not be *aprasiddha-viśẹ*ṣaṇa. Since the causal concept is just that which is in dispute, it serves no purpose to set up an inference like the above to prove that something is caused.

Does the Advaitin then deny causality altogether? No; he does deny its intelligibility and ultimate reality. Viewing ourselves and our environment as finite and changing, there is only one way of rising above our limitations; that is to grasp the identity in the differences, the permanent in the changing. The causal concept is an eminently successful attempt at such apprehension. In the nature of things, however, it cannot claim to be more real than what it seeks to comprehend. The phenomenal world is illusory; the causal concept applicable thereto is also illusory. The causal relation is not ultimately real, because nothing we call cause is ultimately real. What causal explanation seeks is such identity of character between cause and effect as will secure rigid and predictable sequence; the reality of either is for it an irrelevant question. And logically there is no reason for us to insist that any cause or all causes alike should be real. In the first place, all causal factors are not alike; the potter's staff is little like the clay and less like the potter; why should such divergent conditions agree in a claim to reality? True, we call them all causes, just as we apply the notion of similarity to a variety of cases; but the similarity of cow to ox is not the same as that of a cow to the she-buffalo; much less has it in common with the similarity of brother and sister. Why insist on reality being common to such widely divergent factors? Further, by him who says the cause is real, reality is presumably conceived as qualifying the cause. If the cause in every case is that which *has* reality for its qualification, then the substrate (*viśeṣya*), the cause, itself is not real; if, on the contrary, the cause does not have reality for its qualification, then too it is not real. Nor can this dialectical skill be turned against the Advaitin. It may not be said for instance that if *Brahman* be qualified by reality, the substrate of the world would be unreal, and that the same consequence follows, only more so, if *Brahman* be not qualified by reality. For the Advaitin holds *Brahman* to be reality itself, above all distinctions of substrate and attribute. *Brahman* is co-eval with *sattva*, not *antarbhāvitasattva;* and such a claim may intelligibly be made only for what is one, infinite, above space and time, not for the multiple and the limited.

It would follow from this that explanations of the finite as finite would achieve but limited success where they do not wholly fail. For the finite is grounded in the infinite and the latter alone can explain itself or another. Scientific explanations could take us beyond the particular phenomena sought to be known, but not very far; since our particular interests are limited they may and do offer help to satisfy those interests; but if we pressed forward, either because of irrepressible theoretical or satiated and novelty-seeking practical quests, we would find our explanations melting into thin air or doubling back to the starting point. Such an expectation on the part of the advaitin is justified in a measure by what some modern scientists have to say. The name of Eddington is notorious in this connection. And in spite of the disagreement even of some professors of philosophy, it is worth while taking note of his conclusions.

"The determination of the physical laws," says Eddington "reflects the determinism of the method of inference."[5] And the mode of inference he exhibits as strictly cyclic, maintaining its rigidity by cutting away what inconveniently refuses to fit into the scheme. Thus Einstein in his statement of the law of gravitation makes use of the concept of *potentials* which are said to "obey certain lengthy differential equations." *Potentials* are quantities derivable from fundamental quantities called *intervals. Intervals* are relations between events measurable by a *scale* or *clock*. A *scale* is a graduated strip of *matter*. Keeping to the world of mechanics, matter may be defined in terms of *mass, momentum* and *stress*. To the question what these three are, Einstein's theory is claimed to have given an exact answer. "They are formidable looking expressions containing the potentials and their first and second derivatives with respect to the coordinates."[6] And thus we have gone round full circle, or as Eddington diagrammatically represents it, round the pentagon.

The only way to avoid this going round is to stop short somewhere with what you know or what you seem to know. Most people would imagine they know what matter is and would not question further. For them, scientific explanation would appear very sound, simplifying and inter-connecting concepts, making the whole world more intelligible. But the knower, who is he? What is Mr. X? Surely till that is answered, the explanation is not complete. It is because of ignoring this question that systems are maintained and certainty achieved. But neither the metaphysician nor even the scientist has the right to ignore this question.

The cyclic nature of physical inference is illustrated by the children's rhyme of the house that Jack built; only at a certain stage we retrace our steps instead of going on, so that we repeat ourselves indefinitely.[7] And the fact of empirical validity of what we infer cannot guarantee the objective reality of the

---

5. *The Nature of Physical World* (Everyman), p. 262.

6. *Op. cit.*, p. 254.

7. Or, as another interprets it "We are doing what the dictionary compiler did when he defined a violin as a small violoncello and a violoncello as a large violin" (*Limitations of Science*, p. 193, Pelican).

starting point of the inference. "When from an observation of pink rats we infer the presence of alcohol, the validity of the inference lies in the fact that what we infer originates a process which ends in the mental construction of pink rats......But it is not presupposed that the pink rats are objectively real."[8]

Eddington holds that with the advent of quantum physics, the decline of determinism has also set in. The strict reign of causality (the belief in rigid reversible causal relations, as distinguished from the belief in *causation* that any consequent is due to its antecedent or complex of antecedents) is no longer found valid in the domain of physics where it had been supposed to hold undisputed sway. Not all modern physicists are willing to sacrifice determinism. But causality is a positive idea, the burden of proof of which lies on those who advance it; and physicists like Einstein and Max Planck, though they would like to re-establish determinism, see no present means of doing it. Their present failure does not involve failure for all time. Strict causality has not been disproved. But this can give no satisfaction to the physicist whose task it is to prove it, if he can. And despite Planck's emphatic assertion that "natural phenomena invariably occur according to the rigid sequence of cause and effect. This is the indispensable postulate of all scientific research,"[9] we have Eddington's accurance that "Present day physics is simply indifferent to it. We might believe in it today and disbelieve in it tomorrow; not a symbol in the modern text-books of physics would be altered."[10]

If the reaction to determinism among modern physicists is not uniform, the welcome among philosophers has not been all that one might expect. Prof. Stebbing re-acting violently against the idealism as well as the loose language of Eddington will concede only that "the discovery of uncertainty relations does involve a considerable change in our attitude to determinism. But I doubt whether it is quite the change that either Jeans or Eddington supposes."[11] "The dominance of universal causation is felt to be a nightmare. Heisenberg's principle has some part to play in revealing to us what it is we thought we were accepting."[12] A very limited concession! Radhakrishnan holds that "Even freedom of man is not helped in any way by the freaks within the atom. To suggest that electrons possess free will is to degrade freedom itself."[13] "If in order to be

8. *New Pathways in Science*, p. 294.

9. *Where is Science Going?* p. 107.

10. *New Pathways*, p. 302.

11. *Philosophy and the Physicists*, p. 184.

12. *Ibid.*, p. 240.

13. *An Idealist View of Life*, p. 246.

satisfied of the truth of freedom," says Dr. Brahma, "we want it to be proved at the level of mechanism, if instead of rising up to the level of freedom we desire that it may exist at the lower level of mechanism, we are demanding what is nothing short of the impossible. Freedom is not determinism and it can never hold good of determinism."[14] The meaning of this last statement is far from clear, especially in view of what he says later. "The freedom that cannot find any place for necessity and causation but always opposes itself to the latter cannot be ultimate category."[15] Should we not conclude from this that that "real" freedom does not oppose itself to determinism and, to that extent, does hold good of determinism? Dr. Brahma is quite content with the indeterminism or non-determination of *Brahman*; at the level of the phenomenal or empirical, causation may have full sway. But this is just what we as humble logicians in quest of the truth fail to understand. Quite irrespective of what may be true of a transcendent or noumenal background, we found it difficult to grasp the notion of cause or effect in any intelligible or consistent fashion even at the empirical level. We found that try as we might we were landed in self-dependence or infinite regress, defects which strangely enough seemed to find a parallel in physical laws as expounded by Eddington. The cyclic nature of physical law exhibits the self-dependence we have detected in the causal notion. And the scientist today recognises, instead of rejecting, the plurality of causes. "We may think" says Eddington "we have an intuition that the same cause cannot have two alternative effects; but we do not claim any intuition that the same effect may not spring from two alternative causes."[16] And the following quotation from Prof. Davidson will serve as a commentary on this: "The scientific world is full of examples of the same effect proceeding from different causes. An instance from chemistry may be taken. It is well known that formic acid can be obtained from nettles, ants, and other living organisms. It can also be obtained from its elements by simple methods; for instance, potassium formate can be produced from carbon monoxide and caustic potash, and formic acid can be produced from the compound by distilling with dilute sulphuric acid."[17] The measure of agreement makes us suspect that there may be more to the matter than is conceded by Prof. Stebbing or other philosophers, realist or idealist.

Let us consider for a moment the measure of indeterminism now claimed to the credit of the sciences. Each atom is supposed to comprise a nucleus of

14. *Causality and Science*, p. 20.

15. *Ibid.*, p. 22.

16. *Nature of the Physical World*, p. 286.

17. M. Davidson, *Free-Will or Determinism*, p. 44.

positive electricity with one or more electrons revolving round it. The nucleus may consist of a single proton or a number of protons and electrons closely packed together, with a preponderance of protons over electrons so that there is a balance of positive electricity. The electron revolving in its orbit should naturally tend to draw ever closer to the nucleus and the process would be normally presumed to be continuous. It has been found, however, that what occurs is a change by jumps, not a continuous change. We have to assume a succession of orbits; from each of these the electron may jump to a higher or a lower, either absorbing energy or radiating it; it may jump to the next lower or to the next but two; when the electron will jump and how much it will jump we do not know and have no means of knowing; all that we do know for certain is that between the energy levels of the various orbits the relation is constant, being expressible in terms of h (Max Planck's constant, equivalent to 6 ċ 55 $\times 10^{-27}$ erg. seconds) or some integral multiple of h, such as 2 h, 3 h, etc. There is thus an uncertainty within the atom, what Radhakrishnan calls a freak, as to when and how its mobile components, the electrons will change; the time, the quantity and direction of change are all uncertain.

This much can afford little basis for the scientific determinist or indeterminist philosopher. The measurements required may appear present impossibilities but may be future achievements, even like the bombing and disintegration of atoms. To this extent one may sympathise with Dr. Brahma when he says "If future experiments reveal to us that the indeterminism supposed to exist in the movements of the electron is really non-existent, Philosophy would find itself helpless to prove its position if it now accepts the argument of Professor Eddington".[18] But the arguments of Eddington and Schrödinger go a little further than this. They maintain not merely that the movement of the electron is uncertain in the present state of our knowledge, but *can never be certain*, so that scientific prediction such as we used to believe in, is impossible. In order to foretell the motion of the electron you must know both its position and its velocity; but in the nature of things, you can never approach accuracy in regard to the one without receding from accuracy in regard to the other. In order to know the position of the electron you have to look at it or illuminate it with light rays of a smaller wave-length; not even the shortest of ordinary light rays, the violet rays, is short enough for the purpose. We have to use what are called gamma-rays from radio-active substances. When such rays are used, at least one quantum of energy will be involved and this is sufficient to disturb the electron, in an unpredictable manner. We would have very nearly fixed the position but would have disturbed the velocity. If we used lights of

18. *Op. cit.*, p. 20.

long wave-length but little energy, the velocity would be undisturbed, but the position would be uncertain. Accurate prediction requires knowledge of both position and velocity. "But these two factors are so connected that the more accurately we know the one the less accurately we know the other".[19] To put it in terms of Schrödinger's wave-theory, an electron may be taken to be associated with a wave-packet so as to correspond to it in some way. Wave-packets may comprise waves of great or small length. In the former case their velocity will be less than in the latter. The velocity of the electron in the large wave will be not quite determinate, as it may be either in the forward moving or backward moving part of the wave; but since the velocity of the wave itself is low, the indeterminacy will be low compared with the indeterminacy of position due to the length of the wave; the latter indeterminacy is reduced in the case of waves of shorter wave-length; but because of their greater frequency the difference in velocity between the forward and backward parts will be much greater; hence the indeterminacy of velocity is much higher in this case. "We pay for precision in position by uncertainty in velocity and *vice versa.*"[20] The difficulty, to repeat, is not one of present inability, but the impossibility of prediction, given present conceptions.

It may be urged that these conceptions may give place to others, in the light of which prediction may appear possible. The wave theory gave way to the particle theory; now there is a tendency to combine the two and speak of a wavicle; we may in time arrive at some more intelligible synthesis which will do justice to the phenomena and preserve determinism. As against this we have to remember that Eddington and those of his persuasion do not claim to have established indeterminism scientifically. They do claim to have disestablished scientific determinism. Strict causality as understood in the past is neither possible nor necessary for science. We have so far only probability based on statistical laws. These statistical laws are not and need not be grounded on a rigid reversible causal relation.

We may assume for the moment that the principle of indeterminacy (strictly speaking it is uncertainty, and is expressive of the inability of the observer, not of the nature of things) has been established. Even thus, it holds of microscopic bodies, not of macroscopic entities like ourselves or our bodies. Granted the electron is free, what follows for us, endowed with organisms composed of large masses of electrons? The governing law may be statistical in its nature, not a relation of rigid necessity. This, however, means little in practice. By extensive observation we may compute the average longevity of

19. *Limitations of Science*, p. 92.

20. *Ibid.*, p. 93.

the members of a country, community, profession or the like. It will not be possible on the basis of this average to judge the longevity of any particular member of that group; any particular member's length of life may hover about the mean or be far in excess or defect. Despite such uncertainties and aberrations, the average will continue to hold good for the whole as such. Similarly whatever may be the indeterminacy of the individual electron, the general law of causality will continue to hold good of us who are wholes of electrons. Microscopic uncertainties cannot detract from macroscopic certainty. The supposed freakishness within the atom is no guarantee of my freedom.

The argument thus advanced seems irrefutable. And the Advaitin, who is interested not in the empirical, but in the transcendental, ideality of the concept, may well be disposed to accept the argument at its face value. He cannot, however, afford to forget that his own dialectic has convicted the causal concept of self-dependence, reciprocal dependence and so on. The cloven hoof (ideality) would seem to be manifest, however dimly, even at the empirical stage. The philosophic advocate of non-difference cannot afford to recognise water-tight planes or compartments, such that causality is wholly real in one plane and wholly unreal in another. It is in truth neither real nor unreal; this indeterminability, *anirvācyatva*) is manifest in varying degrees in various planes. The Advaitin cannot, therefore, countenance scientific determinism as either actual or possible.

It seems likely that the insurance company analogy is responsible for a confusion. The promoter of such a company, if he accepts reliable statistical figures about longevity, gets the advice of a good actuary, and permits no swindling by himself or by others, is exceedingly likely to prosper in his business despite the uncertainty of any individual's death or survival. In such a case, however, the group or class has no individuality of its own. It is loosely knit; if some die early, others die late and there is a balancing which preserves the average age intact. Suppose we consider instead something like the behaviour of a crowd and the behaviour of a company of soldiers. In the latter case, we can predict for the whole, not in spite of uncertainty about the parts, but because there is no uncertainty about them. In the former case, we may be certain about the parts but uncertain about the whole; while each member of a crowd may be inoffensive, whether because of timidity or a genuine law-abiding nature, the crowd as a whole will often over-ride both tendencies and behave in a thoroughly disgraceful manner. The difference between the insurance statistician and the collective psychologist is that the former studies happenings, while the latter studies behaviour. "Collective security" is possible in the former case in a manner and to an extent impossible in the latter. This is because in *behaviour* as contrasted with *event*, we have to deal not merely with particulars, but with units or individuals; and each unit or individual seems to exhibit distressing symptoms of uncertainty.[21] This is of course most so in the case of the units called individual selves, as is evident from our deliberation as to what we shall do, our regrets for what we did or failed to do and so on. This, however, is to anticipate the question of human freedom.

To return to scientific determinism, it may be argued that with the possible exception of psychology, science is interested in happenings as such, not behaviour, and that if statistical laws can make predictions in those fields, the needs of determinism will be satisfied therewith. This sounds reasonable enough. But let us examine the nature of statistical law. It is based on a number of observations presumably accurate and formulated in such a way as to hold good of the whole constituted of the individuals observed. The proposition "Early marriages produce weaklings" based on observation of A. B, C......Z, who are all progeny of early marriage, is an instance of such a law; again, the proposition "South Indians generally die at 50," based on numerous observations as to the incidence of mortality in a large number of South Indians in all walks of life, is a statistical law. In neither case has a necessary connection been established between cause and effect or antecedent and consequent. But the observations so far as they went, were accurate. There was no doubt of A–Z having been children of parents married early or their being weaklings; the individual South Indians observed did die at the various ages noted by the observer. There is some basis of accuracy to go upon. If similar accuracy were attainable in the case of at least some of these microscopic electrons, we might formulate a statistical law holding good of the macroscopic body though not of any individual microscopic component. This possibility, however, is just what is denied by the Principle of Indeterminacy which says that position and velocity cannot both be accurately determined. And though from a large number of non-accurate observations one may make a guess to a future event, the prediction can never on this basis achieve any better status than that of a guess, more or less lucky.

We may be faced now with the proposition that what is statistically aimed at is a law that applied to microscopic bodies, not to macroscopic ones; with regard to these, there is neither doubt nor failure of the application of the causal law as ordinarily understood. Even on this position there are certain

---

21. After I had completed the paper I came across the following lines in Eddington's latest book: "A study of mob-psychology would be a very unsatisfactory foundation for a theory of the human mind. The molar law, or mob-law, of physics is an equally unsatisfactory introduction to the theory of individual or atomic behaviour". *The Philosophy of Physical Science*, p. 30.

difficulties. What we know as statistical law is such not because its basis is inaccurate, but because though accurate as far as it goes it does not make room for analysis and the establishment of a rigid connection; with the microscopic bodies, however, we find, if Heisenberg is not mistaken, that our observations are and necessarily must remain inaccurate. Statistics deal with inadequate data while here we are faced with inaccurate data. The difference, we grant, is one of degree; this, however, is as little ground for ignoring it, as the tiny size of the baby for ignoring its illegitmacy (in Marryat's story). Secondly, we have to ask whether these microscopic entities occupy a region of their own or are constitutive of the macroscopic bodies supposed to be governed by rigid causality. If they are constitutive, what is the guarantee that the uncertainty of microscopic behaviour will not affect the macroscopic too?[22] It would be ridiculous of course to argue that the larger the whole the greater is the indeterminacy; for the uncertainties may cancel out one another. But is the cancelling out more than a probability? Strictly speaking, should we not say that we cannot be certain as to whether the microscopic uncertainties accumulate or are annulled? And whatever we may judge of *events* as such, should not this uncertainty be our most legitimate conclusion with regard to *behaviour?*

All this seems much at variance with common sense. In looking back on what we know of occurrences or behaviour, we fail to see how any event could have occurred or failed to occur otherwise than as it did. In retrospect at least there seems to be no uncertainty. But this is no problem for the advocate of indeterminacy. In stating the principle, this is how Eddington envisages and answers the difficulty: "There is no limit to the accuracy with which we may know the position, provided that we do not want to know the velocity also. Very well; let us make a highly accurate determination of position now, and after waiting a moment make another highly accurate determination of position. Comparing the two accurate positions we compute the accurate velocity—and snap our fingers against at the principle of indeterminacy. This velocity, however, is of no use for prediction, because in making the second accurate determination of position we have rough-handled the particle so much that it no longer has the velocity we calculated. *It is a purely retrospective* velocity."[23] "Nature thus provides that knowledge of one half of the world will ensure ignorance of the other half, ignorance, which, as we have seen, may

22. *Cp.* "If, however, the components acted quite capriciously why should there be aggregate constancy?" Laird, *Recent Philosophy*, p. 165.

23. *Nature of the Physical World*, p. 295.

be remedied later when the same part of the world is contemplated retrospectively".[24] "It is easy to prophesy after the event".[25]

Between the Eddington picture of the indeterminacy in the atom and our average picture of human indeterminacy there is a close parallel. Most of us feel that, after we have acted, the speculation if we could have done otherwise is idle; but before acting we do feel that there is a choice to be made and that much hangs on this choice. Retrospectively we do admit determinism, but not prospectively. And if a serious-minded scientist finds a parallel for this in intra-atomic behaviour, there is little need for us to look with scorn at "freaks within the atom." Any such parallel is bound to be interesting and illuminating, though, of course, never conclusive. And it is not the claim of the Eddington group to have proved human freedom; rather do they maintain that the supposed obstacle of the exact sciences is no longer there.

It may be thought that the claim to exactitude of certain sciences was never a bar to human freedom. The determinism of external events cannot affect the fact of human responsibility. Prof. Stebbing makes a distinction between responsibility *for* and responsibility *to*. I am responsible *for* my acts *to* some authority, God or the king or my neighbours. When a question of accountability or responsibility *to* some one arises, it may be legitimate to plead determinism as an excuse. But so long as I do not ignore the fact that whatever is done it is *I* that do it, my responsibility *for* the act persists and cannot be got rid of. The notion of responsibility *to* is irrelevant; what matters is responsibility *for* and this does not stand in need of scientific indeterminism. What matters is that *I* act; and our interest should lie in making precise the *I*, not in making the act indeterminate.

---

24. *Ibid.*, p. 296.

25. *Ibid.*, p. 296. It will be interesting to consider here what we know of astrology. It is a matter of common experience among those who consult astrologers that any astrologer worth the name shows uncanny ability in predicting the past while his success as to the future is much more restricted. He may succeed in forecasting certain outstanding events; but the minuteness and accuracy characteristic of the prediction of the past are generally lacking in the prediction of the future. This may be due in many cases to the astrologer's lack of competence; in some cases it is due to inaccuracy of data, the required precision being almost unattainable in the nature of things; to some extent again the lack of accuracy is due to the possible modification of the future by the individual himself; he may offer propitiations and avert malign influences; the planets seem to be responsible only for some tendencies, the effectuation or frustration of such tendencies being, to some extent at least, in the hands of the victim. It is indeed urged that the function of astrology is not to satisfy idle curiosity about the future, but to help the individual to forward good tendencies and avert evil ones, by suitable measures. It is also common belief that astrological predictions of the future fail in the case of yogins, because of their intensive self-culture. However this may be, we find that astrology combines precision as regards the past with a haziness more or less negligible as regards the future; and this combination instead of disentitling it to be a science, seems to bring it into line with other exact science, in its modern developments.

One may sympathise with this clever line of reasoning without, however, being convinced by it. The question of responsibility to God may be irrelevant, but that of responsibility to society and the state is very important. If a person's acts are the result not of choice, but of prior states and those of still prior states and so on, are we justified in intervening at some stage awarding praise or blame, reward or punishment? On such an extremely determinist view even our approbation and reprobation would appear determined; so the question of justification may not arise. But even in regard to responsibility *for,* surely there is a difference between a primary and a secondary sense thereof. I am responsible for my fall, physical or moral, in a way in which the stone is not responsible for falling. If my responsibility consists in this, that it is *I* who act, the stone should be responsible in precisely a similar manner in that it is the *stone* which falls. This however is not what we mean. With regard to this very falling of the stone, both I and the stone may be responsible, I by the fact of displacing it and the stone by the act of falling, but in very different senses. The stone acts as it is acted on. I act because of the forces which act on me and as I choose among these forces. An abstract external calculation of forces, such as is possible or as is assumed to be possible in the case of the stone, is not possible in my case. That is why I am responsible in a sense in which the stone is not. To square this fact of responsibility with scientific determinism we have either to deny that fact or abrogate determinism. The former is what earlier scientists and the materialists did; the latter is what the Eddington group of scientists do.

A third course is perhaps not impossible. One such way would admit determinism in a limited sphere. Determinism is all right in the world of matter, but will not apply to spirit. We are concerned, however, not with the freedom of spirit in the abstract, but with the freedom of human beings, apparently bound in and reacting to a material environment, and embodied in psychophysical frames. If those frames and the environment are strictly determined, there is no sense in claiming freedom for me; my responsibility is no better than that of the falling stone. Am I different from the frame and the mechanism? If not, the determinism of the latter applies to me also. If I am different, in what relation am I to the mechanism, and how is it determined? If there is a relation and that is undetermined we leave the door wide open for the influx of the demons of primitive faith; calculation and determinism, even within a limited sphere, become impossible since this sphere is liable to be disrupted at any time from without. If the relation is determined, it cannot obviously be so unless the other relatum, the *I* is also determined, and no determinate relation is conceivable where one relatum is undetermined and undeterminable. The only relation, if it can be called that, is one of superposition of the mechanical on the non-mechanical, of matter on spirit. This is the Advaita notion which we shall examine presently. But short of this there seems no way of avoiding the extremes of denying human responsibility or scientific determinism. To claim a mysterious sphere for the *I* is only to do violence to science without any corresponding advantage in metaphysics.

Why not then adopt the Advaita doctrine of super-position? The mechanical, the material, the determined is a superimposition on the conscious, the spiritual, the ever-free. So long as we are in the sphere of the super-imposed we gladly concede determinism. We recognise however that it is only a phenomenal plane, the plane of the analytical intellect. When, by a deeper intuition, we rise to the higher plane of spirit, there is no determinism. The Real, the Absolute is neither free nor not-free; the appearance is never free. The fetterless spirit appears as fettered in its own laws; the non-relational appears as the harmoniously related; the uncaused and uncausing appears as a system of rigidly interlinked causes and effects. "The Absolute", says Dr. Brahma, "expresses itself differently at different stages and this infinite variety of expressions also in a way proves the infinitude of the Absolute. It is our limitation which is responsible for the belief that what is causally connected cannot be freely conceived. But if we attempt to reach the deepest levels of our experience and to be directly cognisant of the inexhaustible, autonomous spring that underlies and supports the ever-changing playful states of consciousness, we can realise that what is freely conceived is expressed through harmony, law and system, and that there is no opposition between perfect freedom and spontaneity on the one hand and law and system, causality and determinism on the other."[26]

This passage, I confess, has puzzled me greatly. In some ways its contention seems as patent as it is acceptable. How can the infinite appear finite, the self-luminous as other-illumined, the undetermined as determined? To this our answer must frankly be that as finite consciousness we do not know, and to deny the reconciliation is really to presume an omniscience we do not possess. The reconciliation *may be* for aught we know; it *must be* if we are to conserve the intelligibility of the finite in some measure; therefore it *is*. The adoption of this Bradleian reasoning, however, presupposes a *must be*: a stage which we cannot postulate if the finite causal system were a closed system, if determinism, causality, law, system were intelligible instead of being riddled with contradictions as shown in the Bradleian and advaita dialectic. We may admit that the ever-free can and does express itself as if bound; but if the freedom is real, the bondage can be nowhere near perfect.

---

26. *Op. cit.*, p. 22.

Another idea underlying Dr. Brahma's words may perhaps be expressed thus. *Brahman* is undetermined; it is not a term in a cause-effect series; all the same it is not characterless; the undetermined nature of *Brahman* does not lead to the possibility of anything being anything else; the absolute freedom of *Brahman* is consistent with its being determinate, its being character (though not endowed with characteristics), so that what is abstracted therefrom or superposed thereon is such and such, not something else; and between the various super-positions certain definite laws hold good. This is as it should be. A thoughtful Advaitin would repudiate the characterisation of *Brahman*, refuse to predicate characteristics thereof, but not say that it is characterless. It is that which is at the mercy of all outside influences that has no character; not, however, that which has no inside or outside and is homogeneous. If, therefore, it is this reconciliation that is meant by Dr. Brahma between law and its transcendence, there is no need to disagree.

But here again it must be remembered that the finite is not a plane or sphere apart from the infinite; it is the infinite itself which expresses itself in finitude; hence even on the empirical view the boundaries of the finite cannot afford to be hard and fast; they must have a certain haziness, though the haziness may be negligible when dealing with large numbers. What I wish to stress is this: what you call finite has or has not a hard crust; if *ex hypothesi* you endow it with such a crust you will never make it jump out of its skin into the infinite either now or ever; if on the contrary it has no such crust, but we treat it as if it had, then law, system, determinism are not absolute even in the empirical sphere. Surely this is the only legitimate conclusion, if the deeper intuition is not a *deus ex machina* but the fruition and fulfilment of the disciplined intellect itself. From such a point of view the postulation of indeterminism in science is a conclusion very much to be welcomed. Absolute certainty for the true advaitin, belongs to *Brahman* alone for that alone is both determinate and undetermined. Anywhere short of that, what is claimed to be absolutely certain is only an exercise in tautology more or less successfully camouflaged.

Again, what can be meant by the statement that the "Absolute expresses itself differently at different stages"? Is it that distinctions of space and time have real significance for the Absolute? Does the Absolute really have to pass through various stages? Or is it that in the Absolute, which is one, *we* distinguish stages? Surely this last is the position acceptable to the advaitin. And on such a view, the non-reality of the stages and distinctions has to be admitted, despite their presentation and empirical reality. The admission of this much of reality may be a necessary stage even in the realisation of illusoriness. As the ancient Advaitin asks:

"गौणमिथ्यात्मनोऽसत्त्वे पुत्रदेहादिबाधनात्
सद्ब्रह्मात्मा-हमिति एवं बोधि कार्यं कथं भवेत्?'

gauṇamithyātmano 'sattve putradehādibādhanāt
sadbrahmātmāham iti evaṃ bodhi kāryaṃ kathaṃ bhavet[27]

But what we insist on is only the non-reality, not the unreality (*asattva*) of the empirically real. Even at a level far short of absolute realisation, we find that error has been the gateway to truth; this does not prevent the recognition of the error nor shift the realisation of the more inclusive truth to a higher plane or to a different sphere. The passage from error to truth may follow the laws of wave mechanics or of quantum mechanics. We may insensibly move towards the truth or jump to it in well-marked stages; and our jumps may not all be in a forward direction; however this may be, it can never be maintained that in one sphere or plane the error was true, but not in another. We thought it true at one stage, but now we do not think so; the germ of our present realisation was in it from the outset; it may be a fresh discovery, not a fresh importation; and consistently with this we have to declare not its reality, but its non-reality even in the empirical sphere. The deficiencies of empirical reality are to be made known not elsewhere or at another time in a different order of experience; our finite practical life itself exhibits its self-diremptive character. What is required is not an ecstatic flight to mystic heights but some patient and persistent analysis. The Vedānta says "That thou art" not "That thou wilt become"; oneness with the Absolute is a present experience, not a mere hope of the future; and the imperfections of the phenomenal must be evident to us now, since we are the noumenon even now and do not have to become it hereafter. We cannot admit indeterminism in one plane and system, causality and law in another plane. Indeterminism is not indeterminateness; hence the *possibility of law* to a limited extent; system is relational, and relation being an unintelligible concept in the last resort, can never be complete; hence the possibility of law *only to a limited extent*. Freedom can hold good of determinism, despite Dr. Brahma's assurance to the contrary; it is because determinism can never be complete; in its attempt at fullness and precision it reaches out indefinitely or turns round in a tautologous circle. The self is free energising,

---

27. Śaṁkara's commentary to the Brahmasūtras 1.1.4,, reading "bodhe" for "bodhi." When, because of rejecting sons and body and so forth, given the unreality of the figurative and false self, there is knowledge that my true self is brahman, how will the effect (of that idea which has been rejected) arise? (trans. R Hayes, personal communication)

as it is self-luminous consciousness. This freedom, however, being another name for the fullness of character independent of external conditions, and not equivalent to the indeterminable subjection to influences other than one-self, it is determinate. This determinateness is appreciable by us in our efforts at prediction, which are so successful in regard to the past and achieve a limited measure of success in regard to the future, though our certainty about the future is not and can never be anything more than a high measure of probability. For the ever-free in its appearance can never appear as the merely determined or the merely indeterminable; it must combine both features while rising above both; hence the predictability in retrospect and the probability in prospect. This is one approach to an understanding of reality and for help in this approach, we may be duly thankful to modern scientists, though beyond this we may not go in reliance on their conclusions.

The dismissal of causality does not involve the abolition of all certainty. It is dreary philosophy which can hold out no certainty at least of release. This certainty cannot be taken away by Advaita or by modern science. There is no philosophy possible without the certainty of the philosophising self. This is self-luminous, self-evident, self-guaranteed. And release, according to the advaitin, is the self's own nature. It is that it is; it can never be gained nor lost, though it may appear to be lost and appear to be regained. For us who appear to be searching, the regaining of our own nature is a certainty; it is indeed the only certainty, and the only measure among the probabilities which are all we have left to us in prospect.

A. C. Mukerji, "Śaṅkara's Theory of Consciousness" (1937)

Anukul Chandra Mukerji (1888–1968) succeeded R. D. Ranade as Professor of Philosophy at Allahabad. He was a scholar of Western and Indian philosophy and specialized in Epistemology, with a special interest in idealism and the problem of self-knowledge. He published two books during his life, *The Nature of Self* (1933), and *Self Thought and Reality* (1938). In this essay Mukerji defends Śaṅkara's account of consciousness as an exposition of Advaita Vedānta.

6

Śaṅkara's Theory of Consciousness

THE DEVELOPMENT OF philosophical thought is, not in a small measure, due to the rise of the sceptical spirit which paves the way to sound speculations by exposing the self-contradictory basis of dogmatism. Scepticism, therefore, is invariably a sign of the maturity and vitality of reason. There is, however, an unhealthy type of scepticism which, far from providing a stepping-stone to further progress and maturer growth, has always acted as a clog in the way of rational speculations; it doubts everything without looking at its own foundations, it carries on its destructive campaign against every established belief and institution without stopping to examine the ground upon which it itself stands. Any one who surveys reflectively the main currents of contemporary thought would have no difficulty in detecting that the majority of the currents have an unmistakable tendency towards a position that can hardly be distinguished from this unhealthy scepticism. The result is that a lot of mist has gathered around some of the most fundamental principles of thought and existence. The object of the following lines is to attempt a partial dissipation of the mist with the aid of an Indian analysis of one of these basic principles, namely, the principle of consciousness.

In a well-known passage of his commentary on the *Praśnopaniṣad*, Śaṅkara attempts a classification of the principal theories of consciousness each of which had its enthusiastic exponents in the history of Indian speculation. The advaita theory of consciousness is here distinguished from as many as four other theories which are carefully scrutinized and ultimately rejected as based upon an imperfect analysis of experience. These rival theories are defined as follows:—(1) that which looks upon consciousness as something that is every moment born and destroyed, (2) the theory which denies the very reality of consciousness, (3) that which regards consciousness to be an evanescent property of a permanent self, and (4) the theory according to which consciousness is the quality of matter.[1] It is easy to see that almost every theory of consciousness that is still in the forefront of philosophical discussion today can

1. *Commentary on the Praśnopaniṣad*, VI, 2.

be classified under one or the other of the different heads mentioned here. And an examination of some of the outstanding theories of contemporary philosophy in the light of the Advaita analysis may, therefore, be of fascinating interest for the modern thinkers.

The polemical mood in which Śaṅkara expounds the Advaita theory of consciousness frequently obscures the important hints he gives of a constructive theory, and it will, therefore, be useful to start with an initial statement of the main features of his position. The most important and far-reaching of his contentions is to be found in what may be called the foundational character of knowledge or consciousness. It ought to be accepted as a universal rule, he insists, that there can be no objects of knowledge without knowledge.[2] None can prove something that is not known, and the attempt to prove it would be as absurd as to maintain that there is no eye though the form is apprehended.[3] The objects may change their essence, but consciousness cannot be said to change inasmuch as it witnesses all objects irrespective of the place where they may happen to be; the fact-of-being-known is thus implied by all objects without exception.[4] Even when something is supposed to be non-existent, this very non-existence cannot be proved in the absence of knowledge.[5]

The second feature of the Advaita analysis of consciousness lies in its insistence that consciousness is always distinct from the object of consciousness, the things, therefore, should on no account be identified with the consciousness which makes them its objects. From this follow two corollaries; namely, that consciousness cannot be its own object and that every object of consciousness is unconscious or material.

Out of these four cardinal points of the Advaita theory of consciousness, the first would easily put a modern student in mind of the central contention of an influential school of thought which is generally known as the idealistic school. Since Kant's analysis of knowledge it has been a recognised tenet of the idealistic theory of knowledge that consciousness is the *prius* of reality, inasmuch as all things must be "determined in relation to the conscious self, as the one condition which we can lay down for them *a priori*."[6] In fact, the development of post-Kantian idealism bears eloquent testimony to the vitality

2. *Na hi jñāne asati iñeyam nāma bhavati kasyacit.*

3. *Kincit na jñāyate iti anupapannam, rūpam ca dṛśyate na ca asti cakṣuriti yathā.*

4. *Svarūpavyabhicāreṣu padārtheṣu caitanyasyāvyabhicārāt yathā yathā yo yahpadartho vijñāyate tathā tathā jñāyamānatvādeva tasya tasya caitanyasyāvyabhicāritvam vasiutatvam bhavati.*

5. *Abhāvasyāpi jñeyatvāt jñānābhāve tadanupapatteh.*

6. E. Caird, *The Critical Philosophy*, Vol. I, p. 353.

of the Advaita position, and the former may in this respect be regarded as an elaborate exposition and ramification of the latter.[7]

Consciousness, when regarded in this light, is the ultimate principle of revelation for which alone the world of objects has a meaning; it is not a relation between two elements, on the contrary, it is the light which manifests all objects and all relations between the objects. It is "the centre of the whole world comprising the objects, the senses and the mind, and has neither inside nor outside, it is altogether a mass of knowledge."[8]

This is generally known as the centre theory of self; the conscious self, according to it, occupies the central place of the universe, inasmuch as all objects owe their meaning and significance to the relations in which they stand to the self that essentially is consciousness. It is from this standpoint that the self is also described as the *Sākṣī* which witnesses all objects and all changes in the objects, it is *sarvapratyayadarśī* and *citśaktisvarūpamātra*.[9] The entire world is revealed only through the light of the self, "just as the light of the sun is the condition of the manifestation of all form and colour."[10] This is excellently expressed by Sureśvara when he remarks that the self and the not-self are established in the world through perception and other means of knowledge, but the not-self is in every case established only on the presupposition of the existence of the self.[11] For a surprisingly similar language one may turn to Prof. B. Varisco's observations that objective existence "is *my* cognition, cognition of an experience belonging to myself, and obtained by an activity of my own; it would not exist, if I did not exist."[12] Hence all objects are said to be *ātmapūrvaka*. To put it in the language of modern idealism, existence-for-self is the highest category to which must conform all objects. Matter, mind, electron, proton, etc., have any meaning for us only in so far as they stand in relation to the conscious self whose reality, therefore, has to be presupposed by every intelligible entity. In this sense, consciousness is the prior principle or the foundational fact which cannot be reduced to something other than itself except through a confusion of thought.

---

7. Compare, for instance, Green's remark that "all knowing and all that is known, all intelligence and intelligible reality, indifferently consists in a relation between subject and object," and, consequently, the generic element in our definition of the knowable universe is "that it is such a relation."—*Works i*, 386. See also Lord Haldane, *The Reign of Relativity*, p. 150.

8. *S. B. I.* 4, 19. Compare Lord Haldane's explanation of the sense in which the essence of the panorama of life centres in me as given in the *Reign of Relativity*, p. 169.

9. *Commentary on the Kenopaniṣad*, 12.

10. *S. B. I.* 3, 22.

11. *Naiṣkarmyasiddhi*, IV, 3.

12. *Know Thyself*, p. 2.

A word of explanation may be useful at this place in regard to the precise meaning in which consciousness is said to be the *prius* of reality. This doctrine is often interpreted on the idealistic line and supposed to deny the independent existence of the material world apart from consciousness. This, however, would be to raise a highly controversial and difficult problem, and if the priority of consciousness could not be established till the age-long controversy on the relation between the external world and the knowing mind had been settled once for all in favour of idealism, the Advaita theory of consciousness would naturally stand on a shaky foundation. It is, therefore, important to dissociate the assertion of the priority of consciousness from the idealistic contention, and realise clearly that the doctrine of the priority of consciousness is equally compatible with the realistic belief in an independent world. Even if it be granted that knowledge does not create but only reveal a preexistent reality, yet it would remain unchallengeable that the external reality could not be revealed to us apart from consciousness which is the principle of revelation. We may thus be in a position to appreciate Green's well-known remarks that even if it could be admitted that matter and motion had an existence in themselves, it would still not be by such matter and motion, but by the matter and motion which is known that the functions of the soul can be explained by the materialists.[13] The epistemological priority of the conscious self is thus reconcilable with realism as well as with idealism.[14]

The force and vitality of the Advaita position will be better appreciated through a consideration of the anti-Advaita theories which, as noted above, are classified by Śaṅkara under four heads. The most audacious and apparently paradoxical of all these theories is that of the nihilists who reduce consciousness itself to pure nothing. Not content with the mentalism taught by the Buddhists of the Yogācāra school which reduced everything to momentary flashes of consciousness, the Mādhyamikas seek to cut the ground from under the feet of consciousness itself. This is evidently a very bold and dare-devil position which would easily outbraze a number of modern theories that deny the reality of consciousness. When W. James challenges the existence of consciousness and proves it to be nothing more than a loose name for the relations

---

13. *Prolegomena*, p. 13. Prof. R. B. Perry does not appear to us to have done full justice to the doctrine of the priority of consciousness when he associates it with idealism in his admirable book, *Present Philosophical Tendencies*, p. 105. To limit things to what can be experienced may be groundless and misleading (*Ibid*., p. 316), the things may not require any home, yet the independent reality, call it a thing or a neutral entity, could not be revealed to us and so could not be used in explanation of anything if it had not been *known* at all.

14. For a further exposition of the meaning of independence, I must refer the readers to my *Self, Thought and Reality*, pp. 115–120.

existing between certain events and the life of the organism,[15] he had at least to seek the support of the neutral events for destroying the wide-spread prejudice for consciousness. Consciousness, for him, is a particular relation into which the neutral events enter which, therefore, must be acknowledged to be real entities. The Mādhyamikas, on the other hand, go about their iconoclastic business all single-handed and unaided and will not rest till all philosophical superstitions are finally eradicated including the Vijñānavādin's superstition in favour of consciousness.[16]

Śaṅkara's attitude towards the theory of pure nothing or *śūnyavāda* is generally one of sheer contempt.[17] Yet, however, he has indirectly subjected it to a scathing criticism which, though directed against some of the assumptions of Indian nihilism, may very well be utilized in assessing the merit of the modern theories. One of his contentions against the position of universal nihilism is that a significant denial has invariably a reference to something real as its logical basis; e.g., when the illusory snake is negated as unreal this is made possible only on the basis of the perceived rope which is real.[18] Denial is significant only when something is left; if, on the other hand, "everything is denied, and no real entity is left, the negation becomes impossible and, consequently, that entity which we started to deny becomes real." Turning to the nihilist's denial of consciousness, it is remarked in another context that even if the position of the subjective idealist be left in the region of controversy and it is left undecided whether the object of knowledge is real or unreal, yet the reality of consciousness or knowledge has to be presupposed in either case.[19] Even the nihilists, it is observed elsewhere, have to concede

15. *Journal of Philosophy, Psychology, and Scientific Method*, I, 1904, since incorporated in *Essays in Radical Empiricism*, p. 17.

16. This distinction between the position of the subjective idealist and that of the nihilist is beautifully brought out in the *Sarva-Siddhānta-Saṅgraha*, IV, 6, a work attributed to Śnkara. The only philosopher whose nihilistic perfection approaches the radical scepticism of the Indian Buddhists is F. H. Bradley who has so far been rightly characterised as "a genuine Mādhyamika" by Dr. Th. Stcherbatsky in his *Nirvāna*, p. 52. But the difference between these positions is at least as great as their similarity. Bradley, in spite of his condemnation of the self and self consciousness as mere appearances, is anxious to find a home for them in the life of the Absolute, though they have to undergo transformation and transmutation before they can enter it. Moreover, the self, for him, though not a true form of experience, is the highest form of experience which we have (*Appearance and Reality*, p. 103). For Nāgārjuna, on the other hand, the self is as unreal as the son of a barren woman, and, consequently, has no place in Reality.

17. Compare, for instance, his indignant remark that nihilism does not merit refutation as it is opposed to all types of proof—*S. B.*, II, 2, 31.

18. *Kinviddhi paramārtham ālambya aparamārthaḥ pratisidhyate*—*S. B.*, III, 2, 22.

19. *Ubhayathāpi ghatādivijñānasya bhāvabhutatvam abhyupagatameva*—*Commentary on the Brh. Up.*, IV, 3, 7.

that non-existence or *abhāva* is knowable as well as permanent.[20] And it would be absurd, therefore, to assert the knowability of negation while denying the reality of knowledge.[21]

The modern theories of consciousness, as we have observed above, are less audacious and much less radical than the doctrine of the Indian nihilists. Even W. James who first doubted the reality of consciousness did not doubt the reality of the neutral events which, according to him, were the ultimate stuff of the real world. Similarly, the behaviouristic and neo-realistic doctrines of consciousness, far from committing themselves to the position of universal negation, undertake to reduce consciousness to a particular type of relation between the external stimulus and the organism. That is, instead of reducing consciousness to pure nothing, these modern theories reduce it to something other than consciousness, and so far they escape partly the edge of Śaṅkara's criticism. But this partial escape brings out all the more prominently their weakness when judged in the light of the other part of the criticism. The most fundamental point in the contemporary attempts at denying the reality of consciousness lies in their unanimous rejection of the idealistic procedure of assigning a supreme place to consciousness and knowledge. Things, it is urged, are not only independent of knowledge, but knowledge is nothing more than a specific type of relation into which the things enter under certain conditions. These things are no doubt variously named in the various theories, but the central contention remains identical in all of them, namely, that there is no consciousness outside or apart from the things and their relations.[22]

The internal paradox of the contemporary theories of consciousness may best be exposed by enquiring whether the elements, the neutral events or the bits of pure experience into which consciousness is reduced are themselves unknown or known. The former alternative would evidently render them undistinguishable from pure nothing or mere naught, and, as such, they must repel all predicates. And in that case they cannot be brought in for explaining anything. The only alternative, therefore, would be to admit that they are objects of knowledge and, as such, presuppose the reality of knowledge or consciousness. The scepticism of Descartes, as is well known, was arrested by

---

20. *Commentary on the Praśnopaniṣad*, VI, 2.

21. This argument has found in Prof. Gentile one of its distinguished modern supporters: "It is clear that our very ignorance is not a fact unless at the same time it is a cognition...so that ignorance is a fact to which experience can appeal only because it is known."—*The Mind as Pure Act*, p. 29.

22. The only exception to this general tendency is furnished by Prof. S. Alexander who does not favour the total obliteration of the well-established distinction between the mental and the physical and insists on enjoyment and contemplation as being two fundamentally different types of knowledge none of which can be reduced to the other.

the *cogito*, and it is this very fact which is denied here. When I doubt, I cannot doubt that I doubt, and as doubting is a mode of consciousness, it would be paradoxical to doubt, and more so to deny, the reality of consciousness. It is this fact which, as we have seen above, is emphasised by the epistemological priority of consciousness.[23] All objects, no matter what they are in detail, are, in so far as they are appealed to in explanation of something, known objects, and must have their *prius* in "I think," "I know" or "I am conscious." They are, as put by Sureśvara with his characteristic terseness, *ātmapūrvaka*.

The reason, however, why such an apparently self-evident position threatens to degenerate into the relic of an exploded doctrine is that the majority of the modern theories of consciousness have unwittingly pledged themselves to an altogether unwarranted postulate. This postulate, to put it simply, is that consciousness is an object, and as such can be investigated and explained in the same way in which we explain all other objects of the world. There have been, no doubt, philosophers and psychologists who have protested against the practice of regarding the self as an object, but they have as a rule ended by depriving the self of all its meaning till it dwindles into a bare zero or, as it is disparagingly put by A. S. Pringle-Pattison, the dot upon the i.[24] Thus, Kant and Green, J. Ward and E. Caird have exhibited in their expositon of the self a clear drift to agnosticism. Whether or no some type of agnosticism be inseparable from a true theory of self, the indubitable reality of consciousness provides a brilliant instance of a reality which, though incapable of being known as an object, is yet a foundational fact. This leads us to what we have called before the second feature of the Advaita theory of consciousness.

Consciousness, according to the Advaita thinkers, being the ultimate principle of revelation cannot stand in need of a more ulterior principle for its own revelation. That which is the *prius* of the knowable objects cannot itself be conceived as an object among other objects much as the light which reveals everything does not require a second light for its own manifestation.[25] Hence, consciousness is characterised as *svayamprakāśa*. All things, it is observed,[26] "can be classified as knowledge and knowable, and none except the Vaināśikas

23. In this connection one may recall Professor G. F. Stout's important observation that whatever "it meant, intended, or thought of by the mind, inasmuch as it is meant, intended, or thought of, is the mind's object, whether it be fact or fiction, a mountain or a headache or a geometrical problem." *Manual of Psychology*, fourth edition, p. 8. And they are all objects because they are "presented to consciousness."—*Ibid.*, p. 99.

24. *The Idea of God*, p. 199.

25. *Samvedanasvarūpatvāt samvedanāntarāpekṣ ā ca na sambhavati yathā prakāśasya prakāś āntarāpekṣayā na sambhavah tadvat—Commentary on the Kenopaniṣad*, 12.

26. *Commentary on the Praśnopaniṣad*, VI, 2.

would admit a third knowledge which perceives the other knowledge." In fact the distinction between knowledge and the object of knowledge is inevitable in all cases, and "a hundred Vaināśikas cannot make knowledge itself knowable and this is as sure as they cannot revive a dead man." The knowledge of knowledge (*jñānasya jñeyatvam*) or awareness of awareness is, therefore, a psychological absurdity; and even when it is advanced as a logical theory, its untenability may be shown by the evident conflict it comes into with the admittedly valid principle that all objects are presented to consciousness. "In so far as consciousness is an object of consciousness," it has been rightly remarked by Prof. Gentile, "it is no longer consciousness. In so far as the original apperception is an apperceived object, it is no longer apperception."[27]

A lot of mist that has gathered round the problem of self and that of consciousness would, therefore, disappear as soon as we abandon the logical superstition that all that is real must necessarily be a definite object of thought. And modern philosophy has already prepared the weapons with which one may kill the superstition. Berkeley's distinction between 'idea' and 'notion,' Professor S. Alexander's insistence that knowledge in the way of contemplation is altogether different from what we get in the way of enjoyment, James Ward's contrast of the self from the presentations, and lastly G. Gentile's position that the transcendental ego can never in any possible manner be objectified—these are some of the clear instances in which attempts have been made to widen the domain of reality beyond the world of knowable objects. All that is needed now for a just appreciation of the Advaita position is to see clearly that it is consciousness and consciousness alone which, though not an object, is yet eminently real. And this would certainly disarm the critics who have been but too ready to identify such a position with that of the agnostic.

It ought to be clear from what has been so far said in elucidation of the advaita doctrine of consciousness that any analysis of consciousness which is undertaken without a distinct comprehension of the essential difference between consciousness on the one hand and the objects that are presented to it on the other is sure to be inadequate and uninstructive. That which reveals every object and illumines the entire world of things cannot itself be apprehended as a 'this' or a 'that.' The nearest analogy to it in the physical world is furnished by light which, therefore, has been very frequently appealed to in illustrating the peculiar character of consciousness by the Indian as well as the western thinkers.[28] The light which manifests all material things cannot

---

27. *Ibid*, p. 6.

28. Among the western philosophers, one may remember here Hamilton's comparison of consciousness with "an internal light" (*Metaphysics* I, p. 183) or E. Caird's comparison of the self with "the light which reveals both itself and the darkness" (*Hegel*, p. 147). The advaita literature abounds in this analogy and frequently refers to the self as the lamp-light or the light of the sun.

be appropriately said to be here and not there, it is not a particular thing existing by the side of other things; yet it is the condition of the revelation of the particular things.[29] Hence arise the difficulties which our psychologists experience in defining consciousness, the reality of which they find it necessary to emphasise; it is something, they say, that can be defined only in terms of itself. Hence, again, Yājñavalkya while expounding the nature of the Absolute to Uṣasta insisted on the impossibility of explaining it in the same way in which one shows the cow by holding her by the horn. The Self being the seer of sight, as he puts it, it is not capable of being apprehended as an object, as, e.g., we know the jug, etc.[30]

The initial assumption of the contemporary theories of consciousness is essentially identical with that of Uṣasta, namely, nothing that cannot be presented as a definite object is real. This very assumption was at the root of the imperfect analysis of experience offered by associationism and presentationism; particularly, it formed the corner-stone of Hume's analysis. And if Hume's search for the self ended in a total failure, the relational theories of consciousness of the present century cannot be expected to fare better while the initial assumption is allowed to stand unchallenged. When, that is, consciousness is defined as a species of function exercised by the organism,[31] or as the cross-section of the universe determined by the specific response of the organism,[32] it is not so much as questioned whether consciousness to which are presented all things including the nervous system can itself be adequately conceived as a presentation or a particular type of thing among other things. The result is that the conscious self which in fact is the presupposition of the organism and its function is lost sight of amidst the congeries of objects; and then ingenious attempts are made to evolve it out of that very organism which when separated from a conscious self is devoid of all intelligible meaning. This procedure, in the words of Śaṅkara, is as preposterous as to think that the colour is seen though there is no eye.[33] When the self is reduced to

29. Another favourite instance of the advaita thinkers is provided by space or *ākāśa* which is too ubiquitous to be determined as 'this' or 'that' or 'here' as distinct from 'there.'

30. *Commentary on the Bṛh. Up.*, III, 4, 1.

31. Prof. R. B. Perry, *Present Philosophical Tendencies*, p. 322.

32. Prof. E. B. Holt, *Concept of Consciousness*, p. 170.

33. It is interesting to note that W. James whose analysis has profoundly influenced the realistic theories of our age has sometimes been more careful in this respect than his followers. When the psychologist undertakes an analysis of knowledge, he tells us, he has not only to see the elements and their relations involved in knowledge, but also the relation in which he himself stands to the total situation.—*Principles of Psychology*, I, p. 184. When a philosopher analyses or explains an object, it is as natural as it is disastrous to drop himself out of sight.

the complex of the body, etc., it is significantly remarked by Śaṅkara, what is ignored is that "this complex, not being distinguishable from sounds and the rest in so far as it, like them, is of the nature of the knowable, it is not reasonable to attribute the nature of the knower to it."[34] The colour cannot see the sound, but everything is knowable by the self.[35]

A curious meeting of extremes in this respect is illustrated by the accounts of self advanced by Bradley and Bosanquet. Out of the various meanings of self which Bradley examines in his monumental work, *Appearance and Reality*, there is hardly any reference to the doctrine according to which the self is consciousness or knowledge, though such a doctrine has been strongly suggested and ably explained by Lord Haldane.[36] And the reason seems to be that he starts with the same assumption which vitiated the analysis of Hume and the associationists in general.[37] Even if it be granted that the self is, "where not hiding itself in obscurity, a mere bundle of discrepancies,"[38] it may still be urged that the conscious self *for* which such a bundle exists cannot itself be reduced to a mere bundle of discrepancies. The fact is that all his difficulties about the self as aptly put by Dr. Haldar, "is due to his identification of it with its content."[39] And once this identification is assumed to be true, it would be a comparatively easy task to condemn the self as a gross fiction, a mere monster, or a metaphysical chimera. This identification remains essentially unchallenged in Bosanquet's theory. It is true that he, in spite of his deep sympathy with Bradley's way of thinking, does not go the length of condemning the self as a mere appearance. On the contrary, he insists that the significance of mind should be accepted on its own merits and as *sui generis*. Yet, the description of the self as a world of experience working itself out towards harmony and completeness, or an active form of totality, or, again, as a living world of content, is strongly suggestive of a fruitless search of the conscious self in the wrong place.[40]

---

34. *Dehādisaṅghātasyāpi śabdādisvarūpatvāviśeṣāt vijñeyatvāviśeṣāt ca na yuktam vijñātṛtvam.*

35. *Sarvameva tu Ātmanā vijñeyam—Commentary on the Kathopaniṣad*, IV, 3.

36. Compare, for instance, his article in the *Proceedings of the British Academy*, Vol. IX, and also *The Reign of Relativity*, pp. 150, 288.

37. This is particularly evident from the way in which he asks "whether there is anything which may not become an object, and in that sense, a not-self"—*loc. cit.*, p. 77. Such remarks as that the main bulk of the elements on the side of the self and on the side of the not-self "is interchangeable" illustrate clearly Bradley's tendency to presentationism.

38. *Loc. cit.*, p. 104.

39. *Neo-Hegelianism*, p. 252.

40. Some of his pregnant remarks on the self are to be found in *The Principle of Individuality and Value*, pp. 193, 289, 335. Cp. also *The Nature of Mind*, p. 125 f.

The conclusion that emerges out of these considerations is that no theory of consciousness is likely to survive the light of critical thought which leaves unexamined and unchallenged the identification of consciousness with what is presented to it. And it further follows that consciousness cannot be dismissed as a mere chimera simply on the ground that it cannot be known as an object. Thus, agnosticism and presentationism are the two extremes which should be carefully avoided by a true theory of consciousness. The self, which is essentially consciousness for the Advaita thinkers, is, therefore, frequently described as different from the known and beyond the unknown, and this character, it is urged, does not belong to any other thing.[41] That is, as explained by Śaṅkara, the self is different from the entire world of objects but that does not mean that it is unknown.[42]

The Advaita distinction between the *svayamsiddha* and the *āgantuka* may also be used as an effective remedy against the false theories of consciousness. The conscious self, according to the thinkers of this school, is of the nature of an irrepressible reality which is necessarily presupposed by all proof and disproof, and which, therefore, falls beyond the region of logical justification or refutation. The self in this respect is different from the adventitious' objects, such as ether. These are not beyond the range of proof (*pramāṇanirapekṣa*) or self-established (*svayamsiddha*); the self, on the other hand, is the basis (*āśraya*) of the process of proof, and, consequently, is established prior to the process of proof.[43] You can refute what is adventitious, but not that which is your essential nature; much as the heat of a fire cannot be refuted by the fire itself.

Regarded in this light, the conscious self, according to the Advaita theory, is an irrepressible reality, and what Bradley says with regard to the principle of contradiction may with equal justice be applied to it, namely, that its absolute reality is proved by the fact that, "either in endeavouring to deny it, or even in attempting to doubt it, we tacitly assume its validity."[44]

---

41. *Kenopaniṣad*, I, 3.

42. Ānandagiri illustrates the point by the help of light which, as we have seen above, is the most favourite analogy with the Advaita thinkers.

43. *Ātmā tu pramāṇādivyavahārāśrayatvāt prāge a pramāṇādivyavahārāt siddhyati.—S. B.*, II, 3, 7.

44. *Appearance and Reality*, p. 120. This in fact contains the essence of Kant's transcendental deduction. The necessity and universality of the principles of the understanding are ultimately proved by the fact that they are the ground of the possibility of experience; that which makes experience possible is for that very reason necessary. In this sense the unity of consciousness, according to Kant, is a transcendental condition of all experience and all knowledge, it is the ultimate presupposition of knowledge. The advaita conception of *svayamsiddha* essentially conveys the same meaning; and if Bradley condemns the self as a mere appearance while accepting the absolute validity of the law of contradiction, that is probably due to his assumption that the self, if real, must be an objective content.

From the dictum that there is no consciousness, which has so far been considered, to materialism there is but a short way. The latter does not deny the fact of consciousness, but, accepting it as an indubitable fact, materialism considers it to be a product of matter. But nonetheless materialism and the doctrine of no-consciousness meet on the confusion of consciousness with the content; the only difference is that the latter has the merit of drawing the inevitable consequences of the fundamental postulate which has always been at the basis of the former. And this postulate, it may be worthwhile to urge at the risk of repetition, lies in assuming that consciousness is one object among others. Once this assumption has been swallowed, the wood is sure to be lost in the trees, and, consequently, the relational theories of consciousness may very aptly be styled as the natural nemesis of objectifying the subject.

As the purport of the present essay is to provide an antitoxin for counteracting the ruinous tendency of contemporary thought to what we have called above unhealthy scepticism in respect of the most ultimate principle of thought and existence, a full and detailed examination of the anti-advaita theories of consciousness, however interesting and profitable, is not called for in the present context. In fact, all these anti-Advaita theories may be ultimately traced back to the root-fallacy which has inevitably led to the relational theory of the present century; and the *reductio ad absurdum* which it illustrates in a very piquant and clear manner ought to force philosophical thought to retrace its steps and come to a clearer consciousness of the limits within which alone scepticism can exercise its healthy influence.

V. S. Iyer, Śaṅkara's Philosophy (1955)

V. Subrahmania Iyer (1869–1949) was Registrar of the University of Mysore, Diwan of Trivancore, and Court Philosopher and Advisor to the Maharajah of Mysore. He was a modernist, concerned to interpret Advaita as a doctrine amenable to contemporary philosophy and to strip it of its mystical overtones. The present essay presents his reading of Śaṅkara from this modernist perspective.

7

Śaṅkara's Philosophy

(A MODERN HINDU VIEW)

"Thus engaged in supporting conflicting theories...... they have all been drawn away from truth".
—Śaṅkara's com. on *Praśnopaniṣad.*

ŚAṄKARA, RELIGIOUS TEACHER, mystic, theologian, philosopher, and above all, man of action, has been variously interpreted and estimated by scholars both eastern and western. Apart from the natural tendency in interpreters, unconsciously to read, *at times*, their own thoughts into other's words, the differences in the presentations of the philosophy of Śaṅkara, to a bird's eye view of which this article is confined, are due not only to the difficulty of understanding the abstruse mind of one who lived over a thousand years ago, but also to the circumstance that he has given to this world no work containing what might be called a *systematic* exposition of his own thought, as a modern Kant or Hegel has done. His most authoritative works are but the commentaries on those of others, mainly theological or mystical in character, which necessitates our sifting his philosophy proper from the rest of his thoughts.

A study of Advaita (Non-dualism), as Śaṅkara's system is called, may start from either of the two standpoints of physics or metaphysics and proceed to the other. This Indian thinker like his ancient predecessors, the Vedic Rishis, held that a philosophy should explain in the light of its fundamental doctrine the whole of life or existence.[1] That Advaita aims at such an explanation will be evident from its most characteristic feature the keystone of the system, the method of '*Avastatraya*' which will be adverted to in the sequel.

The mental as well as the material of which we are aware, *appears* to be as few would dispute, one of continuous change. The appearance and disappearance of psychical or spiritual phenomena as well as all physical, including the natural and the social, indicate *movement* of one kind or other. So the basic

1. *Muṇḍaka* I. 1. 1 & 3. *Bṛhadāraṇyaka* IV. 5. 6; *Chāndogya* VI. 1. 3. and VI. 4. 5; Śaṅkara's *Sūtrabhāṣhya* II 1. 14.

philosophical question with which this social also, like many an other, may be said to grapple, is: What does the urge[2], which manifests these several activities and changes in mind and matter, point to and imply?

The two central topics round which all his disquisitions may be said to range themselves in this connection are (1) the problems of Truth, and (2) the problem of Reality, which are necessarily interrelated and therefore inseparable. In the course of his treatment of these two problems he states his views on many others which are usually considered under philosophy.

What distinguishes him from other thinkers of the past is his approach to the subject. A thousand years ago he appears to have held that the battles of philosophy (not religion or mysticism) have to be fought and won on the field of epistemological problem of Truth but not on that of ontology. This is evident from the introductory remarks in his great commentary on Badarayana's *Sūtras* and the commentaries on the most important Upaniṣads, such as the *Bṛihadāraṇyaka* and the *Māṇḍūkya* (with Goudapada's *Kārikās*). While as theologian he is content to start, like Badarayana, with the assumption that Brahman or God is the first cause or Creator, as a philosopher he begins with an enquiry into the meaning of truth. Here he relies on no theoretical hypothesis (as many a modern philosopher does), or ecstatic visions; no scriptural authority or theological dogma, upon nothing beyond the common experience of mankind. Great thinkers have no doubt enquired into logical truth; but what Śaṅkara seeks is philosophical or ultimate truth,—truth which comprehends all other truths i.e., the truth-process which explains all other truth-processes.

Falling into error is among the commonest occurrences in life, which man learns to be due to ignorance. Error brings on suffering, which prompts enquiry. An enquiry into causes and their implications means search after truth. The moment at which one knows that one has fallen into error marks the awakening of the sense of truth. The first point[3] therefore that Śaṅkara considers is, What constitutes error? Then come the questions: How does it arise and how is it removed? These lead to the elucidation of the meaning of truth, which naturally involves the discussion of the problem of reality. It is not unusual to find persons proceeding to the study of 'reality' straight, in Śaṅkara. It is preferable however to follow Śaṅkara's own course. Further some writers have ignored his distinction between 'Truth' and 'Reality' which has led to some misunderstanding of his system. This is probably due in a measure to the use at times of the same word '*Satyam*' in Vedānta in both the senses. The confusion is further attributable to the fact that in the philosophy

---

2. For an explanation of it as impulse *vide* Śaṅkara's commentary. *Baghavad Gītā* VII 4–6 and XIII 19–20. Specially Śaṅkara's com. Bri. Up. I. 4. 7. and II. 7. Reference to *Pravṛtti* and *Nivṛtti* etc.

of non-dualism (Advaita), absolute or ultimate Truth and Reality are identical. That he, however, does make this distinction, till the ultimate (*paramārthika*) point is reached, is evident from what he says in various places in regard to 'Existing or real things' and our 'knowledge of them' as distinct conceptions. In other words, truth here is one's knowledge, thought or conception of something denoted as fact or reality, or, more accurately speaking truth is a mental effort to get at fact or reality. And it must be said that without a clear grasp of Śaṅkara's views in regard to truth it is impossible to understand his philosophy, though one may get at his religion and mysticism without such knowledge.

He holds that not only religious feeling, mystic experiences, theological dogmas but also laws of science rest upon truth and they all reveal but different degrees of it, through which the human mind passes before it attains to the highest or ultimate truth. All these realms of knowledge receive their stamp or imprimatur of truth or more accurately, of the degrees of truth that they contain only from philosophic enquiry (*Tatva-vichara*: Bg. XIII 25). There are any number of doctrines or schools *(mātā)* of religion, theology, mysticism, scientific theory, every one of which without exception seeks a justification of its attitude in the language of truth (*Tatva* or *Paramārtha*). Even when some of them argue the existence of non-rational facts, beyond the reach of the intellect, they do so relying on their sense of truth, for establishing the validity[4] of their convictions. If an adherent of any school or doctrine felt his non-intellectual beliefs, to be false or foolish, he would not stick to them for a moment, whatever others may think of them. What, however, directly led Śaṅkara to tackle the problem of truth may be best indicated in his own words thus: "The followers of Kapila, Kanada, Buddha, Jina, and many others are obstinately firm, each in their individual conviction............so as to hold that truth (paramārtha) in its entirety must be of this form and this alone........ And they are in endless conflict with one another".

Since every one possesses an instinct of truth with which one tests the validity of one's own experience and knowledge, the question arises: Does this sense of truth signify that what is called truth is different for different men or that it is one and the same for all, though there may be various degrees of it. Is there a basic universal standard? Śaṅkara's enquiry leads him to the conclusion that there exists a common standard which is the same for all

3. For his distinction between theological dogma and philosophical enquiry vide his com. *Baghavad Gītā* XIII 25; *Sūtrabhāsya*: Introduction.

4. In Western philosophy 'validity' is held to be more comprehensive than 'Truth'. But in Indian thought such a distinction does not seem to obtain.

men, which 'does not conflict with any'[5] and 'is free from dispute' and 'which' is 'non-antithetical'[6]. In the absence of such a touchstone no discussion will help us to estimate the value of any piece of human knowledge and particularly of philosophical knowledge, nay, even of any human action, not to say anything of the conflict and discord naturally resulting from want of a correct estimate of this kind.

Before proceeding to the enquiry proper, Śaṅkara lays down that a seeker after the standard truth should keep out whatever might disturb the mental equilibrium and clearness necessary to perceive it. And he accordingly says that:

1. the seeker must not be actuated by any motive—such as of gain or of pleasure, temporal or celestial,—other than that of the pursuit of truth;[7].
2. he must possess such control over himself as to secure perfect calmness, patience, attentiveness and concentration;[8].
3. he must be free from all predilections or prejudices even those of a religious or theological character,[9] besides possessing a resolution to accept 'truth' be it agreeable or disagreeable to his preconceived notions.

Now, what does this 'urge' of thought called truth aim at? When I say that I am seeking 'truth' I expect that my thought will correspond to something material or mental that 'exists' but not what does not exist. Since my expectation implies also a comprehension of what exists, intelligence or consciousness is a necessary concomitant. Lastly, when consciousness or intelligence has grasped the existent without any doubts, a satisfaction must be felt which marks the grasping; for, in the absence of such satisfaction there is no knowing whether what I know is true. Or, if a man were asked why he considers a piece of knowledge or a belief true, he would say that he does so because he feels that it tells him of something which is a fact, positive or negative, that actually exists, because he has intellectually comprehended it, and because he feels a satisfaction in having grasped it. 'Existence, comprehension or intellection and satisfaction' are the trio of characteristics that mark the objective of all truth-seeking:—a view which is of Upaniṣadic origin, as we shall see.[10] And these three are indissolubly united though they may according to

---

5. *Avivada.*

6. *Aviruddha.*

7. *Īhamūtra phalabhogavirāga.*

8. *Śama, dama, titiksa* etc.

9. *Uparati* etc.

10. This trio is known as *sat, cit, ānandam.* It has been further elaborated by later Vedāntins into *asti, bhati, priam, nama* and *rupam* with which we are not concerned here (*Vide Drigdrisya Vivekam*).

circumstances be of different degrees of intensity. When the 'urge' attains its maximum limit and the three characteristics are also at their highest degree of effectiveness, we reach the *conceivable* 'goal' of truth-seeking.

In the practical world, this 'urge' which varies with temparaments and intellects, sometimes overemphasises one or two of the three characteristics, which leads to different levels or varieties of truth and to fallacies of various kinds. In mixed philosophy which does not wean itself from religious, theological, mystical, scientific and other bias, there is infinite scope for differences and grades of truth. On the other hand in *pure philosophy*, which seeks 'Absolute truth', the standard common to all, there can be no room for gradation or differentiation. And those who have not the patience to get at the ultimate balance of emphasis do not attain to the standard of 'Absolute truth', though they do get at some aspect of truth, which they very often believe to be ultimate, but which is not such, as is evident, and as Śaṅkara says, from the 'conflicts' we see.

Fallacies of mysticism arise out of an over-emphasis of the 'satisfaction' (*Ānandam*) and 'existence' (*sat*) aspects subordinating 'intelligence' (cit) or reason to use a modern word. Those of religion owe their origin to the stressing of 'satisfaction' more than even the 'existence' feature. Prominence given to the 'intelligence' character subordinating 'existence' and 'satisfaction' leads to inconsistencies of Intellectualism and Idealism and of some of the theories of Science. Attachment of undue importance to the 'existence' character involves us in the contradictions of Realism and Materialism[11]. The more balanced and the greater the degrees of emphasis, the nearer one is to absolute or standard truth. It is, however, Intelligence that is aware of and that determines the degrees of the emphasis on the three aspects. The utmost limit of the emphasis is reached when intelligence sees that it is not possible for the 'urge' to reach a higher level in any of the factors. Hence the supreme importance of intelligence. And it happens that owing to want of intellectual acuteness one is not able to see when this maximum level is reached. And intelligence does not develop as rapidly as one often wishes. Science however quickens its pace. Truth being the effect of thought or knowledge to get at something which is considered real, the 'urge' of truth-seeking has no further function to perform when reality is reached. Next, what Reality is has to be considered.

Truth-efforts being thus subject to various modifications, their objectives which also likewise vary, are classified by Śaṅkara under three heads. The highest or the absolute is called '*Paramārthika*' which admits of no degrees or conditions. Next comes the Relative or '*Vyāvahārika*', the most familiar one,

11. Atheism also.

which contains an infinite number of grades and varieties, such as not only the basic or logical, but also the mathematical, the scientific, the historical, the legal and many others, each determined by the character of the data or facts dealt with, and each governed by subsidiary laws of its own. His last order is the illusory or '*Pratibhāsika*', in which what is taken for truth at first turns out subsequently on enquiry to be untrue as is a dream. *Vyāvahārika* and *Pratibhāsika* truths resemble each other so largely that they are often bracketed and placed under the head Relative by some of the writers. '*Paramārthika*' truth being absolute and beyond all characterisation, the 'Existence, consciousness and satisfaction' formula indicates in varying degrees the objective of the truths of the 'Relative' class only. Many thinkers seem to hold that there is no limit or finality in regard to truth and that ultimate truth is unattainable. They are perfectly correct so far, in as much as their point of view is only the relative. '*Paramārthika*' or absolute truth being beyond characterisation is to them necessarily meaningless. Hence they have no idea of a standard common to all men. Even Śaṅkara quotes one of the Rishis who when asked to put into *language* the absolute truth, answers by maintaining silence.

How then, do we in practice speak of it, in such terms as 'Absolute' or 'Ultimate'? So long as we use language to indicate it, as we have to, by directing our attention from, i. e., by negating the relative, we cannot help having recourse to languages. Using such language, Śaṅkara declares that 'Perfect knowledge has the characteristic mark of Uniformity[12], which implies, as he himself says, 'Permanence'[13] and 'Universality' or an absence of mutual conflict of men's opinions, or rather an impossibility of such conflict regarding it[14]. Such knowledge, however, he adds, it is 'impossible' to attain actually within the limits of the relative. And he also says that the greater the degree of such 'uniformity', the nearer one is absolute truth. Absolute truth as distinguished from relative truths, which are dynamic, is static. But in itself it is neither.

Corresponding to these varieties of truth, tests have been adopted. The Advaitic system recognises, for instance, in the world of relative knowledge, the test of correspondence where the 'Existence' and 'Intelligence' aspects of the objective are emphasised, the test of non-contradictability or consistency where the 'Intelligence' factor predominates; the pragmatic test where the 'Existence' and 'Satisfaction' features are stressed. The test of the inconceivability of the opposite is applied to what is known as the subject or self, where there is a consciousness of subject as related to object. As for absolute truth

12. *Ekarūpam.*

13. *Avasthita.*

14. *Vipratipattiranupapanna.*

viewed from the world of relativity a three-fold test is provided which is essentially one. When this truth is attained (1) there remains no existence unknown, for, 'Everything becomes known'; (2) there is not merely no room for, but no possibility of room for any doubt arising (of intellect); (3) there is no higher 'Satisfaction' to seek; for there is and can be no desire for anything beyond. This corresponds to the three-fold *objective*, 'Existence, intelligence and satisfaction (*satchidanandam*)' of the relative world which is here *negatived*, by saying that of these three characteristics there remains nothing that is distinguishable in absolute truth. Perfect agreement or perfect consistency is possible only when truth is Reality i.e., when both are the same when the urge naturally ceases. This is the oldest three-fold Vedic-test which only 'unity' or better still 'non-duality' can stand. When we look at it from the point of view of negation, we call it non-duality. This non-duality is denoted by Śaṅkara by the unique expression '*Antyam Pramāṇam*' (ultimate measure of truth).

The absolute reality is beyond even 'unity'[15]. Hence non-duality is not the same as 'unity' or 'monistic reality' as applied to truth process. Even unity may imply duality. When we have the *idea* of unity, there is not only the *idea* but also a thinking or consciousness of that idea, i.e., two entities or or existents. Śaṅkara therefore uses the negative 'non-duality' advisedly.

Now, it might be urged that '*Paramārthika*' or absolute truth is only a theoretical or intellectual conception with an equally theoretical 'ultimate measure' corresponding to it. Strictly speaking, what it is is inconceivable. Can it then be actual? Or, is it attainable? In answering this question, Śaṅkara has recourse to what has been referred to as the 'keystone of Advaita Vedānta'. The highest Court of appeal is common experience. The business of truth is to read it aright. Europe and other parts of the world which have no knowledge of 'non-dualism'—which is not 'monism' as has been pointed out—rely upon experience of a *fragmentary* character for the data of their knowledge. Whereas the Advaitic philosopher takes account of the *totality* of experience. Those thinkers of East and West who are not non-dualists base their inference on the experience furnished by the 'waking' state only, while the adherents of the Śaṅkara doctrine cover the entire ground of the three states of the 'waking', the 'dream' and the 'deep sleep'. This is known as the '*Avastatraya*'. Scientists of the West have no doubt studied dream and sleep physiologically and psychologically, but not for epistemological or noetic purposes........'*Avastatraya*' is the core of Śaṅkara's philosophy. Some critics of Śaṅkara have ignored this in the belief that it involves the *fallacy of solipsism*. Without however going into its details, it

15. *Bṛhadāranyaka Upaniṣad II*. 3. 1. Also *Chand Up*. S's com. *Ekam evādvitīyam*.

16. *Vide* Śaṅkara's *Sūtrabhāsya* III. 2. 21.

may be stated that '*Avastatraya*' shows that non-dual experience is no hypothesis, but a fact and reality, beyond all doubt and within the reach of one and all.

Truth-seeking as has been said is a process of thinking. Thought is a movement at bottom. And thinking implies a 'being' that thinks; which 'being' need not be, as some men suppose, a material or tangible entity. Being and thinking cannot be different in essence or stuff. Only the one is static while the other is dynamic. Sometimes the word 'spirit' is used to denote 'being'. Inasmuch as thinking implies 'being', so long as we think we are 'thinking beings'. To get at 'pure being'[17] thinking has to cease. Hegel thought 'pure being' to be nothing because of his intellectual attitude, which while it corrected the fallacious reasonings of those that relied too much on feeling, subordinated the factor of existence. It is not nothing however for Śaṅkara; for to him it is 'Non-duality'[18].

But it will be said that with the cessation of thinking the idea of 'being' also is lost to thought. But this 'being' is beyond not only affirmation but also negation. It cannot be said that it does not exist merely because thinking ceases. Further 'being' is not non-existent because of the awareness of the fact of the cessation of thinking as in the intervals of thinking, when it is said that one has had a blank mind; or, generally speaking, as illustrated by deep sleep. In the reality revealed by 'non-duality', there is no annihilation, as some, nihilists hold, but it is indescribable—indescribable because, 'being' is all that is and is not and could possibly be. In fact there is nothing different from it to think of. *Paramārthika* truth is such that in which 'knowing' and 'being' are not—two: are not different.

The argument of 'unconscious cerebration' and 'subconscious thinking' of certain critics is not to the point. They are never aware of such thinking at the time. We only infer such processes from what appears to us when we become conscious of them. But such phenomena or experience is accounted for differently and more practically by Advaitism into which we cannot go here.

How then do we know that this *Paramārthika*, 'non-dual' standard is ever present, functioning even in the *Vyāvahārika* or *Pratibhāsika* truths as the universal and permanent sense of truth? In the first place, so long as the 'urge' is felt for attaining truth, i.e., the equilibrated, non-conflicting standard, so long is it said to be present in the waking and in the dream states[19]. Next, 'Being' is present in all thinking (including feeling) and Being which

17. Śaṅkara's pure 'being' is beyond thought and therefore beyond Hegel's distinction of 'being' and 'non-being'. Śaṅkara's 'pure being' (Sadeva) is beyond being '*Sat*' as ordinarily known. It is even '*Asat*' non-being from another aspect.

18. *Sat* implies Sat *asat*; therefore pure *Sat* is what is beyond this duality. *Vide* Śaṅkara's Commentary: Goudapada Kārikā 2.

19. There can be no urge towards or no seeking for an object of which we have not some knowledge implicit or explicit.

is un-related, is the non-dual reality or absolute truth. Śaṅkara's 'pure-being' abhors all attempts at reaching it by 'thinking' which only hides pure being from view, though it is ever present. No amount of thinking will ever help us to get at 'being' pure and simple, which alone determines the validity of all the thinking whose object is to get at 'being'. Some philosophers attach no value to 'Pure-Being'........inasmuch as they are so attached to the ego, that its disappearance alarms them. They seem to have no idea of the *totality* of experience, which shows that the ego is only an 'idea' (*kalpana*). The ultimate truth or existence is 'pure-Being' which is called *Ātman*.

Further, what perceives the various degrees and kinds of truth is what comprehends them all. What is ordinarily called truth is the truth of the waking and the dream states, that is, of the relative world. Śaṅkara's analysis of the knowledge of the Relative world gives him an 'awareness' or 'witness' as subject and a two fold object, one internal and the other external. All thoughts are ideas including those of time, space and causality, feelings, volitions, soul or ego, intellect, in a word, what one is mentally aware of constitutes the *internal object*. And whatever is perceived through the senses including the body is *external object*. Both these appear and disappear and are subject to change. Our knowledge of them is neither 'uniform' in all men nor 'permanent'. They are therefore considered to be unlike the constant witness 'awareness' or 'subject' whose nonexistence cannot be conceived of. Even when you think of the absence of awareness you are somehow aware of the awareness. If awareness whose nonexistence cannot even be thought of be called, 'real' what is off and on presented to it and is changing may be denoted by the term 'unreal'. Now if a person says that he feels or sees, conceives, or in any other manner becomes aware of God, he only knows God as an object, which is unreal, being subject to the changes of appearance and disappearance, being not known to be 'uniform' or the same to all. Śaṅkara is therefore in one sense in agreement with Tersteegen who says 'A God comprehended is no God'[20]. Śaṅkara goes a step further. If any one feels that God is external, subject to no changes or conditions, is truth, or that He exists but cannot be thought of or described or comprehended, God must be one with 'Pure Being'. In no other sense can there exist God.

Śaṅkara holds that the characteristics of the *Vyāvahārika* and *Pratibhāsika*, i.e. of the waking and the dream worlds are time, space and causality[21], which are unreal being but creations of thought as is proved by '*Avastatraya*'. Therefore those that talk of a first cause, a ruler, a director, or a saviour, belong to the

20. Quoted from Dr. Otto's "The Idea of the Holy".

21. In this Śaṅkara anticipated Kant about a thousand years before Kant. His proof is however different.

theological stage. As Śaṅkara declares, they alone who can see the truth value of the causal relation are qualified to enter upon a study of *pure philosophy* whose object is the pursuit of the absolute or the ultimate 'non-conflicting' truth.

Now, the truth-seeking effort is a thought process, passing through the *Vyāvahārika* and the *Pratibhāsika* grades of experience, which leaves each step as it rises higher, as soon as it is felt that reality is yet to be reached. But to have the satisfaction that it moves in the direction of reality, it keeps the idea of reality, constantly before it, which forces it to take at first sight anything as real. This reality which is a tentative superimposition (*aropita*) is also called apparent reality or shortly, appearance. This is apparent because it is removed (*apavada*) afterwards. Experience itself shows the character of this superimposed reality by means of the changes and by the contradictions arising in one's knowledge of it. There is thus a combined process of affirmation and negation. The aim of the combined process is the attainment of the unimposed reality, which is 'being' itself, which is always implied in thinking, as the non-dual *Paramārthika* truth. It is by this process of the dialectic of thought, that non-duality is reached. The modern tendency in European Philosophy is more towards construction (*aropa*) based on hypothesis. But the '*apavada*' is left to mysticism, because Europe or the West has as yet no idea of the 'standard' truth as revealed by 'avastatraya'.

Taking it for granted that causality is a *real* relation, men often ask,—How does the 'dual' spring out of the non-dual? The dual may be unreal, even then the question arises: How does the unreal come into existence while the real is held to be unchanging? The usual reply is well known that causality is a characteristic only of the relative or dual world, that no relation can be predicated of the non-dual and that therefore the question is inadmissible. But this does not satisfy; for, it is said that it is only an intellectual reply. Now if we turn to experience and ask how the dual is produced by the non-dual, we get the answer that if it has been produced, we could say how it has been produced. Experience has nowhere given us such production from the 'non-dual'. We only assume or imagine that it has been produced by the 'non-dual' and ask for the cause.

To make this clearer, if we hold a piece of ice in hand, we feel its solidity and hardness. We also perceive its shining surface and its defined shape. But it soon turns into water, when it loses the above features. Water then turns into vapour; vapour may be turned into gases. But at each step the characteristics that we once found disappeared. Where have they gone? Do solidity, hardness, shining surface, shape etc., exist or no? If they do exist where is the proof of their existence? When one asks what is ice one is told that ice is water. And when one asks what water is, one is told that it is vapour, a compound of gases and so on. At each step of seeking the cause, certain features which were so actual as to be perceived by the senses disappear. In other words when we ask an explanation by analysing and enquiring into causes and rising to higher generalisation, if anything ceases to be, this inexplicability is said to be *Māyā*[22], which is assumed to be the cause of the dual existence[23].

Māyā is only a statement of a fact, the most stubborn of facts. It is no theory. And there is no philosopher of the past or present who is more oppossed than Śaṅkara to imaginary, hypothetical and mythical assumptions or inference in the search of the Absolute truth. *Māyā* which is beyond dispute *explains* this duality to be of the nature of ideas or thoughts which disappear when you seek their cause; i.e., when you seek to know the stuff of which they are made; for ideas or thoughts disappear in 'being' when you seek their cause. This we learn from *Avastatraya*', which tells us that we have before us duality consisting of the witness (subject) or Being, and the object (internal and external). When we seek for the cause of the whole of the object we are obliged to fall back upon the subject; for, nothing else exists[24]. The object character must disappear in the subject, i.e., if the object is treated as effect and its cause is sought. The thought world of the waking and the dream states disappear in deep sleep.

Śaṅkara, however, holds that the causal relation is only an idea (*kalpana*) and says[25] that the seeking for a cause is only the urge or craving for the 'real' the 'being', the 'non-dual' which is never an object of thought. And when there is pure being there can be no thinking, for, when there is thinking we have a 'thinking being'. If one knows how one's own 'being' and one's own 'thinking' are related one knows how 'duality' appears or disappears.

The internal object, i.e., the mental world may disappear in sleep, as it is only a world of ideas. What about the external object or the mental universe? How can we dispose it off so summarily? That the external world is also of the same stuff as ideas and are like the world of dreams is made clear by *Avastatraya*. The modern Gentile is a good approach to this part of Śaṅkara here. This subject however must be reserved for a future occasion[26].

---

22. Śaṅkara's com. and Vidyaranya's gloss—*Taittirīya* Upaniṣad: Anandavalli ch. VII.

23. That is, so long as we view from the *Vyāvahārika* or relative world. When there is no causal or any other relation to think of as in the *Paramarthika* world, there is no *māyā* in it.

24. *Vide* Śaṅkara's commentary on *Goudapada Kārikā* II 16.

25. *Vide* Śaṅkara's commentary - *Goudapada Kārikā* Ir 78 et seq.

26. To avoid misunderstanding it must be added that Śaṅkara is neither an 'Idealist' nor a 'Realist' nor a 'Monist' in the European sense of these terms. He is a 'non-dualist'. He admits an internal or mental world and an external or material world like all other men. But both these are of the same stuff as the *Ātman*. They appear to be distinct. Duality or manifoldness is an error of thought. He is the opponent of Gentile in this, that while for Gentile 'thinking' is reality for Śaṅkara 'pure being' alone is reality, for Śaṅkara relies solely upon his definition of truth. Thinking is chimera. While Idealism fails to explain whence comes the *feeling or sense of reality* of external entities, Śaṅkara's Advaita alone gives a rational explanation of the *fact* of such a feeling. In this sense Śaṅkara is a realist.

We may now turn to other provinces of knowledge, to get an insight into the truths they teach. We can only take a bird's eye view by noting the highest generalisations without going into details. Inasmuch as logic furnishes the general groundwork of all rational enquiry, we may ask what does the 'urge' which manifests itself as logical processes, imply? Logic seeks truth in the 'objective' (internal and external) world only, but not the truth of entire existence, which is the province of philosophy. Logical processes are primarily based upon what is known as 'induction' which points to a universal, starting from one or more particulars. What does this 'urge' or movement of thought indicate? It is the effort to realise the ultimate character of thought by abolishing in mind, the distinction of duality and multiplicity. Perfect Induction seeks to attain a universal, i.e., a non-dual principle of thought underlying the manifold which is constantly abolishing itself by its changes. Deduction gives us no new information but only indicates how manifoldness is comprehended in unified knowledge. The way this is done by steps in the two processes, in the various departments of knowledge of the 'objective' (internal and external) world is a matter of detail.

In Ethics only such conduct is held to be good or right as seeks to negate the idea of the Ego and of the objective world as something other than 'being'. The effort at self-sacrifice, selflessness or self-restraint or at renouncing worldly gains would not be thought of and would not be made, nor justified if the ego and the world were real. The desire for self-purification is a desire to divest 'being' of all the acretions which 'thinking' has covered it with, by negating dualistic ideas. If a person utters a lie, his conduct is disapproved because he has one thing at heart and another on his lips. He is affirming 'duality' in thought which is abhorred by the 'urge' towards nondualism. To take another illustration, if one seeks to identify one's self with all by making another's sorrows and joys his own, by widening the circle step by step, by expanding his being till the idea of the duality of the ego and the non-ego disappears, one is said to do what is right.[27] Do unto the world as though all the world was your own self is the highest Advaitic doctrine of Ethics taught by Śaṅkara. In fact it is the course recommended by him for *practice* by every one who wishes to realise the highest truth or reality.

Śaṅkara certainly could not have known the modern developments of knowledge. But the truth of his philosophy may be tested by applications of it to modern knowledge.

---

27. All the affirmation of the unreal by taking it to be real (which is duality) is evil and the seeking of delight in such affirmation is a sinful act.

In Aesthetics[28], the 'urge' of creativeness is the effort of self-expansion by imitating the Creator (*Iśvara*) of the Universe, which leads to a negation of thought, by steps, of the distinction between an external creator and one's own ego. When the ego seeks thus to expand and realise its own greatness as Being, the process makes one forget one's individual self which is being expanded and which gives us the *bliss* of expansion which is but a step towards self realisations[29]. When the thought of self is lost in thought of the infinite, it is the *way* of the realisation of Being or 'non-duality'. The production and the *enjoyment* of all that is beautiful is a process of expansion which implies effort at effacement of ego and gradual negation of duality in thought. How it does this in poetry, music, drama, sculpture, etc., is a question that will take up far outside the scope of this paper to answer.

No school of philosophy would be considered a system in modern times (as in the Vedic times also) unless it explained the facts of life in all aspects. Turn we therefore to the field of physical and social phenomena. Here we must first distinguish between a scientific enquiry and philosophic one. The latter seeks to generalise the generalisations which are called truths of several sciences and to interpret them in terms of some fundamental principle or principles. Science is a handmaid to philosophy as a means of arriving at from the objective side, at the highest truth of non-dualism. For, the phenomena of all sciences form part of the waking experience.

The assertion of individual interests leads invariably to discord in society, while the merging of the same interests in those of the family, and those of the family in the interests of the community and those of the community in those of human society, makes for harmony in increasing degrees. And that is what the social 'urge' points to. It means the negation of the individual interests for realising the oneness or *non-duality* of Being; which is common to all. Similarly, uniting for purposes of common good is the aim of political life. In other words, the effort at gradual abolition of differences and inequalities in their practical aspect so as to ensure undivided action, is the meaning of the urge as it is studied by sociology in all its phenomena. Even here the realisation of the idea and the ideal of non-duality is the *goal*, sought to be obtained, though by degrees, in different social groups. All expansion is negation of limitations. All division and disunion is suffering and is, at every stage, sought to be avoided.

In the world of natural and physical sciences the movement of the urge of forces which manifest themselves as evolution, involution or retrogression, as

---

28. The aesthetic urge according to Śaṅkara's views emphasises or seeks the *ānanda* aspect of the objective; i.e., realises the *paramārthika* truth, or reality by transcending, finally this '*ānanda*'.

29. The index of creative expansion of Being is naturally 'expression' which is said by modern Western philosophers to be the essence of art, which fact also is clearly indicated by Śaṅkara.

integration and disintegration, attraction and repulsion, whatever new forms they may create, points to changes not only from homogeneous unity to heterogeneous variety and multiplicity but also vice versa. The phenomena of assimilation during what is called progress and growth are followed by those of dissolution during what are known as decay and death. But this dissolution means a reunion, in some other way, of the released elements with their own kind or with others to form fresh combination pointing to unity. There are also processes which make one part of nature co-operate with or subserve the purposes of another. These but indicate a basic oneness of matter or energy beneath the manifested phenomenal duality or diversity, which is ceaselessly abolishing itself by constant changes, proclaiming that the objective world as it *appears* is not permanent, while the whole of the physical and natural world is found to be an inter-related unity.

The urge in man to conquer nature so as to make it subservient to his purposes is an attempt at bridging the apparent gulf between the world of man and that of nature. It also shows that the entire existence is a connected or concrete unity.

Thus much modern science has taught us. But the question is what is the process by which this lesson of unity is taught? It is not by affirming multiplicity but *by negating it*. In this sense philosophy is a summing up of all sciences[30].

It may be asked what bearing has the physical world upon the metaphysical beyond enabling us to learn the truths underlying them? Of what significance are the storms and earthquakes to thoughts and feelings? '*Avastatraya*' reveals to every one the great fact that the materiality of the external or sense world and the mental character of the internal or thought world are not different from the same basic entity the 'being' called the *Brahman* or *Ātman*. '*Avastatraya*' points out how "By knowing the *one* everything becomes known". All that exists and all that is felt, thought or perceived is *Brahman* or *Ātman*[31]. The 'urge' seems to point to *Ātman* trying to reveal itself as something as non-dual! The 'urge' itself is but the ceaseless effort of the *objective* world to deny itself by change. The subject—not the ego, but—the witness of all, is beyond all changes[32]. And

30. There are disruptive or multiplying forces in nature. And in the ethical world men are seen impelled to do evil deeds. What do such urges indicate? In all these cases the impulsive process is incomplete; for, all these are but struggles towards a goal of equilibrium or complete satisfaction which points to negation of diversity - a goal *never reached* in the '*objective*' world but only aimed at.

31. *Vide* Śaṅkara's commentary. *Aitareya Upaniṣad* V. 2–3.

32. Self-realisation of the Hegelian school is different from the Advaitic. It is *not* by multiplying ideas, and making existence richer, but by negating and dissolving ideas, that the Advaita gets at self or reality, though all ideas *appear* in the self.

using the same language of relativity, or subject-object relation, the universal 'urge' which manifests all processes including those of thought, which in practical life makes for the good and the beautiful and which moves nature in all its aspects towards the universal goal is but the effort to unfold reality or *Ātman*,[33] by negating duality.[34] But in *absolute* truth which is marked by the cessation of the 'urge' which is technically known as '*māyā*' or '*sakti*', there is nothing moving, causing or thinking.[35] What is, is beyond thought, that is what thought *implies*.

Whether or not one has understood Śaṅkara is best known by the truth-test. When the non-duality implied in the universal urge is seen, Śaṅkara's philosophy has been understood. Or to what extent that truth is seen to that extent Śaṅkara is understood,[36] when all differences speakable and thinkable such as "It is," "It is not" are merged into one "existence".[37]

---

33. *Vide* Śaṅkara's commentary *Bṛhadāranyaka Up*. I. 4. 7.

34. *Vide* Śaṅkara's commentary: *Bg. Gita* XVIII 50; Śaṅkara's commentary: *Taittiriya* II. 1. (last para).

35. This appears to be a perfect contrast to European or Western thought which seeks to pile thought upon thought aiming at affirmation, construction, synthesis and activism in an ever increasing measure. But in reality it is not such. There has not probably been and there cannot be another human being more *active* as a man of the world, than Śaṅkara. His philosophy is only an interpretation of all experience. He shows how 'activity' from one point of view is 'inactivity' from another. It opposes nothing that nature and reason make out as the goal of existence.

36. Advaita seeks universal happiness (*sarvabhuta-hitartha*) which implies most directly individual happiness also. In fact they coincide in Advaita. This system aims, as all systems of philosophy in the East, at a remedy not only for human but also for all sorrow and suffering.

37. Śaṅkara's commentary. *Aitreya Up*. IV Introduction.

P. T. Raju, "Skepticism and Its Place in Śaṅkara's Philosophy" (1937)

Poolla Tirupati Raju (1904–1992) was a significant figure in the modern development of comparative philosophy and did a great deal to bring Indian philosophy to the attention of the American academy. He taught both in India and in the West (for many years at the College of Wooster) and was a prolific scholar. The present essay addresses the relationship of skepticism to idealism in Vedānta.

Poolla Tirupathi Raju

8

Scepticism and Its Place in Śaṅkara's Philosophy

THE QUESTION, WHETHER Śaṅkara is a sceptic, may draw different and even quite opposite answers. It has been usual to regard Śaṅkara as a sceptic and an agnostic for the reason that he time and again declares that the absolute reality is beyond thought. Śaṅkara maintains,[1] like Bradley, that reality is neither substance not attribute, neither cause nor effect; in short, it is none of the things which we perceive and think of. The Advaitin or the Sankarite tells us that perception is not the sole guide to truth[2] and sometimes its deliverances are to be set aside; even inference is unreliable.[3]

On the other hand, it may be maintained that Śaṅkara is not a sceptic because he holds that the ultimate reality can be experienced.[4] Like the Greek sceptic, he does not end in blind subjectivism, but maintains that knowledge is of the object.[5] He does not accept the *syādvāda*, the theory[6] that every cognition is full of contradictory possibilities, of the *ārhata*.

In view of these conflicting possible interpretations it is necessary to determine whether and how far Śaṅkara is a sceptic. It is also necessary to find out whether the scepticism present in Śaṅkara's philosophy, if any, is of a disconcerting type and vitiates his system. Very often we come across critics of absolutism and supra-rationalism questioning how, if an entity is unknowable or unthinkable, it is possible to talk about it, while in the same breath deriding absolutism as unhealthy mysticism, if it is said that some kind of contact with the absolute is possible. It is therefore incumbent on all supra-rational absolutists to answer them.

---

1. We read in Śaṅkara's commentary on *Brahmasūtras* that *Brahman* is the cause of the world. But what Śaṅkara means here by 'cause' is a moot question. Yet it is certain that he does not use the word in the ordinary sense.

2. See *Advaitasiddhi*

3. *Sārīrakabhāshya*, II, 1, 11.

4. *Anubhavaikavedya*

5. *Sārīrakabhāshya*, II, 2, 28.

6. *Ibid*, II, 2, 33.

I

Scepticism is mainly an epistemological theory according to which certainty is not attainable by the human intellect. There are some philosophers, like Descartes, who have adopted scepticism for methodological purposes. They say that it is necessary to doubt before reaching truth. Yet they do not deny the possibility of right knowledge through human intellect. Even Hegel, by considering scepticism to be an essential moment in the dialectical process of reaching truth,[7] follows Descartes to some extent. Yet Descartes' aim is to reach the indubitable by doubting everything that can be doubted, and then reach the latter through deduction from the former. It is in this spirit that he teaches us to analyse everything complex into its simple components and then see that these simples are not deniable without self-contradiction. But the acceptance of scepticism as a moment in his method does not lead Hegel to analyse a concept into its simple components in order to ascertain its truth. Coming after Kant and having the advantage of the discoveries of the critical philosophy, he uses scepticism as a means to eliciting the whole within which the conflict that generates scepticism occurs. Scepticism thus provides the spur to the discovery of a synthesis that quiets the conflict of scepticism. But in this discovery the sceptical spirit, Hegel maintains, is not left back, but is carried up, sublimated, and turned into an essential moment of speculative reason. The conflicting moments, thesis and anti-thesis, become moments of the synthesis.

Even in Advaita we can discern some scepticism which is significant as a method. The Advaitin's denial of every finite concept as not the reality, as *neti, neti,* and consequently the denial of all the instruments of determinate knowledge to grasp the ultimate real has much in common with scepticism. This denial is a gradual process which, if it does not lead to any positive conclusion, would be little different from scepticism of the most morbid type. In fact, the sceptic presupposes some reality; for without this presupposition there would be no meaning in doubting. We doubt the certainty of our judgment only on the assumption of a fact about which the judgment is made. It may be objected that we may doubt whether there is any object at all. But then the doubt about our judgment would be of the form, If there is an object,— and I am not sure of its existence,—then my judgment would be of doubtful validity. But the difficulty would be to understand how the first occasion for doubting whether there is any object at all arises, if from the beginning of our knowledge we were not conscious of the existence of any object. Śaṅkara's

7. Wallace: *The Logic of Hegel*, p. 141.

position is unambiguous on this point. His declaration that cognition is dependent on the object,[8] and that illusion has a positive real basis[9] leaves no room for a controversy. It is the Vijnānavādins who maintain that, because of the relativity of our knowledge of things, there are no objects, and objects are nothing but our ideas. They fail to see that the difference in our knowledge of things is not a sufficient ground for maintaining that there are no objects at all. It is a sufficient ground only to maintain that the innate nature of the object is not revealed to us through our senses and mind. The very presence of error and evil shows that there is something not ourselves in this world.

It is the aim of Śaṅkara to point to the innate nature of the object, and he declares that none of the concepts express it, and none of the means of finite knowledge enable us to grasp it. Thus even in Śaṅkara's system scepticism is made a stepping stone to the attainment of truth. But unlike Hegel, he does not carry up what is discarded and make the sceptical spirit a moment of the Absolute Spirit. The former completely disappears and finds no place in the Absolute.

It is, however, to be noted that Śaṅkara did not consciously recognise the usefulness of scepticism as a method. Its presence in his system is a result of our analysis. In fact, every rationalistic philosophy is more or less sceptical. Rationalism is iconoclastic, it is destructive of all superstitions and falsities. It therefore doubts whenever the slightest contradiction is found. Some philosophers may use the method of doubt, and express it in formulas; others may unwittingly make use of it. Śaṅkara has no formula of doubt to apply systematically. Yet his scepticism of the final certainty of the finite knowledge leads to the view that the Absolute alone carries final certainity and that it is experienceable.

Another important point to note is that Śaṅkara, unlike Descartes, does not begin with doubting. Any interpretation to the contrary conflicts with the advaitin's view that knowledge is its own criterion.[10] For Śaṅkara every cognition is its own test, and is not to be doubted unless some contradiction is perceived. For instance Śaṅkara would not dismiss a cognition as uncertain for the reason that its contradictory is conceivable. Hume draws a distinction between the propositions about fact and mathematical propositions, and treats the validity of the former as always open to doubt as their contradictories are conceivable. But this attitude lands him in absolute scepticism. But Śaṅkara's attitude is quite healthy and realistic and does not lead to the scepticism of Hume.

---

8. *Vastutantra.*

9. *Brahma* is *sadadhishthāna.*

10. *Svatahprāmānyavāda.*

There could be no clear-cut line of demarkation between scepticism as a method and scepticism according to which positive and certain truth is not attainable by human intellect. We have seen how Śaṅkara may be said to have used scepticism as a method; yet he declares that human intellect cannot achieve final certainty. Yet the second kind of scepticism may deny the possibility of certainty in any way, and the difference between the two would then lie in the assumption by the former of the reality and the experienceability of something which cannot be doubted. Śaṅkara, therefore, is not a pure sceptic. He may be called a mystic; yet he is not a mystic of the pathological type. His mysticism is based on rationalism. It is the result of a system of philosophical thought, and is not adopted as a method. We may therefore say that he is a sceptic in method—not forgetting that he differs from Descartes even here—and a mystic in results. Every form of mysticism, by maintaining the truth of an ultimate reality not realisable through the senses and the intellect, may be regarded as a methodological scepticism. In this sense, Plato, Aristotle, Spinoza, Kant, Bergson, Bradley, and a number of other great philosophers are mystics and sceptics. But this scepticism in no way lowers the value of their philosophy. In fact, one who cannot appreciate music is a sceptic with regard to music and its influences. There are different levels of consciousness and different levels of reality corresponding to them. Every level of reality cannot be known by every level of consciousness. Therefore scepticism is an unavoidable phenomenon of our life. Yet this kind of scepticism is not a sign of a morbid intellectual condition.

If we consider Śaṅkara's epistemological theory, our doubt that his is a self-defeating scepticism will be easily dissipated. His theory that truth is self-revealing leaves no room for such doubts. We should of course be careful not to identify his theory with the coherence theory of Western philosophy, which also holds that truth is self-revealing. For the latter view there is only one truth, which as the Absolute, is all-inclusive. This all-inclusiveness makes it impossible for anything else which could be the standard of truth to exist. This view leaves no place for finite truth; and even if finite truth exists, it cannot be self-revelatory, it cannot be its own standard. Thus, as Joachim complains, no way is open between the finite and the absolute truths. The finite truth is made truth only by its coherence with other truths. Thus the standard of finite truth lies outside itself. But according to Śaṅkara, even finite truth could be self-revealing. No truth is made truth by anything external to itself though every untruth is made untruth by something external. The system which could maintain that every true cognition is true by itself, that even at the empirical level every empirical truth, unless empirically contradicted, remains an empirical truth, cannot be reasonably dubbed scepticism. On the other hand, the Naiyāyika, who is a realist and a pluralist, is nearer to scepticism than the Advaitin, by maintaining that no cognition is either true or false by itself, but is made so by other considerations,[11] such as some *guna* or good quality in the instruments of cognition, other cognitions with which it coheres, and the pragmatic tests. This view implies that at first every cognition is doubted and doubtable, and is made truth only by coherence and other considerations. Logically, only coherence counts, for even other considerations result in judgments the coherence of which with the judgment in question makes it truth. But in this chain of coherent judgments the truth of no judgment is self-revealing, and therefore absolute scepticism is inherent in the Naiyāyika epistemology.

II

Thus, paradoxical though it may seem, Śaṅkara appears to have very admirably blended and incorporated into his system both scepticism and its rival, direct realism. But by the presence of direct realism scepticism is made harmless. Speaking of Advaita, Professor Urquhart writes: We are thus left without guidance, and into the emptiness in the house of the intellect thus swept and garnished, undesirable guests may enter. If our fundamental belief presents us with no deterring positive characters, we are at the mercy of arbitrary authority, superstition, and even of our capricious invention. Distrust of our faculties may produce a permanent and disconcerting mood of scepticism in which we despair of arriving at any universal standard".[12] By this objection the presence in Śaṅkara of direct realism seems to be overlooked. True, Śaṅkara distrusts finite intellect as inadequate to grasp the nature of ultimate truth. For him, the ultimate truth is known by a consciousness above finite intellect but continuous with it. This view, one may imagine, leaves room for all kinds of superstition and spiritism. Further, it may be thought that Śaṅkara's view that every cognition is its own standard of truth supports and encourages all superstitions. But no. The other part of Śaṅkara's epistemological theory, that every cognition is made untruth by something other than itself,[13] dissipates all superstitions. The critical or negative function of thought, which turns every cognition contradicted into an untruth, is made good use of by him.

It might be questioned whether the doctrine of *māyā* is not in principle a sceptical doctrine. *Māyā* of course involves some scepticism, but not the scepticism of despair. *Māyā* is the principle of inexplicability, which regards the world as a hard and stubborn fact. We may try to understand the world in

---

11. *Paratah prāmānyavāda.*

12. *The Vedānta and Modern Thought*, p, 227.

13. *Paratah aprāmāṇavāda.*

terms of cause and effect, reason and consequent, creator and created; but we always fail. We fail to understand the nature of even a finite thing fully. There is always some core of individuality and impenetrability left out in our explanations, which is irreducible into terms and relations. The doctrine of *māyā* is the necessary outcome of the view that intellect cannot grasp the ultimate reality. The doctrine results as the postulation of a non-rational element by the intellect as the very condition of explanation. Unless the nature of ultimate reality is known fully and in detail, we cannot understand the nature of the phenomenal world. We have to bring down the Absolute to the level of the phenomenal world in order to fully explain it. But this is an impossible task. So the phenomena have to be accepted without full explanation. Yet we can understand them enough for our practical life. Hence Śaṅkara's scepticism does not land us in despair and inactivity. As we have already noted, Śaṅkara's scepticism is inherent in our very conscious life with its different levels. Every lower level must be sceptical of its powers to grasp the experiences of the higher, unless it rises up. But then it ceases to be what it was at first.

We may repeat that, as regards empirical truth, Śaṅkara is not at all sceptical. He tells us, unlike the Mādhyamika, that illusion or *pratibhāsika satta*, is based on empirical truth or *vyavahārika satta*. He is confident that even this *vyavahārika satta* is directly known and its truth is self-revealed. The doubt about *vyavahārika satta* arises, not because it does not produce any certainty, but because it does not produce ultimate certainty. So Śaṅkara's scepticism is really due, not to epistemological considerations, but to logical and metaphysical. As regards empirical truth, a Śaṅkarite could, consistently with his principles ask, Why should I doubt when my perception is not contradicted? But when the question of final truth is raised, he begins to doubt. The considerations that lead to this doubting are many and various. Sometimes the relativity of our senses, of the medium, etc., and at other times the conflict between senses and reasoning are made the ground for rejecting phenomena as ultimate reality. These can all be reduced to the consideration of the agreement between the object and our conception of it. While examining this agreement logical and normative considerations arise. I do not mean that epistemology has no logical and metaphysical presuppositions; but when the question of these presuppositions is raised, we leave pure epistemology and enter the sphere of metaphysics. My judgment, "The rose is yellow," is false because I perceive later that the rose is red. But the unreality of the judgment, "The rose is red," is not proved by any subsequent empirical perception, but by considerations other than merely epistemological.

Śaṅkara's scepticism,—if, after all the above consideration, we agree to call it scepticism, and some may even refuse to call him sceptic for the reason that the meaning of the word has to be so much extended that it would lose its sting,—is thus a motive force that impels us to move to higher levels of consciousness, always in the hope that final reality is realisable by man. Because consciousness is identified by many of the Western philosophers with thought, when it is said that thought cannot have final certainty, it is understood that man cannot have it. But for Śaṅkara the self is more than the intellect. Final certainty which the intellect fails to have can be had by the self.

III

It may be asked: If the intellect is unable to grasp the final reality, how is it able to recognise its presence? How is it certain of its existence? This has been a very common objection against many kinds of agnosticism and scepticism. Some recent writers seem to satisfy these objectors by unquestioningly yielding to them. Professor C. A. Campbell in his *Scepticism and Construction* accepts the existence of an unknowable principle on logical grounds, but will have nothing to do with it in the moral sphere, for a sceptical and unknowable principle cannot form a standard of morality, which has to be consciously applied. But the sceptical principle or the absolute which Professor Campbell accepts owes its recognition mainly to normative considerations. Only when the question of perfect truth arises is the sceptical principle postulated. Perfect truth, like the perfect man is a normative category. If this principle works as a norm in logic, it should also be able to work as a norm in morals. If the absolute is truth, its presence should be felt not only in the sphere of logic but also in that of morals. Otherwise, the usual charge that idealism is a sublime fairy tale without any basis in fact cannot be met.

Professor Santayana in his *Scepticism and Animal Faith*, approaching the problem from the side of critical realism, admits the unknowable on moral considerations, but rejects thought as having anything to do with it. Existence is an object of animal faith and action and not of consciousness, which therefore should treat it as an unknowable. The objects of consciousness are essences, which have no existence, and between which any and every relation is possible. But even this position cannot avoid the critic, who would urge that if Professor Santayana had not consciously experienced existence, he would not have been able to bring the experience to the level of consciousness and argue about it.

Hence we have to interpret our experience of the unknowable, whether it is the Absolute as in Śaṅkara and Campbell or matter as in Santayana, as certainly due to consciousness, but to a different level of it from thought or pure reason. But all the levels of consciousness are continuous and the conscious subject is the same all through. In absolutism the Absolute and the supra-intellectual consciousness are postulated as the very condition of the phenomena and our intellect. The critic of the unknowable has to be met by saying that our conscious life is too complex to fit into the deterministic explanation of the intellect.

Similarly, the contrary criticism that any experience of the supra-rational is a sign of unhealthy mysticism is also due to deliberately ignoring the complexity of our conscious life and the inordinate desire for deterministic explanations. This criticism too has therefore to be met by saying, as above, that human beings possess different levels of consciousness which are continuous and overlapping. If we were endowed merely with animal faith, we would have wondered how reasoning could be a good guide to existence. Similarly, we wonder from the level of the intellect what pure supra-rational consciousness would be like. Yet in the experience of beauty and in moments of moral conversion, we feel that we rise above ourselves. These facts cannot be deterministically explained. At this point we cannot attach too much significance to the demands of our moral consciousness that we should rise above ourselves and our circumstances. This idea of perfection may be very vague for the intellect; it may take this or that form; yet the human being is dissatisfied with each and is able to say, it is not this, it is not this. He feels the stirrings of the ideal within. This feeling may perhaps be dismissed as a pathological state of mind. Yet that really is at the root of all moral, nay, even all human progress. The presence of the ideal may not be felt by each and every person just as music, painting, philosophy and so forth are not appreciated by every man. Even when felt it is possible to ignore it by not caring to push explanations in logic and ethics to their ends. The presence and the work of this ideal in history and in the individual show that the subject is not a mere counterpart of the object and explainable, like it, mechanistically, but passes beyond it, and is in touch with something more than the object and itself. Our contact with the Absolute is therefore not a sign of unhealthy mysticism, but is an essential fact the truth of which is supported by many rational considerations.

9

*Bringing Brahman Down to Earth: Līlāvāda in Colonial India**

Nalini Bhushan and Jay L. Garfield

1. A Risky and Playful Modernity

It is the dawn of the 20th century. Your task, should you decide to accept it, is to develop a philosophical foundation for India's entry into modernity and a major independence movement. Where do you look? Materialism? Plenty of that on offer in European and Indian marketplaces of ideas. Logicism? Another good, modern idea. How about British empiricism? Or the Cartesian individualism that launched European modernity? You reject all of these as a suitable foundation for modernity. Instead you reach way back into India's past to create the future. You adopt Advaita Vedānta, an orthodox, monistic, an idealist school of thought, with an approach to life and a way of thinking that goes back to the ancient philosopher Śaṅkaracārya. What could possibly motivate such a choice?

This, as we have seen in this section, is no fantasy, but the reality of colonial Indian philosophy. How did Vedānta emerge as the dominant voice in Indian metaphysics in the late 19th and early 20th centuries? In this essay, we explain how Aurobindo's *Līlāvāda* interpretation of Vedānta made so much sense in India at that time as a vehicle for modernity. We explore how Aurobindo understood *Līlāvāda*, and the impact of this understanding on subsequent developments in Indian philosophy and culture.

Let us begin by reminding ourselves of the political and philosophical problems confronting Indian philosophy in this period. First of all, there was the pressing need for a theoretical foundation for modernity. The context of

* Thanks are due first, to Daya Krishna, who insisted on the importance of *Life Divine* to Indian philosophy in the early 20th century, and second to our team of research assistants, Margaret Dodge, Francesca King, Mary Kate Long, Jennifer DeBernardinis, and Shama Rahman, without whom this work would have been impossible.

Indian modernity was determined by the encounter with modern Europe and East Asia. The pressures of global trade and the interchange of ideas initiated by British colonialism made intellectual retreat, even to an imagined golden age, impossible. To insist on a scholastic focus on the *śastras* and on an Indian identity chained to its past would be to guarantee irrelevance. On the other hand, to rush headlong into the embrace of European foundations of modernity would be to forego any hope of national intellectual emancipation or identity. For this reason, the political, scientific, technological, or economic bases of European (or even Japanese) modernity were not live options. Indian philosophy did not compromise here either. Indian philosophers instead developed an altogether different approach to modernity. They erected a metaphysical foundation that at once unifies a modern vision of India with a classical tradition and breaks with that tradition to forge a creative vision of future philosophy.

Such a strategy is fraught with risk. After all, at the core of classical Indian metaphysics is the doctrine of *māyā*—the doctrine that the world is, *au fond*, a grand illusion, and that reality is to be sought in the transcendent. So, to remain faithful to this tradition is to risk a status as an antique culture, at best one more diorama in a contemporary museum of premodern human history. This is not the only risk. To modernize this classical tradition could be to do it serious violence, and to impose contemporary European ideas on an Indian tradition. To navigate between Scylla and Charybdis is to articulate a transcendent idealism that is at the same time an immanent materialism, an ideal of human life that can be lived in the actual world. *Līlā* was the answer. This answer, however, came with its own risk—the risk of communalism in a philosophical context. The fact that Indian philosophy avoided this eventuality is a testament to the success of an unusual secularization of an originally religious tradition.

2. *Līlā and Māyā*

From the beginning, Advaita Vedānta employs both the language of *māyā* and of *līlā*. Both terms, for instance, figure in Śaṅkara *kārikās*. The term *māyā* connotes both *measurement* and *magic*, or *illusion*. So, when the world is represented as *māyā*, it is represented as a magically created illusion, no more real than the snake for which the rope is mistaken; it is the necessarily failed attempt to take the measure of reality, and not reality itself. Śaṅkara does insist that the world is illusory in this sense, and *māyāvāda* has been the dominant strain in Advaita metaphysics since his time. Indeed, the rubric of *māyā* dominates even the early 20th Century Vedānta rhetoric of such figures as Swami Vivekananda.

Nonetheless, Śaṅkara also introduces the term *līlā*. In classical Vedānta thought, *līlā* answers an important question: *Why* did *Iśvara* create the world? To appeal to a motive would be to presuppose a *need*, and hence an *imperfection*; to appeal to a *purpose* would be to presuppose a *duality*, in virtue of the need for an unrealized goal beyond *Iśvara* himself. But to regard the act of creation (or for that matter, the acts of sustenance or of destruction) as *accidental* would be to regard Iśvara as a bumbling fool. The obvious solution is to take the creative, sustaining, and destructive acts of Brahma, Viśnu, and Śiva as mere sport, or play—*līlā*. In this sense, these acts are not purposeful but are yet intentional; not necessary, but good fun. They are represented as the overflowing into action of divine joy (see Isayeva, 1993).

Seen in this way, *līlā* accomplishes a secondary religious and philosophical purpose. It infuses an aesthetic dimension into the fabric of the universe. The world, *ab initio* is a site of *ānanda*, of bliss. As an artistic creation, it is already suffused with *rasa* and cannot be understood even metaphysically without being understood aesthetically. Art, on the other hand, becomes not an incidental human activity, but rather a central arena in which we partake of the divine activity of creation—of the manifestation of *sat*, *cit*, and *ānanda* in the temporal realm.

Inasmuch as the central insight of Advaita Vedānta is *advaita*, or nondualism, *māyā* and *līlā* can be seen as two alternative ways of developing this insight. Until the early 20th century, *māyā* is dominant. It expresses the idea that there is ultimately no duality in reality because all *apparent* duality is just that—mere appearance. When we recoil from the rope taking it to be a snake and then pick up the useful rope, there are not *two* objects to which we react—a snake and a rope, each with its proper grade of existence—but one, a rope, mistakenly regarded as a snake.

Māyāvāda establishes nonduality by removing one of the dual poles, viz., the world. This is all right as far as it goes, of course, so long as one is metaphysically content to reject the entire phenomenal world, including the empirical human subject, as illusory. One might be content to reduce one's own existence to cosmic illusion. The doctrine of *māyā*, however, raises further problems. As Bannerjee (1944) puts it:

> The Absolute Spirit is said to *appear* quite unaccountably as the world of plurality, and not to truly *create* it or *transform* Himself into it. But how can the Absolute Spirit *appear* falsely as a diversified material world and to whom should He appear as such?...The appearance of the Absolute Spirit as a plurality of finite spirits and a world of finite transitory phenomena experienced by them is, therefore, regarded as *inexplicable*. [p. 276]

The point is this: The doctrine of *māyā*, while it secures nonduality, does so at the price of mystery. Not only do we need to swallow the inconceivability of our own nonexistence despite our conviction to the contrary (or even despite our conviction in favor of this doctrine), but we must accept that the very existence of the supposedly explanatory illusion is itself inexplicable. Sri Aurobindo put the point this way: "The theory of Illusion cuts the knot of the world problem, it does not disentangle it; it is an escape, not a solution.... It effects a separation from Nature, not a liberation and fulfillment of our nature." [*The Life Divine*, p. 419]

But suppose one wanted to take the world seriously, while retaining the Advaita insight. *Līlā*, if adopted as an ontological option, as opposed to a mere divine psychology, offers hope. On this understanding, the world is not the illusion that emerges when *we* take the measure of a nondual reality; instead, it is the *manifestation* of that reality, its *play* in space and time. Just as when we watch a dancer perform the role of Krishna in a Bharatnatyam we do not see *two* personae—the dancer and the Lord—but a dancer *playing* the Lord; when we encounter reality, on this metaphor, we encounter not reality *and* its manifestation, but reality manifested—or *played out*—as a universe.

Banerjee explores this rich analogy between performance or art and the manifestation of the universe as divine *līlā* with particular clarity:

> A true sportsman and a true artist give expression to their inner joy and beauty and power and skill in various outward forms with perfect freedom and self-consciousness, without any motive, without any sense of want or imperfection, without any concern about consequences.... A true sportsman thus becomes a creator of beauty and he imports his own inner joy into the hearts of the spectators. A true artist's action is also of similar nature... His aesthetic consciousness is embodied in his artistic productions....
>
> In such cases we find a type of actions, which are essentially distinct from our ordinary voluntary actions, but in which, nevertheless, there is manifestation of free will, dynamic consciousness, creative genius, wisdom and knowledge, power and skill, all these being merged in or unified with a sense of inner joy and beauty. According to the *līlāvādins* actions of this type may give us a clue, however imperfect, to the nature of the divine self-expression....
>
> [The perfect artist—*Brahman*] may be described as a *rasa-raja*—Beauty personified, or as self-conscious and a self-determining Beauty. Whatever he perceives is beautiful; whatever he thinks is beautiful; whatever he does is beautiful. [pp. 278–279]

There is, on this view, no duality between creator and creation, as the creation is the creator as he chooses to manifest himself. This manifestation is spontaneous—as Aurobindo would put it, "an act of free unity," arising not from imperfection or need, but from a pure aesthetic impulse, an impulse that infuses the world not only with being but with primordial aesthetic value. Sri Aurobindo's genius was to elevate this second interpretation of Vedānta as a foundation for modern Indian philosophy.

3. *The Project of The Life Divine*

It is a truism to say that Aurobindo's magnum opus is called *The Life Divine*. But the obviousness of what is printed on the cover can lead us to overlook its significance. In fact, it indicates clearly the nature of his project, a project whose nature is easily obscured by the luxuriant prose within those covers. The dominant *Māyāvāda* development of Advaita sharply distinguishes between the *illusion* we call *life* and the *reality* of the divine. Aurobindo's project is the radical integration of life and divinity in a unitary totality that is at once *jīva* and *jagannāth*, at once immanent and transcendent. This, for Aurobindo, is the true sense of nonduality in Advaita. But why adopt this interpretation?

In many quarters, Aurobindo's interpretive project is read as a Hindu theodicy. On this account, Aurobindo's *līlāvāda* is represented as a solution to the problem of evil. In the Indian context, this is the problem of explaining how a perfect *Brahman* or *Iśvara* could create an imperfect, indeed, deceptive and illusory world, one at that filled with serpents, investment bankers and other forms of evil. On this view, Sri Aurobindo is a kind of Indian Saint Augustine, trying to solve the conundrum posed by a world permeated by evil created by a perfect God. On this reading of Aurobindo, however much he diverges from the Christian tradition regarding the nature of evil itself, regarding the nature of the Divinity (for sure) and regarding the role of evil in the world, he nonetheless follows Augustine in seeing evil as a necessary consequence of a *descent*. In the case of Augustine, that is a descent from divine grace; in that of Aurobindo, a descent from divine consciousness.

The problem of evil is said by many who read Aurobindo in this way (Burtt, 1956; Maitra, 1956; Deutsch, 1969; Herman, 1971; Betty, 1976; Phillips, 1985) to be solved by denying that an illusory world is created in the first place, and by *identifying* the putatively problematic evil with the infinitely conscious, good, and blissful Brahman, either at present or in a future state of world evolution. Since Brahman is possessed of all of these positive qualities, the apparent *evil* in the world, not the world itself, is what is illusory, either a mistaken apparition to ignorant consciousness (Maitra), or a failure to appreciate the teleological character of history in which this illusion and evil will be dispelled (Phillips). Phillips puts the point this way:

> The central argument of *Life Divine* is that two facts, one Brahma's being *Sachchidananda*, particularly *Ānanda*, and two, the presence of evil, together indicate the inevitable emergence of divine life, through the instrumentality of evil. [p. 276]

Despite its popularity, this view is in error. It is a superimposition of a Christian framework on a text that shares neither its ideology nor its problematic. It is easy to be misled, perhaps, by the parallel sets of three that schematize the relation between divinity and the mundane in the two traditions. The Christian God is omniscient, omnipotent, and omnibenevolent; *Brahman* is *sat, cit,* and *ānanda.* Theodicy emerges naturally from the first, Christian, *triguna.* It does not from the second, Indian, one. *Brahman* is, as Dubey (2002) perceptively puts it, *supramoral,* not *good. Brahman manifests* as the universe; he does not *create it.* Aurobindo is concerned not with the conflict between evil and good, but with that between ignorance and knowledge. Christian *man falls* from a state of innocence; the *Brahman* of Advaita *purposefully descends* in the act of creation. Aurobindo himself puts it this way: "The Ignorance is a necessary, though quite subordinate term, which the Universal Knowledge has imposed upon itself that movement might be possible, not a blunder and a fall, but a purposeful descent, not a curse, but a divine opportunity." (*The Life Divine*, Vol. 2, p. 361? Cited in Nikam, within Amalner symposium, 1950, present volume.)

Inder Sen (often cited as Indra Sen) characterizes Aurobindo's problematic as follows: "His *leitmotif* and the first formulation of the philosophical question is, "How is divine life, a full life of the Spirit, possible on Earth? How can Spirit be reconciled to Matter)" (present volume p. 596) This gets things exactly right. *The Life Divine* is not aimed at the *moral* reconciliation of a good god with an evil world but rather with the *metaphysical* and *epistemological* reconciliation of mind and matter, knowledge and ignorance. (This is why the late Daya Krishna remarked in conversation that *The Life Divine* marks Aurobindo as a *philosopher*, not a *religious leader*.) Bannerjee (1944), commenting on the term *līlā* in this context, says:

> ...The perfectly free and delightful, sportive and artistic, self-expression of the One in the many, of the Infinite in the finite, of the Eternal in the temporal, of the Absolute in the relative, is called by the Vaishnava devotees, his *līlā*. [p. 277]

This connection of the term *līlā* to Vaishnava thought is worth further comment, and we will return to this issue in our concluding remarks. For now, though, note that although Aurobindo, like Augustine, is concerned with perfection, and its relation to imperfection, their respective conceptions of perfection, and hence of the reconciliation of it with its opposite, are entirely different. Augustine's perfection is the omnisicence-omnipotence-omnibenevolence variety scouted above; Auronbindo's is the perfection of self-understanding and joy in life. Augustine's perfection is the necessary, but humanly impossible perfection of God; Aurobindo's, the anticipated and possible perfection of human life. Augustine's is, however problematically, already, and essentially, realized; Aurobindo's is the cosmic *telos*. Perhaps most importantly, the dialectic instituted by Augustine's thought demands *distance* between the perfect and the imperfect (hence free will, the serpent, and the fall, which insulate God from evil, ignorance, and responsibility); that instituted by Aurobindo demands the *unity* of the perfect and the imperfect through sublation in the historical, dialectical, ethical, and aesthetic processes of involution and evolution.

The mystery to be solved then, in Aurobindo's words, is this:

> How did an illimitable consciousness and force of integral being enter into this limitation and separateness?... It is the mystery not of an original Illusion, but of the origin of the Ignorance and inconscience and of the relations of Knowledge and Ignorance to the original Consciousness or Super-Conscience. [The *Life Divine, p.* 430]

Aurobindo raises the central philosophical problems in this passage. The first concerns the *metaphysical* relation between the reality of the totality of an unlimited being and its instantiation in finite particulars. On the one hand, the requirement that reality must be an infinite unity appears inconsistent with the reality of its many particular parts; on the other hand, without these parts, there is no way for this reality to be manifest at all. The second concerns the *epistemological* relation between the consciousness to which we aspire and our present cognitive status. We are frankly unable to conceive of the epistemic perspective to which we aspire, while at the same time conscious of it as the intentional object of legitimate aspiration. While Aurobindo casts all of this is in the language of creation and evolution, the fundamental problem he addresses is that of the relation between the finite and the infinite as it manifests in each of these domains.

Let us crystallize this problem further, so as to feel its irresistible pull on philosophical thought. We can always, on the one hand, as Kant and Hegel—both of whom are important influences on Aurobindo—emphasize, conceive reality as an unbounded whole, and we must think ourselves as parts thereof. But on the other, we are always conscious of our particularity and limitation and so think of ourselves not as moments in a cosmos, but as independent original existences. These ontological perspectives are in tension and demand unification. On the epistemological side, we are always committed to the views we in fact hold, and to their warrant. Nonetheless, no matter how committed we are to a view we endorse, we are also always conscious of our own limitation, and so of a higher epistemic standpoint from which what we take to be knowledge is exposed as error. Once again, these perspectives are in tension and demand unification.

The moral and aesthetic domains give rise to parallel tensions. As Kant noted, we are forced to think of ourselves as biological organisms governed by the inexorable laws of a causally closed nature; as moral agents, we are forced to conceive ourselves as free. This is an apparent duality that demands reconciliation, but whose poles each resist treatment as mere illusion. As aesthetic subjects we are simultaneously aware of the particularity of our taste and aesthetic response and of the universality of claims to beauty. This requires us, as K. C. Bhattacharyya so perceptively put it (present volume, pp. 196–198), to be simultaneously engaged with and detached from the object of aesthetic experience.

Aurobindo's resolution of these tensions—the project of *Life Divine*—is distinctive in its creative blend of ideas drawn from Vedānta, Sāṃkhya, and Hegel. Vedānta motivates the project through the conviction that the solution is to be found in a kind of nonduality of the mundane and the transcendent, although, as we will see in our exploration of his conception of *līlā*, Aurobindo was convinced that the then-dominant interpretation of this tradition is untenable. Vedānta also delivers to him the insight that the world we experience conditioned by our own sensibility and conceptual framework (*saguna*) is nondifferent from the reality we also must think as transcendent of those conceptual categories (*nirguna*).

But Vedānta is not the only well from which Aurobindo draws. Sāṃkhya is another principal resource both Phillips (1985) and Dubey (2002) note; Sāṃkhya is the origin of Aurobindo's conception of evolution. From Sāṃkhya, and in particular from the primordial principles of *prakṛti* and *puruśa*, Auronbindo also draws his conception of the regulative and causal roles played by the idea of progress in human history. This idea of progress is inflected by Aurobindo's understanding of Hegel, filtered through the British neo-Hegelians Bradley and Caird, all as interpreted by the Indian neo-Hegelian Haldar (1927) (see also Odin, 1981.) He thus reconstructs Sāṃkhya through the framework of dialectical progress through sublation. This Hegelian reading of Sāṃkhya structures his account of the unity of apparent contradictories in higher moments of understanding. The consequent dialectical understanding of knowledge and reality in turn allows Aurobindo to reconcile the metaphysical and epistemological oppositions he takes to structure our lives and to imagine transcending them in a life divine.

4. Aurobindo's Critique of Māyā

At the core of *The Life Divine* lie two chapters (II: 5 and 6 on cosmic illusion) in which Aurobindo considers and refutes the hypothesis that the phenomenal world is a grand illusion. He sets up the *māyāvāda* hypothesis as follows:

> The cosmic Illusion is sometimes envisaged...as something that has the character of an unreal subjective experience; it...may be...a figure of forms or movements that arises in some eternal sleep of things, or in a dream consciousness, and is temporarily imposed on a pure and featureless self-aware Existence; it is a dream that takes place in the Infinite. [*The Life Divine*, p. 377].

He points out the role of stock analogies such as dreaming or hallucination in classical arguments for this version of Vedānta idealism. Aurobindo then, taking this analogy seriously, argues that it fails as an account of ordinary experience. First, he argues, while dreams may contrast with waking life, that mere fact of contrast is insufficient to justify distinguishing them as unreal as opposed to real; for all we know, dreams and waking life could be equally *real*, though different in *other* respects, or even equally unreal (p. 378). After all, mirages and water, to take another stock Indian example, are both real. But one is a real liquid and the other a real refraction pattern. Similarly, mirages and water in works of fiction are equally unreal. Nonetheless, within those fictional realities, they differ in ontic status. Second, he points out, dreams and waking life are in fact very different, and in specific ways: dreams lack the continuity, coherence, and stability that characterize waking life. So, proposing the dream state as an analogy for waking life seems at least unmotivated, at worst misleading (pp. 378–379).

The most significant critique Aurobindo develops of the metaphor of *māyā* is the third: Aurobindo argues that even if we set aside the first two difficulties, the dream analogy, even if taken seriously, fails utterly to establish the *unreality* of the world; in fact, if it establishes anything, he argues, it is instead, the *reality* of the world. This critique is important not only because of its depth, but also because it constitutes the foundation for Aurobindo's alternative *līlāvāda*.

Aurobindo points out that dreams are in fact *real*: they are *real dreams*. So, to argue that the phenomenal world is a dream is not to argue that it is unreal in the first place; it is only to characterize the mode of its reality. In this context, Aurobindo notes that psychology, in particular, psychoanalysis, takes dreams seriously as real phenomena to be explained and that can explain other psychic phenomena (pp. 379–385) He concludes that "the dream analogy fails us altogether, and is better put out of the way; it can always be used as a vivid metaphor for a certain attitude our mind can take towards its experiences, but it has no value for a metaphysical inquiry into the reality and fundamental significances or the origin of existence" (pp. 385).

Aurobindo then offers a parallel critique of the metaphor of hallucination, arguing that it is no more useful metaphysically than the dream metaphor. He surveys a number of stock analogies for understanding *māyā*:

> The familiar existence of mother-of-pearl and silver, turns also, like the rope and snake analogy, upon an error due to a resemblance between a present real and another, an absent real; it can have no application to the imposition of a multiple and mutable unreality upon a sole and unique immutable Real. (pp. 387)

Here and in his subsequent discussion of a number of other putative metaphors for *māyā*, Aurobindo emphasizes the pervasive disanalogy between a case in which one real entity is mistaken for another, or one possible property is misattributed instead of another, and the case of *māyā*, in which something entirely unreal and impossible is supposed to be projected. He concludes that the metaphor of cosmic illusion is unwarranted and misleading as a metaphysical image. Instead, he urges, to the extent that any of these metaphors is useful at all, they force us to take seriously the *reality* of the world. Taking its reality seriously, Aurobindo urges, should lead us to inquire not into the mystery of its appearance, but rather into that of the precise nature of its reality.

Aurobindo offers a second line of critique, arguing that even if these metaphors could be made to work in some sense, they would still not solve the problem that *māyā* is introduced to solve, *viz*, to explain the relation between the manifold nature of experience and the unity of being as such. We begin with the assumption that *Brahman* (Absolute) is real. If the phenomenal world is a product of māyā rather than of *Brahman*, the question then arises, "Is *Māyā* also real?" This is a difficult question for the *māyāvādin*. If it is real, then it seems that we are committed to a fundamental duality, that of *Brahman* and *Māyā*. But if it is unreal, then it cannot be causally efficacious in generating the world of appearance. A traditional response is to conceive of *māyā* as both real and unreal. Aurobindo agrees that māyā is real in some sense. But in that case, we need an account of the nature of its reality.

There is a deeper, internal problem for *māyāvāda* here: whether we conceive māyā as unreal or as real in some sense, we must ask, "Why does *māya* mediate between us and the ultimately real *Brahman*?" Nothing in the theory of *māyā* explains this. This strikes at the heart of the *māyā* metaphor, for that metaphor is posited as an explanation, as an account of why a nondual reality appears dualistically. But if the theory itself requires a totally inexplicable explanans, it is no explanation at all.

Third, Aurobindo poses an insoluble dilemma for *Māyāvāda*:

> [If] *Brahman* is the sole Reality, and if he is not the percipient, who, then, perceives the illusion? Any other percipient is not in existence; the individual who is in us, the apparent witness, is himself phenomenal and unreal, a creation of *Māyā*. But if *Brahman* is the percipient, how is it possible that the illusion can persist for a moment, since the true consciousness of the Percipient is consciousness of self, and awareness solely of its own pure self-existence? If *Brahman* perceives the world and things with a true consciousness, then they must all be itself and real, but since they are not the pure self-existence, but at best are forms of it, and are seen through a phenomenal Ignorance, this realistic solution is not possible. [p. 397]

Illusion must be someone's illusion, but neither the absolute *Brahman* nor the phenomenal consciousness can be the subject. Nothing is solved by *māyā*. As Aurobindo concludes his refutation, "The theory of *māyā*... does not really solve the problem of existence, but rather renders if forever insoluble" (p. 418). This is why Aurobindo says that taking the entire world of experience to be *māyā* accomplishes nothing so much as rendering it all meaningless and worthy only of escape, effecting "a separation from Nature, not a liberation and fulfillment of our nature" (p. 419). Aurobindo insists that a solution to the problem of existence should *account for* existence, not *explain it away*. This, not theodicy, not a mystical vision of transcendence, is the real point of *The Life Divine* and explains why this frankly impenetrable volume of Vedānta metaphysics has exerted such a powerful influence on modern Indian philosophy.

5. *Aurobindo's Doctrine of Līlā*

What, then, is real? And in what sense is it real? Phenomenal reality is real. That is where we live, and that is where ontology begins. But phenomenal reality is not therefore the measure of all things. As Aurobindo points out (pp. 427–428), it stands corrected both by science, and by rational reflection, each of which can correct its illusions and defects and each of which is of assistance in the evolution of our understanding of reality and its nature. This evolution is what makes possible the attainment of the immanent life divine Aurobindo envisions.

At each level of the dialectic of knowledge (the dialectic of spirit?), our apprehension of reality is enhanced, and more of what is real is manifested. This demands an account of the now central construct of manifestation. Aurobindo's account is strikingly Hegelian: "All manifestation depends on being, but also upon consciousness and its power or degree; for as is the status of consciousness, so will be the status of being." (pp. 427–428) Manifestation, Aurobindo argues, is always manifestation *for* a consciousness. To be, in a Hegelian—not a Berkeleyan sense—is to be apprehended, and so all Being is in this sense dependent upon consciousness; as a consequence, the nature and scope of consciousness is not only of psychological, but also of epistemological and metaphysical significance, determining both the range of objects of knowledge and of beings.

This reading allows us to make sense of one of the more obscure aspects of Aurobindo's ontology, one which, when misunderstood, gives aid and comfort to the Theodicists, viz. his account of *plunging*. Aurobindo poses the question of why there is a material world rather than nothing, or rather even than a world of pure spirit, by asking why consciousness *plunges* into insentience in its manifestation as matter. It is easy to read this as an extravagant metaphysical presupposition of the literal materialization of the psychic. Read in this way, *The Life Divine* posits a "fall" from spirit into matter parallel to Eve's from grace into sin. But Aurobindo is making a different point. He is arguing that for that matter to be a manifestation of being at all, consciousness is presupposed as its ontological ground, and matter must come into existence as its object. The necessary coordination of subject and object entails, he argues, that matter is object consciousness made concrete. This is more Schopenhauer than Berkeley, a Kantian transfiguration of metaphysics into epistemology. He writes:

> This, then, is the mystery,—how did an illimitable consciousness and force of integral being enter into this limitation and separativeness? How could this be possible and, if its possibility has to be admitted, what is its justification in the Real and its significance? *It is the mystery not of an original Illusion, but of the origin of the Ignorance and Inconscience and of the relations of Knowledge and Ignorance to the original Consciousness or Superconscience.* (p. 430; emphasis ours)

The solution to this mystery, the mystery of the nature of the manifestation of reality in experience, is, for Aurobindo, *līlā*. It is worth thinking about the etymology of this term. A. K. Coomaraswamy's comments are useful in this context. He locates the first occurrence of this term in *Brahmasūtra II.1.32,33: "Na prayojanatvāt, lokavat tu līlākayvalyam.* (Brahma's creative activity is not undertaken by way of any need on his part, but simply by way of sport, in the common sense of the word.)" (1941, p. 98). The point here is that *līlā* is introduced as a way of accounting for voluntary, but not purposive, action, action done just for its own sake, but action nonetheless. In the *jātakas,* Coomaraswamy also notes, the term occurs frequently in the context of Buddha's manifestation in virtuous action or miraculous deeds. Of these occurrences, he writes, "the rendering of *līlā* here [in the *jātakas*] and in the Pali Text Society Dictionary by 'grace' is far too weak; the grace of the Buddha's virtuosity [*kusalam*] is certainly implied, but the direct reference is to his 'wonderful works'; the Buddha's *līlā* is, like Brahma's *līlā,* the manifestation of himself in act" [1941, p. 99]. *Līlā,* therefore, in its classical connotation, is not an *attribute* of the divine, but a manifestation of divinity in action. Indeed, this connotation of *līlā,* as manifestation, as opposed to *play,* is reflected in the fact that in the Upaniṣads, the manifestation of the elements in material objects is also *līlā. "Yadā līlāyata hy arciḥ."* (As soon as the point of flame burns upward, *Muṇḍaka Upaniṣad 1.2.2*).

How does this account of *līlā* as manifestation help to solve the problem that *māyā* left insoluble? We are still left with a set of crucial distinctions toward the overcoming of which Vedānta is directed—that between the absolute and the relative; the Divine and the mundane; the unconditioned and the conditioned; the unitary and the manifold; the perfect and the imperfect. *Māyāvāda,* Aurobindo argues, attempted, but failed, to reconcile these by denying the reality of one term in each. *Līlāvāda,* by contrast, *affirms* the reality of the relative, the mundane, the conditioned, the manifold, and the imperfect but sees them as *manifestations* of the absolute, the Divine, the unconditioned, the unitary, and the perfect. The resolution of the tension and the dichotomy is thus achieved through an account of nonduality in which the apparent opposites are reconciled as identical in the same sense that the dancer and the divinity are one and the same in the *nāṭya.* Just as the dance cannot be performed unless we have an imperfect—all-too-human—dancer, and it is not a successful performance unless the divinity is evoked, imperfection and its metaphysical, moral, and epistemological cognates are necessary for the manifestation of the perfect in reality. Aurobindo puts the point this way: "When we say that all is a divine manifestation, even that which we call undivine, we mean that in its essentiality, all is divine, even if the form baffles or repels us" (*The Life Divine,* p. 353).

In Aurobindo's hands, then, *līlā* replaces *māyā* as a way of making sense of the nonduality at the heart of Advaita. Whereas *māyā*, he shows, promises a resolution of the tensions inherent in the apparent duality of *Brahman* and *lokavyavahāra*, it fails in two respects. First, any resolution is achieved at the expense of denying the reality of the world we inhabit, hence not so much solving the problem of existence as wishing it away. But second, even if we were to accept that solution, all of the problems that originally attended the duality of lifeworld and ultimate reality reappear for *māyā* itself.

Līlā explains both the apparent duality and its ultimate unreality. The duality is that of player and role; the dancer is not a *deva*, and we know that. On the other hand, nor is he different from the *deva* we see on stage, and so the apparent duality is unreal. *Līlā* explains this apparent but unreal duality without denying the facts of our ordinary life, which are rejected as illusory in *māyāvāda* but affirmed as an ineliminable aspect of reality in *līlā*. Finally, *līlā* provides an account of why life in the world we inhabit is meaningful; it is in fact potentially divine and is the locus of our potential for transcendence. *Līlāvāda* thus provides a metaphysics consistent both with the Indian philosophical tradition and with modernity.

Whether the critique of *māyāvāda* Aurobindo mobilizes was the point of his *līlāvāda* or merely an incidental consequence, and indeed whether these two viewpoints can be reconciled in the end, is the subject of the fascinating debate held in Amalner in 1950 (the present volume). That question need not detain us here. Instead, we turn to the momentous impact of Aurobindo's līlāvāda on subsequent Indian philosophy of the late colonial period.

6. The Impact of Līlāvāda

When Aurobindo left politics for philosophy, Advaita Vedānta was indeed dominant in Indian metaphysics and indeed was already being appropriated as a medium for the assertion of Indian national identity. But the Advaita that was current was that of Sri Ramakrishna and his *math*, most eloquently articulated by his student Swami Vivekananda. *That* Advaita was *Māyāvādin* through and through. (See the selections from Swami Vivekananda, 1915, present volume, p. 000) Of course, this does not mean that Aurobindo and Vivekananda are philosophical adversaries. For, as a close reading of Vivekananda on *māyā* reveals, in the end he takes *māyā* more in the sense of *manifestation* than of *illusion*. Nonetheless, his metaphors are the metaphors of *māyā*. When he asserts that "This, too is *māyā*," he indicates illusion and not reality, an appearance to be rejected. When Ras Bihari Das follows him in announcing the falsity of the world (present volume), we see the impact of this metaphor of illusion so long dominant in Vedānta. In metaphysics, metaphors are often the most salient and effective expository devices. (As Sellars was wont to say, "In doing philosophy, we stack metaphors one on top the other until, like a house of cards, it all falls down, and then we start again"). It is not surprising that Aurobindo, originally a theorist of poetry, was drawn to these metaphors. In effecting this shift of metaphor from *māyā* to *līlā*, Aurobindo reoriented Vedānta thinking from the transcendent to the immanent and so allowed its discourse to enter that of modernity.

The transmission from Pondicherry to the universities was not entirely literary; it was oral as well. We know (Aster Patel, 2007, personal communication) that numerous professional philosophers were regular visitors to the ashram. Professor Indersen, once he left Delhi to join Aurobindo, was specifically assigned the role of liaison to the academic community. M. Hiriyanna and T. M. P. Mahadevan, among others, were regular visitors, followed later by Daya Krishna. Aurobindo exercised direct influence on academic philosophy in India through these interactions.

We see that influence spreading in the philosophical community in, for example, the work of A. C. Mukerji, distinctive in its development of Vedānta-inflected idealism, redolent with Hegelian themes in a decidedly realistic, scientifically oriented direction. While the line of influence is not so direct in cases like this, there is certainly reason to believe that the *weltanschauung* that makes this philosophical innovation possible derives in large part from the taming of Vedānta accomplished by Aurobindo's *līlāvāda*. The Amalner symposium on Aurobindo's impact on Vedānta reproduced in the present volume is additional evidence of the importance of his ideas in academic metaphysics and epistemology.

Līlā is not new to India. But there is *Līlā* and *līlā*. Indian popular religious culture has for centuries manifested itself in public festivals, such as *Ram līlā*, in which communities gather in mass performances in which deities and *asuras* are *enacted*, and attain concrete reality in that enactment. (Sax, 2002). These festivals and attendant practices are woven into the fabric of popular culture and constitute a shared understanding of *līlā* as a site of divine manifestation in the everyday world. Recasting the central idea of Advaita Vedānta in this language presents the possibility of linking this prima facie abstruse metaphysics to Indian popular culture. Aurobindo may thus have forged, if only in homonymy, a link between the rarefied world of the *math* and the temple and the workaday world of the village and the peasant. This link is reminiscent of that to which Tagore alludes explicitly in his presidential address to the inaugural session of the Indian Philosophical Congress in 1925 (present volume). Tagore and Aurobindo, however much they disagreed about other matters, agreed that Indian philosophy was not the exclusive province of the elite but saturates Indian culture.

Līlāvāda also reinforces the centrality of aesthetics to Indian philosophical activity in this period. As Bannerjee (1944) notes, and as we have argued, a fertile *līlāvāda* metaphor is that of the consummate artist manifesting her skill in creation. This suggests an everyday world pervaded not only by a sense of divine action, but also by a divine beauty produced in the play of reality. To understand Being, therefore, demands an understanding of beauty; to understand the nature of art and of the creative act is to understand the nature of reality. No wonder that so many Indian metaphysicians of this period are also aestheticians!

We should not forget that Aurobindo, before his life as a *rishi* was a political activist and editor of *Bande Mātāram*, an influential political journal of ideas. And even after leaving political life for the ashram, Aurobindo's thought developed and spread in the context of the independence movement and provided a philosophical foundation for the construction of a sense of Indian national identity linking contemporary India with its classical past. At the same time, India was negotiating modernity in the context of a vexed relationship with Europe and its version of modernity. Aurobindo's essays, which became *The Life Divine*, were widely read, and, were widely influential. It is apparent that Aurobindo was taken seriously not merely as a religious figure, but also as a philosophical writer.

Neither for the purpose of nation building nor for that of constructing a distinctly Indian sense of the modern was a doctrine of the unreality of the world an ideal vehicle. Aurobindo's genius was to see that idealism did not disqualify Vedānta from this role, and that Vedānta could be given a startling, realistic twist. *Līlā* provided the framework and the metaphors that allowed India to construct its ideological identity and its engagement with modernity on its own terms.

7. *Conclusion*

Such metaphysical experiments do not come without risk. The great risk of *līlāvāda* was a descent of philosophy into a divisive, sectarian, and even communal popular religion. It is easy to convert the idea of divine manifestation into that of the manifestation of a *divinity*, and once one adopts a nondual, even materialistic metaphysics, the most obvious divinity is the *Brahman* of the Vaishnava sects, whose divine *līlā* is that which brings the world into being. To take this route could be both politically and philosophically disastrous: politically because of its communalist implications; philosophically because of the inevitable reintroduction of duality, illusion, and a difficult-to-sustain theism.

Tagore famously averted the politically disastrous consequences of bringing theism into Indian poetic modernity (see his "Pathway to *Mukti*", 1925, this volume) even as he advocated the reintroduction of Baul folk songs with a Vaishnavite flavor into the modern Indian aesthetic canon. In a stroke of genius, rather than emphasizing the religious sectarian quality of the songs, he showcases their religious cosmopolitanism. Tagore accomplishes this by juxtaposing the texts of Baul songs with the texts of English poetry, which had the dual effect of rendering the traditional folk songs in a contemporary light as it deemphasized its sectarian aspect. In this way, Tagore successfully navigates the risk inherent in giving *līlā* a theistic interpretation.

In the work of Aurobindo, we see an avoidance of the distinctly philosophical risk associated with *līlā*. How does the doctrine of *The Life Divine* avoid this risk? Precisely by proposing not the life of a *divinity*, but a *divine* life for us. Aurobindo urges that the world we inhabit is indeed the manifestation of an ultimate reality, but that reality is not a personal divinity, but consciousness itself; that manifestation is not the projection of one entity by another, but rather the identity of the lifeworld with the spiritual reality that completes its dialectical development. The promise of *The Life Divine* is simply the promise of our own potential realized.

References

Sri Aurobindo. (1949). *The Life Divine*. Pondicherry: Sri Aurobindo Ashram.

Bannerjee, A. K. (1944). "The Philosophy of Divine Leela," *Prabuddha Bharata* 49, pp. 275–281, 311–316.

Betty, L. S. (1976). "Aurobindo's Concept of Līlā and the Problem of Evil," *International Philosophical Quarterly 16*: 3, pp. 315–329.

Burtt, (1956). "East and West in Sri Aurobindo's Philosophy," *Philosophy East and West 6*: 3, pp. 231–238.

Coomaraswamy, A. K. (1941). "Līlā," *Journal of the American Oriental Society, 61:2*, pp. 98–101.

Deutsch, E. (1969). *Advaita Vedānta*. Honolulu, HI: East-West Center Press.

Dubey, V. K. (2002). *Absolutism: East and West (A Comparative Study of Sri Aurobindo and Hegel)*. Delhi: New Bharatiya Book Corporation.

Haldar, H. (1927). *Neo-Hegelianism*. London: Heath Cranton.

Herman, A. (1971). "Indian Theodicy: Śaṁkara and Rāmānuja on Brahma Sūtra II.1.32–36," *Philosophy East and West 21*: 3, pp. 265–281.

Isayeva, N. (1993). *Śaṅkara and Indian Philosophy*. Albany: State University of New York Press.

Maitra, S. K. (1956). *The Meeting of East and West in Sri Aurobindo's Philosophy.* Pondsichery: Sri Aurobindo Ashram.

Odin, S. (1981). "Sri Aurobindo and Hegel on the Involution-Evolution of Absolute Spirit," *Philosophy East and West 31*: 7, pp. 179–191.

Patel, A. (2007). Personal interview, New Delhi.

Phillips, S. (1985). "The Central Argument of Auronbindo's 'The Life Divine,'" *Philosophy East and West 35*: 3, pp. 271–284.

Sax, W. (2002). *Dancing the Self: Personhood and Performance in the Pandav Līlā of Garwhal.* New York: Oxford University Press.

PART FOUR

Metaphysics and Epistemology

I

*The Plato of Allahabad: A. C. Mukerji's Contributions to Indian and to World Philosophy**

1. The Philosopher's Predicament

"I will say that philosophy written in English is not Indian Philosophy. Indian philosophy is not written in English, but in Sanskrit" (Krishna, interview with the authors, 2006). Daya Krishna poses a dilemma here for anyone who wishes to understand Indian philosophy as it was practiced in Indian universities during the British colonial period. For if he is right, there *was no Indian philosophy* in Anglophone universities during the British Raj.

We disagree with the deprecation of the Indian philosophy of this period, and we trust that this volume documents the probity of that disagreement. But we are not the first to have been disturbed by this attitude. The presidential address in 1950 to the 26th session of the Indian Philosophical Congress delivered by the late A. C. Mukerji of Allahabad inspires the case we build against the dominant view expressed above. Mukerji says:

* Thanks to the late Daya Krishna, Arvind Mehrotra, Tapati Guha-Takhurta, and Kapila Vatsyayan and the members of the University of Allahabad Philosophy Department for conversations that generated the ideas developed in this paper. In particular, we thank Professor Narendra Singh for granting us access to the department library and to Mukerji's library and for facilitating our collection of materials and our visit to Allahabad. We are grateful to G. C. Pande for introducing us to the work of A. C. Mukerji, to Francesca King, Jeanette Smith, Margaret Dodge, Kendra Ralston, Shama Rahman, and Thomas J. Leach for invaluable help assembling material for this paper, for discussion of the issues, and for reading early drafts of this paper and to members of the International Vedānta Congress for useful discussion and encouragement. This paper was presented earlier as the Lal Radha Joshi India Lecture at the University of Connecticut in October 2007. We thank the participants in that discussion for useful comments. Thanks also to Richard Millington and Andrew Rotman for valuable discussion of a more recent version. We also gratefully acknowledge the support of a Smith College Faculty Development grant that made this research possible. Portions of this material appear in our contribution to the memorial volume for R. Gandhi and Daya Krishna edited by S. Mayaram.

> I would like to avail myself of this opportunity to give expression to my genuine admiration and appreciation for the work my colleagues in the Indian colleges and universities have succeeded in doing in the sphere of philosophy notwithstanding a hundred handicaps and formidable difficulties. I am fully aware of the general attitude of scorn and contempt, of distrust and discouragement, that has brought discredit upon the contemporary Indian thinkers from within and outside India; but I shall not enquire into the nature and cause of the circumstances responsible for this growing volume of suspicion. Of one thing, however, I am pretty sure and it is this that the adverse critics have neither the inclination nor the courtesy of spending on the Indian attempts a hundredth part of the time and attention they devote to the study of the currents of foreign thought. Philosophical convictions grow through the spirit of cooperation and helpful mutual criticism; it is positively unfair to refuse cooperation and yet wail over languishment. I for one do believe that the philosophers of contemporary India have already given sufficiently convincing evidence of the virility and strength of Indian thought which, given favourable atmosphere, would gradually develop into world views of far-reaching consequences whose value in the context of world philosophy would not be negligible. What is needed is a concerted effort on the part of our countrymen to help the growth of Indian thought rather than harp on the discordant tune. I have long felt that, far from providing an incentive, this apathy and indifference are the symptom of a dangerous disease that produces intellectual paralysis and a moral anesthesia. (S. Dubey, 1994, volume I, pp. 181–182)

At the end of his career, Mukerji gives voice to the legitimate frustration that must have been experienced by so many of his colleagues and also to the deep ambivalence felt by Indian intellectuals regarding the quality of cross-culturally grounded writing, especially works written in English. Mukerji is correct in all respects. Indian philosophy under the Raj was treated with scorn and contempt. And it is at least as true today as it was a half century ago that the critics of Indian philosophy systematically ignore in their reading and reflection the very literature they do not hesitate to disparage. Mukerji's assessment of the genuine strength and creativity of Indian thought of this period is also correct. We endorse his conclusion that to continue to ignore this body of work is both an intellectual and a moral failing.

Mukerji himself has suffered the fate he so eloquently laments in these remarks. Despite the brilliance of his work, few outside of Allahabad have heard of him, let alone have read his work. Mukerji is far from alone in this fate. Indeed, even those who acknowledge the greatness of particular figures from that period, such as K. C. Bhattacharyya, have often read little, if any, of their actual writing. In this essay we argue that there was in fact a renaissance underway in Indian philosophy during this period, in some ways analogous to the renaissance that occurred in art, although it was not recognized as such. We intend to indicate—through a detailed case study—that Indian philosophy was pursued creatively in English during the British colonial period, and that it represents an important contribution to world philosophy. We do not mean to suggest, however, that this period is monolithic in its character. While we present only a single case study in this essay, this anthology presents a variety of voices, each with its distinctive philosophical view, in dialogue with one another, and in dialogue with a global philosophical community.

In Indian art and aesthetics, a curious dilemma between authenticity and creativity frames the evaluation of art during the colonial period. Nonetheless, Indian colonial art has subsequently been reassessed and this false dichotomy put aside ("An Indian in Paris," the present volume). However, while that same dilemma structures the reception of Indian philosophy during that period, it has not yet been set aside in this domain. In the art case, despite decades of critique, we now witness a resurgence of interest in and appreciation of Ravi Varma, as well as Bengal School and Company School art. There is no parallel resurrection of Indian philosophy. Finally, the discussion and debates so clear in the art community, about what it means to generate a new but still authentically Indian art, are almost entirely hidden from view in the field of philosophy. The renaissance in philosophy is still not recognized.

There were, to be sure, critical differences between the two communities that partially explain this divergence in attitude to the bodies of work produced in each of the disciplines. While the community of artists and art critics were bound by well-known journals and enjoyed a receptive public, there was no analogous visible community of Indian academic philosophers. *Sri* Aurobindo, *Nobel Laureate* Tagore, *Mahatma* Gandhi, and *Swami* Vivekananda all worked outside of the academy, and those within the academy who came into public consciousness, like *Dr.* Radhakrishnan, were few in number, standing as prototypes of philosophy rather than as members of a community of academic philosophers. Not only has philosophy no *public* canon of criticism comparable to that of art, but Indian academia—and a fortiori, philosophy—was subject to a regionalism that structured the discipline during this period. As a consequence, philosophy flourished in microcommunities that were tied to specific geographic regions and to members of philosophy departments in universities of those regions.

Despite these differences between the disciplines of art and philosophy, we find two striking similarities. First, central in each case is the trope of the authentic versus the creative in colonial India. A philosopher writing in that period faced the following the challenge: how was one to do philosophy at once authentically Indian and creative? How could a Sanskritist engage with Russell? How could a Hegelian draw on Śaṅkaracārya? There is a second similarity: A single genius and perhaps his disciples, and his school, got credited with avoiding the dilemma. K. C. Bhattacharyya was philosophy's Abanindranath Tagore. In his lifetime, and to this day, the one academic philosopher from this period who has name recognition and respect for his philosophical work is K. C. Bhattacharyya (see, for instance, Raghuramaraju, 2006).

In the case of art, we saw that the contrast between the "genius" A. Tagore and the "cheap lithographer" Ravi Varma had much less to do with the actual content of their work and everything to do with a certain national romantic narrative in the context of which that work was appropriated ("An Indian in Paris," the present volume) So too in philosophy. The writings of many other philosophers of this period, such as M. Hiriyanna and A. C. Mukerji, are as creative as the work of K. C. Bhattacharyya. In the narrative of the history of philosophy of this period, K. C. Bhattacharyya gets the genius pass. He alone is imagined to have accomplished the practically impossible task of transcending the dichotomy between the authentic and the creative. As a consequence, as Raghuramaraju (2006) has noted (though in a different register, and for different reasons), the diversity of views in play during this period, and hence the philosophical creativity and fertility of the period, and important contributions go unremarked. And just as a vision of classical Indian culture as available to elite aesthetes issued in the disparagement of art available to the populace, a vision of classical Indian culture as enshrined in a literature only available to a Sanskrit-literate elite issued in the disparagement of philosophy written in English.

There is, however, a striking difference between the ways that the narratives of these two disciplines segue from the colonial into the postcolonial era. While we now give a multitude of artists of that time and of today freedom to work creatively in continuity with an ancient tradition, this has not been the case in philosophy. Further, there is no recovery effort underway to restore to public consciousness the high quality work of other philosophers of that period. And tragically, the dichotomy of the authentic versus the creative as it applies to philosophy is as unbridgeable as ever in the attitude of present-day Indian philosophers. Daya Krishna's lament (see present volume xiii–xiv) is testament to this state of affairs. It is high time to provide a corrective.

We do so by undertaking a study of the work of a contemporary of K. C. Bhattacharyya who worked and taught at the University of Allahabad, A. C. Mukerji. This will provide evidence that there were other philosophers prosecuting philosophy continuous with the Indian philosophical tradition in an innovative and exciting way. A. C. Mukerji, however, is only the tip of the iceberg. There were many others working in the universities of India during the British period who did not themselves see tradition and innovation as mutually exclusive categories, who creatively and successfully overcame this divide but who were not, and still are not, recognized for their efforts. The perception that the ninety years of the Raj constituted a period of sterility in Indian philosophy is a mere perception. Its inaccuracy has tragic consequences for our appreciation of Indian intellectual life and of the engagement of India with modernity.

2. *A Case Study in Philosophy*

We now begin our case study of the work of A. C. Mukerji of Allahabad who, despite his considerable genius, does not get the *genius pass* in the collective memory of Indian philosophy in the colonial period. Very few remember or have read his work. But in Allahabad, people in the philosophy department still refer to the trio of eminent philosophers who dominated that department for decades—R. K. Ranade, the great mystic; A. C. Mukerji, the Kantian Vedānta scholar; the positivist A. N. Kaul—as the Socrates, Plato, and Aristotle of Allahabad.

We quoted earlier from A. C. Mukerji's presidential address to the Indian Philosophical Congress in 1950. We would now like to explore some of his philosophical work. His corpus is substantial, spanning a quarter century (1925–1950) comprising two books, and about a dozen essays, one of which could constitute a book in its own right. Unfortunately for his reputation, most of his essays were published in *Allahabad University Studies*, a scholarly journal not generally read outside of the gates of Allahabad University at the time, and now, not at all. (This pattern of local publication was typical of this period.) His two books, *Self Thought and Reality* (1933) and *The Nature of Self* (1938), were also published in Allahabad, and are long out of print.

There is of course, insufficient time in a short essay to survey all of his contributions to philosophy. But we want to say enough to establish four claims: First, A. C. Mukerji was a philosopher of great accomplishment and his ideas merit serious attention. Second, while A. C. Mukerji was thoroughly conversant with and attentive to the European philosophical tradition, he was also deeply immersed in the Indian tradition. Third, while early in his career he takes comparative philosophy seriously as an enterprise, in his mature thought he rejects *comparison* in favour of *systematic* philosophy, drawing on Indian and Western sources indifferently. Finally, A. C. Mukerji sees himself first and foremost as an *Indian* philosopher prosecuting philosophical problems that emerge from a classical *Indian* tradition, but in an international forum; and his frequent use of *Western* material is generally in the service of that global philosophical project. That is, although we will be emphasizing ways in which Mukerji's thought anticipates that of certain important Western figures, we are not claiming that that anticipation is what makes his work important; rather, it is the fact that he develops these prescient ideas—ideas that are clearly philosophically important in their own right—in the context of an articulation of Advaita Vedānta that marks his contribution as a development of *Indian* philosophy.

It is hard to overstate Mukerji's creativity. Most of us would regard Wilfrid Sellars and Donald Davidson (of course along with W. V. Quine) as the most significant exponents of American pragmatist and neo-Kantian thought of the 20th century. We would cite as being among their principal contributions to our discipline, in Sellars' case, the identification of and attack on the "myth of the given" and the harnessing of Kant's idealism in the service of realism, and in Davidson's, the attack on the possibility of alternative conceptual schemes, and of the scheme/content and world/word distinctions. These contributions were made between 1956 and 1980. The circulation and later publication of "Empiricism and the Philosophy of Mind" (Sellars, 1963) and "On the Very Idea of a Conceptual Scheme" (Davidson, 1984, pp. 183–198) transformed Anglo-American philosophy and set entirely new agendas for generations of Anglophone philosophers. Indeed, some of the most important philosophical books of the last few years are direct descendants of these seminal essays.

Mukerji identified each of these themes and anticipated these conclusions and their arguments long before his better-known American colleagues, and with a distinctively Vedānta motivation and inflection. Advaita Vedānta came to dominate colonial Indian philosophy in the wake of the renaissance for two reasons. First, it was the inspiration that drove the work of Swami Vivekananda of the Ramakrishna mission, as well as Sri Aurobindo, both of whom were prominent religious, philosophical, and national figures. Second, Advaita Vedānta bears a striking affinity to the neo-Hegelianism that was then so popular in England and that was brought to India by British educators. While this school achieved a kind of hegemony in Indian philosophical circles, it was not monolithic, and serious debates within Vedānta, particularly between advocates of the *māyāvāda* and *līlāvāda* interpretations, divided Indian philosophers of this period. (See "Bringing Brahman Down to Earth," present volume.)

In his 1927 paper, "The Realist's Conception of Idealism," Mukerji writes:

> In the thinkers of the Enlightenment, the desire to be clear at any cost grew into such a master-passion that they could not admit the truth

> of anything except what would stand out with clear-cut features and hard immutable outlines, the consequence being a wide-spread disorganization in the different departments of life. This led Kant to ask for a "further analysis" of the so-called facts. So, if we are to retain the terms Idealism and Realism, we *must give up the old method of contrasting them, and define Realism as he habit of accepting the facts as out there, unconditioned and absolute. Idealism, on the contrary, insists on the conditioned nature of the ordinary facts of experience and holds that apart from their conditions, the so-called facts are reduced to non-entities.* (the present volume, p. 475)

In the defense of Kant that follows, Mukerji develops a sustained critique of givenness. He argues that neither facts about the external world nor facts about inner experience can coherently be understood as self-presenting, or as having factual structure independent of descriptive or explanatory interests and schemes. This, he argues, is the real content of Kantian idealism, and of the idealism of Vedānta. The structure of reality, and hence its factual content, is determined by the faculties of the subject. Nonetheless, he argues, this is not to say that either the external world or the inner world so conditioned is therefore nonexistent, or existent in some second-rate sense. To exist, Mukerji argues, just is to exist in this way. The empirical world as well as the inner world of experience is all the facts there are. There is no "higher reality" lurking behind a veil of illusion.

The idealism he endorses is hence neither individualistic and subjective nor hostile to the reality of the external world. Instead, Mukerji defends a robust realism about the natural world and an intersubjective account of the constitution of our ontology. This intersubjective, as opposed to ego-based, account of the sources of the structure of experience set his own understanding of Kantian and Vedānta idealism apart and reflect the idea that the reality we inhabit is collectively constituted, a joint play of cognitive activity. A quarter century later, he was to return to this theme, saying in his ironically entitled address "Traditional Epistemology" (1950), while exploring the quaint traditions of Western empiricism:

> In reverting to Hume's dualism, and accepting his verdict as final, the logical empiricists, along with the majority of contemporary thinkers, appear to have completely ignored the value of an alternative theory of knowledge, according to which neither the *a priori* nor the empirical knowledge is a species of knowledge by the side of the other species; on the contrary, what is called *a priori* knowledge is nothing more than the knowledge of the universal elements involved in the very existence

> of an empirical object or an empirically given event. *If, for instance, it is assumed that sense data are the ultimate materials of experience, our analysis, according to this theory, is defective, for it does not take into consideration the conditions of there being a world of sense data at all.* (pp. 588–589 of the present volume)

Mukerji, anticipating Sellars' own Kantian critique in "Empiricism and the Philosophy of Mind" of sense datum theories and the foundationalism they represent, argues in this essay that sense data cannot even be granted epistemic status without taking them covertly to be already intentional objects of conceptually rich cognitive states. That is, he argues, there is no nonconceptual foundation of knowledge. For sense data, for instance, to be such a foundation, other knowledge would have to be deductively derived from it. But inference is always a transition from statements to statements; statements represent structured, conceptualized facts, inasmuch as they must have predicative structure, and sense data, or any nonconceptually given foundations, are presented as unstructured, nonconceptual. They hence would be useless as epistemic foundations.

This view, of course, is closely tied to Mukerji's understanding of idealism and realism we discuss above: the fact that all knowledge is conceptual knowledge and hence that all facts are understood conceptually means that our individual and collective conceptual resources determine the character of even our most basic knowledge. We cannot escape the world as conditioned by our own consciousness. This late essay is also redolent with themes to be developed three decades later by Donald Davidson, including (a) the impossibility of drawing a scheme/content distinction (1984, pp. 183–198), (b) the requirement of broad agreement as a background for disagreement (1973/1984, pp. 65–75) and (c) the centrality of truth to meaning (1967/1984, pp. 17–36; 1977, pp. 199–214), and (d) the impossibility of distinguishing between reality and our accounts of it (1974/1984, pp. 183–198; 1977/1984, pp. 215–225). Mukerji writes:

> *Every theory of reality…lays claim to truth and consequently challenges the truth claim of a rival theory.…That there is a reality which refuses to be represented by conflicting theories is, therefore, one of the common assumptions uniting the new with the old theory. If reality, as philosophical perversity has sometimes claimed, had been in its ultimate nature the subject of conflicting and mutually destructive judgments, there could be neither science nor philosophy.* Even the most radical skeptics or a confirmed misologist, insofar as he claims truth for his assertion that knowledge is unattainable or that reality is inscrutable, makes the unconscious

> assumption that reality has a positive nature by virtue of which it repels conflicting formulations. Thus, radical skepticism or total agnosticism is a disguised parasite that feeds upon the sap supplied by the parent tree of absolute knowledge.
>
> *One of the results of these considerations is to disclose the utter futility of an unbridgeable dualism of knowledge and reality.* (1950, p. 586 of the present volume)

Mukerji argues that it is incoherent to talk about alternative conceptual schemes or versions of reality standing against a reality with respect to which they represent alternative versions. This, he argues, is because of the centrality of the idea of *truth* both to the idea of reality and to that of representation. Because any version of reality is only a version to the degree that it is *true*, then competing claims really compete. Even to say that there are *two* equally good versions of reality is to make a *third truth claim*, one that supersedes the two it ostensibly vindicates. As a consequence, Mukerji argues, although our conceptual schemes determine the reality we live in, they do so not from outside—there is no dualism of concept and world—but rather from the inside. Concept and conceptualized are one. This is the content of Advaita Vedānta in Mukerji's very modern reading. It is hard to read this material, as well as the rest of Mukerji's corpus, and deny that we are reading the work of a first-rate intellect.

So far, we have been emphasizing Mukerji's conversation with Western thought, and of course his chosen philosophical medium was English. In discussions with contemporary Indian philosophers about their colonial forbearers, we often hear the refrain that the philosophers writing in English during this period did not know their Sanskrit and were not truly conversant with classical Indian philosophical thought. We have found this perception in general to be baseless, and indeed it is false of Mukerji. His two books as well as his articles on Śaṅkara are replete with Sanskrit quotation, copious references to Sanskrit literature, and detailed and nuanced commentary on Indian philosophy. Mukerji was every bit as at home in the Sanskritic tradition of his homeland as he was in the European tradition in which he was also educated. Indeed, this is not surprising, given that his immediate teachers were Baghavan Das and P. P. Adhikari of Benares, both widely respected as Sanskritists.

In addition to using English as his philosophical medium, as he worked on metaphysical and epistemological problems, Mukerji also used comparison as a method to both illuminate and complicate received philosophical views within each philosophical tradition. It is a conceit of contemporary metaphilosophy that "comparative philosophy" is a phrase of deprecation, indicating the mind-numbing enterprise of itemizing points of similarity and difference between canonical texts of disparate traditions, the stuff of an undergraduate "compare and contrast" assignment made into a pseudospecialty of our profession in mock deference to excluded others. And indeed much of what goes under that head is fairly so characterized, and we are arguably at a historical moment where the comparative enterprise has passed its use-by date.

It is, however, useful to step back for a moment to the origins of the phrase itself and of the enterprise it denotes. The phrase itself was first used by the patriarch of Indian Anglophone philosophy, B. N. Seal. Seal (1899) writes that "historical comparison implies that the objects compared are of co-ordinate rank" (quoted in McEvilley, 2002, p. ix). Many Indian and Western philosophers followed Seal in this path, preeminently in India Dr. S. Radhakrishnan and P. T. Raju. Mukerji's philosophical career, on the other hand, was marked by a persistent critical engagement with the very *idea* of comparison. He opens his volume, *The Nature of Self*, with the following remarks:

> Comparative philosophy has so far been either predominantly historical and descriptive, or it has contented itself with discovering stray similarities between the Western and Indian thought. No serious attempt, as far as I know, has yet been made to undertake a comparative study for mutual supplementation of arguments and consequent clarification of issues. Yet, this alone can suggest the paths to new constructions and thus help the development of philosophical thought. (1938, pp. v–vi)

The book itself, as several contemporary reviews in the Western press note (Pratt, 1939; Schrader, 1936), is remarkable in its systematic eschewal of comparison in favor of the dramatic joint use of philosophical texts and insights for systematic ends. The remarks above indicate the trajectory of Mukerji's concern about comparison: that underscoring similarities in argument or viewpoint between traditions may well have the happy consequence of making a case for equality in value—an important political point—but does not necessarily *supplement* those arguments or push joint thinking in new directions. Serious philosophy that brings together texts from disparate traditions must be philosophy aimed at the solution of live problems, pursued in openness to the contribution of multiple traditions; texts from disparate traditions in such a venture are brought not for the *purpose of comparison*, but for the purpose of philosophical progress.

His 1928 essay, "Some Aspects of the Absolutism of Śaṅkara" ("A comparison between Śaṅkara and Hegel") addresses the methodology of cross-cultural philosophy. In this essay he criticizes the attempts by some philosophers (citing Radhakrishnan most prominently) "to infuse the spirit of the latest systems of European philosophy into the old bodies of Indian metaphysics" (p. 375). He writes instead,

> The object of the comparative study of philosophy, we believe, is to discover the dialectic movement of universal thought; but this will remain a far-off dream or a mere pious wish till the different interpretations are dragged out of their subjective seclusion in the enjoyment of an oracular prestige into the region of objective criticism. [ibid.]

In this essay, Mukerji argues persuasively and meticulously that if there are useful comparisons to be made in the history of philosophy, they require the juxtaposition of entire textual traditions to reveal the dynamics of philosophical dialectic and progress, and not the juxtaposition of individual texts. He writes:

> If...we want to profit by thinking modern problems of European philosophy in Indian terms, without misrepresentation of either and yet with a considerable clarification of both methods of thought, *we must give up the practice of finding Kant and Hegel for instance in the Upaniṣads; these are misrepresentations which do not clarify but confound problems.* (p. 379)

In Mukerji we see an example of a genuine cross-cultural philosopher, adept at philosophizing with Hegel, Śrīharṣa, Kant and Śaṅkara and conversant with the psychology of his time as well. He is no comparativist, not due to isolation, but because he sees philosophical *problems* and not *texts* as the business of philosophy.

Indeed, Mukerji's philosophical agenda, despite his concerted engagement with Western philosophy and his masterful command of English as a medium, is Indian through and through. In keeping with his own proscription on finding the solutions to modern problems in ancient texts and vocabulary, Mukerji builds upon but does not rest content with the conclusions of the classical and medieval Advaita Vedānta tradition. His central project has its origins in the *Bṛhadhārañyaka-Upaniṣad* and the voice of Yajñavalkya. Much, though to be sure not all, of Mukerji's philosophical energy was devoted to developing and defending a version of idealism that he regarded as thoroughly *realistic.*

Mukerji's formulation of this problem and the direction of its solution are related to that of Wittgenstein in the *Tractatus* (1961). That is, like Wittgenstein, Mukerji recognizes that any version of transcendental idealism, including the Kantian/Vedānta version he defends, distinguishes a transcendental *subject*—the condition of the possibility of knowledge—from the *objects* of knowledge. The subject must then be unknowable, just as the eye that is the condition of the visual field stands outside of that field, invisible to itself. Mukerji never read Wittgenstein. Nonetheless, there is an affinity here, as Wittgenstein arguably came to his thought about this problem via Schopenhauer, who acknowledges Vedic and Upaniṣadic sources of his own views about this matter. Mukerji shares these Indian roots. It is illuminating to consider Mukerji's formulation of what he took to be the central problem of philosophy—the problem of the nature of self-knowledge, posed by the idealistic conundrum: the self is at the same time that to which we are most immediately related, and so the best known of all things, and at the same time, in virtue of not being an object, is unknowable. He begins not with Descartes, as one might think on a cursory reading of Mukerji's corpus, but with the Upaniṣads:

> The doctrine that the Self the existence of which none can seriously doubt is yet essentially unknowable through the ordinary avenues of knowledge is as old as the Upaniṣads. The puzzle was started by Yajñavalkya...: That, through which everything is known, he urged, cannot itself be made an object of knowledge, none can know the knower.... This puzzle has remained ingrained in the Vedānta philosophy of a later age, and has found in Śaṅkara one of its most powerful exponents. (1938, p. 22)

Mukerji insists that the proper structure of this problem is not what it is taken to be in much of Western philosophy, viz., to navigate the choice between excluding the self from the domain of knowledge and taking it to be one more object in that domain (e.g., Kant vs. Locke). Instead, he takes up the project of understanding *how* the self is to be known *despite* not being an *object* of knowledge, exploring the possibility of a paradoxical, nonconceptual, inexpressible, but nonetheless primordial, self-knowledge.

In the West, only those few Vedānta-influenced philosophers—Schopenhauer and Wittgenstein—follow Mukerji this far. But Mukerji's thought is more Indian, more Advaita, than even theirs. For in the end, *their* self remains only a transcendental subject and a transcendental agent. The *aesthetic* dimension of transcendental subjectivity remains unexplored by Western protagonists of special self-knowledge, with the exception of a single cryptic remark in Wittgenstein's *Tractatus* (6.421). (It is ironic that Kant, who denies the possibility of this kind of transcendental *self-knowledge*, but who was deeply respected by Mukerji, is the European figure who devotes the most attention to the transcendental dimension of aesthetic experience in *The Critique of Judgment*.) Mukerji goes further and emphasizes, in his two monographs, the importance of the self as *enjoyer*. His emphasis on the centrality of what we might call the aesthetic dimension of transcendental subjectivity and its role in self-knowledge, consistent with, and possibly influenced by, the *līlāvāda* of Sri Aurobindo, is a uniquely Advaita Vedānta insight.

There is a deeper sense in which Mukerji's project is Indian. His account of self-knowledge is neither agnostic (like that of Kant) nor naturalist (like that of much contemporary cognitive science). Mukerji instead proposes that self-knowledge requires a distinct form of objectless self-understanding to be gained in philosophical reflection, a form of intentionality *toto genere* different from ordinary perception, more akin to *yoga-pratyakṣa* than to any cognitive attitude to be found in the post-Kantian tradition.

For all that, however, Mukerji is not a traditionalist, not an advocate of a "return to the Vedas," or of reviving ancient doctrines in the 20th century. He is sharply critical of this tendency in Radhakrishnan. His use of Śaṅkara, Śrīharṣa, and other Indian sources is like the use a contemporary Western philosopher such as McDowell might make of Aristotle, of a touchstone for thinking in a way appropriate to the present. In particular, Mukerji is a realist about the external world and is deferential to science as a measure of the empirical. His idealism is consistent with realism. He argues that, while consciousness might have *epistemological* priority, as the condition of knowledge, it has no *ontological* priority over the external world. While as *object*, any object of knowledge can be known only subject to the conditions of consciousness, objects do not depend for their existence per se on minds. *This* Advaita position is hence a critique of the transcendent view from nowhere, as opposed to a rejection of the reality of the external world.

3. The Fate of Mukerji: Pan Indianism versus Regionalism

What made Mukerji and his colleagues possible? And why are philosophers of Mukerji's stature unremarked today, and indeed why were they of such limited repute even in their own days? To answer these questions, we must recall the pan-Indian context in which academic philosophy was practiced as well as the curious regionalism of Indian philosophy during the period of British rule. We have already referred to a bit of the pan-Indian story. The *academic* philosophers were profoundly influenced by those national intellectual leaders but themselves had more limited spheres of influence. This was for multiple social and logistical reasons, and also due to the prevalence of in-house academic journals to which we referred earlier. As a consequence, there are a host of specific regional stories to be told, each with its own account of influences, central ideas, and political engagement. Mukerji and his colleagues, while working in the context set by Aurobindo and his colleagues, led local lives. So did the Bhattacharyyas of Calcutta, Das of Benares, and Mahadevan, Iyer, Sastri, and Hiriyanna in Madras and Mysore. National interaction occurred only at annual IPC conferences or at the occasional seminars at Amalner. Such journals as *Allahabad University Studies* (or *Mysore University Magazine*) were never distributed nationally and now exist only in seriously moth- and termite-infested *almirahs* scattered throughout India. This is a reason for the obscurity into which so much of the work of these figures has lapsed, while the work of their nonacademic contemporaries who set their agenda remains so well known. It is also the reason for the urgency of detailed research into their work so that these regional stories can be stitched together to provide a comprehensive history of Indian philosophy in English.

Let us return again to the art world for some final comparative points. First, the disanalogies. In the case of art, we see an active and public critical comparison; in the case of philosophy, whatever public attention gets paid to it is often within a religious context (e.g., its affinity vs. contrast with Christianity, or with Hinduism), with relatively little attention paid to the work of the scholars in the academy (though note the remarks in Mukerji's presidential address that refer to active disparagement). In the case of art, the discourse is contemporary and has evolved to a very different position; in the case of philosophy, the discourse develops much later and has gone nowhere. In the case of art, alliance with a particular social movement is clearly in play; its role in the case of philosophy is at least much more obscure. Nonetheless, there are important analogies, and it is to these analogies that we here draw attention: In each case, a difference is marked between the solitary genius and a run of putative failures; in each case, the failures fail by being impaled on the same dilemma between creativity and authenticity; in each case, for extraneous reasons, the genius is accorded a pass that exempts him from this dilemma. In each case, reevaluation and attention to a broader literature is imperative.

A. C. Mukerji was indeed brilliant, but he was not unique. This period saw many individuals in the academy in a vibrant engagement with philosophical ideas and questions grounded in the Indian Vedic tradition, and reformulated in a modern context. Indian philosophers under the Raj were conscious of that classical history, as well as of the resources European philosophy could supply to its future. Colonial India was home to a creative community of philosophers in dialogue with one another, internally diverse and preoccupied with problems that are at the same time immanent in and transcendent of that Indian context.

References

Davidson, Donald. 1984. *Inquiries into Truth and Interpretation*. New York: Oxford University Press.

Dubey, S., Ed. 1994. *The Metaphysics of Spirit: Presidential Addresses of the Indian Philosophical Congress, v. I*. New Delhi: Indian Council of Philosophical Research.

Guha-Thakurta, T. 2007. *The Making of a New 'Indian' Art: Artists, Aesthetics and Nationalism in Bengal, c. 1850–1920*. Cambridge, UK: Cambridge University Press.

Krishna, Daya. May, 2006. Personal interview by Bhushan and Garfield. Jaipur.

McEvilley, Thomas. 2002. *The Shape of Ancient Thought: Comparative Studies in Greek and Indian Philosophies*. New York: Allworth Press.

Mukerji, A. C. 1928. "Some Aspects of the Absolutism of Śaṅkara" ("A comparison between Śaṅkara and Hegel"). *Allahabad University Studies vol. IV*, pp. 375–429.

Mukerji, A. C. 1938. *The Nature of Self*. Allahabad: The Indian Press.

Pratt, James. 1939. "Descriptive Notices: *The Nature of Self* by AC Mukerji." *Philosophical Review* 48:3, p. 343.

Raghuramaraju, A. 2007. *Debates in Indian Philosophy: Classical, Colonial and Contemporary*. New Delhi: Oxford University Press.

Schrader, Otto F. January, 1940. "Review of *Self, Thought, and Reality* by A.C. Mukerji." *Philosophy*. 15, pp. 211–212.

Seal, B. N. 1899. *Comparative Studies of Vaishnavism and Christianity*. Calcutta: University of Calcutta.

Sellars, Wilfrid. 1963. "Empiricism and the Philosophy of Mind" in *Science, Perception and Reality*, 127–196. London: Routledge & Kegan Paul.

Wittgenstein, Ludwig. 1961. *Tractatus Logico-Philosophicus*. London: Routledge.

A. C. Mukerji, "The Realist's Conception of Idealism" (1927)

Anukul Chandra Mukerji (1888–1968) succeeded R. D. Ranade as Professor of Philosophy at Allahabad. He was a scholar of Western and Indian philosophy and specialized in Epistemology, with a special interest in idealism and the problem of self-knowledge. He published two books during his life, *The Nature of Self* (1933), and *Self Thought and Reality* (1938). In this essay he develops an intersubjective, realistic idealism drawing creatively from Kantian and Vedānta philosophy.

2

The Realist's Conception of Idealism

TRANSCENDENTALISM.—IT HAS BEEN aptly said that the terms realism and idealism are "traditional battle-cries and watchwords rather than names of precision."[1] This is only natural. Every thinker has, of necessity, to accept certain facts as given, and no amount of theorizing is equal to the task of driving them out of existence. If then the distinction between idealism and realism is, as is ordinarily supposed, to rest on the acceptance by the latter of facts denied by the former, then the sooner we cease to talk of the distinction the better, for no one who has ever approached the facts of experience with an appreciative outlook could reduce them to nothing. So, on the one hand, Berkeley's system has been supposed to be thoroughly realistic in its intention[2] and, on the other hand, it has been said that Reid's realism "might pass into the most extreme idealism."[3] To realise the lack of precision and the difficulties in the conception of this distinction, one need only look at the different *fundamenta divisionis* that have been proposed by different thinkers. Realism, it is sometimes said, must insist on the independence of the objects of experience in general over against the idealistic contention of their dependence on the experiencing mind. More frequently, the distinction is supposed to rest on a more restricted basis, namely, the relation between the perceiving mind and the external world revealed in perception. It is this narrower problem which generally comes to the foreground in controversies, and then realism is thought to consist in the assertion that the external world which is before the mind in perception is not dependent on the perceiving subject. This general position again is accepted by different realists with different degrees of qualification, some insisting on the independence of the external world in its existence as well as qualities, others making the qualities dependent on the perceptual context. As thus defined, it is difficult to distinguish realism from that type of idealism which is represented, say, by T. H. Green who urges unambiguously that "the fact that there is a real external world... is one which no philosophy disputes."[4] The demarcation line

1. Dr. Bosanquet: *Contemporary Philosophy*, Preface.

2. See Prof. Laird's article in *Mind*, 1916.

3. Dr. Bosanquet: *The Essentials of Logic*, p. 10.

4. *Works*, Vol. I, p. 376.

is sometimes drawn at a different place, and the centre of emphasis is shifted from the external world to the conception of time. Realism maintains, while idealism denies, that the universe as a whole is in time, evolution or change; yet thinkers like Croce, Gentile and Ward are claimed to be idealists. Finally, the term idealism has been made to cover "all those philosophies which agree in maintaining that spiritual values have a determining voice in the ordering of the universe";[5] yet Prof. Alexander is widely known as a prominent realist of our time. We are not substantially helped out of this confusion by Mr. J. Laird when he defines realism as "a theory of knowledge whose essence is to supply a complete phenomenology of knowing and of things known [in a] peculiar and distinctive way";[6] and the confusion is still more increased when it is claimed that the main assumption of realism is that things can be known as they really are, that "the object of true knowledge is in a certain sense independent of our knowing of it,...the fact of being known does not imply any effect upon the character or existence of thing which is known....All idealists, in spite of their differences dispute this independence of the objects of knowledge."[7] That our knowledge does not falsify reality and that the object is independent of the act of knowing in a certain sense, are not disputed by the idealist. Every idealist who knows his business must admit that, "when I use the word 'red,' I mean a colour...which I think of as not dependent either for being or for quality on my happening to know it";[8] on the contrary, "the sun means the sun; and whatever that may be, it is not anything *merely* in my mind,......not a psychical fact in my individual history."[9]

It is amply evident from the above that all attempts at defining the contrast between realism and idealism by reference to the facts supposed to be accepted by the former and rejected by the latter must be futile. And in so far as the reality of the external world is concerned, even Berkeley, while arguing for the mind-dependent character of the material world, maintained emphatically that nothing which was considered real by common sense had been banished by his system. To appreciate the real contrast then, we may revert once more to Green. In continuing the thought, to which reference has been made above, he observes that no philosophy disputes the fact that there is a real external world "of which through feeling we have a determinate experience...The idealist merely asks for a further analysis of a fact which he finds

5. N. K. Smith: *Prolegomene to an Idealistic Theory of Knowledge*, p. 1.

6. J. Laird, *A Study in Realism*. Cambridge University Press (1920), p. 3.

7. *Ibid*., p. 14.

8. Bosanquet: *Logic*, Vol. I, p. 17.

9. *Ibid*., p. 73.

so far from simple."[10] That is, while the realist takes the facts "at their face-value," the idealist asks for the conditions involved in the factual nature of the so-called facts. If this is made the criterion of idealism, then we must look to Kant rather than Berkeley for a true lesson in idealism; for it was Kant who for the first time raised, and attempted a solution of, the question:—how is nature possible? It will be unprofitabte at this place to hazard any opinion on the success or failure of Kant's task—a task which is universally admitted to be extremely difficult. But what can be said positively is that it was he who first realised the importance of striking this "hitherto untravelled route" and brought philosophy to transcendental investigations. This Fichte considered to be the epoch-making achievement of Kant. His works have been compared to a bridge by which we pass from the spirit of the eighteenth to that of the nineteenth century, and the great change which this latter brought into the intellectual outlook of man has been aptly described as the "substitution of the idea of organic unity and development for the idea of the mechanical combination of reciprocally external elements."[11] In the thinkers of the Enlightenment the desire to be clear at any cost, grew into such a master-passion that they could not admit the truth of anything except what would stand out with clear-cut features and hard immutable outlines, the consequence being a wide-spread disorganization in the different departments of life. This led Kant to ask for a "further analysis" of the so-called facts. So, if we are to retain the terms Idealism and Realism, we must give up the old method of contrasting them, and define Realism as the habit of accepting the facts as out there unconditioned and absolute. Idealism, on the contrary, insists on the conditioned nature of the ordinary facts of experience and holds that apart from their conditions the so-called facts are reduced to non-entities. As thus defined, Kant in his reply to Hume, undermined the basis of realism, and laid the foundation of a system of idealism which is as opposed to subjective idealism as any system of realism has ever been.

The Cognitive Relation.—We have deliberately omitted so far the consideration of an eminently suggestive definition of realism, for it raises an issue of really vital importance—an issue the right understanding of which goes a great way to mould one's final view of the universe. In defining the general characteristic of realism, Prof. Alexander maintains that mind has no privileged place in the democracy of things, "in respect of being or reality, all existences are on an equal footing...... This attitude of mind imposed by the empirical method is and may rightly be called in philosophy the attitude of

10. Green, *Works*, Vol, I, page reference lost.

11. E. Caird: *The Critical Philosophy of Kant*, p. 46.

realism."[12] Judged by this standard, Locke together with his followers should, we believe, be considered as realists. That the finite mind is only one object among others distinguished from them by the attribute of thought was a belief which pervaded Locke's investigations from the start to finish. Now this belief, or rather attitude, which is called realistic here, has been elsewhere[13] considered as the attitude of psychology, and Prof. Alexander thinks that the study of mind in metaphysics "must be borrowing a page from psychology."[14] This is evidently a bold step, for even William James, the modern protagonist of this attitude, did not think it justifiable except from the standpoint of psychology, thus suggesting that the metaphysics of mind could not be coterminous with the psychology of mind.[15]

This levelling down of mind to the status of other things is carried further by the American realists. Thus Mr. E. B. Holt considers the mind to be the cross-section of the environment, and in this sense mind or consciousness belongs to the totality of objects. All objects are portions of a mass of object which the neural response selects from the world, and these objects are not simply the so-called physical objects, but sensations and memories, thoughts and volitions, have as much claim to the name as the rest. Here the realistic attitude leads to pure objectivism, and the introspective psychology is reduced to 'behaviourism.' Mind has no privileged place in the democracy of things, because mind in the traditional sense is an outworn superstition, while in the realistic sense it belongs to the totality of objects. Here, in this materialism of the American realists, we find an illustration of the *reductio ad absurdum* of the psychological or empirical method which is not less instructive than what was illustrated in the course of pre-Kantian empiricism. Following the introspective method which Locke introduced into epistemology, Hume reduced mind into a bundle of perceptions which led to the denial of mind not only in the sense of a substance persisting through the continued flux of conscious states, but in the sense of a thinking subject too. But the modern feat of reducing the mental to terms of the physical organism was unknown to him.

It has been pointed out by the critics of this cross-section view of mind that it does not explain one vital fact in the cognitive relation. The crucial error of New Realism, according to Mr. L. A. Reid, is that it has no way to the admission that "*I* am in *thee* and *thou* in *me*."[16] Similarly, Prof. Alexander,

12. *Space, Time and Deity*, Vol. I, p. 6.

13 Dr. E. Caird: *Critical Philosophy*, Vol. I, p. 11.

14. *Ibid.*, p. 9.

15. *Principles of Psychology*, Vol. I, p. 183.

16. *Knowledge and Truth*, p. 50.

while admitting the simplicity of the theory—a theory to which he finds himself "perpetually being drawn back and persuaded to adopt"—admits that it "fails to account for a vital feature in the cognitive situation, as we experience it, namely, that in being aware of the fire, the fire is before *me*, or it is *I* who see it, or it is in a sense *my* fire."[17] This is really the vital feature which cannot be accounted for by any theory which is realistic in the above sense. It is not only the theory of search-light, but every theory of mind which adopts the abstract method of empirical psychology in its analysis of the cognitive relation must fail to offer an ultimate explanation of the fact that a common world is revealed to a plurality of minds. If idealism rejects the realistic analysis of experience, the ground of the rejection is not to be found in the so-called idealistic prejudice that mind is somehow superior to all other existences; but it is rejected because its analysis is inadequate and superficial. The ultimate test of a sound philosophy, we are persuaded to believe, is its capacity to explain how the *fire* is before *me*. The fire is an object having a unity and permanence, as against the multiplicity and transitoriness of the cognitive acts through which it is grasped; it has its 'date' and position, a past and a future; it, together with other objects, constitutes parts of one world; it reveals itself to many minds, each claiming it own experience as *mine*, while referring it to one identical object. These are some of the aspects of experience which a metaphysical analysis must not ignore.

That the behaviouristic analysis of the cognitive relation is utterly inadequate, is clearly seen by Prof. Alexander. But is it not the legitimate conclusion which must be ultimately drawn whenever experience is analysed by means of a false method? His great merit no doubt consists in realising that the 'mental' cannot be put in terms of the 'non-mental'; yet he is essentially on the verge of the dangerous ditch from which he is trying to keep himself off, so long as cognition is taken to be a particular instance of the general relation of compresence. To behaviourism there is an easy, and perhaps an inevitable transition from the assertions that "the behaviour of finites to one another in this relation of compresence is determined by the character of the finites. The plant lives, grows, and breathes, and twines around a stick. The material body resists, or falls, or sounds when struck, or emits light when touched by the sun. The mind knows."[18] The cognitive situation remains substantially the same, the mind on the one side, and the objects on the other entering into a temporary mechanical relation. While this is not challenged, it is immaterial whether we consider the knowing mind as a qualitatively distinct kind of

17. *Ibid.*, p. 111.

18. *Ibid.*, Vol. II, p. 81.

physical thing possessing a unique type of response, or the object as a kind of existence which is in some sense mental either as a 'state of consciousness' or a mere 'idea' in the mind. That is, the problem of knowledge is unaffected whether we are landed in an unqualified objectivism or an unqualified subjectivism. A few remarks of Lord Haldane's are so pertinent here that we cannot help quoting them at some length: "We have ever to avoid the stereotyping of a general principle into the form of an image.......Two of the most dangerous kinds of these have their origin in an unduly loose use of the conceptions of cause and of substance.......The full meaning of what we experience may be something very different from the relation of cause or of thing with its properties that we assume ourselves to observe. The self-determining operation of an end, for example, is not causal in the ordinary sense. The cause does not here pass over into the effect as a new aspect of the originating energy....Nor is the relation of mind to its manifestations that of a substance to its accidents....Knowledge is the highest category, and it is not a merely meticulous criticism of expressions. The whole of the Berkeleian theory, and the essence of what is now called Mentalism, seem to depend on mind being regarded as a substance, and knowledge as an activity or property of that substance. But the New Realists generally appear to make the same sort of assumption as the Mentalists about the adequacy of the category of substance, for they treat knowledge as the causal result of the operation of one set of things in the external world on another set of things there, the nervous system, imaged as compresent with them in a fundamentally real time and space....Most of the controversy between Subjective Idealism and Realism seems to arise out of the metaphorical view of the human mind as something that looks out through the windows of the senses. The Subjective Idealists say that beyond the activity of the mind in this outlook there lies nothing, and that what is real is just the mind and this activity. The Realists...discover knowledge to be just an additional external relation, superinduced on that in which my arm-chair, for example, stands to the fire which I see near me while I am writing, and consisting in a special kind of causal operation of that fire upon my nervous system."[19] To understand the origin of this mistaken conception of the subject-object relation, it is necessary to consider some of the difficulties besetting the problem of external perception.

What is an Idea?—How we perceive external objects, Reid points out,[20] is a difficult problem with many ancient and modern philosophers. Plato's

19. An article in the *Proceedings of the British Academy*, Vol. IX. See Green's explanation of Locke's confusions as due to the misapplication of the conceptions of cause and substance—*Works*, Vol. I, p. 109.

20. *Works*, Hamilton's edition, Vol. I, p. 262.

illustration of men bound to a dark subterraneous cave and knowing only the shadows of reality gave rise to this problem. These shadows of Plato represent the species and phantasms of the Peripatetic school, and the ideas and impressions of modern philosophers. Descartes, while rejecting only a part of the Peripatetic system—namely, that images come from the external objects, adopted the other part—that the external object itself is not perceived. For this adoption, however, Reid contends, Descartes does not give reasons. All philosophers from Plato to Hume agree that we do not perceive external objects immediately. It is owing to this "original defect" that the "ideal system" leads to scepticism. Our analysis, therefore, must discard that doctrine, and should be inspired by the belief that our knowledge involves from the very beginning certain "judgments of nature—judgments not got by comparing ideas and perceiving agreements and disagreements, but immediately inspired by our constitution." This, as explained by Prof. A. Seth, means that "we do not have sensation first, and refer them afterwards to a subject and an object; our first having of a sensation is at the same time the knowledge of a present object and of that object as somehow related to me."[21]

It is not our present purpose to enquire how far Reid is justified in assimilating Plato's view on our knowledge of the external world to that of Hume, or why Kant's speculations about the external world did not lead to scepticism in spite of the fact that he never questioned, as has been sometimes maintained,[22] the fundamental assumption of the "ideal system." All we can do here is simply to remember that it is possible in the one case to think that Plato "does not volatilise, so to speak, our world of facts and externality, but accepting for it all that it claims of existence and reality, then passes on to interpret its conditions, and assigns its significance more profoundly."[23] And in the other case, it is equally possible so to interpret Kant's thoughts as to distinguish them from the false view of idealism according to which the external world is merely the creation of our own minds—"a doctrine expressly rejected by Kant and which has had no place since his time in any idealism that knows what it is about."[24] It must be however admitted that the idealistic contention that the world is my idea is extremely liable to misinterpretation, owing to the association the term "idea" has acquired in our minds. By an idea we ordinarily mean a mental picture, a representation or copy of a thing outside the mind. As thus understood, it is manifestly absurd to reduce the outside thing

21. *Scottish Philosophy*, p. 78.

22. Prof. A. Seth: *Scottish Philosophy*, p. 150.

23. Dr. Bosanquet: *Contemporary Philosophy*, p. 2.

24. Green: *Works*, Vol. I, p. 386.

to the idea, we should rather think the thing to be the antecedent condition of the idea. We may go further and admit that the difficulty in this case arises to a large extent from the conditions of our discursive thought which understands by division, and defines by exclusion. Owing to this dichotomous intellect we have to make our notion of 'idea' definite only by contrasting it with what is *not* an idea; and evidently the most natural candidate for such a contrast is the ideatum or the thing which the idea is said to represent. That is, the ideas have for adult consciousness a reference beyond themselves to something non-mental in contradistinction from which they are defined. Hence the realist has always the advantage of this popular distinction whenever the idealist speaks of the world as my idea; and in spite of the indignant protest of the latter that he should be so grossly misunderstood, the former continues to consider idealism to be a doctrine which, somehow or other, attempts to spin the world of reality out of psychical existences. Without essaying the difficult task of presenting idealistic contentions in a way which will not be open to misinterpretation, let us turn to the advocates of the "ideal system" and see why they used the term 'idea' for the object of immediate experience. And to make this point clear we should turn to the system of Hume, not only because he is the most consistent of the advocates of what Reid calls the ideal system, but also because Hume's scepticism is supposed to be the legitimate outcome of the doctrine of ideas.

The immediate object of knowledge Hume calls perception which he divides into impressions and ideas, and the difference between these, he says, consists in the degrees of force and liveliness with which they strike upon the mind. Impressions are those perceptions which "enter with most force and violence," and in point of time they are prior to the ideas. Impressions again are divided into those of sensation and those of reflection, but the second is derived in a great measure from our ideas, and so the impressions of reflection are "posterior to those of sensations and derived from them." Hence the simple impressions of sensation are the ultimate material of all knowledge. In illustration of these impressions of sensation and their relation to ideas Hume says that "to give a child an idea of scarlet or orange, of sweet or bitter, I present the objects, or in other words, convey to him these impressions," but "wherever, by an accident, the faculties which give rise to any impressions are obstructed in their operations, as when one is born blind or deaf, not only the impressions are lost, but also their correspondent ideas." The characteristics of the impressions of sensation Hume states more precisely in the famous section of the *Treatise* on "Scepticism with Regard to the Senses." He seeks to examine here the belief in the *continued* existence of objects even when they are not present to the senses, and the belief in the existence of objects *distinct* from the mind; and his conclusion is that the opinion of a continued and of a distinct existence never arises from the senses or the reason but from imagination. Everything, he says, "which appears to the mind is nothing but a perception and is interrupted and dependent on the mind." All impressions are "perishing existences." Certain impressions are involuntary, e.g., our pains and pleasures, and the impressions of figure and extension. Those impressions "which we regard as fleeting and perishing have also a certain coherence or regularity in their appearances." Our broken and interrupted perceptions resemble each other. "All our perceptions are dependent on our organs and the disposition of our nerves and animal spirits," e.g., "when we press one eye with a finger, we immediately perceive all the objects to become double, and one half of them to be removed from their common and natural position.... This opinion is confirmed by the seeming increase and diminution of objects according to their distance; by the apparent alteration in their figure; by the changes in their colour and other qualities, from our sickness and distempers, and by an infinite number of other experiments of the same kind." "We clearly perceive the dependence and interruption of our perceptions." With regard to the characteristic of dependence Hume says later that there are certain "variations of the impressions"; but "when different impressions of the same sense arise from any object, every one of these impressions has not a resembling quality existent in the object. For as the same object cannot, at the same time, be endowed with different qualities of the same sense, and as the same quality cannot resemble impressions entirely different; it evidently follows, that many of our impressions have no external model or archetype." But "when we talk of real distinct existences... we think an object has a sufficient reality when its being is uninterrupted and independent of the incessant revolutions, which we are conscious of in ourselves." "I am naturally led to regard the world as something real and durable, and as preserving its existence, even when it is no longer present to my perceptions," because "this supposition" is the "only one upon which I can reconcile these contradictions of observations."

One point in this extraordinarily suggestive psychological analysis of external perception needs special emphasis. On the one hand, Hume characterises the immediate object of perception as transient, variable and contradictory. On the other hand, he describes them as given, though dependent on our psychophysical conditions. Hume appears to have received from his critics less than justice in both these respects. The realists point out that the immediate objects of our perceptual knowledge are erroneously called ideas which shut us off from an immediate perception of an external world. The idealists complain that he ascribes to the mere sensation a factual existence which it cannot have except through the works of thought. To begin with the former, the original assumption of the "ideal system" appears to be based on a profound logical insight.

The world of experience is for the adult mind split up into a multiplicity of worlds with varying grades of reality; we habitually make the experiences of waking consciousness the standard of reality, and then seek to explain dreams by reference to that standard. Within the waking experiences again it is customary to distinguish between experiences which are real and those that are illusory or abnormal. Descartes, determined to assume nothing which cannot arrest doubt, discovers that these divisions which we make within experience are due to reflections the validity of which can be doubted and so stands in need of proof. The immediate objects presented to us in dreams, illusions and the so-called real experience are perfectly similar. Something is apprehended, the subject not yet judging what that something is—this is immediate experience. The starting point of knowledge then is furnished by given facts devoid of all interpretations. This is the truth which the 'ideal system' seeks to convey by its original assumption. It is of course another question how far its advocates have consistently adhered to the standpoint of immediate experience. In fact, it is the very simplicity of the data which makes it a difficult task to essay a description without clothing them with the categories of interpretation. This difficulty has led many to deny their existence altogether. There is, however, a more serious difficulty, which has prevented the critics of the ideal system from recognising its true merits. Most of the philosophers from Descartes onward, in their description of the data, have either consciously or unconsciously introduced concepts of doubtful application, e.g., 'mental,' 'state of consciousness,' 'mind-dependent,' etc. Thus their description becomes a curious mixture of logical sagacity and philosophical confusion. "Ideas" are said to be whatever we are conscious or percipient of, when viewed without respect to truth or falsehood; and in this respect they are rightly described as transient existences. But they are further classified as mental or mind-dependent. That they are presentations is beyond doubt, and this must be admitted by realists and idealists alike. As so regarded they have all the characteristics by which the realists describe the sense-data. It is said[25] that the "particular sense-data here and now cannot be doubted. Taken thus abstractly, they assert nothing, they mean nothing. They simply *are*.... They are, occur, are 'had' or experienced. In this sense, of course, their 'reality' is not in debate. But as soon as they are taken to mean something, are classified in some way... ...they are caught up in a network of theory, and their reality in *this* sense is at once open to doubt, but open also to confirmation." So, the really debatable part of the "theory of ideas" is how far the ideas as the immediate sensible objects are mental existences. To call them mental, to start with, is apparently to commit the "psychologist's fallacy." But to deny

---

25. Hoernlé: *Studies in Contemporary Metaphysics*, p. 76.

their existence altogether is to commit what may be called the "epistemologist's fallacy." Facts in order to be interpreted must be first apprehended as given, however short the interval may be between these two phases of knowledge. It is needless to labour this point—a point which has been pressed with relentless acuteness by the critics of idealism.[26] Kant's "*natura materialiter spectata*" can no more be reduced to mere relations than the ideas and perceptions of pre-Kantian empiricism or the sense-data of contemporary philosophy.[27] If the post-Kantian identification of form and content is interpreted as a polemic against the distinction of the given facts from their interpretations, we must reply in Kant's words that our understanding is not intuitive. The recognition of the immediate objects of perception then, we claim, is the true merit of what is generally known as subjective idealism. In so far as Hume's opponents have failed to do justice to this aspect of his teachings, the real difficulties of external perception are simply flung to the winds. Yet, the superiority of Reid has been often supposed to lie in rejecting simple apprehension in favour of apprehension accompanied with belief and knowledge, as a true description of the beginning of experience.[28] This theory, it must be admitted, has an appearance of simplicity by which it readily recommends itself to our ordinary ways of thinking. But appearances may be deceptive. This much at least is unquestionably true that all the theories about primitive experience are necessarily of a conjectural character. Consequently, to those who think that the only remedy for subjective idealism is the recognition of the belief in external existence from the start of experience, we must point out that this method of dealing with subjective idealism cannot be ultimately effective. As an account of the psychological genesis of our belief in the external world, it is purely conjectural; and secondly, even granting the truth of this psychological account, it does not solve the problem of validity. All our beliefs have their psychological conditions, but in spite of their necessity as events in the history of the individual's mind, many of them are false, and are in fact found to be mere "fictions of imagination." Even if we grant that Hume was wrong in deriving the fiction of external existence from the constancy and coherence of the perceptions, instead of recognizing its presence from the start, it must make us wonder why this primitive fiction is not rejected by us with the

26. *E.g.*, by Prof. A. Seth in his *Hegelianism and Personality*, pp. 79–83. It is however claimed that even Hegel did not mean to reduce the matter of intuition to pure thought—McTaggart: *Hegelian Dialectic*, second edition, p. 18 n.

27. This however does not mean that we can *know* these ideas, in the strict sense of the term 'knowing,' without and apart from all relations. We can surely feel the tooth-ache without being dentists, but to know the feeling in the totality of its conditions under which alone it is real, is entirely different from knowledge in the way of feeling.

28. *Cf.* A. Seth: *Scottish Philosophy*, p. 78.

growth of experience in view of the fact that in dreams and hallucinations this fiction unmistakably betrays its fictitious character. We are, therefore, unable to follow those psychologists who, like Mr. Stout, insist that presentations always involve the thought of that which is not itself a presentation. We are obliged, in view of the limited space at our disposal, to put off the consideration of the question how far Kant can be bracketed with Reid[29] in this respect. The distinction between the question of genesis from that of validity, as is well-known, is one of the most reiterated warnings of his criticism and it would be surely strange if he should weaken the force of his transcendental deduction in favour of an extremely questionable theory of external perception.

The philosophical confusion mentioned above, which is mixed up with the logical sagacity in Hume's analysis, arises from an apparently ambiguous way in which the advocates of the "ideal system" use the words "idea," "perception," etc. On the one hand, they are called transient existences, but, on the other hand, they are frequently described as mental or mind-dependent appearances. But why should they be called mental at all? It is apparently unquestionable that the bare knowledge of their existence need not necessarily include the belief that they are mental. It has been, however, pointed out[30] that this question drives the subjective idealist to a quandary; for "he can only prove things perceived to be subjective by proving them to be externally related to objects as their mechanical effects, and yet this can only be done by simultaneously interpreting the things perceived in a manner which the realist standpoint can alone justify." This contention may in fact be substantiated by numerous quotations from their works. It is specially true of Locke that his theory of sensation is "chiefly influenced by the physiological standpoint." And it is also true that Hume frequently talks of external objects "becoming known to us only by those perceptions they occasion." But they do not, as he himself points out, represent his true views; for "when the mind looks further than what immediately appears to it, its conclusions can never be put to the account of the senses," nor is it possible that our reason "ever should, upon any supposition, give us assurance of the continued and distinct existence of body." In fact, neither Locke nor Hume could seriously accept the physiological theory of sensation.[31] Their

29. *Ibid.*, p. 88.

30. N. K. Smith: *Prolegomena*, p. 53. *Cf.* also his *Commentary to Kant*, p. 587.

31. The problems arising out of Locke's 'new way of ideas' could not be solved by physiology. No critic who does not see this is in a position to do justice to the subjective idealists. See Green's *Introduction*, sec. 198; also Adamson on the ambiguity of the term 'idea'—*Modern Philosophy*, p. 113. Indeed the mistake of confusing these two standpoints has been very common among the exponents and the critics of the theory of ideas. *Cf.* Broad: *Scientific Thought*, pp. 256, 510; and Bergson: *Mind Energy*, p. 196. For a similar confusion between the physiological method and the critical method of Kant, see Adamson: *Philosophy of Kant*, pp. 23, 77, 78.

problem being to explain how our belief in the external thing grows out of the immediately given sense-data, it was not open to them to start with that belief and explain the sense-data as the effect of external things. So it has been emphatically maintained[32] that in this respect, "Hume is as much a Berkeleian as Berkeley himself, and they effectually exclude any reference to body from those original impressions, by reference to which all other modes of consciousness are to be explained." It must be however admitted that the real problem raised by Locke is never kept clear of the confusion arising from the physiological theory. Even Descartes, though attempting to approach all varieties of experience with a perfectly impartial attitude, is, when the problem of external perception is at issue, chiefly influenced by physiological considerations. And in so far as this is the case, Mr. Smith's observations are entirely justified. But what we contend for is that their confusions on this head were due to the difficulty of keeping consistently to the standpoint of immediate experience to which it was their merit to draw the attention of the thinkers for the first time. It is only when we come to Hume that we see a genuine attempt made to keep clear of that confusion; and so Hume, in spite of his occasional lapses, detects that "properly speaking it is not our body we perceive when we regard our limbs and members, but certain impressions which enter by the senses." More precisely he ought to say "impressions which are ordinarily supposed to enter by the senses."

We cannot enter at present upon the current controversies regarding the nature and status of the sensa. The question whether they are mind-dependent or not is a difficult one, and this is amply evident from the historical movements of the different theories, concerning the nature of the qualities. Reflections on the nature of motion at the dawn of the modern period led to the distinction between the world as it appears to us and as it is in itself. As a consequence, Galileo declared the mind-dependent nature of a number of qualities which are ordinarily referred to the physical world. This theory passing through Descartes and Locke, falls into the hands of Berkeley as a weapon against the independence of the primary qualities. The latter points out that the same considerations which disclose the mind-dependent nature of the secondary qualities may be equally applied to the primary ones which have been therefore falsely declared as independent. Contemporary realism, in making the alternative trial, finds that the considerations which disclosed the independent nature of the primary qualities could in fact be extended to the secondary qualities as well. Previous philosophers, in their opinion, did not

32. Green: *Works*, Vol. I, p. 163. It is true that Hume's restricted use of the term 'idea' was, as pointed out by Dr. J. Ward (*Psychological Principles*, p. 46), a retrograde step; yet, in excluding any reference to body from the original impressions, he was unquestionably truer to the 'new way of ideas' than its author.

see that it was impossible to confer independence upon the primary qualities without at the same time emancipating their ordinary associates. But, some of the modern realists (e.g., Mr. Alexander in considering the tertiary qualities as mind-dependent) have not been able to join this philosophical struggle for independence as whole-heartedly as their more enthusiastic comrades and thus have furnished an occasion to the enemy. For, a future Berkeley may take this as a clue and force the primary and the secondary qualities once more into the state of tutelage or servitude. Others however are more prudent and so cry out that all the things of earth and heaven, all qualities and all relations, are perfectly independent and have no need for a guardian.

Fortunately, however, this question of dependence or independence is not so material at the start as is often thought by the disputants. The representative theory of perception which forced itself upon Descartes who sought to go from mind to matter must also be the only refuge for those who seek to go from the transient and contradictory to the permanent and self-consistent. "Many of our impressisons," says Hume, "have no external model or archetype," for, the impressions are transient and conflicting existences, while, the external objects are permanent and self-identical. Similarly, Berkeley asks in the Dialogue:[33] "How then is it possible that things perpetually fleeting and variable as our ideas should be copies or images of anything fixed and constant?" Berkeley, therefore, substitutes what is now known as epistemological monism for "a two-fold existence of the objects of sense."[34] But he never dreamt that it could ever be possible for realism to give a coherent account of "nature as it is disclosed to us in sense-awareness, without dragging in its relations to mind."[35]

Hume's difficulties then, we claim, arose ultimately not from the "original assumption of the ideal system," but from the interrupted and variable nature of those perceptions which are revealed to immediate experience. He brings the impressions of figure, bulk and motion as well as those of colour, taste and smell, together with pain and pleasure, and declares that though "both philosophers and the vulgar esteem the third to be merely perceptions, and consequently interrupted and dependent beings," yet closer inspection reveals the same characteristics in the first and the second varieties of perception. It is true that "all of us at one time or other" become unthinking and unphilosophical and suppose that our perceptions are the only objects "and never think

33. Fraser: *Selections,* p. 160.

34. *Cf.* Prof. A.N. Whitehead: *The Concept of Nature*, Ch. II.

35. *Ibid.*, p. 27. Contrast Bosanquet's position that "the world cannot be a coherent whole without mind"—*Logic II*, p. 321.

of a double existence, internal and external, representing and represented." But when we philosophise, it is not enough to refer to the common sense of mankind or to an implanted instinct for the justification of the belief in the continued existence of the external objects. As our perceptions are transient, interrupted and conflicting, it is necessary to enquire into the origin of the belief in a continued uninterrupted external world which is independent of the fact that somebody experiences it.

The substitution of the terms sensa or sense-data, perspective or appearance for impressions, perceptions or ideas does not materially help us to solve the difficulties of Hume; and this is amply evident from the conflicting theories propounded to explain the nature and position of sense-datum. The perplexities in the modern account of the distinction between sensations, sense-data and physical objects, and the difficulties thence arising in the selective theory, creative theory and the mixed theory respectively can never be satisfactorily solved, until it is recognised that all contradictions ultimately spring from the false ascription of absolute existence to that which in reality has a complex of conditions all of which are equally important determining factors in its existence. It is immaterial whether we should *call* the sensa mental or physical, created or selected. What really matters is whether we should consider them to be conditioned or unconditioned existences, and this, as suggested above, is at the root of the controversy between realism and idealism. On closer inspection, it will appear that Hume's difficulties ultimately arose from his atomism. The impressions he regarded as so many isolated atoms making their appearance on the animal sentiency and then disappearing, without being in the least affected by the entrance or disappearance. Taking it for granted that the impression of colour, for instance, has an intrinsic nature of its own unaffected by its relation either to other impressions or to the mind, his only means of escape from the interrupted and variable impressions was to reduce our belief in the continued existence of the external world into a fiction of imagination. The perplexities which inevitably arise from separating nature from mind are perhaps nowhere more apparent than in connection with the categories to which we make a short reference in the remaining part of this essay.

The Realistic Conception of Categories.—The contrast of empiricism with criticism, and consequently the distinction between realism and idealism, appears in its vital form in connection with the ultimate principles of knowledge and existence. The merit of the "ideal system," as indicated above, consisted in reaching, in its analysis of external perception, the standpoint of immediate experience. But Locke, in his zeal against all forms of *a priori* philosophy and the theory of innate ideas, was prevented from reaping the full fruits of the position so assiduously reached by his predecessors. Instead of recognising the part played by the "understanding" in transforming the chaotic manifold of sense-presentations into a world of permanent objects, he sought to derive the ultimate principles of knowledge from the sense-manifold and finally reduced them to mere creatures of the mind. In reviving the doctrine of *entia rationis* of the Schoolmen, Locke was merely giving expression to the spirit of the time. His *tabula rasa* is only the mystic's "globe of light" passed into the hands of a philosopher. The purely receptive understanding of the mystic is freed from the encumbrance of divine influence, and the theologian sinks into a philosopher. But it was not open to the philosopher determined to emancipate thought from the extravagances of *a priori* speculations to indulge in the idea of an eternal understanding, and hence his only alternative was to show the empirical origin of all the eternal verities and the so-called innate ideas. As was to be expected, it is David Hume who perceives the legitimate consequence of this empirical method, and so he raises the problem which he claims to be both important and new, "little cultivated either by the ancients or moderns."[36] What is the nature of that evidence, Hume asks, which assures us of any real existence and matter of fact, beyond the present testimony of our senses? All transcendence of immediate experience, the answer comes, is due to a subjective tendency arising from repetition of similar instances. By means of the relation of cause and effect, Hume thinks, we go beyond the evidence of our memory and senses. But the knowledge of causal relation is not attained by *a priori* reasonings. It is ultimately due to the customary transition of the mind from one presentation to its usual attendant. This conclusion, Hume admits to be extraordinary yet inevitable.

We must avoid at this place the difficult task of estimating the merits of Kant's answer to the difficulties raised by Hume. The widely divergent interpretations of the transcendental deduction of the categories, and the equally divergent views on the merits of the deduction still prevailing among his critics and commentators leave no room for a summary account which will be free from dogmatism. We have undertaken here the humbler task of enquiring whether some of the tenets of contemporary philosophy are not due to the thinkers not appreciating the exact nature of the movement from Hume to Kant. The contrast of the selective with the creative function of the mind, the adoption of the psychological standpoint against the epistemological, the rigid separation between knowledge and reality—these and similar other features which characterise contemporary thought appear to depend on a false view of the first principles of knowledge. Till this error is got rid of, Hume's difficulties will remain unsolved. Indeed the very fact that the thinkers of the

36. *Enquiry*, Green's edition, p. 23.

present-day sometimes pretend to miss Hume's difficulties is a proof that their systems are founded on a false basis. A consistent empiricist must be able to swear by the legacy bequeathed by the Scottish sceptic, and is expected to have the courage to found the first principles of thought and reality on the observation of the psychical habits of man. They are to be exhibited as certain habits or tendencies of our minds acquired by a process of sensitive experience in the individual or the race. This conclusion, however, is never drawn explicitly, though it is strongly suggested by some of the characteristic tenets of current realism.

As a protest against the idealist's attempt to consider the entire universe as contents of the mind in some sense or other, the modern realist is bent upon eviscerating mind of all its contents and, if possible, wiping the mind itself out of existence. So he looks about to examine the different things with the label "mental" and his judgment in each case is the same, *viz*., "away with the impostor." He takes up one by one the abstract and the unreal, dreams and illusions, relations and universals, laws of thought and facts of feeling, and finally the mind itself. On examination it is found that all these items have been erroneously labelled "mental." They must take their seats out there among the objects; and lastly the mind itself must follow suit. Thus current realism aspires to be called objectivism, and its theory of mind, behaviourism. The realist's account of the categories is inspired by the same ideal. The categories are described as pervasive features as distinct from the variable ones,[37] and if Kant referred them to the mind that was because in the age in which Kant and Reid lived, this was the only way of indicating that the world of experience contains pervasive features as well as variable ones. Is this a right interpretation of the doctrine of categories as held by Kant?

To identify the categories with the pervasive features of the world of experience is to put the transcendental enquiry in an extremely misleading light, for it prevents us from seeing the real problem to which Kant's entire labour in the *Critique of Pure Reason* was devoted. The fundamental problem to which it was the merit of Descartes to draw the attention of thinkers for the first time, and in solving which philosophers were led to propound widely divergent theories, is much darkened by this identification. The theories of Occasionalism, Pre-established Harmony and Parallelism are the different attempts to solve this basic problem of modern philosophy, while the pantheism of Malebranche and Spinoza, the monadology of Leibniz, the phenomenalism of Kant, and even the theories of Identity and Panlogism of the post-Kantian period arose out of reflections upon the same problem. This, as is well known,

37. *Space, Time and Deity*, Vol. I, p. 192.

is the problem of the real and the ideal, which Descartes brought to consciousness for which he has been claimed to be the father of modern philosophy. Except in relation to this problem, the Kantian doctrine of categories must remain as the strangest offspring of philosophical perversity. To the subjective idealist he points out that the categories are not mere "creatures of the mind" or "fictions of imagination"; on the contrary, they enter, in the words of Prof. Alexander, as constituent factors into every existent. In opposition to the realist's position, on the other hand, he points out that they are not in Nature abstracted from Spirit, and that if they had belonged to abstract Nature our knowledge of Nature would never go beyond the habits of expectation to which Hume reduced all our inferences from experience. That is, the mentalist and the realist both begin with separating the logical from the metaphysical necessity, and end with reducing the former into mere psychological necessity. The new theory, on the other hand, germinated in the Aristotelian conception of the categories as both "kinds of predicate" and "kinds of being." It is not then a superficial observation that Kant's philosophy is a half-way house to the Hegelian idealism. It is, however, incontestable that Kant was far from identifying his synthetic unity of apperception with the Absolute of the later philosophers. In fact, he protests against this identification in the most emphatic terms; and is equally emphatic against the extraction of a real object from pure logic. But it is no less incontestable that one of the most vital points which he sought to make clear for all time was that the logical and the metaphysical aspects of the categories are inseparable. Nature which is "self-contained for thought"[38] may be a useful postulate for natural science; but in the philosophy of nature, we cannot accept without examination that postulate which is justifiable only from the abstract standpoint of the natural sciences. The pervasive features of the world of experience and the laws of Nature, when we consider it as externally related to mind can be nothing superior to the mental habits of a species of individuals who are doomed to know Nature through the transient presentations of the senses. These considerations confirm the observations we made on another occasion, and they are so relevant to the present topic that we need not apologize for quoting them here. The idealistic position "is all the more inevitable for a theory of immediate perception of the world, for, representative perception is a necessary accompaniment of realism, however clearly the fact may be disguised under the cover of an ambiguous expression... The embarrassments which the new realists feel in determining the status of the sensum are the inevitable consequence of the abstraction of mind from the objects... This does not amount to the denial of a possible abstraction of Nature from

38. *Cf.* Whitehead: *The Concept of Nature*, p. 3.

mind temporarily...and thinking homogeneously about Nature. But then it is to be constantly borne in mind, that this is after all a useful make-shift, and so in dealing with a nature 'closed to mind,' we have to use words and phrases that cry out for the concrete whole."[39]

Kant, therefore, in his theory of categories seeks to steer clear of the Scylla of absolute idealism and the Charybdis of atomistic sensationalism. The ultimate presuppositions of knowledge are also the ultimate conditions of the world of experience, for, Nature exists only for a rational individual who is constantly guided in his investigations by the *ideal* of a unitary system. Nature reveals herself to man because he is more than beasts and less than God. An intuitive understanding, as Kant says, is the prerogative of God alone, while animals are condemned to merely sensitive experience. Man, on the other hand, has both sense and understanding, and so Nature exists for him only in so far as the chaotic manifold of sense-presentations which are alone *given* in the strict sense suffers gradual transformation under the intellectual ideal of a thorough-going unity.

We are not at this place concerned with examining how far Kant's account of categories as suggested above can be ultimately maintained without developing it further and carrying it on to the dangerous precincts of absolute idealism. We are only trying to remove some of the misapprehensions and misgivings which appear to cluster round his theory of knowledge owing perhaps to its historical connexion with a widely accepted interpretation of Hegel's philosophy. A student of Kant has no hesitation to offer the warmest reception to the realist in so far as he teaches that the world of reality is not the mere contents of the universal mind, nor is it the unrolling of mental events by a creative imagination or æsthetic activity as taught by neo-idealism.[40] He may accept the realist as a fellow combatant against the attempts to leave the sure ground of experience. His only complaint is that the realist does not sufficiently and always realize that Nature the deciphering of which is the object of natural sciences is not given as a complete fact like colour or sound to the purely receptive sensibility or, to borrow a modern phrase, anœtic consciousness. Nature of course is given in another sense, i.e., in the sense of being independent of the chance movements of individual fancy arising from, say, the laws of association. The laws according to which we consciously or unconsciously interpret Nature are not due to arbitrary impositions of

39. An article in the *Educational Review*, December, 1921.

40. It may be permissible to observe here that if he is ever asked to choose between the orthodox Hegelian position and the creative idealism of Croce and Gentile, he will surely prefer the former as more in keeping with the transcendental teachings of Kant.

mental forms on a foreign material. Understanding has its inherent laws which it can no more violate than water can refuse to flow downwards. These ultimate laws are obeyed by all scientists though they may not be conscious of the fact that they are obeyed, e.g., every scientist must admit that nature is a system. All his attempts to revise and remodel knowledge are actuated by the belief that Nature is a complex whole. Every new theory which is but an admission that we failed so far to understand Nature is born of the incapacity of the old theory to present Nature as a systematic whole. So far the idealist and the realist must go together. But here the question inevitably arises: how do we know that Nature is a whole? This knowledge surely cannot come from sense which only presents us with fleeting and conflicting sense-data. We might be tempted here to say that Nature is there completely independent of the scientist's mind, but it is revealed to him only because he is a sensitive as well as a rational being. Kant however goes a step further, and insists that Nature about which the scientist forms his theory is not *given in any other way* than through the theory, and so it is impossible to compare the theory with something external to it in order to see how far his knowledge corresponds to natural facts. The criterion by which he can judge whether he has correctly known Nature or not is to be found in the laws of understanding itself. So, in this connexion what is revelation from one side is realization or construction from another.

To pursue further the suggestions made above will be to expound the Kantian theory of knowledge as a whole which is far from our present object. It is widely admitted by the exponents of the critical philosophy that the dream of making Kant consistent will never be realized. Every student of Kant is compelled to follow what he thinks to be the main drift of the master's teaching. The above suggestions are meant to indicate the particular line of interpretation which the critical philosophy admits of, and which may be necessary at a time when distinguished thinkers are offering a completely realistic interpretation of Kant's categories. The perplexing and apparently contradictory statements in which Kant has couched his thoughts may be open to diverse interpretations equally plausible and sound. But to read realistic meaning into his doctrine of the categories is to transfigure his position beyond all recognition. The students of Kant have so long been taught to guard themselves against that false view of the categories which was made current by such logicians as J. S. Mill. The 'summa genera' of the scholastic logicians are *not* the Kantian categories. The confusion was due to the Schoolmen not realizing the profound significance of the Aristotelian theory which had necessarily passed through their hands. But it is now equally necessary to avoid the other misconception which probably has its source in the criticism which the Hegelian Dialectic has received from the critics like Trendelenburg, Von Hartmann and

Haym.[41] The chief complaint of Trendelenburg against the claim of the Dialectic Method is that every step of the advance is empirically conditioned. Each of the categories is only an abstraction from the fulness of actuality, and so craves to escape from this forced position; and the dialectic method is simply the act by which we retrace our original abstraction.[42] We are not in a position to judge how far Hegel really meant what his critics attribute to him. It is at least strange that he should have taught a doctrine which is ultimately based on a confusion between thought and existence, knowledge and being. But one thing is certain, namely, that he, coming as he did after Kant, could not have meant his categories to be mere abstractions. In fact, the reduction by Hume of the general or universal elements of experience into the contingent psychological result of the particular "perceptions" was due to the abstract method initiated by Locke; and the wrong conception of the categories was ultimately born of this abstraction. There is, as Green points out,[43] a wrong view of the categories and a right one. "The right one regards them as the relations or formal conceptions, without which there would be no knowledge and no objective world to be known. They are not the end but the beginning of knowledge, not ultimate truths, but truths which we already know in knowing anything, though the correct disentanglement of them is in one sense the great problem of philosophy...The wrong view goes along with the false notion that the essential of thought is abstraction....According to one they are really apart from the objects of ordinary knowledge and experience, and are known by abstraction from these; according to the other, all objects of ordinary knowledge and experience are determinations of them, so that we know them in knowing the former, though we do not know that we know them." This brings out clearly the deficiencies of the empirical attitude towards experience, an attitude which is characteristic of all minds so long as they do not care to step beyond the "face-value" of the things of experience. It is the distinctive feature of empiricism to take experience as an ultimate fact without enquiring into those conditions which make experience possible, and the consequence is that these transcendental factors of experience are supposed to be either mere

---

41. In fact, there are striking resemblances between some of the tenents of current philosophy, and what Trendelenburg taught in his *Logical Investigations*. Motion, Space and Time, for example, are declared by him as undefinable. Space and Time are further thought to be products of Motion or sides of it obtained by abstraction. *Cf.* Whitehead, *Ibid.*, p. 33, and the following pages, where he too calls Space and Time abstractions from the passage of events. There are naturally striking differences between their views arising chiefly from the current conception of the creative advance of a four-dimensional world; but the resemblances are no less striking.

42. For a criticism of this view, see McTaggart: *Studies in Hegelian Dialectic*, Ch. II.

43. *Cf. Works*, Vol. II, p. 207.

"creatures of mind" or mere "features of the world." In fact, Locke's view of categories as mere creatures of mind to which nothing corresponds in nature, and Prof. Alexander's interpretation of them as mere pervasive features of the world to which nothing corresponds in mind, are based on a common assumption—an assumption which was expressly rejected by Kant.

The point which calls for special emphasis in this connection is that the empiricists before Kant conceived the relation between the knowing mind and the known object as purely mechanical and accidental. Locke, for instance, takes mind as something existing independently of the material world which come into relation with each other in perception. The material world causes certain ideas in the mind which the mind analyses, combines and recombines in various ways, thus producing the complex ideas corresponding to which there are no objective archetypes. This abstraction of the subject from the object became current in philosophy since the Cartesian doctrine of *cogito ergo sum*, and Locke had simply to purge it of its rationalistic implications in order to fit it into his system. So, he retained the mind-substance of Descartes, but rejected the latter's assumption of innate ideas. The *tabula rasa*, in the first instance, passively receives the simple ideas and then works upon these materials in diverse ways. Kant's originality here consists in exposing the groundlessness of this assumption, and in pointing out the perfect correlativity of the subject and the object. A subject which waits for the material world to produce ideas in it is a logical abstraction as much as an object apart from the subject. The various powers which Locke attributes to the mind can belong to it only in so far as it is a self-conscious individual; but self-consciousness implies consciousness of an objective world and hence experience must be already a fact before the mind can operate upon it and then derive the complex ideas. The necessary relations which empiricism explained as born of repeated observations through the laws of association are imbedded in that very experience, apart from which there can be no mind to make those observations and no object to be observed. So, the laws of association, far from accounting for the origin of experience, presuppose a conscious subject and a world of objects, that is, the associative faculty can operate only when there is a mind which consciously apprehends the data to be associated, and this conscious apprehension is possible only in so far as those data conform to the transcendental conditions of experience. If then the categories are these conditions, they make association possible, and cannot therefore be themselves due to association. "Were cinnabar, for instance, sometimes red and sometimes black, sometimes light and sometimes heavy;...there could be no empirical synthesis of reproduction," because the representations would not be subject to any rule and so could not fit into a unitary experience. This is Kant's central polemic against the empirical method of approaching experience. Empiricism explains those factors as later derivations which being at the basis of all knowledge and experience make this derivation itself possible.

It will appear from these considerations that the fundamental distinction between the empirical and the transcendental treatment of the categories consists in this that empiricism takes experience as a given fact without further explanation of that fact, and hence the categories for him are but empirical generalizations which are abstracted from experience; transcendentalism, on the contrary, discovers in the categories the very conditions of experience, and not mere empirical concepts or contingent products of experience. As a matter of fact, the empirical concepts depend upon the categories in so far as experience from which the former are derived is made possible by the categories. The categories may also be called the indispensable condition of a unitary experience which makes possible the unity of apperception. As Mr. N. K. Smith puts it, the categories may be regarded as expressing the minimum of unity necessary to the possibility of self-consciousness. "If sensations cannot be interpreted as the diverse attributes of unitary substances, if events cannot be viewed as arising out of one another, if the entire world in space cannot be conceived as a system of existences reciprocally interdependent, all unity must vanish from experience, and apperception would be utterly impossible."[44] The ultimate necessity of the categories, therefore, is due to its connection with self-consciousness. They are the modes of unity under which the sense-manifold must stand in order that subject-object experience may be possible. Empiricism, then, entirely misunderstands the nature of the categories when it looks upon them as the most abstract generalizations from experience. This misunderstanding leads to an important consequence. Once we look upon the categories as abstract concepts, they cannot be held to have any necessary connection with experience, and so they become mere "creatures of mind" or "fictions of imagination." Now, if we probe a little deeper into this empirical view of the categories, we tumble upon one of the fundamental assumptions of neo-realism, namely, that the relations into which the different parts of experience enter are purely arbitrary and adventitious, that the particular parts exist in their own right which are afterwards forced into different complexes. The mind apprehends the different sensa in their distinctness and then combines them into various things, so that the latter are but clusters of sensa which go together we do not know why. Similarly, the mind receives two sensations in succession which being repeated several times generates a tendency of the imagination to pass from the one to the other, and here also there is no necessity why one should follow the other.

44. *Commentary*, p. 253.

The same line of thought when applied to the unity of consciousness must result in the assertion that this unity also is purely a fiction generated by the different elements which are real apart from this unity. This is the *reductio ad absurdum* of the original dogma of empiricism—the dogma, namely, that the elements are real apart from the whole, into which they may happen to enter. It is hardly necessary to state in detail the points of agreement between Hume and contemporary realists in this respect. It is enough to remember that the conception of mind as a mere continuum of acts without an agent to whom those acts belong has been forced by the "empirical" method even upon such a realist as Prof. Alexander who has found it necessary to part company with those realists who "look at their mind from the outside and do not, as it were, put themselves into the place of their own minds."[45]

Ideal Construction.—It may be pointed out in conclusion that, even if we suppose the physical world to be independent of mind, there are difficulties in considering the pervasive features of that world as either objective or subjective exclusively; and these difficulties increase in proportion to the pervasiveness of those features. This may be illustrated, e.g., from the Law of Contradiction. Is it a law of thought or of thing? In rejecting what he thinks to be the Kantian account of the *a priori* elements of experience, Mr. Bertrand Russell[46] observes that there are strong reasons for thinking that the view which led to the "laws of thought" being so named is erroneous. For, "what we believe when we believe the law of contradiction, is not that the mind is so made that it must believe the law of contradiction. *This* belief is a subsequent result of psychological reflection, which presupposes the belief in the law of contradiction." Mr. Russell, however, does not say explicitly that it is a law of things in abstraction from thought. On the contrary, he insists that "the belief in the law of contradiction is a belief about things, *not only about thoughts*."[47] In so far as this is the case, he really subscribes to the Kantian view. Kant could never be persuaded to imagine that the *a priori* forms of experience are mere subjective beliefs. On the contrary, he waged a continued warfare against this doctrine. When, therefore, it is said that the *a priori* forms belong to the constitution of the mind, what is meant is, *not* that they are purely subjective, but that they are the ways in which we are compelled to think in thinking of any object of experience. And it must be acknowledged that the only criterion, in the last resort, by which we can distinguish between the fanciful and the objective is whether we are obliged to think in a particular way. To such critics of Kant as

---

45. *Space, Time, and Deity*, Vol. II, p. 109.

46. *The Problems of Philosophy*, p. 136.

47. Italics not in the original.

think that "ideal construction is a contradiction in terms, unless it refers solely to mental imagining,"[48] we must respectfully reply, in the words of Green, that "it is not understood that his doctrine of *a priori* forms of experience refers not to subjective beliefs but to those relations of phenomena which are necessary to the existence of a knowable objective world."[49]

The failure to appreciate the place of ideal constructions in our knowledge, and the consequent separation of the ultimate laws of nature from the fundamental laws of thought are then intimately connected with the realistic interpretation of the doctrine of categories. This interpretation, we must insist at the risk of repetition, does not bring out the correlativity of the real and the ideal which it was one of the chief aims of Kant's doctrine of categories to establish. Yet, this aspect of the doctrine it is important to recognise not only on its own merits, but also to understand Kant's historical position. The problem of the Ideal and Real has been called "the axis on which the whole of modern philosophy turns."[50] It is one of the chief results of Kant's transcendental investigations that the ordinary conception of the relation between knowledge and reality is untenable. The categories are not merely the universal features of facts of experience, but also the universal modes or forms of thought involved in experience. The result of this view is, as put by Mr. Green, "to overcome the separation, which in our ordinary thinking we assume, between the faculty or capacity or subjective process of experience on the one side and the facts experienced on the other."[51] Much of the mystery that enshrouds ideal construction disappears when it is observed that by calling understanding the source of the categories which from the side of the objects are their pervasive features, Kant was trying to make clear a truth which was indicated by Aristotle when the latter called the categories both "modes of being" and "modes of predicate." Whatever is real or can be thought of as real, must come under one of the categories, and that which is neither a substance, nor a quality, nor any of the other categories, is indistinguishable from nothing; it is matter without form, and hence unknowable and incapable of standing, to borrow a current expression, as the subject of significant propositions. Similarly, the result of Kant's investigation was to bring out the essential identity of the forms of understanding and the forms of object. In other words, he exploded the false basis, upon which the separation between the subjective and the objective elements of knowledge was made by his predecessors, and this he did by showing

48. *E.g.*, H. A. Prichard: *Kant's Theory of Knowledge*, p. 244.

49. *Works*, Vol. III, p. 129. *Cf.* Lotze: *Logic*, II, p. 314; Bosanquet: *Contemporary Philosophy*, p. 176.

50. Schopenhauer's Essay: *The Doctrine of the Ideal and Real*, p. 15.

51. *Prolegomena*, Sec. 34.

that the laws according to which thought works in knowledge are inseparable from the universal laws according to which objects or Nature as a system of things can exist for us. The necessity of thought and objective necessity are inseparable, so that to understand the fundamental laws of objects is also to gain an insight into the basic laws according to which thought works. Prof. Alexander's account, then, we are inclined to believe, ignores this aspect of Kant's doctrine, and it is this which is responsible for the widespread misunderstanding which he shares with Kant's critics like Mr. H. A. Prichard who think that Kant was unconscious of a fundamental objection to his account of knowledge, though the objection is "so obvious as to be hardly worth stating; it is of course that knowing and making are not the same."[52] It is hardly necessary to add that this, far from being an obvious objection, is one of the most permanent intellectual conquests that was ever achieved by a thinker.

52. *Kant's Theory of Knowledge*. p. 236.

Hiralal Haldar, "Realistic Idealism" (1930)

Hiralal Haldar (1865–1942) was largely responsible for the popularization of British neo-Hegelianism in India. He studied at Calcutta University, where he later assumed his chair as Professor of Philosophy. Haldar's massive *Neo-Hegelianism* (London, 1927) is the most extended study of the neo-Hegelian movement in English, discussing the work of Bradley, Caird, Greene, Stirling, and McTaggart among others. This essay is important because it provides a window into the philosophical education and development of early Indian philosophical scholars and their relationship to their missionary teachers.

Hiralal Haldar

3

Realistic Idealism

MORE THAN FIFTY years ago, when I entered Calcutta University as an Undergraduate, there was very little of what can rightly be called philosophical teaching in the University. Certain text-books, mainly on psychology and ethics, were prescribed and all that the Professors generally did was to expound them and to dictate to the students short summaries of them. Very often the exposition was wanting and the dictation of notes everything. One conspicuous exception to this method of teaching was that of Dr. William Hastie, who was Principal of the General Assembly's Institution affiliated to Calcutta University when I became a student of the College in 1882. But I was a freshman, and as Dr. Hastie's lectures were delivered to the higher classes only, I had not the opportunity of being benefited by his stimulating teaching. Dr. Hastie was one of the few real teachers of philosophy that ever came out to this country. But by the time I reached the B.A. Classes he had quarrelled with his home authorities and resigned. The usual sort of teaching did not suit me at all. I had a perfect horror of taking down dictated notes. I longed for instructive and inspiring lectures but none was available. Under such circumstances I was forced to ignore college teaching altogether and to acquire such knowledge of philosophy as I could by means of private study only. This reliance on my own efforts probably did me a great deal of good by compelling me to think a little on my own account. At first I had not much taste for philosophy. But fortunately my attention was drawn to a series of short articles in a weekly journal of Calcutta inculcating an idealistic doctrine of the Berkeleian type. These articles awakened my interest in Berkeley and I turned to his writings. I read his *Principles of Human Knowledge* and *Three Dialogues between Hylas and Philonous* and was very much impressed by them. But I was enabled to avoid a subjectivist bias by reading almost simultaneously expositions of Kant by Stirling, Green, Caird and Adamson. The *Critique of Pure Reason* I studied a little later. Hegel I tried to read but without success. Such expositions of him as came into my hands were perfectly useless. I remember spending hours one evening over Ueberweg's account of Hegel in his *History of Philosophy*. Not a single line was intelligible and I closed the book in despair. This, I suppose, is the usual experience of those who first approach Hegel. The book which first enabled me to comprehend something of the meaning of Hegel was Edward Caird's *Hegel* in Blackwood's Philosophical Classics Series, a book which is justly described by Professor Watson as "small but golden." William Wallace's Prolegomena to his translation of the *Encyclopaedia of the Philosophical Sciences* was also of immense help. By and by I managed to read the *Encyclopaedia* itself. The philosophical movement known as Neo-Hegelianism was in my student days gathering strength in Great Britain and I was one of the very few, not improbably the only one, who then felt its power in India. I eagerly studied everything that appeared from the pens of J. H. Stirling, the two Cairds, Green, G. S. Morris, R. Adamson, J. Watson, A. Seth, afterwards Pringle Pattison, D. G. Ritchie, F. H. Bradley, B. Bosanquet, R. B. Haldane, afterwards Viscount Haldane, Henry Jones and others. I was very powerfully influenced by these writings, particularly by those of Green and Caird. Bradley's *Ethical Studies* also very deeply impressed me. A new heaven and a new earth seemed to be disclosed to my eyes. In later years Hegel was studied with much difficulty and slowly.

I should add that in the Proceedings of the Society for Psychical Research and Myers' *Human Personality and its Survival of Bodily Death* I have found much that is informing and suggestive.

I have seen myself described as a Hegelian. The basis of my thought is undoubtedly Hegelian, but in the course of years, as this sketch may show, I have been led to modify in many ways what I have learned from Hegel. No man, however poor a thinker he may be, can exactly reproduce the views of another. The very essence of individuality is its uniqueness and therefore the angle of vision of one man is bound to be somewhat different from that of another. In the process of making my own the ideas acquired from Hegel and others, I have inevitably transformed them more or less.

Alexander Bain was perfectly right when he said that the ingenuity of a century and half had failed to see a way out of the contradiction exposed by Berkeley. The contradiction is that of supposing that the objects all around us, the things which we see, smell, taste, hear and touch exist on their own account independently of their being perceived. To be, argues Berkeley, is to be perceived. Take away from things the relations in which they stand to the perceiving mind and they lose all meaning, simply cease to be. The objective world can no more exist apart from mind than can the outside of a thing exist in isolation from its inside. The self is the very centre of being of whatever can be called real, the life and soul of all that is. The experienced world has its support in mind. This argument is by no means of modern origin and Berkeley was not the first to use it. It was well known to the sages of the Upaniṣads nearly three thousand years ago. In the *Bṛhadāraṇyaka Upaniṣad*, for example, probably the oldest of the Upaniṣads, Yājñavalkya tells his wife Maitreyi that all things forsake him who supposes that they are separate from mind. As the sound of a musical instrument cannot be taken hold of apart from that instrument, as the sound of a conch-shell cannot be apprehended separately from the conch-shell, but if the musical instrument and the conch-shell are cognised the sounds emanating from them are necessarily cognised along with them, so none of these things issuing forth from the self can be known independently of the self. It may be said that the plausibility of the idealistic argument is due to a confusion between a thing and the thing as known. A man with whom I am shaking hands is necessarily related to the act of hand-shaking but this does not mean that his very existence depends on it. The food I am eating implies the act of eating, but eating is not the necessary condition of the existence of the food. So a thing *as perceived* is dependent upon perceiving, but the thing as perceived is not identical with the thing. The latter has no necessary relation to knowledge. The contention of the idealist is that no such distinction can be made between object and object of knowledge. The very essence of an object is its being known. As Yājñavalkya says, all things flee from him who attempts to separate them from the self. Food which is not eaten is possible, a man with whom no one is shaking hands is possible, but a thing which no mind knows is impossible. It is the outcome of false abstraction.

But however sound and unassailable Berkeley's fundamental principle, in its essence, may be, the conclusions he draws from it are not all tenable. In the first place, he gives a too restricted meaning to it. Perception is not the only mode of knowledge and it is therefore not possible to say that what is perceived is alone real. It would have been better if he had said that the *esse* of a thing is its *intelligi*. In his earlier writings he ignores almost completely the universal forms of knowledge and takes cognisance of its contents only consisting of particular sensations and ideas. In the *Siris* this view is to some extent corrected and the importance of universality in knowledge realised. Even in the *Principles* he admits that the self is an object of thought, not of perception. In the second place, from the right premiss that nothing is real apart from mind the wrong conclusion is drawn that everything is reducible to ideas of the mind. So far from it being true that things are only ideas, ideas have no meaning, as Reid urged, without their reference to things. The *opposition* of mind to its object is the very basis of knowledge and without this duality no sort of cognition can take place. If to be is to be perceived it is equally true that to be perceived is to be. In all knowledge the distinguishable but inseparable factors opposed and irreducible to each other are the mind that knows, the object that is known and the act or process of knowing. Imagination also has this three-fold character. The imagined world is as much opposed to the imagining mind and its activity as the solid world of perception in time and space. This being so it is the images of the mind, the ideas that are to be brought into line with things and not the latter with the former. The imagined world is quite as objective as the physical world of perception to which we belong. Things therefore are not mental ideas, they are objects of mind. Instead of things being ideas, it is ideas which have the status of things. This truth is clearly realised by the idealist philosophers of India. Śaṅkara, for example, who is commonly but wrongly supposed to be an illusionist, a thinker who denies the reality of the world, lays the utmost stress on the opposition of what is known to the mind that knows. In the absence of something distinguished from mind and opposed to it knowledge is no more possible than it is possible for a dancer to dance on his own shoulders. Epistemologically, Śaṅkara is a thorough-going realist. He does not say that the empirical world is in any way dependent for its being on the finite mind. All that he maintains is that ultimately, from the highest point of view, it has no independent existence apart from *Brahman*. Both Śaṅkara and Rāmānuja maintain that even illusions are not unreal and merely subjective. They are as objective as the things of ordinary perception, the only difference being that they are not common to all, but individual and last only as long as they are experienced.

The objective world then is wider and more comprehensive than the world of common cognition and contains numberless extensions in the shape of the products of the imaginative activity of the mind. What is imagined is not one whit less objective and opposed to the mind than what is perceived. It is not more mental than the latter and has no specially intimate connection with the subjective process of knowing. It is on the same footing with sensible realities and differs from them not in essence but in respect of detailed characteristics only. Imagined things are not of common experience and are peculiar only to those who conceive them. Unlike perceived substances they have no tangible qualities and do not offer any resistance to movement. They are not enduring and are in being only as long as the activity of imagination continues. The error of the subjective idealist is to suppose that images, ideas, representations are purely mental and to maintain that perceived objects are like them. The subjective processes of cognition alone are mental. The contents of the mind to which they refer, no matter whether they are perceived or only imagined, are all equally objective and antithetical to mind and constitute ingredients of different kinds of what is called the external world. It is not things that are to be reduced to ideas but ideas are to be assimilated to things. There is nothing that belongs specially to the knowing mind except its own activities.

In what has been said above stress has been laid on the opposition of the experienced world to the mind that knows it. It stands over against the subject on its own legs and is in no way reducible to it. Its existence is not dependent upon the finite minds which are included within it except those portions of it that are the products of their imaginative activities. On the opposition of subject and object all knowledge is founded. There is no such thing as an insulated mind contemplating only its own internal states. The whole content of mind, percepts as well as ideas, belongs to objective experience. What are specifically mental are its own activities of knowing and willing. But the opposition of subject and object does not mean that they are separable from each other. The error of realism is to make this opposition absolute, just as the error of subjective idealism is to ignore or minimise it. There the opposition is undeniably, fundamentally and glaringly, but it presupposes an ultimate unity from which it arises and of which it is the other side. In the realisation of this truth consists the strength of idealism. Berkeley's doctrine is an inadequate and misleading expression of it. The South Pole is not the North Pole or a locality within it; it is diametrically opposite to it. Nevertheless the being of the one pole is implicated with that of the other and they exist only as two necessarily connected sides of the earth. Similarly the front and the back of my body do not look at each other. They are not on speaking terms with each other, but in spite of this they are the inseparable parts of my entire organism. Just in the same way mind and its object are the two opposed aspects of the one all-embracing unity which also is mind. The term "mind" has two meanings. It is the knower opposed to the object of which it is conscious. Further, it is the unity presupposed in the distinction of subject and object and manifested in that distinction. This all-inclusive spirit within which distinctions of every kind arise, which is bifurcated into subject and object is the ultimate reality—the universe in its last interpretation. It is not mere mind nor abstract matter but the source and presupposition, the truth of both.

To superficial observation nature seems to be but a vast aggregate of independent entities existing side by side with one another in space and time without being in any way essentially connected. It is by pure chance that a thing is what and where it is. Remove it from its place and there is no change whatever anywhere in the world except in itself. What necessary connection is there between the individual bricks heaped together there on the ground? May not the earth vanish into nothing to-morrow owing to some catastrophe and the rest of the universe remain exactly as it is? What modest man does not think that his coming into being and passing into nothing makes no difference whatever to the world to which he happens to belong unaccountably for a few years? Self-subsistent realities are somehow put together and to the totality thus formed we give the name of nature. This view seems to be plausible at first sight but on reflection it turns out to be quite erroneous. According to Spinoza it is imagination, not knowledge. Things exist in virtue of the relations in which they stand to one another. These relations are not external to the things. They constitute their very nature, make them possible, sustain them and are inseparable from them. Lotze has shown that if things were isolated no interaction between them would be possible. How could one thing affect another if there were a breach of continuity between them? A influences B. What is this influence? If it emanates from A then in being detached from A and passing on to B, it momentarily at least enjoys independent existence and becomes a third thing C giving rise to the problem of its relation to A and B. Bradley's argument against external relations is in spirit the same. If a relation be outside the related terms how does it get itself connected with them? The truth is that things are not self-subsistent and independent. They have being only in so far as they are essentially related to one another. It is not that things first exist separately and then casually enter into relations. Apart from the relations they are mere abstractions as unreal as the top of a thing separated from its bottom. Relations are the very pith and marrow of the related entities, their foundation and support. Science brings this truth to light. It regards the universe as a unitary system of which individual objects are constituent elements. Everything is real only in its own place necessarily connected with other things by means of definitely ascertainable relations. Everywhere in the Cosmos isolation means death.

> Nothing in this world is single,
> All things by a law divine in each other's being mingle.
> (Shelley, P.B, Love's Philosophy)

Objects are continuous with one another and because of this continuity they are also different. They are one because they are many, many because they are one. Unity finds expression in difference and difference has its presupposition in unity. Undifferentiated unity and mere difference are the products of abstract thinking. In the concrete world unity and difference go together. They are complementary aspects of the whole—the universe. If things ceased to be different they would coalesce with each other and vanish into a geometrical point. On the other hand if they absolutely flew apart from each other they would be dissipated into nothing. It is because they attract and also repel each other, are one as well as many, that they exist as integral parts of a single spatio-temporal world. The world undoubtedly looks like an aggregate of independent units. But this is superficial appearance only. In its true nature it is an organic whole realised in the difference of its members. It is the concrete reality of which finite beings and the so-called things are only fragments kept apart by false abstraction. These fragments scientific reflection shows to have being only as elements of the whole—the Cosmos.

But what is the ultimate nature of the unity of all things? Is it some form of the universe itself or some supra-cosmic essence into which the world is absorbed and from which it emanates alternately? The latter view, in spite of the support it has received in the history of thought, is untenable. The unity of the world is the world itself in its ideality, the world regarded as the spirit in which it is centred and of which it is the expression. Inter-connected things which exist in virtue of the influence which they reciprocally exert upon one another are one, not as this or that thing is one but as the universal principle that pervades them, connects them and at the same time maintains their difference. Their unity, in short, is not a numerical unity, for a numerical unity presupposes other similar unities from which it is excluded. It is ideal unity, the unity of a principle common to them, realised completely and indivisibly in each of them but limited to none of them. It is the universal mind at the root of things manifested in them and their mutual relations. In the words of the *Bhagavad Gītā* it is the supreme *Brahman* that "exists in the world pervading all things and having hands and feet everywhere, eyes, heads and faces in all directions and ears on all sides." It is "without and within all things and beings, the unmoving and also the moving. Though undivided it yet exists as if divided in them."

We thus see that from the highest point of view the universe is spirit self-distinguished into the knower and the known, the cognising mind and its own other, namely the object-world that is cognised. The distinction of self and not-self, mind and matter, is fundamental and inescapable. It is not by obliterating but by maintaining and transcending this distinction that the Absolute is what it is. Neither can matter be evaporated into subjective impressions nor can mind be regarded as a byproduct of matter. They are opposed to each other as correlated aspects of the one ultimate reality.

The mind in which the universe finds its truth and explanation is not foreign to it. It is the mind of the universe itself, its own highest form. What at a lower level of interpretation is a system of mutually determining things in space and time is at a higher level of interpretation mind—mind that does not exclude the physical world but takes it up into itself. The material world is inwardised in mind and mind is externalised in matter. They are the correlated phases of the one all-inclusive spirit. In preaching this truth idealism is in no way inconsistent with realism. It does not make it its business to deny the reality of the world. On the contrary, it strongly affirms it. It goes as far as realism does but goes farther, maintaining that the world is indeed real, even what are called ideas are component parts of it, but that in order to know that it is real it has got to have mind. What is the use of being real if mind, without which consciousness of reality cannot be, is wanting? It is not enough that you or I are aware of it. The real world ought to have its own mind so that it may enjoy the abundance of its wealth which is never completely known to any finite being. Surely the idealist who says that the objective world is spiritual without ceasing to be physical is a better realist than he who denies mind to it and thereby makes its reality worth nothing.

The spiritual whole is internally divided into subject and object, self and not-self. The object-world again as related to intelligence involves the distinction and inseparable union of the universal and the particular, the forms of thought and the contents of experience. The relation between the universal and the particular has always been a subject of controversy among philosophers. It was Plato who first realised the importance of the universals, ideas as he called them, and saw that without them neither knowing nor being is possible. But he separated the ideas from sensible phenomena and thought that they were imposed upon the latter *ab extra*. The empiricists, on the other hand, think that they consist of the common features of experienced facts obtained by means of abstraction. Kant's great achievement was to show that experience is richer than what the empiricists take it to be and involves both the categories of thought and the particulars of sense. Like Plato he separates the universal from the particular but perceives that so separated they are names only, the one empty and the other blind. The empiricists suppose that experience consists of particular phenomena only. Kant does not deny that they have independent being, but argues that they are as good as nothing unless they are subjected to the categories. He undertakes the impossible task of showing how the forms of thought and the matter of sense are brought into relationship with each other and of course fails. But the solid result of his philosophical thinking was to demonstrate that apart from the principles of the understanding experience is not possible. In actual knowledge the universal and the particular are never found cut loose from each other. Sensible phenomena are never merely discrete and disconnected but are always pervaded and sustained by universal forms of thought as connected members of the intelligible and orderly cosmos. Nature is not made by the understanding but is the outer expression of reason. A firm grasp of this truth is the merit of Hegel. In his eye, the material universe, always involving the duality but not the dualism of the universal principles of reason and the particular facts of experience, is the embodiment of the Infinite mind. It is this mind "that is the ultimate nature of life, the soul of the world, the universal life-blood which courses everywhere, and whose flow is neither disturbed nor checked by any obstructing distinction, but is itself every distinction that arises, as well as that into which all distinctions are dissolved; pulsating within itself, but ever motionless, shaken to its depths, but still at rest."[1]

Kant regards the categories only as instruments used by the self for the purpose of producing knowledge out of the data of sense. In themselves they are but empty forms not essentially related to one another and to the self.

---

1. *Phenomenology of Mind*, Baillie's Tr., George Allen & Unwin, vol. i, p. 157.

Hegel, on the contrary, views them as at once forms of thought and modes of being, subjective as well as objective. They are not airy abstractions but comprehensive systems implying particularity. They are all essentially related to one another as vital parts of the whole of reality. The organised whole of which they are members is the Absolute. Each of them is implicated with and has no being apart from the rest. They form a graded system and the business of philosophy is to show how thought necessarily passes from the lowest of them step by step through the intermediate stages to the highest. Each category incorporates the immediately lower one into itself and is taken up into the immediately higher, and the highest, the Absolute Idea, therefore contains them all as necessary elements of itself. It is to them what the living body is to its members. For Hegel this view implies that the Absolute Idea is a completed and closed system and that human knowledge is co-extensive with reality. There cannot in his view be anything in thought or reality which has not a definitely ascertainable place in the system of the Absolute Idea.

Now it is not easy to avoid being overpowered by the persuasiveness of Hegel's argument. The methodical procession of the categories produces an immense effect on the reader's mind. But in the end few are able to accept the view that the Logic exhaustively discloses the contents of reality. The really valuable work which Hegel does is to demonstrate that the universe is an orderly and intelligible system with mind at its centre, but this does not mean that we know in detail what its constitution and contents are. If the categories specified by him were the only elements of this system, if human intelligence penetrated reality to the very core, omniscience would be the necessary consequence and there would be no room for doubt and hesitation of any kind. It sometimes looks as though Hegel actually claimed omniscience. But the revisions to which he himself subjected the arrangement of his categories, the alterations he made in their list from time to time, show that he by no means knew all that there is to be known and that reality after all very largely eluded the grasp of his intellect. The truth, of course, is that human knowledge is not co-extensive with reality and the categories of Hegel's *Logic* do not furnish a complete exposition of it. They are only a section of the contents of Absolute thought detached from the whole. The fragmentary character of our knowledge is obvious. It bears unmistakable marks of its narrowness and incompleteness. The breach of continuity which is everywhere apparent in the world, the abrupt manner in which facts of one order are marked off from those of another order, the immense blanks between the bright spots of knowledge, the failure of the universals of thought and the particulars of sense to fit in with each other smoothly and without hitch, the inability of time and space to attain the completeness at which they aim, the antinomies and contradictions of which experience is full, the unreason obtruding upon us on all sides in a world which theory forces us to regard as rational through and through, the evils that mar the beauty and orderliness of the cosmos, the angularities and rough sides of things, the trials and tragedies of life, all plainly indicate that the world to which we belong is not the whole, but only a fragment of the real universe the major part of which is beyond our ken. It is in Kant's words but an island in the vast ocean of reality, only the ocean is not something unintelligible but the rational whole of existents.

The categories of human knowledge do indeed express the nature of reality but only partially. They are valid so far as they go, but in the Absolute they must be supplemented by others not at present known to us. Of them organised into a complete whole the objective world, both seen and unseen, is the expression. What we call nature is only a tiny fragment of this greater universe, if we may call it so, and in it alone the Absolute mind finds its full content. The unseen world or worlds, it must be remembered, is not psychical. There is nothing purely psychical or purely physical. All the *contents* of the mind are objective and opposed to the self that knows. The unseen universe, therefore, although not material, is of a piece with what is material. It is spiritual exactly as *this* world, the material world, is spiritual. Whatever is, is the expression of mind. There is nothing which is out of relation to intelligence. As Bradley says, "Outside of spirit there is not and there cannot be any reality." All the worlds, the visible material world and the invisible immaterial but objective worlds, are parts of one stupendous whole and in this whole the Absolute mind is completely embodied. A purely spiritual or psychical world is as much a fiction as a purely material world. What is real is also ideal and the genuinely ideal must be real.

The Absolute mind is one but it is not a monadic unity. In it the minds of the things that constitute the world are fused into a single whole or, what is the same thing viewed from the other end, it is pluralised in them. The universal mind is immanent in all things. This means that it is present in each of them undivided and as a whole, which cannot be unless it is in it as its inner soul. To be a self-complete whole, to be in all parts of it equally and yet to remain a whole in each part is the prerogative of the universal. The mind for which the universe is, is not apart from it; it is its own central principle. Its relation to things, therefore, is not an external relation like that of one thing to another. It is the ideality of each of the things themselves, the very core of its being. In being externalised in the multifarious objects of the world, the Absolute mind goes forth to them and dwells in them as their own individual minds. It becomes manifold and yet remains one. Were it not so it would be external to them and being limited by them would be just like one of them. The self of the world is one and yet many. In it many minds, the minds of the myriads of objects that are comprised within the world, are gathered up and, on its part, it is diversified in them. There is nothing unintelligible in this notion of minds being many and yet one. The self of every one of us is such. A is a distinguished statesman, a great metaphysician and an expert player of cricket. These are distinct personalities with different characters and yet they are fused into a single whole in the self of A. Pathological cases of multiple personality prove this. In them the process of disintegration goes so far as to give rise to distinct personalities sometimes of opposite characters and very hostile to one another. The case of Sally Beauchamp is an example. We speak of the conflict of the better self and the worse self in us. Why should this be regarded as only a metaphor and not literal truth? What every man is that the Absolute itself is. Is not man made in the image of God? The self is our ultimate principle of explanation. In analogy with it we think of the Absolute. But our self is never a solitary unit. It is not only composite in itself but is always a member of the social whole. The concrete actuality is the social mind. If therefore the Absolute is spirit, its nature must be analogous to the composite mind of society. It is on one side mind consisting of many minds and on another the physical world consisting of inter-related objects. There are thirty-three millions of Gods in the Hindu pantheon. This need not be denied; only it must be remembered that they are all integral parts of the supreme Brahman. An infinite number of selves, the selves of the constituent members of the objective world, go to form the Absolute mind. This is what Arjuna sees in *Viśvarūpa* (the cosmic form of the Lord) in the *Bhagavad Gītā*: "O Lord of the Universe, O thou whose form the Universe is, I behold thee of countless forms everywhere with many arms, bellies, mouths and eyes. I do not see thy end, nor thy middle, nor yet thy beginning."

Things existing in time and space and excluding each other are limited, but in their ideality, as minds, they are all-pervading and omniscient. A finite object is marked off from others, repels them, but this is possible because it is also continuous with them and includes them in its own being. Such inclusion takes the form of the consciousness of them. What is distinguished from others is in the very process of distinction joined with them. That is to say, it transcends the distinction between them and itself as inclusive mind. Nothing, therefore, as ideal can be limited to the place where it is as a reality. It encompasses all being, is everywhere. A strong point of the pluralistic systems of Indian philosophy, Jainism, the Saṁkhya and the Nyāya Vaiśeṣika, is their conception of the many selves as omnipresent and eternal. These, however, cannot be regarded as independent and self-subsistent but must be viewed as component factors of the one Absolute mind. The many are one and the one is many. Each of the particular selves into which the Infinite mind is differentiated represents, because of its all inclusiveness and omniscience, the whole world. But it does so in its own unique way, from its own special point of view. It is the merit of Leibniz to emphasise this truth. But unfortunately he distinguishes the ideation of the world from the world and isolates the monads from each other, thereby making the unity of the world inexplicable. The Jain doctrine of *Syādvāda* has a clearer perception of the truth. The one world is known by many minds, the minds of the things that constitute it, in various ways like different triangles standing upon the same base. Their world-pictures are different. The universe presents itself in different perspectives to them, but they are all fused into a composite whole. Different views of things obtained from different standpoints become complementary to one another in the final synthesis. What is seen with the right eye is also seen with the left eye in a slightly different way but the two visions are merged in one and do not remain apart from each other. See a word consisting, say, of five letters with attention mainly focused on each of the five letters successively and you will get five somewhat different appearances, but they are all amalgamated with each other in the ordinary appearance of the word. Nothing is as simple as it seems to be. A lump of sugar is no doubt sweet, but who will undertake to prove that it is sweet to me in precisely the same way as it is to you? Its real sweetness may be the synopsis of the sweetnesses felt by all those who taste it. As no two faces are alike, so it may be that no two perceptions, no two ideas of the same thing are alike. The vulture finds enjoyable repast in a rotten carcass, but to men it is noxious. This ought to give us food for reflection. The truth is that relatively things are different from different standpoints, but absolutely they combine in them all these variations. There is no contradiction in this, for the essence of contradiction is the confusion of standpoints. The Absolute cognises the world in an infinite number of ways from the standpoints of the countless things the minds of which are confluent in it without detriment to their distinctness. Its knowledge therefore is infinitely rich and complex. The universe is not only diverse in composition but knows itself in diverse ways.

Finite beings belong to nature; they are rooted in it and arise out of it. They in no sense create it. By means of their cognitive processes, they merely select certain elements of reality which go to constitute the world we experience and live in. They have been regarded as partial reproductions of the Infinite mind, emanations from it conditioned by organic processes. But as the Absolute mind is a unity of many minds, finite selves can only be fragmentary expressions of these constituent minds and not of the Absolute as a whole. Except the contents of their experiences there is nothing additional in the Absolute. Human bodies are among the things whose minds enter into the composition of the Absolute. Each of it is the objective side, the outer expression of an omniscient mind having its abode in the Absolute as one of its members. Consisting of millions of cells it is itself highly composite.

In one body, consequently, there are many bodies and many minds. One self has not many bodies, and many selves, as is sometimes supposed, do not belong to a single body. The many cells that compose the body are the many bodies of the many selves unified in the one mind of the whole body which is the ideality of the body itself. It is a constituent element of the Absolute mind. Finite selves are detachments from these deeper selves, assuming new forms, relatively independent and setting up their own households. They are sustained by the Absolute but not swayed by it from outside. They participate in its being, share in its freedom and are not mere excrescences upon it. Finite selves no doubt derive the materials of their life and experience from the Absolute but are not useless repetitions of what already exists. They give rise to novelties in being limited and in the course of the changes they undergo as they grow and seek to realise their purposes, to work out the ideals of their lives. They do not revolve round and round the same point but move on from freshness to freshness, from one stage of life to another and newer. They do not stagnate but alter and progress, do not perpetuate the existing but create the non-existing. In them the Absolute attains new modes of being, new outlooks on existence. In their knowledge they carve out only a small section of the whole of reality. The things we experience are not the things as they are in the knowledge of the Absolute but selections made from them for the purposes of life. Only so much of them is known as our organs of sense are fitted to take in and the sense-organs as they are at present are constructed not to reveal to us the total wealth of existence but to enable us to adapt ourselves to our existing environment and thereby to live. The table before me is not the table as it is in Absolute knowledge possessing an infinite number of properties but only the sum of a few of its characteristics that come within the range of my knowledge. Even of these characteristics a very small part only is perceived at any particular moment. What *we* perceive may therefore be said in one sense to depend on us for its existence, but as it is an ingredient of the true reality, it is in another sense independent of our cognition. Besides the features selected from the whole the perceived object may in virtue of its relation to our knowledge have new elements added to it. These, of course, exist as percepts only as long as they are perceived. But even here their support is not the human mind by itself but that mind in commerce with the object.

Finite minds necessarily seek to be the infinite that they potentially are. The Infinite immanent in them goads them on and does not allow them to rest. Even the shoemaker wants sovereignty over the whole universe. But self-realisation is not possible in isolation. Only in fellowship and co-operation with one another can human beings move forward towards the goal of life. In their ordinary lives and achievements as finite beings in time they are seldom aware of their greatness, but sooner or later they are bound to be conscious of their true nature, to be united with the source of their being in knowledge and love. God is not without man and man is not without God. The Divine spirit manifested in the community of men and the community of men rooted in the Divine spirit, God in man and man in God—this whole is the Absolute Spirit.

K. C. Bhattacharyya, "The Concept of Philosophy" (1936)

Krishna Chandra Bhattacharyya (1875–1949) is perhaps the best-known academic philosopher of the colonial period. He held the King George V Chair (now the B. N. Seal Chair) in Philosophy at the University of Calcutta and trained many of the eminent philosophers of the postindependence period. He is best known for his highly technical and even forbidding work on metaphysics, epistemology, aesthetics, and the philosophy of Kant. The present essay is widely regarded as among his most important philosophical works. Bhattacharyya distinguishes different grades of theoretic consciousness, connecting the hierarchy of cognitive attitudes to an account of the limits of language.

4

The Concept of Philosophy

1. An explication of the concept of philosophy appears to me more important than the discussion of any specific problem of philosophy. The possibility of philosophy as a body of knowledge distinct from science is nowadays called in question. I may indicate my general position by stating wherein I differ from the Kantian view of the subject.

I. Orientation to Kant

2. With regard to the knowability of the self as a metaphysical entity, Kant holds that the self is a necessity of thought and is the object of moral faith, but is not in itself knowable. My position is, on the one hand, that the self is unthinkable and on the other that while actually it is not known and is only an object of faith, though not necessarily only of moral faith, we have to admit the possibility of knowing it without *thinking*, there being a demand, alternative with other spiritual demands, to realise such knowledge. This is practically reopening the entire epistemological question of the meaning of thought and knowledge.

3. In taking the self to be unthinkable, I understand Kant's Idea of the Reason to be not only not knowledge, but to be not even thought in the literal sense. The so-called extension of thought beyond experience and the possibility of experience means to me only the use of the verbal form of thought as a symbol of an unthinkable reality, such symbolising use not being thinking. I go further and hold that a form of thought as understood by itself in logic and apart from its symbolising use is not literally thought. Some present-day positivists who deny not only metaphysical knowing, but also metaphysical thinking, would not go so far as to deny logic itself to be a body of thought. They rely in fact on logic, which they take to be pure thinking, in order to deny metaphysical thinking. I take logic to be a philosophical and not a scientific subject: the logical forms are shadows of metaphysical symbolisms and are as such themselves to be understood as symbolisms.

4. On the negative side then I go much further than Kant. On the positive side, however, I would tone down his agnosticism. That the self is believed in and is yet actually unknown is itself to me ground for holding that it is

knowable without thinking and has to be so known. The self or freedom is taken to be a moral postulate, but why is a moral postulate formulated at all? Neither morality nor metaphysical theory gains anything by the formulation in theoretic form. A moral postulate is not simply an Idea of the Reason, nor is it a construct of the aesthetic imagination. It appears to me to be formulated for the contemplation of it not as a moral good or as an enjoyable value but as a truth to be known. Such contemplation cannot be a spiritual luxury or make-believe, but must have behind it the faith that it is just the process of reaching the truth without thinking. It is not indeed a duty to contemplate, but the contemplation being already there, it demands fulfilment in knowledge. The contemplation of the self as truth may start from consciousness other than the moral, nor need moral consciousness develop into it. A distinctively spiritual activity comes spontaneously and has no necessary origin. The contemplation of the self as truth demands fulfilment in knowledge only by one in whom this activity has already started. It is an absolute demand co-ordinate with other absolute demands.

5. What applies to the self applies with necessary alterations to other metaphysical entities. Metaphysics, or more generally, philosophy including logic and epistemology, is not only not actual knowledge, but is not even literal thought; and yet its contents are contemplated as true in the faith that it is only by such contemplation that absolute truth can be known.

II. Grades of Theoretic Consciousness

6. Whether philosophy is knowledge or embodies literal thinking may be open to dispute. But in any case it presents beliefs that are speakable or systematically communicable and is like science an expression of the theoretic consciousness. Theoretic consciousness at its minimum is the understanding of a speakable. What is spoken must be in the first instance believed. What is disbelieved must be, to start with, a believed content. The meaning of a sportive combination of words like the "hare's horn" or "square circle" is only not believed and cannot even be said to be disbelieved. Nor is such combination said to be spoken except as an example of what is not spoken. To speak is to formulate a belief. Even imperative or exclamatory speech expresses some kind of belief of the speaker, though the belief is not primarily intended to be communicated. A lie which is not believed by the speaker is not felt by him to be informatively spoken, being felt to be spoken only as incorporated in the implied prefix of all speech, viz. the imperative "believe me." It is the believed content that is spoken and it is the understanding of what can be spoken that constitutes the theoretic consciousness.

7. Such understanding may not be knowledge, but it involves belief in something as known or to be known. The belief may not be explicitly an awareness of the actual or possible known-ness, but it can always be made explicit as such. The belief in knowledge may be implied in the explicit awareness of unknown-ness. The agnostic or the anti-rationalist or the absolute sceptic is primarily conscious of unknown-ness, but to be conscious of unknown-ness is to be conscious of known-ness also. They may not be said to *know* the unknown as such but they *believe* it and impliedly believe also in something as known, even though it may be speakable only as unspeakable. They are said to present a philosophy so far as they express the theoretic consciousness which implies belief in something as known.

8. All forms of theoretic consciousness as involving the understanding of a speakable are sometimes called thought. Of these, as will appear presently, only one form is literal thought, the others being symbolistic thought which should not be called thought at all. Four forms or grades of thought may be distinguished. They may be roughly called empirical thought, pure objective thought, spiritual thought and transcendental thought. Empirical thought is the theoretic consciousness of a content involving reference to an object that is perceived or imagined to be perceived, such reference being part of the meaning of the content. There are contents that are objective but have no necessary reference to sense-perception and the consciousness of such contents may be called pure objective or contemplative thought. The content of spiritual thought is no object, nothing that is contemplated in the objective attitude, being subjective in the sense of being appreciated in a subjective or "enjoying" attitude. Transcendental thought is the consciousness of a content that is neither objective nor subjective, the further characterisation of which will come later. The contents of the four grades of thought may be provisionally called fact, self-subsistence, reality and truth. Science deals with fact, the content of empirical thought. Philosophy deals with the last three, the contents of pure thought in the objective, subjective and transcendental attitudes.

9. All contents of the theoretic consciousness are speakable. The so-called grades of thought are really grades of speaking. Fact in science is spoken of as information and understood without reference to the spoken form. It is what need not be spoken to be believed. Speakability is a contingent character of the content of empirical thought, but it is a necessary character of the content of pure or philosophic thought. In philosophy, the content that is spoken is not intelligible except as spoken. Pure thought is not thought of a content distinguishable from it and is accordingly sometimes regarded as a fiction, philosophy being rejected as a disease of speech. Philosophical contents are indeed believed to be self-evident and the self-evident means what is independent of the spoken belief of an individual mind. This independence of

speaking is, however, a part of their meaning. It is not part of the meaning of a scientific content which is understood without reference at all to the linguistic expression of it.

10. Now a believed content that has necessary reference to the speaking of it is not spoken of as information. Self-subsistence or enjoyed reality or truth is not assertable as fact. Belief in it may be expressed in the form of a judgment but the form would be only artificial or symbolic. Fact is always expressible as a judgment of the form "A is thus related to B," this being the only judgment-form that is literally intelligible. A judgment of the form "X is," if it expresses belief in a fact of science, is only a periphrasis for a judgment of the above relational form. In "X is," if X stands for "A as related to B," the assertion means either only that A is related to B or that A that is thus related is related to something else. Fact is always a fact related to facts. If anywhere "X is" means something other than the relational assertion, it means that X is self-subsistent, real or true, which is only an apparent judgment. The subject is here understood as presupposing the predicate. The predicate does not, as in a judgment proper, amplify or explicate the meaning of a subject that is already believed. The subject is here believed as a self-evident elaboration of the predicate that is already believed to be self-evident.

11. Philosophy is such self-evident elaboration of the self-evident and is not a body of judgments. The self-evident is spoken, but is not spoken *of*. Of what is only spoken and contains a necessary reference to the speaking of it there are three forms according as it is spoken in the objective, subjective or transcendental attitude. The difference between the first two forms is the difference between the imports of the apparent judgments "The object (-in-general) is" and "I am." In a judgment proper "A *is* thus related to B," if the word *is* by itself means anything, if in other words the assertion means any content more than "A related to B," the content as isolated would be objectivity. It may be expressed as an apparent judgment "the relation of A and B is." In a judgment proper, the word "is" expresses only the objective attitude of the subject, but in this apparent judgment, "is" means an objective content which is self-subsistent but not fact. To express or formulate this content is still to retain the objective attitude. The attitude is explicitly dropped in saying "I am." The content here also is spoken and not spoken *of*, but it is explicitly understood as not objective and as only apparently objective or symbolised by objectivity. What the word "am" means is not contemplated in the objective attitude, but is subjectively enjoyed and only spoken *as though* it were objectively contemplated. If fact is spoken of and the self-subsistent object is only spoken—both being spoken as *meant*, reality is spoken not as meant but as only *symbolised*.

12. All the three are literally speakable. To say that the object is not the subject and that the latter is symbolised by the former is still to speak literally.

The word that is used as symbol is not indeed literally understood, but what is symbolised by it (and that it is symbolised) is literally spoken. The subjective is a positive entity through which the objective is understood. The concept of the object is not reached through a generalisation of the objective facts of science. Were it not for the direct consciousness and speakability of the subject *I*, the concept of the object would never be precipitated. The first person *I* is the primary instance of a content that necessarily refers to the speaking of it. It is in fact the spoken that is understood as the same as the speaking function. In "I am" then, the predicate is a symbol of a literally spoken subject. What is taken as self-subsistent or real is literally spoken and understood. What, however, is taken as true is not literally understood.

13. How then is truth as beyond reality spoken? To answer the question, the connection between the notions of fact, self-subsistence and reality has to be further elucidated. The denial of each of these is possible. The judgment "A is thus related to B" may be denied in the form "that A is so related is not fact," "That A is so related" is no judgment, but what is nowadays called a proposition. The enunciation and denial of it are possible because we have already a belief in the self-subsistent. If the proposition is understood as not fact, it is because we cannot deny it self-subsistence.[1] So we may deny the self-subsistent in the form "object is not," meaning "What is other than the subjective is not a definite or self-identical content for contemplation"—a recognised philosophical view that is not *prima facie* meaningless. The denial is possible because we already believe in the subjective as enjoyed reality. We may also deny reality in the form "I (as individual subject) am not." This too is *prima facie* intelligible and it represents a new grade of negation, for the individual subject is understood to be real as subject and not as object though it may be individual through some sort of identification with the object. Even as individual, the *I* is enjoyingly believed and the denial of such a content is possible because we have already the notion of truth beyond reality.

14. Taking a sentence of the form "X is," it is a judgment proper if "X," "is" and their combination (or the judgment-form) are each literally understood. Where X stands for the self-subsistent, both X and *is* are literally understood but the combination is not, since X is intelligible only through *is*. Where X stands for the (individual) self as enjoyed, it is literally understood, but the word *is* is only an objective symbolism for enjoyed reality and the combination therefore is also symbolic. Where X stands for the negation of the (individual) self, it is not literally understood, because no positive is understood as

1. The term self-subsistence instead of subsistence is used because we *mean* only in reference to a belief. The believed subsistent is the self-subsistent as meant. A meaning that is not a believed content of one grade is a believed content of a higher grade.

equivalent to it. The self is unintelligible except as the subject *I* or as what the subject *I* is not. There is no consciousness of an absolute or transcendental self without reference to the subject *I*. If such a self is understood, it is only as the implication of the enjoyed *I* and never by itself. It is indeed positively believed, but there is no positive formulation of it independent of the notion of *I*. Thus here X is only symbolically understood and consequently the word *is* and the judgment-form also are symbolically understood. "Object is" is no judgment, being tautologous as a judgment and "I am" is no judgment because *am* is only symbolism, but both are literally spoken because the subject is literally understood as positive. But the sentence "the absolute self is" is not only no judgment but is not even literally spoken. Still, it is not meaningless, and symbolises what is positively believed, viz. truth. What is believed and is not literally speakable (and is as such undeniable) is truth.

15. So there are the four grades of speakables. There is the primary distinction between what is only symbolically speakable and what is literally speakable. The literally speakable comprises what is spoken of as information and what is only spoken and not spoken *of*. Of these, what is only spoken is spoken either as symbolised or as meant. Truth is only symbolically spoken, reality is literally spoken as symbolised and the self-subsistent is literally spoken as meant. None of these are spoken *of* as information, while fact is spoken of as information. These correspond to what were roughly called empirical, contemplative, enjoying and transcendental thought. It is only what is spoken of as information or fact that is or can be meant literally. In contemplative, enjoying and transcendental thought, the content is not spoken *of* but is only spoken. If it is put in the judgment form "X is," the form is only symbolical. In the first two, X being literally understood, the content though not literally thought is still said to be literally spoken. In contemplative thought, the judgment-form is only symbolical, even in enjoying thought, the word *is* is also used symbolically. In transcendental thought, X also being symbolical, "X is" is not only not literally thought but not also literally spoken.

16. A content that can be literally spoken of is the content of a judgment. The content of a judgment is information or fact that is intelligible without reference to the speaking of it. A content that is necessarily understood in reference to the speaking of it is in some respect at least symbolically understood and is not information, fact or content of judgment. Beliefs in science alone are formulable as judgments and literally thinkable. If a content is literally thinkable in a judgment, the belief in it as known is actual knowledge. If it is only symbolically thinkable, it is said not to be known but to be only believed as known.

17. Theoretic consciousness was said to be belief in a speakable content involving belief in a content as known. When the content is spoken

symbolically, it may not be believed as known, but is at least understood as pointing to what is believed to be known. In science, the content is spoken literally, and is just the content that is believed to be known and is as such actually known. In philosophy, the content is spoken as at least partially symbolised. The self-subsistent content meant by "object is" where the judgment-form is symbolical is not actually known and demands to be known in absorbed contemplation (or intuited) as simply "object." The real *I* similarly demands to be known not only without the judgment-form, but also without the objective intuitive attitude, i.e. in pure enjoyment. Yet in all these cases something is literally spoken and there is no demand to know the content without the speaking attitude. Truth, however, which is not literally speakable at all demands to be known without even the speaking attitude. The speaking function is the final form of individual subjectivity and even the pure form of spiritual thought implies it. Transcendental consciousness starts by regarding all speaking as only symbolising, and is accordingly conceived as completed when this symbolising speech also is dispensed with. What transcendental consciousness amounts to and whether it remains consciousness at all when it frees itself from speech or individual subjectivity we do not know, for absolute or impersonal consciousness is only conceivable in a negative way. All that can be said is that truth which consciousness starts by symbolising continues to be believed and becomes more and more self-evident as the symbolising accomplishes its purpose.

18. Theoretic consciousness is embodied in science and philosophy. Science alone speaks in genuine judgments, the content of which is fact intelligible without reference to speaking and is alone actually known and literally thought. Philosophy deals with contents that are not literally thinkable and are not actually known, but are believed as demanding to be known without being thought. Such contents are understood as self-subsistent object, real subject and transcendental truth. We have accordingly three grades of philosophy which may be roughly called philosophy of the object, philosophy of the subject and philosophy of truth.

III. Science and Metaphysics

19. The philosophy of the object requires to be further distinguished from science. Both deal with the object understood as what is believed to be known in the objective attitude as distinct from the subjective, enjoying or spiritual attitude. The object in science, however, is understood as fact and not as self-subsistent. By fact is meant what is perceivable or has necessary reference to the perceivable, is speakable in the form of a literal judgment and is believed

without reference to the speaking of it. The self-subsistent is an object that has no necessary reference to the perceivable, is not literally expressible in a judgment and is believed only as it is spoken. A speakable is understood in necessary reference either to sense-perception or to the speaking of it. What is believed and understood in necessary reference to the speaking of it is, however, believed as self-evident or independent of the belief of any individual mind. As understood in the objective attitude, the self-evident is the self-subsistent. Fact in science is not believed as self-subsistent, as what would be even if no one believed it.

20. The self-subsistent object is a concept of philosophy, and it is not only not a concept of science, but may be even denied by science. Science has no interest to formulate the concept of the self-subsistent object; and it apparently believes that the object *must* be knowable or usable. The self-subsistence of the object implies that the object *may be* in its very nature inaccessible to the mind. To contemplate the object as what would be if there were no subject to know it is to believe that it may be unknowable, that in any case it is not known as of right. Science would not only take this suggestion to be gratuitous but would positively deny it. The notion that truth freely reveals itself and is in itself a mystery or even that it is its very nature to reveal itself would be scouted by science as obscurantist or anthropomorphic. To science, there is nothing in the object to make it known; it is just what is known and though it may be unknown, there is no question of its being unknowable.

21. The implicit belief of science then is that the object is knowable and usable *as of right*. This belief is at least questioned in philosophy to which it is an expression of solipsistic self-sufficiency on the part of the subject. In normal practical life, nature is not consciously exploited as a tool but is negotiated in the primitive spirit of sociableness. It is the arrogant exploiting attitude of science towards the object that provokes a self-healing reaction of the spirit in the form of philosophy or some cognate discipline. The spiritual demand is that nature should be contemplated and not merely used or manipulated. Science even as theory is evolved in a practical interest. What is more significant is that its very intellectual method is practical, being the use of actual or ideal *contrivances*. It is the wrong spiritual attitude of science towards the object rather than the so-called contradictions and problems left unsolved in scientific theory—as imagined by the philosopher but never felt by the scientist—that suggests the need for a speculative theory of the object. The concept of the self-subsistent object is the first corrective that philosophy offers of the predatory outlook of the scientific intellect. Realism is a philosophical faith among faiths: the creed of science, if formulated, would be a pragmatist form of solipsistic idealism.

22. The relation between science and the philosophy of the object may be brought out by a reference to certain problems which have been wrongly taken

to be philosophical. There is the problem of piecing together the results of the sciences into a world-view. The synthesis wanted is sometimes imagined to be the generalisation of the primary laws of the sciences into more comprehensive laws. To suppose, however, that it can be accomplished by philosophy without the employment of the distinctive technique and methods of science would be nothing short of a presumptuous folly. If a law as distinct from a loose descriptive concept could be thus established, philosophy might well take in hand the entire work of science. All that can be achieved in this direction is an imaginative description of the world, which would be not only not actual knowledge, but not even a hypothesis that is intended to be turned into knowledge. Nor could it claim the *a priori* certitude of a theory of logic or of metaphysics. Philosophical contents, if not known, are at least theoretically believed, but a world-view of this kind cannot even be claimed to be believed. It can be only an aesthetic view, having at best a suggestive value for science and an illustrative value for philosophy.

23. As an example of such speculation, I may refer to what is called evolutionary philosophy as distinct from the scientific account of evolution. Metaphysics may discuss the general concept of evolution which is but the concept of life and its materialistic, spiritualistic or other interpretations. For this, however, it does not require to piece together the results of science, all the data needed—matter, life and mind—being presented in the knowledge of oneself as in the body. The details and specific generalisations of science are utilised in the so-called philosophy of evolution not as evidence but as only illustrative material intended for visualising the metaphysical theory on the subject. The scientific account of evolution is knowledge or hypothesis, the metaphysic of life in relation to matter and mind is believed, if not known, but the so-called philosophy of evolution, so far as it is different from either, is only an organised presentation of the known or supposed facts of evolution *as though* they constituted the history of a single cosmic life. Cosmic life is not known as a fact, but may still be believed as self-subsisting. The single significant history of this life, however, as rounding off the jagged groupings of facts in science and bridging over the gaps left by it, is only imagined, and is understood to be neither self-evident nor verifiable. The significant story of cosmic evolution then is neither science nor philosophy, but only a species of imaginative literature.

24. There is another problem, viz. the formulation of the postulates or structural concepts of science, which used to be regarded as a philosophical problem. Pure physics, for example, was taken by Kant as a branch of knowable metaphysic established by deduction from the *a priori* principles of synthetic knowledge. There is a similar confusion of thought at the present day in the romantic philosophy that has sprung up round the physico-mathematical

theory of relativity, although here the confusion is of science with philosophy and not of philosophy with science as in the other case. In both the impassable gulf between fact and the self-subsistent is ignored. The so-called axioms of science are but postulates, the formulation of which is the work of science itself. The postulates are hypotheses of a kind which are intended not for the anticipation of facts, but for the organisation of them into a system. They admit of rival hypotheses and may be rejected though not as contradicted by fact, but only as clumsier and less expeditious to work with than the rival hypotheses. Again there is no passage from a postulate of science to a concept of the object in itself. Whether the real world is four-dimensional or is intrinsically indeterminate in its behaviour can never be determined from the basic conceptual devices that happen to organise the facts of science at the present day. The postulates of science neither lead to nor are deducible from any metaphysical conception of the object.

IV. Philosophy of the Object

25. What then has philosophy to say about the object? The objective attitude is understood only in contrast with the subjective or enjoying attitude. What is believed in the objective attitude, viz. the object, need not, however, be understood in reference to the subject. Where the reference to the subject is no part of the meaning of the object, the object is called fact and is dealt with in science. Philosophy deals with the object that is intelligible only in reference to the subject. By subject is meant the individual subject or *I* which is understood in the theoretic consciousness as the speaking function that is symbolised by itself as spoken. The object that has necessary reference to the speaking of it is the self-subsistent object for philosophy.

26. Philosophy formulates and elaborates the concept of the self-subsistent object. What is common to such object and scientific fact is objectivity which is itself no fact, being only the circumstance of being understood in the objective attitude. This is just the form of the object, the self-subsistent form that is elaborated in logic. It is indeed the form of spoken fact, but as it is the form of the self-subsistent object also, it cannot be said to have necessary reference to fact or the perceivable. Logic as the study of this form is thus no science, but a branch of the philosophy of the object. The form is itself a pure object and is also the form of pure object. The pure object of which logic is the form or shadow is the metaphysical object. The two branches of the philosophy of the object then are logic and metaphysics.

27. Logical form or objectivity is not a concept reached by a comparison of the objects or facts of science. The concept of the object is reached in the first

instance by contrast with the subject as the self-evident content of the spiritual consciousness. It is in the theoretic consciousness of the spiritual grade that one is first explicitly conscious of the object as such. In the consciousness of "I am," one appreciates the objective attitude of judgment as distinct from the enjoying attitude and understands it to be assumed only as a necessary make-believe. The consciousness of the asserted being (*am*) or object as such here emerges as the consciousness of a necessary symbol of the subject *I*. That object is symbol of subject implies that object is not subject. The consciousness of negation as such in fact emerges only in this symbolising consciousness. One may be conscious of the object without being explicitly conscious of the subject, but object has no meaning except as the negation and the symbol of the subject. The symbolism here is necessary, and hence when the reference to the subject is only implicit, the object appears as the immediacy of the subject, as implicitly real. Thus object is understood as self-subsistent before fact is understood as object. Hence objectivity or the form of the object is intelligible in reference to the object that is taken to be implicitly real or what is called metaphysical object. Logic in this sense presupposes metaphysics.

28. Metaphysics is philosophy of the object and involves theoretic consciousness in the objective attitude. There is properly speaking no metaphysic of the subject. What passes as such is either the metaphysic of the mind understood as a particular type of object or is no metaphysic but a self-symbolising form of spiritual activity. Metaphysics elaborates the concept of the object in reference to the subject. The rationale of any distinction of metaphysical contents is to be found in an introspectively appreciable distinction within spiritual experience. Even the crude division of the object into matter, life and mind is not intelligible as an inductive classification of fact. That these are *all that is* can at least never be known by induction. The notion of the objective universe is that of an infinite singular and not of a universal; and an *exhaustive* division of such a singular into items that are *all positive* can only be reached if the singular self-evidently unfolds itself in them, if in other words each item means every other item or means the entire system. Such a system is self-evident only as the symbol of an introspective or enjoyed content, as the symbolic analysis of the simple or unitary consciousness of oneself living in the body. The analysis is symbolic because the so-called constituents of the content—matter, life and mind—are intelligible not by themselves but only in reference to this consciousness. Their difference is such as is immediately felt and every apparently factual characterisation of them is understood in reference to this feeling.

29. No metaphysical concept is intelligible without reference to the subject or spirit which itself goes beyond metaphysics. The characteristic abstractions of metaphysics which are supposed on the one hand to be of an "extra

high grade," and on the other to be only diseases of speech are really symbolic meanings which derive their whole value for belief from the spiritual experiences that they symbolise. There are no judgments, accordingly, in metaphysics and, paradoxical as it may sound, the metaphysical beliefs are not reached by inference. The elaborate parade of deductive proof in metaphysics is only a make-believe, unless proof is taken, as it is sometimes taken, as the exposition of an unperceived tautology. Metaphysical reasoning is only the *systematic exposition of symbolic concepts*, concepts that are implicitly taken as symbols of contents that are enjoyingly believed.

30. Fact and the self-subsistent are both literally spoken and in both the believed content is figured by being spoken. Fact is understood as independent of this figuration while the self-subsistent is presented as constituted by it. What is common to these spoken contents is this speech-created form. There are accidental forms of speech, but there are also certain structural forms that are unavoidable in the communication of belief and which are believed to belong to the understood content and not to the speech only. When a fact is spoken, there is a peculiar dualism in the understood content of the meant and the believed, the latter being meant as beyond meaning or as perceivable. When a self-subsistent is spoken, the dualism lapses, the meant and the believed being coincident. The unavoidable forms of speech are constitutive of the meaning. Logic presents a system of speech-created forms of meaning. There may be alternative systems, for logic presupposes metaphysic which presents alternative theories. The fundamental disputes in logic are unavowed metaphysical disputes. Apart from the question of accidental inconsistency within a logical system, whether one logical system is better than another is settled not by logic but by metaphysic. Metaphysical dispute, however, is not settled by logic, for apparently every metaphysical system has its distinctive logic.

31. The suspicion that the subject is not believed in in the same sense as the metaphysical object does not arise within metaphysics. Metaphysics is unaware of the distinction between the self-subsistent and the real. There seems to be nothing wrong, for instance, in the characterisation of matter or mind as real. The distinction is suggested by a contrast of logic with metaphysics. The forms of meaning as discussed in logic are a kind of entity that must be said to be believed in, but it would be absurd to say that they are real. They are believed in as not real and yet not nothing or in other words as self-subsistent. If logical form or objectivity is self-subsistent, has the object of metaphysics any higher status? The distinction of abstract and concrete has meaning only within fact and hence the object cannot mean anything more than objectivity. The metaphysical object is defined, in contrast with fact, as objectivity or self-subsistent meaning. Metaphysic defines itself into logic.

V. Philosophy of the Spirit

32. The suggested distinction of self-subsistence and reality is explicitly verified in the spiritual or enjoying consciousness of objectivity as a symbol of the real subject. As already pointed out, in "I am," *am* meaning self-subsistent being as understood in the objective attitude is the symbol of *I* as understood in the subjective attitude. Enjoying understanding of a content in fact is the consciousness of it as symbolised by an objectively contemplated meaning. Without such a symbolism, the subject would be enjoyed but not enjoyingly understood. It is not only understood like the self-subsistent in necessary reference to the speaking of it: it is understood further as symbolised by its spoken form. This enjoying understanding is what we mean or should mean by introspection. Introspection proper is a form of the theoretic consciousness that implies an abjuration of the objective attitude. Its content is not understood as objective fact nor even as self-subsistent object. The content is not the "interior" of the body which is fact nor is it the "mental" which as unintelligible without reference to the speaking of it is a self-subsistent object. The content is *I* or implies *I*, and although it is spoken as though it were an object, it is understood as what object is not, as the speaking subjectivity.

33. To introspect is actually or ideally to speak in the first person. To speak in the first person may not be to be explicitly conscious of the *I* as what the object is not. When it involves such consciousness, it amounts to introspection. Again introspective speaking may or may not involve the explicit consciousness of *being* what is spoken. When it involves such consciousness, it may be called spiritual introspection. The consciousness of being what is spoken (*I*) is itself a new achievement of the subject, its realisation or deepening of being. All introspection involves such achievement: introspection cannot be like the knowledge of objective fact, which leaves the fact unaffected in being. But there is a form of introspection which *apparently* leaves the content thus unaffected, where really there is an alteration of subjective being which is enjoyed only in the non-theoretic way. This may be taken to be an implicit form of spiritual introspection. Sometimes there is a conscious suspension of theoretic consciousness about such alteration, a deliberate exclusion of it from introspection. In such a case, introspection tends to degenerate into objective consciousness of the mind as distinct from the *I*—what is ordinarily called psychological introspection.

34. The subject *I* is never accepted by itself in spiritual introspection. Something else is always enjoyed along with the subject and enjoyed in reference to it. This may be of three grades. There is in the first place the explicit consciousness of the subject as *unaccountably* embodied, this being the same as the consciousness of the subject as what the object including the mind is

not. Next there is the consciousness of personal relation to other selves. Lastly there is the consciousness of the over-personal self. The over-personal self is enjoyingly understood not only in reference to the subject *I* but as implying the specific experience of communion, the felt form of identity with the *I*. Such enjoying identity is what is called concrete identity or identity-in-difference, a relation that is unintelligible in the objective attitude. Identity in the philosophy of the object is conceived as abstract identity of the form "A is A" and there is no place for the *relation* of identity in the sphere of fact. The consciousness of the over-personal self as thus one with the *I* is the religious form of the spiritual consciousness. The study of all contents enjoyed in explicit reference to the subject *I* may be called the philosophy of the spirit.

35. Spiritual consciousness is not mere consciousness of reality but is reality itself. Except in the specifically religious form of it, however, it involves some consciousness of reality as distinct from what may be called empty subjectivity. In the enjoying consciousness of the self as embodied or symbolised by the object, the object is conceived not as self-subsistent, but only as a shadow or symbol of the *I*, the consciousness of the shadow as such being said to be empty. In the consciousness of personal relations—the moral consciousness, for example—*I* and the other person are each not the other, each the symbol of the other, there being an alternation of symbolisms. The other person is to me "another *I*" which taken literally is a contradiction through which alone, however, he is understood. Or I (first person) am aware of being "this person" (third person) to him, which too is symbolising by a contradiction. Each alternative is real in being but contradictory or empty in meaning or theory. The experience of religious communion or worship is the consciousness of the over-personal reality as symbolised by *I*. The conscious symbolising by *I* is a non-theoretic experience of self-abnegation: it is consciously *being* nought and not consciousness *of I* as nought. What emerges to theoretic religious consciousness is the over-personal reality alone. In this sense the religious consciousness is said to outgrow all empty subjectivity and to be the enjoyed fulness of being.

36. Religious experience as conscious fulness of being is simple and admits of no variation within itself. There is, however, an infinite plurality of unique religious experiences. Their relation is determined by themselves and not by any external reflection. Each experience by its self-deepening gets opposed to or synthesised with other experiences. One experience may enjoy another as a stage outgrown or as in absolute conflict with it, where a third experience may emerge as adjusting them to one another. There is no possibility of systematising them by secular reason and so far as they systematise themselves, they present themselves in many alternative systems. Each experience in fact is a revelation and we believe in a system only so far as

it is actually revealed. Extensive internally coherent systems with indefinite boundaries are actually revealed, though there is no *a priori* necessity of a system and still less of a system admitting of no alternative systems. The Hegelian notion of a single and exclusive gradation of religions would appear from this stand-point to be intrinsically irreligious.

37. The theoretic form of a religious system is a philosophy of religion, there being as many forms of this philosophy as there are religious systems. This form expresses itself in the lower grades of philosophy—in the theory of the sub-religious spirit, in the metaphysic of the object and even in logic. Every system of religious philosophy has its distinctive theory of the spirit, metaphysic and logic. The fundamental differences within logical theory are, as has been suggested, implicitly metaphysical, those in metaphysic are implicitly spiritual and those in the theory of the secular spirit are implicitly religious. Religions may indefinitely multiply and indefinitely get synthesised. So is there indefinite scope for differences and syntheses in philosophical theory in general. There is no question of philosophy progressing towards a single unanimously acceptable solution. All philosophy is systematic symbolism and symbolism necessarily admits of alternatives.

VI. Philosophy of Truth

38. In religion, there can be no theoretic denial of the subject *I*. In worship, indeed, the subject abnegates itself but the abnegation is there an affair of enjoyed being and not of theory. There is, however, a theoretic consciousness of "I am nought," of the possibility at any rate of the subject or the individual self being unreal. The denial of the *I* is possible because we already believe that the absolute is. The absolute is not the same as the over-personal reality that is enjoyed in religion. It means what the subject *I* is not, but the reality of religious experience while it is enjoyed and symbolised by *I* does not mean such theoretic negation of *I*. What is called the absolute is a positively believed entity that is only negatively understood. It is an entity that cannot be understood as it is believed, and is speakable only by way of symbolism. Reality as apprehended in religion is indeed symbolised by *I*, but so far as it is expressed as a self, it is expressed literally. The positive character of the absolute, however, is expressible only by the negation of *I* (or more accurately by "what I am not") and as such is not literally expressible at all. If then we say that the absolute *is*, we mean by *is* not reality but truth. Reality is enjoyed but truth is not. The consciousness of truth as what is believed in but not understood either in the objective or in the subjective attitude, as not literally speakable

at all but speakable only in the purely symbolistic way, is extra-religious or transcendental consciousness.

39. What is believed in and understood as literally unspeakable may be said to be self-revealing. Reality is still literally speakable and may be taken to depend on the speaking for its revelation, though the speaking (which means the *I*) is not there empty subjectivity. Truth is believed or revealed *as* independent of it, as *self*-revealing, what is true being spoken as what the speaking *I* is not. At the same time, to be even symbolically spoken, it has to be believed as a distinct. As a positive to which even the *I* is but a symbol and therefore nought in itself, it has nothing to be distinguished from and is absolute. If, then, truth as absolute is distinguished, it can only be distinguished from itself. The self-distinction of the absolute cannot mean self-identity as it appears in the religious consciousness in which the identity-indifference is conceived to be necessary. There is no necessity in this self-distinction. The absolute may be truth or it may be what truth is not or it may be their mere distinction without any unity in the background, which means their indeterminate togetherness which cannot be denied to be either of them. What truth is not and is yet positive is the absolute freedom beyond being (the absolute freedom of the will) and what is indeterminately either truth or freedom is absolute value. There is no sense in speaking of the absolute as the unity of truth, freedom and value. It is *each* of them, these being only *spoken* separately but not *meant* either as separate or as one. The theoretic consciousness of truth, then, is the consciousness of truth as distinct from itself as freedom and from this identityless self-distinction or value. The absolute as transcending the enjoyed reality of religion is positive being (truth) or positive non-being (freedom) or their positive indetermination (value). The absolute is conceived rigorously as truth in (Advaita) Vedānta. What is loosely called nihilistic Buddhism apparently understands the absolute as freedom. The Hegelian absolute may be taken to represent the indetermination, miscalled *identity*, of truth and freedom which is value. All these views belong to what may be called the transcendental grade of philosophy.

40. This triple absolute is apparently the prototype of the three subjective functions—knowing, willing and feeling. These functions are primarily the self-distinction of the transcendental consciousness. The distinction of the functions does not emerge in the spiritual consciousness. Spiritual experience is simple and integral in its very nature. The consciousness of *I* is not only not the consciousness of a complex unity of these functions, it is not even the consciousness of a unity revealing itself in each of them. It not only does not analyse itself: it supplies no motive for such analysis. The tripartite elaboration of consciousness is not introspective but transcendental. The absolutes reveal themselves and the *I* appears trinal only as their shadow or symbolism.

As the absolutes are not related into a unity, neither can their subjective shadows be said to be related. The simple *I* has no enjoyed elements or aspects to be related. Nor are the so-called functions intelligible as pure acts or interests *of the I*. They cannot be defined in subjective terms nor can they be taken as unique subjective experiences, being not presented as distinct to introspection at all. Their whole meaning is derived from the self-revealed absolutes.

41. The theory of truth is the theory of the other two absolutes also. At the same time it recognises the possibility of elaborating a primary theory of each of them in reference to the other absolutes. We have shadows of these primary theories in the lower grades of philosophy. The theory of truth, for example, as conceived in its explicit transcendental form has its shadow in the theory of knowledge which belongs to the philosophy of the spirit and in the theory of objective categories which is somewhere intermediate between metaphysics and logic in the philosophy of the object.

M. Hiriyanna, "The Problem of Truth" (1930)

Mysore Hiriyanna (1871–1950) is best known as a historian of Indian philosophy. His text *Outlines of Indian Philosophy* (1932) is still a standard text worldwide. He also made important contributions to Vedānta studies and to ethics and aesthetics. Hiriyanna taught for many years at Mysore University. In this essay Hiriyanna addresses the nature of absolute truth, which he regards as the principal human cognitive aim but approaches it through an analysis of empirical truth and the relation of the empirical to the absolute.

5

The Problem of Truth

THE LOGICAL ASPECT of knowledge is now commonly discussed with exclusive reference to the nature of ultimate truth. There is no doubt that this is the question with which epistemology is finally concerned, but it may be asked whether we cannot advantageously begin by having before us a less ambitious aim. Irrespective of the final solution we may arrive at about the nature of truth, there is knowledge which is distinguished as either true or false from the common-sense point of view; and we may start by asking what this distinction means. Our answer to this question may not satisfy the ultimate epistemological test, but we need not occupy ourselves with that consideration from the beginning. "Confusion often results," it has been said, "from proceeding at once to large and complex cases." If we thus restrict the scope of the enquiry, we shall be simplifying the problem to be solved; and its solution, though it may not furnish the complete explanation of the nature of ultimate truth, may be expected to throw considerable light upon it. We propose to adopt this plan of treatment in the sequel.

Let us begin by analysing an act of perception. When a person opens his eyes (say) and sees a table before him, there are, as ordinarily supposed, three elements that can be distinguished in the situation: First, the percipient who sees; secondly the object, viz. the table; and lastly the sense-data or sensa, as they are described—a certain shape, colour, etc., which he associates with the table and regards as its actual characteristics. These sensa he takes as revealing the nature of the table but partly, for, while he may be seeing only its shape and colour, he believes that it has also other qualities like hardness and weight. It may appear that the common man does not distinguish between the last two of the three elements just referred to; the fact, however, is that he only does not attend to the distinction between them particularly but passes over swiftly from the sensa to the object which is what practically interests him. The process has been compared to our overlooking the peculiarities of the print in reading, because it is the meaning of what is printed that interests us.[1] This is the popular notion of the perceptual situation; and it implies belief in (1) the presence of the self, (2) the givenness and the direct apprehension of

1. *Mind* (1921), p. 389.

the object and (3) the partial revelation of its character by the sensa, which are likewise given and directly known. Of these, the ultimate nature of the self or the knowing subject is not relevant to our present purpose. It is a problem for metaphysics. All that we have to remember is that it is a factor which enters into the cognitive situation. The same observation holds true in the case of the final nature of the object also. The points that chiefly matter for us now are the nature of sense-data, their relation to the object and the manner in which they both, viz. the sense-data and the object, come to be known.

I

According to the above analysis, the sensa are actual features or "literal aspects" of objects; and they both are directly apprehended by the self. We should now ask to what extent this analysis stands the test of reflection. If it be correct, it should apply to all perceptual knowledge; but it seems that, though it may be right as an analysis of perception that is true, it does not apply to illusion and error[2] where we apprehend an object or some aspect of it which is not there. Without prejudging the question, however, we shall try to find out whether errors can be at all explained by assuming that even they do not involve a reference to anything that is not actually given. Such a view was maintained not only in respect of perception but also all knowledge (excepting only memory) by certain thinkers in ancient India,[3] and it will serve as a convenient starting-point for our enquiry. The illustrations usually given in explaining their theory are those of a white crystal which is mistaken for red when placed by the side of a red flower, and of a conch which is seen yellow by a jaundiced person. We shall select the latter for consideration, but with a slight alteration. We shall suppose that the conch is seen through a sheet of yellow glass instead of by the jaundiced eye, and that the fact of the existence of the glass is for some reason or other lost sight of. Here we have, according to this theory, the perception of the conch *minus* its true colour, viz. white, and the sensation of the yellowness alone of the glass. They are two acts of knowing, but they quickly succeed each other; and we therefore miss the fact that they are two. Each of them is valid so far as it goes, for neither the yellowness nor the conch as such is negated afterwards when we discover the error. But we overlook at first that they stand apart; and it is only this deficiency in our

2. We shall, in what follows, overlook the distinction between errors of perception and illusions, as the only difference between them is that while the judgment is explicit in the former, it is implicit in the latter. Illusions have been described as "errors in the germ."

3. Prābhākaras.

knowledge that is made good later when we find out our mistake. Thus discovery of error only means a further step in advancing knowledge. It confirms the previous knowledge and does not cancel any part of it as false, so that to talk of "rectification" with reference to error is a misnomer. In admitting that error is incomplete knowledge which needs to be supplemented, the theory grants that ignorance is involved in it; but the ignorance, it maintains, is purely of a negative character and does not import into erroneous knowledge any element which is positively wrong. In other words, it holds that the mind may fail to apprehend one or more aspects of what is presented, but that it never *mis*apprehends it and that all errors are therefore only errors of omission.

There is no need, on this view, to verify any knowledge. All knowledge is true in the sense that no portion of what it reveals is contradicted afterwards; and to question whether it agrees with reality in any particular instance is therefore to question its very nature. But truth being commonly distinguished from error, it is necessary to give some explanation of the distinction. The so-called error may be partial knowledge; but we cannot characterise it as such, for human knowledge is always partial in one sense or another. So another explanation is given, and it is indirect. Though all knowledge is alike incomplete, error is more so than truth. It is *relatively* incomplete, and its relative incompleteness is determined by reference to an extrinsic standard, viz. a pragmatic one. All knowledge, according to this school, leads to action; and the success or failure of the activity prompted by any particular knowledge is regarded as constituting its truth or error. In other words, that knowledge is true which works; and that which does not, is erroneous. Though this school upholds a pragmatic view of truth, it should be noticed that it is essentially unlike modern Pragmatism. Epistemologically speaking, the latter amounts to a sceptical attitude, for it teaches that absolute truth in any matter is unattainable because it does not exist. Every truth is provisional—true only so long as it furthers human purposes. But here knowledge is admitted to have a logical, apart from a practical or guiding, value. Though it may be false on its purposive side, it is theoretically quite true and never fails to agree with the outside reality which it reveals. If we still speak of knowledge as sometimes false, we mean that it is not useful—thus transferring to it a feature which is significant only in reference to the practical consequences that follow from it. All knowledge in itself being thus regarded here as true, we may say that while current Pragmatism denies truth in the sense in which it is ordinarily understood, the present theory denies error.

This theory merits commendation for its simplicity as well as for its complete consistency in explaining the logical character of knowledge. It may be said to represent the extreme form of realism, for it not only upholds that external objects are independent of the knowing mind and are directly apprehended; it even denies error. But it is far from convincing. The indirect manner, for instance, in which it explains the familiar terms "true" and "false" is hardly satisfactory. But even waiving this consideration, it must be said that a purely negative explanation cannot account for error which, as a judgment, presents the two elements in it as synthesised though they may be actually unrelated. Its distinction from "doubt," which lacks such synthesis as shown by its alternative suppositions, and is not a judgment but a suspension of it, points to the same fact. In our illustration, the knowledge of the conch cannot accordingly be assumed to arise separately from that of yellowness; there is only a single psychical process, and the resulting knowledge includes a reference to a positive element which is false. Error is therefore misapprehension and not mere lack of apprehension. Such a view, we may add, is implied even in the explanation given by the school of thinkers mentioned above. It will be remembered that, according to that explanation, discovery of error means only an advance from less complete to more complete knowledge. But there may be incomplete knowledge which we do or do not know to be so at the time; and it is only the latter that can be regarded as an error, for surely nobody that *knows* that his knowledge is incomplete can be said to make a mistake when that knowledge, so far as it goes, is admitted to be right. It will be wrong only when there is an implicit, if not an explicit, identification of it with truth or adequate knowledge. That is, if our knowledge is to be viewed as erroneous, it is not enough for us to be merely unaware of one or more aspects of the presented object; we should also take the knowledge as complete or adequate. And in so far as what is incomplete is taken for the complete or the less adequate for the more adequate, there is misapprehension. Thus the mind may not only misapprehend presented objects, but it invariably does so in error; and all errors are, therefore, errors of commission. Errors of *mere* omission in the sphere of knowledge are strictly not errors at all. There is, however, this much of truth in the previous view when it insists on the validity of all knowledge, that, so far as its perceptual form at least is concerned (to which we are now confining our attention), it always points to some reality or other, and that there can, therefore, be no complete error. That is, though a part of the content of knowledge may be false, the whole of it can never be so.

The outcome of the above reasoning is that there is always in error some element which needs to be recanted later, although it may be only the element of relation as in the above example; and, so far, the contention that no portion of what knowledge reveals is ever negated afterwards has to be given up. Before we enquire into the precise status of this element, it will be desirable to consider another type of error. We have hitherto spoken of errors in which, even after they are detected, the two elements involved, taken separately—or, to state the same in a different manner, the subject and the predicate of the propositions expressing the corresponding judgments—continue to be presented as before. Even the false localisation of the predicate ("yellow") persists, though it no longer misleads the person who has seen through the error. But there are other instances in which the predicate is contradicted—and necessarily the relation also along with it—the moment the error is discovered. This happens, for example, when we find out that we mistook a block of crystal for ice on seeing at some distance a certain shape and colour which are common to both.[4] The difference between the two cases is that in the one the predicative element ("yellow") is actually within the field of visual sensation, while in the other it ("ice") is not so. What we come to know as false in the latter case, when we fail to find that the given object is neither cool nor moist (say) as we expected, is not, therefore, merely the element of relation but also the predicate. Our perception of "ice" here, as if it were bodily present, when it does not form part of the given situation needs a satisfactory explanation. All that we know for certain is that there is *something* given, and that the sensa actually apprehended—a certain shape and colour as we have assumed—are of that something,[5] and not of the object to which they seem to pertain. Two explanations of this "presence in absence" are possible:

(1) It may be argued that the object in question, though not present in the given situation, is still to be reckoned as a physical existent because it is found elsewhere and should have been actually experienced at some other time. While the force of this argument may be admitted so far as it means that only things resembling those experienced before can be seen in such errors, it has to be observed that the question here is not merely about the *being* of the object but also about its presence at a particular place and at a particular time. In error, it is experienced as here and now; and the experience in this determinate form is contradicted later. The reality of the object *in itself* may be conceded, but it has no bearing upon this fact; and the contradiction, therefore, remains wholly unexplained by it. It may be said that what is meant by the above contention is not that the object is merely external and real but also that it somehow comes to be actually presented, though remote in time and place.[6] That would be to credit

4. The Prābhākara school, mentioned above, explained this class of errors also on the same principle, the two consecutive mental acts here being the perception of the subject and the recollection of the predicate.

5. This statement requires modification as, for example, in the case of the moon which looks vastly smaller than it actually is. But it will be better to postpone the consideration of this point for the present.

6. As is maintained, for example, in the Indian Nyāya-Vaiśeṣika system and, in a somewhat different form, by Professor Alexander (see *Space, Time and Deity*, vol. ii, p. 254).

physical objects with what has been described as "a somewhat surprising mobility." But even granting the supposition, there is the difficulty of explaining how, if the object be given, its givenness comes to be negated later. The other element, for instance, in the error, viz. the one represented by the subject ("this")[7] in the judgment—"This is ice"—is also given; but it is not contradicted later. Its presence, on the other hand, at the place where it appears is reaffirmed when we replace the wrong judgment by the correct one—"*This* is a crystal." The distinction in the way in which the correcting judgment affects the two elements indicates that, although what is predicated may be taken as out there, it cannot be regarded as real *in the same sense* in which the subject is. The fact is that those who give such explanations confound likeness with identity. They forget that, while the erroneous object may be similar to what has once been experienced, it need not be the same. They are right in urging that knowledge is self-transcendent and always implies a content that is known—something beyond or other than itself, and that error forms no exception to this rule. But if the reasoning should be free from all prepossession, the only conclusion we can draw from it is that that content here is a mere presentation, and not that it is also physically real.

(2) If the erroneous content is merely a presentation and not a physical reality, it may be thought that it is either a memory-image or an ideal construction. But this conclusion again clashes with experience. If it were a memory-image, it would involve a reference to past time and to a distant place, and would not, therefore, be apprehended as immediately given. In other words, if the presentation were an ideal revival, one would realise it as such at the time. There being no such realisation here, it cannot be explained as a memory-image. It is not denied, we should add, that the false "ice" would not have been presented at all, had not real ice been experienced before. The mental disposition left behind by past experience is, indeed, an indispensable condition of the occurrence of such errors; but it only helps to determine the nature of the presentation, and does not, for the reason just stated, make it a memory-image. A similar kind of reasoning applies to the second alternative of an ideal construction. The "ice" in that case would be experienced as related to the future, or it would appear without any special reference to time at all. In either case, the apprehension of it as a *present* existence would be inexplicable. The mental attitude, besides, would then be one of supposal and not of belief, as it is here.

---

7. As we have already seen, the "this" in such cases signifies not merely present time and proximate place, but also some sensa like shape and colour.

The considerations which singly or in combination prevent us from accepting the above explanations in regard to the status of the object in error are its felt immediacy, its determinate position in the objective sphere, and its later sublation. Both the explanations possible being thus ruled out, we are obliged to regard it as a presentation which is quite unique. Its uniqueness consists in this, viz. that its nature cannot be fully expressed in terms known to logic or to psychology. A necessary condition of its emergence is that a real object should be apprehended, but only in its general aspects, and that the percipient, while being ignorant of its specific features, should be unaware of his ignorance. A sense of ignorance would perforce prevent the occurrence of error. In the case of "doubt," for instance, only the general features of the object presented are grasped; and yet there is no error, for one is *conscious* at the time that one does not know its distinctive features, as is clear from the wavering of the mind between two alternative possibilities. It is this dependence of the wrong object for its appearance upon a defect characterising an individual percipient[8] that explains why it is private to him and is not public or open to the view of others. Similarly, it is the position in the outside world of the thing mistaken, or the source from which the sensory stimulus comes, that determines the position of the wrong presentation there. The "ice" appears where the crystal is; and a change in the location of the thing mistaken would, other conditions remaining the same, result in a corresponding change in the external location of the wrong object. Ignorance, however, is not by itself sufficient to account for error; and it is always found associated in producing it with some fortuitous circumstance or other like the flash of similarity between the given thing and another. But it is difficult to detail these circumstances, for they vary so much from one instance to another. We can only characterise them generally by saying that, in the matter of giving rise to error, they are altogether subsidiary to ignorance and that their nature is such that the removal of the latter simultaneously renders them inoperative. Thus in the present case, the resemblance between the crystal and the ice is a necessary factor in producing the error; but the removal of ignorance, which means a knowledge of the specific features of the crystal, at once makes it ineffective. The resemblance, of course, continues thereafter, and may remind one of real ice; but it cannot aid the false presentation of it as before. It means that ignorance, as characterised above, is what sustains error; and we shall refer to it alone hereafter, disregarding additional causes like the one just mentioned.

Thus in all errors of the kind we are now considering, the subject ("this") and some of the sensa that characterise it are actually given; but the predicate

8. Ignorance also might be general or common to all; but the resulting misapprehension would not, in that case, be ordinarily recognised as an error by any one.

("ice") and the relation between it and the subject are unique presentations. The content of erroneous knowledge is, therefore, a medley of the true and the false. According to the principle on which we have explained the wrong presentation here, the element of relation in the case of the "yellow conch" also should be reckoned as unique. It is experienced immediately and as actually obtaining between two external objects; it is also later discovered to be false. Thus in both classes of error there is complete correspondence between knowledge and content. This does not imply the acceptance of the view that knowing involves a psychic medium which is *like* its object. Knowledge, on the other hand, reveals reality directly; and by its correspondence with content, we here mean that no part of what it reveals is ever sheer non-being. There may be disparity in the nature of the elements included within its content, for, while some of them are real, others may be unique in the sense explained above. But the latter, though not physically real, are felt as confronting the mind and cannot therefore be absolute nothing. There is resemblance between the two kinds of error[9] in other respects also. Both are forms of misapprehension traceable to ignorance of the actual character of the given objects, and both are private to the erring observer. To an important difference which they exhibit, we have already had occasion to allude. In the case of the crystal mistaken for "ice," the discovery of error or the knowledge that the given reality is not ice, means the total disappearance of the wrong presentation.[10] The presentation is due to ignorance and the removal of the cause removes the effect. But in the other case, the knowledge that the conch is not yellow has no such effect, and the relation *appears* to persist even after it is contradicted. This appearance should consequently be traced to a circumstance other than ignorance which is the source of the error, viz. a particular disposition of the conch and the yellow glass relative to the point of space occupied by the observer. It is a conclusion which is corroborated by the fact that the apparent relation vanishes as soon as the disposition of the objects in question is changed.

II

True knowledge, by contrast, is that whose content is free from such unique presentations. Here also we may, and ordinarily do, go beyond the given as in error; but, on account of the apprehension of the sensa constituting the

---

9. Other forms of error, like dreams and hallucinations, fall under one or other of these two; or they partake of the character of both.

10. The "ice" may appear there again, but it only shows that a man may fall twice into the same error.

specific features of the object presented and not its general ones only, our knowledge does not become erroneous. Since sensa, according to what we have stated, are the very basis of our knowledge of the external world, they should be regarded as directly known; and it seems to follow from this that the object, of which they are the actual aspects, is also known directly. But this latter point cannot be properly argued without reference to the question of the ultimate nature of objects, which we are not considering here.

According to the description just given, knowledge is true when no part of its content has to be discarded as false. That is, it does not come in conflict with the rest of our experience, but harmonises with it.[11] This signifies that it is coherence with other experience, and not correspondence with reality, that makes it true. The rejection of the correspondence hypothesis does not mean the denial of the self-transcendent character of knowledge. It only means that since *all* knowledge, as we have pointed out, equally satisfies the condition of agreement with an objective counterpart, correspondence cannot be regarded as a distinguishing feature of truth. The conclusion that truth is coherence may be reached somewhat differently by considering the manner in which error comes to be known. Error, as we have seen, is a judgment that is self-discrepant; but its self-discrepancy remains unknown until it is revealed by another judgment which contradicts it. Now while one judgment may confirm or supplement another, it is difficult to see how it can correct or annul it, for there is no reason to prefer either of them to the other. The only circumstance in which it may do so is when it forms part of a body of knowledge which, as a whole, is, for some reason or other, regarded as well established. That is, a judgment can correct another or claim to be true, not by itself, but as belonging to or as implicated in a system of judgments. Since without the evidence of such a system, no one can know reality from unique presentations, we may say that error also, like a judgment which is true, becomes intelligible only in connection with a body of coherent knowledge which is taken as the standard of reference. The standard is ordinarily furnished in the case of each individual by the totality of his experience. When, however, any doubt arises and the individual's experience, even at its widest, is inadequate for settling it, an appeal to the experience of others becomes necessary. It is this collective experience or the commonsense of mankind that, in the end, serves as the standard. That knowledge is true which fits into it perfectly; and that which does not, is false. Herein consists the social or general character of truth, as distinguished from error. We share truth with others; and it is

11. Old truths may need to be modified in the light of new experience. But we are not taking such details into consideration here.

therefore public, while error is private. The elements constituting the content of a true judgment are mutually compatible, since all of them are alike public. Error differs from truth in this respect, for it involves a reference not only to an object of common experience but also to unique presentations which are private and are not therefore endorsed by that experience.

We have so far assumed that all sensa correctly reveal the character of the object given, if only partially, and are never false. But it does not seem to be always so, for we know from experience that the precise form in which they appear depends, for instance, upon the point of space occupied by the percipient with reference to the object in question. It shows that sensa are not only partial in their bearing upon the nature of the object given, but that they may also vary though the object remains the same. A coin, for example, presents a round or an oval shape according to the position from which it is viewed. Similarly, a change in the position of an object may affect the sensa. A ship, which is seen as but a speck on the horizon, seems to increase in size as it approaches the shore, although there may be no change in the standpoint of the observer or in the objective situation as a whole. It may therefore appear that sensa also, like objects and relations, may be false. These altered sensa, it should be admitted, are not verifiable. A coin, to take one of our examples, cannot be both oval and round. But yet such appearances are not to be regarded as false; for, unlike erroneous presentations, they can be deduced from the actual sensa according to well-known physical laws. These secondary or derivative phenomena, as we may call them, may not literally qualify the object; but, owing to the fact that their altered form is determined by strict laws, they indicate correctly, though only indirectly, the nature of the object to which they refer. It is in this indirect, and not in a literal, sense that we characterise the data in such cases as true. The fact is that they are the result solely of the physical conditions under which normal human perception takes place, and do not in any manner depend upon the idiosyncrasies of the percipient mind to make them erroneous. Hence we should place these presentations on a footing which is quite different from those in error. Seeing a tree stump, which is at a distance, to be smaller than it actually is, is very much different from taking it to be something else (say), a human being. Besides, these phenomena do not commonly deceive us like erroneous presentations. A ship is not understood to undergo actual increase of bulk as it approaches the shore from a point on the horizon. All of them, no doubt, contain the seeds of error, and may therefore prove deceptive. A child may believe that the moon is really only as small as it appears, or that railway tracks actually converge towards a point in the distance. But then the essential condition of error, viz. ignorance of the true character of the objects in question, is also present; and its removal, though it shows the beliefs to be erroneous, does not lead to the removal of the presentations. In other words, they disappear as errors but persist as appearances of the real. These appearances may not, in themselves, be real; yet they are not false in the sense in which erroneous presentations, like the "ice" in our former example, are. For the same reason, the *apparent* relation also, noticed before in connection with errors of the first type like the "yellow conch," is not to be regarded as false.

We may designate these secondary phenomena as "perspectives of the real" or, briefly, "perspectives."[12] The distinction between them and erroneous presentations, as already indicated, is that the latter are rooted in ignorance which is a defect of the knowing subject, while the former are purely the result of certain physical conditions under which an object happens to be apprehended. The term "perspective," no doubt, implies relation to the standpoint of a particular observer; and, so far, the presentations are personal. The point here, however, is not that the phenomena in question are unrelated to the individual, but that they are in no way due to his oddities. In this latter respect, they are like sensa proper; but, unlike them, they do not directly belong to the objects to which they seem to belong. Hence in determining the true character of any perceived object or objects from such phenomena, we should apply a suitable correction taking into account the nature of the physical context in which they appear. In simple cases we make such corrections ourselves, as, for instance, when we see a coin as oval but interpret it as circular; in more intricate ones, however, the aid of science is necessary as in ascertaining the true magnitude of the moon from its apparent size. The truths so determined are impersonal because they reveal objects as they are in themselves, not as they appear, and are therefore independent of the point of view of the person or persons asserting them. While a part of empirical knowledge may be impersonal, the whole of science is so, for the one aim of the scientist is to find out the actual features or normal aspects of things. The extent to which this difference affects the correctness of common knowledge, where the phenomena concerned are of a complicated nature, may be very great; and what are only "perspectives" and, as such, are not literally true, may often be mistaken by us for sensa or actual features of the external world. Hence empirical knowledge, as a whole, stands far lower, in point of accuracy, than the scientific. Its primary function is to subserve the purposes of everyday life, and it does not therefore ordinarily aim at greater accuracy than is needed for their fulfilment. Its value lies in its practical utility, not in its theo-

---

12. This term, which is used by more than one modern philosopher (e.g. Professor Alexander), is intended here to stand, though not in every detail, for the phenomena underlying what is described as *sopādhikabhrama* in the philosophy of Śaṅkara.

retical certainty; and the saying that "thought is the slave of life" is therefore essentially true here.

III

The conclusion thus far reached is that the common-sense analysis of knowledge, with which we started, requires to be modified in two important respects. There are some instances, viz. "perspectives" which only indirectly disclose the character of external objects; and there are others, viz. errors which, while they may reveal reality, also include presentations that are not genuine parts or aspects of it at all. Objects and relations may thus be erroneously presented, but never sensa. It may seem that, if proper allowance be made for these two kinds of discrepancies, the system of common knowledge, taken as a whole, will give us the final or absolute truth sought after in epistemology; but it does not, because it has other limitations. In the first place, it obviously refers only to a small portion of the whole of reality, and is therefore fragmentary. In the second place, it leaves out even from this portion a great deal as not relevant to the carrying out of common human purposes which is its pre-eminent function. Scientific knowledge is without this latter limitation, since it aims at expounding phenomena in terms of the non-human; but even that cannot be regarded as giving us the final epistemological solution, for it also is selective, though in a different way. No science treats of the whole of reality, but each is concerned only with particular aspects of it; and, since it studies these aspects apart from their concrete accompaniments, it may be said to deal more with abstractions than with reality. Moreover science, in spite of the indefinite expansion possible for it, will never arrive at an exhaustive knowledge of reality because its selective method will always leave for it a field which is still to be explored. Although the view of truth formulated above cannot therefore be regarded as final, it will yield the solution which epistemology seeks when its implications are fully worked out. We shall now point out how it does so; but, within the limits of this paper, we can do so only very briefly.

The possibility of its furnishing the final solution is contained in the conception of knowledge as a system, and of truth as coherence with it. A strict adherence to this view may seem to lead one to the conclusion that truth is relative. For there may be two or more coherent systems of knowledge which are at variance with one another, and what is true from one standpoint may not be so from another. All our so-called truths may thus turn out to be equally false relatively, not excluding the results of scientific investigation. We have explained the common notions of truth and error, it will be remembered, by reference to the body of knowledge that bears the stamp of social sanction. But it is really only one of the standards by which truth may be distinguished from error; and we should take into account the possibility of there being also other types or systems of knowledge, relatively to each of which a similar distinction can be made. These systems may be many; and every one of them, according to the view taken of knowledge here, corresponds to a self-consistent whole of objective existence—the sphere of reference, which is common to all the judgments making up that system. Hence it is not only the world in the ordinary sense that exists; there may be others also, so long as they are systematic or are wholes constituted of inter-related parts, making it possible to distinguish the true from the false in statements relating to them. The world of Shakespeare's *Othello*, for example, is such a system, since it admits of right as well as wrong statements being made about it. It would be false, for instance, to represent Desdemona in it as in love with Cassio. As a consequence of such an enlarged view of objective existence, there will be not one type of truth only, but several—each order of existence, constituting the basis for a distinct type of it. "Our beds are not stained," it has been said, "by the wounds of dream scimitars"; but our dream beds may well be.

It may, on such considerations, be held that there is no absolute truth at all and that we may regard any truth as relatively false, if we choose to do so. But it appears that the very notion of *relative* truth suggests the recognition of an absolute standard by which all knowledge is judged; and we have to accept such a standard, giving up "relativist epistemology," if we are to avoid universal scepticism. Only it is necessary to further define truth, if it should be absolute. This can be done by bringing in the idea of comprehensiveness, when the systematic coherence which is our definition of truth will be perfect. The fulfilment of this new condition means the possibility of conceiving absolute truth as the expansion or development of one of the above truths such that it will, in some sense or other, include within its sphere of reference the whole of existence—not merely objective worlds but also conscious subjects. To leave out any portion of it would be to admit two or more truths, none of which, on account of their mutual exclusion, can be taken as absolute. But it may appear that there is no means of determining which of the relative truths is to be elevated to this rank. If, however, the sceptical position is to be avoided, a choice has to be made; and there is every consideration, short of logical certitude, to recommend common truth for the purpose. We may now divide all the subsidiary truths into two groups—one consisting of those that relate to the everyday world, though they may not all refer necessarily to the same aspects of it; and the other consisting of the rest which relate to the world of fiction or even to the region of dreams and illusions, so far as they are self-consistent. Of these, the former may be viewed as lying on the way to absolute truth; and since they may approximate to it more or less, we may speak of them as representing degrees of truth, a higher degree of it meaning greater completeness in the view it gives of reality. The truth of science as well as that of empirical life is of this kind. They mark relatively higher and lower stages on the path leading to ultimate truth. All such truths are integrated in the absolute one which is self-complete. The others cannot thus be integrated, owing to the divergence in their objective reference. But when we remember that, whether they refer to ideal constructions or to unique presentations, they are dependent for their subject-matter upon the reality which forms the content of the first group of truths, we find that they have their ultimate explanation, through them, in the absolute truth, even though they cannot be said to actually endure in it. They may be described as lower kinds of truth to distinguish them from the degrees of it already referred to. These two groups or classes of truth correspond to two orders of existence, one less real than the other. The world of morals implied by ethical truth, for example, belongs to the common order of existence, because of its direct bearing on actual life. But the world of art, though the truth at which it finally aims may be the very highest, stands lower than that. This is evident, for instance, from the fact that, as observed by A. C. Bradley,[13] "we dismiss the agony of Lear in a moment if the kitten goes and burns his nose."[14]

It is this absolute truth that is the goal of epistemology; and it yields a unified view of the whole of reality. All the elements of the universe—whether they be knowable objects or knowing subjects—appear in it as internally related; and each of them reveals itself there as occupying the place that rightly belongs to it within the whole. That is, the ultimate truth is entirely impersonal. Further, these elements are seen in it not merely as they are at any particular moment, but in the perspective of their entire history—as what they were in the past and as what they will be in the future. Or rather there can be no distinctions of time in it—"no future rushing to the past," but one eternal now. A temporal world when viewed in its wholeness, it has been remarked, must be an eternal one. In this concreteness and completeness it differs from scientific truth, though impersonal like it. It also differs from truth as commonly understood by us which is neither comprehensive nor wholly impersonal. There is one important point to which it is necessary to draw attention before we conclude. If the absolute truth should really comprehend all, it cannot exclude the self of the person that contemplates it. It will not therefore do if he stands apart, regarding himself as a mere knower and

13. *The Uses of Poetry*, p. 12

14. This preference, however, implies that we realise at the time the relative status of the two realities. There is such realisation generally in the case of art, but not in illusions.

therefore distinct from what it points to. He should, on the other hand, view himself as inseparably one with it. The subject and the object would still be distinguished in his view, but there would not be that opposition or disaccord which we commonly feel between them. It means a profound transformation in the ordinary conception of the knowing self and of the objects known. Here naturally arises the question of the precise nature of the transformation in each case; but, as our present concern is with truth rather than with reality, we shall not attempt to discuss the possible answers to it. We shall only make one observation: though we left undetermined at the start the ultimate character of the self and of the object, we assumed that they were distinct. This initial dualism has to be abandoned now, for, according to the final conception of truth at which we have arrived, the knower and the known, though distinguishable, are not separable. Knowledge begins by assuming that they are different, but it culminates in the discovery of a latent harmony between them in which the difference is resolved. It is not merely the notions of the subject and object that are thus transmuted; the knowledge also which relates them must be of a higher order than any we are familiar with—whether perceptual or conceptual. But this higher experience, which may be described as insight or intuition, is not altogether alien to us, for we get a glimpse of it whenever for any reason we rise above the distractions of personal living. Only it is too faint and fitful to enable us to understand what the exact character of the experience will be when the absolute truth is realised. All that we can say is that for one who attains to such experience, through a proper development of this intuitive power, there will be nothing that is not immediately known and that no part of what is so known will appear as external. What the means of developing intuition are, and whether the ideal of absolute truth can be completely realised, are questions whose consideration lies outside the scope of the present paper.

G. R. Malkani, "Philosophical Truth" (1949)

G. R. Malkani (1892–1977) was longtime director of the Indian Institute of Philosophy at Amalner and was editor of the *Philosophical Quarterly*. He was influential both in his role as a convenor of all-India philosophical conferences at Amalner and in his role as editor of the then premier Indian philosophical journal. Malkani studied at the University of Bombay and began his career at Almaner. He was a noted Vedānta scholar who drew on Hegelian insights to expound and to defend Advaita. We present here a metaphilosophical essay in which Malkani identifies the nature of philosophical questions and the role of philosophy vis á vis science, religion, and human affairs.

Ghanshamdas Ratanmal Malkani

6

Philosophical Truth

I

1. *Introductory*: I do not know whether I should be thankful to the Executive Committee for the honour they have done to me. I know my limitations; and if the post of the General President were merely a post of honour, I would have thankfully refused it. But I associate with it something more than honour. It carries a certain responsibility,—to serve the cause of philosophy in India. As I happen to have something of the missionary spirit for philosophy in me, I could not well refuse the call to make my contribution to those ends which I so strongly cherish.

2. *Too many technicalities and logical subtleties unnecessary*: I am one of those who believe that philosophy should be freed from unnecessary technicalities, and made intelligible to all those intelligent lay persons who have not made of philosophy their profession. It should cease to become a purely academic affair, and descend into the life of the people. It is only then that it can regain something of the popularity which it has naturally lost in recent years. I often believe that too many technicalities conceal a fundamental lack of clarity and depth in thought. When we cannot find our way to the solution of vital problems, we revel in the pleasant game of coining new words, new phrases and new names, and we clothe our thought in these to conceal our failure and our ignorance. There is enough scope in the ordinary language of an intelligent person to express the very highest and the best ever conceived by man in his philosophical adventure. Simplicity here, as perhaps nowhere else, is of the essence of truth. Abstruseness in philosophy is a sin. A philosopher also need not be very learned. What is required of him is only a certain earnestness of mind and a capacity for thought. He must be able to formulate an intelligent question, and bent upon finding a perfect answer to it which will completely resolve it. The ideals of scholarship are different from the ideals of philosophic truth. Similarly, logical subtleties are one thing and truth another. It is a pity that some of the best read philosophical writings both in the East and

---

Address of the General President to the Indian Philosophical Congress, XXIV Session, Patna, 1949.

> in the West are loaded with unnecessary logical subtleties, which have a very remote relation to the truth, and which make the study of philosophy an arduous and uninteresting job. Philosophical questions have, in my opinion, quite a romantic and personal touch of their own. They belong to a realm of thought which lies nearest to the highest ideals of life. The pursuit of their solutions can certainly be made more interesting than the pursuit of the solution of questions connected with the neutral realm of nature that serves only our physical needs.
>
> 3. *Is Indian philosophy stagnant?*: Most men think that Indian philosophy is stagnant and unprogressive. Our greatest philosophers lived and did their work in the distant past. Their tradition has not been kept alive. The flame has died down and is only dimly visible. There are no men of equal stature in the India of today who can keep alive the Indian tradition through fresh contributions in line with present-day needs and intellectual demands. I agree with this view only to a limited extent. I agree that the best among us are neither here nor there in the field of philosophic creativeness. I do not agree that we have lost touch with the ancient masters, or that we necessarily need to progress beyond them. To a large extent, we have been creatures of circumstances. It was part of our political subjection that our intellectual and cultural ideals should undergo a change. We were overcome by the flood of the many-sided intellectual activities of the Western countries. Perhaps it was all to the good. We have certainly the feeling of being intellectually more enlightened than our forefathers. But intellectual enlightenment is not the whole of life. What is more important are the ideals which inspire the intellect. It is these ideals that have undergone change to our detriment.

The philosophy of ancient India was tied to religion. It was part of religion, and a necessary part. There was no great religion which sprang from the native soil, that did not tackle some of the more important philosophical problems. It tended to be more philosophical, and less dogmatic. It emphasised right knowledge as an integral part of religion. Philosophy was not a mere intellectual game of concepts to be pursued for its own sake. It justified itself in a certain type of life. It started with faith, but aimed at knowledge, or at least intellectual confirmation. It had a definite purpose, namely to educate and to instruct thought for the higher life of the spirit. It was like the back-stroke of the forward movement of religion.

It is different with modern European thought. It draws its inspiration from science. There is quite a natural alliance between the two, and only an artificial bond between philosophical thought and religion. The result is that science has infected our philosophy. The ideals of philosophic truth are supposed to be unattainable like the ideals of science. Science, with its method of hypothetisation, can only reach probable and practical truth, never absolute truth. This can be condoned in science. It cannot be condoned in philosophy. *The very problems of philosophy are problems that are not capable of a solution that is only probably true.* Philosophy seeks truth that is true literally and absolutely. It is this or it is nothing.

It is conceivable that different philosophers have different conceptions as to what is absolute truth. They may all be wrong. But they have a right conception as to the sort of truth that philosophy ought to seek. To maintain otherwise is to degrade philosophy to the level of one of the sciences, without the advantages which a natural science enjoys. A natural science is checked by facts, its theories can be tested and verified, and its truths serve the purposes of life insofar as they give us control over nature and facilitate the handling of natural forces. Scientific truth, hypothetical though it may be, has a biological value. Philosophy has no biological value. It has, in fact, a negative value in this sphere. It often makes us unpractical and vacillating in action,—a laughing-stock of our fellow-men. If it has any value, it is to serve the ends of spirit,—to remove ultimate doubts, and to make life at a higher level possible, more harmonious, more self-contained and more enlightened. But if doubts remain and we are not quite sure of the truth, this purpose cannot be served. The removal of doubt, even through erroneous reasoning, will serve the purpose, so long as the error in reasoning is not detected. It may be *bad* philosophy. But, it *is* philosophy. A philosophy that vacillates between alternative views, or that regards Ultimate Truth as unattainable, is no philosophy at all. It is merely a sort of intellectual pedantry, having no practical value for life. The progress of philosophy is from one absolutism to another absolutism. In between we philosophise, but we have no philosophy yet.

Some learned people, impressed, or perhaps depressed, by the conflicting opinions of philosophers, think that philosophising itself has a value greater than that of any fixed system of thought. Philosophising, they say, gives us a balanced view of things. There is no need to have ultimate convictions, which are invariably short-lived and dogmatic in character. To be open-minded, to be always weighing and evaluating issues, to be ready to retract from a position and equally ready to advance to another,—this appears to them to be the very essence of the life of reason. But it is reason, in our opinion, that does not know its philosophical business. Reason is only an instrument of truth. We reason in order to get at the truth, not for the sake of reasoning itself. *To doubt its capacity to lead us to the goal is to de-rationalize reason.* A philosopher who distrusts reason should not philosophise at all. It is another story how this reason is to be handled for its proper tasks.

Philosophical truth is absolute truth. But, as we said, it is necessarily connected with the spiritual needs of mankind. There is in fact an internal connection between the ideals of life we hold precious and our theoretic consciousness.

Every type of life has a theoretic background of its own. It is difficult to think of a form of philosophical thought which has grown out of the pure light of reason, and which has not drawn its inspiration from life. There is a deep and intrinsic connection between life and thought. It would therefore be wrong for us philosophers to suppose that truth is an isolated entity, which we can pursue intellectually, while we let our life run its course just as it pleases. We live the truth, we do not merely know it. Truth may be true for all times. But it cannot be appreciated as true without the appropriate kind of life. The Advaitic system of philosophy, for example, appeared quite convincing when the spirit of man was dominated by religious ideals and yearned for the Unseen, the Whole and the All, and when science with its purely secular interest was not developed. It is quite out of tune with the type of life that scientific interest or interest in visible nature has inspired in us. A *māyā-vādin* in the twentieth century appears strangely unconvincing and out of form. This is the age of science; and science goes hand in hand with technology and with Industry. It encourages a type of life that is fully extrovert and this-worldly. Humanism, with its materialistic bias, is the kind of philosophy that the modern man needs. Thus, philosophical thinking, aiming at absolute truth, is not a fixed and rigid affair. It is tied to the changing times. It has to keep pace with the cultural needs of man and the spirit of the age. What is absolute truth now may be discarded in the next generation. But that is no argument against the possibility of a truth that is true for all time, if the requisite cultural atmosphere is forthcoming.

Indian philosophy is not progressive, just because the types of religious life out of which it grew, are more or less fixed and cannot be multiplied indefinitely. European philosophy, in comparison, is progressive, because philosophy is conceived as a purely theoretical activity that must satisfy the intellect, but that has no necessary or intrinsic connection to religion or to life. Every philosopher is a small-scale creator. He thinks out his philosophical system in his own individual way, borrowing something from here, something from there, adding something of his own, and making the whole thing appear new and original. With so much freedom to the imagination, philosophy can never be stagnant or unprogressive. New systems of thought are always on the horizon, claiming our attention. This certainly is movement. We can legitimately have a history of European philosophy. There is no such legitimate history of Indian philosophy. Instead we have a number of more or less fixed traditions and types of philosophical thinking, continuing side by side throughout the ages. There is little or no progress. Our best philosophers seem to suffer from theological bias and from servility to the word of the scripture. The result is that philosophy as it is done in the West interests us much more than philosophy as it was done in ancient India. We do not care so much for the substance, the philosophic content and its meaning for life, as we do for the method through which that substance is presented to us. We belong to a different age, in which theology and the scriptures take a back-place, and free thinking, which we exalt as rational thinking par excellence, the place of honour. We find it difficult to recapture the cultural atmosphere of ancient Indian philosophy. It is no wonder that Indian philosophy interests us only distantly. It is not a living thing. It appears to have no relevance to present-day philosophical problems and the accepted methods of their solution. We do not ask the real question,—does any system of ancient Indian philosophy solve problems of philosophy for us in the only way they are capable of being solved? If it does, it is a living thing? If it does not, let us at least cease talking cant about the greatness of ancient Indian philosophy, Vedānta and all. There is only one test of a system of thought, modern or ancient,—does it dissolve our ultimate doubts, and make life in the truth possible? It is not unlikely that we may have to revise our opinion of Indian philosophy, stagnant though it may appear to be, if we search within it the key to the highest form of living truth.

4. *The problems of philosophy are eternal problems:* A philosopher should be able to distinguish eternal truth from truth that is temporal. Every age has its own special problems. They may be called sociological problems in a general way. Philosophy is often called upon to tackle them. These tasks, valuable though they are, are outside the province of philosophy proper. Sociological problems are capable of various solutions and various approaches, according to the group-interests involved. There can be no single panacea for society, unless man as such is regenerated and his inner freedom is fully realised. Philosophy should therefore keep aloof from any involvement in social matters. There is no need of a race of philosophers, who should take upon themselves the dubious and unwelcome task of giving advice and guidance to politicians and social workers who do not ask for it, and who are quite sceptical about it when it comes from persons who are trained and nursed in a sort of artificial summer-house protected from the heat and the cold of social climate. The philosopher should not assume the role of a demi-god to his fellow men. It is nothing but ridiculous, for instance, for philosophers to hold up the ideal of pacifism or of non-violence before nations that find themselves, *nolens volens,* in a struggle of life and death in an embrace which can only be loosened at the peril of self-destruction and the destruction of all those human values which a society lives for. It is also tempting for a philosopher to preach some form or other of socialism as a cure for social ills, and in general to preach idealism of every sort in order to justify his own existence. All this outside business philosophers have taken upon themselves in ignorance of their own proper tasks and their own proper problems. I do not know

> whether I should like to see a philosopher as a king. Perhaps if I see one, I shall either doubt that he is a good philosopher or that he is a good king. Raja Janak was indeed both. But then his kingship went with his philosophical enlightenment as any kind of *natural profession* might go with that enlightenment. But persons who are philosophers by *profession* should not be forced into offices which they are ill-equipped to discharge. The ridicule often poured upon the philosopher by men of affairs is only merited when the philosopher forsakes his own proper tasks and invades fields where he has no special jurisdiction, and where he is considered an intruder without experience and without expert opinion.

The tasks of philosophy are not the tasks that the *zeitgeist* sets the human family to solve. The tasks of philosophy are to solve certain perennial problems, that arise for man, because he is man, not because he belongs to this age or that. There are questions that arise in every reflective mind in every age, for the simple reason that the spirit of man demands their solution for its own emancipation. If he can achieve this, his whole life undergoes a radical change. He can stand up to the world. All other problems of life are automatically solved. It is because of this inwardness of philosophical truth that philosophy is rightly called the kingly science.

This is not to deny that the cultural requirements of each different age demand a different kind of philosophy. We have accordingly Greek philosophy, mediaeval philosophy, renaissance philosophy, and modern philosophy of the maturer age of science. But behind these differences of approach, there are certain perennial questions which do not change. They appear from age to age under a different guise, and may be said to be implanted in human nature as such. What changes are the dress and the ideological bias, not the theoretical need for a higher truth. While the questions are the same, the answers too are not new. They are invariably old answers in a new dress. No philosophical question is ever solved in an altogether new way without any affiliations to the past. We only dress up the old answers in a language which is more up-to-date and therefore more intelligible to the people of that age.

Human spirit finds no joy except in creative activity. Stereotyped questions and stereotyped answers are as repugnant to it as liturgical formulae. It seeks to know the truth on its own, and in complete freedom from any outside authority. This is only possible when it has a *real question*. Very often we have no question *ourselves*. We adopt a question proposed by another. An adopted question, like an adopted son, may not elicit the reality of feeling and interest. The question hangs loosely from our mental life; and since it is not a very insistent question, no answer seems to satisfy us, or one answer appears to be quite as satisfactory as another. Our mind is confused by different answers.

The fact is that truth is not a free gift to anybody. We must evolve it out of ourselves. Others can only help us to look within and look well. But we must see it for ourselves. It is not the sort of truth that is in the keeping of a professional philosopher who must communicate it to us. To know it, we must be philosophers ourselves. In this sense, philosophical truth is the most subjectivist and personal species of truth. Everyone must learn it the hard way. He must go through the whole process of personal doubt and error. A person who has not passed through this inner travail will find philosophy a useless and dull study, that leads nowhere and gives no clear and definite answers. But if we go to philosophy in the right spirit, there will be nothing hackneyed, stale or insipid about it. The truth we come to know may be old and well-worn. But my seeing of it is something new and intimately personal. Nobody can see exactly as I see; for the previous schooling is part of the seeing. When philosophy is pursued in this spirit, in the spirit of a real philosopher, it will have a charm which no other human subject of study can ever have, although our achievement may be very humble indeed. It is true about philosophical truth as it is of no other truth, that the old is ever new, and the new never becomes old.

II

5. *Philosophical knowledge, like all knowledge, must be an answer to a question:* Philosophical thinking is evidently a species of theoretic activity. Theoretic activity has for its object some kind of knowledge. But every species of knowledge constitutes an answer to a question. The question may be quite explicit to us or it may be only implicit. But if there is no question, there is no knowledge. In fact, all knowledge derives its cognitive character from the fact that it is an answer to a question. No statement in the indicative mood conveys any sense, if we cannot see to what question it would be an answer. What then is a philosophical question? And can it be solved completely?

We tackle the latter question first. A philosophical question, if it is a legitimate question, must be capable of a complete solution. A question which cannot be answered completely is an illegitimate question; and an illegitimate question is only answered when it is seen to be illegitimate. But can a legitimate question have different answers? That too does not seem possible. Different answers may no doubt satisfy different people. But that is because their questions are different, which they fail to recognise. I may have a question which you do not have. The verbal form of the question may be the same, but we mean different things by it. All philosophical controversies may in this sense be said to revolve round the interpretation of the question. If yourself and myself are asking the same question, then it is rationally impossible that different answers should satisfy us. There is an inevitableness about a philosophical question as well as about its answer. Often our questions are vague, and therefore they cover many meanings. Naturally several different answers seem to fit them and to satisfy them. Sometimes, they even look insoluble, because we are not sure what exactly we are asking. Perhaps we are asking many things in one question; and so there is no wonder that no particular answer seems to us to be *the* answer. Rarely, in fact *never*, do we have an identical question both in form and in spirit, and the answers different, which are equally true and satisfactory. We know the story of Indra and Virochana who went to Prajāpati with an identical question. But the same answer did not satisfy both. Were they really asking the same identical question? Certainly not. Otherwise, there was no reason for Indra to become dissatisfied with the answer on reflection. A philosophical question, once made clear and definite, is only capable of a single and indubitable answer. We might even say that the answer is immanent in the question itself, and that it is delivered readymade into our hands as the question itself is clarified and analysed. The question is resolved from within. It is rational certainty in a very special sense. What do you ask? The more certain you are about what you ask, the more certain is the answer. We never need go out of the question itself. It is an epitome of a certain confusion of the understanding. The analysis of the question removes the confusion. The question is seen not to arise. Where the expectation is for an outside answer, the answer can never fully satisfy. It is bound to be dubitable. But where there is no such expectation, and we are merely seeking to get at the bottom of the question itself, there can be no such doubt. We are seeking to understand our own mind so to say. Why are we asking this question? What exactly are we asking? These are simple enough questions. But they are the very life and soul of philosophical thinking. Naturally, the answer, properly pursued, cannot fail to satisfy. It is a kind of absolute certainty.

This certainty is to be distinguished from the sort of certainty that the mystics might be supposed to have. The mystic certainty is psychological or subjective. They have seen something ineffable and luminous, and they simply cannot make up their mind to doubt it. They feel powerless before their vision. Their reason has forsaken them. We common people have a similar certainty about the physical world which we can contact sensibly. The mystic is only a greater subjectivist than the common man. The philosopher's certainty is in a class by itself. His reason never forsakes him. He can doubt what the mystic cannot doubt. He certainly doubts what the common man cannot doubt. Such being the scope of his doubt, the certainty he demands can never be a subjective certainty. It is rational certainty par excellence. It is the realization on the part of reason that the limit of doubt has been reached, that truth is not made true by a certain state of our mind, but that *truth reveals itself as true and as self-effulgent*. Reason here surrenders and is satisfied. This is the goal; and philosophy goes about it quite confidently.

In this connection, we may refer to a common misunderstanding. We are prone to think that philosophical truth is either mystic truth, something unusual and uncommon, or it is something common, hum-drum and on the whole unimpressive. We think it is neither. It is the perception of the common in an uncommon way. It is a new illumination of meaning. Facts of experience are what they are. Only their meaning has changed. Philosophy neither gives us a mass of new information about a reality which we know, nor does it put us into contact with a reality which we do not know and which is in a sense transcendent. It merely works its alchemy of meaning on the commonplace and transforms it for our understanding into something uncommon. Every question is alluring. It has its roots in the infinite. If we could answer it decisively,—why!, we could answer every other question of philosophy decisively. There is an interconnectedness about them which a superficial view is sure to miss. Philosophy is not a mass of opinions on different subjects. There is a unity running through all its questions. But it requires a certain philosophical sense to appreciate a decisive theoretic issue, and to formulate a philosophical question. And it requires the reputed swan or the pearl-tester in a new role to resolve the question.

6. *The limitations of scientific knowledge provide the basis for a higher kind of knowledge:* We said that every species of knowledge is an answer to a question. What now is a philosophical question? The fundamental question of the theoretic consciousness is the question of truth. Science also pursues truth. But its approach to the problem is unreflective. It does not *consciously* seek truth. It consciously seeks to know the *object*. It takes the object for granted. It does not doubt the object as such. All its questions are about the object. This knowledge can have no end or limit. What we come to know becomes only the basis for a new question. The goal can be nothing less than objective omni-science, which is ruled out by the very method of science, which is the method of trial and error. Scientific truth is *factual truth* only. And all factual truth can be questioned. If we want to have a theory of truth for science, it can be no other than that of coherence. Facts may be said to pursue facts and to reduce them to consistency and coherence. But the whole coherent system is still a fact of another kind, which can be questioned.

What we call an objective perceptual fact comes to us mediated by the whole apparatus of our knowledge. We therefore accept it with an instinctive reservation. Since the mediated fact claims to be a transcript of reality in knowledge, we have a problem. Is it true? Does it correctly represent reality to us? We may investigate the so-called real facts of experience with all the rectitude of scientific precision; and yet in the end, we are confronted with a big question-mark. There is a demand to go beyond science. Those who do not find in the facts of science any challenge to our notion of truth are those practically-minded and theoretically-free souls who have no need to philosophise. They do not look deep within their souls. Or perhaps pure truth, which has no biological value, does not interest them. They are contented and self-complacent souls, who are not tortured by the pangs of a second birth.

The philosopher is, in comparison, an unlucky species of mankind, who suffers from what may be called divine discontent. He is conscious that what divides him from the animal is not that lower reason which pursues the knowledge of science. The most materialistic of men know the uses of science better than anybody else. The *rākṣasās* of mythology were quite the equals of the *devās*, if not superior to them, in the skills of war and of diplomacy. It is not science that is the glory of man. Science, in fact, has always the tendency to turn man into the worst of animals. It is the symbol of physical power, not of any spiritual power. We add no great quality to animality by reasoning more efficiently than the mere animal does. The mere animal infers from habit. We infer more methodically and to greater purpose. But the practical ideals of this kind of knowledge, or *bhautic vidyā*, are the same,—adaptation, success and self-aggrandisement. The philosopher is the animal seeking to be God-like. He reasons to know the true from the false, the real from the unreal. Truth in its purest light is for him the highest value, in fact Divinity itself.

7. *Speculative Philosophy is an exalted science:* Some philosophers suppose that philosophy is only an extension of science. It seeks the most universal kind of knowledge. It seeks what is called a world-view or *weltanschauung*. Philosophy thus understood as a speculative or constructive activity of thought is a species of philosophy that apes the method of science, without the advantages of that method in science. A philosophical world-view is a product of pure imagination. It is not knowledge in any sense. Imaginary things can never be true. Those who indulge in the pastime of theorising in philosophy can take all possible attitudes, and put all possible interpretations upon facts of experience with perfect freedom, and without the possibility of being exposed or effectively contradicted, unless they contradict themselves, which they need not do flagrantly. Philosophy is not a higher science in any accepted sense of that term. It is a science of the spirit, if we may so call it. It is *adhyātmic-vidyā*. This *vidyā* has nothing hypothetical or speculative about it. It is more properly a way of direct

seeing or *darśan*. Imagination misleads. The pure light of reason does not mislead. Philosophy is the operation of this pure light of reason. This is the concept of philosophy that was current coin in ancient India. We need to revert to it, if philosophy is to justify its place of honour among all other human activities, both theoretical and practical.

Unlike science, philosophy does not go out to tackle objective reality. Its business only begins when the realisation comes that the object as such is open to negation. This business is all within. It is to put our understanding right with things. It is the understanding that is at the root of our bondage. Reality practises no deception upon us, our understanding does. Reality does not hide its face from us. We have hidden it away through the screen of our own misunderstanding. If we can clean up the understanding, correct it and reform it, the task of philosophy is over, and we are intellectually free. It is the negative task of correction, not the positive task of a search after a missing and unknown reality. For there is no positive way of knowing reality, if reality does not by its very nature reveal itself within our experience as it is. The truth which philosophy seeks is known automatically on the removal of error.

It must be remembered in this connection that philosophical truth is not a distinct variety of truth. There is only one kind of truth. It is truth in its wholeness and completeness. What is called partial truth is only a form of error. The distinction between truth and error is a qualitative distinction. There can therefore be no degrees of truth. We may speak of degrees of error for convenience. For error can be more radical or less. It may come nearer and nearer to truth, till it is almost indistinguishable from it. But truth must be absolute truth or it is no truth. This is the truth that philosophy seeks; and when it finds it, there is no subjectivity about it. Truth speaks, and we listen. Verily is *śruti* or hearing the way to truth.

8. *Where our understanding goes wrong: The answer of Logical Positivism:* We said that the cause of error lies in us. What is this cause? It is imagination or *Kalpanā*. But how can we get rid of it?, it is argued by some philosophers. It colours all our knowledge. There is no pure knowledge without any element of imagination. It is this that makes our knowledge subjective; and there is no way of getting rid of our subjectivity. We can only look at things through our subjectivity. We may commit errors. But these errors must be capable of being exposed by the facts themselves. True facts chase away false facts. Facts that stand the test of time, and have necessarily to be taken cognizance of, are true facts. Philosophy has no special claim to knowing truth. In fact, science alone is competent for the purpose. It can sift evidence, and determine its proper value. Philosophy

has no scope here. It has a different job, and a more onerous one. It is not to correct our errors of knowledge as such, but errors of another kind which are peculiar to philosophy. Philosophers have often raised questions which are unanswerable, just because they are meaningless. And yet they never realise this. They are always in search of an answer, and that in the wrong way. They are tricked by language. They are under an illusion of meaning. It is the true business of philosophy, through analysis of the logical forms of language, to dissipate this illusion.

We use words and sentences with meaning. But sometimes we make a combination of words which appears to have a meaning, but which really has no meaning. The syntax deceives us. All purely metaphysical statements have this character. The way to rid ourselves of these non-sensical statements is to remind ourselves of the right use of words. This right use we all know when we are *not philosophers*. Language is a medium of communication and of common understanding. There is a correct and legitimate use of words which we all understand in social intercourse. The traditional philosopher has unnecessarily involved himself in trouble, misled by syntax, into a wrong use. He needs to be extricated out of himself. We must *remind* him of the right use. The modern philosopher, of course of this particular persuasion, who has seen through the antics of his predecessors, must remove the dust of the centuries from philosophical discussion by insisting upon the sobriety of lingual expression and usage. Philosophy is certainly a form of home-cleaning and slum-cleaning, but the slums are of the philosopher's own making. There is no other positive truth which philosophy can aim at. All systems of speculative thought are so much meaningless verbiage. Philosophical truth is a more hum-drum affair. It does not lift us to the seventh heaven as some would like to imagine. It is a purely formal or logical affair of elucidating meanings of words and forms of language which are philosophically misused through an illegitimate extension of their legitimate meaning. There is no such thing as absolute truth. All truth is relative; and it is the privilege of science to pursue it. Philosophy is not concerned with the knowledge of reality, but only with the misuse of language in asking certain supposedly ultimate, but meaningless, questions. This is what I consider to be the view of Logical Positivism in rough outline.

9. *The theory of truth to which Logical Positivism is driven by its own logic:* This pre-occupation with lingual problems leads to a theory of truth which is in conformity with its general standpoint. Our knowledge begins and ends with propositions. We cannot get out of them to reality, or compare them with reality. Even when we so attempt, we only succeed in getting

to other propositions about reality. We only know what the proposition states, or the meaning-content of a statement. But if that is so, truth of a proposition cannot be determined by an appeal to a non-lingual reality. 'Statements are compared with statements, not with experiences of such reality.' It is thus possible to have different systems of propositions, systems which are mutually incompatible but internally coherent, all claiming equal truth. The decision between them cannot depend upon any logical considerations, but merely upon the historical fact that a body of propositions is accepted as true by the 'scientists of our culture circle',—Neurath, quoted from Russell. There is accordingly no ultimate validity of any particular body of propositions; and we can conceive that one body of propositions gives place to another almost endlessly.

If once we concede that all our knowledge is confined to propositions, a form of solipsism is inevitable. The word is not significant of a reality beyond it which we know directly in experience; the reality beyond it is significant in the word. The word is all in all. Speaking is knowing. A non-lingual reality beyond the spoken word is meaningless.

This view may be controverted. It may be argued that 'language is an empirical phenomenon like another, and a man who is metaphysically agnostic must deny that he knows when he uses a word,'—Russell. But if to know is to use words meaningfully, how can anyone persuade me that I know in any other sense? There is nothing that I know, including the empirical phenomenon called language, that does not put on this lingual dress. Otherwise, it should be possible to know something without speaking it or expressing it in language. This has been denied.

The question naturally arises, how are words, used meaningfully? If the meaning of a non-logical word is derived ostensively,—i.e. by perceiving a situation and hearing the appropriate word that designates it,—then evidently we can know before we have learnt the use of words, and extra-lingual knowledge becomes possible. This however can be questioned. It may be argued that we cannot perceive a situation unless we are *already* in a position to use words meaningfully. The meaning of words in the end consists of the use made of them in society. The use is governed by certain rules. When we have learned these rules, we have learned the right use. The meaning of words thus has no reference to a non-lingual reality, but merely to the rules which govern their right use. Logical Positivism thus reduces itself to lingual formalism. Not only metaphysics, but even science cannot reach out beyond the spoken word.

This form of extreme lingualism can be made self-consistent. It has a logic of its own. We use words meaningfully before we can discuss their right use. There is always a common basis of agreement about the rules of syntax which give meaning to words in a proposition. If anybody disagrees here, his language is different from ours. This different language is also possible, if there are people who agree that it serves their purpose of mutual understanding and communication. Language is after all a social affair. That is the only restriction upon its meaningful use. There is no question here of right use in itself or wrong use in itself, but only a question of accepted use and not accepted use. The only way therefore to convince a person that he is in the wrong is to show to him that he himself does not *use* words in the way he *describes* their use, and that there is an incompatibility between his use and his description of the use.

> 10. *Where Logical Positivism fails: The real function of language*: We contend that language cannot be a closed circle. We must distinguish the word from the meaning of the word, the symbol from the symbolised. This meaning cannot be another word. Words cannot mean other words. To give verbal equivalents is not to give the meaning. The primary meaning refers to something beyond the word, or something that is in a sense known. Knowledge is the original fact. The word has meaning in it. If there is no knowledge, there is no function of language. *Language merely fixes what is said to be known and what is essentially a non-verbal reality.* Language is not the whole and the entire thing. It is only a function of knowledge. If there is nothing non-verbal that may be known, language has no meaning.

Indeed, this may be denied. Language may be said to be all in all. What the word *means* may be the function of the word itself. As the Hegelians say, thought realises itself through the other; but the other is the function of thought itself, and its reality is part of the reality of thought. We need only substitute 'word' for 'thought' in the present context. The word is thus all-powerful. It is the very creative power of God. As the Bible says, 'In the beginning was the Word, and the Word was with God, and the Word was God....All things were made by him; and without him was not anything made that was made,' St. John. But the power of God is not the same thing as God. It demands the person of God that has power. God creates the world through the word. But He alone creates, not the word. What is called Veda is just the word or *śabda*. It is eternal. Brahman creates the world through the utterance of the word at each new *Kalpa* or creative era. There is thus a reality beyond the word and higher than the word that uses the word as an instrument of action. This reality may be *spoken*. But it cannot be literally *meant* by any word. For the word has meaning *in it*.

In the context of knowledge we might say that the *reference* beyond the word is only substantiated *in knowledge*. This knowledge itself must be a non-verbal awareness. As we commonly say, it is not the word that means, it is *I* that mean by the word. The word taken by itself is neutral and has no meaning. It is no more than mere sound or a visual mark. It is I that use the word meaningfully. The word has meaning *for me*. It has no meaning *in itself*. The I is the higher reality beyond the word. The word cannot be the last word in reality. The last word in reality is a non-verbal awareness which knows the word and the meaning of the word.

The inadequacy of Logical Positivism is shown by the fact that there can be reality that is beyond the word, but that cannot be literally expressed by the word. All reality is speakable, but all reality cannot be literally meant. If something is not speakable, it is nothing to us. It has no kind of reality. But it may be spoken and yet not meant. Here the word has a function, but it is only a symbolic function,—i.e. it points to something beyond the word, which may be symbolised, but not meant. Let us take the metaphysical entity called 'I'. The word 'I' is used meaningfully to stand for the speaker. It does not stand for a common or socialised object. It is not a character which can be shared by many things, as the character 'dog' can be shared by many individual dogs. The 'I' stands for one entity only at a time, and that a whole and entire entity that communicates itself to the hearer in all its unique and spiritual significance. There can never be many 'I-s' at a time, but only one 'I', namely the speaker. We can never point to several things, and say, this is an 'I', that is an 'I', etc. Indeed, we may have our problems and our doubts about the nature of the entity called 'I'. What is not in doubt is the meaning itself, which is absolutely unique and unmistakable, since it cannot be confused with any other meaning that refers us to a socialised object, or a 'this'. So far the word 'I' has a real and literal meaning. We mean by it the speaker.

But the word has also a symbolic meaning. It stands for something which is spoken as 'I', but which is not meant by the word. Or as we might say, paradoxically speaking, it points to a meaning beyond all meanings. The speaking 'I' is still an entity that can be meant. It distinguishes itself from the hearer. The 'I' is meaningful only in contradistinction from the 'you'. To that extent it has an objective content which can be contemplated as the 'not-I' or as 'this'. This contradiction in its meaning requires to be removed; and it can only be removed when we negate its literal meaning, and through the negation, rise to its symbolic meaning. This symbolic meaning refers to nothing that can be known in the objective attitude. The word 'I' is used in both the senses; but the latter sense is the more important sense. It is the sense in which the word 'I' stands for something that is absolutely immediate, non-objective and self-evidencing. It is something that is truly metaphysical and non-empirical. It may be called the ultimate Self or *ātman*.

IV

11. *Problems of reflective thought*: Philosophical problems do not relate to the right use of language. They arise only after this use has been fixed and determined. Language is an instrument of truth. We should not therefore be engrossed in the instrument without regard to the ulterior purpose for which the instrument has been devised. Philosophical problems are problems of reflective thought which arise through consciousness of a conflict in the meaning of experience, and in the beliefs based upon it. There are distinct types in experience itself. We confuse one type with another. This confusion must be resolved in order to regain a healthy mental perspective and spiritual freedom.

We are familiar with the logic of the idea. It seeks, through internal analysis of the idea, to bring out its inadequacy and its self-discrepancy, and to make it more adequate and harmonious through transition to a higher concept. This is the Hegelian logic, which is supposed to give us the ultimate truth about reality. But the idea is not reality itself. It is only our way of grasping reality. It, is necessarily abstract, one-sided and schematic. It can never be adequate to reality, and so above criticism.

Experience on the other hand is essentially concrete. If reality is contacted anywhere, it is only in experience. This experience therefore ought never to deceive us. If it deceives us, what can save us? It should be taken to be always in the right. What deceives us is our own understanding, which confuses different types, leading to endless questions. It is this understanding that we must put right. *There is a logic of experience.* It is the logic of discriminating the types, negating the foreign elements that are 'confused' with each type, and in general purifying experience from within. We have no need to go outside experience, to conceptualise experience, or to construct a world-view. The so-called *synthetic* view or the *integral* view is pure imagination. Truth is given in experience from the very beginning. Only we do not see it, because it is hidden under a mass of half-truths and fanciful interpretations put by our understanding upon it. We need to remove these through a form of self-criticism, and truth ought to reveal itself for what it is. We must in particular remember that every conceptual dress, which the philosophers so often love to put upon reality, is a fancy dress that hides the naked truth.

12. *Does philosophy explain?:* We often expect philosophy to explain facts of experience. But philosophy does not really explain. All explanation is rational explanation. But what is rational explanation? There is the causal explanation. But it explains nothing. Whitehead makes much of it.

> The causal event, according to him, is the only possible reason, if reason there is, of the successor event. We cannot start from pure potentiality or from mere possibility, which is tantamount to non-being, and explain an actuality. Only the actual can explain the actual. If we want to explain the world as a whole, we must still postulate a God who is actual and not a mere potentiality. But whatever may be said of a voluntaristic explanation which involves a creative act, it is not a rational explanation. Reason cannot accept one actual event as a *reason* for another. It involves an irrational jump. *The cause is not the same thing as the reason.*

A voluntaristic explanation explains only euphemistically. There is no necessity for the cause to transform itself into the effect. The effect is a matter of free creation; it need not be, and yet is. It has no reality co-ordinate with the reality of the cause. The cause is really real, while the effect is real only in a transferred and dependent sense. This cause cannot in its turn be an effect. It must in some sense be the primary cause or the first cause. The first cause explains only in the sense that it wills the effect *without any reason for it.* Where a reason can be given, the effect is not freely created, and the voluntaristic explanation fails.

Rationalists have been at pains to justify the causal explanation. By cause they mean reason. The causal relation is to be conceived on the analogy of the relation of the ground and the consequents. But this reduction is clearly artificial. The causal relation is essentially a temporal relation. The effect is never contained literally in the cause. It is an emergent. The causal relation is not a rational relation. Reason can only understand the logic of identity. This logic does not apply to the explanation of factual reality.

A sort of rational explanation has been evolved by Hegel. But that, it appears to us, has been achieved by sacrificing facts. Reason is supposed to supply both the *form* and the *matter* of experience. Reason is all the reality there is. What is real in the facts is their rational content; and this is of the stuff of the idea. Accordingly, we need not go outside reason at all. We can study its inner movement from one concept to another in a purely rational way. Reason has its own law, the law of negation, by which it seeks to perfect the idea. No idea is found on analysis to be self-consistent and stable in itself. It contains within itself the seed of its own self-transcendence. Any position is found on analysis to lead to the counter-position. Reason cannot accept this contradiction, and it is forced to move up to a higher concept which is more inclusive, and which reconciles the contradiction. It rejects nothing and includes everything in a rational whole. This is the Absolute Idea. Reason here is dynamic. Its logic is not the static logic of identity, but the logic of self-realisation. It supplies its own content, its own law of progress, and its own goal of fulfilment of the idea. Reason can explain the world, because reason *is* the world.

That all reality is rational is an assertion, which, it appears to us, is dogmatic. We are conscious of the limitation of the concept as such. No mere concept, which is necessarily of the nature of a generality or a pattern of thought, can ever be the real concrete Whole or a synthesis of all possible opposites. It partakes of the nature of all one-sided views of reality. To call something an idea and to call it absolute is a self-contradiction. An idea is significant only in its relatedness to other ideas. And then the process of deduction of the categories is anything but rational. Each positive step forward involves a leap which no purely rational considerations can justify. Critics have accordingly pointed out that Hegel is merely drawing upon his experience in order to make the so-called deduction of the higher categories possible. The transcendental logic derives what plausibility it has, not from the inner necessity of the process, but from our normal experience where certain concepts are found to be more complex and wider in scope than others. The self-evidence of a purely deductive process is quite absent. We are not literally deducing, but really hypothesising. The process has all the uncertainties of an adventure in thought, which can have no finality about it. It is just another instance of a constructive effort of the imagination, which is doomed to failure.

> 13. *Philosophy evaluates:* Philosophy does not explain facts. It evaluates them. This evaluation is dependent upon certain ideal forms that are immanent in experience. Each type of experience has its own ideal form. It defines the highest value of that particular type. We often identify philosophy with ontology. There is some justification for it. The problems of ontology are perhaps the most important problems of philosophy. They decide for us the question of truth. Truth is certainly the most important value. Other values are in a sense dependent upon it. But at the same time, problems of truth belong only to one type of experience, namely cognitive experience.

There are three clearly defined forms of relationship between the subject and the object, and each form gives rise to its own peculiar problems. There is the cognitive type of experience in which the object is all-important and ought to determine the subject. There is the volitional type of experience in which the roles of the subject and the object are reversed, and the subject determines what the object is going to be. And lastly, there is the aesthetic type of experience in which the subject and the object co-operate in equal measure to give rise to a unitary form of experience. The problems arise because the pure form of these types is difficult to find. We confuse the types, and this is at the bottom of all our misunderstanding. The demand is to get at the pure form, which would remove all doubts and questions pertaining to that type, and thus lead to a form of Absolute Experience. When we have achieved this for each different type, we have come to the end of our philosophical adventure. We have no further problem of an ultimate unity, or a problem about *the* Absolute. For the logic of experience, with which philosophy is concerned, the Absolute has alternative forms; each type of experience has its own absolute or ideal form, which is immanent in it from the very beginning, and the non-realization of which in actual experience gives rise to the problems peculiar to that type. Beyond philosophy is, mystic experience, where the Absolute of one type may not be distinguished from the Absolute of another type. But that unity cannot be argued about. It poses no problem to reason. All the problems of reason belong to one type of experience or another, and not to experience in general; and they must be resolved on their own ground. The business of philosophy ends here. Ontology, ethics and aesthetics have different problems to tackle, but the goal is always the Absolute of that particular type. This leaves the ground open for mystic experience where truth, freedom and joy or truth, beauty and goodness are simultaneously realised in what may be called *sat-chit-ānanda mukta-svabhāva Brahman*.

The function of reason in philosophy is analytic, not constructive. It adds nothing to experience. It merely *elicits* it in its pure form. It aims at the consummation of an ideal implanted in experience from the very beginning. The ideal is in this sense the always-old and the always-known. Only the recognition of it is new. Instead of *reminding* ourselves of the right use of certain concepts through philosophical analysis, as the Logical Positivists would have it, we remind ourselves of certain ideals of experience which are always present and always operative, but always mixed up and confused by our understanding or conscious thinking. If that is so, philosophical knowledge is only the conscious recognition of what we possess already in ignorance. It is re-finding the found, or the re-discovery of what is in our possession already.

V

14. *Truth is the pre-eminent value:* It will be generally admitted that truth is the highest value for philosophy. It dominates the rest of our life. Our will and our feeling automatically conform to the state of our knowledge. If we feel and act in ignorance of the truth, we can never realize the highest value in those spheres of our experience. We shall be internally in bondage to certain false conceptions of reality, and thus act and feel wrongly. Hence the pre-eminence of right knowledge or *samyak-darśan* for the realization of all other values. We can only love truly when we know truly. To see the face of truth is to rejoice in the truth. Similarly, we can only act truly,

when we know truly. Knowledge destroys all impure desires and blind passions. It makes us truly free in all that we do. Knowledge alone can make us free,—*jñānāt eva tu Kaivalyam. Bhakti-yoga* and *Karma-yoga* are not mere alternatives to *jñāna-yoga*, but they are subsidiary to it and attain their highest consummation only *after it*. This explains the preoccupation of the typical Hindu philosopher with metaphysics to the almost complete exclusion of ethics. His metaphysics swallows up ethics. Ethics is like a post-script in a metaphysical enquiry.

The problem of truth arises because what we know is something to *us* only; it is not *in-itself*. Reality is something in itself, not relative to us. It is only such reality that is the proper subject-matter of knowledge. Phenomenal reality or reality that is relative to us is not, properly speaking, known at all. It is conceived, not known. We are in the habit of thinking that metaphysics seeks the knowledge of ultimate reality or super-sensible reality. This is only a faulty way of stating the true business of metaphysics, which is to achieve knowledge that is true to reality as it is in itself or knowledge that is *vastu-tantra*. When this is done, the problem of knowledge is solved, and there is no ultimate reality left that demands to be known.

Truth belongs to the theoretic consciousness. When we purge this consciousness of all volitional and affective elements, we ought to get at the truth. That there are these elements mixed up with cognition is proved by the epistemological theories of realism and idealism, which emphasise just those non-cognitive elements, and thus give us a warped account of knowledge. According to idealism, thought gives form to reality,—informs it and makes it knowable. It is the intelligible element in reality, the rest is all darkness and is not known at all. As a consequence of this view, knowledge is held to be an internal relation, so that knowing makes a difference to the object known. This is clearly the case in the volitional type of experience, where the agent determines the act, the subject determines the object. Thus idealism confuses cognition with volition, and still boasts of a theory of knowledge and of truth.

Again, the idealists hold that reality is neither subject nor object, but a unity of both; it is subject-object. This is the character of all feeling. Feeling is just a unity of this sort. It is found in aesthetic appreciation. An object is not beautiful *in itself* and independently of all subjective appreciation; nor does this appreciation *create* beauty in the object. Here then the idealists confuse knowledge with feeling. They over-emphasise the non-cognitive elements, and thus misinterpret knowledge. They have a theory of knowledge based upon a perverted view of knowledge.

The realists shift the emphasis to the object, which is all to the good. But they commit other sins. The intrinsic unrelatedness of the object, assumed by them, is only a dogma. It is not known, and can never be proved. As Prof. K. C. Bhattacharyya says, 'There is no knowledge of the circumstance of unrelatedness but only an extra-cognitive awareness of it.' The object, according to the realists, is externally related to knowledge. If they were right, perceptual error should become impossible; for the object of perception is in-itself and independent of the perception of it by definition. 'If this is a perception, then this is true.' He will be a bold man who will subscribe to this dogma. The independence and the unrelatedness of the object therefore which is *not known*, but only believed, and believed falsely, is taken by the realists to be an actual and accomplished fact of knowledge. The whole problem of knowledge would be solved, if we could show a simple case of perception where the ideal of knowledge was completely realised, i.e. where subjective interference was wholly absent and our awareness was determined by the object and nothing but the object after the well-known conception of the *tabula rasa*. We could then have, in perception, the absolute standard of truth, and the problem of truth would no longer be on our hands.

It might be argued that there are after all certain limitations inherent in our human situation. We cannot be omniscient. Nor can we jump out of our subjectivity and contact things as they are in themselves. We must therefore accept the appearances of things as they come to us with the humility appropriate to our embodied and finite existence. Any knowledge is true, and objectively true, till it is proved otherwise by further experience. We consider this an argument of despair. It cuts at the very root of a philosophical approach to the problem. We philosophise, in order to get rid of our subjectivity, not to accept it resignedly. If, as Plato says, we are confined within the cave of our subjectivity, and can only perceive the shadows on the walls of our mind, let us at least agree not to call the shadows 'truth,' till we have had an opportunity to look beyond the walls of our cave, and compare the shadows with the reality in all its wholeness and nakedness. It is the business of philosophy to strike down the walls of the cave, and to free the individual from his self-imposed shell of ignorance.

15. *True knowledge must be self-evidently true:* We contend that truth is not an extraneous character of knowledge, so that one piece of knowledge should require to be confirmed by another. Knowledge ought to be self-evidently true. It is different with falsehood. No piece of knowledge can reveal its own falsehood. Falsehood is only revealed by another piece of knowledge which corrects it. In other words, falsehood is revealed by truth, but truth itself is self-revealed. If truth itself required to be revealed by another piece of knowledge which was true, there would be the fallacy of *regressus ad infinitum:* 'Each piece of knowledge is true, because another

piece of knowledge which confirms it is true, and so on ad-infinitum; and since there is no last term in this series which is true in itself, the truth of any particular piece of knowledge cannot be established.' The coherence theory of truth, which involves mutual support of propositions in a systematic whole, is equally vicious for the same reason. Falsehoods can be no less coherent than truths. The fact is that truth does not require to be coherent with anything. It is *svato-pramāṇa*, not *parato-pramāṇa*. Any piece of knowledge therefore which is open to doubt, or which requires confirmation, is less than the truth, and is not the truth.

But what *is* the truth? Empirically, we can only get truth, which is *probable*, and which is true *now*. It is always open to cancellation. Empirical knowledge is mediated knowledge. It is knowledge through the idea. Such knowledge can never be *vastutantra*. It is *kalpita* or determined by the idea. The idea gives form to the object, creates the dualism of the subject and the object, and makes any direct contact of our awareness with reality impossible. In other words, knowledge at the level of discursive thought cannot be true knowledge. There must be some other kind of knowledge which is qualitatively different from it. We may call it for convenience the level of rational intuition. For thought here ceases to idealise, and becomes intuitive. It no longer functions through the senses, and is not associated and mixed up with imagination. It is pure thought reflecting reality as such. It rejects every sensible and every ideal element in our contact with reality; and through this negation, it rises to the direct perception of a higher reality that reveals itself as self-evidently true. The object as such is negated; and truth shines as true for all time, or eternally true. It is knowledge *sub specie aeternitatis*. We know the world *in* God, and *as* God. *Sarvaṃidaṃ Brahmaiva*.

16. *Subjective illusions:* Our condemnation of all knowledge of objective reality may appear exaggerated. Objects of external perception have been doubted by most philosophers, but not objects of internal perception or mental objects as they are called. When Descartes doubted everything, he did not doubt the fact of thinking. A conscious or mental fact cannot be doubted. But it appears to us that introspection is not a superior form of knowledge. Introspection involves mediation no less than any other form of supposed direct awareness; and as such its testimony is open to doubt. As a matter of fact, its object is never co-present with it. It only knows the recreated image of a past event which was never known in the past. The idealistic dictum that all knowledge is mediated knowledge has no exception in the phenomenal sphere; and Kant showed that mental facts were no less phenomenal than facts of nature.

Mental facts may be no exception to the almost universal subjectivity of all our knowledge. But can they ever be *illusory* like objects of external perception? We think they can be equally illusory. *What is taken to be a case of knowledge for example may be only an illusion of knowledge.* Knowledge ought to be true knowledge. That is the only real knowledge there is. And yet we have doubted all so-called knowledge of objects. Is it anything more than an illusion of knowledge?

It may here be argued that knowledge itself can never be illusory. It is only an object that can be illusory. The snake-appearance may be illusory; but the fact that I *saw* the snake-appearance cannot be illusory. We think that this is a wrong analysis of our knowledge of the snake-appearance. If that appearance is illusory, my belief that I really *saw* it is a false belief. I never really saw it, I only *imagined* it. I confuse this imagination with seeing.

What is true about knowledge can be shown to be true about feeling and willing as well. There too we suffer from illusions. We may believe, and believe falsely, that we are really willing i.e. willing freely, while in truth we are being determined by the dead weight of desire, etc. Our freedom may be illusory only. We conclude that scepticism has scope over all facts, whether subjective or objective, physical or mental. What it cannot touch is what cannot be known in the objective attitude, if anything is left for knowledge after we have negated both the subjective and the objective which are necessarily correlated.

17. *Beyond the subject and the object.* All theories of truth given by European philosophers are based upon the idea that we know truth when we know anything empirically. They merely seek to justify what is taken to be true knowledge in one way or another, through science or commonsense, but which philosophical reflection condemns as subjective, open to doubt, and a species of untrue knowledge. How can we have a *theory* of truth, unless we first *know truth?* Knowledge of the truth is the primary object, a theory of truth is secondary and even superfluous.

The question which we should ask is, is anything left of reality when we have negated both the subjective and the objective? It appears to us now that negation is never absolute and that we cannot negate everything. If we merely negate, there is at least the negating. If we negate the negating, we are either setting up another level of un-negated reality, or we are in the region of pure non-being where negating has no meaning. This non-being, which is the negation of all negation, cannot be a matter of knowledge or intuitive realization. Or if it is so conceived, as Mādhyamika Buddhists do, it can only be a *state of being* induced by withdrawing from both affirming and negating.

All negation is relative. When we negate, we take up a position which remains un-negated. If, for example, we negate an illusory appearance, we do not negate objectivity as such. The snake-appearance, being realised as illusory, is negated. But we still believe that there is some object there, which illusorily appears. We may go a step forward. We may negate objectivity as such, because we realise that it is a product of an act of the mind, or that it is ideal in character, being defined by thought. This creation of the mind cannot be reality, and it cannot be a fit subject for knowledge. We negate it. But when we have negated all objectivity as such or the pure object, we have not negated the negating. The negating is the logical function of thought. We may negate even this as a subjective phenomenon, that is not literally known, but only ideally reconstructed. When however we have negated the logical function of thought, the 'I' that negates still stands. It is reality that nobody can deny or disown. Nobody meaningfully says, 'I am not', while he would be quite prepared to deny the existence of everything else. But we can go beyond the assertion of the 'I', and reduce it to a phenomenal object that can be negated. The only significant use of the word 'I' is in respect of the speaker, who distinguishes himself from the bearer, i.e. from 'you'. I am aware of myself only as I distinguish myself from the 'not-I'. The 'I' is a phenomenon, an object of a kind, although a most intimate object which passes as my very true ultimate Self. 'It is always found either in identity with this Self, or it is not found at all and remains in abeyance.'

Kant went as far as this in his epistemological account. The empirical 'I' was not the reality itself, but only a phenomenon. The non-phenomenal and transcendental functions of reason might be the ultimate reality behind the 'I'. But they could not be known in the ordinary sense. They were more logical than metaphysical. Hegel merely carried this argument to its logical conclusion. The logical forms were transformed into metaphysical entities, and metaphysics was reduced to logic. For Kant himself, there was no reality behind the empirical 'I'. The transcendent, permanent and substantival Self was only an idea of reason. This is, in our opinion, sheer dogmatism and lack of critical thinking. When I have become aware of the empirical ego, or *ahaṁkāra*, and negated it as a phenomenon, have I not retreated further inwards? I have rejected the ego itself as external to my real Self, as a mere object that emerges and also disappears, and which I have wrongly confused with the true Self. When everything is negated, this Self is not negated. It is the limit of negation; for it is the supreme subject, which does not present itself to thought and is no phenomenon of any kind. It is beyond the duality of the subject and the object which it illumines or reveals. If there is a sense in which this could be said to be known, a reality which is by its very nature immediate and not open to the mediating activities of thought, there would be a level of knowledge which ought to reveal the self-evident truth to us.

> 18. *Can there be an unmediated awareness of reality?* It is often argued that any kind of immediate awareness, even if it is possible, cannot be reliable or true. Our knowledge begins with judgment. What is prior to judgment is nothing to us. We can only go forward and develop the judgment. If the judgment is false, we should correct it; if it is one-sided, we should supplement it. The ideal of truth can only be a mediated and discriminated awareness made immediate. This is only possible when the process of supplementation and transformation has reached its limit, and we know the Whole. The mediating idea may then be found to be superfluous. Reality may be known as an all-inclusive Whole above the level of thought in a sort of Absolute Experience on the analogy of feeling. Alternatively, the idea itself becomes concrete, because it is the very Whole. To know reality as the Concrete Universal is to know it for what it is. All the content of reality is ideal content; and in the end, the idea as object is known as the reflection of the idea as subject. This ideal of self-consciousness is the ideal of ultimate truth.

We cannot agree with this view. The idea does not require to be supplemented, it requires to be cancelled. No amount of ideal content can add up to reality, which is qualitatively distinct from the idea. The idea is ours and subjective, reality is in itself. Every idea, therefore, however inclusive, is just false. It requires to be negated. Supplementation is out of the question. If we add one erroneous view to another, they will not cancel each other out. Errors can cohere and confirm each other as we often find witnesses do in law-suits. Besides, a mediated awareness can never be made immediate through supplementation. An infinity cannot be covered by any number of finite distances, and must always remain undiminished how-so-ever far we carry the process; even so, reality cannot be grasped in its concreteness through one-sided views or abstract ideas. How-so-ever much we may claim to know in terms of the idea, an infinite distance still divides us from reality. It is the distance that divides reality in itself and the appearances of it manufactured by the mind, or the distance that divides truth from falsehood.

We reject this idealistic approach to the problem of truth. It is based upon our knowledge of nature which is necessarily mediated. But this is not the only knowledge that we have. There is another kind of direct knowledge which we have, and it has very different implications. It is the intuition of 'I' or *ahaṁ-pratya*. This intuition is quite common-place; in fact so common-place, that no-one seems to take it very seriously, and few appreciate its significance. This significance consists not in the correlativity of 'I' to 'this', which is generally admitted, but in the absolute opposition of the two. This opposition is so clear-cut and unmistakable that it has been compared to the opposition of light and darkness *(tama-prakāśa-vat)*. The two can never reside in the same locus. It is impossible therefore for any one to assert consciously 'this is I'. No doubt, we often quite carelessly and recklessly identify ourselves with some kind of object, such as the body and its characteristics, thought, etc. But a little reflection immediately corrects us. Anything that we can contemplate as object is just what we call the 'not-I'. Here then is a form of reality that never does present itself before our thought. If we want to know it, we can never know it in the objective attitude, or as mediated by the idea. It is essentially something immediate by its nature. It is because we seek to know it in the objective way, as something that can be presented to thought, that it appears to us as a mythological entity. Many have sought to deny its existence or to explain it away. We however contend that it is the key to the higher form of knowledge which we seek. 'Know Thyself' may be found to be the very quint-essence of philosophic wisdom. The Self may be the Truth that shall make us free.

> 19. *Truth consciousness is a higher level consciousness that is yet to be born:* The common intuition of the self or *ahaṁ-pratya* is only our starting point for the knowledge of the truth. There is no simple awareness of Truth. Truth is only born through a great effort of thought or rational mid-wifery. It is the result of discrimination, criticism and negation. Truth is a *value*. It is not a *fact*. A fact is something crude. Any believed content would be a fact. We know facts without being conscious of it. We can never know Truth without being conscious of the same. Truth is the product of reflective thinking or a crisis in theoretic life. It involves therefore a new awakening, or a new birth, the birth of a self-conscious awareness of Truth as such. It is the end of our philosophical adventure, not its beginning. The common intuition of the self, on which we have laid so much emphasis, merely provides a new dimension for our reason. Reason, ordinarily, is concerned with the study of the object. It has scope in physical, biological, mental and social sciences. It has no vital question about the subject as such. It treats the subject, at best, as some kind of ultimate fact to be accepted, but which has no content that we might seek to know. It is taken as a kind of attenuated object, too thin, too subtle, and too evasive for explicit awareness. The least said about it, the better.

This evaluation of our ordinary empirical thinking has got to be reversed. We have become reflectively aware that all science, with its subjective approach, can never give us the truth in a literal sense; and anything less than literal and pure truth is ultimately a form of error. The intuition of 'I' opens a whole new realm of the spirit to us. *Adhyātmic vidyā* has its own different problems and its own methods of tackling them. It does not seek to build up or imagine a *theory* of truth. All theories are mere conceptual structures which have a use for science, but no use for philosophy. Philosophy seeks to know the truth itself. It is an effort not at *explaining*, which is always misguided, but at seeing the truth. This it does, not through any abstract argument, but through the inwardisation and the deepening of our experience, so that what everybody knows becomes more significant and more luminous.

If philosophical thinking aims at a higher kind of knowledge or a species of seeing, it is more akin to what may be called transcendental or rational psychology than to transcendental logic; for we can only see what is there already by a shift of attention, we cannot see what thought has imported into reality. There are various species of seeing, but the seeing which philosophy aims at is different from them all and in a class by itself. We see the sensible object. But this seeing is mixed up at all stages with interpretative elements, so that we cannot say what is the object in itself and what is contributed by the subject. In fact, there is no such thing as object in itself. The poet and the mystic are also said to see. But they only see what they have visualised vividly in their imagination. They have high-strung temperaments. The scientist sees, but he sees only in a metaphorical sense. It is a flash of imagination in which a mere mental suggestion or hypothesis clears up the mist of thought.

The philosopher has no use for poetic imagination. He subordinates imagination to the pure light of reason, in order to see what *is*. Imagination gives us a sense of freedom. It is at the basis of most of our joys. But it is no instrument of truth in its nakedness. It has its use in philosophy as in all theoretic activities. It accentuates certain issues, visualises possibilities, invests problems with a new meaning and importance, and it provides the over-tones of joyful appreciation and wonder when the truth is seen. But as a *method* of philosophical knowledge, it must be rigidly suppressed and kept under control. The philosopher sees the truth, because the truth has caught him, enslaved him. He cannot but see it. He has no option. His seeing is pure. It imports nothing into what is seen, but gets everything from it. There is no other seeing like it. It is seeing the truth face to face. The philosopher and the seer are not two persons, although a line can be drawn between them in a loose way: The true philosopher must be a seer, although a seer may not be a philosopher. The philosopher-seer is in fact the greatest among the seers. His reason is disciplined to the highest standard, and it accepts nothing which is not absolutely true. The seeing is not divorced from reason, but it takes reason with itself, and transforms it into a higher form of intuition, the so-called intellectual intuition of God.

20. *The place of sādhanā*: It is sometimes argued that spiritual discipline or *sādhanā* is something more precious than philosophical knowledge. It supervenes after the business of philosophy is over, and it carries the philosopher a step further in the realization of the truth. I cannot agree with this view. There are certain spiritual qualifications no doubt (*sādhanā catuṣṭaya*), which are pre-supposed by a serious philosophical enquiry, or what may be called *Brahma-jijñāsā*. But they are subsidiary to the enquiry itself, and by themselves they carry us nowhere. There is another kind of discipline which comes after the truth is known, and which is called *niditdhyāsana*. This too is in a sense a subsidiary affair. It is merely the humbler effort of the mind to keep in tact what has been attained through philosophic effort, to persist in the philosophic vision, and to transform it into a living and all-embracing feeling. It is a form of drilling of thought to stick to the game right to the end. Truth does not *reveal itself* through this discipline. It is merely made to *rule over* the mind by reforming and transforming the rebellious tendencies and the false ways of thought. It is because of this high conception of philosophy, as giving us the saving knowledge, that it is regarded in India as the apex of all other forms of knowledge. It is not an empty intellectual game to please the curious, or to provide tricky arguments for the mere logician, or to dazzle the simple-minded with learned discourses on high and abstract themes. It is the instrument for the highest kind of enlightenment for the more serious-minded and the more reflective species of mankind, that seek in truth the satisfaction of their highest ideal of theoretical and practical life. It is that truth, which, when realized, leaves no other value unachieved, or yet to be achieved. We can close the chapter of our life with the happy ending that our very will, the source of all our restless activities, is rendered submissive and peaceful, because there is nothing left that it can aspire after. Verily, Truth is the summum bonum; and if we, as philosophers, are true to our profession, there lies our goal.

My stand throughout has been that of Advaita Vedānta of Śri Śaṅkarācārya; and if any of my arguments are found similar to those of Prof. K.C. Bhattacharyya, it may be taken for granted that I am to that extent indebted to him.

A. C. Mukerji, "Traditional Epistemology" (1950)

Anukul Chandra Mukerji (1888–1968) succeeded R. D. Ranade as Professor of Philosophy at Allahabad. He was a scholar of Western and Indian philosophy and specialized in Epistemology, with a special interest in idealism and the problem of self-knowledge. He published two books during his life, *The Nature of Self* (1933), and *Self, Thought and Reality* (1938). Mukerji argues in this Presidential address to the Logic and Metaphysics section of the Indian Philosophical Congress against the cogency of sense-datum theories and against foundationalism in epistemology generally.

7

Traditional Epistemology

PRESIDENTIAL ADDRESS

Section: Logic and Metaphysics

About a couple of decades have passed since I had the privilege of first presiding over this section and acquainting my learned colleagues with the reasons why, notwithstanding my deep respect for a particular philosophical tradition, I felt then dissatisfied with its modern form in which an apparently abrupt turn has been given to an analysis of experience which, if pursued more resolutely and boldly; would yield a richer harvest than what has so far been reaped. I would very much like to use the present opportunity for presenting before you some of the considerations that have further deepened my allegiance to that old, mistakenly fancied dead, tradition in spite of my profound admiration for the overwhelming scholarship and remarkable ingenuity with which some of the comtemporary theories of epistemology and metaphysics have been, and are still being, worked out. But this being impossible in a brief presidential address I shall try to give here the barest outline of my views against the background of some arbitrarily selected new orientations in epistemology and metaphysics.

That every new reorientation in the field of logic and metaphysics necessarily represents a forward step opening the way to a hitherto unattained insight into the nature of experience and reality has been a disastrous assumption in the history of philosophy. The assumption is disastrous for it promotes an unhealthy craze for originality and encourages a sort of dilettantish attitude to the achievements of the past. Personal initiative is, no doubt, a great virtue in philosophy as in the other spheres of life; but it must be admitted at the same time that this virtue, when completely divorced from an intelligent appropriation of the heritage of the past, degenerates into a perverse crotchet, and sometimes even a deceitful conceit, that is ill-suited for furthering the cause of truth. I have often asked myself if some of the recent developments in logic and metaphysics, not-withstanding the remarkable ingenuity with which they have been, are not born of the craze for novelty rather than a genuine speculative impulse. When, for instance, it is proclaimed that all philosophers from

Plato and Aristotle down to Kant and Hegel, have only erected the pillars of aberration in their efforts to analyse experience, it would *prima facie* arouse the suspicion that such a presumptuous generalization could not be the result of any fairly sympathetic or thorough study of the great thinkers of the past. Before proceeding to justify this suspicion, it may be useful to start with what may be called the common platform of the warring theories.

Paradoxical as it may appear, a total discontinuity between a new theory and the old would render its critical weapons totally ineffective against the latter. To put it from the other side, the underlying unity and continuity of views is the very reason why they come into clash in respect of certain specific problems and particular situations. In a philosophical controversy it is but natural for the disputants to be oblivious of the solid core of knowledge which supports and lends force to the weapons of offence and defence, much as in the heat of the battle the combatants remain unconscious of the solid common ground under their feet. If they had not been absolutely certain about the general features of what reality must be, the participants in the controversy would not so much as feel the need of differing from one another in regard to the specific formulations of their respective positions. The assertion "The virtuous are happy" does not come into conflict with the assertion "All crows are black," because there is no common concept uniting them; similarly, "You are just" and "He is unjust" are not conflicting assertions, because the predicates, though mutually exclusive, lose their opposition when they are ascribed to different subjects.

Every theory of reality, for example, lays claim to truth and consequently challenges the truth-claim of a rival theory. That there is a reality which refuses to be represented by conflicting theories is, therefore, one of the common assumptions uniting the new with the old theory. If reality, as philosophical perversity has sometimes claimed, had been in its ultimate nature the subject of conflicting and mutually destructive judgments, there could be neither science nor philosophy. Even the most radical sceptic or a confirmed misologist, in so far as he claims truth for his assertion that knowledge is unattainable or that reality is inscrutable, makes the unconscious assumption that reality has a positive nature by virtue of which it repels conflicting formulations. Thus radical scepticism or total agnosticism is a disguised parasite that feeds upon the sap supplied by the parent tree of absolute knowledge.

One of the results of these considerations is to disclose the utter futility of an unbridgeable dualism of knowledge and reality. Even when reality is taken to lie beyond the frontiers of knowledge, the position owes its plausibility to a confusion between the general and the specific features of reality, and then our obvious ignorance of the details is misconstrued as total ignorance including that of its general features. What is not clearly realized by those who make this mistake is that a completely unknowable reality, being a contentless vacuity cannot be intelligently used for demarcating or limiting the sphere of human knowledge. Existentialism, when viewed in this light, has only revived an old fallacy, by creating an impassable gulf between knowledge and existence. Even if-it be granted that existence cannot be resolved into mere logic and that it is best illustrated in the spontaneity or creative resolve and in the attitude of men, it does not follow from this that "existence" is, on that account, beyond knowledge or beyond the principles involved in a systematic presentation. In fact, the existentialistic mistrust of system which is supposed to stifle spontaneity and human personality would make existentialism either speechless or senseless. If personality and spontaneity are to convey any definite meaning they must conform to the principles of significant assertions and systematic presentation; and so to condemn the rationalistic practice of building up an impersonal objective system, far from preparing the ground for an alternative formulation of reality, would knock off the ground from under the feet of "existence" itself. The need of a philosophical or scientific reform arises when a particular theory is found to be inadequate for the purpose of complete systematization and a new theory comes to establish itself by reason of its greater systematizing capacity. Thus, system being the most fundamental demand that unites the new with the old theory, an initial distrust of system is utterly incompatible with the claim to reform or improve upon the old doctrines of epistemology or metaphysics.

To discard system is, in fact, to eliminate the universal from an analysis of experience and reduce knowledge to incommunicable flashes of extreme subjectivity which render all questions of truth and error as irrelevant as unmeaning. That some existentialists have perceived this paradox in an extreme type of subjectivism is apparent from the super-existential philosophy of Heidegger with its emphasis on the human-being-in-general by which he has sought to remove the paradoxes in the existential philosophy of Jaspers. The reduction of truth to a mere subjective attitude of man may no doubt display an excessive zeal against the objectivation of existence, but it betrays at the same time the *reductio ad absurdum* inherent in a one sided emphasis on the abstract particular.

These observations, of course, are not intended to belittle the importance of recognizing an unobjectifiable principle for a sound and systematic theory of knowledge, and so far the contention that human personality contains a principle that does not admit of objectivation may be essentially right. But from this it does not follow that the unobjectifiable principle is beyond the region of coherent thought; all that follows is the inapplicability to it of the specific characters that belong to the objectifiable facts. Indeed, this inapplicability is accepted as much in the interest of coherent thought as any other discovery in science or philosophy; and it would, therefore, be a very serious confusion of issues to extol the virtue of incoherent thinking, as some existentialists have actually done, in formulating the doctrine of existentialism. It is one thing to insist that existence cannot be objectified, but it is an entirely different thing to deny on that ground an objective system of knowledge born of coherent thought.

Another new departure in epistemology is represented by what is called logical positivism, analysis, or logical empiricism. Like every type of positivism it dismisses all metaphysical problems as pseudo-problems due to linguistic confusion and proceeds to solve afresh the problems of epistemology which are supposed to be insolvable without a strictly logical analysis of language designed to clarify the meaning of words. It would be an endless task to go into the considerations which have led to the conclusion that the meaning of words is determined by syntactical and semantic rules of the language. But what is significant is the acute difference of opinion in the camp of the logical positivists themselves about the truth or falsity of empirical propositions, particularly of the "Protocol" sentences, some holding that truth or falsity of these sentences is determined solely by the formal relation each of them has to a given system of sentences, and thus enunciating a modified form of the coherence theory of truth, while others questioning the possibility of any sentence, howsoever coherent and consistent, conveying knowledge about matters of fact simply on the ground of its formal self-consistency. Thus an old dispute has received a new lease of life, and one would not be far wrong if it is surmised that the importance of the logical analysis of language for solving the problems of philosophy has been considerably exaggerated by the modern positivists.

If this is an instance of the exaggerated claims of contemporary positivism to solve an old problem, the renewed emphasis it has laid on the dualism of *a priori* and empirical knowledge may be taken to be an instance of its uncritical acceptance of an old questionable solution of another important problem of epistemology. This dualism to which the empiricists of all grades of perfection have persistently clung, as is well known, was thrown into prominence by Hume by his famous distinction between the truth about the relations of ideas and that about the matters of fact. It is only in the case of the former that, according to him, there may be demonstration while our knowledge of the matters of fact is bound to remain in the region of probability. In reverting to Hume's dualism and accepting his verdict as final, the logical empiricists, along with the majority of contemporary thinkers, appear to have completely ignored the value of an alternative theory of knowledge, according to which neither the *a priori* nor the empirical knowledge is a species of knowledge by the side of the other species, on the contrary, what is called *a priori* knowledge is nothing more than the knowledge of the universal elements involved in the very existence of an empirical object or an empirically given event. If, for instance, it is assumed that sense-data are the ultimate materials of experience, our analysis, according to this theory, is defective, for it does not take into consideration the conditions of there being a world of sense-data at all. Every sense-datum, for example, must be identifiable in different contexts, and must, at the least, be distinguishable from the other sense-data by its spatio-temporal and other relations. These formal relations being involved in their very existence, to abstract them from the sense-data is to reduce the latter to what would be as good as nothing for us. When considered in this light, the distinction between the formally true or formally false and the factually true or factually false propositions would be found to be based upon an unfortunate mistake in interpreting the meaning of *a priori* knowledge.

No careful exponent of *a priori* knowledge has denied the substantial truth of Hume's contention that we can never be quite sure of the truth of a given inductive generalization. But at the same time it would be a blunder to infer, as has been done by the logical empiricists, that one never has a good reason for believing that any event will occur rather than any other. This is a blunder because the conception of an objective order of succession, which no empiricist can doubt except through a confusion of thought, implies that every event has a definite place in the spatio-temporal system. What the past has taught us may be untaught by the future. Such an uncertainty is conditioned by the absolute certainty that the past is necessarily followed by the future, but this necessity is after all the necessity with which one event follows another. Here, once more, we come upon the truth, explained above, that our ignorance of the special features of reality is based upon our absolute certainty about its general features. That is, to put it in the present context, the validity of objective succession is necessarily presupposed by, and consequently cannot be derived from, or assailed by, particular inductions of doubtful validity.

A modified form of the same confusion has been at the root of the logical positivists' dualism between the world of meanings and the structure of reality. Criticism of the rules of logic is not a new venture in the history of philosophy; nor is there much room for adding to the points that have been historically made out to meet this misological challenge. One may, therefore, afford to be brief in bringing out the self-contradiction in the positivists' attack on the logical rules on the ground that their application is restricted to the field of discourse organizing our meanings and, as such, has no ontological significance. The simplest way of realizing the inherent paradox of this criticism would be to enquire whether or not this itself is an assertion claiming to be absolutely true, and, as such, possessing a meaning which, though expressed in language, is not determined by the syntactical rules of the language; and whether or not its truth claim is an implicit rejection of the truth of any other assertion that is its contradictory. It will then be evident that the positivists' criticism of the logical rules cannot be left standing except on the basis of those very principles it seeks to deprecate. The law of contradiction, for instance, regulates, not only the use of words, but also every significant assertion, and every systematic formulation of our views. What defies systematic formulation, as we have urged in the context of existentialism, is not a profounder reality than the logical reality but a contentless vacuity, a mere word emptied of the least shred of meaning. Even the distinction between the field of discourse and the structure of reality, like every other distinction, has for its ultimate sanction the logical demand for coherent and systematic thinking. The conclusion, therefore, seems to be unavoidable that all attempts to deny, or restrict the application of, the principles of logic are but the offspring of an illegitimate particularization of the universal and a consequent co-ordination of the transcendental principles with what they condition. A new theory, a new analysis, a new orientation,—these are all alike dictated by the principles of logic, and so far they may be called foundational principles as distinct from the superstructural rules. The latter are certainly subject to change and revision; but these changes being always dictated by the former, it would be as insane to condemn the logical principles as mere tautologies as to expect that the superstructure will not collapse on the removal of its foundation.

A similar conclusion would follow from a careful and impartial examination of the other empirico-sceptical re-orientations of epistemological and metaphysical thought of the present day. The hunt for the pure data isolated from the transforming activity of thought, the phenomenological description of the data of consciousness in their original purity and immediacy, the attempt to replace the *Critique of Pure Reason* by the *Critique of Historical Reason* or by the biographical studies of great men's lives, are but new bottles containing old wine. None of them, when every thing is said and done, can afford to ignore the conditions of systematic thought and, inasmuch as the logical principles provide these conditions, every criticism of the older types of epistemological analysis which unearthed the foundational principles of knowledge is bound to be ineffectual and abortive.

PART FIVE

A Session of the Indian Philosophical Congress at Amalner, 1950

Symposium: Has Aurobindo Refuted Māyāvāda? (Amalner, 1950)

Indra Sen, N. A. Nikam, Haridas Chaudhuri, and G. R. Malkani

In 1950, the Indian Institute of Philosophy at Amalner convened a symposium on the question, "Has Aurobindo refuted *Māyāvāda*?" This is a significant event in the recent history of Indian philosophy because of its explicit acknowledgment of the pervasive influence of Aurobindo's thought on Indian philosophy in the colonial period, an instance of the regular but often unacknowledged interaction between academic philosophers in India and those who pursued philosophy in public or religious contexts.

Indra Sen (1903–1954) studied at Freiburg under Heidegger, was Professor of Philosophy at Delhi University, and resigned his position at the university for a life at the Aurobindo ashram. **N. A. Nikam** was a President of the Indian Philosophical Congress. **Haridas Chaudhuri** (1913–1975) studied and taught at the University of Calcutta. **G. R. Malkani** (1892–1977) was longtime director of the Indian Institute of Philosophy at Amalner and was editor of the Philosophical Quarterly. He was a follower of Sri Aurobindo and founded the California Institute for Integral Studies. In this symposium divergent views are expressed regarding the relation between *Līlāvada* and *Māyāvāda* (between Aurobindo's realistic challenge to the traditional doctrine of the illusory nature of the world due to Śaṅkara).

Indra Sen

Haridas Chaudhuri

I

SYMPOSIUM II of the Indian Philosophical Congress Silver Jubilee Commemoration 1950

Has Sri Aurobindo Refuted Māyāvāda?

I by Indra Sen

The word *'Māyā'* is as ancient as the *Ṛgveda*, but *'Māyāvāda'* as a philosophical school came into being with Śaṅkara in the 9th century A.D. The author of this Weltanschauung was a most dynamic personality and even during his life-time, which was exceedingly short, his thought had become fairly dominant in this vast sub-continent. The succeeding centuries witnessed a growth in the power and influence of it and the philosophers who appeared on the stage of Indian life during this time, on the whole either accepted him and wrote elaborative commentaries on his works or rejected him and wrote refutations of the view that the world is *māyā*, an illusion, *mithya*, false, and *asat*, non-existent or *vyavahārika*, purely empirical and phenomenal. However, it continued to be the major and the dominant trend of Indian thought, with of course many vicissitudes, up till about the middle of the 19th century, when primarily through impact with the West a new ferment started in Indian life. A reaction appeared against the idea of *'māyā'* and the world and life-denying attitude and thinkers and leaders of Indian life, one after the other, emphasized action and the value of life in the world. Under this changed cultural atmosphere the old *'Māyāvāda'* or illusionism itself tended to become more or less a *'Sattavada'*, a positive creativity justifying life in the world.

The classical critics of Śaṅkara have often called him a *'Pracchanna Buddha'*, a disguised Buddhist, meaning that he was virtually reaffirming the same Buddhist position regarding the world process, with the difference that he affirmed a Supracosmic Absolute too, regarding which Buddha had chosen to remain silent. This is, however, only a historical antecedent of *Māyāvāda*, which is hardly of any direct significance in considering the philosophical value of the doctrine.

We have said that since the middle of the 19th century, thinkers and leaders of Indian life have repeatedly rejected *Māyāvāda* and stressed life and world-affirming attitude. However, a full-fledged philosophical system, which offers a complete *Weltanschauung* involving a revaluation of *Māyāvāda* has found expression in Sri Aurobindo. But a refutation of *Māyāvāda* is no essential objective of his. His leitmotiv and the first formulation of the philosophical question is: How is divine life, a full life of the Spirit, possible on earth? How can Spirit be reconciled to Matter? These are the two practical and theoretical issues of his philosophy, which receive a comprehensive ontological, epistemological and axiological treatment at his hands. Obviously there are some assumptions here, but were there no assumptions in Kant's question: How is knowledge possible? Or Hegel's fundamental affirmation that reality must be rational. It is not necessary for us to go into the validity or otherwise of the assumptions involved. What we wish to show is that Sri Aurobindo's philosophizing starts independently with an original question of its own and in seeking to work out its answer the refutation of *Māyāvāda* becomes an incidental circumstance, virtually an aid to evolve a fuller Monism free from the necessity of a negativist attitude towards any sphere or part of experience. The positive part of the system, its fundamental philosophical approach and the substantiation and correlation of its constituent elements have reinforced this refutation with a constructive alternative. Now assuming that the doctrine, as traditionally represented, is still held by some we can consider and discuss, "Has Sri Aurobindo refuted *Māyāvāda?*" or rather "How Sri Aurobindo's philosophy refutes *Māyāvāda?*"

Māyāvāda is essentially an expression of a sense of inexplicability, *anirvacaniya*, in the presence of a contradiction between, on the one hand, the normal experience of the world or multiple finite objects and, on the other, the super-normal spiritual experience of an undifferentiated infinite existence. The quality and the intensity of the latter, its undifferentiated unity in contrast to the multiplicity of the normal experience and a rigid adherence to the logical law of contradiction are sufficient to show *Māyāvāda* as an intelligible philosophical consequence. Unity being undifferentiated, in fact absolutely featureless, and then more intense as an experience, multiplicity must naturally become unreal and illusory. Yet the multiplicity does exist, our practical life is intimately bound up with it, we cannot deny it altogether. Therefore it exists, but only as *vyavahārika satta*, a practical and empirical reality. Now this must somehow be related to the real reality, the transcendental or the *paramārthika* reality. That is obviously the crux of monistic philosophy, which, in essential impulse and character, Śaṅkara's system is and, in fact, one of the best known to the history of thought. Now the *Māyāvāda's* solution of this critical issue is that the world only appears to be, actually it is not. The world is no more than the jugglery of the juggler, the snake in the rope or the silver in the shell. It is like the dream, which appears to be real while it lasts but on waking we know it definitely as unreal. The world too we come to know as absolutely unreal when we awaken to the reality of the *Brahman*, which is the supreme, undifferentiated Unity, one and sole, without a second.

This world of variety and colour is an *adhyāsa*, a super-imposition, on the one and the uniform reality of the *Brahman*. But how does this come about? On account of *'Māyā'*. But then what is *'Māyā'*? This proves to be a very uncomfortable question. *Māyā* is supposed to be the solution of the greatest difficulty of monistic philosophy, that of the relation between the apparent 'many' and the real 'one', yet it in itself becomes a more serious problem. Metaphysically it cannot be admitted as another principle of existence besides the *Brahman* therefore it cannot be said to be real. Yet unreal it is not. Therefore it is declared as real as well as unreal, *sat* as well as *asat*. It is in fact *anirvacanīya*, inexplicable. Epistemologically it determines our ordinary cognitions, which being of the apparent 'Many' involving relational judgements are all false. The cognition of the absolute undifferentiated 'One' alone can be knowledge, which is an intuition.

A most wonderful crop of dualisms was the result of the great monistic sowing of Śaṅkara. Yet it answered to the metaphysical needs of the people of those times in such an abundant measure that it found a ready acceptance with them. The spiritual reality of the Absolute *Brahman* afforded such a great satisfaction that the difficulties due to *'Māyā'* were ignored. Or perhaps *'Māyā'* and the unreality of the world were themselves positive satisfactions to the people nursed on Buddhist view of life. But this general satisfaction did not last long and the dualisms so sharply brought into play by Śaṅkara's Monism and, in particular, his concept of *'Māyā'*, as it were, provoked new orientations of Vedāntic thought. Ramanuja, Nimbarka, Vallabha and Madhva are the chief of such creators and they uniformly reject the idea of *Māyā*. To all of them the world is real. None of them resorts to the idea of illusion to explain one or the other part of experience, whether normal or supernormal. Ramanuja (12th century), in particular, evolves a powerful philosophy and a more powerful religion, which is also the more dominant trend of contemporary Hinduism. His philosophical approach to reality is truly monistic, i.e. all-embracing and all-inclusive. He accepts the experience of the 'one' as well of the 'many' as equally real and then proceeds to reconcile them in a whole-hearted manner. It can be said that his account of unity is rather weak but he is not prepared to achieve a unity by rejecting plurality as illusory. His seven arguments, *Saptavidkanupapatti*, against *'Māyāvāda'* constitute the classical and the most authentic criticism of the doctrine. He asks for the locus of *Māyā* or *Avidyā* (Ignorance) and says that it cannot be the human individual, because he is himself the product of it. Nor can *Brahman* be the locus, because It is absolute self-luminosity in which there is no ignorance. *Avidyā* can also not hide away the *Brahman,* which is absolute knowledge. It can also not be a third thing from existence and non-existence. It can also not be a positive factor, since ignorance means want of knowledge. And if we admit it as positive, then it will be impossible to destroy it. Lastly, an *Avidyā*-beset universe contradicts moral effort and religious aspiration, because it negates human individuality and offers for an ideal an impersonal existence. Nimbarka (13th century) urges one special argument, i.e. "If the world were not real, it could not be superimposed on another".[1] And Vallabha (16th century) insists that if those who accept the force of *Māyā* as the explanation of the world are not mere Advaitins, since they admit a second to *Brahman*".[2]

The *Māyāvāda* thus became an issue for centuries but in spite of all the polemic raised against it, it continued to be influential. However, the successors of Śaṅkara, whether in consequence of the criticisms levelled against *Māyāvāda* or independently, felt obliged to modify their position in a number of ways. With the author of the *Śanksepasdriraka*, for example, the '*Māyā*' becomes "a *modus operandi* (*vyapadeśa*) which coming itself from the material cause (*Brahman*) brings about the material product, i.e. the world."[3] In connection with the Īśvara, a concept accepted by Śaṅkara, *Māyā* is even for him the power which creates the world. *Māyā* as creative power, on the whole, acquired emphasis during this later period.

Some contemporary interpreters of Śaṅkara too have either been much struck by some special passages in his commentaries or otherwise felt inclined to give new meanings to old terms and passages but in every case the result is that Śaṅkara's abstract non-dualism tends to be changed into a concrete absolutism.[4]

However the Śaṅkara of these contemporary exponents is not the Śaṅkara known to and accepted by his classical exponents or critics. Sri Aurobindo accepts the classical Śaṅkara and regards his *Māyāvāda* a legitimate

---

1. Radhakrishnan, *Indian Philosophy,* Vol. II, p. 753.

2. *Ibid,* p. 756.

3. *Ibid,* p, 571.

4. (1) "There are in the world many *sāmānyas* with their *viśeṣas,* both conscious and unconscious. All these *sāmānyas* in their graduated series are included and comprehended in one great *sāmāyana,* i.e. in *Brahman's* nature is a mass of intelligence", (*Śaṅkara-bhāsya* on *Bṛhadāraṇyaka Upaniṣad,* ii. 4.9, *Indian Philosophy,* Vol.11, p. 534). (2) *tajjanyatve sati, tajjanyajanako vyāpārah. Māyā* is only a *modus operandi* (*vyāpāra*), which coming itself from the material cause (*Brahman*) brings about the material product, i.e., the world (*Sankṣepaśārīraka* [*ibid* p. 571]) (3) *Yathā kāraṇaṃ brahma triṣu haleṣu sattvam na vyabhicarati, tathā kāryam api jagat triṣu kaleṣu tattvaṃ na vyabhicarati.* Just as the *Brahman* as cause is eternally real, so is the world as effect eternally real. (*Śaṅkara-bhāṣya on Brahma-sūtra, Outline of Indian Philosophy,* Chatterjee and Datta, p. 425.)

philosophical alternative and examines it as such. As we have said before, he uses it often to develop and state his own position. Now the most fundamental and crucial attack of Sri Aurobindo against *Māyāvāda* consists in his formulation of the philosophical problem itself. Spirit and Matter are to him the two undeniable decisive facts of experience and, therefore, to reconcile them is the proper philosophical issue. And, says he, "True reconciliation proceeds always by a mutual comprehension leading to some sort of oneness".[5] The same thought is stated in a variant form like this: "As in science, so in metaphysical thought, that general and ultimate solution is likely to be the best which includes and accounts for all so that each truth as experience takes its place in the whole."[6] A unification of Spirit and Matter or the discovery of that "ultimate solution" which "includes and accounts for all" becomes the aim of philosophical inquiry. Such unification has to proceed by a systematic "mutual comprehension" or intimate inter-relatedness so that in the end the whole of experience becomes perfectly intelligible. Here the attitude towards all experience is one of acceptance and seeking to interpret and explain it.

Śaṅkara's approach to the philosophical problem was much different. He sought for the "foundational" in experience, which, he thought, must be eternal, unchanging and uniform. He came to regard the "undifferenced consciousness alone" (*nirviśeṣacinmātram*) as real and then naturally the rest became unreal and illusory. Here too a unity is achieved, but as Sri Aurobindo says, "Illusionism unifies by elimination."[7]

It is hardly necessary to comment on the relative merits of the two approaches, as we now regard it as almost axiomatic that to interpret experience is the proper business of philosophy and that means really to account for all the principal facts of experience. Anything given in experience is existent and not illusion or unreal and surely illusion is no valid form of explanation either. Our sole concern regarding each fact of experience is to determine the nature and the character of its reality in the scheme and the unity of the whole, for truly are "all problems of existence essentially problems of harmony."[8]

Now the one general consequence of this difference of attitude is that, while both, Śaṅkara and Sri Aurobindo are monists by philosophical seeking, the one constantly dichotomizes while the other always reconciles, in the one you suffer divisions, rejections and eliminations, in the other enjoy growing orientations and ever larger harmonies.

---

5. *The Life Divine* (First Edition), Vol. I, p. 39.

6. *Ibid*, vol. II (i), p. 265.

7. *The Life Divine*, Vol. II (i). p. 265.

8. *Ibid*, I, p. 3.

Obviously, according to Sri Aurobindo, illusion will be an illegitimate term to be applied to any fact of experience. If so, falsehood can only be partial truth. Ramanuja had rightly stressed against Śaṅkara that error cannot exist and this indeed threatened to knock the bottom out of the case of *Māyāvāda*, because it would make illusion impossible. But Ramanuja had overstated his case. When he said that all knowledge is true (*yathdṛtham sarva-vijñānam*) he failed to see that even if all things admitted to be composed of the same constituents, they might yet differ in the relations of those constituents. *Anirvacanīya-khyāti-vāda* of Śaṅkara and *Satkhyāti-vāda* of Ramanuja, both have their respective short-comings. The one theory of error ends in inexplicability and the other in the affirmation that even in the so-called illusion, the real appears. Virtually error is best explained as 'relative in nature' dependent on the 'perversion' and 'contradiction' of Truth[9] and as "an indispensable step or stage in the slow evolution towards knowledge."[10] It is a consequence of the cosmic ignorance conceived as a self-limitation of its absolute knowledge so as to produce the divided action of the mind and the ego.

Now if absolute falsehood or error does not exist then we should be obliged to consider and examine his principle of non-contradiction (*abādhitatva*), which rests upon a complete opposition of truth and falsehood and which governs his thought from one end to the other. The experience of a snake in the rope is false, because our normal experience of the object contradicts it. Things seen in the dream are untrue, because waking life does not confirm them. And our entire normal waking experience of the world is invalid because experience of spiritual intuition (*anubhāva*) contradicts it. Firstly, it can be questioned whether there is really a contradiction between the experience of 'a snake in a rope' and that of 'a rope as a rope'. Is there not a continuity and link between the two which makes the relating possible and hence the perception of the difference possible. Similarly, if there were really no relation between the world and the *Brahman*, the apparent and the real, the relative and the absolute, it could not have been possible to think of the two together as we actually do. The illusory appearance is surely not absolutely contradictory of the real object. That is a psychological impossibility. The terms 'dream', 'illusion', 'jugglery', etc. connote unreality in the very limited sense of practical objectives of life. As facts and phenomena by themselves they are not unreal. And a right use of them as analogies (even though the best analogies are no reasons to prove a thing) cannot suggest unreality but only a different order of reality.

9. *Ibid*, II (i), p. 474.

10. *Ibid*, II (i), p. 491.

Secondly, whether the law of contradiction can have a valid application to questions of total reality, which by its essential nature and concept involves inclusion and affirmation of all facts rather than exclusion and rejection of any, which is the necessary method of this logical principle. Sri Aurobindo argues that "A law founded upon an observation of what is divided in Space and Time cannot be confidently applied to the being and action of the indivisible: not only it cannot be applied to this spaceless and timeless infinite, but it cannot be applied even to a Time Infinite and Space Infinite."[11] The lesson of the Eleatic Zeno must come back to our mind in this connection. From discrete moments of rest a unitary process of motion cannot be produced. A logic which is at home in dealing with discrete finite objects gets entangled in contradictions when it attempts to take up the infinite as its subject-matter. Positively delineating the scope of the law of contradiction Sri Aurobindo trenchantly says that "the law is necessary to us in order that we may posit partial and practical truths, think out things clearly, decisively and usefully, classify, act, deal with them effectively for particular purposes in our divisions of Space, distinctions of form and property, moments of Time."[12]

Obviously if Śaṅkara had recognized the proper sphere of application of this law he would surely have been spared all the dualisms and sharp divisions which so tenaciously pursued his search for a monism. In the West, it has been the merit of Hegel to have clearly recognized that the Absolute Idea must reconcile the very last contradictions and antinomies. It was, indeed, a supreme perception which showed him the necessity of a larger synthesis inherent in the nature of two contradictions. And it was surely a feat of philosophical genius, which enabled him to conceive of synthetic reason and the dialectical process as a higher function of thought indispensable to the consideration of the Absolute Reality.

Sri Aurobindo's perceptions in this connection are in fact clearer and more definite. "An Omnipresent Reality", says he, "is the truth of all life and existence, whether absolute or relative, whether corporeal or incorporeal, whether animate or inanimate, whether intelligent or unintelligent.... All antinomies confront each other in order to recognize one Truth in their opposed aspects and embrace by the way of conflict their mutual unity. *Brahman* is the Alpha and the Omega. *Brahman* is the one besides whom there is nothing else existent."[13] Such ultimate Reality in which all antinomies confront and realize their 'Unity' will obviously lie beyond our Intellect and Reason, which

11. *The Life Divine*, Vol. II (i), p. 51.

12. *Ibid*, II (i), p. 130.

13. *Ibid*, I, p. 51.

rely upon the law of non-contradiction. Says Sri Aurobindo: "Our way of knowing must be appropriate to that which is to be known."[14] Now a greater reason than ours is obviously operative in the ultimate reality which being all-inclusive must reconcile all contradictions and whose "essence is a higher spiritual unity" and, therefore, a higher spiritual reason or intuition is necessary to know it. Such reason must be "more vast, subtle, and complex in its operations"[15] so as to be able to comprehend the "unbounded variability" of the life of the Infinite. Our normal reason works indirectly through representative ideas and has to infer and build up constructs of reality on the basis of fragmentary gathered data. The larger and higher reason must necessarily be an instrument of direct knowledge and essential truth. If we are able to recognize that our normal reason in its search after truth is limited to an indirect approach and can at best achieve constructs of reality and obviously this faculty is a great advance on the perception of the animals and the continuation of evolution is a fact then the possibility of a direct instrumentation of knowledge becomes fairly obvious. Now the data of facts that this instrumentation might yield can be of immense importance to philosophical thinking. Such data will probably give us new unities in place of the distinctions and oppositions of our intellectual reason. But our intellect too is, to an extent, capable of a larger action, as in the West, Hegel had shown; and that by itself can prevent the catastrophic consequences of sharp mutilations of reality as has happened in *Māyāvāda*. "Our intellect", says Sri Aurobindo, "must consent to pass out of the bounds of finite logic and accustom itself to the logic of Infinite," and continues he, "if we insist on applying finite logic to the Infinite, the omnipresent reality will escape us and we shall grasp instead an abstract shadow."[16] This is exactly what happens in *Māyāvāda,* which is a perfect demonstration of the incapacity of our common logic, born out of our practical handling of the finite objects of the world, to deal with the issues of ultimate reality.

Thus ultimate reality must be Integral Reality and it will be wrong to suppose that such Reality will be a relational whole involving the fallacy of infinite regress. Bradley was right in affirming that if Reality were constructed on the basis of relational judgement, absolute knowledge would be impossible. But the view here presented is not of such a relational whole; it is of an intimate unity, which however being not abstract blankness but real unity involves inner relations, presented to it in a perception of self-identity.

---

14. *Ibid,* Vol. II (i), p. 437.

15. *Ibid.* II (i), p. 52.

16. *Ibid.* II (I), p. 43.

Śaṅkara's severe conception of identity and his exclusive prepossession with the *Upaniṣadic* descriptions of the Unity of the *Brahman* in negative terms proved absolutely determining for his philosophy. The Absolute Reality should be to him nothing but just Identity. Any difference meant a denial of it. Every determination, as in Spinoza, meant a limitation of the Absolute Substance.

To Sri Aurobindo, however, identity necessarily involves difference and the higher the identity the richer its content and the more complex its organization. Surely things of the world cannot be attributed to the *Brahman,* because He is more than the world. Therefore, the *Upaniṣads* describe Him by the terms *"neti neti"* not this, not this, but they also described him positively in the terms *"sarvam khalu idam brahma,"* All this is *Brahman,* or "annam brahma," Matter is *Brahman, "pranam brahma,"* Life is *Brahman,* etc.

Here are the two basic positions and perceptions, which make all the difference between the two philosophies.

To Śaṅkara the *Brahman* is also the supreme universal in which no particulars can have any place. "*Brahman* is devoid of anything of a like kind or of a different kind and has no internal variety".[17] This universal obviously becomes a supracosmic transcendent reality. But the nature of relations between the particular, the universal, and the transcendent as conceived here could not but lead to *Māyāvāda* and we must carefully examine them. This again implies an old controversy which has raged long and furiously both in the East and the West and we are conscious of the abstractions that vitiated the old discussions. Sri Aurobindo affirms, "The Universal particularizes itself in the individual; the individual contains in himself all the generalities of the Universal,"[18] and they both represent the Immanence of the Absolute, which must rest upon the Transcendence of the Absolute. "The transcendent", says Sri Aurobindo, "contains, manifests, constitutes the cosmos and by manifesting it manifests or discovers as we may say in the old poetic sense of that word, its own infinite harmonic varieties."[19] The individual, the universal, and the transcendent are thus necessary to one another and they together constitute the three poises of the Absolute. Now if this relation between them is correct then the individual and the universal can certainly not be sundered from the Transcendent; but if they are, the consequence irresistibly will be, on the one hand, the unreality of the world including all the moral, religious and spiritual effort of man and, on the other, a complete poverty of the Transcendent.

---

17. *sajātīya-vijātīya-svagata-bheda-rahitam.* (*Indian Philosophy,* II. p. 353.)

18. *The Life Divine,* II (i), p. 129.

19. *Ibid,* II (T), p. 129.

We know that the spiritual experience or *anubhāva* of *nirviśeṣacinmātram* (undifferenced consciousness as such) represents to Śaṅkara the ultimate reality because it is not contradicted by anything further. It is most interesting that Sri Aurobindo has a full appreciation and understanding of this experience. Says he, "the mind, when it passes those gates (the gates of the Transcendent) suddenly, without intermediate transitions, receives a sense of the unreality of world and the sole reality of silence which is one of the most powerful and convincing experiences of which the human mind is capable."[20] Buddha's basic spiritual experience was different. Now while each spiritual experience is intense and powerful, we have to recognize that in the spiritual realm too, perhaps more than the intellectual, there are large ranges and varieties of experiences. Sri Aurobindo's contribution in this connection is of the highest importance to the interpretation of Indian philosophy. He has given us an ascending order of these experiences and also a criterion of their relative valuations. Śaṅkara's experience, says he, is higher than Buddha's, but if Śaṅkara had taken a step further he would have arrived at an experience which presents the *nirguna Brahman* and the *saguna Brahman* in a single unity. To Sri Aurobindo's philosophy this fact of spiritual experience is basic and determining, as that of the *nirguna Brahman* was to Śaṅkara. Obviously this contradicts, contradicts in Śaṅkara's sense of the term, his own experience. Applying his own criterion of Truth then shall we not say that this special experience of the unity of the *saguna* and *nirguna* must be taken as the final until a yet higher experience becomes available.

Between this experience of the supreme unity of the *saguna* and the *nirguna Brahman* and our normal experience of plurality Sri Aurobindo describes a spiritual experience of a unique character and significance. This is his well-known Supermind. In it the unity is presented in and with plurality as a fact of immediate experience. In mind the plurality is the more marked and evident experience and the unity has to be constructed through piecing together of detached data. In Supermind the unity is the direct experience but the plurality is, as it were, nascently present in it. It is the instrumentation which creates out of the spaceless and timeless Absolute through self-extension the world of space and time.

Sri Aurobindo says that in the *Ṛg-veda* the description of the *ṛta-cit,* Truth-Consciousness, seem to suggest the Supermind and this is, he affirms definitely, the proper solution of illusionism as it is "the intermediate link" between the Absolute and the world, which "can explain them to each other".

The fact of Supermind is equally a matter of logical inference. We have already shown how a higher instrumentation of knowledge than mind is implied in and suggested by it. Now the Supermind is really the stage and form of the cognitive

20. *Ibid*, I, p. 34.

action which may best be described as the experience of the 'many-in-one' or the 'one-in-many'. As a universal principle it would represent the consciousness which holds the divided 'many' of the mind in an essential unity. Looked at from above the Transcendent Absolute must needs have an instrumentation through which the unity begins to translate itself into a plurality.

If we recognize our responsibility to accept all experience as valid, the Spirit as well as the material world, then Supermind is the best idea to explain their relation. And it is an idea, as much supported by logical need as by experience, present and Vedic.

Śaṅkara had said that his Absolute undifferenced consciousness was a fact of his experience. But an absolute Being is to him equally a necesssity of common experience. All unreal and passing things imply to him something abiding. Buddha could deny the world process as unity (a passing show) but for Śaṅkara the unity of the *anitya* (passing) world must imply a *nitya* (abiding) *Brahman*. Says he, "Wherever we deny something as unreal, we do so with reference to something real."[21] Śaṅkara's thinking here is very cogent. The temporal implies the eternal, the apparent, the real, the relative the Absolute. He apparently saw the inter-relatedness of these pairs and the impossibility of thinking of the one without the other. But was it then not arbitrary to call one member of these pairs unreal, virtually the one which was the starting-point and which led on to the other. If he had faithfully followed the trend of his original thinking, which had relied upon the inter-relatedness of these pairs, then he would have logically arrived at the concept of a *Brahman*, which in its rich unity must have comprehended both the aspects of these pairs.

The whole-hearted monist that Sri Aurobindo is, he naturally asks "If *Brahman* is the only reality, why speak of *Māyā* at all?" And if you do it, says he, "there will always be some form of ultimate dualism". And is the *Māyāvādin*, with all his subtle logic, really able to escape an ultimate dualism? Sri Aurobindo also urges that "the world cannot be all an illusion" since "it has real objectivity for us in any conceivable sense of the term". But "if the world is an illusion, then illusion in some sense is". And, therefore, the *Brahman* cannot be the only reality.

However the world is not the full reality of the Brahman and, therefore, an element of illusion, ignorance, *Māyā* or *Avidyā* has to be admitted as operative in the cosmic process. But it can only be conceived as a power of the *Brahman* through which he creates a world in space and time. The mind and the ego, which are the limited terms of knowledge and being subject to division, can also be nothing but willed creations, serving as transitional stages in the process of cosmic evolution. The purpose of cosmic evolution, and of the original

21. *Śaṅkara-bhāṣya*, iii, 2.22, (*Indian Philosophy*.)

involution, its necessary correlate, can only be the delight of becoming. The original involution and the self-withdrawal implied in it released the force of *Avidyā*, necessary for the joy of the rediscovery of the *Brahman* through evolution. It created the possibility of a superficial, partial and divided regard of things in the world. Ignorance is, therefore, only "a half-knowledge evolving towards knowledge".[22]

The concept of the Īśvara is a most curious phenomenon in *Māyāvāda*. It is the lord and the creator of the world and the *Māyā* is a real power to it. This supreme immanence in the world is perhaps an admission of the need and demand of the religious nature of man. But the *Māyāvadin* refuses to recognize that the religious need in itself requires an eternal principle of experience and that an Īśvara which is as illusory as the world it creates, cannot satisfy it.

Māyāvāda, we will concede, affords much satisfaction to the logical reason for the subtlety and sharpness of thinking and to the spiritual instinct for a fundamental reality, even though it leaves us in a sharp contradiction. But so far as our religious and the active aspects are concerned, it completely disappoints.

There is also another way of looking at this phenomenon of the Īśvara. The Īśvara is the representation of the Absolute *Brahman* in the world or the *Brahman* itself as It appears to us in the world. Looked at from the world It is real as immanent *Brahman*, so is his power of *Māyā* or *Avidyā* and so is the world. But looked at from the transcendent *Brahman* all this becomes unreal. Evidently, as Sri Aurobindo says, there is "a missing link between the transcendent and the immanent *Brahman*." Should Śaṅkara have seen the necessity of a positive relation between the two, the whole picture of his philosophy would have been different.

The individual human existence too is as unreal as the world for *Māyāvāda*. The Vedāntic thought and the seeking for *Brahman*, which takes place in this world would also then be unreal. Is this not a consequence as suicidal as that of scepticism, which saying that no knowledge is possible affirms something and thereby refutes itself? The *Māyāvāda* philosophy is obviously destructive of its own seeking (*vijñāsa*) for the *Brahman*, its supreme objective. And Liberation or *Mukti* too, which is oneness with the *Brahman*[23] involves a most interesting contradiction. Says Sri Aurobindo, "The individual soul can only cut the knot of ego by a supreme act of egoism, an exclusive attachment to its own individual salvation". Other souls seem to be of no consequence because they "who were equally myself remain behind in bondage."[24]

---

22. *The Life Divine* II (t), p. 282.

23. *brahmaiva hi mukti-avasthā* (*Indian Philosophy*, II, p. 639).

24. *The Life Divine*, Vol. I, p. 60.

We may now bring our consideration of *Māyāvāda* to a close. The question with which we started "Has Sri Aurobindo refuted *Māyāvāda*" will recur to us. *Māyāvāda* is an old subject and many of the objections which Sri Aurobindo's philosophy raises are bound to appear familiar. But there is an evident freshness and originality about them, because they arise out of the present-day cultural situation and answer to the curiosity of the modern mind. However the greater strength of a criticism must always lie in the constructive solutions it can offer for the same problems and herein consists the true originality and the unique satisfactoriness of Sri Aurobindo's philosophy. These constitute also the more powerful refutation of *Māyāvāda* and in this connection we would repeat that we have to carefully consider and recognize whether the "mind" and the "ego"[11] are just "intermediate representations" and "transitional stages" or not. If they are, then philosophical thinking must no longer take them as final in the cosmic evolution and should rather seek to determine the nature and the conditions of the higher instrumentations of knowledge as an epistemological inquiry precedent to the ontological determinations. The "Larger Reason" with an understanding for "the logic of the Infinite is a function and ready possibility of our normal rationality. It can easily pave the way to an appreciation of the other instrumentations of knowledge leading to the decisive "Supermind". Philosophy limited to the mind and intellect will always have to proceed upon an exceedingly partial data and will always have to remain content with a construction or a reconstruction of reality. A knowledge of reality will always remain denied to it. Our philosophical divergences under such circumstances will always remain ununderstandable and irreconcilable. Philosophy can surely show greater progress than it has done, but then we must be able to recognize that besides sense and reason there can be other cognitive processes, which may yield fresh data and suggest new explanations. Thus the advance of philosophy and the solution of its many insoluble problems lie, as Sri Aurobindo says, in "an extension of the field of our consciousness and an unhoped-for increase in our instruments of knowledge".[25]

Has Sri Aurobindo Refuted Mayavada? II by N. A. Nikam

1. Dr Indra Sen observes that Śaṅkara and Sri Aurobindo are both monists, but Śaṅkara "constantly dichotomizes" and Sri Aurobindo "always reconciles". Śaṅkara's position is: "*brahma satyam jagan mithya*

25. *The Life Divine*, I, p. 31.

jīvo brahmaiva na parah": *Brahman* is the only Reality; the world is an illusion or a false appearance; the individual soul is identical with *Brahman*"; *Brahman* is one "without a second". The two main points of Śaṅkara's teaching are: (a) that *Brahman* undergoes only an "apparent modification" in creating the world; (b) that the appearance of a world of multiplicity is due to *Avidyā;* an original or 'primitive' Ignorance, which is *anadi* or is beginning-less but has an end. In discussing the question of this symposium the main point on which it is necessary to dwell is to see whether: (a) in Sri Aurobindo's philosophy of the Life Divine this sense of "apparent modification" is also present, or whether it is transcended; and, (b) whether Sri Aurobindo does, or does not, find it necessary to postulate, also like Śaṅkara, an 'original' nescience or *Avidyā* or ignorance in his philosophy. It will not be sufficient merely to accept or reject Sri Aurobindo's weighty arguments against *māyāvāda* in chapters V & VI in Vol. II of *The Life Divine* but to make a survey of the general features of the philosophy of *The Life Divine.*

2. Throughout Sri Aurobindo's philosophy of the Life Divine there is present a certain logical distinction which I shall call the distinction between 'Appearance' (or illusion) and Manifestation; and, I shall analyze the logical presuppositions of the Appearance-Theory and the Manifestation-Theory. While Śaṅkara's Advaita may be called Appearance-Theory, the Advaita of Sri Aurobindo may be described as Manifestation-Theory. From among the several meanings of the term appearance in Western and in Indian philosophy I shall arbitrarily select one meaning: appearance "must belong to reality and yet it cannot belong to reality."

So Appearance is in its nature essentially inconsistent and self-contradictory and complex and false: it is *sat-asat-vilakṣaṇa,* "other than real and unreal" (*Essentials of Indian Philosophy*, by M. Hiriyanna p. 161). Secondly, 'appearance' is always due to a "misperception or wrong judgment; and, in either the term 'misperception' is used by McTaggart in *The Nature of Existence*, Vol. II, chapter XLVI: "Some percepts are perceived as having characteristics which they do not possess". So, error is "in the observing subject". "But when the error is one which is believed to be shared by all thinking beings in the universe and when the effects of the error are not such as to prevent the formation of an orderly and uniform system of experience, it often happens that the error is called phenomenal truth." (p. 206)

In this case appearance presupposes error. If there is no error within there is no appearance of multiplicity without. Thirdly, the Appearance-Theory implies the conception of a transcendental Reality which is above and behind appearance and the true nature of Reality is correctly stated by the logical law of non-contradiction or Identity which says: A is A; or, its true nature is correctly stated by excluding negatives: *neti, neti,* 'not-this', 'not-this.' Sri Aurobindo designates his philosophy "realistic advaita" or realistic non-dualism and the nature of Reality is to him *saccidānanda* (existence-consciousness-bliss) but the world is not an "appearance" of *saccidānanda.* It is a real Manifestation of *saccidānanda.* "The pure existent is then a fact and no mere concept; it is the fundamental reality. But, let us hasten to add, the movement, the energy, the becoming are also a fact, also a reality" (*Life Divine,* Vol. I, p. 99). The relation of *saccidānanda* to the world in Sri Aurobindo's philosophy is not "that of an original reality and phenomenal unreality, but of an original to a resultant and dependent, a temporal and manifested reality" (*Life Divine,* Vol. II, p. 197).[26]

So what are the logical implications of this theory of Sri Aurobindo which defines the relation between the world and *saccidānanda* as Manifestation? The following are some of the logical implications of the Manifestation Theory; these implications progressively define the relation between Reality and the world of manifested phenomena in Sri Aurobindo's philosophy. (1) B may be said to be a manifestation of A, when B is 'dependent upon' A and is dependent upon no other. (E.g. the world is a real creation of *Brahman* and is dependent upon it.) (2) If B is a manifestation of A, B 'belongs to' A, and B 'reveals' A; it reveals A's essence. In the Manifestation Theory, if B is the manifestation of A, then, A is the material cause of B. In the Appearance-Theory this is not the case: e.g. *Brahman* is not the material cause of the world. (3) In the relation of Manifestation A is never without B, where B is a manifestation of A. A is never without some Manifestation. As Sri Aurobindo puts it: there is "an eternal recurrence" but not an "eternal persistence" of Forms. (4) In manifestation there is an integral relation between opposites: the Eternal in the Temporal, Spirit in Matter, Unity in Multiplicity, the Static in the Dynamic, the Divine in the Human. This relation is integral in the sense that one is necessary to the other and does not contradict the other, while, the Advaita of Śaṅkara "definitely denies that there can be any relation at all between two such disparate entities as spirit and matter." (*Essentials of Indian Philosophy* by M. Hiriyanna, p. 160) So the Law of Integral Manifestation is not the Logical law of Identity which says A is A, but the comprehensive and inclusive Law: A is both A and not-A. (5) Since there is an integral relation between Reality and its manifestations all manifestations of Reality are real, because all manifestations are of the same Real. "If *Brahman* alone is", says Sri Aurobindo, "then, all that is, is Brahman". (6) Manifestation is a Process; it is a 'yet to

26. See Śaṅkara's *Vivekacūḍāmaṇi,* st. 109: *sannāpy asannāpy ubhayatmikā na.*

be'; Reality is "laboring to realize the Idea"; and the Process of Manifestation is an Evolution; thus the tremendous importance of the idea of evolution and of its application to spiritual life in the philosophy of Life Divine. In this evolutionary process the Future is of overwhelming importance and so Sri Aurobindo's vision is described as a "Vision of the Future". (7) There are two aspects of Manifestation: Descent and Ascent: Manifestation of A in B is a "Descent". It is a "Veiling". By an act of self-oblivion Spirit has 'veiled' itself in Matter, according to Sri Aurobindo. If the Descent of Spirit in Matter is a "Veiling" the self-discovery of Spirit in Matter is an Ascent; and the Path of this Self-discovery in Sri Aurobindo's philosophy of Life Divine is not *jñāna* as in Śaṅkara or *bhakti* as in Ramanuja, but an integral yoga which is "a labour of self-discipline and self-perfection, which is a sacrifice to the Supreme"; "a sacrifice of works, a sacrifice of love and adoration, a sacrifice of knowledge." (*The Synthesis of Yoga* by Sri Aurobindo, p. 103) The two processes of Descent and Ascent are always going on, and they constitute the cycle of cosmic existence; thus we are brought to the fundamental problem of the why and how of Existence and of the Cosmic Process of Sri Aurobindo's philosophy. (8) It may be noted that there is a distinction between the being of things and their becoming. Why is there Being at all and why is there any Becoming at all are two distinct questions and need distinct answers. Existence is not an inscrutable mystery, but is a delight of existence. "For who could live or breathe if there were not this delight of existence as the ether in which we dwell? From Delight all these beings are born, by Delight they exist and grow, to Delight they return". (*Taittiriya Upaniṣad*, II, 7; III; 6)[27] Existence is a Delight because "absoluteness of conscious existence is illimitable bliss of conscious existence; the two are only different phases of the same thing. All illimitableness, all infinity, all absoluteness is pure Delight". (*Life Divine*, Vol. I, p. 115) "Delight of being is universal, illimitable and self-existent and not dependent upon particular causes. (*Life Divine*, Vol. I, -p. 123)

The particular problem which the subject of this symposium raises is not the why of Existence but the why of Becoming. The philosophy of the Life Divine says that Becoming is a *Līlā*, a Play: "the play, the child's joy, the poet's joy, the author's joy, the mechanician's joy of the Soul of things eternally young, perpetually inexhaustible, creating and re-creating Himself in Himself for the sheer bliss of that self-creation, of that Self-representation, Himself the Play, Himself the Player, Himself the Playground," (*Life Divine*, Vol. I, p. 129). Supposing this is true, the play must imply a method; as there is 'a

27. *tapasvibhyo 'dhiko yogī jñānibhyo 'pi mato 'dhika. karmibhyaś cādhiko yogi tasmād yogī bhāvārjuna.* (*Bhagavadgītā* 6:46).

method in madness' so there is a method in everything; there is a method in play. So we come to the how of cosmic becoming. According to the philosophy of the Life Divine, the method of cosmic play is: "the Formless imposes Form upon itself"; this self-imposition is in the nature of a 'formative', 'limiting', 'measuring' consciousness which is a consciousness of self-division and self-oblivion. "It is to find himself in the apparent opposites of his being and his nature that *saccidānanda* descends into the material nescience and puts on its phenomenal ignorance as a superficial mask in which he hides himself from his own conscious energy, leaving it self-forgetful and absorbed in its works and forms" (*Life Divine,* Vol. II, p. 361). "The Ignorance is a necessary, though quite subordinate term which the Universal Knowledge has imposed upon itself that movement might be possible, not a blunder and a fall, but a purposeful descent, not a curse, but a divine opportunity". (*Life Divine,* Vol. II, p. 36) So there is an original ignorance in the philosophy of the Life Divine as in *Māyāvāda* which is the cause of phenomenal multiplicity. The point is not that the multiplicity is real in Sri Aurobindo's philosophy and is unreal in Śaṅkara's philosophy; the point rather is that *Līlāvāda* has the same metaphysical pre-suppositions as *Māyāvāda,* and uses the same method as *Māyāvāda* to explain cosmic Becoming. Sri Aurobindo distinguishes between two senses of the term *Māyā*: (a) a measuring, limiting and formative consciousness: (b) a certain cunning or fraud or illusion or enchantment (Vol. I, p. 127). It is in the second sense that the term *Māyā* is used, he says, in Māyāvāda.

Now, if the *doctrine* or the *Līlā* has refuted *Māyāvāda,* it has 'refuted' it in the Hegelian sense in which a lower category is refuted by including it in the higher. The philosophy of the Life Divine implies both the meanings of *Māyā*. The first possibility of there being any cosmic becoming consists in a measuring, limiting and formative consciousness; while the actuality of the descent of spirit in matter is possible by a "Veiling" which is another name for 'cunning'. It is the 'cunning' of *saccidānanda* that it "loses itself in the appearance of non-being and emerges in the appearance of discordant Rhythm of varied pain, pleasure and neutral feeling, love, hatred and indifference; infinite Unity loses itself in the appearance of a chaos of multiplicity and emerges in a discord of forces and beings which seek to recover reunity by possessing, dissolving and devouring each other. In this creation the real *saccidānanda* has to emerge" (*Life Divine*).

3. It is asked: where is the Ignorance? On what plane of Being does this occur? The answer in *Life Divine* is: on the plane of mind. (Vol. II, p. 303) Yes, the real saccidananda could emerge only from a real saccidananda. Real *saccidānanda* is at the end because it is at the beginning. So the

question is: Has *saccidānanda* undergone a real or only an "apparent modification?" There is no unambiguous and straight-forward answer to this question because, two different standpoints, the empirical and the transcendental, are involved in it; and, on this point, *Līlāvāda* is in no better position than *Māyāvāda*, which says that the world is empirically real and transcendentally ideal. The motive of realistic *Līlāvāda* is to "justify the presence of reality in all its appearances." which F. H. Bradley said is 'the last word of philosophy'; so according to *Līlāviida* everything is real because it is of the same Real. Realistic *Līlāvada*, after all, asserts, like *Māyāvāda*, the Law of Identity: A is A: 'All this is *Brahman*', because *Brahman* is the All: *Brahman* "alone is; nothing else is."

4. Between the *Māyāvāda* of Śaṅkara and the *Līlāvāda* of the *Life Divine*, there is a Major premise which is common to both. *Māyāvāda* says:

The world is a dream
Dreams are unreal
Therefore, the world is unreal.

The *Līlāvada* of *Life Divine* says:

The world is a dream,
dreams are real.
Therefore, the world is real.

In refuting the *Māyāvāda* doctrine that the world is a dream, the philosophy of the Life Divine does not merely discuss this theory but constructs an elaborate metaphysical (and not a psycho-analytical) theory of dream to prove its minor premise: 'Dreams are real'. The outlines of this metaphysical theory of dream are as follows:

(i) In sleep, the waking activities are in abeyance, but the "inner consciousness is not suspended but enters into new inner activities."
(ii) The whole of this inner activity we do not remember; we remember only what is near the surface.
(iii) Near the surface there is "an obscure subconscious element which is a receptacle or passage for our dream experiences and itself also a dream-builder." (*Life Divine*, Vol. II, p. 155) (It is the subconcious that is the dream-builder.)
(iv) But behind it is the "subliminal" self which is the totality of our inner being and consciousness; this subliminal self "is quite of another order."

From this it would look as if the subconscious which is intermediate between the waking self and the subliminal self is the dream-builder. The philosophy of the *Life Divine* observes: "But the sub-consciousness is not our sole dream-builder." (Vol. II, p. 156). The substance of the difficult and rather paradoxical argument on p. 157 in *The Life Divine* is: "we dream not only in dreams, but in dreamless sleep." "We are dreaming there but unable to grasp or retain in the recording layer of subconscious these more obscure dream figures." (Vol. II, p. 157) If this argument is correct then the implication is that, the deeper we go into our inner being the more we discover that we dream: "If we develop our inner being, live more inwardly than most men do, then the balance is changed and a larger dream consciousness opens before us; our dreams can take on a subliminal and no longer a subconscious character and can assume a reality and significance." (*Life Divine*, Vol. II, p. 159) This may be true; but the meaning of the term 'dream' has changed and it seems that we ought to substitute for the Cartesian *Cogito ergo sum* the proposition: I dream, therefore, I exist.

5. Throughout the philosophy of the *Life Divine* there recurs the term 'the logic of the Infinite'. The extraordinary merit and charm of the philosophy of the *Life Divine* is that, while it denies the logic of idealistic *Māyāvāda*, it does not deny the reality of its spiritual experience. It recognizes that the experience which *Māyāvāda* "formulates into a philosophy accompanies a most powerful and apparently final spiritual realization." (*Life Divine*, Vol. II, p. 212) What *Līlāvāda*, however, denies is the logic of *Māyāvāda*. Like Modern Realism, *Līlāvada* denies the ultimate validity of the Law of Contradiction. Speaking of Realism and of mathematical logic Professor C. D. Broad says that it does "not welcome contradictions as proofs that such and such features in the apparent world are unreal." (*Contemporary British Philosophy*, First Series, p. 781) Likewise, but in a different manner, the philosophy of the Life Divine: "But what appears as contradictions to a reason based on the finite, may not be contradictions to a vision or a larger reason based on the infinite." (*Life Divine*, Vol. II, p. 229) "To understand truly the world-process of the Infinite and the Time-process of the Eternal, the consciousness must pass beyond this finite reason and the finite sense to a larger reason and spiritual sense in touch with the consciousness of the infinite and responsive to the logic of the Infinite which is the very logic of being itself and arises inscrutably from its self-operation of its own realities, a logic whose sequences are not the steps of thought but the steps of existence." (*Life Divine*, Vol. II, p. 219–220) This must bring us after all, to a sense of "dichotomy" between the logic of the finite and the logic of the infinite between thought and existence. So, there is a dichotomy in Sri Aurobindo's philosophy as there is alleged to be in Śaṅkara's philosophy. This dichotomy is such that it leaves *Māyāvāda* unrefuted.

6. But there is no treatise which has urged such powerful arguments against the doctrine of the unreality of the world and has endeavoured to present to us the true philosophy of our Upaniṣads with a logic and a light all its own, which conveys so successfully the sense of the reality of the Divine and the divine operation in things than the profoundly important two volumes of Sri Aurobindo's *Life Divine.*

Has Sri Aurobindo Refuted Māyāvāda? III

by Haridas Chaudhuri

There is a sense in which none of the ultimate standpoints of thought or representative philosophical positions can be finally refuted. Logical refutation in the usual acceptation of the term can hardly be expected to knock the bottom out of a philosophical theory; to the opponent's mind, it only underlines the necessity of a better and more accurate formulation of his own particular point of view. That is why all such basic metaphysical positions as Realism and Idealism, Monism and Pluralism, Materialism and Spiritualism, and the like, survive up to the present day, all opposition and refutation notwithstanding. Realism repudiates Idealism, and Idealism hits back, and both go on merrily expanding their respective spheres of influence; Pluralism attacks Monism with its "atomic weapons," and Monism seeks to conquer Pluralism in its inclusive embrace; Materialism pours contempt on Spiritualism as idle day-dreaming or wishful thinking, and Spiritualism quietly sets aside Materialism as no better than a kind of enlightened animalism. And thus the same old conflict that started with the history of philosophical reflection perpetually goes on. Every philosophical system, in so far as it embodies an important aspect of truth, or a definite perspective of reality, survives by reason of its own inner vitality. Apparently vanquished or finished with, it always re-appears with renewed vigour in ever fresh forms. Every great philosopher realizes that synthesis or harmony is the very essence of philosophical truth. Consequently, every philosophical system endeavours to achieve some sort of synthesis within itself by exhibiting the opposed standpoints as subordinate factors in its own *Weltanschauung.* But the real harmony can hardly be achieved at the logical level, because no rigidly logical scheme of thought or conceptual formulation can fully articulate the integral truth, or do full justice to the truth of the opposite standpoint.

Māyāvāda is one such fundamental philosophical position. No conclusive refutation of it is possible at the logical level, because seldom do logical arguments carry conviction to the human heart. There have been critics of *Māyāvāda* in the past, there are critics at the present day, and there will be critics in future, but still *Mayavada* is sure to survive. No intelligent supporter of *Māyāvāda* can have any difficulty in finding an answer to every point of criticism that may be made against it. It has its own peculiar standpoint and framework of fundamental assumptions. All refutation, therefore, quite naturally appears to it as external, and, consequently, inspired by a greater or lesser degree of misunderstanding of its own real position. Now, it should be stated at the very outset that *Māyāvāda* is not simply refuted but transcended and sublated in Sri Aurobindo's philosophy. Philosophical criticism is, for Sri Aurobindo, not a purely logical affair, but an evaluation of fundamental metaphysical or spiritual insights in the light of his own integral spiritual experience. He places before us a higher metaphysical insight such as is inclusive, not exclusive, of the truth inherent in *Māyāvāda*. He appeals to an integral spiritual realization such as discloses the deepest secret of reconciliation of all philosophical conflicts. The arguments which he advances against *Māyāvāda* are, in the last analysis, the negative side of a rational articulation of his supra-intellectual truth-vision. They are indeed perfectly reasonable, but reasonable with a deeper rationality of the reality that transcends the intellect, and as such they embody what has been described by him as "the logic of the Infinite." It has been said that when in the Upaniṣadic age of ancient India one seeker of truth met another, the main question which they put to each other was, not "What is your theory and your argument?", but "What is your spiritual realization?" That was followed by a comparison and evaluation of different forms of spiritual experience. Sri Aurobindo believes that if a particular form of spiritual experience is found to include within itself and illumine another form of spiritual experience, then the former must be accepted as a greater revelation of the supreme truth. Self-luminous or self-coherent inclusiveness is indeed the criterion of ultimate truth.

In the present paper, I should like first of all briefly to indicate what according to Sri Aurobindo is the value, importance, or significance of *Māyāvāda*. Next, I shall turn to a consideration of the various misunderstandings to which *Māyāvāda* has been subjected at the hands of its critics, and then to a critical examination of the various modes of interpretation to which *Māyāvāda* has lent itself at the hands of its advocates. I shall conclude with a few observations on Prof. N. A. Nikam's criticism of Sri Aurobindo's position.

The Significance of *Māyāvāda*

Māyāvāda represents one of the ultimate standpoints of philosophic thinking. It is noted for its logical charm and simplicity and its speculative boldness, in consequence of which it has a great intellectual appeal. But, what is of much greater importance, *Māyāvāda* embodies a very deep spiritual insight into the nature of ultimate reality. The enunciation of *Māyāvāda* was indeed a historical necessity in the course of India's varied spiritual experiments with the Truth. Prior to an integral realization of the Spirit in its multiform richness of content it was of vital importance that the Spirit should have been clearly grasped in its transcendent purity. *Māyāvāda* is a clear logical formulation of an unfettered realization of the Spirit, the Self, *Brahman*, in its aspect of supracosmic transcendent only, in its eagerness to perceive Reality in its highest height, it turns a blind eye to its extent or comprehensiveness; in its eagerness to know the Self in its full freedom it fails to take note of its immeasurable opulence. But still viewed from the perspective of the history of spiritual evolution, it was imperatively necessary that *Brahman* should have been grasped in its utmost purity before being experienced in its full integrality.

Consideration of some misunderstandings about *Māyāvāda*

It has already been observed that *Māyāvāda* has been subjected to various misunderstandings at the hands of its critics. In order to form a correct estimate of *Māyāvāda* it is essential that its true meaning should be carefully disentangled from all such misunderstandings.

The fundamental contention of *Māyāvāda* is that the world is essentially a product of *Māyā* it is *mithya* or unreal. It is in the nature of an illusory superimposition on the basis of *Brahman* which is pure, unobjective, undifferentiated consciousness. But, what is the precise meaning of the term '*mithya*' or 'unreal'? It does not surely mean that the variegated world of our experience is a mere non-entity or void, a metaphysical zero, an *asat* or *śūnya*. Śaṅkara's scathing criticism of the Sautrantika school of Buddhism is clear evidence of that. It is meaningless to suggest that the world which is a positive fact of our experience emerges out of nothing. Nor can it be reasonably held that a mere non-entity or void functions as the positive content of our experience.

Secondly, the world is assuredly not unreal in the sense of being '*tuccha*' or formally self-contradictory like 'round square' or 'barren mother'. Such self-contradictory entities which owe their origin to some sort of verbal juggler, and cannot really be even so much as thought of by us, can no more function as the object of our experience than a mere non-entity.

Thirdly, the world is not said to be unreal in the sense of being *alika*, i.e., imaginary or fanciful like the sky-flower. It cannot obviously be a free creation of our fancy, because it is obstrusively thrust upon us, and is "given" to our perceptual experience.

Fourthly, *Māyāvāda* does not imply that the world is a mere externalization or objectification of our subjective cognitions. That is evident from Śaṅkara's refutation of the *Vijñānavāda* school of Buddhism. Had there been no objectively real facts at all, it would have been impossible even to mistake internal cognitions for external facts. Epistemologically considered, Śaṅkara is an uncompromising realist. He assigns some kind of objectivity even to our ordinary illusory experience. He speaks of *pratibhāṣika satya*, and expounds what is known as *anirvacanīya-khyāti-vāda*, having energetically repudiated *asat-khyāti-vāda* and *ātma-khyātivāda*. Śaṅkara's *Māyāvāda* must, therefore, be carefully distinguished from all forms of mentalism or subjective idealism. While, according to Berkeley, the essence of a thing consists in being perceived, according to Śaṅkara, the perception of a thing is conclusive proof of its objectivity. Śaṅkara agrues much with the emphasis of a modern neo-realist that the object of perception, by reason of the very fact that it is perceived by us, must be admitted to have some kind of reality of its own. He is, however, unyielding on one point, namely, that everything short of *Brahman* is real only relatively to the standpoint of ignorance (*Avidyā*.)

Finally, it should also be noted that the world is not unreal in the sense of being a pure sense-illusion. Śāṅkara makes a clear distinction between the illusory and the phenomenal, the *pratibhāṣika* and the *vyavahārika*, even though both of them may be equally unreal from the standpoint of Brahman. While the illusory is private and short-lived, the phenomenal is universal and relatively permanent. While the illusory is not only useless but also harmful from the practical point of view, the phenomenal is undoubtedly endowed with practical usefulness or pragmatic validity. From this it should not, however, be concluded that *Māyāvāda* looks upon the *pratibhāṣika* and the *vyavahārika* as different degrees of truth and reality in the Bradleyan sense of the term. They are, as we have already observed, equally unreal from the standpoint of ultimate reality. The distinction between them is pragmatic, not ontological.

Thus we find that when *Māyāvāda* declares the world to be unreal, it does not mean that the world is a void or non-entity (*śunya* or *asat*), or that it is formally self-contradictory (*tuccha*), or that it is fanciful or imaginary (*alika*), or that it is a subjective idea (*vijñāna*), or that it is a pure illusion (*bhranti*).

An Examination of *Māyāvāda*

What then is the exact meaning of the statement that the world is unreal (*mithya*)? Eminent authorities on the Śaṅkara Vedānta are agreed that the world is unreal in the sense that it is logically indeterminable (*anirvacanīya*), so that the categories of being and non-being are simply inapplicable in the determination of its ontological status. The world cannot be said to be nonexistent, because it functions as the positive content and objective terminus of our perceptual experience. The world cannot also be said to be existent, because it is flatly contradicted (*badhita*) on our realization of the supreme truth, *Brahman*. Nor is it open to us to hold that the world is at once existent and non-existent, because that would be a flagrant violation of the fundamental law of contradiction. While from the standpoint of *Avidyā* or *Māyā* the world is real and endowed with pragmatic validity, it is assuredly unreal from the standpoint of ultimate reality. It is *sadasadvilakṣaṇa*.

Now, it will be evident from the *Māyāvādin's* elaboration of his concept of unreality (*mithyatva*) that he finally takes his stand upon a fundamental duality of standpoints, the empirical and the ultimate or transcendental. And yet he leaves that duality unresolved and unreconciled. What is the logical transition from the higher standpoint to the lower? In other words, how are we to understand the logical derivation of the empirical standpoint from the ultimate or transcendental standpoint? A failure to answer this question is extremely unsatisfactory in a monistic system of thought. The *Māyāvādin's* usual reply in this connection is: "Oh, that is a question which ought not to be asked at all, because it proceeds from abysmal ignorance!" Now, to explain everything in terms of Ignorance and yet make no attempt to derive ignorance from knowledge is as irrational as it is inimical to the monistic outlook. The *Māyāvādin* will perhaps retort by saying that the demand for an explanation of ignorance in terms of knowledge is prompted by a total failure to understand the very meaning of ignorance. For, is not ignorance a final irrationality, about which no further question should be asked? That is indeed a very curious position. In order to avoid dualism, the *Māyāvādin* says that *Māyā* is an eternally cancelled falsehood (*sanatana mithya*); in order to account for the world of our experience, he declares that *Māyā* is beginningless and positive (*anadi* and *bhāvivarupa*); and in order to avoid the necessity for a rational explanation of the principle of *Māyā*, he describes it as a final irrationality, a logically indefinable mystery (*mahadbhuta anirvacanīya-rūpa*). And it passes one's comprehension how an eternally cancelled falsehood and irrationality can function as a beginning-less positive entity productive of a highly significant world of experience.

It has been observed that according to *Māyāvāda* while the world is real from the standpoint of *Avidyā*, it is unreal from the standpoint of *Brahman*. There seems to be some difference of opinion on this point among the interpreters of *Māyāvāda*. According to some, the world is unreal in the sense that it is not as real as *Brahman*, from which it follows that the world possesses a subordinate and inferior type of reality intermediate between *Brahman* and non-being. Whereas *Brahman* is permanent and non-temporal, the world is impermanent, evanescent or ephemeral; whereas *Brahman* is the embodiment of the highest values of life, the world is void of any enduring worth or value. Now, the world so understood is either related or not related to *Brahman*. If the world be in any way related to *Brahman*, then the necessity is imposed upon the *Māyāvādin* for precisely determining the nature of that relationship consistently with the differentiated unity of *Brahman*. If the world, supposed to enjoy a peculiar subordinate type of reality, be not in any way related to *Brahman*, then we are landed in a position of unmitigated dualism.

According to a second school of interpretation, the world is unreal in the sense of being absolutely non-existent (*asat* or *tuccha*) from the standpoint of ultimate reality. On such an interpretation, no satisfactory explanation of the world of our experience can evidently be sought in the nature of *Brahman*. *Brahman*, which is void of any power of self-determination (*nirguna*), can have nothing to do with the world of determinations, which is a mere nothing to it. The *Māyāvādin* will no doubt reply by saying that the world being essentially unreal, the question of its explanation does not arise at all. But it must be noted that even though the world be unreal or illusory, the fact of its being so remains and demands explanation. The appearance of an unreal world as a real world is no less in need of explanation than the creation of a real world by a real power. The *Māyāvādin* will perhaps say that the appearance of the world is itself false or illusory because the world being illusory there can be only an illusory and no true perception of it. How can there be a true perception of a false world? But this will appear on examination to be an evasion of the real difficulty. Taking for granted that we have only a false perception of a false world, there is no getting away from the fact that there is the appearance of a true perception of a real world. Taking for granted that the world and our perception of it are equally false, the fact of a false world falsely appearing to false perception must itself be admitted to be an eternal truth. It is an eternal fact, or an eternally true proposition which has got to be explained. If this eternal fact also be declared to be false, then the *Māyāvādin* would be confuted out of his own mouth. If this eternal fact be accepted as true, then the *Māyāvādin* must provide some explanation of this eternal truth in terms of its ultimate principle *Brahman*. But can the *Māyāvādin's Brahman* be treated as a source of explanation of this eternal truth? If so, then *Māyā* conceived as a power of presenting a false appearance to some false percipient must be accepted as a power inherent in *Brahman*, in which case *Brahman* would cease to be absolutely *nirguna*. If, on the contrary, no explanation of this eternal truth is to be found in the nature of *Nirguna Brahman*, then the latter ceases to be the sole ultimate reality, and must be accepted as only a particular poise of being of the supreme Reality, as Aurobindo maintains.

Again, the question may be raised: Does the world have even a false appearance from the standpoint of *Brahman?* According to some, the world appears as unreal only to the *Jivanmukta* and to *Īśvara*, but not to *Brahman*, from whose standpoint the world as a pure nonentity is less than a false appearance. On the realization of *Brahman*, the world entirely vanishes into nothingness, just as the false snake completely disappears on the true perception of the rope. So, viewed from the standpoint of *Brahman*, not only is the world unreal, there is not even any appearance of an unreal world. On such an interpretation, *Brahman* must suffer from some limitation of knowledge in so far as it is unaware of the eternal fact of a false world falsely appearing to the false perception of false individuals. According to others, *Brahman*, who is the ultimate ground-consciousness, must indeed be aware of the world, but then *Brahman* is aware of the world as a false appearance just as the scientifically enlightened human mind is aware of the sun's movement in the sky as a false appearance. In that case, what is it that is responsible for the presentation of a false appearance to *Brahman*? It cannot be a power of ignorance inherent in *Brahman*, because *Brahman* is *nirguna*. It cannot be a power of ignorance inherent in *Īśvara*, because from the standpoint of *Brahman*, *Īśvara* does not exist as a separate reality. It cannot also be regarded as a self-existent power, because that would militate against the undivided unity and sovereign reality of *Brahman*.

Finally, there is another question that may be put to the *Māyāvādin*. Is *Īśvara* in any way affected or deluded by *Māyā*? *Īśvara* is the creator, sustainer, and destroyer of the world. But does *Īśvara* labour under any false impression that the world is ultimately real, or that the qualities of being creator, sustainer, and destroyer are his limiting determinations? If so, then *Īśvara* is not the Lord of Māyā in the strict sense of the term, but is as much a victim of *Māyā* as the *Jiva* is. If, on the contrary, *Īśvara* is free from any such self-delusion, then why regard *Īśvara*hood as a mere illusory superimposition (*adhyāsa*) on the basis of *Brahman*? Why consider *mokṣa* or absorption in *Brahman* as a higher ideal than *Līlā-sāhacarya*, i.e., blissful communion and conscious co-operation with the dynamic Divine for the fulfilment of His purpose in the world? If *Īśvara* is the Lord of *Māyā* in the full sense of the term, then he can by no means be regarded as a mere phenomenal manifestation. So Sri Aurobindo rightly contends that *Brahman* and *Īśvara*, supra-cosmic silence and cosmic creativity, are equally real and eternal terms of existence. It follows from this that dynamic co-operation with the divine will for the fulfilment of the divine purpose immanent in the world is a far greater ideal of life than that of static absorption in *Nirguna Brahman*. That is why Śrī Kṛṣṇa emphatically declares in the *Gītā* that a yogi, or a man dynamically united with the Divine, is by far preferable in his eyes to all other categories of spiritual aspirants.

Prof. Nikam's Observations examined

Prof. N. A. Nikam has brought out with admirable clarity and precision the full significance of Sri Aurobindo's view that the world is a genuine manifestation of *Brahman*, and not an unreal superimposition on its basis. As Sri Aurobindo views it, the variegated world of our experience is indeed an expression of some imperative truths in the nature of ultimate reality. Prof. Nikam is also perfectly right when he observes at the conclusion of his article that Sri Aurobindo's two profoundly important volumes of *The Life Divine*, more than any other treatise, have endeavoured to present to us the true philosophy of the Upaniṣads and convey to us the all-pervasive and dynamic presence of the Divine in all things. But the comments which he makes on Sri Aurobindo's philosophical position seem quite encompatible with the aforesaid appreciation. Dr Indra Sen has said that while Śaṅkara "constantly dichotomises," Sri Aurobindo "always reconciles." Prof. N. A. Nikam points out by way of criticism that in Sri Aurobindo's philosophy also there is a dichotomy, the dichotomy between the logic of the finite and the logic of the Infinite, the dichotomy between thought and existence. But had Prof. Nikam looked a bit closer into Sri Aurobindo's philosophy, he would have certainly noticed that whatever dichotomy or antinomy one comes across in that philosophy is not left unresolved, but is reconciled in the harmony of an inclusive unity. True, there is according to Sri Aurobindo an essential difference between the logic of the Infinite which constitutes the deeper rationality of Reality itself and the logic of the finite which is characteristic of our rational thinking. But there is, in his view, no yawning chasm or unbridgeable gulf between the two. He shows how the supra-mental self-knowledge of the Infinite expresses itself at a lower level in the form of the rational intellect as its own subordinate instrumentation or inferior mode of operation, and how again the rational mind, by casting off its vanity and rigidity and through adequate self-opening and self-surrender, can pass over into the infinite consciousness of the Supermind. There is not only a continuous passage between the logic of the Infinite and the logic of the finite, between supra-rational Being and rational thinking, between the Supermind and the Mind, but the latter can even be more and more expanded and heightened and finally transformed into a flawless medium of self-utterance of the former.

Then again, Prof. Nikam says that between the *Māyāvāda* of Śaṅkara and the *Līlāvāda* of Sri Aurobindo there is a common premise, namely, "The, world is a dream." Prof. Nikam supposes that Sri Aurobindo considers the world to be real, because although the world is a dream, dreams are in his view real. Now, such a presentation of Sri Aurobindo's view about the world appears to our mind to rest upon a misunderstanding. In Sri Aurobindo's view, the world is real, not because dreams are real, but because it is a genuine self-manifestation of the supra-cosmic Spirit. It is an expression of some imperative truths embedded in the nature of the Infinite. It is an outcome of the fullness of joy that is in the heart of God, a manifestation of His delight of becoming (*anandam hy eva khalv imam bhutani jayante*). The question of dream crops up in Sri Aurobindo's philosophy in connection with his critical evaluation of *Māyāvāda*. *Māyāvāda* considers the world to be as unreal as a dream. Just as dreams disappear into nothingness on the attainment of wakeful experience, so also the world is supposed to be revealed as an unreality on the realization of the self-shining truth. But Sri Aurobindo points out that dreams, rightly understood, provided no real support to the contention of *Māyāvāda*. Dreams are not unreal simply because they are excluded from waking experience. Waking experience is as much excluded from dream experience as dream experience is excluded from waking experience. The truth about the matter is that waking and dreaming represent two different orders of one and the same Reality; they constitute different grades of our self-experience and world-experience.[28]

Modern Psychology in course of its exploration of the unconscious regions of the mind has come to discover that dreams have a profound truth and connected significance of their own. In modern European philosophy, such extremes of thought as Neo-Realism and the Absolute Idealism of Bradley and Bosanquet, agree in holding that dreams can hardly be dismissed as unreal and arbitrary constructions of fancy, and Aurobindo maintains that besides the bulk of our ordinary dreams which are significant creations of the subconscient, there are "subliminal dreams," some of which occur to us in the shape of warnings, premonitions, prophetic utterances, glimpses into the future and the like, and some of which again are records of happenings seen or experienced by us on other planes of our own being or of universal being into which we may enter on the automatic stilling of the surface mentality during sleep.

The point to be particularly noted here is that the dream analogy is not, according to Aurobindo, available as an illustration of the lack of significance and reality of the external world. Both the dream world and the waking world (*Jagrat* and *Svapna*) are in truth different forms of manifestation of the same ultimate Reality. What is unreal is not the world as such but the world ignorantly supposed to be self-existent and real apart from *Brahman*. The world as it wrongly appears to the eye of Ignorance is a distorted perspective of the world which is revealed to the eye of Knowledge as a genuine self manifestation of the supreme Reality. In Sri Aurobindo's view, the world is not only real, but is deeply significant as the field of progressive self-revelation of the Divine in such apparent contraries of his nature as discord and division, darkness and distress, death and disability. But be it observed that the reality

---

28. *The Life Divine*, Vol. II (i), p. 202.

of the world does not in any way detract from the full freedom, eternal self-sufficiency, and infinite opulence of the supreme Spirit. Just as on the one hand Sri Aurobindo does not accept the position of Śaṅkara that the world is unreal from the standpoint of ultimate reality, so also on the other hand he would not agree with Bradley that the Absolute Spirit "has no asssets beyond the appearances" such as constitute the very stuff of its existence, or with Hegel that the Absolute depends on the world for its own perfection and self-fulfilment. Although in respect of his delight of becoming *Brahman* descends into the world of manifestation as infinite creativity, in respect of his delight of immutable being, he is eternally self-sufficient as supracosmic silence. Although by virtue of his superconscient creative energy, the *śakti,* he is the creator and lord of the universe, yet he is absolutely free either to allow or not to allow his *śakti,* the divine mother, to embark upon her creative adventures. To be at once freedom and creativity, transcendence and universality, silence and activity, that is indeed the profoundest mystery of existence, the standing miracle in the nature of the spirit.

Has Sri Aurobindo Refuted Māyāvāda?
IV by G. R. Malkani

1. I hold the view that Sri Aurobindo has not refuted *Māyāvāda.* My positive contribution to the subject is offered elsewhere. Here I merely tackle certain points raised by my esteemed friends, with all of whom I disagree.

2. According to Indra Sen, the fundamental attack of Sri Aurobindo consists in his formulation of the philosophical problem itself. This is the reconciliation of spirit and matter, which are both taken to be real. The idea is that all experience is to be accepted, and no form of it is to be rejected. Acceptance and reconciliation certainly. But reconciliation must not be artificial or forced. The fundamental fact of experience is that the spirit is known to us only in the intuition of 'I' (*aham-pratyāya*); and matter is only known to us in the intuition of 'this' (*idam-pratyāya*). These two intuitions are absolutely opposed to each other like light and darkness. Nothing accordingly can ever have the character of both I-ness and this-ness. How is the reconciliation to be achieved without rejection? Aurobindo looks at the matter from a neutral standpoint, and sees no opposition. We cannot agree with this external view of spirit. It degrades spirit to the status of an object. The reality of matter is a challenge to the integrity of spirit. The so-called duality of the subject and the object is not a higher form of reality inclusive of both. It is still presentable as object, and is thus reducible

to the category of 'this-ness', which is the category of matter. The purity and the integrity of spirit demand the rejection of matter as an illusory appearance in all its forms, gross and subtle.

3. The same argument is to be pursued strictly with regard to the reconciliation of unity and multiplicity. Both can never be true, and both can never be reconciled. It is no real unity, which is not a pure undifferentiated unity. The moment we introduce multiplicity within it, and conceive a differentiated unity, we take away from its unitary character and disrupt it from within. We wrongly ask, unity of what?, as though the unity must include a multiplicity. But if the multiplicity thus included is real, no amount of unification can avail against it or unify it. We are misled by teleological unities, which are only functional or subjective. Such unities are, ontologically speaking, quite fictitious. We cannot therefore agree with the view of Sri Aurobindo that "identity necessarily involves difference and the higher the identity the richer the content and the more complex its organization" (Indra Sen). This makes the conception of identity meaningless. We have the perception of identity only in the case of the self, I am the same person today as I was yesterday. This perception of self-identity, which is never annulled, can only be true, if the differences of today and yesterday are completely eliminated from the unity of the self.

4. Another form of attack against *Māyāvāda* is on the basis of a superior spiritual experience. Nikam and Chaudhury hold opposite views in this respect. Nikam says, "The extraordinary merit and charm of the philosophy of the Life Divine is that, while it denies the logic of idealistic *Māyāvāda* it does not deny the reality of its spiritual experience. ..." Chaudhury, on the other hand, avers that no conclusive refutation of *Māyāvāda* is possible at the logical level. "Sri Aurobindo places before us a higher metaphysical insight which is inclusive, not exclusive, of the truth inherent in *Māyāvāda*. He appeals to an integral spiritual realization such as discloses the deepest secret of reconciliation of all philosophical conflicts".

I cannot agree with Nikam that the main difference is about the logic of *Māyāvāda*, and not about the spiritual experience at the back of that logic. The real difference is here, Sri Aurobindo concedes that the experience of undifferentiated unity is an intense spiritual experience which tends to wipe out multiplicity or at least to make it appear unreal or illusory. But he contends that it is one-sided. There is a more inclusive experience, an experience that presents the *Nirguna Brahman* and the *Saguna Brahman* in a single unity.

There is, it appears to me, some confusion here. I can understand that there is an experience of *Brahman* as undifferentiated unity, or *Brahman* understood as wholly transcendent and giving no place to the multiplicity of experience. I can also understand an experience of *Brahman* as the indwelling Spirit qualified by the multiplicity, the position of Ramanuja. But how are the two experiences to be reconciled so as to constitute a single experience of both *Saguna Brahman* and *Nirguna Brahman* passes my understanding. *Saguna Brahman* must either lose its differentiating character and coalesce with *Nirguna Brahman*, or it must stand out and thereby qualify or limit the latter in some way. In the former case, *Nirguna Brahman* constitutes the only reality; in the latter case, *Nirguna Brahman* is degraded and replaced by *Brahman* that is qualified. How is any experience possible which can keep them what they are and still bring them into a unity? To call the experience of *Nirguna Brahman* as one-sided does not make sense.

There is another verbal subterfuge by which this contradiction is sought to be resolved. It is said that *Nirguna Brahman* is only a certain poise of Ultimate Reality. Ultimate Reality sometimes retreats within itself to a deeper stratum where it loses all differences, and becomes to all appearance *Nirguna Brahman*. But then does not this deeper stratum represent its true Selfhood? Are there any differences there? If they are present in a nascent form and are not wholly abolished, let us at least admit that here is no genuine experience of *Nirguna Brahman*, and that what appears to be such is quite illusory in character. There can be no compromise between reality that is qualified and reality that is unqualified. The one cannot be a real poise of the other. We can only mistake the one for the other.

5. In this connection, I cannot agree with Indra Sen's contention that falsehood is partial truth. The distinction between truth and falsehood is logically absolute. Truth is one and indivisible. There can be no degrees of it. There can be degrees of error, and that for practical purposes only. For error can take different forms almost indistinguishable from truth. It can take us farther and farther away from truth, or bring us nearer and nearer to it. But on a strictly theoretical plane, the distinction between truth and error is complete and absolute. The only true experience is that which cancels all other forms of experience as erroneous, but itself remains uncancelled. By this test, the experience of undifferentiated unity cannot be partially true. It must be wholly true, or not at all.

6. Indra Sen finds fault with the principle of non-contradiction or *abdahitatva* as he calls it, which rests upon a complete opposition of truth and falsehood. He thinks that there is a continuity and a link between the experience of 'a snake in a rope' and the experience of the rope itself. This is a complete misunderstanding of the experience of *abhāvaddha* or cancellation. The illusory appearance is to be wholly rejected or negated. It has no place in the truth. Its only link with the truth is the ground or *adhisthana*; but

this is a complete negation of it. We must not confuse a logical evaluation of the truth-value of a fact with the fact itself as a psychological occurrent. The illusory snake is part of a misperception, but it is wholly non-existent as objective truth.

We are told that the law of non-contradiction does not apply to the whole or to the infinite, and that *Māyāvāda* is based upon the universal validity of this law. But can any intelligence accept a contradiction? Can reality for instance be both qualified as well as unqualified? If it can be both, then we do not know what we are talking. The so-called logic of the Infinite cannot annul the law of non-contradiction. All that it can possibly show is that there is no contradiction in the Infinite, not that the law itself is abrogated there and that contradictory elements can both be housed in it. Logic itself may be superseded; for the very distinctions and conflicts on which logic is based are unavailable in the Infinite. But if logic is applicable, the law of non-contradiction is also applicable. The logic of the Infinite can only consist in the recognition that the Infinite is wholly transcendent and unrelated to the finite, and that the latter is only an erroneous formulation of the former that requires to be negated. There is no higher or larger reason that can reconcile the two, or abrogate the law of non-contradiction itself.

7. In this connection, we may also note that *Māyāvāda* is not an expression of a sense of inexplicability in the presence of a contradiction between the normal experience and the supernormal experience, as held by Indra Sen. It is not a case of frustration of our intelligence and the acceptance of a contradiction which we cannot get over. The higher experience cancels the lower as untrue. Where then is the contradiction? Where is the mystery or inexplicability? If *Māyāvāda* is true, the riddle of existence is completely resolved. The world is an illusory appearance; and no intelligent question can be raised about the why and the wherefore of this appearance. It is wholly explained by erroneous perception. An erroneous perception is an irrationality that we can get rid of through right knowledge but can never explain. For an error is never necessitated, and what is not necessitated has no real cause. It is an irrationality that has got to be recognized; and when it is recognized, it is simply transcended. This is all the explanation that it is capable of. In other words, we reject an error; we cannot explain it. No legitimate question accordingly can be raised about the illusory.

8. It is contended by Indra Sen that *Māyāvāda* explains through rejection. Once we adopt this method, we are faced with an ultimate dualism, which conflicts with the main thesis of *Māyāvāda*, namely that

Brahman alone is the reality. The right method of explanation would be the method of integration. It alone can lead to a true monism. Everything is real and has its place in Ultimate Reality. This reality is a harmonious whole. "All problems of existence are problems of harmony," we are told.

We contend that *Māyāvāda* does not entail any kind of ultimate dualism. In fact, it is the only view possible consistently with the non-dualistic character of *Brahman*. *Māyā* is not something real that is "second" to *Brahman*. That would be the Sāṃkhya position. But if *Brahman* is the only reality, and *Brahman* is completely opposed in nature to the world, the latter, together with its cause can only be an illusory appearance; and an illusory appearance never can qualify or limit the underlying reality. It is quite as non-existent as the purely imaginary or the self-contradictory or *tuccha*. It never was at any time and shall never be. Can we still speak of an ultimate dualism?

Let us however try the alternative process of explanation, namely that of integration. This means that we can deduce the world from *Brahman* alone. But how is this possible? *Brahman* is self-luminous knowledge, pure joy, etc. The world is full of division, discord, evil and pain. Such a world cannot be literally contained in *Brahman*. Even according to Sri Aurobindo, it is the result of cosmic ignorance "conceived as a self-limitation of Absolute Knowledge so as to produce the divided action of the mind and the ego." Is this language intelligible? Can Absolute Knowledge contain within itself the principle of its own limitation? Briefly, can ignorance reside in knowledge as a certain action of knowledge itself? Can darkness be a function of light, pain a function of joy, etc.? Is this any kind of monism? Is not monism disrupted from within? As against this, *Māyāvāda* offers us the purest form of monism there can be. For there is no dualism, including the dualism of *Brahman* and *māyā*, that is not the result of ignorance. This ignorance itself, in the last analysis, is not a reality, but a principle of explanation only, that explains itself away. Like the mythical monster, it first devours its children, then it devours as much of itself as it can bite on, and that means the whole realm of objectivity, leaving pure *Brahman* alone.

The positive approach to *Brahman* that takes for its text the Upaniṣadic saying "All this is *Brahman*" can only be understood to mean that 'all this' is not 'all this', but that it is in truth and in reality nothing but *Brahman*. It is as much negative in its import as the text "*neti, neti* (not this, not this)." There is no difference in their meaning.

9. *Māyāvāda* may be wrong. But what is the alternative? We are offered in its place a theory of creation and of evolution. We are told that the purpose of cosmic evolution, and of the original involution, can only be the delight of becoming or *Līlā*.

Nikam in his paper makes *Līlāvāda* appear similar to *Māyāvāda*. He says,.... So according to *Līlāvāda* everything is real because it is of the same real. And this realistic *Līlāvāda*, after all, asserts, like *Māyāvāda*, the Law of Identity: A is A. 'All this is *Brahman*', because *Brahman* is the all." The real issue between the two theories is not the acceptance or the rejection of the Law of Identity. The real issue between them is the conception of *Brahman*, and the relation of the world to *Brahman*. For *Līlāvāda*, *Brahman* is both the material and the efficient cause of the world. *Brahman* so to say spins out the world out of Himself just as the spider does his web. *Māyāvāda* emphatically denies this. *Brahman* does nothing. He does not undergo any modification, real or apparent. He is merely the support or *adhisthana* of the world-appearance or *vivarta-upadāna*. While therefore the *Brahman* of Sri Aurobindo is liable to real modification through the exercise of His power or *śakti* which is part of him, no such charge can be made against *Māyāvāda*. As to the delight of becoming or playfulness, which is attributed to *Brahman*, it is only intelligible in relation to an inner tension and the release of suppressed energy. Will that not make for a certain deficiency in Him, and for a real change or mutation? A playful *Brahman* is conceived wholly on the analogy of the finite man.

10. I agree with Nikam that Sri Aurobindo has not refuted *Māyāvāda*, but I do not agree with his reasons for saying so. He attributes to both the theories the view that the world is a dream. This is quite wrong. The world is not a dream for Sri Aurobindo. It is real. It is quite a different matter that, according to Sri Aurobindo, dreams too happen to be real in their own way. And then Nikam's conclusion that Sri Aurobindo has urged very cogent arguments against the doctrine of the unreality of the world leaves me amazed. If Sri Aurobindo has not refuted *Māyāvāda*, then the reason can only be that his arguments are not cogent or convincing. We cannot have it both ways. It appears as though Nikam does not want to dissatisfy either side, and prefers therefore to sit on the fence.

11. Chaudhury says, "It passes one's comprehension how an eternally cancelled falsehood and irrationality can function as a beginningless positive entity productive of a highly significant world of experience". Here we are confusing two different stand-points. An eliminated or cancelled snake-appearance does produce fear in me. Indeed, the snake-appearance is cancelled in time. But so is *māyā*. And yet there is a sense in which the snake did not exist in the rope at any time, and can therefore be taken to be cancelled for all time or eternally cancelled. Those who see *Brahman* see nothing beside *Brahman*. There is no māyā for them. But those who see the world cannot altogether disown the function of *māyā*. For them *māyā* is undeniable as a principle of explanation. The ontological status of

māyā is one thing, and the fact itself at a certain level of our experience is another. There is no conflict between the two.

12. It is admitted by Chaudhury that the world ignorantly supposed to be self-existent and real apart from *Brahman* is indeed unreal. But then what are the logical implications of this view? I contend that the only thing real is the self-existent real. If the world is not self-existent then it is not real at all. That which is created can have no appearance of reality if it is not confused with the self-existent.

Creation involves volition. But what is willed is so dependent upon the willing that it can have no appearance of existence or being to the person who wills. What is willed is always an act which is put forth and also retracted. Our acts seem to effectuate something that is real and that continues to exist even after we have ceased to act. The arrow that has once been released will go to its target, even though we have ceased to have any connection with it. But then we are here dealing with self-existing arrows and self-existing targets in which our act is embodied. Let arrows and targets be all matters of our creative will. Can they appear to us as given or as real independently of us? Evidently not. The same is true about the world and its creator. Nothing real is ever created. If the world is created, it is for that reason alone incapable of existing in itself; and it can only appear to exist whan it is confused with a self-existing and abiding reality. The evanescent is confused with the enduring, the willed with the known, the imaginary with the real. That is the position of *Māyāvāda*. The world is my creation. So is any illusory appearance. Can it be real?

A Bibliography of Significant Work in Indian Philosophy from the Colonial Period and the Immediate Postindependence Period

Abhedananda, Swami. *Thoughts on Philosophy and Religion*. Calcutta: Ramakrishna Vedānta Math, 1989.

Anand, Mulk Raj. *The Hindu View of Art*. London: George Allen & Unwin Limited, 1933.

Atmarprana, Pravrajika. *Sister Nivedita on Ramakrishna-Vivekananda*. Hollywood, CA: Vedānta Press, 1961.

Aurobindo. *Essays on the Gita*. New York: The Sri Aurobindo Library, Incorporated, 1950.

Aurobindo. The Renaissance in India with a Defence of Indian Culture. Pondicherry, Sri Aurobindo Ashram Trust, 1997.

Aurobindo. *On Education*. Pondicherry: Sri Aurobindo Ashram, 1953.

Aurobindo. *Savitri: A Legend and a Symbol*, Pondicherry: Sri Aurobindo Birth Centenary Library, 1970.

Aurobindo. *Sri Aurobindo and the Mother on Education*. Pondicherry: Sri Aurobindo Ashram, 2004.

Aurobindo. *Sri Aurobindo International Centre of Education Collection, Volume IX: The Human Cycle, The Ideal of Human Unity, War and Self-Determination*. Pondicherry: Sri Aurobindo Ashram, 1962.

Aurobindo. *The Foundations of Indian Culture*. Pondicherry: Sri Aurobindo Ashram Trust, 1968.

Aurobindo. *The Future Poetry*. Pondicherry: Sri Aurobindo Ashram, 2000.

Aurobindo. *The Life Divine*. Pondicherry: Sri Aurobindo Birth Centenary Library, 1970.

Aurobindo. *The Mind of Light*. New York: E.P. Dutton & Company, Incorporated, 1953.

Aurobindo, Sri. 1910. "The National Value of Art." *Webside Literaturen*. Web. 01 Feb. 2011. <www.odinring.de/eng/art.htm>.

Bannerjee, A. K. "The Philosophy of Divine Leela," *Prabuddha Bharata* 49, pp. 275–281, 311–316 (1944).

Bhattacharya, G. *Essays in Analytical Philosophy*. Kolkata: Sanskrit Pustak Bhandar, 1989.

Bhattacharya, Gopinath. *Studies in Philosophy*. Delhi: Motilal Banarsidass, 1983.

Bhattacharya, H. D. *Proceedings of the Seventh Indian Philosophical Congress*. Patna: Patna University, 1931.

Bhattacharya, Kalidas. *The Fundamentals of K.C. Bhattacharyya's Philosophy*. Calcutta: Saraswat Library, 1975.

Bhattacharya, Krishnachandra. *The Subject as Freedom*. Amalner: The Indian Institute of Philosophy, 1930.

Bhattacharyya, H. M. *The Principles of Philosophy*. Kolkata: The University of Calcutta, 1969.

Bhattacharyya, K. *Philosophy, Logic and Language*. Kolkata: Allied, 1965.

Bhattacharyya, K. C. *Search for the Absolute in Neo-Vedānta*. Honolulu: The University Press of Hawaii, 1976.

Bhattacharyya, K. C. *Studies in Philosophy vols. I and II*. (Ed. G. Bhattacharyya.) Kolkata: Motilal Banarsidass, 1958.

Biswas, Dilip K. and Prabhat C. Ganguli. *The Life and Letters of Raja Rammohun Roy*. Calcutta: Sadharan Brahmo Samaj, 1962.

Bose, D. N. and Hiralal Haldar. *Tantras: Their Philosophy and Occult Secrets*. Calcutta: Oriental Publishing Company, 1981.

Brunton, Paul. *Indian Philosophy and Modern Culture*. New York: E.P. Dutton & Company, 1939.

Coomaraswamy, Ananda K. *Art and Swadeshi*. New Delhi: Munshiram Manoharlal Publishers Private Limited, 1994.

Coomaraswamy, Ananda K. *Christian and Oriental Philosophy of Art*. New Delhi: Munshiram Manoharlal Publishers Private Limited, 1994.

Coomaraswamy, Ananda K. *Essays in National Idealism*. New Delhi: Munshiram Manoharlal Publishers Private Limited, 1981.

Coomaraswamy, Ananda K. *Figures of Speech or Figures of Thought*. New Delhi: Munshiram Manoharlal Publishers Private Limited, 1981.

Coomaraswamy, A. K.. "Līlā," *Journal of the American Oriental Society*, *61*:2, pp. 98–101 (1941).

Coomaraswamy, Ananda K. *Perception of the Vedas*. New Delhi: Indira Gandhi Centre for the Arts, 2000.

Coomaraswamy, Aanada K. *The Arts and Crafts of India and Ceylon*. London: T.N. Foulis, 1913.

Coomaraswamy, Ananda K. *The Dance of Shiva: Fourteen Indian Essays*. New Delhi: Munshiram Manoharlal Publishers Private Limited, 2003.

Coomaraswamy, Ananda K. *The Transformation of Nature in Art*. New Delhi: Munshiram Manoharlal Publishers Private Limited, 2004.

Dalmia, Yashodhara. *Contemporary Indian Art: Other Realities*. Mumbai: Marq Publications, 2002.

Dasgupta, Surendranath. *A History of Indian Philosophy, (Five volumes)* Delhi: Motilal Banarsidass, 1922.

Dear, John. *Mohandas Gandhi: Essential Writings*. New Delhi: New Age Books, 2004.

Desai, S. K. and G. N. Devy. *Critical Thought: An Anthology of 20th Century Indian English Essays*. India: Oriental University Press, 1987.

Dubey, S. P. *Facets of Recent Indian Philosophy, Volume 1: The Metaphysics of the Spirit, IPC Presidential Addresses*. New Delhi: Indian Council of Philosophical Research, 1994.

Dubey, S. P. *Facets of Recent Indian Philosophy, Volume 2: Indian Philosophy and History, IPC Presidential Addresses*. New Delhi: Indian Council of Philosophical Research, 1996.

Dubey, S. P. *Facets of Recent Indian Philosophy, Volume 3: Problems of Indian Philosophy, IPC Presidential Addresses*. New Delhi: Indian Council of Philosophical Research, 1996.

Dubey, S. P. *Facets of Recent Indian Philosophy, Volume 4: The Philosophy of Life, IPC Presidential Addresses*. New Delhi: Indian Council of Philosophical Research, 1998.

Gandhi, M. *Hindu Dharma*. Ahmedabad: Navajwan Publishing House, 1950.

Gandhi, M. *Hind Swaraj, or Indian Home Rule*. Ahmedabad: Navajwan Publishing House, 1962.

Gandhi, M. *Satyagraha*. Ahmedabad: Navajwan Publishing House, 1951.

Gandhi, M. *The Moral and Political Writings of Mahatma Gandhi*. (Ed. R. Iyer.) New York: Oxford University Press, 1986.

Haldar, Hiralal. *Essays in Philosophy*. Calcutta: University of Calcutta Press, 1920.

Haldar, Hiralal. *Hegelianism and Human Personality*. Calcutta: University of Calcutta Press, 1920.

Haldar, Hiralal. *Neo-Hegelianism*. London: Heath Cranton Limited, 1927.

Havell, E. B. *The Art Heritage of India*. Bombay: D.B. Taraporevala Sons & Company, 1964.

Hiriyanna, M. *Art Experience*. Mysore: Kavyalaya Publishers, 1997.

Hiriyanna, M. *Indian Conception of Values*. Mysore: Kavyalaya Publishers, 1975.

Hiriyanna, M. *Indian Philosophical Studies, Volume 1*. Mysore: Kavyalaya Publishers, 1957.

Hiriyanna, M. *The Essentials of Indian Philosophy*. London: George Allen & Unwin Limited, 1949.

Hiriyanna, M. *The Quest After Perfection*. Mysore: Wesley Press and Publishing House, 1952.

Hogg, A. G. *Karma and Redemption*. Madras: Diocesan Press, 1970.

Joshi, Vijaya C. *Lala Lajput Rai: Writings and Speeches. 1888–1919*. Delhi: University Publishers, 1966.

Mahadevan, T. M. P. "Can Difference Be Perceived?" *The Philosophical Quarterly*. pp. 142–151 (1938).

Mahadevan, T. M. P. "Can There Be Ethics without Metaphysics?" *Indian Philosophical Congress*. Presidential Address (1952).

Mahadevan, T. M. P. *Collected Papers of Professor S. S. Suryanarayana Sastri*. Madras: University of Madras, 1961.

Mahadevan, T. M. P. *Contemporary Indian Philosophy*. New Delhi: Sterling Publishers Private Limited, 1983.

Mahadevan, T.M.P. "Indian Ethics and Social Practice." *Philosophy East and West* vol. 9. nos. 1,2. pp. 62–63 (1959).

Mahadevan, T. M. P. "Interpreting Indian Thought to America." *The Indian Review* 51 pp. 53–56 (April–July 1950).

Mahadevan, T. M. P. *Superimposition in Advaita Vedānta*. New Delhi: Sterling Publishers Private Limited, 1985.

Mahadevan, T. M. P. *The Philosophy of Advaita with Special Reference to Bharatitirtha-Vidyaranya*. Madras: Ganesh & Co. Private Limited, 1957.

Mahadevan, T. M. P. *The Philosophy of Beauty with Special Reference to Advaita-Vedānta*. (Ed. K.M. Munshi.) Chowpatty: Bharatiya Vidya Bhavan, 1969.

Mahadevan, T. M. P. *Time and the Timeless: Principle Miller Lectures, 1953*. Madras: Central Art Press, 1953.

Mahadevan, T. M. P. "Value and Reality: A Comparative Study." *International Philosophical Quarterly* 6. pp. 22–32 (March 1966).

Maitra, S. K. *The Meeting of the East and the West in Sri Aurobindo's Philosophy*. Pondicherry: Sri Aurobindo Ashram, 1956.

Mill, James. *The History of British India*. London: Piper, Stephenson and Spence, 1858.

Mukerji, A. C. "The Realism of David Hume in Relation to Contemporary Philosophy." *Allahabad University Studies*, vol. 1. pp. 213–234 (1925).

Mukerji, A. C. "James Ward's Analysis of Experience." *Allahabad University Studies*, pp. 337–368 (1931).

Mukerji, A. C. "Reality and Rationality." *Review of Philosophy & Religion: A Quarterly Journal*, vol. 2. no. 3. pp. 7–20 (July 1942).

Mukerji, A. C. "The Puzzles of Self-Consciousness." *Allahabad University Studies* pp. 105–162 (1933).

Mukerji, A. C. "Thought and Reality." *Allahabad University Studies*. vol. 6, pt. 1. pp. 359–455 (1930).

Mukerji, A. C. *Self, Thought and Reality*. Allahabad: The Juvenile Press, 1933.

Mukerji, A. C. "Some Aspects of the Absolutism of Śaṅkaracharya." *Allahabad University* Studies. vol. 4. pp. 375–433 (1928).

Mukerji, A. C. *The Nature of Self*. Allahabad: The Indian Press, Limited, 1938.

Nivedita "Unpublished Letters of Sister Nivedita." *Prabuddha Bharata*. vol. 42. no. 2. pp. 53–54 (February 1937).

Parameswaran, C. *Dayananda and the Indian Problem*. Lahore, Swami Vedānanda Tirtha, 1944.

Pratt, James. "Descriptive Notices: The Nature of Self by AC Mukerji." *Philosophical Review* 48:3: 343 (May 1939).

Pringle-Pattison, A. S. *The Idea of God in the Light of Recent Philosophy: The Gifford Lectures: Delivered in the University of Aberdeen in the Years 1912 and 1913*. Oxford: The Clarendon Press, 1917.

Pringle-Pattison, A. S. *The Idea of Immortality: The Gifford Lectures: Delivered in the University of Edinburgh in the Year 1922*. Oxford: The Clarendon Press, 1922.

Radhakrishnan, S. *An Idealist View of Life: Being the Hibbert Lectures for 1929*. London: George Allen & Unwin Limited, 1932.

Radhakrishnan, S. *Indian Philosophy* Delhi: Oxford University Press, 1993.

Radhakrishnan, S. "Presidential Address: Silver Jubilee Session." *The Indian Philosophical Congress* (1950).

Radhakrishnan, S. *The Bhagavadgītā with an Introductory Essay: Sanskrit Text, English Translation and Notes*. New York: Harper & Brothers Publishers, 1948.

Radhakrishnan, S. *The Brahma Sutra: The Philosophy of Spiritual Life*. London: George Allen & Unwin Limited, 1960.

Radhakrishnan, S. *The Concept of Man: A Study in Comparative Philosophy*. London: George Allen & Unwim LTD, 1966.

Radhakrishnan, S. *The Hindu View of Life: Upton Lectures Delivered at Manchester College, Oxford, 1926*. London: George Allen & Unwin Limited, 1927.

Radhakrishnan, S. "The Indian Approach to the Problem of Religion." *Philosophy East and West* vol. 9. nos. 1,2. pp. 36–38 (1959).

Radhakrishnan, S. *The Philosophy of the Upaniṣads*. London: George Allen & Unwin Limited, 1924.

Radhakrishnan, S. and J. H. Muirhead. *Contemporary Indian Philosophy*. New York: The Macmillan Company, 1936.

Radhakrishnan, S. and P. T. Raju. *The Concept of Man*. London: George Allen & Unwin Limited, 1960.

Rai, Lajpat. *Young India: An Interpretation and History of the Nationalist Movement From Within*. London: British, Auxillary, 1917

Raju, P. T. *An Extension Lecture on East and West in Philosophy*. Jaipur: University of Rajputana, 1947.

Raju, P. T. *East-West Studies on The Problem of the Self*. Netherlands: Martinus Nijhoff, 1968.

Raju, P. T. "Idealisms: Eastern and Western." *Philosophy East and West 3* pp. 211–234 (1955).

Raju, P. T. *Idealistic Thought of India: Vedānta and Buddhism in Light of Western Idealism*. London: Allen and Unwin, 1963.

Raju, P. T. *Idealistic Thought of India*. Cambridge: The Harvard University Press, 1953.

Raju, P. T. *Indian Idealism and Modern Challenges*. Chandigarh: Panjab University Publication Bureau, 1961.

Raju, P. T. *Introduction to Comparative Philosophy*. Lincoln: University of Nebraska Press, 1962.

Raju, P. T. *Lectures on Comparative Philosophy*. Poona: University of Poona, 1970.

Raju, P. T. "Religion and Spiritual Values in Indian Thought." *Philosophy East and West* 9. pp. 38–40 (1959).

Raju, P. T. *Spirit, Being and Self: Studies in Indian and Western Philosophy*. New Delhi: South Asian Publishers, 1982.

Raju, P. T. "The Absolute and Negation." *Review of Philosophy and Religion*. Vol. 5, no. 1, pp. 47–60 (1934).

Raju, P. T. "The Principle of Four-Cornered Negation in Indian Philosophy." *Review of Metaphysics* 4. pp. 694–713 (1954).

Raju, P. T. "The Reality of Negation." *The Philosophical Review*. vol. 50. pp. 585–601 (1941).

Raju, P. T. "The Western and the Indian Philosophical Traditions." *The Philosophical Review* 56 pp. 127–155 (1947).

Raju, P. T. *Thought and Reality: Hegelianism and Advaita*. London: George Allen & Unwin Limited, 1937.

Ranade, R. D. *A Constructive Survey of Upaniṣadic Philosophy*. Poona: Oriental Book Agency, 1926.

Ranade, R. D. *Pathway to God in Hindi Literature*. Karnatak: Shri Gurudev Ranade Samadhi Trust, 1997.

Ranade, R. D. *The Bhagavadgītā as a Philosophy of God-Realisation: Being a clue through the labyrinth of modern interpretations*. Bombay: Bharatiya Vidya Bhavan, 2001.

Roy, R. *The English Works of Raja Ram Mohan Roy, Calcutta*: The Baptist Mission Press, 1820.

Roy, R. *The Precepts of Jesus: The Guide to Peace and Happiness*. Calcutta: Baptist Mission Press, 1820.

Sarkar, Benoy K. *The Futurism of Young Asia and Other Essays on the Relations between the East and the West*. Berlin: Julius Springer, 1922.

Sarkar, Benoy K. *The Political Philosophers Since 1905, Volume II: The Epoch of Neo-Democracy and Neo-Socialism (1929–), Part II*. Lahore: Motilal Banarsidass, 1942.

Sarkar, Benoy K. *The Political Philosophies Since 1905: Their Origins and Their Tendencies: An Objective and Chronological Survey: Outline of a Course of Lectures Given at the Kashi Vidyapitha, Benares in October 1927*. Madras: B.G. Paul & Company, 1928.

Schrader, F. Otto. "Reviewed Work: Self, Thought, and Reality by A.C. Mukerji." *Philosophy*. vol. 2, no. 41, pp. 103–104 (January 1936).

Schrader, F. Otto. "Reviewed Work: The Nature of Self by A.C. Mukerji." *Philosophy* vol. 15, no. 58, pp. 211–212 (April 1940).

Seal, B. N. *Comparative Studies of Vaishnavism and Christianity*. Calcutta: University of Calcutta, 1899.

Sen, Keshub C. *Lectures in India*. London: Cassel and Company, Limited, 1904.

Seth, Andrew. *Hegelianism and Personality*. Edinburgh, UK: William Blackwood and Sons, 1897.

Seth, Andrew. *Man's Place in the Cosmos and Other Essays*. New York: Charles Scribner's Sons, 1897.

Seth, Andrew. *Scottish Philosophy: A Comparison of the Scottish and German Answers to Hume*. Edinburgh, UK: William Blackwood and Sons, 1890.

Tagore, Rabindranath. *Creative Unity*. New Delhi: MacMillan, 1922.

Tagore, Rabindranath. *Lectures and Addresses of Rabindranath Tagore*. (Ed. A. X. Soares.) Kolkata: MacMillan, 1970.

Tagore, Rabindranath. *Sadhana: The Realisation of Life*. Tucson: Omen Press, 1972.

Tagore, Rabindranath. *The English Writings of Rabindranath Tagore* (Ed. S.K. Das). Delhi: Sahitya Akademi, 1994.

Tagore, Rabindranath. *Sadhana: the Realization of Life*. New York: The Macmillan Company, 1915.

Upadhyaya, Ganga P. *The Light of Truth: English Translation of Svami Dayananda's Satyartha Prakasha*. Allahabad: The Kala Press, 1956.

Vivekananda, Swami. *A Study of the Muṇḍaka Upanisha*. Calcutta: Advaita Ashrama, 2000.

Vivekananda, Swami. *Chicago Addresses*. Kolkata: Advaita Ashrama, 2005.

Vivekananda, Swami. *Practical Vedānta*. Kolkata: Advaita Ashrama, 2004.

Vivekananda, Swami. *Swami Vivekananda on India and Her Problems*. Kolkata: Advaita Ashrama, 2006.

Vivekananda: The Yogas and Other Works Including the Chicago Addresses, Jnana-Yoga, Bhakti-Yoga, Karma-Yoga, Raja-Yoga, Inspired Talks, and Lectures, Poems, and Letters. New York: Ramakrishna-Vivekananda Center, 1953.

Yadav, K. C. *Autobiography of Dayanand Saraswati*. New Delhi: Manohar Publications, 1978.

WORKS ANTHOLOGIZED IN THIS VOLUME

National Identity

Tagore, Rabindranath. "Nationalism in India," in The English Writings of Rabindranath Tagore. Delhi: Macmillan, 1976., pp 453–465.

Ghosh, Aurobindo. *The Renaissance in India with a Defence of Indian Culture*. Pondicherry: Sri Aurobindo Ashram Press, 1997.

Coomaraswamy, Ananda K. "Indian Nationality." *Essays in National Idealism*. New Delhi: Munshiram Manoharalal Publishers, 1981. 7–13.

Rai, Lajpat. "Reform or Revival?" *Lala Lajpat Rai Writings and Speeches Volume 1: 1888–1919*. Ed. Vijaya Chandra Joshi. Delhi: University Publishers, 1966. 45–54.

Das, Bhagavan. *The Meaning of Swaraj or Self-Government*. Banaras: Gyan Mandal, 1921. 1–25.

Bhattacharya, Krishna C. "Svaraj in Ideas." *Indian Philosophical Quarterly* 11:4 (1984): 383–393.

Aesthetics

Coomaraswamy, Ananda K. "Art and Swadeshi." *Art and Swadeshi*. New Delhi: Munishiram Manoharlal Publishers, 1994. 1–6.

Sarkar, Benoy K. "View-Points in Aesthetics." *The Futurism of Young Asia and Other Essays on the Relations between the East and the West*. Berlin: Julius Springer, 1922. 116–143.

Aurobindo, The Future Poetry cs. 1–5. Pondicherry: Sri Aurobindo Ashram Publication Department, pp. 3–40.

Tagore, Rabindranath, "Pathway to Mukti," Facets of Recent Indian Philosophy vol. 1, R. Balasubramanian. New Delhi: Indian Council for Philosophical Research. 1994, pp. 323–339.

Bhattacharyya, Krishnachandra. "The Concept of Rasa." *Studies in Philosophy*. Delhi: Motilal Banarsidass Publishers, 2008.

Hiriyanna, M. "Indian Aesthetics – 2." *Art Experience*. Mysore: Kavyalaya Publishers, 1997. 33–47.

Hiriyanna, M. "Art Experience – 2." *Art Experience*. Mysore: Kavyalaya Publishers, 1997. 48–60.

Vedānta

Ranade, R. D. "The Problem of Ultimate Reality in the Upaniṣads." *A Constructive Survey of Upaniṣadic Philosophy Being a Systematic Introduction to Indian Metaphysics*. Poona: Oriental Book Agency, 1926. 246–279.

Vivekananda, "Jñāna Yoga," The Yogas and Other Works, (ed. Swami Nikhilananda). New York: Ramakrishna-Vivekananda Center. 2953. pp 201–399.

Mukerji, A. C. "Absolute Conciousness." *The Nature of Self*. Allahabad: The Indian Press Limited, 1938. 43–59.

Das, Ras Bihari. "The Falsity of the World." *The Philosophical Quarterly, 1940*. 80–90.

Shastri, S. "Advaita, Casuality and Human Freedom." *Collected Papers of Professor S. S. Suryanarayana Sastri*. (Ed. T. M. P. Mahadevan.) Madras: University of Madras, 1961. 201–232.

Mukerji, A. C. "Śaṅkara's Theory of Consciousness." *Allahabad Studies University*, Vol. 13, 1937. 43–55.

Sen, Indra, N.A. Nikam, Haridas, Chaudhuri and G.R. Malkani, "Has Aurobindo Refuted Māyāvāda?," *Indian Philosophical Congress Silver Jubilee Commemoration Volume. Almalner*: Indian Philosophical Congress. 1950.

Iyer, V. Subrahmanya. "Śaṅkara's Philosophy: A Modern Hindu View." *The Philosophy of Truth: Or, Tatvagnana. A Collection of Speeches and Writings*. Salem: Mrs. R. Kuppanna, 1955. 310–337.

Raju, P. T. "Scepticism and Its Place in Śaṅkara's Philosophy." *The Philosophical Quarterly*, 1937. 46–57.

Metaphysic and Epistemology

Mukerji, A. C. "The Realist's Conception of Idealism." *Reader in Philosphy*. Allahabad: Allahabad University, 1927. 207–243.

Haldar, Hiralal. "Realistic Idealism." *Contemporary Indian Philosophy*. (Ed. S. Radhakrishnan.) London: G. Allen & Unwin, 1952. 215–232.

Bhattacharyya, K. C. "The Concept of Philosophy." *Contemporary Indian Philosophy*. (Ed. S. Radhakrishnan.) London: G. Allen & Unwin, 1952. 65–86.

Hiriyanna, M. "The Problem of Truth." *Contemporary Indian Philosophy*. (Ed. S. Radhakrishnan.) London: G. Allen & Unwin, 1952. 235–254.

Malkani G. R. "Philosophical Truth." *The Philosophy of G.R. Malkani*. (Ed. Sharad Deshpande.) New Delhi: Indian Council of Philosophical Research, 1997. 20–53.

Mukerji, A. C. "Traditional Epistemology: Presidential Address." *The Indian Philosophical Congress Silver Jubilee Commemoration Volume*. Bangalore: Indian Philosophical Congress, 1950. 37–42.

Sen, Indra, N.A. Nikam, Haridas, Chaudhuri and G.R. Malkani, "Has Aurobindo Refuted Māyāvāda?," Indian Philosophical Congress Silver Jubilee Commemoration Volume. Almalner: Indian Philosophical Congress. 1950.

Index

CPSIA information can be obtained
at www.ICGtesting.com
Printed in the USA
BVHW031731160819
555729BV00039B/1/P